T
HELLER CASE:
GUN RIGHTS AFFIRMED!

A Defining Moment in History
The Supreme Court Embraces the Second Amendment

— ◆ —

Including summaries of all 96 gun-related cases

Alan Korwin
David B. Kopel

BLOOMFIELD PRESS
Scottsdale, Arizona

BLOOMFIELD PRESS

4848 E. Cactus #505-440 • Scottsdale, AZ 85254
602-996-4020 Offices • 602-494-0679 Fax
1-800-707-4020 Order Hotline
gunlaws.com

Mr. Kopel's material is used by permission and is Copyright 2008 David Kopel. Mr. Kopel can be reached at Independence Institute, 13952 Denver West Parkway #400 Golden, Colorado 80401, 303-279-6536 davekopel.org, independenceinstitute.org

Cover photograph of the Court building courtesy of Franz Jantzen, Collections Manager, United States Supreme Court Cover photo-illustration and design by Ralph Richardson Photograph of Mr. Korwin by Michael Ives

ISBN-10: 1-889632-21-X ISBN 13: 978-1-889632-21-6
Library of Congress Control Number: 2008935707

ATTENTION
Contact the publisher for information on quantity discounts!

Printed and bound in the United States of America
at Color House Graphics, Michigan

First Edition

TABLE OF CONTENTS

ACKNOWLEDGMENTS

When Dave Kopel and I first engaged in this project back in 1997 neither of us could begin to guess where it would lead. Now, with the nation's 96th Supreme Court gun case under its belt, we can only guess where it is headed. A lot of very well-educated guesses and deep insights on that point are included in this book, thanks to a host of true experts whose thoughts grace these pages in a special chapter. Dave and I contributed the time, effort, skill and content without which there would be no *Supreme Court Gun Cases* or this logical sequel.

The *Heller* case brought together the greatest minds in Second Amendment scholarship, and I was beyond fortunate to have interacted with many, and in some small measure to have earned a place in that august crowd. Many people had a special place in guiding this journey, which for me began in 1996 when I first conceived of *Supreme Court Gun Cases*. Friends and strangers alike encouraged me, filling in the blanks, keeping me in line, answering my innumerable questions and being there for moral and technical support. This book could not have come out as it did without every ounce of help and guidance from every one of them:

Aaron Zelman, Alan Gottlieb, Alan Gura, Becky Fenger, Bill Sumner, Bob Blackmer, Bob Cottrol, Bob Dowlut, Bob Levy, Brad Beebe, Brad Harper, C.D. Tavares, Candice DeBarr, Cheryl Korwin, Christopher Conte, Chris Cox, Clayton Cramer, Craig Cantoni, Dave Hamel, Dave Hardy, Eugene Volokh, Gary Christiansen, Gary Marbut, Irving and Shirley Korwin, Jennifer Perkins, Jim Willinger, Larry Pratt, Mark Moritz, Mike Anthony, Mitch Wayne, Nick Gillespie, Paul and Cari Updike, Ralph Richardson, Richard Gardiner, Richard Korwin, Richard Stevens, Roy Miller, Sandy Venitt, Sharyn Grobman, Stephen Halbrook, Tim Lynch, Tom Jenney, Tyler Korwin.

I am especially indebted to Ryan Turner, a talented and hard-working third-year law student who, while he prepared for his bar exams, found time to assemble the *amicus* summaries.

FOREWORD

WARNING! • DON'T MISS THIS!

This book is not "the law," and is not a substitute for the law. The law includes all the legal obligations imposed on you, a much greater volume of work than the mere Supreme Court decisions contained in this book. You are fully accountable under the exact wording and current official interpretations of all applicable laws, regulations, court precedents, executive orders and more, when you deal with firearms under any circumstances.

Many people find laws hard to understand and gathering all the relevant ones is a lot of work. This book helps you with these chores, by gathering information on the entire set of gun-related cases heard by the U.S. Supreme Court, including the text of the most recent cases.

A variety of scholarly and popular analysis and description of the High Court's rulings are included for your convenience. However, legal interpretation of Supreme Court decisions is a matter for the courts, **no guarantee of accuracy is expressed or implied, and the explanatory sections of this book are not to be considered as legal advice or a restatement of law.**

In explaining the general meanings of various cases, using plain English, differences inevitably arise, so **you must always check the actual cases. Some of the cases reproduced in these books are edited excerpts only.** The actual and complete cases are published by the U.S. Government Printing Office and by commercial publishers. The authors and publisher of this book expressly disclaim any liability whatsoever arising out of reliance on information contained in this book.

New laws and regulations may be enacted at any time by the authorities, and courts at every level are constantly interpreting the laws and regulations. **The authors and publisher make no representation that this book includes all cases, requirements, prohibitions and rules that may exist.**

FIREARMS LAWS AND PRECEDENTS ARE CONSTANTLY CHANGING. You are strongly urged to consult with a qualified attorney and local authorities to determine the current status and applicability of the law to specific situations you may encounter.

Some people may feel that certain laws are unconstitutional and invalid, but remember that while they are laws they are enforceable, and remain so until overturned by legislatures or future test cases. Being able to cite the perfect test case may not matter to a police officer at the side of your car.

Guns are deadly serious business and require the highest level of responsibility from you. Firearm ownership, possession and use are long-recognized rights that carry awesome responsibility. Unfortunately, **what the law says and what the authorities and courts do aren't always an exact match.** You must remember that each legal case is different and may lack prior court precedents. A decision to prosecute a case and the charges brought may involve a degree of discretion from the authorities involved. A defense on constitutional grounds may not be allowed in some cases or by some courts. Sometimes, there just isn't a plain, clear-cut answer you can rely upon. Abuses, ignorance, carelessness, human frailties, political agendas, get-tough policies and plain fate subject you to legal risks, which can be exacerbated when firearms are involved. Take nothing for granted and recognize that legal risk attaches to everything you do. **ALWAYS ERR ON THE SIDE OF SAFETY.**

The Second Amendment to the United States Constitution

"A well regulated Militia,
being necessary to the security of a free State,
the right of the people to keep and bear Arms,
shall not be infringed."

The Heller Case: Gun Rights Affirmed is a followup to our prior book:

Supreme Court Gun Cases (SCGC), 2003

Backgrounder—A unique reference book, six years in the making; SCGC includes 44 cases unedited and another 48 in pertinent part, for a total of 92 gun cases. No one ever realized there were so many cases—previous estimates suggested a set of cases not exceeding perhaps a dozen. Includes plain-English summaries of every case, more than 1,000 highlighted quotations for easy reading; essays on the subject matter by the three co-authors; a special "descriptive index" that reduces each case to the questions it answers about firearms.

WHO: *Supreme Court Gun Cases* is the work of three co-authors: Attorney David B. Kopel, Research Director of the Independence Institute in Colorado; Attorney Stephen P. Halbrook, Ph.D., attorney in private practice in Virginia who has won three gun-related cases before the Supreme Court; author Alan Korwin, nationally recognized expert on American gun laws and the originator of the project.

WHEN: Official release occurred on September 18, 2003. The case list and case summaries were posted on the web on April 2, 2006. Work began in 1997, when it was believed that a mere few cases could be compiled and studied in a short period of time. Boy was that notion wrong.

WHERE: Book release events were held simultaneously in Phoenix, Ariz., where the book was published, and in the Washington, D.C., area in association with civil rights groups concerned with the Second Amendment. The American Enterprise Institute held a forum addressing the issues raised by Supreme Court Gun Cases. Phoenix ceremonies took place at an event sponsored by the Goldwater Institute think tank.

WHY: This book sheds light on a contentious American political issue. Before the release of *Supreme Court Gun Cases* it was common for the news media and the public to believe the High Court had been relatively quiet on the subject of guns. With the release of this definitive reference book, it becomes plain that the Court has been very vocal on the subject. The debate about gun rights can take place now with hard factual information to help illuminate the issues.

WHY IT'S IMPORTANT: It turns out the High Court has been consistently supportive of the individual right to keep and bear arms, and the right of armed self defense. Mythologies surrounding these points can be laid to rest, and public policy can be established on a more factual and rational basis.

Supreme Court Gun Cases, Kopel, Halbrook, Korwin (2003)
Published by Bloomfield Press, ISBN 1-889632-05-8
Trade paperback, 672 pp., $24.95, Library/Lawyer's Hardcover $49.95

Supreme Court Gun Cases garnered praise:

"Right in the face of unrelenting media distortion and anti-gun propaganda, *Supreme Court Gun Cases* proves beyond any doubt that the Court has explicitly upheld the legal and historical record of private firearms ownership and armed self-defense. This book proves what NRA has been saying all along—the Second Amendment protects an individual's right to keep and bear arms—a freedom existing before America's founding and enshrined in our Bill of Rights." –**Wayne LaPierre, Executive Vice Pres., National Rifle Association**

"...a political earthquake... an exceptional piece of research... the anti-freedom crowd is not going to like Supreme Court Gun Cases."
–**Larry Pratt, Executive Director, Gun Owners of America**

"...wonderful... groundbreaking... belongs on the bookshelf of every practitioner of constitutional law... Gun rights are an integral part of each American's fundamental constitutional liberties."
–**Thomas C. Patterson, M.D., Chairman, Goldwater Institute**

"...dynamite... Sometimes people need to defend themselves while we're responding to a 911 call. Law enforcement officers know that firearms in the hands of decent people are a deterrent to crime... It's good to know the Supreme Court has been this positive about gun rights and self defense... pulls the rug out from under politicians who want you to believe you have no right to defend yourself or own a gun." –**Joe Arpaio, "America's Toughest Sheriff"**

"Academics and judges will be surprised (no actually shocked) by how many times the Supreme Court has issued decisions bearing on private gun ownership. The extremely careful attention to documenting all the decisions will make it very difficult for future court decisions not to be affected by this work. The number of precedents is truly overwhelming."
–**John R. Lott, Jr., Ph.D., Resident Scholar, American Enterprise Institute**

"...a stunning accomplishment... will change the political landscape on the gun-rights debate." –**Evan Nappen, Attorney and Author**

"The dream team of American gun-law experts has driven a stake through the heart of the anti-rights gun-ban lobby... gun haters will need to manufacture new lies... The individual right to keep and bear arms is an American tradition with roots as deep as the nation itself."
–Alan Gottlieb, Chairman, Second Amendment Foundation

"...shows that scores of Supreme Court decisions recognize the legal, theoretical and practical logic of private firearms ownership... entertainingly explains the amazing true stories and profound ideals that rise from time-honored American gun rights."
–Aaron Zelman, Jews for the Preservation of Firearms Ownership

"It is fundamentally sound, sorely needed research that supports the basic human and civil right to protect what's yours."
–Lawrence E. Tahler, Executive Director, American Self-Defense Institute

"...the rights of man are endowed by their Creator, but ensured by the state... Each responsible citizen must consider himself to be the custodian of his own liberty, and thus it is incumbent upon him to understand the processes by which such liberty is ensured. This text covers that subject at appropriate length." **–Lt. Col. Jeff Cooper, USMC (Ret.), "The Father of the Modern Techniques of Shooting"**

"While the Supremes have directly acknowledged the Second Amendment as an individual right, this new book unearths 92 gun-related cases where the High Court upheld, among other things, armed self-defense of person, family and community—the heart of the Second Amendment. The synopsis of the Miller case is the best I have ever read."
–Neal Knox, Gun-Rights Activist and Writer, The Firearms Coalition

"...strikes a powerful blow for freedom... I'm particularly gratified to learn how vigorous the Court has been in supporting the right to self defense. If more states accepted this, countless innocent lives would be saved. My hope and prayer is that your book will supply the brain-cell ammunition necessary to continue our battle against those who would deny Americans such a basic human right." **–Suzanna Gratia Hupp, Texas State Representative, Survivor of Luby's Massacre and Mother**

"My interviews of gun-control spokespeople show they either don't know or won't tell the truth about how the Supreme Court has consistently ruled in favor of a strong Second Amendment. This book, in the Court's own words, should convince anyone that the right to own firearms is at least as strong as the right to free speech. Bravo on an important scholastic work that is easy to read and understand."
–Tom Gresham, Nationally Syndicated Radio Host of "Gun Talk."

Dedicated in the hope that we preserve
the good thing we have here in America, and
to the memory of David I. Caplan, a meticulous scholar
and a tireless supporter of the Second Amendment.
His work for over three decades and encouragement of others helped
create the solid foundation on which the *Heller* decision is built.

Supreme Court Gun Cases
Excerpts from the book, written in 2003

One of the biggest problems with law today is that there is so much of it. Congress doesn't stop legislating, it seems, sometimes heedless of its delegated authority or any real need to do so. The federal courts at every level churn out stupefying quantities of interpretation of legislative activity, practically legislating on their own in case after case. All 50 states do the same. Every county and every city contributes to the glut.

Law is an institution of the most pernicious tendency. The institution, once begun, can never be brought to a close. No action of any man was ever the same as any other action, ever had the same degree of utility or injury. As new cases occur, the law is perpetually found to be deficient. It is therefore perpetually necessary to make new laws. The volume in which justice records her prescriptions is forever increasing, and the world would not contain the books that might be written. The consequences of the infinitude of law is its uncertainty. –William Godwin

All the components that constitute law have already grown so large they are functionally inaccessible to the general public on which they act. The informed electorate that the Founding Fathers hoped for, in too many respects, has fallen beyond the pale of human endeavor:

It will be of little avail to the people that the laws are made by men of their own choice, if the laws be so voluminous that they cannot be read, or so incoherent that they cannot be understood; if they be repealed or revised before they are promulgated, or undergo such incessant changes that no man who knows what the law is to-day can guess what it will be to-morrow. –James Madison, The Federalist Papers, #62

The Supreme Court's steady activity contributes to this difficulty, though its work is perhaps more well organized and (sometimes) better thought out. The full official bound set requires 95 feet of shelf space.

It is the goal of *Supreme Court Gun Cases* (SCGC) to make accessible one tiny fragment of that august body's work, namely the High Court's decisions that have a bearing on private gun ownership in America today. What does the Supreme Court say about your right to keep arms and your right to bear arms?

11

Few other subjects have sparked such a firestorm of debate—but a mostly recent debate it turns out, which takes place all too often in abject darkness, or replete with lies, deceit, myths, politically motivated balderdash, statistical work from The Three Stooges and outright self-evident silliness.

It is the self-evident silliness that is hardest to accept—if we are ever to reach any rational conciliation on crucial issues, surely it must be by exercising our intellect. Even absent an infallible agreed-upon set of facts, we should be able to apply our critical thinking to proceed in a straight line.

Nowhere are the self-evident errors more pronounced than in the new (recent decades) argument that the Second Amendment does not protect the rights of individual people, but rather protects the "right" of the states to run a militia. The ability of a state to organize its militia is not a right, it is a power delegated to the state by the people.

Even a casual glance at history shows there are and have always been gun dealers selling to citizens who are not in the National Guard (which didn't even exist until 1903). More than 94,000 words of federal statute regulate well this activity (q.v., *Gun Laws of America*). How could all the people and all the authorities possibly have gotten it so wrong for so long, and only now be discovering their mistake?

The answer of course is that we and they didn't get it wrong. Through the efforts of Stephen Halbrook we know that the collective-rights argument—the one that proclaims you have no rights—first appears out of nowhere in the federal judiciary in *U.S. v. Tot,* as he noted in SCGC (citations omitted here):

> **The "collective rights" theory originated in *U.S. v. Tot,* (1943). The historical references in *Tot* simply do not support its thesis. See Halbrook, *That Every Man Be Armed* 189-191 (1984). Subsequent cases merely string cite to earlier cases which are ultimately traceable to *Tot*.**

Another source of distortion over the years has been flagrant use of out-of-context quotations, and with this book that farce ends. For too long, *Cruikshank* has been held up as flatly dismissing your rights, with these pulled phrases referring to the Second Amendment:

> **The right there specified is that of "bearing arms for a lawful purpose." This is not a right granted by the Constitution.**

Sure, the Supreme Court actually said that. What is all too frequently omitted however is the very next line:

> **Neither is it in any manner dependent upon that instrument for its existence.**

The High Court goes on to explain, in its now-awkward nineteenth century legalese, that the individual right to arms embodied in the Second Amendment (as well as certain other basic individual rights), existed before the Constitution. These are inherent natural rights of free people, recognized but certainly not created by the Founders, which the Constitution merely established as off-limits for federal intrusion.

The United States operates the way it does because the Second Amendment means what it always used to mean—individual people can and do indeed keep arms and bear arms for their personal safety, defense of the common good, and every other legitimate purpose, if they so choose. The idea that you don't have these rights is something new and aberrant, and represents a total reversal of what has been the case in America so far. Feel how you wish about an armed people's deterrence to tyranny, or personal gun possession in public, or resisting crime, or firearm education at school, or safety measures for anything you keep at your home. But in order to adopt the logically bankrupt notion that the Constitution does not protect your individual right to arms, you must deny the reality surrounding you.

The individual right to arms is clearly borne out in the copious decisions of the Supreme Court, which have been obscured from public view until now. The Supreme Court's gun cases were not heretofore referred to as plentiful in public discourse. That is one of the breakthroughs of this book. It is also the reason this book took six years to complete.

I thought myself pretty clever when I first approached Dave Kopel at a convention with my concept for an easy and unique book about the Supreme Court. We would take the popular essays Dave had already written for Mike Dillon's magazine-catalog ("magalog") the *Blue Press,* reproduce the actual cases he discussed, and create a relatively thin text pretty quickly. Dillon's publication of those fascinating essays was the genesis of the book you now hold. The early burst of enthusiasm that set this task on its course anticipated an easy compilation of less than a dozen cases, believing, as we all did back then, that the Supreme Court has said little with respect to guns. The number of cases to be included unedited was small enough to be pitched on the draft of the back cover from 1997:

U.S. v. Cruikshank, 1876
Presser v. Illinois, 1886
Miller v. State of Texas, 1894
U.S. v. Miller, 1939
Lewis v. U.S., 1980
U.S. v. Thompson/Center, 1992
U.S. v. Lopez, 1995
Printz v. U.S., 1997

The shocking realization that this was in fact an enormous body of work (44 cases are included unedited in SCGC) pulled the rug out from under the effort. The project alternately languished behind every other pressing exigency of modern life, or pressed ahead in fits and starts as batches of new cases were unearthed. In the interim I used my discovery of a dozen self-defense cases for a section of Tanya Metaksa's book, *Safe, Not Sorry* (Harper Collins). David published "The Supreme Court's Thirty-Five *Other* Gun Cases," in the *St. Louis University Public Law Review* (1999), and other material based on our unfinished research crept into scholarly and popular work for years.

On top of 36 cases that actually mention or quote the Second Amendment, we began to recognize that guns are a bigger subject than the Amendment itself. We kept discovering cases that addressed firearms from other perspectives—search and seizure, sentence enhancements, taxes, states' rights, double jeopardy, definitions, statutory interpretation, due process and more. My faith and motivation waned more than once. Finally, I could no longer stand the continued darkness and applied the afterburners in mid 2002. I thought for sure I would finish by New Year's, but the project just soaked up the hours and I sit here in July 2003 still trying to nail it all down.

My friend Steve Cascone has advice that rings true here—you don't finish a book, you declare an ending. But I couldn't do that until I had examined every case for quotable lines (and found 1,068). Then I felt compelled to simmer each case down to the identifying questions in the special Descriptive Index. And of course a few new cases sprang up near the end (*Simpson* on armed robbery, *Busic* on armed assault of officials, and even *Terry v. Ohio*, on frisks).

It was common for writers of every stripe to refer to the mere few pronouncements of the High Court, but now that ends. As you can see for yourself, 92 decisions have a bearing on the issue, and at least seven others (see *Miranda*) are often cited. Reduced to a common measurement, these 337,141 words with a bearing on your gun rights are three times more case law on guns than federal statutory law (a tidy 94,333 words as of 2003).

Interesting word counts within the case text (first 92 cases only):
(all variant spellings are included)

firearm	1,380	ammunition	77
arms	621	shotgun	61
gun	362	handgun	53
rifle	134	revolver	47
pistol	135	keep and bear arms	37
armed	125	Second Amendment	38
self defense	123	bear arms	27
machinegun	112	Winchester	5

The "few" cases most writers were referring to was just a mass mental blockage passed down from one lazy parrot to another, and I include myself in that class. How much other claptrap passes for fact unobserved, you have to wonder. The few-cases fallacy perhaps reflects an interest by some people in seeing this inconvenient Amendment up and leave—an interest so strong mere facts are not normally enough to contain it.

•

The centuries-old inherent acceptance of the right to arms is evident in the practically forgotten Supreme Court self-defense cases from the 1890s, where time after time the Justices take for granted that the people have guns. The Court focuses instead solely on when and how the people used their guns, and if such use was proper.

It was understood as normal, reasonable and expectable for a small man to go home and get his gun, as in *Gourko*, when publicly threatened with death by a much larger man. And no, it was not premeditated murder when Gourko used his gun in the ensuing confrontation. Time and again, the Court easily and calmly presumes that gun ownership is normal, permissible behavior. American people own and use guns for all the legitimate purposes that make guns so important in a peace-loving society. That's them talking, not me.

No less than nine fundamental elements of self defense are defined by these cases, and can be categorized roughly thus:

Innocence
Logan 1892; Beard 1895; Rowe 1896; Brown 1921

Reasonable Belief & Grounds For Belief
Beard 1895; Allen, Acers, Alberty, Wallace 1896

Intent
Gourko 1894; Thompson 1894; Allen, Wallace 1896

Actions Not Words
Allison 1895; Allen, Acers, Alberty 1896

Necessity
Logan 1892; Starr 1894; Beard 1895; Rowe 1896

Equal Force
Logan 1892; Beard 1895; Allen, Alberty 1896

Immediacy Ends
Acers 1896; Brown 1921

Retreat
Beard 1895; Rowe, Alberty 1896; Brown 1921

Chase
Garner 1995

Garner has not been previously thought of as a self-defense case, but it exists nonetheless on an important fringe of that issue. When a criminal exits your home at a high rate of speed carrying your valuables, is deadly force permissible to retain your property, as so many staunch gun owners wish? A continuum exists on types of criminal flight, from kidnapping and car-jacking where innocent life is at risk, to escape of known dangerous characters, to the mere loss of property or escape of suspects. *Garner,* which applies specifically to police, is the only Supreme Court case known to address this at all. Many states have codified the use of deadly force to prevent escape, but folk wisdom has a place here. "Better a criminal goes free than a lien on your home."

Later cases generally have better English, at least to the modern ear, but all the important things were settled early on. Cases in modern times often pick at minutiae related to statutory construction, the constitutionality of a provision, or quite often, the possession of guns in connection with the war on some drugs. That war takes up much of the back half of SCGC. Statements about the rights each American has with regard to personal possession and use of firearms were established matters of law by the early 1900s.

Cases since then restate or reinforce the American right to arms, directly and by implication. The question now seems to be how much infringement is tolerable, a question that unfortunately will always dog us. The relationship between rights and controls is a dynamic balance, not a bright line.

When you think about it, no rights are limitless. Put simply, your right to swing your arms stops where my nose begins. The right to arms does not include a right to wave a gun around wildly and terrify people, or to stick up a liquor store. Even the absolute pronouncement at the front of the First Amendment, "Congress shall make no law…" allows for laws against fraud, slander, impersonating an officer, threatening the President, bomb jokes in airports and the classic, falsely shouting fire in a crowded theater and creating a panic. Justice Holmes created the wonderful theater metaphor in a case that convicted a man for circulating leaflets about resisting the military draft, a less than beautiful example in retrospect.

With the word *gun* used in some form in these decisions 2,910 times, they can't all be part of the holding in each case. Many expressions of the individual right to keep arms and to bear arms are in *dicta*, the discussion portions of the decisions that are not legally binding. Serious lawyers scoff at *dicta*, uh, except when it strongly supports their cases. They dismiss it totally when the other side claims the Court's words mean something.

I guess I'm the champion of *dicta*. I like *dicta*. In it I find the life of America, the depth of the decisions, a window into what reality was like at the time. I give great credit to those writers of words, they had something to say, and they could turn a phrase. The statute might give you the rules about liquor, cigarettes and guns, but *dicta* tells you what it was like at the party.

Experts don't always agree on where *dicta* ends and the holding begins, except for occasional brief statements such as, "The holding of the court below is reversed." While *dicta* is not binding, it is persuasive, and that is the nub. With so much "between the lines" evidence available and all basically pointed in the same direction, it can only logically be read to support the decisions themselves, which are consistent with the individual private gun ownership in place in America since Day One. A portion of the record may only be *dicta*, but have mercy, there are 500 pages of it.

Whether you "have" any legal rights or not is immaterial in the larger picture of human survival. You *can* defend against predatory attack, you *can* slay an adversary, and if you survive in today's world, you get to take what comes next from the people generally known as officials, for better or worse. Your neighbors, being by and large rational, will typically celebrate your survival, when you persevere in the stark face of unprovoked assault, regardless of law books on a shelf somewhere. And so it has been since time immemorial. Nothing in the natural order of the jungle can require you to stand idle and let the lion eat you or your family, with or without some musty old parchment curtain between you and the powers that be.

The Supreme Court has upheld the legal tradition and historical record of self-defense in both law and logic, which has existed as a principle, unbroken, since the Code of Hamurabai, the first written law drafted, 4,000 years ago. In America, you have a right to armed self defense. The Court describes it explicitly, repeatedly.

Those well buttressed pronouncements are under assault, as increasingly strident calls are made to denounce the protection the Second Amendment has traditionally afforded us, e.g., police need guns but you don't, because they face dangerous criminals and you, umm, well… that line of thought does fall a bit short in the logic department. Such arguments are generally designed to incrementally disarm the freely armed public we observe today, and to ban or severely discourage personal responsibility for your own safety.

Three main reasons are put forth in advocating such a radical departure from the historical and legal record. The first simply suggests that you're too stupid and guns are too dangerous for a citizen to handle. This requires accepting a bizarre paradox—guns should be banned because they make murder easy but are way too complex for effective self defense. (See dozens of similar paradoxes by M.Z. Williamson posted at KeepAndBearArms.com).

The second reason is seemingly benign and sometimes presented as the "common sense" approach to public disarmament—as an attempt to control crime. Since guns cause crime, or so the thinking goes, ban the guns and crime will go away. The fact that guns are already totally banned for criminals doesn't enter the equation, and only the guns of people who don't commit crimes are targeted. Both arguments are easily dismissed on common sense grounds.

The mainstream media, though, inexplicably adopts these as a frame of reference and abandons any semblance of balance, casting nearly all gun-related reports to imply that guns and crime are inextricably linked, and that firearms serve little other than criminal purposes. Research showing millions of DGUs (defensive gun uses) each year are completely suppressed by America's "unbiased" mainstream reporters.

John Lott's recent book, *The Bias Against Guns,* documents how *The New York Times,* for example, ran 50,745 words about crimes with guns in 2001, and one story of 163 words on a gun being used (by a retired cop) to prevent a crime. The "paper of record" shamelessly deceives the public. The hand-wringing scandal caused by and endlessly debated about one lying reporter on its staff is meaningless in comparison, a smokescreen that obscures its institutionalized distortions.

Certainly, the gun-friendly sense of early Americans and their Supreme Court is not what appears on nightly news broadcasts or the morning newspaper. The facts that guns save lives, guns stop crime, guns keep you safe, and guns are why America is still free, are not found in the "news." This contributes to why tens of millions of gun-friendly people today have good reason to distrust the media. And why many unsuspecting members of the public have come to dislike—or have even been manipulated into viciously hating guns—the very thing that helps guarantee their freedom.

The third and darkest motive, according to an increasing number of observers, is for more sinister purposes involving stricter management of the population and the incremental demise of a self-governing republic that was founded with populist arms two-and-a-quarter centuries ago. Nah, couldn't possibly happen here.

Still, no issue as large as this is absolute. The anti-rights argument can draw some support from cases like *Lewis, Maryland, Miller* (which everyone claims as their own) and a few others, plus occasional dissents that take a strong statist view.

The question of what might occur in the future if the Supremes were to hear a case about the personal, individual, historically extant right to the means of self and national defense that you and your forbearers have always had, is addressed next.

The question of where the Supreme Court has stood thus far on the issue is addressed in the body of this work (i.e., SCGC), for all to see.

The Fall of the Second Amendment

The past speaks for itself. In this country, individual free people have always had the right and the ability to keep arms and to bear arms. In recent times, restrictions on this right and ability have grown. Challenges to the civil right itself have been introduced in courts and the public debate.

Things change. Why not the Second Amendment? We asked if slavery should continue and said no. We asked if women should be allowed to vote and said yes. We asked if liquor should be outlawed and said yes, then no. We even asked if sovereignty should stand in the way of forcing the Bill of Rights on the several states and eventually said why not. So why not private gun ownership—should "they" allow "us" to keep and bear arms?

What if the Supreme Court were to hear yet another case addressing the Second Amendment's current protection of the individual right to both keep arms and to bear arms? Should people continue to have the right to arms they currently have, or should the right be taken away by the very government this right is intended to keep in check?

And let's assume the High Court unequivocally answers the question to the satisfaction of the most skeptical critic, instead of being unclear, waffling around, or addressing only tangents, as the most ardent critics might argue they have done, even in the face of the research presented in this book. I can't even find a perfect way to frame the bottom-line question if that case appeared today. Are the people the militia? Do individual people in the United States have a right to keep and bear arms which shall not be infringed? Yes or no?

The results of such a case are so intense, and could so shift or rend the fabric of America—adjusting the balances of power in ways no one can foresee—that both sides in the gun-rights debate have been reluctant to take the chance. They have actually backed off when cases presented themselves, arguing the case wasn't airtight enough, or the Bench was not in their favor. They each have too much to lose.

The Court itself has shown repeated reluctance to address the issue, refusing to review many cases that might answer, from its desk at least, The Big Question. So the status quo remains—most anyone can stroll into a gun store and go shopping, while infringements of all flavors continue to mount.

The Supreme Court is unlikely to one day jump in and decide that, yes, the Second Amendment does indeed protect an uninfringeable right to individually arm yourself if you so choose, and any laws violating that freedom would be invalid. That's not going to happen because, as we've already seen, reasonable boundaries are defined around all rights. There's also the practical problem of defining each word, not just answering some single question— what are arms, how does "regulated" differ from "well regulated," what exactly is "keep," and "bear"—the human condition, and the rules by which we govern ourselves, do not conveniently reduce down to a yea or nay.

Even if the Court once again says yes, the Second Amendment basically means what the gunnies say it means, nothing substantial is invented. Gun stores will open the very next day, the same as the previous day. Here comes the new boss, same as the old boss.

The loudest of the "gun bigots," from huge non-profits to people who are actually in Congress sworn to uphold the Constitution, would be missing their main subject matter. The mass media would be out on a limb trying to spin the decision to the masses, since it would conflict with the bulk of what the "news" has been saying for the past several decades.

The valid debate must then become how much regulation constitutes infringement. This is in fact the direction policy debates are now taking, as overwhelming scholarly evidence and the book you are holding begin to force anti-rights advocates into rethinking their untenable positions. Disarmament advocates would have to shift to the less deceitful policy question of whether people should *continue* to run around with this right to keep arms and right to bear arms intact.

Otherwise, and here's the surprise, life after an unambiguous 2A decision would pretty much be business as usual, with guns for sale during regular business hours, shooting ranges handling the usual crowds, honorable people handling firearms in honorable ways, and 99+% of all guns involved in no wrongdoing or inherent evil, exactly as things are today. Oh, I suppose some people would drink beer till dawn, and feel woozy for a few days.

Crooks would essentially be unaffected, since guns are already totally prohibited as far as they're concerned, and all the existing anti-criminal laws would still be in place, with neither more nor less resources for enforcement than are available now.

Challenges would be mounted against many of the more egregious infringing laws at the state and federal levels, and there are some real doozies. The juggernaut of social fabric would ponderously lumber ahead. People terrified of guns (*hoplophobes*, from the Greek *hoplites*, weapon) would shriek about blood in the streets, gun owners would remain skeptical of course, and we'd all get to see what really happens.

On the other hand, well-meaning Justices sometimes choose to use their power and perceived notions of the public good, instead of plain evaluation of law or the Constitution, as a basis for their decisions. A High Court peopled with enough Justices of that philosophical bent could conceivably decide that, no, there is no protection in the Second Amendment for individuals to keep arms, or to bear arms, or at least there won't be anymore, despite the historical, social and judicial record. The Supreme Court can essentially decide to reverse what is.

If you doubt this possibility, see the dissenting opinion in *Adams v. Williams*, where Justices Douglas and Marshall see no problem with outright bans. With three more similarly oriented people on the Bench, gun rights could be abolished, on paper at least, regardless of precedent.

Voices of increasing authority and volume are grousing that the Constitution no longer adequately constrains the Congress. Why should the uninfringeable right to arms be any different.

There would be elation in some circles, a euphoria of perceived safety, and I suppose some folks would sip tea and converse in giddy tones until quite late. And we might expect that a substantial and already discomfited armed portion of the public would feel further alienated. The political right would be sweating bullets, and the far right, armed to the teeth, might begin to figure we're doomed.

But one of the surprising results if the personal protection of the Second Amendment were to fall by Supreme Court decree (or even by legislative decree, for a bill to repeal the Second Amendment has been introduced by a Congressman from New York) is that all of the honest gun ownership, possession and use we see in every fiber of American life today would not suddenly become illegal. The collapse of the Second Amendment is not a ban on anything.

It might open a floodgate of attempts at new regulation, but the current status quo rights would not, of themselves, up and disappear. The complex bundle of rights merely become vulnerable to attack on the grounds that they are no longer specifically protected by the Second Amendment as they had always been thought to be. We would be back to floor fights in all the legislatures over every new proposal for either side. Just like now.

If the Second Amendment is suddenly found to only guarantee the gun "rights" of the state, or only the gun "rights" of the National Guard, or some sort of gun rights of organized collectives of people, then the Constitution suddenly falls almost totally silent on the gun rights of individual people and privately held arms.

Then the Ninth Amendment suddenly rears its forgotten head, and reminds us that any rights that aren't specifically granted (which the fall of the Second could be interpreted as), belong to the people. The people. That's us. It's hard to imagine a winning argument proposing that "the people" in the Ninth Amendment means the National Guard or the states:

> **The enumeration in the Constitution of certain rights shall not be construed to deny or disparage others retained by the people.**

Then too, states have their own Constitutions, most of which embed their own rendition of the Second Amendment, and often in far more direct terms. These would remain standing, wholly unaffected by any abrogation of the Bill of Rights' apparent protections of gun ownership. Consider Arizona's take, where I currently make my home:

> **The right of the individual citizen to bear arms in defense of himself or the state shall not be impaired, but nothing in this section shall be construed as authorizing individuals or corporations to organize, maintain, or employ an armed body of men.**

It's hard to imagine a court exercising legitimate authority and determining that the Second Amendment does not mean what it always used to mean, with language like Arizona's in a Constitution drafted as late as 1912 (the last of the 48 contiguous states). If you consider each states' statements and their historical evolution—the list compiled by Professor Eugene Volokh of UCLA Law School is included in this book—it leaves little room for rationally arguing against the individual rights to arms. These may give rise to a debate on the degree to which privately held arms may be regulated, but they are simultaneously clear that such a right exists. For example:

> **Connecticut: Every citizen has a right to bear arms in defense of himself and the state.**

Delaware: A person has the right to keep and bear arms for the defense of self, family, home and State, and for hunting and recreational use.

Wyoming: The right of citizens to bear arms in defense of themselves and of the state shall not be denied.

Never forget that a complete collapse of 10% of the Bill of Rights (the Second Amendment) would leave untouched and unaffected the Constitutions of the individual States.

There is also the inconvenient question of what to do with all the existing gun laws. For just as laws regulate what you cannot do, they often stipulate what's allowed as well. Federal statutes would be subject to refreshed attack from pro-rights and anti-rights groups and individuals. But those 94,333 words of federal gun law describe how to become a gun dealer, what age you must reach before you can buy this gun or that gun, ammunition sales, and even how to buy, sell and trade fully automatic firearms like the Army and National Guard routinely use.

Statutes tell you how to walk into your local gun shop on a nice sunny day and buy pretty much anything that's legal to own, even if that legality was no more guaranteed by the Constitution than buying chewing gum or floor tile. Owning nice cars isn't specifically constitutionally guaranteed but you certainly can build quite a collection.

The analogy is a strong one. The Court cannot today meaningfully say you have a right to own a car, and be saying anything of substance, since that right is endemic to citizenry, and well manifested. It can only say you have no right to own a car, and affect change. Imagine a world gone to such a weird future place that for reasons of safety, or crime control, or speed control, or to avert some other perceived disaster, a Supreme Court might consider finding citizens have no right to own a car, and having to defend your commute to work on Ninth Amendment grounds.

The work necessary to unhinge all the federal and state laws that guarantee and administer private ownership of arms could take decades, against a populace that might appear somewhat less than receptive and who are, after all, heavily armed. All this contributes to making sudden dramatic change from the centuries-long status quo of a free fully armed public unlikely. The true specter of loss of our rights and freedom comes from more subtle foes:

There are more instances of the abridgment of the freedom of the people by the gradual and silent encroachment of those in power, than by violent and sudden usurpation. –James Madison

The greatest dangers to liberty lurk in insidious encroachment by men of zeal, well-meaning but without understanding.
–Justice Louis Brandeis

If a nation values anything more than freedom, it will lose its freedom; and the irony of it is that if it is comfort or money that it values more, it will lose that, too. –Somerset Maugham

The saddest epitaph which can be carved in memory of a vanished liberty is that it was lost because its possessors failed to stretch forth a saving hand while yet there was time. –Justice George Sutherland

They that can give up liberty to obtain a little temporary safety deserve neither liberty nor safety. –Benjamin Franklin

Guard with jealous attention the public liberty. Suspect everyone who approaches that jewel. Unfortunately, nothing will preserve it but downright force. Whenever you give up that force, you are ruined. –Patrick Henry

Today, we need a nation of Minutemen: citizens who are not only prepared to take arms, but citizens who regard the preservation of freedom as the basic purpose of their daily life and who are willing to consciously work and sacrifice for that freedom. –John F. Kennedy

The natural progress of things is for liberty to yield and government to gain ground. –Thomas Jefferson

It kind of makes the Second Amendment seem a little less vulnerable, because ultimately, the right to defend what's yours doesn't depend on the Constitution for its existence, as *Cruikshank* makes so elegantly clear. It depends on the valiant courage of the people, and the forces of nature, which the Constitution merely recognizes in this particular case.

Life, liberty, and property do not exist because men have made laws. On the contrary, it was the fact that life, liberty, and property existed beforehand that caused men to make laws in the first place. –Frederic Bastiat

Understanding the Citation System

When you first come upon Supreme Court cases you have to marvel at the craftsmanship. These are not idle musings, or the "opinions" that, like part of the anatomy, everyone has. No, these are meticulously crafted and scholarly renderings of the highest order. They actually take into account every case that has ever come before and which they feel has a bearing on the matter at hand, naming each one with exquisite precision. These citations are flatly inserted into the text with no other indication at all, which is startling to the newcomer, but eventually become second nature and are remarkably efficient. Just the system necessary to catalog each prior case, and the precedent it sets for the future, is a science and artform without equal.

Majority decisions become the law of the land, as much as any signed piece of legislation. You can only hope we have the most competent people up there acting to the highest order of performance. Though the majority carries the day, dissenting opinions are usually as well reasoned as the majority decisions, and often quite as compelling. These may even more closely reflect the prevailing beliefs of the public, if such a thing could be known. The dissenting Justices have a point, just not the numbers to sway the determining vote. In some cases, the dissent is compelling enough to sway future arguments. In more than one case, a previous dissent has been adopted verbatim in a later decision, making it law.

The overall logic and precision of the dissents can be as hard to ignore as the holding of the majority. They *both* have a point. It's like the old joke where, on hearing the defense argument, a trial judge says, "You're right," and then on hearing the prosecution, the judge says, "You're right." "But they can't both be right, your honor," the bailiff implores. "You're right too," comes the dry judicial reply.

A tad of tempest can occasionally be seen in the Justices' remarks toward each other's conclusions. The Justices circulate and review all the drafts before a final version is released, and sometimes address each others' concerns in the published document.

In producing the decisions, these individuals we call Justices don't merely decide the fate of the people in the case before them, although those folks' fates are as bindingly sealed as we can make them in this society. No, these nine people decide what the very fabric of America looks like, where the different weaves and colors and textures are to be placed. They are defining who we are as a people, and they bring to it a level of thought and care that is unmatched anywhere in our national being. The controversies are as fundamental as any we know.

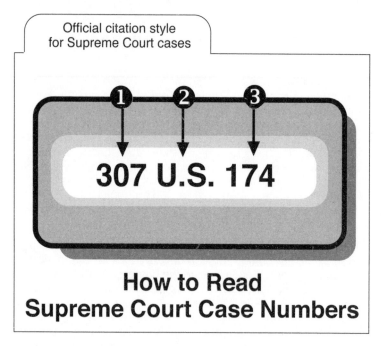

Official citation style
for Supreme Court cases

① ② ③

307 U.S. 174

How to Read
Supreme Court Case Numbers

❶ The Volume Number   **307** U.S. 174

Every Supreme Court case is printed and bound into an official set of books by the U.S. Government. Once bound into the set, the book number of each court case never changes, and becomes the first point of reference. The case cited above is found in volume number 307. The volume numbers are printed on the book spines.

❷ The Book Name Abbreviation   307 **U.S.** 174

Many of the numbering systems in U.S. law use a three-part notation like Supreme Court citations, where the middle element is an abbreviation for the name of the series of books. "U.S." stands for *United States Reports*, the official set of Supreme Court cases. Many of the abbreviations seem alien at first, with mixtures of numbers, capital and lower case letters, and punctuation no public school class ever hinted at, but they become eminently familiar with use, and you get to know most of the main ones by heart. Law libraries have lists of all the abbreviations used.

Since 1879, the bound set of Supreme Court decisions has been abbreviated simply "U.S.". The earlier sets, however, were known by the name of the person who assembled them. So the earliest case citations have a volume number, the name of the "reporter" and a page number. The very first case is *1 Dallas 1* and, as it was produced on a volunteer basis for a court that in its infancy didn't require written decisions, it isn't even a Supreme Court case—it's a Pennsylvania state case that this ambitious entrepreneur was also busy reporting, and included in the same volume.

The volume names following Dallas are Cranch, Wheaton, Peters, Howard, Black and Wallace, after which the "U.S." designation is used exclusively. No records from some of the earliest cases exist, and some of the earliest committed to writing are known to be unreliable. Wheaton was the first reporter to be federally paid, and is generally credited with upgrading the reporting system to a reliable professional science, a process that continues to this day.

Only one Supreme Court gun case in this book dates back before the "U.S." terminology, and that is 5 Wheaton 1, (abbreviated, as many of the reporters' names are, 5 Wheat. 1). It is the case of *Houston v. Moore*, 1820, that establishes when an individual person leaves private citizenship and becomes a member of the nationalized militia for purposes cited in the Constitution, subject to the President's call.

❸ The Page Number   307 U.S. **174**

Because each Supreme Court case is permanently bound into the official set of books, its starting page number never changes, and this is the third and final element needed to zero in precisely on any given case.

To summarize, the case cited here will be found in volume 307 of *United States Reports* on page 174. What could be simpler.

When writing their opinions, the Supreme Court Justices refer frequently to other cases by using this system, and indicate the precise page they are referring to. So while the citation for this example case (which happens to be *U.S. v. Miller*, 1939) is correct as shown (307 U.S. 174), it would also be valid to cite 307 U.S. 177, to make a point about something that appears on that page, or more commonly (though perhaps less intuitively) 307 U.S. 174, 177. After identifying a case, subsequent consecutive references may simply refer back to a page number by simply saying, "at 177."

Also imbedded within many cases are indicators for the original page breaks, where they fall in the official version. This allows you to make sense of any internal references a case makes to its own pages. The "imbedded page numbers" are contained within brackets, are not part of the language of the decision, take the form, "[307 U.S. 176]" and are placed precisely where the original page breaks occur (making for some occasionally weird looking typesetting). For complex technological reasons, these are not included in *Supreme Court Gun Cases,* though you may see them in online or other printed versions of the cases.

Other Systems

The numbering system described above, used by the government, is the primary one used in this book. To keep things interesting, it turns out there are fully three printed editions of Supreme Court decisions, each with its own numbering system.

It seems that several companies have figured out that with something as important as the Supreme Court, there was room for more than just the government version, and it turns out they were right.

The other editions added their own head notes—summary comments preceding the official decision, prepared by the company instead of the Court's staff (the official summary is known as the *syllabus*). This is not law but is usually easier to read than the decisions and is all that some people review (including many lawyers, and often the news media) when trying to figure out the sometimes voluminous decisions of the Court.

So there are three different sets of head notes, all fascinating, all offering slightly different takes on what the cases are about. With the publication of this edition there is a fourth version, at least on the cases included here. Our system attempts to be the most convenient for use and reference by our audience, but only the official U.S. version counts in matters at law.

Each of the published editions are typeset slightly differently. Sometimes the break of a paragraph or the arrangement of the remarks affects the sense of the words. Sometimes the words themselves are different, though not by much (one version says "Justice Soandso dissents," another says "Justice Soandso dissenting,") and typos are known to occur in all three versions.

In what appears to be the worst typo in this entire set of cases, Justice Story quotes the Second Amendment in a proper context, yet refers to it as the Fifth, in *Houston v. Moore,* 18 U.S. (5 Wheat.) 1 (1820).

Whenever there is a discrepancy, the *United States Reports* version rules. That version is the most spacious, with large type and wide margins, taking four times the number of pages for the same content. For example, *Houston v. Moore* fills 75 pages in U.S., but only 19 pages in S.Ct., the West Co. edition.

Our version attempts to be as compact as reasonable, using slightly less ink on smaller characters, and conveniently saving trees in the process. By editing each case to its essentials for the theme of this book, *Houston v. Moore* is a scant three pages in SCGC. This is a sword that cuts both ways, and if you haven't read the unedited originals, you don't know what you're missing. The very same financial forces that motivate other commercial publishers and which the government seems to more or less ignore, affect Bloomfield Press and its comparatively small scope of operations.

When making citations,
the official government edition is:
United States Reports
307 U.S. 174

The West Co. edition is:
Supreme Court Reporter
59 S.Ct. 816

The Lawyer's Edition is:
United States Supreme Court Reports
83 L.Ed. 1206

The citations above all refer to the same case, *United States v. Miller*, 1939, and in many contexts you will see this cited as simply *Miller*. Sometimes cross-references within a case will include more than one citation to be thorough. Citations appear without warning or controlling punctuation, imbedded in the text right where they apply, in an off-putting, confusing but highly efficient way. Footnote reference numbers are similarly bluntly inserted. Hey, they didn't ask me if I thought it made good sense. Try to think of it as style.

To the novice eye, the text has an imposing impossible look to it. Once you acclimatize however, the eye has a natural ability to scan past the numbers and follow the threads of text. When you get *really* good at it, you take notice of the cite, quickly recollect the essence of the case it refers to, and read on, adding an entire dimension to your understanding of these marvelous writings.

Rumor has it that law students and even attorneys use whatever's available online, and then cite to *U.S. Reports*. The difference between the versions can be pronounced, and though we considered documenting some of the more interesting anomalies we found, we left that task for someone else.

Bloomfield Press refers to its own books by acronyms:

Supreme Court Gun Cases: SCGC

Gun Laws of America: GLOA
(unabridged edition of federal firearms statutes)

The Arizona Gun Owner's Guide: AGOG
(comprehensive guide to state firearms laws)

and when specifying a page:
SCGC-357, GLOA-223, AGOG-38

Another great challenge for newcomers, or the average member of the gun hobby, is all the Latin that gets thrown around in these decisions. As if 100-year-old legalese isn't bad enough, the Justices rely on a language that has been on life-support for centuries for added clarity. The obvious solution, as I began this project, was to build a glossary of terms. When it became obvious I was recreating *Black's Law Dictionary*, I instead got one, and you should too.

With time and care you can spot the Court's bewildering uses of actual English words like defendant, respondent, petitioner, prisoner, plaintiff, plaintiff in error, and victim to mean the same thing. Don't be surprised to learn that some cases cannot be read, they must be studied. In a few, I had to make a cast of characters and draw diagrams to get it straight. Don't worry, be happy. Look at it this way— it keeps life interesting.

The Supreme Court's Thirty-Five *Other* Gun Cases:

What the Supreme Court Has Said About the Second Amendment
(Excerpted from SCGC, 2003, footnotes omitted)

by David B. Kopel

Among legal scholars, it is undisputed that the Supreme Court has said almost nothing about the Second Amendment. This article suggests that the Court has not been so silent as the conventional wisdom suggests.

While the meaning of the Supreme Court's leading Second Amendment case, the 1939 *United States v. Miller* decision remains hotly disputed, the dispute about whether the Second Amendment guarantees an individual right can be pretty well settled by looking at the thirty-five other Supreme Court cases which quote, cite, or discuss the Second Amendment. These cases suggest that the Justices of the Supreme Court do now and usually have regarded the Second Amendment "right of the people to keep and bear arms" as an individual right, rather than as a right of state governments.

Chief Justice Melville Fuller's Supreme Court (1888-1910) had the most cases involving the Second Amendment: eight. So far, the Rehnquist Court is in second place, with six. But Supreme Court opinions dealing with the Second Amendment come from almost every period in the Court's history, and almost all of them assume or are consistent with the proposition that the Second Amendment is an individual right.

Part I of this Article discusses the opinions from the Rehnquist Court. Part II looks at the Burger Court, and Part III at the Warren, Vinson, and Hughes Courts. Part IV groups together the cases from the Taft, Fuller, and Waite Courts, while Part V consolidates the Chase, Taney, and Marshall Courts. (See SCGC for this material.)

[David's exceptional analysis of the Court's cases that name or quote the Second Amendment originally appeared as "The Supreme Court's Thirty-Five Other Second Amendment Cases." 18 St. Louis University Public Law Review 99 (1999).]

SUPREME COURT CASES THAT NAME OR QUOTE
THE SECOND AMENDMENT TO THE U.S. CONSTITUTION

Case name and year.	Main issue in case	Opinion by	Type of opinion	Supportive of individual right in 2d Amendment?	Main clause of 2d A. quoted without introductory clause?
Spencer v. Kemna. 1998	Article III case or controversy.	Stevens	Dissent from denial of cert.	Yes, but could possibly be read as referring to rights under state constitutions	No quote.
Muscarello v. U.S. 1998	Fed stat. interp.	Ginsburg	Dissent	Yes.	Partial quote.
Printz v. U.S. 1997	Federalism	Thomas	Concur	Says that *Miller* did not decide the issue. Thomas appears to support individual right.	Full quote.
Albright v. Oliver. 1994	14th A. and § 1983	Stevens	Dissent	Yes.	Partial quote.
Planned Parenthood v. Casey. 1992.	14th A.	O'Connor	Majority	Yes.	Partial quote.
U.S. v. Verdugo-Urquidez. 1990.	4th A. applied to foreign national.	Rehnquist	Majority	Yes.	Partial quote.
Lewis v. U.S. 1980.	Statutory interp. of Gun Control Act of 1968	Blackmun	Majority	Ambiguous, but probably not. If an individual right, less fundamental than some others.	Full quote.
Moore v. East Cleveland. 1976.	14th A.	Powell	Plurality	Yes. (But contrary opinion expressed by Justice Powell after retirement.)	Partial quote.
" "	" "	White	Dissent.	Yes.	Partial quote.
Adams v. Williams. 1972	4th A.	Douglas	Dissent	No.	Full quote.
Roe v. Wade. 1973	14th A.	Stewart	Concur	Yes.	Partial quote.

Laird v. Tatum. 1972.	Justiciability	Douglas	Dissent	Ambiguous.	Partial quote.
Burton v. Sills. 1969.	Challenge to state gun licensing law	Per curiam	Summary affirm.	Ambiguous.	No quote.
Duncan v. Louisiana. 1968.	Incorporation of 6th Amendment.	Black	Concur	Yes.	Partial quote.
Malloy v. Hogan. 1964.	Incorporation of 5th Amend.	Brennan	Majority	Yes.	No quote.
Konigsberg v. State Bar. 1961.	1st Amendment	Harlan	Majority	Yes.	Partial quote.
Poe v. Ullman. 1961.	14th Amendment	Harlan	Dissent	Yes	Partial quote.
" "	" "	Douglas	Dissent	Yes, but implicitly abandoned in *Adams*.	No quote.
Knapp v. Schweitzer. 1958.	Incorp. of 5th Amendment	Frankfurter	Majority	Yes	Partial quote.
Johnson v. Eisentrager. 1950.	5th A. applied to trial of enemy soldier.	Jackson	Majority	Yes	Partial quote.
Adamson v. Calif. 1947.	Incorp. of 5th Amendment	Black	Dissent	Yes	Partial quote.
Hamilton v. Regents. 1935.	Conscientious objector.	Butler	Majority	No, but not necessarily inconsistent with an individual right.	No quote.
U.S. v. Schwimmer. 1929.	Immigration laws	Butler	Majority	Ambiguous	Full quote.
Stearns v. Wood. 1915.	Article III case or controversy.	McReynolds	Majority	Ambiguous, since court refuses to hear any of plaintiff's claims	No quote.
Twining v. N.J. 1908.	Incorp. of 5th A self-incrim.	Moody	Majority	Yes.	Partial quote
Trono v. U.S. 1905	5th A. in the Philippines.	Peckham	Majority	Yes.	Partial quote.
Kepner v. U.S. 1904.	" "	Day	Majority	Yes. Same as *Trono*.	Partial quote.
Maxwell v. Dow. 1899.	Incorp. of 5th A. jury trial	Peckham	Majority	Yes.	Partial quote.

Robertson v. Baldwin. 1897.	13th Amend.	Brown	Majority	Yes.	Partial quote.
Brown v. Walker. 1896.	5th Amend.	Field.	Dissent	Yes.	Partial quote.
Miller v. Texas. 1894.	14th Amendment	Brown	Majority	Yes.	Partial quote.
Logan v. U.S. 1892.	Cong. Power from 14th A.	Gray	Majority	Yes.	Partial quote.
Presser v. Illinois. 1886.	2d A.	Woods	Majority	Yes.	Full quote.
U.S. v. Cruikshank 1876.	Cong. Power under 14th Amendment	Waite	Majority	Yes. A basic human right which pre-exists the Constitution, and is guaranteed by the Constitution, exactly like the 1st A. right to assembly.	No quote.
Scott v. Sandford. 1857.	Citizenship; Cong. powers over territories.	Taney	Majority	Yes.	Partial quote.
Houston v. Moore. 1820.	State powers over militia.	Story	Dissent	Yes, but also supportive of a state's right. (A later treatise written by Story is for individual right only.)	No quote.

In addition to the oft-debated case of *United States* v. *Miller*, the Supreme Court has mentioned or quoted the Second Amendment in thirty-seven opinions in thirty-five other cases, almost always in *dicta*. One of the opinions, Justice Douglas's dissent in *Adams v. Williams*, explicitly claims that the Second Amendment is not an individual right.

Three majority opinions of the Court (the 1980 *Lewis* case, the 1934 *Hamilton* case, and the 1929 *Schwimmer* case), plus one appeal dismissal (*Burton v. Sills*, 1969), and one dissent (Douglas in *Laird*) are consistent with either the individual rights or the states rights theory, although *Lewis* is better read as not supportive of an individual right, or not supportive of an individual right worthy of any serious protection. (And knowing of Justice Douglas's later dissent in *Adams*, his *Laird* dissent should not be construed as supportive of an individual right.) *Spencer v. Kemna* refers to right to bear arms as an individual right, but the opinion does not specifically mention the Second Amendment, and so the reference could, perhaps, be to the right established by state constitutions.

Two other cases are complicated by off-the-bench statements of the Justices. The 1976 *Moore v. East Cleveland* plurality opinion supports the individual right, but in 1989 the opinion's author, retired Justice Powell, told a television interviewer that there was no right to own a firearm. In an 1820 dissent, Justice Story pointed to the Second Amendment to make a point about state authority over the militia (although this would not necessarily be to the exclusion of an individual right). Justice Story's later scholarly commentaries on the Second Amendment only addressed the individual right, and did not investigate the Amendment as a basis of state authority.

Concurring in *Printz*, Justice Thomas stated that *United States v. Miller* had not resolved the individual rights question; the tone of the concurrence suggested that Justice Thomas considered the Second Amendment to be an important individual right.

Twenty-eight opinions remain, including nineteen majority opinions. Each of these opinions treats the Second Amendment as a right of individual American citizens. Of these twenty-eight opinions, five come from the present Rehnquist Court, and on the Rehnquist Court there has been no disagreement that the Second Amendment is an individual right.

Of course that fact that a right exists does not mean that every proposed gun control would violate that right; indeed, many of the opinions explicitly or implicitly endorse various controls, and, except for Justice Black, none of the authors of the opinions claim that the right is absolute.

In the face of this Supreme Court record, is it accurate for gun control advocates to claim that the non-individual nature of the Second Amendment is "perhaps the most well-settled" point in all of American constitutional law? The extravagant claim cannot survive a reading of what the Supreme Court has actually said about the Second Amendment. In the written opinions of the Justices of the United States Supreme Court, the Second Amendment does appear to be reasonably well-settled—as an individual right. The argument that a particular Supreme Court opinion's language about the Second Amendment does not reflect what the author "really" thought about the Second Amendment cannot be used to ignore all these written opinions— unless we presume that Supreme Court Justices throughout the Republic's history have written things about the Second Amendment that they did not mean.

While the Warren Court and the Burger Court offered mixed records on the Second Amendment, the opinions from the Rehnquist Court (including from the Court's "liberals" Ginsburg and Stevens) are just as clear as were the opinions from the Supreme Court Justices of the nineteenth century: "the right of the people to keep and bear arms" is a right that belongs to individual American citizens. Although the boundaries of the Second Amendment have only partially been addressed by Supreme Court jurisprudence, the core of the Second Amendment is clear: the Second Amendment—like the First, Third, Fourth, Fifth, Sixth, and Fourteenth Amendments—belongs to "the people," not the government.

Setting the Stage

by *Alan Korwin*

No analogy exists for the buildup to The *Heller* Case.

In recent decades, the gun-rights struggle had been fought in lower courts and legislatures. It had been waged as a practical matter daily in gun stores and gun shows and shooting ranges by tens of millions of practitioners.

It had been fought by all sides in barroom rants, activist meetings, rallies, marches, demonstrations, political campaigns, the print and broadcast "news" media, radio talk shows, law journals, pop-culture books, official-sounding pronouncements, Hollywood fantasies, pundit pontifications, classrooms, formal debate and speeches, scholarly texts, websites, blogs, podcasts and eblasts—no venue was spared the often rancorous, emotionally charged enterprise that was the gun-rights debate, except one. The United States Supreme Court.

So much power resides in those nine chairs in that stone chamber that everyone was afraid to take the debate there. One word from the Supremes might end the debate, and throw the entire cast of the pro-rights or anti-rights show out on its ear. It was too great a risk. The consequences too dire. The result too devastating to chance finding out what that result might be. All the "I'm right" "No I'm right" would grind to a halt. Someone would be out of business. Better to let it rest in every inferior forum known, than to finally determine who's right.

A handful of cases were pretenders to that throne of decision. In the 1990s a few raised their heads, but the powers that be on both sides of the rights divide decided not to chance it. Prior to that time, the clamor against long-cherished gun rights was too low to force the matter up that high, and the rights themselves too robust and widely acknowledged to merit such ultimate review (although admittedly, infringements were mounting). The sleeping dog slept, while half of America bought ammo at dirt-cheap prices and went to the range on Father's Day. And every other day.

The anti-gun mood among some segments of the public, including the media in the late 1960s, was very intense. Anti-rights forces did manage to shut down gun carrying in a lot of the country, and they got the 1968 Gun Control Act passed. The Supreme Court response was basically to step aside while lower courts incrementally ate away at the Second Amendment. To some extent the High Court sent a signal that this was OK with its summary affirmance in *Burton v. Sills,* a lower-court decision that had upheld New Jersey's gun-licensing law.

Often, the cases that pleaded for hearings involved the lowest dregs of society, bottom-dwelling violent criminals desperately seeking a way out of some gun-related crime or other. Out of options, they would hope the Second Amendment might somehow protect otherwise heinous acts, and immunize them from richly deserved punishment.

Many of the Court's 96 gun-related cases do revolve around the disposition of hardened repeat-offender criminals. The pro-rights side bristles at the thought. The *Heller* case was, among other things, an effort to examine gun-rights in the context of decent people seeking their civil liberties. In that respect, it was a refreshing change.

The High Court itself did take a few cases where it conceivably could have addressed the core issues, but even the Justices chose to let that dog lie. *Silveira* looked possible for a while (largely to people who believed fundraising efforts from lawyers promoting the case), and *Emerson* was right on point. But *cert* was denied again and again. People perpetually debated how the then-current Justices would handle a case, as if we were a nation of lawyers, not laws (which, few like to admit, we are). The four-out-of-nine Justices needed to agree to take a case could not be found by either side.

Despite discord in the lower courts, which show a decided hostility toward Second Amendment rights, and confusion and inconsistency in many decisions, the High Court's extant pronouncements in firearm-related cases can only be consistently read as recognizing an individual right to arms. The early cases, for the first 150 years, blithely presume that of course individual American citizens keep and bear arms, and can use them judiciously, and wrestled instead with the use of those arms, and interpretation of laws that regulated such affairs, for perfectly acceptable limits—like disarming criminals when they're arrested. Here an analogy works well.

It is true, as the "news" media is fond of blaring, the Supreme Court never said you have an individual right to keep and bear arms—but context is sorely missing. Similarly, in a much greater body of work, the Court has never said you have the right to own a pen. They have never said that. They never had to. It has simply always been presumed. There was never any reason to make such a blatantly self-evident statement. It would have been, well, silly. Of course you have the right to a pen. The question has always been: did you use your pen in a just and legal manner.

Did you commit libel or fraud with your pen, limits on free speech that have been recognized as legitimate since Colonial days. Did you commit plagiarism, a limit on your pen recognized in the Constitution itself, or treason, which could incur the death penalty for circulating written words. "Congress shall make no law...," and free speech in general, are very well litigated, but pens have not been declared legal. Just like guns, gun ownership, possession and use, it's like the right to breathe, the Court has had no need to address such simplicities.

The right to keep and bear arms is only an issue because, in recent decades, an outcry from anti-rights activists, hoplophobes, and some legislatures have called the "question" of your rights under the Second Amendment into question. Against a historical background where anyone could buy any sort of firearm with no government controls whatsoever, to a modern day where federal oversight of the whole business has become intrusive in most aspects, that this question of "Do you have any rights at all under this part of the Bill of Rights" became an issue. The Court addressed this very point in the *Heller* decision (citations omitted):

> It should be unsurprising that such a significant matter has been for so long judicially unresolved. For most of our history, the Bill of Rights was not thought applicable to the States, and the Federal Government did not significantly regulate the possession of firearms by law-abiding citizens. Other provisions of the Bill of Rights have similarly remained unilluminated for lengthy periods.

> This Court first held a law to violate the First Amendment's guarantee of freedom of speech in 1931, almost 150 years after the Amendment was ratified (*Near v. Minnesota ex rel. Olson*), and it was not until after World War II that we held a law invalid under the Establishment Clause (*Illinois ex rel. McCollum v. Board of Ed.*). Even a question as basic as the scope of proscribable libel was not addressed by this Court until 1964, nearly two centuries after the founding (*New York Times Co. v. Sullivan*)...

> It is demonstrably not true that, as Justice Stevens claims, "for most of our history, the invalidity of Second-Amendment-based objections to firearms regulations has been well settled and uncontroversial." For most of our history the question did not present itself.

Supreme Court Gun Cases, written after six years of research with two of the top Second Amendment attorneys in the country, conclusively showed that the Supreme Court has recognized an individual right to arms consistently for two hundred years. Can you use the shotgun you travel with, for defense when you get back home (1895)? Of course. Can a kangaroo trial in Japan remove your right to arms (2005)? Of course not. Can the government disarm a felon? Well, of course it can.

The 95 prior gun cases reach that type of conclusion—without ever specifically saying "you have the right" in the first place. It's that flat-out statement—and the accumulating hoplophobic detritus to the contrary—that *Heller* finally addresses. If the antis had not created such well publicized fabrications since the 1960s, the so-called "question" might still not have been addressed. And gun ownership, possession and use would simply continue as it had since before the country's Founding.

Stephen Halbrook addresses the point in his latest book, *The Founders' Second Amendment* (2008), after scrupulously analyzing the 27-word Amendment:

> This exhaustive textual analysis of the Second Amendment would never have been necessary for most of the first two hundred years of the republic. It was only beginning in the second half of the twentieth century that the Orwellian view gained currency that "the people" means the states or state-conscripted militia, that "right" means governmental power, that "keep" does not mean to possess, that "bear" does not mean carry, that "arms" do not include ordinary handguns and rifles, and that "infringe" does not include prohibition.

> But the Founders intended to, and did, word the Second Amendment in an easy to understand manner. Individuals have a right to have arms in their houses and to carry them, and the government may not violate that right. Recognition of the right promotes a militia composed of the body of the people, which is necessary for a free society.

One *amicus* brief for D.C., seeking to preserve the city's gun ban, suggested the High Court should look to legislative acts of Congress for guidance on what a proper course should be. They had in mind all the gun laws the federal legislature has seen fit to pass, viewing that as justification for broad, nearly unrestrained dominion over this right of the people to keep arms and to bear arms.

What they overlooked is that Congress has in fact *directly* addressed the nature and applicability of the Amendment. Again, thanks to Halbrook's work, we know this has occurred five times, and in each case Congress has specifically recognized 2A as an individual right:

> The Freedman's Bureau Act of 1866
> The Property Requisition Act of 1941
> The Firearm Owner's Protection Act of 1986
> The Protection of Lawful Commerce in Arms Act of 2005
> Disaster Recovery Personal Protection Act of 2006

In that sense, *Heller* cannot establish the right to keep and bear. That right is firmly established, with two centuries of backup. Think about it—you don't have to enlist to walk into a gun store, right? The long list of "reasons" used by the antis suffer from similarly gaping logical holes. All the Court could do, really, is reverse all our extremely well-established precedent.

The anti-rights activists and their sympathizers in the "news" media have been enormously successful in promoting, in recent decades, this idea that one right in the Bill of Rights doesn't protect people's rights, suggesting instead it protects government, or separate states, or people as a collective something or other. I know, it sounds absurd, and it is.

But after banging away long enough and finding cool ways to demean and denigrate the cherished American right to keep and bear arms, the newly created ideas began to hold sway. These inventions began to erode what was previously a deeply held, completely unregulated, *fundamental* right represented by, for example, twelve pages of guns in the Sears Roebuck mail-order catalog, and staple products available in hardware stores across America.

This Is The 96th Gun Case, Not The First

Please understand that I do not accept the almost universally promoted characterization of *Heller* as the first 2A case in 70 years, or that it is the only case to directly address the central issue of individual rights. I am in a small minority perhaps, but those widely circulated sentiments don't meet my tests for validity. The most important case? Perhaps. The only one? No.

In *dicta* and holdings, there is no body of cases that are inconsistent with the idea that 2A is a long extant right of people—the same people found in 1A, 4A, 9A and 10A. Of the 92 decisions in our original *Supreme Court Guns Cases*, 89 flatly support the American right to arms, even if they focus on rightly imprisoning felons for crimes. The remaining three can be timorously clung to by those hoping to eradicate a human right, but the support is fragile (*Schwimmer* in 1929, *Lewis* in 1980, and *Dickerson* in 1984).

The right to arms has been regulated and tweaked, especially for felons, too often for the public, and perhaps unfairly at times, but it is always an adjustment to a recognized right whose boundaries are and may always be in judicial flux. This must be what people mean when they say, "The fight for freedom never ends."

Two of the most recent cases illustrate this flux—and what a wonderful pair of cases they are. In one (*Bean*, 2002), a man loses his RKBA, which he depended on for his livelihood as a gun-show vendor. He had crossed the Texas border into Mexico for dinner with friends after a gun show, and a forgotten box of shells in his vehicle got him a Mexican felony arrest. Through a loophole, the High Court upheld the ban on his rights as a convicted felon, and he needed to change careers, never to handle firearms again. Poor Mr. Bean.

In a similar case with a different outcome (*Small*, 2005), a man lost his RKBA due to what we would call a kangaroo-court decision in Japan.

Here, the High Court decided this was *not* sufficient to remove his private and individual right to keep and bear arms, with no mention or concern whatsoever for a nexus to militia or military service or any of the other anti-rights excreta. Lucky Mr. Small.

The Bean case was not technically a 2A case—it was a question of jurisdiction. The federal agency for reinstating an individual's rights didn't rule against him, they just refused to review his case at all, for a lack of funding (which Congress has refused to renew since 1992). So the poor schlub with his rights denied had no standing to sue to regain his rights, and he was plumb out of luck.

The second case was a statutory language question of whether "any court" included foreign courts. The Supreme Court decided that, no, a felony conviction was insufficient when it came to a Japanese court in that specific case. You should see the injustice this man was subjected to—including 23 days of interrogation without a lawyer present.

Here were two men who had this right "the Supreme Court has never ruled upon," then lost this right "the Supreme Court has never ruled upon," and sued to regain this right "the Supreme Court has never ruled upon," and one got it back—and one did not.

It's easy to see these cases do not rule on the meaning of the Second Amendment, so the naysayers are correct, especially if you want to twist words and meanings. But these cases simply take the Second Amendment in stride, and presume it's there, real, and deal with it. Of course you have this right going in, but do you get to keep it under the given circumstances? Virtually all the cases match this model in effect. I can hear some of my lawyer friends objecting already. Let them.

In 1990, the Supreme Court said:

> "the people" protected by the Second Amendment are the same "people"—individual human beings—protected by other portions of the Bill of Rights: "[T]he people" protected by the Fourth Amendment, and by the First and Second Amendments, and to whom rights and powers are reserved in the Ninth and Tenth Amendments, refers to a class of persons who are part of a national community or who have otherwise developed sufficient connection with this country to be considered part of that community. (*United States v. Verdugo-Urquidez*, 494 U.S. 259)

How do you square that with "no pronouncements in 70 years"? Some lawyers actually can, and with very little guilt or doubt. Quoting from a 1961 case, the Court in 1992 explained the "liberty" protected by the Fourteenth Amendment:

> This 'liberty' is not a series of isolated points pricked out in terms of the taking of property; the freedom of speech, press, and religion; the right to keep and bear arms; the freedom from unreasonable searches and seizures; and so on. It is a rational continuum which, broadly speaking,

includes a freedom from all substantial arbitrary impositions and purposeless restraints... *Planned Parenthood v. Casey*, 1992

A dozen nearly forgotten self-defense cases dating from the 1890s (and one more in 1921) expressly recognized people's right to use personally owned firearms in defense of self, family and property. For example:

• Going home to get your handgun for protection after being threatened was a reasonable act under the given circumstances. (*Gourko*, 1894)

• Using your deer rifle for protection after you were threatened was a reasonable act under the given circumstances. (*Allison*, 1895)

• Using the shotgun you travel with for protection, to defend yourself and prevent theft of your cow on returning home is permissible. (*Beard*, 1895)

• Defending yourself against a criminal attack, in a place where you had a right to be, matching force with force, was perfectly legal under the given circumstances. (*Brown*, 1921)

• Standing your ground against a criminal attack is justifiable, and although you can run if you are able or prefer to, there is normally no duty to retreat under American law. (*Alberty*, 1896)

• Being held under arrest, where you are deprived of 'all means of self defense' carries with it a right to be protected from harm and a matching duty to ensure your safety by those maintaining custody, and these rights are natural, inalienable and predate the Constitution. (*Logan*, 1892)

The statement that *Heller* is the first case bearing on the Second Amendment in 70 years is *false*. The idea that the High Court has been inconsistent on this issue is *false*.

And most of all, the idea that the High Court has been silent on the issue is false, and terribly ignorant, as its 95 prior gun cases show.

The High Court used the word *firearm* in some form more than 2,900 times in its first 92 gun-related decisions, and the decisions are consistent with an individual right to arms. As much as the anti-rights forces would like gun rights to go away, guns are why America is still free, and will remain free while its citizens retain power.

Heller is the 96th gun case to reach the Supreme Court. Like the examples above, only some are directly 2A cases, the rest deal with RKBA from other vantage points—taxes, regulations, statutory interpretation, states' rights and more. Co-author Dave Kopel found 35 cases that name or quote the Second Amendment. I counted 92 gun-related cases at the High Court (including his 35) through 2003, and hence *Supreme Court Gun Cases*. *Heller* is the 64th case since *Miller*.

Enter, stage left. D.C. was the anti-rights dream town. You could only have a firearm if it was disassembled or locked up. It could not be loaded regardless of circumstance, even if you were under attack. This simple approach to regulating an individual person's gun rights would be called a perfectly reasonable, common sense, legally permissible approach in 19 Friend-of-the-Court briefs, filed by politicians and some police officials, lawyers, doctors, activists and others. To find out who's against the right of the people to keep and bear arms, just look at who wrote those briefs.

When the High Court announced it would take the case, Sen. Barack Obama's presidential campaign said, in the *Chicago Tribune* (Nov. 20, 2007) that the candidate believed in "the rights of law-abiding gun owners," and in the same breath that, "Obama believes the D.C. handgun law is constitutional." There could hardly be a more hypocritical anti-rights statement—*gun rights* means *no guns allowed.*

If nothing else, the cat was out of the bag—a total ban on the right to keep and bear arms was the goal on the anti-rights side. Years of hiding behind slippery or just flatly deceptive statements about "reasonable" gun laws were washed away forever. Nothing less than a total ban was what was reasonable. You could not even move an unloaded and locked or disassembled gun from room to room in your own home without a permit—and they, uh, didn't issue permits.

Thugs, gangs and the assortment of criminals on the streets were largely unaffected by the D.C. gun bans, and they roamed free, illegally armed (which of course was illegal before the city's special infringements). With innocent people disarmed by law, the "ban" subsequently turned the nation's capital into the murder capital of the nation.

That's not completely correct. The bad actors turned not the city but the "bad parts of town" into a theater for murder. The murder centers were brightly defined geographically, demographically, and largely related to the government's war on some drugs—making these war deaths, not mere random acts of violence as portrayed in the media.

This is a point generally omitted in the gun debate. So-called "gun deaths" aren't random or homogenously disbursed in the population. They typically have social, economic, geographic and demographic components and hopelessly lack diversity. This ugly underbelly of the problem, and government's complicity in it through its long running war on some drugs, is not discussed in polite company. Do not look at a dot map of where the war deaths occur, or uncomfortable truths will appear.

The District, in its filings, portrayed the 1976 gun ban as a resounding public-policy success, as well as repeatedly and falsely calling its all-guns ban simply a handgun ban (a piece of spoiled meat swallowed without chewing by the media). It's not clear what sort of Kool-Aid they were drinking when they drafted those papers. Like so much else in the decades of anti-rights arguments, pure fabrication was a key component.

This is seen in many myths offered by the anti-rights community. For example, if the D.C. law falls, they claimed, all gun laws in the nation will be lost, which is utterly absurd. Pure scare tactics without a shred of truth is admissible evidence on that side of the debate.

The Violence Policy Center actually said in its brief that, if you are confronted with a criminal threat, a handgun makes it more likely that you'll kill yourself, a family member or an innocent bystander. And the notion that an individual right to arms means a citizen can own F-16 jets or nuclear weapons is beyond preposterous—but tenaciously clung to by individuals with an irrational fear of firearms acting irrationally.

An individual right to arms gives you no more right to own a battle cruiser than religious freedom gives you a right to conduct human sacrifice. The fact that you don't have to enlist before buying a rifle at WalMart doesn't stop the collectivist arguments concocted from thin air about militias. The idea that the Second Amendment is meant only to protect the National Guard is ridiculous on its face, since the Guard was only founded in the early 1900s. A ludicrous argument does not deter the prohibitionists, it just make them look ludicrous.

Enter, stage center. Shelly Parker, a software designer and former emergency-room nurse living in D.C., organized her neighbors to combat rampant drug crime near her home. The city government had failed miserably in providing any controls. Drug dealers didn't take kindly to this and one, a seven-foot-two-inch dealer pounded on Ms. Parker's door at night and tried to pry it open. "Bitch, I'll kill you, I live on this block, too," he bellowed.

The police didn't come to her aid. She drove him off by setting off an alarm, but that was obviously too close a call and an inadequate plan for the future. One police officer later told her to "get a gun," but the only way to even have a handgun in D.C. was to have obtained it prior to 1976 when the infringement law was passed. And that didn't matter anyway, because any gun had to be unloaded. While unloaded, it had to be locked up or in pieces. The anti-rights dream was firmly in place—guns are OK as long as they don't work.

Enter Bob Levy. This well-to-do scholar, author and attorney, a senior fellow with the Cato Institute think tank, decided it was time to bring it. The impetus for the case came from his co-counsel, Clark Neily, a senior attorney at the Institute for Justice. Neily was the first to suggest bringing a suit, and together they selected Alan Gura as lead attorney.

The Court's makeup seemed fair. The issue had been coming to a head. Levy coordinated and funded an effort to find the right plaintiffs, suitable attorneys and an eminently proper case upon which to examine, and perhaps settle once and for all, the pro-rights and anti-rights battle over the Second Amendment.

Despite school-taught principles that the Supreme Court is a court of laws and not men, men who know, know better. The Court is and has always been a function of who sits on the Bench. Despite any idealistic desire to believe anything else—the people on a court determine its direction. While this case was fermenting, everyone concerned was busy counting votes and conjecturing about the members' prejudices.

Levy chose the District of Columbia, the nation's capital, as the battleground. It had enacted the country's most encompassing infringements on the right to keep and bear arms. It is not a state, so certain precedential complications were absent. This wasn't a narrow question about some forbidden gun type or other, or a shopping limitation, or permits for carrying while out and about town. In D.C., a citizen could not have an operable firearm at home, under any circumstances, even while being assaulted by hoods breaking in. Seems impossible in America. It was routine in D.C.

Levy financed the entire case out of his own pocket, hired Gura to lead the charge and served as co-counsel. Cato has been sometimes incorrectly identified as the sponsor behind the case, but it's just coincident that that fine organization is among Levy's long list of credentials. The Institute generally agreed with what Levy was doing, but was not a party to the case.

Levy reasoned that the time could not be better for a long-overdue challenge to some gun ban somewhere, on purely Second Amendment grounds. With four strongly principled conservatives seated, and tolerance among the others for civil rights at some level, a very narrow explicit exploration of what the Second Amendment was originally intended to mean had the best chance it has had in, well, a really long time. The scholarship on that meaning is about as clear as a thing can get, while the balderdash invented to denounce the protected rights grew louder daily.

With his hand-picked team, Levy and company convinced Parker to join in a lawsuit with other victims of the D.C. disarmament law, to challenge the legitimacy of the ordinance. They chose six plaintiffs in all, including Dick Heller, Tom Palmer, Gillian St. Lawrence, Tracey

Ambeau, and George Lyon. Normal D.C. residents, they all sought to keep guns in their homes for defense against criminals.

The case was originally filed in the U.S. District Court for the District of Columbia as *Shelly Parker et. al. v. District of Columbia*. Parker, the female activist, had already been threatened with death. Palmer, a gay man, had defended himself with a gun in another state but could not do so in D.C. St. Lawrence wanted to keep a shotgun at home for safety but couldn't. Ambeau similarly was prevented from keeping a gun in her apartment for personal protection. Lyon couldn't bring guns he already owned to his home in the District.

Dick Heller, a private licensed security guard, called a "special police officer" under D.C. law, was empowered to carry a firearm at work, and did so, as a guard to federal employees at the time the case was brought. But when he filed for a permit to keep his firearm at home, the city turned him down.

District Court judge Emmet G. Sullivan granted the city's motion to dismiss the case, on the grounds that the Second Amendment, if anything, only granted a person's right to bear arms to serve in the militia. The six, Sullivan said in February, 2004, had no constitutional right to challenge D.C.'s ban. This was not unexpected at the lower court level, and they appealed.

The U.S. Court of Appeals for the District of Columbia Circuit, in accepting the appeal, examined the *standing*, the legal grounds of the plaintiffs, to bring the case, and found five of them lacking. Although D.C. had threatened them all with prosecution, it had only taken action against Mr. Heller by denying his application for a permit. The case moved forward with Heller as the sole plaintiff. The other five were unsuccessful in their subsequent effort to rejoin the case or pursue their cause independently.

It was in March of 2007 that Appeals Court Judge Laurence Silberman found in favor of Heller, and struck down D.C.'s gun ban on Second Amendment grounds. In that historic, 58-page, two-to-one decision, he wrote:

> The Bill of Rights was almost entirely a declaration of individual rights, and the Second Amendment's inclusion there strongly indicates that it, too, was intended to protect personal liberty.

He went on to say, amidst a wonderful mountain of research and citations, "the phrase 'the right of the people'... leads us to conclude that the right in question is individual."

This left a difficult split at the Appeals Court level nationally, on what the Second Amendment meant, and was the final weight needed to lift the curtain.

Mayor Adrian Fenty became party to the case when he replaced the previous mayor, Anthony A. Williams, automatically attaching his name to this landmark case. His government, in requesting a stay of the Circuit's elimination of their cherished gun ban (while they developed their appeal), was sternly warned that asking for such a stay, if they did not actually file an appeal, would be taken as a bad-faith abuse. Such a warning was almost unheard of—but any agency that could so blithely and totally deny a civil right for so long might just need such a slap upside the head.

The Supreme Court granted *certiorari*, review of the Appeals case, in November 2007, and along with several hundred others, Dave Kopel and I observed oral arguments first hand on March 18, 2008, he from the Respondent's table, and me from the second row. We then sat, along with the rest of the world, awaiting the decision announcement, which we imagine and hope will be precisely on point:

Does the Second Amendment to the U.S. Constitution guarantee a right to keep and bear arms to individual people?

Do the people have to be part of a collective or state or any other militia to exercise this right?

Is the District of Columbia's ban on possession of any operable firearm at home unconstitutional and thus invalid?

What standard of review do gun laws have to pass in order to be constitutionally valid?

Can Dick Heller—or anyone—exercise the right to keep and bear arms in Washington, D.C.?

The decision was issued on June 26, 2008.

DATELINE: Washington, D.C., Mon., March 17, 2008
24 Hours Prior to Oral Arguments in *D.C. v. Heller*.

More people are on line in front of the U.S. Supreme Court for the D.C.-gun-ban case tomorrow than there are seats available, and the temperature is hovering above freezing, but that's not stopping them.

Bob Blackmer and I were the first to arrive, on Sunday night March 16th at about 5 p.m., answering the big questions: Would two nights in advance be enough lead time to guarantee a seat? And did we have the endurance to pull that off?

A few moments later, twenty-somethings Jason McCrory and Dan Mott arrived from Pennsylvania with sleeping bags and the same question in mind—would they be in time for the biggest Second Amendment case in the nation's history, and yes, they were.

With no one else around, and the lone Supreme Court police officer pumped for all the info he might have (precious little, including some pompous nonsense about how the D.C. ban goes back to Colonial days), Bob (who turned away to hide his laughter) and I left for our hotel, confident that we would be in time sometime after the crack of dawn.

Before boarding our train, we decided to make the one-mile round-trip walk in the windy freezing cold to Union Station, to bring the two intrepid line sitters some hot food, coffee, and a relief bottle. All we asked in return of our soon-to-be friends was a cell phone call if a long line began forming in the dead of night, while we were comfortably ensconced in out hotel. No call was made.

Jason and Dan became numbers one and two in line, a distinction the media would dwell on the next day. Reporters kept zeroing in on Jason since he was number one, and fortunately, he was articulate, a poli-sci grad and not the bubba the media so often isolates as a "typical" example.

Because the line formed two nights in advance (kind of), and because local ABC-TV carried that news (with images) and bloggers spread it, people did begin arriving first at midnight, and then at the crack of dawn, panicked about gaining access. Bob awoke and left the hotel in time to arrive well before 8 a.m., making him lucky number seven, while I made calls and ran around looking for propane for his porta-heater (the airline had allowed the heater but not the fuel).

I was very fortunate to have secured a reserved seat in advance, as a guest of the Marshal of the Court, so it didn't matter that I arrived at 10 a.m., and that didn't matter either, since I was now #16. I was the only person, the whole day, schmoozing on the line, running errands for people, enjoying the atmosphere, chatting a blue streak, but with a reserved seat and a bed waiting for me at night. My feet throbbed from standing almost the entire time.

People had full-blown lounge chairs, sleeping bags, blankets, food... a regular shanty town developed and as police had advised, the line self-regulated. Physical position was a non-issue, since everyone knew their place, and Sarah, a Harvard law student, took it on herself to start a list and gather everyone's arrival time and position number. People milled around at will, confident they would not lose their cherished place in line. It was a community. Woodstock in Washington.

Almost everyone was a law student, almost no one would qualify as a "gunnie" (well, maybe a small handful) but nearly everyone was on the side of Heller, advocating for a strong Second Amendment and defense of the Bill of Rights. This surprised everyone, the lack of antis on line. The conversations were electric, a bunch of well educated, thoughtful, intelligent people self-selected for a historic moment. When was the last time you saw a long line of people hanging out reading legal briefs?

The promise was for 50 seats for the public, but the Marshal's office made it clear to me that this number could change, and would only be known in the morning, giving a distinct feeling it would shrink as "dignitaries" decided to attend at the last minute. Rumors found fertile ground, and baseless tales ran rampant of more and less available seats until the very end—when the full 50 got official hand-numbered slips and got in. There were 240 people (according to "news" reports) who, lacking seats, found themselves in the three-minute-visit line. I still don't know how they rotated them in and out of the Court chamber without causing a ruckus—I heard nothing.

By 2:30 p.m. Monday, today, the day before the case, 32 people were in line, neatly numbered thanks to Sarah (and everyone in line ahead of them). The lucky (maybe) 50th person arrived at 4:45 p.m., and folks continued to arrive and queue up, hoping against hope for a greater number of seats, or line abandoners. No paid place holders were apparent, though I heard later there was one.

The most novel legal theories were:

• The case could be decided on standing, with the Court concluding Heller didn't really have any after all, and the case falling apart on those grounds (highly unlikely, but it shook up conversations);

• The Court would parse "keep" and "bear," finding an individual right, but applying strict scrutiny to "keep" and rational-basis standard of review for "bear," effectively gutting the Second Amendment;

• A decision narrower than everyone expects would get a surprising nine to zero affirmation of an individual right (a seven-to-two split got a lot of voice);

• The Solicitor General would recant his position (calling for reduced scrutiny and a remand of the case), artfully saying that position was a mistake or oversight, an extremely unlikely but appealing (to some) possibility that would get Clement out of supposed hot water and be talked about, well, forever;

• No one expects anything but an individual-right finding, but the level of scrutiny for any law anywhere was up for grabs;

• Obviously, no one has a clue, but you get an idea of what was going on in the cold, windy, sleep-deprived, hard-scrabble concrete world of Hellertown in front of the Court.

In their enthusiasm, no one mentioned the shocks delivered in the *Kelo* decision, or the McCain-Feingold political-speech-suppression case, both of which so offend constitutional principles that jaws hung slack all across America when they were issued—and still do.

As for me, I'm sunburned, exhausted, undernourished, but at least in a hotel lobby, working on an older machine that times out every 20 minutes, getting ready for what sleep I can get and an early start to what will be an amazing day tomorrow. I'll relieve Bob so he can use the Court restroom to shuck his thermals, freshen up, stash his goods in the Court lockers, grab some chow in the Court cafeteria (great food, low low subsidized prices), and join the rabble in the cheap seats upstairs.

Written without adequate review or a spell checker (but subsequently spiel-checked and fine tuned), I reserve the right to change any of this... I will attempt a swift review of the orals tomorrow as soon afterwards as I can muster tomorrow.

DATELINE: Washington, D.C., Tue., March 18, 2008
Recovering from the whirlwind of the day
Heller case goes better than expected

The bottom line is, I think we're going to be OK.

When Justice Kennedy flat out said he believes in an individual right under the Second Amendment, there were no gasps in the hush of the High Court, but you could tell that the greatest stellar array of gun-rights experts ever assembled, all there in that one room, breathed a sigh of relief—we had five votes to affirm the human and civil right to arms, and to defend the Bill of Rights from attack.

The transcript will be a key for analysis going forward until June, when the decision is expected, and I'm working without the benefit of that at the moment. Digesting the fleeting and immensely complex speech that took place for one hour and thirty-eight minutes a few hours ago, it's hard to see how any line of thought could be strung together to support the idea that the D.C. total ban on operable firearms at home can be seen as reasonable regulation, even though Walter Dellinger, the city's attorney, tried to suggest it was. He was shot down on this repeatedly, found little quarter from any of the Justices, though several found room to move on what amounts to reasonable restrictions.

And it is easy to see, from the non-stop rapid-fire comments and questions of eight of the Justices (Thomas asked nothing, extending his legendary running silence), how even the most permissive standard of review imaginable for gun-ban laws, could not tolerate the District's level of intolerance toward some sort of right to keep and bear arms.

That would give the pro-rights side what it so sorely wants—an open admission that the Second Amendment protects at least something for "the people" it mentions, and the rest of that pie can be baked later.

Dellinger tried to suggest that rifles, shotguns and handguns had different usefulness, actually implying rifles are better for self defense in an urban home.

But that plays very naturally into the thinking of the handgun-ban movement, a subset of the gun-ban movement and anti-self-defense movement, which lives in mortal paranoia of normal sidearms. Dellinger argued that because handguns were so inherently bad or dangerous or something, that cities had a legitimate interest in banning them, and the Constitution doesn't stand in their way.

The Court was buying none of it, and firmly noted that D.C.'s ban banned everything, not just sidearms. Historically, sidearms have been used for personal self defense since they were invented, and are responsible to this day for saving countless lives.

Packed into that short, extremely intense session, the Court examined:

• Original intent, and actions and writings of the States at the time of adoption of the Bill of Rights;

• The meanings of the words, though not to the extent some people had anticipated;

• Separability of the terms *keep* and *bear*, whether they represented one right or two, how one could exist without the other, if they had civilian meanings or military ones, if you can "bear" arms to go hunting and more;

• The scope of the right covered, and whether personal or military protections stood alone, were dependent or had preference over each other;

• The "operative" and preamble clauses, and their relationship, meaningfulness, and interaction with each other;

• The types of weapons that might be covered by the term *arms*. The Justices seemed to accept the idea that some weapons fall outside a sense of militia arms, like "plastic guns" (that's what they called them) that could escape airport metal detection, or "rocket launchers" (actually a commonly used modern militia arm in some countries experiencing insurgencies, a point that did not come up when rocket launchers were mentioned). Machine guns were repeatedly mentioned and were a subject left unresolved, especially since, as the Court noted, these have become standard issue for our modern armed forces, and have confused the *Miller* doctrine of commonly used arms;

• The rise and meaning of *strict scrutiny*, a doctrine that evolved around the First Amendment and had no explicit root in the Constitution, and whose actual definition was fluid and with little consensus. Chief Justice Roberts questioned why the Court needed to reach the question of future scrutiny at all, against a backdrop of the Solicitor General seeking a low level of review, and various players and briefs wrestling at length with how strictly a gun law must be examined for its constitutionality.

Scalia asked if permissible limits could restrict you to one gun, or only a few guns, or if a collector couldn't complete a set like a stamp collector because of a quantity restriction. He then launched into a demonstration of his familiarity with firearms by suggesting a need to have a turkey gun, and a duck gun, and a thirty-ought-six, and a .270, which sent Thomas into a fit of off-mic laughter that most observers missed because they were focused on Scalia, and the world missed because the Court has no cameras. No one outside saw Breyer holding his head with both hands, at an impossible angle.

Noting that Massachusetts in colonial times regulated the storage of gunpowder (it had to be kept upstairs as a fire precaution), Breyer asked if there isn't a lineage to permissible restrictions, and the Court generally agreed. The point of contention, and it would not go away, was where that line was drawn, and again and again the D.C. absolute ban was found violative in its absoluteness. The decision to test the protection of 2A against this law in particular was a brilliant stratagem, thank you Mr. Levy.

Mr. Dellinger either deliberately misled the Court, or didn't understand the D.C. gun-ban law, as hard to believe as that is, and it could come back to bite him. In trying to make it appear less odious than it was, he tripped himself up more than once. I'll cover that later.

OK, I recognize that this is a bit disjointed, and I'm working on an unfamiliar machine, in a hotel lobby, at the end of a grueling endurance test that involved outrageous hours, little sleep, lousy diet, dire cold, miles of up and downhill walking, and I'm getting pretty hungry. I'll do a better job over time, but I wanted to share some inside scoop you might not otherwise get. Let me, before pausing for some chow (which we'll have to go out and find), convey some ambience.

Guests of the Court were ushered into the ground floor early on, milling around (line waiters including my friend Bob were prepped for more than an hour on the white marble steps outside). It was a who's who inside and non-stop on-your-toes meet and greet. Long-time friend John Snyder, lobbyist for the Citizens Committee for the Right to Keep and Bear Arms, had read my blog entry from last night, said nice things about it that made my day, and introduced me to his nondescript companion on the marble lobby bench... Dick Heller, of the *Heller* case. A smile peeled across my face.

A nice mild-mannered guy, he told me, "I just want to be able to keep my guns."

He said when they started this so long ago they had no idea what they were getting into, and eventually they began entertaining the idea that it could go all the way and started raising funds. Now it had taken on a life of its own and barely involved him. That remark was quite telling and has stayed with me. At 9:30 last night, he walked the wait-to-get-in line and passed out cough drops. No one knew who he was. He sat just behind me in the Courtroom. I lucked into the second row.

Stash your stuff in the lockers quickly when your handlers say "go" and get back out right away, it will improve your seat. You need quarters to operate the lockers, and you can use more than one (Bob and I both needed two).

Seated directly in front of me was... mayor Fenty, and I sat in the bright reflected light of his pate. He turned, and in typical smiling politician fashion extended his hand, shook mine, and said warmly, "It's nice to see you," as if we knew each other. Well at least, I knew him. One seat to my right was Ann Dellinger, the city's lawyer's wife, who turned out to be fascinating and a wealth of information. In a few moments, the mayor relinquished his seat to D.C. chief of police Cathy Lanier, but she didn't turn and say hi. Heady stuff. Everybody was a somebody.

Familiar faces were strewn about—there's David Hardy on the other side of the aisle, and Bob Dowlut had a front row seat. Stephen Halbrook, one of my co-authors on *Supreme Court Gun Cases* had an early spot on the Supreme Court bar-members line, which was let in early. My other co-author, Dave Kopel, who previously told me he would not be attending, turned out to be a last-minute addition to the Respondent's table at the head of the Courtroom. He came hustling by with Clark Neily, and I managed a quick snapshot. Cameras were only banned in the Courtroom, not in the waiting areas, so I snapped away, see the photo gallery at gunlaws.com. People who I think were on a better "tier" than I, like Joe Olson, Clayton Cramer and others, didn't luck into a seat and listened to disembodied voices in the lawyers lounge outside the Courtroom.

Three calls for "sshhh" from a clerk at the front instantly dropped the growing anticipatory cacophony to silence which then ramped up gently until the next hiss for quiet. Three minutes to go and a call for silence left everyone sitting calmly with their own thoughts until a tone sounded... the aides signaled us to rise... a great rustle of risers arose...

"The Honorable the Chief Justice and the Associate Justices of the Supreme Court of the United States; Oyez! Oyez! Oyez! All persons having business before the Honorable the Supreme Court of the United States are admonished to draw near and give their attention, for the Court is now sitting. God save the United States and this Honorable Court." The Nine appeared from behind the curtain (there was no "ahhs"), we were waved to sit... obediently did... gave our attention, and we were underway.

By a stroke of luck, Justice Thomas was assigned the reading of a decision of a prior case, and we got to hear his flawless reading in baritone voice, which often remains mute throughout. New members of the Supreme Court bar were sworn in, and Justice Roberts asked Mr. Dellinger to begin, which he did promptly. More later.

DATELINE: Scottsdale, Ariz., Thu., March 20, 2008
Offices of Bloomfield Press

It is a most dangerous game we're playing here.

The major news outlets seemed to agree with my assessment (and I went out on a limb with that, 12 hours before any of them), that the High Court seemed ready and willing to unequivocally affirm an individual right to keep and bear arms.

But it doesn't end there—it barely starts there. If the Court affirms, does that mean *Gun Laws of America* (listing every federal gun law, with plain-English descriptions), is erased? How much of it becomes null and void? What about *The Arizona Gun Owner's Guide*, or the Texas guide, or any of the others? Are they history?

"Gun laws will be over" is the hysterical cry of the antis—that a pro-rights finding will wipe out every gun law in the country and plunge us into bloody terror. And those are almost the fears of the pros too—any finding less than total uninfringed keep-and-bear will jeopardize 200+ years of firmly established cherished rights.

That's why the NRA and the Brady bunch were beyond reluctant to touch this thing initially. There's no telling where it could end up. And the prospects, as I see them, are pretty scary stuff.

Not a single Justice or *amicus* brief suggested that all or even many gun laws must go away; that's just irrational raving. But whatever standard comes out, the Bradys will be able to make some claims that, "See, this falls within reasonable regulation." And the pro-rights people will have openings to challenge some of the more odious rights restrictions, and see if they can prevail. No one knows where any of that will lead. We're back to square one: legislatures, local courts and the ballot box.

New laws that ban your rights may be tougher to enact or even introduce, and pro-rights arguments may have more fuel. Rights-supportive laws may have some obstacles removed—though Texas managed to pass ten of those good laws in their most recent session (2007), without the *Heller* case. So who wins in that scenario?

I used to think that a mere 30 minutes for each side's oral argument was hopelessly small—how could you possibly address a subject adequately in so little time? I no longer believe that. It's more like the adage, "Work expands to fill available time," and when time is short—like before a vacation, or at the Supreme Court—you get an enormous amount done in a day or an hour, that otherwise takes weeks.

The level of intensity in that courtroom defies description. The brain power those nine people brought to bear, on top of the months of prep from the litigants, was exhausting. Any more time than we spent would have been overwhelming. It's a good thing it's kept to an hour (and this case ran 38 minutes longer, including the special 15-minute presentation granted in advance to the Solicitor General, quite rare on all counts). You just fit everything in, then declare an ending.

It's like twilight magic when the Justices walk in through those crimson curtains. There, in one room at one table are the names you know, the faces you recognize, right in front of you clear as day, the most powerful legal minds (politically speaking) in the country, on the planet.

And let me tell you, they knew their stuff. I was able to follow most, but not all, the proceedings. A minor wave of mental fatigue ran over me and passed in about a minute at 11:10. Some legal wrinkles were absolutely new to me, some connections they drew I couldn't follow (but have begun to unravel in studying my notes and the transcript), and some parts I may never adequately connect. Those of you studying the transcripts (many wrote to say you are) are ahead of me.

The closing gavel bangs. Everyone rises. The nine nattily attired natives exit without delay. They retire behind those crisp curtains—and though their actual procedures are a closely guarded secret, the process is roughly understood.

In the Court's conference room, at a time the Justices set (which in recent times has been on Wednesdays and Fridays), they conduct business, including a review of the most recently argued cases. The Chief Justice runs the meeting, and the Associate Justices participate based on seniority. Former Chief Justice Rehnquist preferred that each Justice speak in turn, without interruption. In his book, *The Supreme Court, How It Was, How It Is* (1987), he said, "the true purpose of the conference discussion of argued cases is not to persuade one's colleagues through impassioned advocacy to alter their views, but instead by hearing each justice express his own views to determine therefrom the view of the majority of the Court."

Each Chief Justice handles it differently, however, reflecting their personalities. Chief Justice Earl Warren is known to have adopted an "unstructured discussion" in seeking consensus. However the current Chief Justice runs the meeting, when it concludes, those nine people (no one else attends the meeting once it begins) know where the chips have fallen—exactly what we all want to know—and cannot. In this case, he needs to find out:

1. How many of you are with an individual right existing outside any sort of militia service? Probably gets five, some observers suggest maybe even seven, no one I know sees all nine, Stevens being the hardest holdout if it comes to that. Of course all this is speculative, on our side of the man behind the curtain.

2. Does the D.C. gun ban fail on Second Amendment individual-rights grounds? Everyone (out here) seems to think it must. No way to guess how many in there will find space to toss the 100%-total-ban-on-operable-guns-at-home-in-the-District as an unreasonable limit. But remember the Kelo.

3. Is this individual right to arms (assuming they find one) a fundamental right, making it subject to so-called "strict scrutiny"? Here's where it gets fuzzy, and concurrences and dissents will tear this apart. Here's where the NRA types and the Brady types get to sweat, and probably spin whatever decision emerges to suit their ends.

4. What about off-point issues that came out in the orals and briefs? What exactly is an *arm* for Second Amendment purposes? (This doesn't matter to decide solely the D.C. issue, unless they want to adopt D.C.'s position that sidearms can "reasonably" be excluded.) Are handguns, rifles and shotguns equal?

How much further than keep-and-bear-only-at-home-for-only-the-District-of-Columbia does this case reach? Not at all if the Justices stay on point, but they could stray if they wish. These will not have simple tabulations adding up to nine. These will become non "holdings" of the case, that will fire discussions for a long time to come. My guess is that every Justice will weigh in on these and similarly fudgy points until the next case arises. And a next case will arise.

5. Who's going to write this one? The Chief Justice decides, receptive to the wishes and predispositions of his cohorts, er, colleagues. Scalia maybe, perhaps Thomas whose interest is already in the prior written record. Smart money says Roberts will write it, it's just too seminal, too golden an opportunity for posterity. Whoever pens it, they're all going to get in their say.

6. Maybe the biggest question is—who's going to dissent, and what'll that say. The losers (out here in the public) will latch on to every word. A future Court, with different members, will use a dissent in fashioning subsequent holdings. How will the concurrences add or detract to the main holdings?

How much red meat will the red- and blue-leaners on the Court throw their fans? Know this: the Bradys will come out screaming, as will the rights advocates—that we got this, that, the other, and the rest is judicial activism that must be overturned.

The most eager (and knowledgeable) Court watchers will, when the decision is released, look immediately at the syllabus, the Court's unofficial summary that precedes the decision text, and look for the word *remand*—meaning nothing is settled, or *affirmed*—and the fun really begins in earnest.

Many Court watchers are wondering how, or if, the Court will use *Heller* to set some sort of guidelines for evaluating the constitutionality of existing or future gun laws. The very high standard of *strict scrutiny* is on many tongues, a doctrine developed by the Supreme Court in the 1940s, related to equal protection. It is used in some cases where the Court is evaluating the constitutionality of certain, but not all, restrictions on fundamental rights (e.g., freedom of the press, free exercise of religion). Generally speaking, for a law to pass strict scrutiny, the law must:

1. Serve a "compelling" state interest: An easy example is preventing the enemy from learning about troop movements during wartime.

2. Be "narrowly tailored" to that compelling interest: For example, a law which censored all reporting about the military, rather than merely information about troop movements would not be narrowly tailored.

3. Be the "least restrictive" means to protect the compelling interest: A law that allowed military officers to read press dispatches from the front would be a less restrictive means than a law which required newspapers to have military officers present in their main offices.

Sometimes, the Court introduces a multiple-step test for future courts to use in determining if a law in question is constitutional. Can we expect to see some similar test in *Heller*, or an acknowledged level of scrutiny to help lower courts and law makers? A variety of lower levels of scrutiny, i.e., less restrictive ones, exist and could be adopted.

The reason U.S. Solicitor General Paul Clement (the man who argues the government's position at the Court) was granted time, was to fight to preserve a level of scrutiny that would allow existing "reasonable" federal gun laws. How many? Who knows. Which ones? No one can say—but machine guns and undetectables were mentioned repeatedly. Will he succeed in preserving the federal structural framework on guns? Undoubtedly. Will it all survive or will parts of it fall? No one knows. Yet.

A felon in prison will not be able to successfully argue—even under the wildest fantasy—that the right to arms extends into prison even though, for example, the right to due process or a fair trial does. No doubt, some will try. The ban on arming a vessel of a foreign power at war with an ally (18 USC §961) will remain standing, no worries mate. Many gun laws serve a legitimate purpose, are constitutionally permissible and not infringements, and will not be compromised, despite some rather lunatic ravings to the contrary.

But what about laws against some type of firearm currently banned to the public? How about a normal capacity magazine the exact same as any police officer might be issued? How about bans on where you can carry—the known-to-be-dangerous so-called gun-free zones? Can bans on tasteful, discreet carry in public by innocent women (or men) withstand strict or even intermediate scrutiny? Is a required license-tax-test-expiration-date-required-papers-fingerprint-photo-magnetic-stripe-biometric-data a "reasonable" limit on the exercise of a fundamental right? There's almost no end to such speculation. For these we must wait until June and then, it doesn't end, it begins.

My guess—it's unlikely the Court will go to such points. This time. They don't have to, and if reaching the greatest consensus possible is important, they won't. Locally however, these points will be inescapable in years to come. Legislators at all levels will be quoting *Heller*, count on it. Elect good representatives next time you vote.

Don't worry, as some people are, about machine guns and how quickly Mr. Gura "wrote them off." 1– They're not at issue in this case, so it's immaterial in context. 2– You don't want to or need to push a court too far, so just stay on point, concede a pointless point, it's moot. Get Mr. Heller (along with the rest of the city) his rights back, that's your job, that's all, tomorrow's another day. 3– Mr. Gura's remarks are not the deal maker, the Justices' are. Some of them were just fishing for something to grouse about. It's fine to tell them, "Sure," and get back to the business at hand.

The machine-gun issue is also particularly sticky because, as the Court pointed out, MGs are standard issue for soldiers and so very neatly meet a definition of arms the public should have as related to potential militia service and readiness. It's way too big and convoluted to go into in *Heller*, and simply not needed, yet.

It seems to me that the machine-gun issue would be easy for the Court to sidestep if for no other reason than because MGs are not technically banned, they're taxed. The main controls of the National Firearms Act are under Title 26, the tax code, not under Title 18, the criminal code, and again, neither matter in examining the D.C. ordinance.

When Congress first enacted the NFA limits in 1934 the record shows they suspected they had little authority to ban guns because of the Bill of Rights, and they had not yet acquired the broad latitudes under the Commerce Clause they use today to ban simple interstate possession of property. But they reasoned they might be able to get away with implementing a stifling tax (the $200-per-gun tax was a fortune at the time). Through that mechanism they attached controls, paperwork, financial burdens and tax-evasion penalties that were almost as good as a ban for their purposes then.

The courts acquiesced (and that's a whole 'nother story, see our description of the *Miller* case). The 1986 ban on no-new-full-autos might be more difficult to justify, but it is just not at issue here at all. Some experts told me Gura was right on the mark, handling that as he did. I also bridled though, when the words first passed my ears. It's easy—and meaningless—to Monday-morning quarterback.

Justice Roberts did ask if we even have to go anywhere near these things to settle the issue at hand, and he's right of course, and will be prudent (read, very narrow) in the scope of this decision. I think they'll duck all the chaff we out here like to chew, leave those to digest later. They've got enough on their plate without it.

Will the presidential election affect those future outcomes? You bet it will, and that may be the biggest question mark of all. Note that the "news" media has not raised the point much. I wonder why.

That will have to hold you for now. I need to get to the 580 emails I found on my return from SCOTUS (don't worry, a lot are "anatomy enhancement" ads and similar crud), post my first two eyewitness reports and do the stack of interviews I've agreed to give.

I plan to review the "news" media's coverage of this (some great subtle deceptions and bias I could only pick up by having been there, along with the usual blatant lying and distortions); Bob Blackmer's revealing perspectives from his overnight vigil in front of the Court and his mug in full color on page one (B section) of the *Washington Times* with the protest sign I crafted; the skinny on how we actually got in and what that was like; a photo gallery and more. Now, my wife wants sushi. Sounds good to me.

DATELINE: Scottsdale, Ariz., March 26, 2008
Offices of Bloomfield Press

Pre-Decision Wrap-up and Analysis

Like everyone, I'm on pins and needles to see the decision, all the speculation is fun but meaningless, but fun. Yes, the Court seemed favorable to an individual right and overturning the D.C. total gun ban, even the lamestream media picked that up. But then you have to think about the *Kelo* decision (eminent domain) and McCain-Feingold (free-speech ban before an election), and it's got to worry you. There's no crystal ball.

The biggest problem I see is difficulty the Court faces in recognizing Second Amendment rights to invalidate the D.C. law, and somehow limiting that decision so laws don't fall nationwide—the Solicitor General's concern. OK, so D.C.'s total ban goes too far. Just how far can D.C. go when it rewrites its law and not offend the Second Amendment? How do you describe that?

Whatever direction the Court provides, D.C. will end up as a model for the rest of the nation, and the Pandora's Box is open. If D.C.'s law falls, they'll pass something new, knowing full well it won't make it to the Supreme Court for another long long time.

It's lunacy to think there are no legitimate gun laws, as some wackos suggest, and that all gun laws are doomed. Disarmed prisoners, sentencing enhancements, threats, assaults, reckless endangerment, smuggling—the hard-core criminal laws are not at risk, because those bans are not infringement. Those are reasonable, common-sense gun laws everyone wants—except the hard-core criminals.

But concealed carry, public possession, prohibited-places lists, travel, bureaucratic discretion, licenses, registration schemes, shopping limits—these are indeed put in jeopardy by a robust finding for 2A. Maybe the Court will limit itself narrowly to a person at home in D.C. and go no further, which would be a good first step but awfully hollow. And it would of course address the questions posed, and follow SOP for the Court.

Remember, the Bradys wanted this answered:

"Whether the Second Amendment forbids the District of Columbia from banning private possession of handguns while allowing possession of rifles and shotguns."

And Heller's team proposed this as the question:

Whether the Second Amendment guarantees law-abiding, adult individuals a right to keep ordinary, functional firearms, including handguns, in their homes."

But the Supremes, in a rare move, posed the issue themselves:

"Whether the following provisions—D.C. Code secs. 7-2502.02(a)(4), 22-4504(a), and 7-2507.02—violate the Second Amendment rights of individuals who are not affiliated with any state-regulated militia, but who wish to keep handguns and other firearms for private use in their homes."

Good Things

1. The case unequivocally informs the record. All the solid research the pro-rights people are familiar with can no longer be conveniently denied or lied about by the antis, the Bradys, the lamestream media, the politicians, the U.N. and the rest—it is certifiable public record. This is a good thing. The tremendous value of this cannot even be known yet, but it will be substantial in years to come. It has gotten the best scholarship in the open. I'm guessing the "news" media hates that (and will ignore it to the best of its ability).

2. We have some good new words and phrases injected into the debate, like "remote settlers" whose need for arms was personal, fundamental, oriented to family, food and self defense, and not militia related (thank you Justice Kennedy); "lineage" of both rights and limitations; "reading glasses delays" which Chief Justice Roberts used to humiliate D.C.'s lawyer (thank you Mr. Dellinger for your 3-second-trigger-lock hooey), and perhaps most important, "operative clause" which describes the part of 2A that says, "the right of the people to keep and bear Arms, shall not be infringed.").

3. With luck, the case denies the antis what they want most—a ban. They talk junk guns, cheap guns, assault guns, high-capacity guns,

registered guns, low-melting-point guns, but what they really want is a total ban. If you have a right to have a real gun in your home, their hopes for a ban are dashed.

4. That would have international implications as well, because it would undermine all the globalists, anti-Americans, rogue states, human-rights offenders, NGOs, tyrants and collectivists aligned with the U.N., seeking to preserve a universal declaration of rights that doesn't include your right to protect yourself or the means to do so. The U.N. has glaringly omitted any right to self defense or to possess arms from its controversial declaration of rights.

5. The bogus collectivist inventions are exposed as the fraud they are. In recent decades, the hoplophobic antis have fished around for arguments to deny this right Americans have always enjoyed. They went from collectivist, to statist, to limited individual, to militia-ist, to hybrid—all concoctions now dismembered.

Loose Notes—Including Dellinger and Gura Recaps

Eight security people with curly cords in their ears stood stone-faced facing the audience as we entered chambers and after we were seated. They moved aside before the Justices entered. The D.C. police chief (on the side arguing to disarm the public) was rather poetically disarmed before being allowed to enter. Armed Supreme Court Police were everywhere (the federal government now has more than 70 armed police forces, including egg inspector police, print shop police (not the place where money is printed, those are different police) and environmental protection agency police).

I keep trying to dissect the oral-argument transcript but I find I can't add anything to all the commentary that's been done, and all the public records that have accumulated. What was said that day is precisely known. What it means is speculative, and everyone's got an opinion, why muddy the waters with my own waves.

My initial impressions, good and bad, have been softened, adjusted, modified, better digested, added to and subtracted from, and have matured with time, the counsel of learned friends, reading, and time for reflection. All that matters now is waiting for the next set of official words, the decision.

It seemed to me like Gura did get the job done, which was to get the Justices to recognize that the D.C. law can't stand in the face of an individual right embodied in the Second Amendment. That's all that was on trial in the thinly sliced baloney of the Supreme Court's regular diet.

Machine guns, a thinly veiled tangent and effort to subvert the main question, was neatly sidestepped by Gura, and likely prepared for in advance, although this raised some hackles and definitely has a downside—even though it was not material to the solitary goal of overturning D.C.'s ban on guns at home.

The things that stuck with me on the "ugh" list in Gura's arguments, which got far less mouth in public commentary but left me cold when the words first passed my ears in that Courtroom:

1. Safe storage provisions would be reasonable even under strict scrutiny (except that... "A gun that's safe isn't worth anything" according to Col. Jeff Cooper; and this would satisfy one of the anti's main goals—guns are OK as long as they don't work.)

2. There's no problem with a required license depending on the terms (but... there's no way a writer's license would ever pass muster, is there; and a license implies an immediate (and then expanding) tax scheme, tests, regulatory framework, registration, privacy denial, criminalization for failure to have papers, bureaucracy and (double ugh) expiration dates—all totally unacceptable in the proper operation of a right. Open carry where I live requires absolutely none of that and it's fine, because it harmonizes perfectly with laws outlawing criminals. I might lose that freedom?)

3. Unreasonable infringement (what a horrific idea, introduced by Stevens) might be OK in theory, but *unreasonable* is not defined. Don't even get me started. Laws addressing criminal activity and rights infringement are not the same thing—the former is fine, the latter is unacceptable. Scalia and Roberts both jumped to Gura's aid and tried to take the sting out of that.

4. Crime statistics can be used to determine what's reasonable and set policy, but the statistics are known to be unreliable—what was he hoping to accomplish with that? It stands—but only if you believe rights are subject to cost-benefit analysis. I tend to reject that.

And on Dellinger's side for the city, I did like how he got caught in various varieties of what's technically called BS:

1. He suggested D.C. would carve out an exception for an operable gun if it were used in self defense—which the law flatly does not abide, and the Bench let him know they knew. And it was thoroughly undercut by Gura, who pointed out that the District had such an opportunity twice and did not do so, and in fact did the opposite. Boy that felt good, watching him get caught.

2. For use in self defense, a gun could be easily and quickly unlocked and brought to bear, a point shredded by Chief Justice Roberts, who

had to wrestle to get an admission that the gun had to be reloaded as well, since the D.C. law banned loaded and unlocked arms. Dellinger said it depends on where in the ordinance you put the parenthesis.

3. That lead to a wonderful exchange in which Dellinger said a gun can be simply unlocked quickly. He actually said he could do it in three seconds, after demonstrating a poor understanding of how a lock works ("You—you place a trigger lock on and it has—the version I have, a few—you can buy them at 17th Street Hardware—has a code, like a three-digit code.") I got the impression sitting there, watching as he moved his hands in awkward demonstration in the cameraless room, it seemed he didn't know what he was speaking about; come to think of it, it would have been illegal to actually try that in D.C. if he even had a gun to try it with; he may have never actually unlocked a locked gun in preparing for the case; does he have a friend out of the District who let him try?

4. That lead to Scalia asking about first turning on a lamp next to your bed so you could see the numbers before turning the dials;

5. To which Roberts noted that, after you first turn on the light you then pick up your reading glasses—which got the biggest audience laugh of the day (there were only a few other soft chuckles during the proceedings);

6. He said a rifle is better for home self defense than a sidearm—first time I ever heard that—and in a crowded city no less—which member of his team gave him that delicious bit of advice;

(I later learned this line of reasoning, if you can call it that, sprang from a line cited by the Violence Policy Center, from Chris Bird's book, *The Concealed Handgun Manual*. In it, Bird references the wry humor of Clint Smith, owner of the Thunder Ranch firearms training academy, that the only purpose of a handgun is to battle your way back to your rifle. Few self-defense instructors propose rifles as a first choice for home defense in a city, as D.C. tried to establish. Talk about grasping at straws.)

7. Handguns may be more dangerous than machine guns (well, if you really *really* know what you're doing and you're facing an idiot, maybe), but we sure don't train soldiers that way. Perhaps he got that from Hollywood gun follies, where machine-gun battles last forever and no one can hit Willis or Stallone even at close range if they're running and leaping with their teeth clenched.

The young city lawyer sitting a seat away from me seemed to be keeping a ball score, (I glanced over and kept track) putting what looked like Justices' initials under the headings "CR" and "IR" which I took to mean Collective Right and Individual Right. Under CR he only had two, JS and DS, the rest were under IR. He didn't have a happy look.

Thomas didn't have anything to say in open court, as is his style, but he had plenty to say. He leaned over to Breyer as Mr. Clement began his presentation, and they conversed for perhaps three minutes, and then again at least once. Both of them missed key elements of Clement while talking and listening to each other. Thomas did most of the talking. He was also inclined to hold his face in both hands and rub it, as if refreshing himself, staying alert. Breyer held his slumped head in his hands as if he were in an awful class. Since there are no photos, and the artists work hard to make everyone look good, these images do not emerge from the High Court.

News Distortions

As usual, "news" coverage was loaded with spin, slant, bias, gaffs, hyperbole, misunderstandings, pack-think and editorial where the news is supposed to go. Clips and photos are on the Bloomfield Press website. Here are some highlights.

THEM: "People have been waiting in line all night for front row seats," usually with pictures of people lined up on the white marble steps of the Court.

REALITY: People who had to line up overnight ("the rabble" as a lawyer friend called them) sat in the back, not the front row, lucky to get in at all. Front row seats were packed with honchos. No one waited on the steps, this was forbidden. Just before being led in, the wait-ers were assembled on the steps and then directed inside.

US, to AP: Why is the Associated Press so consistently anti-rights in its gun reporting, and why do they refuse to correct any of the egregious or even self-evident errors they make on the subject constantly?

AP (Mark Sherman): I have no idea what you're talking about and we make error corrections rapidly all the time. And no, I forgot to bring any business cards.

US: Well have you ever done any stories on the good that guns do?

AP: Uh, what do you mean exactly?

THEM: The District of Columbia has a ban on handguns at home.

REALITY: The District of Columbia has a ban on *any* operable gun at home. They also ban transporting any gun through the city, so you can't get a gun to your home, which will remain even if the laws under examination here are overturned. The city *does* allow handguns in the home, if they were obtained more than three decades ago and are unloaded and locked up or in pieces.

THEM: *The Washington Post* saw fit to mention that the "commands" of the Second Amendment were "written more than 200 years ago."

REALITY: A similar derogatory slap at free speech, speedy trials or any other guarantees of the Bill of Rights seems unthinkable, but for guns belongs on page one.

THEM: *The New York Times* used every shibboleth about gun rights in the book—it's a subject the Court has not addressed since 1939 (this is the 64th gun case since then, many with direct 2A implications); how far this "newly recognized right" might go (you just want to smack these bigots); this is the first time in history an individual right will be "embraced" in 2A; and I haven't gone past their introduction (on page one, 3/19/08).

THEM: *USA Today* says the Court may find (for the first time in history) that 2A "gives people an individual right to own guns."

REALITY: The Second Amendment doesn't "give" rights, as the informed portion of the public widely knows, it guarantees existing rights against government interference. *USA Today* also saw fit to bring up the argument, which it at least identified as from "recent decades" that 2A is somehow related not to "the people" named in the Amendment, but to the National Guard (which, uhh, began in the early 1900s).

THEM—A full half page called: "News To Use: Current Events for Classroom Learning and Homework (provided by "Newspapers In Education," a division of *The Arizona Republic*, owned by Gannett)

Set the stage with a demeaning opening line about your civil rights in the Second Amendment:

"The sentence is an English teacher's nightmare."

Continue with a lie:

"What that comma-filled, awkwardly worded sentence means has been debated almost since it was first approved by the nation's founders."

There was virtually no confusion or "debate" until a few decades ago, when anti-rights zealots began fabricating arguments to destroy this well understood right—"Americans have the right and advantage of being armed," as James Madison put it. In America, we the people have always had the right to keep and bear arms, we have routinely bought arms as free citizens, and we treat them as a fundamental right in every walk of life, until these rights-attacks recently began and were propagated by a compliant press. And "founders" takes a capital letter.

Continue by contradicting yourself:

"Everyone agrees that the Second Amendment ensures the right 'to keep and bear arms'"

(and leave out the part about "the right of the people").

Then backtrack and question yourself by bringing up the popular anti-rights argument:

"Or does that right only apply to people who are connected with militias?"

Switch gears to the 1939 *Miller* case:

"the last time the Supreme Court looked at the amendment nearly 70 years ago..."

All right, so they don't know better, way too many people believe in that myth.

Then mis-state that case completely:

"In that case the High Court ruled only that the constitutional right to bear arms did not include the right to carry a sawed-off shotgun across state lines as part of an illegal liquor operation."

In *Miller*, the Court pointed out that there was no evidence in the record (nothing "within judicial notice" as they put it) as to whether a sawed-off shotgun is "ordinary military equipment," so they couldn't decide if it was legal to possess. And since the Supreme Court doesn't take evidence, they remanded to the lower court for a finding of facts regarding sawed-off shotguns. Because Miller had been murdered by his cohorts by that time, the point was moot, the findings were never made, and a final conclusion was never reached. But that's too complex to deal with, isn't it?

"The case involves a special police officer..."

I don't know what to make of this deception. It's the same difficulty the media had in characterizing Jeanne Assam, a private citizen with a carry permit who shot that would-be mass murderer in the mega-church in Colorado. In all the published reports they had this need to call her a security guard, as if a normal person couldn't take such action.

It was doubly wrong, because Ms. Assam carried a modern semi-auto pistol, and in her particular situation, a security guard by law would only be allowed to carry a revolver. Maybe it's related to what an AP bureau chief once told a reporter I know, about a man who defended himself with a firearm—he wouldn't run the story because he didn't want to encourage copy-cat behavior.

Technically the title is accurate, but it's misleading, or belongs in quotes. An insider puts it this way, "Heller is a private security guard for a contractor which provides armed security throughout D.C., and to do that job, he is a "special police officer" of the District of Columbia." If you look at the statute, in order to be a private security guard who carries a firearm, you must comply with red tape, and then the city brands you as a "special police officer." Bob Blackmer, who is a police officer, looked at the requirements and scratched his head, because what a police officer is, and what Dick Heller is, well, they're not the same thing. OK, it's a small point.

Close with a warning that "gun-control efforts" could be put into jeopardy:

"If the High Court rules that individuals have the right 'to keep and bear arms,' cities and states will have to rethink efforts to restrict gun ownership, even if the goal is public safety."

Don't you just hate it when the threat of threats to public safety is the *raison detre* for justifying the denial of your civil rights? Isn't there any cognizance that disarming criminals has no bearing on the issue? (No.)

That disarming criminals is not an infringement, perfectly OK under any scenario, already on the books, and unrelated to innocent possession of firearms? (No.)

Don't the writers, or editors, or teachers being fed this tripe realize that "efforts to restrict gun ownership" from law-abiding Americans is unjust, immoral, dangerous and focused in the wrong direction? (No.)

Don't they realize that "gun control" is a euphemism for rights denial, and civil-rights bans? (No.)

And don't they know that the real issue is gun rights and the right to self defense, and civil rights, and human rights, and a right that pre-exists the Constitution? (No.)

Are they going to issue any sort of correction? (No.)

Will the next story be any better? (No.) Are readers abandoning this balderdash being passed of as news, in droves? (Yes.)

Getting Seats

Here's what it took to get into the Court for the *D.C. v. Heller* case on March 18, 2008, including how Bob and I managed it:

Heller and his two attorneys were originally allotted six seats total, including for themselves, and had to disappoint people who believed they should be there. I wasn't able to find out how many seats D.C. secured but I suspect it was more (three at the Petitioner table, the mayor and police chief who sat right in front of me and had aides; Dellinger's wife was to my right, but not sure how her seat was obtained).

A special section reserved for the Supreme Court press corps filled as fast as the case was announced, no surprise there.

An allotment of 50 seats for members of the Supreme Court bar also filled nearly immediately, and may have been expanded for this special case. Personal friends of the Justices get preference, and other court and government officials with "pull" manage to secure an unknown number of seats. It was by far the hottest ticket in town—history in the making—the *Roe v. Wade* of the gun issue except Roe wasn't as important.

A total of 50 seats are reserved for the public, on a first-come-first-served basis, though a reference book I have falsely says there are 170. Eugene Volokh in his blog responded to numerous requests on when to arrive and opined that a) no one really knows, which is correct, and b) get there early or abandon all hope.

In my case, the picture included:

• spend six years researching and writing *Supreme Court Gun Cases* with two of the top Second Amendment attorneys in the country;

• get involved with the Goldwater Institute free-market think tank in Phoenix which brought me into contact with Bob Levy of the Cato Institute at a book signing;

• become friends with Bob who spearheaded this case, funnel him what case-related info I can, and meet others at Cato including attorney Tim Lynch who, as a fan of my book, was able to place copies into the Supreme Court's library;

• listen hard as my friend and fellow Cartridge Family Band member Bob Blackmer convinces me we ought to go to D.C. to see this historic case with our own eyes;

• allocate a thousand dollars each for airfare, pocket money and a cheap but pricey Washington hotel;

• breathe a sigh of relief when the airfare locks in 60 days in advance at around $400, and a few weeks later has risen to more than $800;

• call every contact I could think of for weeks, for a strategy to obtain seats; Levy says don't even try it will be a total zoo;

• find out about the seat allotments and historical cases of camping out overnight;

• get details from Court Police, the PIO office, Court gift shop and others on what's allowed on the waiting line (like a chair and blanket, though not even an overcoat may enter the Courtroom and must be checked or abandoned);

• prepare to arrive two nights ahead to ensure the trip is successful;

• learn from one highly placed attorney friend that the Marshal of the Court has an allotment of seats for guests of the Marshal, and here's the direct phone line;

• get a ton of insider info from that office, including a suggestion to write a short letter requesting a seat for Bob and myself, which took more than a day to compose to my satisfaction;

• get elated—but also get depressed—when the Marshal faxes a reply granting me a single seat;

• give the good/bad news to Bob, and continue with preparations to support the overnight vigil effort now only for my friend, who has located and purchased military-grade thermals and a portable heater;

• remain with him all day on line Monday (for moral support but it was totally fun and exciting and the place to be) until well past when the line was longer than the available seats;

• make runs for caffeinated sodas and food and relieve him for a few pit stops;

• wish him well and leave for the hotel room five Metro stops away as night was falling, to write and post a digital pre-game report, rejoining him bright and early the next day;

• socialize briefly in line with everyone who knew me from the day before (they looked like they weathered the night fairly well);

• revel in the media/activist circus in front of the Court and do some quick interviews;

• enter through the Maryland Avenue entrance to present my letter of passage from the Marshal's office, while Bob was being issued pass #7 outside;

• bump into Bob on the Court's ground floor and make some introductions (including to Mr. Heller), snap photos, and watch the honchos before Bob's quick departure to get back on the line to get in;

• and make my way upstairs as instructed, have my name checked off the official list (man that felt cool), quickly check everything I had in two lockers, and put my butt in a chair. Easy.

Bob Blackmer had his own experience and a half, spending more than 24 hours outdoors waiting to get it:

March 17, 2008. Alan left the line around sundown, and the media left by about 11:15 p.m. the night before oral argument. By 12:01 a.m. 94 people were logged in to wait in line for a seat in the Court chamber. Up to this point, the weather was as good as I could hope for in Washington D.C. in March—and thankfully, unlike last night, there was almost no wind.

My stool didn't have a back and in hindsight I should've had Alan get me a folding chair when he picked up propane for my heater at Target. About 2:30 in the morning, I had noticed that the girl next to me hadn't been in her chair for several hours so I asked her friend if he thought she would mind if I sat in it for a while, and he said go ahead. I sat down, relaxed and my eyes closed.

It seemed like only a few minutes when I was awakened by raindrops on what little of my face was exposed. It was starting to rain and I thought oh no! This is going to just ruin this adventure for me—and my umbrella somehow did not make it into my gear. The drizzle only lasted a couple of minutes—just long enough to make me panic.

At 4:22 a.m. the first of the media circus arrived. All morning we kept asking different police officers what time they were going to start moving the line and each time we asked we got a different answer. Around 6 a.m. we were told they were going to move the line in about 30 minutes. 6:30 a.m. came and went and so did 7:00 a.m. At 7:07 a.m. we finally got the okay to move to the plateau in between the lower and upper steps of the Supreme Court. As we got up there, it finally set in that this was really going to happen—we had survived the night and were going to be among the lucky few who would see history in the making.

Standing there, they handed out what I thought of as my "golden ticket," like in *Charlie and the Chocolate Factory*. Of the many instructions they called out, this one burned into my mind: If you are not in line when the line starts to move, it will not matter what number is on your ticket, you will not be getting in. Even though it was almost three hours before the arguments were scheduled, everyone near me was somewhat paranoid, afraid to go anywhere—and jeopardize everything we had waited for for so long.

At 8:25 a.m. I decided to chance a trip to the Court's restroom through the side entrance, so that Mother Nature wouldn't call when I was in the courtroom. At 8:35 a.m. I was back in line and was relieved that nothing had changed.

At 9:00 a.m. they let the first 50 of us into the foyer between the outer doors and the inner doors that led to the lobby area. They gave us more instructions, mandatory rules—we were allowed one writing utensil, a small notepad, no overcoats or heavy jackets, no electronic devices of any kind and no bag of any type. Once we were in our chairs we had to remain seated and had to keep any talking to a minimal whisper. Any type of disruption would result in removal.

Once we cleared the first metal detector, we had to stash our overnight stuff in the lockers and coatroom. We then got in another line where we spent more anxious moments waiting to go through another metal detector that led into the courtroom and we were instructed exactly where to sit. Our section was on the left side of the court as you face the Bench, perpendicular to it. The chairs were wooden wicker-types, obviously temporary accommodations.

The first six people were in this side front row and had decent or fairly good views. Starting with my row, the second row, it was partially to mostly obstructed because we were in between two very large pillars. I was sitting behind Jason (Mr. #1 in line) and he noticed that my view was obstructed. He graciously offered to lean forward, back or scooch down. I told him if he just leaned forward a little, I could do the same and would be able to see all nine Justices. It worked out fine.

I noticed Alan on the other side of the court in the second row. I tried to get his attention, he even stood, scanning the crowd, was he looking for me? and I tried to send him a thought, but just as he turned my way he changed his glance and our eyes never met.

At 10:00 a.m. we were given the signal to stand while the Justices entered the courtroom. We had the unique privilege of hearing Justice Clarence Thomas speak at length as he read a ruling regarding

Washington State's primary system. Some lawyers were sworn in to the Supreme Court bar and at 10:06 a.m. the main attraction started...

When orals ended we were told to depart quickly, got our stuff from the lockers, and joined the circus that was happening on the sidewalk below the courthouse steps. When it seemed like there was no more fun to have, I went to lunch with Jason and Dan so we could compare notes. After lunch, I headed back to the hotel and took a nap—this trip was not about getting adequate sleep. Alan and I treated ourselves to steak at Ruth's Chris that night.

After a good night's sleep, we skipped breakfast and headed uptown to have lunch with the folks at Accuracy In Media, the news-media watchdog group that Alan works with. It started to pour on the way back to the hotel, and we felt so lucky—as we got drenched—that it had held off till our mission was accomplished.

The only touristy thing I was able to do was stop by the Jefferson Memorial on the way to the airport, take some pictures and have my picture taken by the statue of him.

At the airport, we grabbed whatever newspapers we could find and sat down for a snack. I saw the picture of the line leading up to the court on page one of *The Washington Times* and, knowing I was there, tried to spot myself, but couldn't really say for sure. Then I was shocked when I turned to the B Section and saw a close-up picture of me— holding one of Alan's signs—the one that says Guns Save Lives. I went back and bought four more copies.

Alan was as thrilled as I was because of the good publicity the sign gave our side. In hindsight, those signs were one of the best ideas of this adventure. The media took countless photos and videos of them— they looked professional and they all had great messages. The return flight went well and Alan and I were just basking in the glow of this adventure and how well everything went.

The Case That Almost Wasn't

Most people don't realize that the pro-rights *and* anti-rights lobbies were against bringing a Second Amendment case to the U.S. Supreme Court. There was just too much to lose to risk a win.

Pressure was brought to bear on D.C. mayor Fenty's office to not appeal the D.C. Circuit Court's ruling that voided the District's draconian gun ban. They were counseled to lick their wounds, accept their fate, and not appeal. The case had potential to permanently overturn the ban, but worse, it could improve the status of other challenges to infringements nationally, as the *Washington Post* had noted on May 17, 2007:

Gun-control advocates are quietly acknowledging that Fenty is in a difficult spot. Across the country, many of them and their attorneys have been meeting in conference rooms to analyze the potential damage that could be done nationwide if the D.C. law falls apart. Some fear that an adverse Supreme Court ruling could lead to more gun lobby challenges and the collapse of tough gun regulations in New York, Chicago and Detroit. Other potential casualties include federal laws that require background checks for gun buyers or ban the manufacture of machine guns for civilian use.

"Making the right choice is going to be a very difficult decision," said Joshua Horwitz, executive director of the D.C.-based Coalition to Stop Gun Violence. "Despite all the rhetoric about 'We're taking this all the way to the Supreme Court,' you have to really think this one through. Everyone is cognizant of the fact that this is probably the high-water mark for Second Amendment cases."

Brady president Paul Helmke added:

> "The D.C. law is an easy one to shoot at. Factually, it's a tougher one to get behind and defend. Background checks and assault weapons ban— you can defend all day long... Why is this the one we're going to be taking up to the Supremes?"

But in the final analysis, D.C.'s gun ban was history anyway if they didn't appeal, because the Circuit Court's ruling would stand, D.C. would endure a hard slap to the face, and the government would relinquish the iron grip it had placed on people's rights since 1976—a prospect government doesn't generally take kindly to. And they had their bruised egos to think about too. Factors were at play behind closed doors that may never be revealed.

For their part, some gun-rights lobbyists did everything they could to prevent the case from going all the way. Teams of lawyers argued with everyone that it was a bad idea. My phone rang with such pleadings, and my opinion hardly mattered. Even though the case looked good on many grounds, I was told the Court was not a reliable pro-gun-rights Bench, or even a strong constitutional Bench.

An alternate case called *Seegars* was introduced that would allow the High Court to sidestep the Second Amendment issues yet lift D.C.'s ban on 5th Amendment, statutory civil rights or other grounds. In one of the many pre-trial filings, Levy's team wrote (internal cites and footnotes omitted):

> Halbrook and the NRA no doubt sympathize with the substantive arguments raised in *Parker*, but they do not share at least one important goal which motivated *Parker* plaintiffs and counsel to take action, and which guides the intended prosecution of this action by the plaintiffs. *Parker* plaintiffs want a timely clarification of the Second Amendment by the United States Supreme Court.

The NRA has made clear that it wishes to avoid such review at this time. So strong is the NRA's opinion on the matter that it sought to dissuade the filing of *Parker*, to alter the litigation's goals, and even to have the litigation designed in such a manner as to avoid or curtail appellate review. Only when *Parker* plaintiffs and counsel refused the NRA's goals was *Seegars* filed.

In August of 2002, Levy was contacted by George Mason University law professor Nelson Lund, who holds the Patrick Henry Professorship of Constitutional Law and the Second Amendment, which is funded by the National Rifle Association Foundation. Lund requested that Levy meet with him and Charles Cooper, a partner at Cooper & Kirk, P.L.L.C. in Washington, DC, who has represented the NRA, to discuss the planned *Parker* litigation.

On August 29, 2002, Lund and Cooper came to the Cato Institute, where they met with Levy and fellow *Parker* counsel Clark Neily and Gene Healy. Lund and Cooper said they were speaking on behalf of the NRA and expressed reservations about a Second Amendment challenge in D.C. federal court.

Specifically, they were concerned that *Parker* might be successful before the appellate court but meet a more hostile reception at the Supreme Court—not because Lund and Cooper thought that *Parker's* legal theories were wanting, but rather because they were skeptical about the near-term composition of the Supreme Court. *Parker* counsel specifically disclaim any ability to predict how the Supreme Court (or, indeed, any court) would rule.

Lund and Cooper encouraged *Parker* counsel either not to file the case, or, if the case were filed, to build in a "trap door" that would give the court a basis, if it chose, to avoid a four-square holding on the Second Amendment and thereby minimize the likelihood of the Supreme Court reaching that issue. Neily, Healy and Levy agreed to give some thought to the NRA's concerns and advice, but ultimately rejected the NRA's suggestions as to how their case should be litigated.

Parker counsel decided that the non-Second Amendment arguments were without merit and even prejudicial. Moreover, a prime objective of *Parker* is to obtain judicial clarification of the Second Amendment's scope. *Parker* plaintiffs are alarmed that against the background of a clear-cut circuit and now intra-circuit split, as well as burgeoning academic debate, Second Amendment claims are being raised largely in criminal contexts that have little bearing on the rights of law-abiding citizens such as plaintiffs.

The NRA, which believes the Second Amendment lacks majority support in the Supreme Court, is plainly interested in depriving *Parker* plaintiffs of this key litigation objective. For an effective political organization, this may be a rational course of action. The NRA may believe that it can adequately secure Second Amendment rights through its extensive lobbying activities, and therefore not wish to risk the Supreme Court's determination of the Second Amendment's scope. See, i.e. Opp., p. 8 ("the wish existed by the many interested persons in the subject that every effort be made to avoid an adverse precedent, particularly in the court of appeals.")

Respectfully, *Parker* plaintiffs are entitled to disagree. They are entitled to act on their beliefs that the best course for securing Second Amendment rights is through carefully measured litigation on behalf of the *Parker* plaintiffs. Two months after the filing of *Parker*, despite its concern about an unfavorable Supreme Court holding on the Second Amendment, the NRA funded its own case, *Seegars*, which was filed by Stephen Halbrook and Richard Gardiner. Clearly, the NRA, frustrated by *Parker* counsels' unwillingness to adopt its recommendations, decided to take matters into its own hands. And by its motion to consolidate, it has attempted to foist on *Parker* legal theories that were explicitly considered and rejected by *Parker* counsel as adverse to their clients' interests.

The extraneous causes of action included in *Seegars* are without merit and are counterproductive to the *Parker* litigation. Moreover, the inclusion of such claims might foreclose a final clarification of the Second Amendment question, which is a major objective of the *Parker* plaintiffs.

It was one heck of a dangerous, winner-takes-all roll of the dice the Parker team was cavalierly taking. The NRA had every reason to be afraid of chancing the entire nation's rights, and everything its membership stands for, on a wobbly vote or two at the Supreme Court. How fragile these precious rights are.

Only in hindsight will we know if the NRA's cautious prudence was the correct position, and if Levy's approach with *Parker* was reckless or ill-advised. And then it will be too late. If the Second Amendment is harmed by *Heller*, the wish to change the past and retract the case will be great, and that train will have left the station. Even if the decision comes down solidly in favor of Mr. Heller, the fallout and aftermath will be felt for decades, with actual results probably quite a mixed bag.

To its great credit, and predictably, once it was clear the case would proceed, the NRA stood four-square behind the effort and poured in resources. Halbrook, portrayed in a less-than-flattering light in the brief above, wrote the brief for the U.S. Vice President, the first time in history a VP has ever signed on to an *amicus* filing. A *majority* of both Houses of Congress signed on to that brief, another historic first and a pretty sweet addition to Halbrook's already stellar *curriculum vitae*.

Legitimate worries were flying—what about the *Kelo* decision? Wasn't everyone stunned that clear constitutional private property rights fell to a city's desire for tax revenue, and the Fourth Amendment was found to provide no protection for a person's home?

What about the "incumbent protection policy" of *McConnell v. FEC*, the McCain-Feingold campaign-finance-reform case? Didn't the Court leave everyone stunned to learn that the Constitution somehow didn't allow you to mention the names of candidates in a broadcast within

60 days of an election, unless you were an authorized pseudo-agent of government? Can we tolerate that kind of risk with our Second Amendment rights?

The NRA went so far as to introduce a bill and drum up support in Congress for a legisled repeal of the D.C. gun ban, which would have made the Supreme Court challenge moot and derail it entirely. The idea had merit. The District's residents would regain their rights, and the extreme risks involved in a Supreme Court challenge could be avoided. They came close to passage too, with impassioned speeches on the floor and a groundswell of support.

Despite some predictable rancor which a big dog is bound to attract, the NRA's weight was absolutely critical because, without them, John Kerry might be President, and he would have appointed Justices like Cass Sunstein and Sonia Sotomeyer, who would virtually guarantee a loss. Despite any disagreements between Gura and NRA at the District Court level, the NRA's level of effort in the Supreme Court was gigantic. Of the 20 most important *amicus* briefs on the pro-rights side, the NRA was an important player in the large majority.

Plenty of extremely fine *amici* were developed with no connection to NRA at all. But there's a big difference between a good brief, or even an excellent brief (SAF's for example, by Nelson Lund), and being able to put together *a bipartisan majority of both houses of Congress* (for the first time in Supreme Court history), *and* the Vice President, *in opposition to his own Department of Justice*.

It's alright on a philosophical level, or a level of legislative tactics, for people to agree with GOA and say that the NRA is too compromising. But in the final analysis, as my co-author Dave Kopel puts it, NRA ranks second only to the Gura team itself as deserving the credit for the win. No NRA, no win in *Heller*. Some people might have preferred the satisfaction and ideological purity of losing this Supreme Court case in a 9-0 martyrdom instead of eking out a win. The authors of this book are not among them.

In the end, the effort to stop the Court challenge through congressional action and other strategies ground to a halt, in a drama as complex and odoriferous as any sausage maker has ever produced.

The case moved inexorably forward thanks to the Herculean efforts of a few people, confirming one oft-cited pearl of wisdom—politics and society move forward based on the dedicated efforts of a small number of individuals.

One of those special few, hidden from the limelight, was the late David Caplan in his role as a Director of the NRA, and perhaps even more so, as a Trustee of the NRA Civil Rights Defense Fund. Unsung in the popular arena, he played an enormous role for three decades in paving the way for *Heller*. He made the NRA a better, more effective, more pro-rights organization, *especially* on Second Amendment law. Among many, many other things, Caplan and the Civil Rights Fund have been huge supporters of high-level scholarly work, and without that tremendous research, we might never have built the array of top scholars who now see the light still shining from the late 1700s.

DATELINE: Washington D.C., June 26, 2008, 10:17 a.m.
Gun Law Update—FLASH—*Heller* Case Affirmed!

5 to 4 Decision Saves Gun Rights In America;

D.C. Gun Ban Is Unconstitutional and Overturned;

Second Amendment Protects an Individual Right Unconnected with Militia Service, and is preserved by a single vote;

Use of firearms for traditional lawful purposes such as self defense at home is a protected right;

The history, precedents, scholarship and wording of the Second Amendment support the Court's decision;

The idea that a lawful firearm at home must be locked up or disassembled prevents a core legal use of self defense and is unconstitutional;

The High Court instructs D.C. to let Heller have a firearm at home.

Less than three hours ago, the U.S. Supreme Court released its 157-page decision in *District of Columbia v. Heller*, the landmark case on the Second Amendment. The Court affirmed the decision of the Circuit Court below it, overturning the D.C. gun ban, and recognizing an individual right to keep and bear arms.

BUT:

The Second Amendment, like most rights, is not an unlimited right and some "longstanding restrictions" on what you can carry, where you can carry (schools and government buildings are mentioned), concealed carry, existing laws regarding felons or the mentally ill, and laws "imposing conditions and qualifications on the commercial sale of arms" are permissible.

Because Heller conceded at oral argument that a gun license would be OK if it wasn't arbitrary or capricious, a D.C. license would satisfy his request for relief, the Court tells D.C. it must permit him to register his handgun and must issue him a license to carry it at home. Any other possession or use appears to not be directly addressed, including carrying it to or from home. Conditions for such registration and license are not addressed, and are apparently left up to the city.

Lack of time frame on D.C. to act to remedy Heller's situation, and lack of directions on what they should do could lead to bizarre results or endless delays and further legal action. The cost, duration and conditions for Heller's (and other residents') license are unknown, skeptical guesses aren't pretty. Mayor Fenty has already said in a "news" conference they won't allow semi-automatics, the most popular sidearm and standard issue for the armed forces.

Full-blown gun bans around the nation are now in jeopardy, but there are few of those. Challenges to other laws, and proposals for new laws are likely, as the debate continues unabated. There are no time frames for action, which will fall to legislative process and court cases, and will likely take years.

Support for specified gun controls is dangerously great, but will be met with also robust supports for individual rights to arms, self defense and lawful gun use.

Both sides get something; Antis are expected to simply walk away from concocted "collectivist" inventions and promote the "reasonable, common-sense goal" of more and stronger gun-control laws, many of which are expressly supported in the opinion, to limit rights Americans currently enjoy.

There will be little "final result" and the struggle will continue at every level.

A loud sigh of relief for recognition of an individual right was heard nationwide, but so was hope for creative new limits on the rights of the people to keep and bear arms. Both sides will be busy issuing demands, "definitive" statements, and arguing their side with vigor. Only one side will be concerned with preserving the right of the people to keep and bear arms in an uninfringed manner.

Three Justices joined in a 46-page dissent expected from Stevens, and three joined a separate 44-page dissent by Breyer, making the dissents longer than the 64-page majority opinion.

Stevens quickly abandons the individual v. collectivist theories, saying of course there is an individual right, and focuses on perceived historical errors by the majority and allowable gun-rights limitations. It clings to the militia-purpose argument for the Second Amendment.

Breyer objects on two grounds—that the Second Amendment is about the militia and not self defense, and that gun controls are "within the zone" of legislative action. He argues that a total ban on handguns in high-crime areas is a "permissible legislative response." This is a very hasty sketch of the dissents in the interest of an early posting of the findings.

My analysis of the complete decision and dissents is ongoing and will be released soon. Sign up for this and related posts at gunlaws.com.

CAUTION: Quickly surveyed news reports show, as predicted, little news and plenty of opinion are being shoveled; pretty (or handsome) talking heads in front of the Supreme Court building are making it up as they go with little depth of understanding of what just happened; promotion of "acceptable" gun control a common theme; ignorance of guns and gun issues abound; video loops of gun pictures (many taken from evidence lockers) and people at target practice proliferate; few of the factual points in my headlines above are included.

No one has read the entire opinion yet, so all comments are subject to revision and likely contain errors, omissions and oversights, lack of nuance, reasoned projections, etc.

Online poll results from SCOTUSblog:
Who's watching the Court's results in real time today—
Lawyer 19%; Student 13%; Other 68%
Owns no guns 26%, one 6%; two 4%; more 63%
NRA member 47%; not 53%
Watching for the *Heller* case 95%; other 5%
Pleased with the decision 86%; No 14%

DATELINE: Scottsdale, Ariz., June 30, 2008
Heller Decision—Deeper Analysis

"Strictest Scrutiny" Found in the Fine Print
Many Other Assets Revealed After Study
Gura Takes Another Case

Do NOT gratuitously yield ground on any points that may be debatable—take the highest ground concerning what the *Heller* decision means, and make the antis fight uphill against you. You may be right despite your own doubts.

FIRST, THREE NEWS ITEMS:

June 26, 2008: "An 'outraged' Chicago Mayor Daley this morning denounced a U.S. Supreme Court ruling overturning Washington D.C.'s handgun ban as a 'frightening decision' and a 'return to the days of the Wild West.'"

Adding salt to the wound, Chicago was immediately sued over its own tyrannical handgun ban and licensing tax scheme, by a coalition of pro-human-rights groups including the Second Amendment Foundation, the NRA and the Illinois State Rifle Association. Quoting from the SAF announcement (saf.org):

"Chicago's registration scheme cries out for common-sense reform," ISRA Executive Director Richard Pearson said. Under Chicago's gun law, firearms must be re-registered annually. Alan Gura, lead attorney in the *Heller* case, is in charge of this lawsuit.

"Each time," Gura said, "a tax is imposed, forms must be filled out, photographs submitted. A person who owns more than one gun will be constantly in the process of registering each gun as it comes due for expiration. If registration is to be required, once is enough."

He further noted that Chicago's bizarre requirement that guns be registered before they are acquired frequently makes registration impossible. Failure to comply with the scheme means that a gun not re-registered on time can never be registered again. Some anti-rights advocates are reportedly happy because gun registration is being accepted as if it's a restoration of rights, which it is not.

Daley's "Wild West" comment refers to a bogus notion used by every anti-rights zealot in the country. It's usually used to resist carry-permit legislation, which has been proven to reduce crime, not revert society to the days of Dodge City. "Why let facts get in the way of a good red-faced rant," said my alter ego The Uninvited Ombudsman, to no one in particular. "Registering honest gun owners lacks a crime-fighting component, and allocates scarce funding in the wrong direction— tracking the innocent." Criminals cannot be registered, due to 5th Amendment self-incrimination rules. More here: gunlaws.com/gunreggie.htm

2. I was going to do a lengthy review of news coverage of the decision, but it has been so biased, distorted, misleading and prejudicial I just don't have the stomach for it. Our local paper (Gannett's #2 rag, *The Arizona Republic*) put it below the fold, giving a daily change in the stock market more prominence. They ran the famously anti-rights *Washington Post* "news" which began, ran and ended with editorial comments and balderdash.

The McClatchy chain closed their completely conjectural Q&A approach by calling SAF, the second largest gun-rights group in the nation "small." Reuters, overlooking that the RKBA has been enshrined, exercised and respected for more than two centuries, called it new. It was dastardly.

3. Against the consistent cry of gun-crazed journalists, clamoring post-*Heller* for an end to what they call "gun deaths," it's time to finally expose the realities of criminal gun homicides. The media is not complaining about the medical problems of the elderly and other suicides. They're euphemizing crime-related "gun deaths" that are in large measure *war deaths*—in the government-sponsored war on some drugs. Police have a term quietly used for this phenomenon—the good riddance factor. Gang-bang murders are war deaths in that war, and are not subject to phony "gun-control" measures aimed squarely at the innocent law-abiding public. D.C.'s failed laws prove this.

The American gun-involved murder rate has major components that are demographic, geographic, and related to social and economic conditions, not a new design by Winchester, Colt or Glock. The anti-rights claims about gun deaths are as false as the now discredited myths from their *Heller*-case arguments.

In 2007 in D.C., *The Wall Street Journal* notes that 80% of the homicides (there were 181 in all) occurred in the NE and SE sectors, what you and I would easily call the bad side of town. A full 30% took place in the single baddest part of town, the notorious 8th Ward. In contrast, the murders in Ward 3, with its upscale suburban homes, were zero, as in nada and zip. A dot map of the incidents would clearly show what law enforcement knows but the "news" media refuses to reveal—so-called gun deaths are in large measure a cultural thing lacking diversity.

The ugly underbelly of gun crimes must be exposed. Gun crime is overwhelmingly concentrated in inner-city neighborhoods. We need new policies to help protect the many decent people in those neighborhoods, and to alter those neighborhoods so they stop creating such large numbers of criminals. The crimes of a small number of vicious people preying on inner city residents must be disassociated— from 100 million legitimate law-abiding gun owners who have nothing whatsoever to do with it.

We can no longer stand by and allow journalists and their leaders, or misguided politicians, to place blame for failed social policies on cherished human rights that have kept this nation a shining beacon of freedom for more than two centuries.

WARNING:

The big hurdle, with *Heller* now in place, will be control of the court of popular opinion. National "news" media, led by the clever and decidedly anti-rights *Washington Post*, will be bending over backwards to characterize any D.C. event that can be twisted to imply:

a) D.C. experienced a crime and it must be due to the dangerous *Heller* decision and its subsequent flood of permit applications,

b) the exercise of your rights is hurting society,

c) politicians should reverse the trend by finding new ways to enact the old failed policies, and

d) you should elect Obama because he will fix everything with some spare change from his campaign (and his 64-page platform document, which doesn't mention guns at all).

The Wall Street Journal says Paul Helmke (president of the Brady group) sees a possible silver lining, "Because the decision eliminates the specter of gun confiscation, advocates will be more willing to come to the table and discuss other gun-control issues."

Additional Aspects of The Heller Decision

June 26 was a great day for human rights and freedom and a terrible day for *The New York Times*. (*The Times* has promoted an anti-rights agenda for decades.)

Bogus anti-rights arguments we have endured for about four decades have had a stake driven through them. Collectivism, the militia requirements, uselessness of sidearms, improper readings of 2A, revisionist history, rights-denial as a crime remedy, "the gun lobby lies about 2A," even "an individual right means you can own an atom bomb," all dead. Did I mention hoplophobia is irrational?

The human right to self defense has received unequivocal support. This is especially important since the U.N. doesn't recognize this right.

Criminals and crazies remain under strict legal controls, despite lunatic claims to the contrary.

Handguns are now recognized as "the quintessential self-defense weapon."

Future efforts to deny these crucial civil rights will be severely chilled (though their advocates are as energized as we would be if we had lost).

The list of weapons useful for a militia—armed citizens capable of being called up in an emergency to serve with their own weapons— remains ambiguous. To wit:

Some legal-eagle friends are confused, in disagreement and debating what the actual holdings are exactly, such as whether the Second

Amendment is incorporated against the states, and similar fine points. I take an expansive view and encourage rights advocates to do the same.

Do NOT yield ground on any points in your preliminary positions— take only the highest ground concerning what the decision means, and make anti-rights advocates fight uphill against you. Push the envelope in the direction of greater freedom.

The finding of a "specific enumerated right" of course means other jurisdictions are affected even if the 14th Amendment isn't specifically invoked—it doesn't need to be. And future cases will continue to move that ball down the field.

June 26 has been proposed as National Right to Keep and Bear Arms Day by Tom Liddy, author, talk show host, politician and son of G. Gordon Liddy.

The decision will provide cover for politicians, who can now reject anti-rights bills by saying their hands are tied by the individual-rights declarations in *Heller.* Obviously not all will, but many will be able to duck a thorny issue without alienating their constituencies, bolstering pro-rights efforts toward new bills and helping to stop bad bills.

I just finished studying the decision, the dense legal text is not easy reading. Much of the commentary I've seen seems based on guesswork, emotion and the syllabus. The case is better than we think, but still, the struggle goes on as it always will. Freedom is not a place you get to, it's a path you travel.

The Truly Tremendous Advance for RKBA:

The core issue of "judicial scrutiny" is well on its way—better than we had dreamed—in what will be known as Famous Footnote #27. Laws impinging on the Second Amendment should receive no lower level of review than any other "specific enumerated right" such as free speech, the guarantee against double jeopardy or the right to counsel (the Court's list of examples).

This is a tremendous win, and overlooked in all initial reviews I've seen. Attorney Mike Anthony was the first to spot it, way to go Mike (see his detailed review of this crucial aspect in the chapter by the experts). "Strict scrutiny," which many folks sought, is a term without formal definition that could prove problematic, and was not applied. I was hoping for a test of some sort and got more than I hoped for. By recognizing 2A as a "specific enumerated right" the majority ties 2A to the rigid standards and precedents of our most cherished rights. That's as strong as there is. Very clever indeed.

Coupled with the Court's dismissal of rational-basis scrutiny, and destruction of a low scrutiny scheme invented by Breyer in his dissent, 2A protection now appears extra robust (but antis will continue their attacks, and not everyone on our side agrees). The big hammer drops, though, with the Court's "clear and penetrating" recognition (Mike's phrase) of self defense as a "core" human right, underpinning one reason for the Second Amendment. Gun-control laws will have to be measured by whether they deny a person's legal right to self defense. Lower courts might not reliably follow the High Court's lead.

It's an interesting coincidence that this quintessential test raises its head in footnote 27, for an amendment with 27 words. What will not be simple coincidence are the coming efforts to deny the importance with an offhanded, "Oh, it's just a footnote." People have already noticed that, while the majority used 29 footnotes, and Stevens used 39 in dissent, Breyer used none in his dissent—because footnotes are a mere matter of style. Breyer chose to put his voluminous statistics in the body of his text, rather than the more typical footnote approach. This choice matters not a whit in terms of the weight of the words. It's the words and their meaning that count, not how the author specifies the typesetting. Writing off meaning in the decision, based on typography, is a sign of desperation.

Seeking to justify the total-handgun-bans-are-perfectly-OK school of thought (the one B. H. Obama supported until this decision came out and he immediately reversed himself), Justice Breyer proposed a brand new level of scrutiny, not just the familiar strict, intermediate or rational-basis levels (from highest to lowest). He invented a new low he calls "interest-balancing inquiry." The Court calls it a "judge empowering... freestanding" approach wholly without merit or precedent and dismisses it completely as a worthless subterfuge.

It's worth noting that, after the decision and Obama's public reversal on the issue, his staff disavowed his anti-gun stance as the mistake of a campaign worker. Unfortunately for the Illinois senator, his anti-rights record on guns is unbroken, and recorded. Removing all the wiggle room, he was asked personally on ABC's local Washington, D.C., station, by anchor Leon Harris, "One other issue that's of great importance here in the District as well is gun control. You said in Idaho recently... 'I have no intention of taking away folks' guns,' but you support the D.C. handgun ban." He had a one-word answer. "Right." When asked further "And you've said that it's constitutional?" He keeps his mouth shut and shakes his head yes.

The *Heller* decision works hard in many ways to preclude further abuses, to establish the primacy of the fundamental rights in the Second Amendment, to foreclose future mischief against the rights protected, and to take certain policy choices off the table—like banning handguns for self defense at home—regardless of how bad criminals are or how they do their dirty work. A gun ban is unconstitutional. Government has other tools to fight crime, and has to use those.

Critics and anti-rights advocates are almost gleeful at the Court's acceptance of Mr. Heller's request for registration and a license to carry his gun in his own home, as long as the terms aren't arbitrary or capricious. Agreed, this is a weak and unsavory intermediate step with potential for abuse, while on the way to greater freedom than D.C. currently has. It has a very dangerous potential for abuse that will be exploited. Antis will try to imply that registration and licensing are more than OK, they are the new standard. This is completely false:

• It is not some national requirement, it is only a response to a specific request from Mr. Heller.

• Heller's request applies specifically to his case, at home, in D.C., to be acted upon by D.C. for its residents.

• Because RKBA is now recognized as a "specific enumerated right" (a phrase you should start using), laws related to it will be subjected to stringent standards like those protecting freedom of speech, protection against double jeopardy or the right to counsel (among the most safeguarded rights we have).

• Registration and a license to practice free speech would obviously never be permissible, so Mr. Heller's request should hold little sway, if any, outside the context of his "prayer" (the Court's word) for relief from the onerous disability he suffered as a D.C. resident. Anti-rights lawyers and legislators will try to argue otherwise, but the ammunition is piled high in the pro-rights arsenal. Our argument is compelling, do not yield. To wit again:

From the Counterintuitive Department: The antis are actually trumpeting our side—People will want less restrictions! Gun bans will fall! Gun-free-zones will come under legal attack! And we're promoting their side for Pete's sake—More licensing and registration is coming! Assault-weapon bans are around the corner! The Court has put another nail in the gun-rights coffin! Be careful about turning a win into a loss, and giving voice to what the other side wants. Don't be a gloomsayer. Watch your neurolinguistics.

The biggest issue for me perhaps is the fact that, on June 25, the day before this decision, not knowing which way it would go, I had this right to keep and bear arms intact. I had it in my home, in my environs, on my steed. I cherished this right, exercised it every day with the keeping and from time to time with the bearing.

It is a right I consider mine, and my country's, and a sign of my status as a free man. And I relish that it's unique in the world—that this country had advanced this right for me, from well before my birth to the present day. I do not care to relinquish this long-held right of mine on some unknown tomorrow. And I cannot see a valid reason even if nine people sitting in a room thousands of miles away say I've been mistaken all this time, or never had it in the first place, or have to give it up for some reason they can imagine, concoct or deem worthwhile.

Certainly, the fact that criminals are doing their nefarious work is not cause or grounds for me to give up my human and civil rights (yet this is the essence of Breyer's dissent).

It is a cruel hoax to seek to persuade the American people that the Bill of Rights should be watered down in response to rising crime rates.
–Nicholas Katzenbach.

And I practically resent, even though I accept the nature of our system, that those nine people actually have the power to deny me the rights my countrymen and I have held since birth, and have held since the birth of this nation. Thank God we dodged this bullet and won. The consequences of a loss are too dire to contemplate.

The Dissent

As is so often the case when reading Supreme Court holdings, after absorbing and agreeing in large measure with the elegant treatise of the majority, the dissent reads well and holds some sway on its own grounds. This is true in *Heller*, and the dissent is compelling in spots (though absurd in other spots), making some points as you would expect a team of top experts to do. There is a little room to wonder, what if the minority of dissenters is actually the right decision? The opposition will do everything in their power to raise that specter of course, just as we would if the single vote went the other way.

The startling realization is that both sides don't *really* know with absolute certainty which argument is correct or how to determine that beyond any doubt, and they cannot. What did the Founders and the public during the period between the Revolution and the drafting of 2A really think about gun ownership, possession and use? Hint: Always choose freedom if such doubts arise.

Each side nips at the surviving documents, assembles the evidence their own way, sprinkles it with clever scholarly wiggle phrases like, "it seems certain that," or "it is unreasonable to assume otherwise," and draws their summation. Argument aside, the historical record leaves little doubt that Americans clung to their gun rights with bitter tenacity.

What is also clear is that the nation has enjoyed private firearms ownership and use for all of its history, and for most of that time, objections have been few, peripheral, and have not negated those rights. In recent times, various government entities have encroached on those rights, in niggling or great ways, and we find ourselves today trying to decide if we should continue to exercise the rights we have always previously enjoyed.

Should we somehow justify the removal of the hundreds of millions of guns Americans presently own? And do all those people have to get Fifth Amendment compensation for their taken property (an issue never raised)? By a single vote in *Heller* we decided no bans, no confiscations, not at this time. And those who have attempted such must reverse their course. They will do so grudgingly at best.

If Stevens' dissent is actually somehow the better assessment, and 2A is all about the militia only, then what of it? Are we no longer the militia armed and ready to serve?

The fact that we have not recently had to take up our arms and repel invaders, suppress an insurrection, execute our laws or resist tyranny from within, are we no longer the impregnable force the Founders expected us to be when the clarion moment arrived? In the grand scheme, if Stevens' dissent controls, we would and should still retain our arms. It might be prudent to promote training with a militia purpose in mind, whatever that might look like.

As a practical matter, one facet of being an American is that you agree, implicitly, if the ship is sinking you will pick up a bucket and bail water. This loyalty is owed in principle to any nation with which you align, where you enjoy its fruits, and serve as a thread in its fabric— but especially so here, where it is codified in statute (10 USC §311 et. seq.). You can abandon ship and run at the slightest wave, but this is without honor. This brings disgrace to you and your house. In this country at least, aside from principle, it's the law. No part of the *Heller* results touch on this, but it's no less true for the omission.

Breyer's dissent cannot be reviewed so favorably, for he admits you "may" have this right, but it can be regulated into oblivion because criminals are bad, guns are dangerous, and government has or should have the power to deny your rights if it thinks a greater purpose is served. It is so off target it is hard to address. Acknowledgment of the values of freedom are absent. His alliance with the principles that make American go are missing in action. He spends inordinate time invoking stats on how bad criminals are, since he holds that this justifies denial of your rights, and believes that a gun ban will stop criminals and save lives (despite the massive evidence to the contrary, which he refutes ambitiously but poorly).

A step-by-step assessment of both the majority opinion and the points made by the dissent are incorporated in the gist introducing the text of the case, later in this book.

The Next Act In This Play

Heller is just the overture. The gun-rights drama will play itself out everywhere. All the world's its stage. International opinion and actions will make their voices heard. Every domestic jurisdiction and channel of communication will be rife with rumor, fear, fact, reason and actions taken with and without logic or common sense. Only some people will hold freedom and human rights in high esteem. Others, many of whom should know better, like the old media, will trounce these precious liberties without mercy.

• While the Court allowed for gun restrictions at schools, it clearly did not make them mandatory. This now becomes a policy issue. Guns at school were normal and routine for most of the nation's history, and could be again under proper circumstances. History can't be taught properly without that component, and show-and-tell is as perfectly valid today as it was when many of us were in grade school. Rights denial at school causes all sorts of harm and should not be easily accepted (or tolerated at all). The well known dangers of fraudulent so-called gun-free school zones are front and center in the national debate, and *Heller* sheds little light upon this.

• Prior restraint is virtually unacceptable with freedom of speech. It remains to be seen whether many gun-control laws will fall under this doctrine as well. Laws banning criminals are not at issue, but many gun laws do in fact ban constitutionally protected activity under the discredited notion that you can restrain a person from something they haven't done for a misguided notion of some professed common good. You can't arrest a person whose car can exceed the speed limit unless and until they do. The degree to which this applies to RKBA remains to be seen.

• Incorporation of RKBA against the states will have to be hammered out, and early cases are already underway, with the Chicago area and San Francisco filings making headlines. A potentially seminal case handled by attorney Evan Nappen in New Jersey (*Peterson*) addresses that state's long-standing intolerance for gun ownership. As a specific enumerated right, states and local jurisdictions have an uphill battle arguing for carte blanche to deny those highly protected rights. Still, they will try, and the boundaries of who has what power will be drawn as we move forward.

• It seems unlikely to me that a bright line will develop around firearm types. What we currently have we will need to fight to continue to have. New cases, many unfortunately involving criminals, will no doubt be promoted by the antis to proscribe what we may own, possess and use.

• The argument may be made that new guns are "unusual" and hence unprotected under *Heller*. Nothing could be further from the truth. Just as newfangled email has become the "usual" form of modern communication, worthy of every protection a Guttenberg press is entitled to, so too an Officer's Class Three Phaser deserves similar protection. The idea that the militia must make do solely with muskets is now on the trash heap of abandoned schemes.

• Any gun litigation or legislation could probably have *Heller* brought to bear on it, but this should be done prudently and with great measured care. As future actions define the scope of *Heller*, harm as well as good can be done. No doubt, as in the past, the worst of the worst criminals will use novel arguments and the Second Amendment to attempt to squirm out of just punishment. These cases should not move forward with *Heller* at the helm, since they can weaken or demolish the strengths that otherwise reside there.

• Defense attorneys around the country are already citing to *Heller* in attempts to exonerate murderers, rapists, armed robbers and other miscreants. A public defender with a long-shot gamble on behalf of an unsavory defendant may have virtually zero chance of success, but does have an obligation to make any plausible argument on behalf of the client. These lawyers play a very important role in keeping the government honest about search and seizure, due process, and much of the rest of the Constitution. It was precisely such an attorney who won *Emerson* in the trial court. Still, this represents a somewhat unexpected consequence of the strong 2A ruling in *Heller*. Don Kates addresses this (as will many others, I'm sure) in a recent law review article (summarized in the chapter by the experts).

• Presidential hopeful Barack H. Obama would consider banning gun stores in America, through the novel suggestion of a five-mile no-store-zone around schools and parks (eliminating virtually every gun store in the nation). Washington D.C. suffers this currently, since there are no gun stores in the city, the Council has publicly announced its reluctance to approve any, and D.C. residents cannot buy and take delivery of a gun across state lines under federal law. The *Heller* decision is extra hollow if D.C. residents can have a firearm, but cannot obtain one. This perfect Catch-22 will need to be addressed.

• The dissenters introduced a number of serious errors and these are examined in the chapter by the experts, especially by Dave Hardy. Let me add a remark in that regard:

Stevens says few Second Amendment cases were heard at the High Court during the 19th Century. There were nine (see Kopel's chart in the first chapter) that touched upon 2A. He also says the legislature had few Second Amendment concerns enacting the National Firearms Act in 1934. In fact, the concerns were great enough that Congress enacted a circuitous taxation scheme, hoping this might squeak past the infringement restriction, whereas an outright ban might not pass scrutiny. Backed by some questionable court maneuvering—like the uncontested "hearing" in *Miller*—they got away with it. The lower court had found no difficulty in dismissing the complaint against Miller and his partner Layton on Second Amendment grounds.

Late Breaking Hubris

As expected, the District of Columbia is doing everything possible to undermine the Supreme Court ruling in *Heller*, to make it virtually (instead of completely) impossible to use a firearm for self defense in the home, and place registration requirements so abusive that few may wish to act under the new dictates and "amnesty" program. WARNING: Governments everywhere will try to use the stunning hubris of the D.C. policy as a model for their own actions, and make *Heller* the precursor to the worst gun restrictions the nation has ever seen proposed. Read the rules yourself, be sure you're sitting down, you'll find them linked at gunlaws.com/supreme.htm.

The horrifying, law-avoiding details issued by D.C.'s rulers include (at present, much of this is expected to be challenged with uncertain results):

• No semi-auto handguns of any kind will be allowed—revolvers and derringers only (completely ignoring the guns "in common use for lawful purposes" requirement);

• Guns in your own home must be unloaded and locked up or disassembled (exactly what the Supreme Court overturned) except "while it is being used to protect against a reasonably perceived threat of immediate harm to a person within the registrant's home";

• Only one gun may be registered in the first 90 days, and it must be brought in for ballistics testing while you are fingerprinted, vision tested and databased.

In other words, if the gun you keep for self defense in your home is not kept useless and inoperable you will be subject to criminal penalties. In the event you do shoot an intruder in legitimate self defense, the city won't indict you for having a working gun. And that's not all:

• Three separate taxes totalling $60 per gun;

• "Rights testing" with a 20-question multiple choice test (no details on the contents or passing grade have been released);

• A 180-day "amnesty" period to register people (voluntarily) who already own guns (that were illegal under the old D.C. law);

• Special "runaround" procedures requiring pre-application approval, paperwork presentation to a gun dealer (and there are none currently operating for the public in D.C., a separate issue concerning federally banned out-of-state gun sales), and immediate return to the only approved police station;

• Instant disclosure requirements to street officers if stopped enroute;

• Two passport photos required (a built in delay and hidden tax);

• No prostitutes allowed (really!). One commentator says that this will prevent some politicians from applying.

It is a blatant effort to deny and harass exercise of rights the High Court declared are fundamental. Gang bangers and other criminals need not apply and are *specifically excluded* from all these requirements.

D.C. says it won't allow any handguns that load "from the bottom," because these could conceivably take a magazine that holds more than 12 rounds. Under D.C. law, though this is irrational, that's a machine gun. I am not making this up. ("'Machine gun' means any firearm which shoots, is designed to shoot, or can be readily converted or restored to shoot: (B) Semiautomatically, more than 12 shots without manual reloading.") By this definition, the D.C. police I saw were carrying machine guns in their holsters. Not.

Dick Heller was near the front of the line on July 17 when the police began taking applications, and he was denied because he sought to register a Colt Model 1911 semi-automatic pistol with a seven-round magazine (which he did not bring along, to avoid confiscation). The High Court decision *specifically* said he must be allowed to register "his handgun" but the bureaucrats and anti-rights zealots in the city turned him down. The denial will give him standing for more legal action. Ugh. This is not good-faith compliance on the part of elected officials or the result Mr. Heller deserved.

The phrase "his handgun," though undefined in the decision, most reasonably refers to the handgun he was originally denied registration for, which gave him legal standing in the first place. That firearm is a nine-shot, .22 caliber, Harrington & Richardson "Longhorn," a cowboy-style piece in blue steel with a six-inch barrel. When interviewed by the *Washington Post,* Heller said it's one of his favorites, "like the kind Matt Dillon used on 'Gunsmoke'" (though it's unlikely a town sheriff would stake his life and a town's safety on the smallest caliber in common use, even on a fictional TV drama).

Heller successfully registered this firearm on July 18, 2008, according to the *Post*. Later reports indicated Heller is indeed pursuing a suit against the city for their semi-auto ban. His winning case had been specifically structured around the revolver to avoid the bogus machine-gun controversy and D.C.'s inane definition of plain pistols.

News reports were widely inconsistent on the events surrounding the initial registrations. The *Post* said that only four other attempted registrations had been made by the time Heller got his gun government approved. Of those, one gun had been confiscated, the *Post* reported, because the applicant had a criminal record. That had to be one pretty stupid criminal, or an error on someone's part.

Virginia Citizens Defense League member Amy McVey apparently became the first person to register a gun in D.C. in 32 years. As she tells it, "I went downtown yesterday with my revolver in a blue grocery bag and managed to walk right past the press... I didn't fit the profile! I thought that the rush would be over by the time I went to police headquarters, but as it turns out, there was no rush! I was it! It was quite comical. I have the "01" property ticket that all the news channels were showing as being unclaimed by midday on Thursday. It has been suggested I put it on eBay. So my revolver was the first to be tagged and tested and I came home with the first legal handgun in D.C. in 32 years. I am one happy camper!"

The city's attitude, with little effort at disguise, is "so sue us." They will spend buckets of our money (taxes,) fighting our sacred and affirmed rights, instead of obeying their oath to preserve, protect and defend the Constitution, and to virtuously follow the rule of law. Meanwhile, criminals are unaffected, and the public remains unarmed.

"We have crafted what I believe to be a model for the nation in terms of complying with the Supreme Court's Second Amendment decision and at the same time protecting our citizens," according to the city's interim Attorney General Peter Nickles.

He's far from alone. In Chicago, the Supreme Court's ruling, "does not apply to state and local governments," according to Benna Solomon, a government official (deputy corporation counsel) involved in trying to preserve Chicago's total gun ban.

"The decision affirms the right of states to regulate gun ownership in order to preserve public safety," according to David Wald, speaking for the New Jersey attorney general's office, another place with little regard for the civil right to arms. (Note that though officials like to speak of the "right" to regulate the public, they have no such thing, they only have specifically delegated powers.)

The poor misguided public non-servants in D.C. and elsewhere conflate crime and honest gun ownership. They are blind to the truth. To them, there is no difference between decent human beings in possession of this private property, and murderers loose on their streets, beyond any semblance of their control. Impotent against the real problem, they lash out insanely at the only available (and cooperative) target, decent citizens. This looks very much like the government the Founders warned us about.

President Bush, who has been something of a disappointment to gun-rights supporters, said in a statement, "As a longstanding advocate of the rights of gun owners in America, I applaud the Supreme Court's historic decision today confirming what has always been clear in the Constitution: the Second Amendment protects an individual right to keep and bear firearms." He asked D.C. to "swiftly move" in protecting residents' rights. (Note: The Second Amendment protects the right to keep and bear *arms*, a broader category than "firearms.")

The Justice Dept., also in a statement, made it clear it will not all of a sudden become a champion of gun rights, but that it, "will continue to defend vigorously the constitutionality, under the Second Amendment, of all existing federal firearms laws." Under its direction (or with its approval tacit or otherwise) it has perpetrated hellacious abuses on citizens for paperwork violations, dubious infractions, and at times, arbitrary enforcement of the laws it is responsible for. Their published guide to firearm laws includes the laws you must obey, but none of the laws that control them. The Department's record on *defending* the right to arms is, well, there isn't one.

In other news, several suburbs of Chicago, sued immediately after the *Heller* decision by a coalition of pro-rights groups, have capitulated and agreed to suspend or repeal the gun bans against their residents. The town of Morton Grove, the poster child of anti-rights gun-banners—where gun-ban advocates had prevailed in media-hyped legal challenges in the early 1980s—is among the capitulators.

Hailed in some quarters as a victory, it is a mere expedient by shrewd politicians acting in their own self interest. Why spend scarce funds defending their gun bans, when they can just sit back and let Chicago's mayor and his underlings do the heavy lifting. If they lose, case closed (after endless appeals, expense and conniving in back rooms). If they win, hey, the genie is out of the bottle and the minor players can just pile on.

This brings up the most frightening aspects of *Heller*. What the Supreme Court said will be defined in large measure not by what

Heller says, but by tiny functionaries in tiny courts with small mindsets and a decidedly hostile attitude toward Second Amendment rights. When Mr. Heller or others attempt to have their rights enforced against government encroachments, even encroachments showing a blatant disregard for the clear terms, requirements and spirit of the SCOTUS decision, they will face low-level officials with power. There is little more dangerous than little bureaucrats with a little power.

It's not unlikely that, when Dick Heller or someone eventually faces the disputed issues with an unsympathetic judge in D.C. who is on the D.C. payroll and works for D.C. masters, he will hear, "Well, the new D.C. law seems reasonable to me, and it seems to comply with the letter of the Supreme Court ruling." The fight against city hall will just drag on. This freedom fight is particularly onerous, because people die or lose heart as their substance is eaten out, but government lingers.

The winning appellate decision before Heller's case was a two-to-one squeaker. The next one could squeak the other way. If there's yet another appeal to on high, who knows if they'll take it, or who might be on the Bench at that time, or what decision it may yield. The fat lady hasn't sung yet.

But she is warming up. Dick Heller, represented by Stephen Halbrook and Richard Gardiner, has filed suit in the U.S. District Court for D.C., against Mayor Fenty and the District of Columbia. They plan to rectify abuses in the D.C. law, which prevent Mr. Heller from full enjoyment of his right to keep and bear arms and the explicit terms of the *Heller* decision. He is joined by Absalom F. Jordan, Jr., a D.C. resident, in case 1:08-cv-01289 before judge Ricardo M. Urbina.

They seek "to redress the deprivation, under color of the laws, statute, ordinances, regulations, customs and usages of the District of Columbia, of rights, privileges or immunities secured by the United States Constitution." Specifically, the narrowly focused suit claims:

1– D.C.'s ban on semi-autos is impermissible ("The Supreme Court explicitly articulated that handguns are constitutionally-protected arms because they are in common use at this time, are typically possessed by law-abiding citizens for lawful purposes, are considered by the American people to be the quintessential self-defense weapon, are the most popular weapon chosen by Americans for self-defense in the home, and are the most preferred firearm in the nation to keep and use for protection of one's home and family");

2– Defining semi-autos that can shoot more than 12 rounds as machine guns, so they may not be registered, is infringement;

3– The requirement that guns at home be kept unloaded and locked except when is use to protect against "a reasonably perceived threat of immediate harm" unduly burdens the right to self defense and infringes the right to keep and bear arms;

4–Requiring any fee, and especially a fee whose size is arbitrarily set by the chief of police, infringes the right to keep and bear arms;

5–Requiring that firearms be submitted for ballistics testing prior to registration infringes the right to keep and bear arms; and

6– In general, while the D.C. Code allows "usual and reasonable police regulations" concerning firearms and other weapons, D.C.'s actions are highly unusual and unreasonable, and hence they are impermissible.

Only time will tell where the suit goes, how many appeals it may take, how much taxpayer money D.C. will spend trying to strip rights from its citizens, and if the courts will settle the various matters favorably, from a constitutional point of view.

Freedom requires eternal vigilance. The ultimate irony here may be that *Heller* enraged and motivated the anti-rights forces, while the pro-rights side is still busy shouting, "Hooray, we won!" That's a dangerous chant to chant for too very long, with your freedom on the line. Is it time to re-up memberships, forge new ones, and refresh your commitment to the cause of liberty? This writer certainly thinks so.

Text of the Cases

Notes and Cautions

The four gun-related cases heard at the Supreme Court since *Supreme Court Gun Cases* (SCGC) was released in 2003 are included in this volume. Summaries and a descriptive index of all 96 cases are also included, making this a stand-alone reference to the entire body of Supreme Court jurisprudence on the subject of guns.

The 92 cases reproduced and described in SCGC will remain available while supplies last. After that, the entire work will be available as a downloadable pdf file at gunlaws.com. Forty-four decisions are presented complete and unedited. The rest are excerpted to preserve gun-related portions only.

Online copies, upon which *Supreme Court Gun Cases* is largely based, are known to have some small differences from the official court decisions, and these will be faithfully reporduced, such as typos, spellings, or occasionally unusual typesetting styles (ellipses, em dashes, hyphenation, etc.). The only official copy is *U.S. Reports*, which should be used exclusively for any legal matters. See the disclaimer in the front section of this book for other important warnings and information.

Omissions within cases are noted by a set of five dots at the left margin. (This volume has no omissions, SCGC has many in its excerpted cases.)

Editorial comments are in <angle brackets> and are not part of the opinions.

The syllabus is a non-binding abstract prepared by the Court, and appears in italics in cases that have one included.

Gists were prepared specifically for these books, precede each case, and are intended to provide an easily readable overview in regular conversational terms for your convenience. The casual reader should be able to enjoy this book by reading the gists and passing over the sometimes complex verbiage of the cases themselves. However, while great care has been taken to produce the gists with a high degree of accuracy, no guarantee of accuracy is expressed or implied, and none of the explanatory sections of this book are to be considered as legal advice or a restatement of law.

Highlighted quotations have been edited for readability and appear right before the paragraph in which they occur verbatim. Highlighted quotations are never drawn from the syllabus. No attempt to sum up or distill the meaning of a case is made or intended by the highlighted quotes. That is the function of the Gists.

The highlights serve to showcase the juicier, more dramatic passages of the Court's published decisions **irrespective of the case outcome**, and to aid in navigation, and to help alleviate what some might inexplicably be inclined to criticize in spots as a rather dry text.

Experts can disagree on what the core holding of a case and its effect may be (just consider the 1939 *U.S. v. Miller* decision), and it is certainly not something attempted by the highlighted quotes. Many times, the key judicial phrase has all the charm and illumination of "reversed and remanded."

In contrast, the Court's history and indeed the nation's is held within the pages of its High Court records. It is this captivating essence the highlights aspire to illuminate. A strong sense emerges of how very gun-conscious the Supreme Court has consistently been over the centuries.

Serious effort was made to highlight quotations evenly on all sides of the gun debate, but the material was simply lopsided. For the collectivist and anti-rights arguments, there isn't very much in the first 95 cases to get excited about. There are several opinions in the last few decades that express a very negative view of guns, or that question where the limits of infringement rest, but that was about it. The dissent in the *Heller* case increased the number of anti-rights quotes significantly, introducing by itself far more anti-rights arguments than the entire history of Supreme Court jurisprudence had previously.

You must take special care to note from within context whether a given highlighted quote is part of the decision of the Court, dissenting opinions, concurrences, the facts of the case, the arguments of the parties, pleadings, *dicta* statements by the Court, quotes from other cases, jury instructions, footnotes, reference material quoted in the case, or other language included in the official published decision.

You should also keep an eye out for inconsistent or potentially confusing nomenclature, since the person at the center of a case might be called the plaintiff, respondent, petitioner, appellee, accused, defendant or prisoner.

More difficult still is the resolution of comments that don't agree with each other, and the question of whether a comment is still valid or even meaningful in light of later cases, recent statutes and a new day. Some subjects experience wholesale reversal, like the applicability of the Bill of Rights to the states, or the changed legality of slavery. **If you decide to run off and mouth quotes without carefully checking context you're at great risk of making a fool of yourself.** Always check the *in situ* verbatim language in the paragraph immediately after highlighted quotes, and other indicators, for context, relevance and meaning.

Although an effort was made initially to highlight gun-specific language, which turned out to be quite revealing if for nothing else than in its copious breadth, all eye-opening passages became candidates for the highlighter as the review process wore on. This being a human endeavor, the reader will no doubt find sections that definitely should or should not be included to personal taste. Permission to use a marker in your own copy of the book is granted.

Complaints regarding the highlighted quotes should be directed solely to Alan Korwin as this element of *Supreme Court Gun Cases* and *The Heller Case: Gun Rights Affirmed*, as well as final responsibility for the Gists, rests upon his desk. He readily admits he could not have done it without invaluable assistance and direct contributions from Dave Kopel and others, duly noted in the acknowledgments, but the buck for the final product stops with him.

BROSSEAU v. HAUGEN

(FULL CASE)

543 U.S. 194

December 13, 2004, Decided

GIST: This case touched upon excessive use of force by police in apprehending a suspect, but the Court sidestepped that issue to only resolve the question of *qualified immunity*, which protects police from lawsuits in certain cases. Because there is a "hazy border between excessive and acceptable force," police are immune to lawsuits, even if their actions are unconstitutional, if they reasonably misapprehend the law under the specific situation they face when a confrontation occurs. These rules for police do not apply equally to the public.

Officer Rochelle Brosseau shot Kenneth Haugen in the back, through his Jeep's window, while he was trying to flee. A criminal with an outstanding warrant who was in a fracas with one of his criminal cohorts, Haugen claimed that officer Brosseau used excessive force that violated his 4th Amendment rights. Although the District court agreed with Brosseau, the 9th Circuit sided with Haugen, but the High Court reversed—because the law in place at the time did not clearly make Brosseau's conduct a violation of the Constitution, and she was found immune. The earlier case of *Tennessee v. Garner* said that shooting an unarmed nondangerous suspect to "seize" the person is unconstitutional, but when the officer has probable cause to believe the person poses a serious threat to the officer or others, deadly force is permissible.

In this case, Brosseau's actions were not in clear violation of the standard from *Tennessee v. Garner,* so Officer Brosseau was entitled to "qualified immunity." Qualified immunity protects a government employee whose actions were in a constitutional gray zone; even if the employee's actions are later determined to violate the Constitution, she is protected from civil liability.

The case begins with a vivid description of the perpetrator's behavior, other parties involved, his attempt to escape and Brosseau's shot through the rear driver's side window.

Per Curiam.

He alleged that the shot fired by Brosseau constituted excessive force and violated his federal constitutional rights.

Officer Rochelle Brosseau, a member of the Puyallup, Washington, Police Department, shot Kenneth Haugen in the back as he attempted to flee from law enforcement authorities in his vehicle. Haugen subsequently filed this action in the United States District Court for the Western District of Washington pursuant to Rev. Stat. §1979, 42 U. S. C. §1983. He alleged that the shot fired by Brosseau constituted excessive force and violated his federal constitutional rights. n1 The District Court granted summary judgment to Brosseau after finding she was entitled to qualified immunity. The Court of Appeals for the Ninth Circuit reversed. 339 F. 3d 857 (2003). Following the two-step process set out in Saucier v. Katz, 533 U. S. 194 (2001), the Court of Appeals found, first, that Brosseau had violated Haugen's Fourth Amendment right to be free from excessive force and, second, that the right violated was clearly established and thus Brosseau was not entitled to qualified immunity. Brosseau then petitioned for writ of certiorari, requesting that we review both of the Court of Appeals' determinations. We grant the petition on the second, qualified immunity question and reverse.

n1 Haugen also asserted pendent state-law claims and claims against the city and police department. These claims are not presently before us.

The material facts, construed in a light most favorable to Haugen, are as follows. n2 On the day before the fracas, Glen Tamburello went to the police station and reported to Brosseau that Haugen, a former crime partner of his, had stolen tools from his shop. Brosseau later learned that there was a felony no-bail warrant out for Haugen's arrest on drug and other offenses. The next morning, Haugen was spray-painting his Jeep Cherokee in his mother's driveway. Tamburello learned of Haugen's whereabouts, and he and cohort Matt Atwood drove a pickup truck to Haugen's mother's house to pay Haugen a visit. A fight ensued, which was witnessed by a neighbor who called 911.

n2 Because this case arises in the posture of a motion for summary judgment, we are required to view all facts and draw all reasonable inferences in favor of the nonmoving party, Haugen. See Saucier v. Katz, 533 U.S. 194, 201, 150 L. Ed. 2d 272, 121 S. Ct. 2151 (2001).

Brosseau heard a report that the men were fighting in Haugen's mother's yard and responded. When she arrived, Tamburello and Atwood were attempting to get Haugen into Tamburello's pickup. Brosseau's arrival created a distraction, which provided Haugen the opportunity to get away. Haugen ran through his mother's yard and hid in the neighborhood. Brosseau requested assistance, and, shortly thereafter, two officers arrived with a K-9 to help track Haugen down. During the search, which lasted about 30 to 45 minutes, officers instructed Tamburello and Atwood to remain in Tamburello's pickup. They instructed Deanna Nocera, Haugen's girlfriend who was also present with her 3-year-old daughter, to remain in her small car with her daughter. Tamburello's pickup was parked in the street in front of the driveway; Nocera's small car was parked in the driveway in front of and facing the Jeep; and the Jeep was in the driveway facing Nocera's car and angled somewhat to the left. The Jeep was parked about 4 feet away from Nocera's car and 20 to 30 feet away from Tamburello's pickup.

Brosseau believed that he was running to the Jeep to retrieve a weapon.

An officer radioed from down the street that a neighbor had seen a man in her backyard. Brosseau ran in that direction, and Haugen appeared. He ran past the front of his mother's house and then turned and ran into the driveway. With Brosseau still in pursuit, he jumped into the driver's side of the Jeep and closed and locked the door. Brosseau believed that he was running to the Jeep to retrieve a weapon.

On the third or fourth try, the window shattered. Brosseau unsuccessfully attempted to grab the keys and struck Haugen on the head with the barrel and butt of her gun. Haugen, still undeterred, succeeded in starting the Jeep. As the Jeep started or shortly after it began to move, Brosseau jumped back and to the left. She fired one shot through the rear driver's side window at a forward angle, hitting Haugen in the back.

Brosseau arrived at the Jeep, pointed her gun at Haugen, and ordered him to get out of the vehicle. Haugen ignored her command and continued to look for the keys so he could get the Jeep started. Brosseau repeated her commands and hit the driver's side window several times with her handgun, which failed to deter Haugen. On the third or fourth try, the window shattered. Brosseau unsuccessfully attempted to grab the keys and struck Haugen on the head with the barrel and butt of her gun. Haugen, still undeterred, succeeded in starting the Jeep. As the Jeep started or shortly after it began to move, Brosseau jumped back and to the left. She fired one shot through the rear driver's side window at a forward angle, hitting Haugen in the back. She later explained that she shot Haugen because she was "'fearful for the other officers on foot who [she] believed were in the immediate area, [and] for the occupied vehicles in [Haugen's] path and for any other citizens who might be in the area.'" 339 F. 3d, at 865.

Despite being hit, Haugen, in his words, "'st[ood] on the gas'"; navigated the "'small, tight space'" to avoid the other vehicles; swerved across the neighbor's lawn; and continued down the street. Id., at 882. After about a half block, Haugen realized that he had been shot and brought the Jeep to a halt. He suffered a collapsed lung and was airlifted to a hospital. He survived the shooting and subsequently pleaded guilty to the felony of "eluding." Wash. Rev. Code §46.61.024 (1994). By so pleading, he admitted that he drove his Jeep in a manner indicating "a wanton or wilful disregard for the lives . . . of others." Ibid. He subsequently brought this §1983 action against Brosseau.

* * *

When confronted with a claim of qualified immunity, a court must ask first the following question: "Taken in the light most favorable to the party asserting the injury, do the facts alleged show the officer's conduct violated a constitutional right?" Saucier v. Katz, 533 U. S., at 201. As the Court of Appeals recognized, the constitutional question in this case is governed by the principles enunciated in Tennessee v. Garner, 471 U. S. 1 (1985), and Graham v. Connor, 490 U. S. 386 (1989). These cases establish that claims of excessive force are to be judged under the Fourth Amendment's "'objective reasonableness'" standard. *Id.,* at 388. Specifically with regard to deadly force, we explained in *Garner* that it is unreasonable for an officer to "seize an unarmed, nondangerous suspect by shooting him dead." 471 U. S., at 11. But "[w]here the officer has probable cause to believe that the suspect poses a threat of serious physical harm, either to the officer or to others, it is not constitutionally unreasonable to prevent escape by using deadly force." *Ibid.*

We express no view as to the correctness of the Court of Appeals' decision on the constitutional question itself. We believe that, however that question is decided, the Court of Appeals was wrong on the issue of qualified immunity. n3

n3 We have no occasion in this case to reconsider our instruction in *Saucier* v. *Katz,* supra, that lower courts decide the constitutional question prior to deciding the qualified immunity question. We exercise our summary reversal procedure here simply to correct a clear misapprehension of the qualified immunity standard.

Qualified immunity shields an officer from suit when she makes a decision that, even if constitutionally deficient, reasonably misapprehends the law governing the circumstances she confronted.

If the law at that time did not clearly establish that the officer's conduct would violate the Constitution, the officer should not be subject to liability or, indeed, even the burdens of litigation.

Qualified immunity shields an officer from suit when she makes a decision that, even if constitutionally deficient, reasonably misapprehends the law governing the circumstances she confronted. *Saucier* v. *Katz,* 533 U. S., at 206 (qualified immunity operates "to protect officers from the sometimes 'hazy border between excessive and acceptable force'"). Because the focus is on whether the officer had fair notice that her conduct was unlawful, reasonableness is judged against the backdrop of the law at the time of the conduct. If the law at that time did not clearly establish that the officer's conduct would violate the Constitution, the officer should not be subject to liability or, indeed, even the burdens of litigation.

It is important to emphasize that this inquiry "must be undertaken in light of the specific context of the case, not as a broad general proposition." *Id.,* at 201. As we previously said in this very context:

"[T]here is no doubt that Graham v. Connor, supra, clearly establishes the general proposition that use of force is contrary to the Fourth Amendment if it is excessive under objective standards of reasonableness. Yet that is not enough. Rather, we emphasized in Anderson [v. Creighton,] 'that the right the official is alleged to have violated must have been "clearly established" in a more particularized, and hence more relevant, sense: The contours of the right must be sufficiently clear that a reasonable official would understand that what he is doing violates that right.' 483 U. S. [635,] 640 [(1987)]. The relevant, dispositive inquiry in determining whether a right is clearly established is whether it would be clear to a reasonable officer that his conduct was unlawful in the situation he confronted." Id., at 201-202.

The Court of Appeals acknowledged this statement of law, but then proceeded to find fair warning in the general tests set out in Graham and Garner. 339 F. 3d, at 873-874. In so doing, it was mistaken. Graham and Garner, following the lead of the Fourth Amendment's text, are cast at a high level of generality. See Graham v. Connor, supra, at 396 ("'[T]he test of reasonableness under the Fourth Amendment is not capable of precise definition or mechanical application'"). Of course, in an obvious case, these standards can "clearly establish" the answer, even without a body of relevant case law. See Hope v. Pelzer, 536 U. S. 730, 738 (2002) (noting in a case where the Eighth Amendment violation was "obvious" that there need not be a materially similar case for the right to be clearly established). See also Pace v. Capobianco, 283 F. 3d 1275, 1283 (CA11 2002) (explaining in a Fourth Amendment case involving an officer shooting a fleeing suspect in a vehicle that, "when we look at decisions such as Garner and Graham, we see some tests to guide us in determining the law in many different kinds of circumstances; but we do not see the kind of clear law (clear answers) that would apply" to the situation at hand). The present case is far from the obvious one where Graham and Garner alone offer a basis for decision.

We therefore turn to ask whether, at the time of Brosseau's actions, it was "'clearly established'" in this more "'particularized'" sense that she was violating Haugen's Fourth Amendment right. *Saucier* v. *Katz,* 533 U. S., at 202. The parties point us to only a handful of cases relevant to the "situation [Brosseau] confronted": whether to shoot a disturbed felon, set on avoiding capture through vehicular flight, when persons in the immediate area are at risk from that flight. n4 *Ibid.* Specifically, Brosseau points us to Cole v. Bone, 993 F. 2d 1328 (CA8 1993), and Smith v. Freland, 954 F. 2d 343 (CA6 1992).

n4 The parties point us to a number of other cases in this vein that postdate the conduct in question, *i.e.*, Brosseau's February 21, 1999, shooting of Haugen. See *Cowan ex rel. Estate of Cooper* v. *Breen*, 352 F.3d 756, 763 (CA2 2003); *Pace* v. *Capobianco*, 283 F.3d 1275, 1281-1282 (CA11 2002); *Scott* v. *Clay County*, 205 F.3d 867, 877 (CA6 2000); *McCaslin* v. *Wilkins*, 183 F.3d 775, 778-779 (CA8 1999); *Abraham* v. *Raso*, 183 F.3d 279, 288-296 (CA3 1999). These decisions, of course, could not have given fair notice to Brosseau and are of no use in the clearly established inquiry.

a car can be a deadly weapon

Smith **is closer to this case ... It noted that the suspect, like Haugen here, "had proven he would do almost anything to avoid capture" and that he posed a major threat to, among others, the officers at the end of the street.**

In these cases, the courts found no Fourth Amendment violation when an officer shot a fleeing suspect who presented a risk to others. *Cole* v. *Bone, supra*, at 1333 (holding the officer "had probable cause to believe that the truck posed an imminent threat of serious physical harm to innocent motorists as well as to the officers themselves"); *Smith* v. *Freland*, 954 F. 2d, at 347 (noting "a car can be a deadly weapon" and holding the officer's decision to stop the car from possibly injuring others was reasonable). *Smith* is closer to this case. There, the officer and suspect engaged in a car chase, which appeared to be at an end when the officer cornered the suspect at the back of a dead-end residential street. The suspect, however, freed his car and began speeding down the street. At this point, the officer fired a shot, which killed the suspect. The court held the officer's decision was reasonable and thus did not violate the Fourth Amendment. It noted that the suspect, like Haugen here, "had proven he would do almost anything to avoid capture" and that he posed a major threat to, among others, the officers at the end of the street. *Ibid.*

Haugen points us to *Estate of Starks* v. *Enyart*, 5 F. 3d 230 (CA7 1993), where the court found summary judgment inappropriate on a Fourth Amendment claim involving a fleeing suspect. There, the court concluded that the threat created by the fleeing suspect's failure to brake when an officer suddenly stepped in front of his just-started car was not a sufficiently grave threat to justify the use of deadly force. *Id.*, at 234.

this area is one in which the result depends very much on the facts of each case.

These three cases taken together undoubtedly show that this area is one in which the result depends very much on the facts of each case. None of them squarely governs the case here; they do suggest that Brosseau's actions fell in the "'hazy border between excessive and acceptable force.'" *Saucier* v. *Katz, supra,* at 206. The cases by no means "clearly establish" that Brosseau's conduct violated the Fourth Amendment.4

The judgment of the United States Court of Appeals for the Ninth Circuit is therefore reversed, and the case is remanded for further proceedings consistent with this opinion.

It is so ordered.

Justice Breyer, with whom Justice Scalia and Justice Ginsburg join, concurring.

I join the Court's opinion but write separately to express my concern about the matter to which the Court refers in footnote 3, namely, the way in which lower courts are required to evaluate claims of qualified immunity under the Court's decision in *Saucier* v. *Katz*, 533 U. S. 194, 201 (2001). As the Court notes, *ante*, at 198, n. 3, 160 L. Ed. 2d, at 588-589, *Saucier* requires lower courts to decide (1) the constitutional question prior to deciding (2) the qualified immunity question. I am concerned that the current rule rigidly requires courts unnecessarily to decide difficult constitutional questions when there is available an easier basis for the decision (*e.g.,* qualified immunity) that will satisfactorily resolve the case before the court. Indeed when courts' dockets are crowded, a rigid "order of battle" makes little administrative sense and can sometimes lead to a constitutional decision that is effectively insulated from review, see *Bunting* v. *Mellen*, 541 U. S. 1019, 1025 (2004) (*Scalia, J.*, dissenting from denial of certiorari). For these reasons, I think we should reconsider this issue.

Justice Stevens, dissenting.

In my judgment, the answer to the constitutional question presented by this case is clear: Under the Fourth Amendment, it was objectively unreasonable for Officer Brosseau to use deadly force against Kenneth Haugen in an attempt to prevent his escape. What is not clear is whether Brosseau is nonetheless entitled to qualified immunity because it might not have been apparent to a reasonably well trained officer in Brosseau's shoes that killing Haugen to prevent his escape was unconstitutional. In my opinion that question should be answered by a jury.

I

Law enforcement officers should never be subject to damages liability for failing to anticipate novel developments in constitutional law. Accordingly, whenever a suit against an officer is based on the alleged violation of a constitutional right that has not been clearly established, the qualified immunity defense is available. *Harlow* v. *Fitzgerald*, 457 U. S. 800, 818 (1982). Prompt dismissal of such actions protects officers from unnecessary litigation and accords with this Court's wise "policy of avoiding the unnecessary adjudication of constitutional questions." *County of Sacramento* v. *Lewis*, 523 U. S. 833, 859 (1998) (*Stevens*, J., concurring in judgment). When, however, the applicable constitutional rule is well settled, "we should address the constitutional question at the outset." *Ibid.;* see also *Siegert* v. *Gilley*, 500 U. S. 226 (1991). The constitutional limits on the use of deadly force have been clearly established for almost two decades.

In 1985, we held that the killing of an unarmed burglar to prevent his escape was an unconstitutional seizure. *Tennessee* v. *Garner*, 471 U. S. 1. We considered, and rejected, the State's contention that the Fourth Amendment's prohibition against unreasonable seizures should be construed in light of the common-law rule, which allowed the use of whatever force was necessary to effectuate the arrest of a fleeing felon. *Id.*, at 12-13. We recognized that the common-law rule had been fashioned "when virtually all felonies were punishable by death" and long before guns were available to the police, and noted that modern police departments in a majority of large cities allowed the firing of a weapon only when a felon presented a threat of death or serious bodily harm. *Id.*, at 13-19. We concluded that "changes in the legal and technological context" had made the old rule obsolete. *Id.*, at 15.

Unlike most "excessive force" cases in which the degree of permissible force varies widely from case to case, the only issue in a "deadly force" case is whether the facts apparent to the officer justify a decision to kill a suspect in order to prevent his escape.

In *Garner* we stated the governing rule:

"The use of deadly force to prevent the escape of all felony suspects, whatever the circumstances, is constitutionally unreasonable. It is not better that all felony suspects die than that they escape.

A police officer may not seize an unarmed, nondangerous suspect by shooting him dead

"The use of deadly force to prevent the escape of all felony suspects, whatever the circumstances, is constitutionally unreasonable. It is not better that all felony suspects die than that they escape. Where the suspect poses no immediate threat to the officer and no threat to others, the harm resulting from failure to apprehend him does not justify the use of deadly force to do so.... . A police officer may not seize an unarmed, nondangerous suspect by shooting him dead.... .

Where the officer has probable cause to believe that the suspect poses a threat of serious physical harm, either to the officer or to others, it is not constitutionally unreasonable to prevent escape by using deadly force.

"Where the officer has probable cause to believe that the suspect poses a threat of serious physical harm, either to the officer or to others, it is not constitutionally unreasonable to prevent escape by using deadly force. Thus, if the suspect threatens the officer with a weapon or there is probable cause to believe that he has committed a crime involving the infliction or threatened infliction of serious physical harm, deadly force may be used if necessary to prevent escape, and if, where feasible, some warning has been given." Id., at 11-12.

The most common justifications for the use of deadly force are plainly inapplicable to this case. Respondent Haugen had not threatened anyone with a weapon, and petitioner Brosseau did not shoot in order to defend herself. n5 Haugen was not a person who had committed a violent crime; nor was there any reason to believe he would do so if permitted to escape. Indeed, there is nothing in the record to suggest he intended to harm anyone. n6 The "threat of serious physical harm, either to the officer or to others," *ibid.*, that provides the sole justification for Brosseau's use of deadly force was the risk that while fleeing in his vehicle Haugen would accidentally collide with a pedestrian or another vehicle. Whether Brosseau's shot enhanced or minimized that risk is debatable, but the risk of such an accident surely did not justify an attempt to kill the fugitive. n7 Thus, I have no difficulty in endorsing the Court's assumption that Brosseau's conduct violated the Constitution.

n5 Although Brosseau attested that she believed Haugen may have been attempting to retrieve a weapon from the floorboard of his vehicle sometime during the struggle, a fact which Haugen hotly contests, there is no evidence in the record to suggest that, at the time the shot was fired,

Brosseau believed, or any reasonable officer would have thought, that Haugen had access to a weapon at that moment.

n6 At the time of the shooting, Brosseau had the following facts at her disposal. Haugen had a felony no-bail warrant for a nonviolent drug offense, was suspected in a nonviolent burglary, and had been fleeing from law enforcement on foot for approximately 30 to 45 minutes without incident. At the behest of Brosseau, the private individuals on the scene were inside their respective vehicles. Haugen's girlfriend and her daughter were in a small car approximately four feet in front and slightly to the right of Haugen's Jeep; Glen Tamburello and Matt Atwood were inside a pickup truck on the street blocking the driveway, approximately 20 to 30 feet from Haugen's Jeep. The only two police officers on foot at the scene were last seen in a neighbor's backyard, two houses down and to the right of the driveway.

n7 The evidence supporting Haugen's allegation that Brosseau did "willfully fire her weapon with the intent to murder me," 1 Record, Doc. No. 1, includes a statement by a defense expert that Brosseau had "clearly articulated her intention to use deadly force," *id.,* Doc. No. 24. Moreover, the report of the Puyallup, Washington, Police Department Firearms Review Board stated that Brosseau "chose to use deadly force to stop Haugen.," 2 *id.,* Doc. No. 27, Exh. H.

II

An officer is entitled to qualified immunity, despite having engaged in constitutionally deficient conduct, if, in doing so, she did not violate "clearly established statutory or constitutional rights of which a reasonable person would have known." *Harlow,* 457 U. S., at 818. The requirement that the law be clearly established is designed to ensure that officers have fair notice of what conduct is proscribed. See *Hope* v. *Pelzer,* 536 U. S. 730, 739 (2002). Accordingly, we have recognized that "general statements of the law are not inherently incapable of giving fair and clear warning," *United States* v. *Lanier,* 520 U. S. 259, 271 (1997), and have firmly rejected the notion that "an official action is protected by qualified immunity unless the very action in question has previously been held unlawful," *Anderson* v. *Creighton,* 483 U. S. 635, 640 (1987).

Thus, the Court's search for relevant case law applying the *Garner* standard to materially similar facts is both unnecessary and ill-advised. See *Hope,* 536 U. S., at 741 ("Although earlier cases involving 'fundamentally similar' facts can provide especially strong support for a conclusion that the law is clearly established, they are not necessary to such a finding"); see also *Lanier,* 520 U. S., at 269. Indeed, the cases the majority relies on are inapposite and, in fact, only serve to illuminate the patent unreasonableness of Brosseau's actions. n8

n8 In *Cole* v. *Bone*, 993 F.2d 1328 (CA8 1993), an 18-wheel tractor-trailer sped through a tollbooth and engaged the police in a high-speed pursuit in excess of 90 miles per hour on a high-traffic interstate during the holiday season. During the course of the pursuit, the driver passed traffic on both shoulders of the interstate, repeatedly attempted to ram several police cars, drove more than 100 passenger vehicles off the road, ran through several roadblocks, and continued driving after the officer shot out the wheels of the fugitive's truck. *Id.,* at 1330-1331. Only then did the officer finally resort to deadly force to disable the driver. Similarly, in *Smith* v. *Freland*, 954 F.2d 343 (CA6 1992), the suspect led a police officer on a high-speed chase, reaching speeds in excess of 90 miles per hour. When the officer initially cornered the suspect in a field, the driver repeatedly swerved directly toward the police car, forcing the officer to move out of the way and allowing the suspect to continue the chase. *Id.,* at 344. Only after additional officers cornered the suspect for a second time, and after the suspect smashed directly into an unoccupied police car and began to flee again, did the officer finally shoot the driver. *Ibid.*

In stark contrast, at the time Brosseau shot Haugen, the Jeep was immobile, or at best, had just started moving. Haugen had not driven at excess speeds; nor had he rammed, or attempted to ram, nearby police cars or passenger vehicles. In sum, there was no ongoing or prior high-speed car chase to inform the probable-cause analysis.

Rather than uncertainty about the law, it is uncertainty about the likely consequences of Haugen's flight—or, more precisely, uncertainty about how a reasonable officer making the split-second decision to use deadly force would have assessed the foreseeability of a serious accident—that prevents me from answering the question of qualified immunity that this case presents. This is a quintessentially "fact-specific" question, not a question that judges should try to answer "as a matter of law." Cf. *Anderson,* 483 U. S., at 641. Although it is preferable to resolve the qualified immunity question at the earliest possible stage of litigation, this preference does not give judges license to take inherently factual questions away from the jury. See *Hunter* v. *Bryant,* 502 U. S. 224, 229 (1991) *(per curiam)* (*Scalia,* J., concurring in judgment); *id.,* at 233 (*Stevens,* J., dissenting) (quoting *Bryant* v. *U. S. Treasury Dept., Secret Service,* 903 F. 2d 717, 720 (CA9

1990) ("Whether a reasonable officer could have believed he had probable cause is a question for the trier of fact, and summary judgment or a directed verdict in a §1983 action based on [the] lack of probable cause is proper only if there is only one reasonable conclusion a jury could reach")). The bizarre scenario described in the record of this case convinces me that reasonable jurors could well disagree about the answer to the qualified immunity issue. My conclusion is strongly reinforced by the differing opinions expressed by the Circuit Judges who have reviewed the record.

III

The Court's attempt to justify its decision to reverse the Court of Appeals without giving the parties an opportunity to provide full briefing and oral argument is woefully unpersuasive. If Brosseau had deliberately shot Haugen in the head and killed him, the legal issues would have been the same as those resulting from the nonfatal wound. I seriously doubt that my colleagues would be so confident about the result as to decide the case without the benefit of briefs or argument on such facts.[5] At a minimum, the Ninth Circuit's decision was not clearly erroneous, and the extraordinary remedy of summary reversal is not warranted on these facts. See R. Stern, E. Gressman, & S. Shapiro, Supreme Court Practice 281 (6th ed. 1986).

In sum, the constitutional limits on an officer's use of deadly force have been well settled in this Court's jurisprudence for nearly two decades, and, in this case, Officer Brosseau acted outside of those clearly delineated bounds. Nonetheless, in my judgment, there is a genuine factual question as to whether a reasonably well-trained officer standing in Brosseau's shoes could have concluded otherwise, and that question plainly falls with the purview of the jury.

For these reasons, I respectfully dissent.

SMALL v. U.S.

(FULL CASE)
544 U.S. 385
November 3, 2004, Argued; April 26, 2005, Decided

GIST: Gary Sherwood Small was, as the Court describes him, an international gunrunner, having been convicted by a Japanese court of smuggling rifles, handguns and ammunition into Japan in a hot-water heater (the third one he had shipped, which is what raised the authorities' suspicions and led to his capture). After his release, at the end of his probation, he bought a handgun from a retail shop in Pennsylvania, his home state, and was subsequently arrested and convicted as a felon in possession of a firearm.

The case turned on whether the law, which bans anyone convicted "in any court," of a crime with a prison sentence exceeding one year (except for two-year state misdemeanors) included conviction in a Japanese court. In an unusual turn of events, the Court's more liberal members, led by Justice Breyer, successfully argued that a person's ability to possess firearms remains intact despite foreign convictions. The conservative leaning members, in a dissent written by Justice Thomas, argued for disarming people found guilty of the described crimes "in any court."

The majority made the persuasive point that if "any court" conviction with a penalty exceeding one year counts, then many decidedly unAmerican convictions would cause a person harm. In Soviet Russia, for example, a conviction for buying and selling goods for a profit (a crime to the communists), would make you a prohibited possessor, as would simple vandalism in Singapore (where it carries a three-year sentence). It would also offend the

American sense of fairness in, for example, a country where "the testimony of one man equals that of two women."

Conversely, the dissent points out that the majority result is absurd, because it defines "any" as "a subset of any," and because a person convicted of murder, rape, assault, kidnapping and terrorism abroad is not barred from buying, possessing or using firearms here.

Unmentioned in the decision, Small, who could reasonably be called a ne'er-do-well, had endured what we might call a kangaroo trial. He had been arrested at a Japanese airport not in possession of any alleged evidence, held without bail, denied due process and interrogated by police for 23 days straight without a lawyer. The Japanese prosecution relied on sworn statements with no cross examination or witnesses present; his Japanese lawyer barely spoke English and mainly tried to get him to confess (which he refused to do); he was brought to trial without a jury, and his silence to outrageous questioning, in Japanese style, was held as proof of guilt. His attorney had briefed the Justices on these points.

The case presents a striking contrast with *Bean v. U.S.*, just three years earlier. In that case, a federally licensed firearms dealer convicted of an innocent mistake on his way to dinner in Mexico lost his right to arms and his livelihood, and could not get his rights restored due to a technicality. In this case, a potentially dangerous criminal was made whole through some unusual reasoning. The *Small* decision works in support of gun rights, but in a controversial way.

Petitioner Small was convicted in a Japanese Court of trying to smuggle firearms and ammunition into that country. He served five years in prison and then returned to the United States, where he bought a gun. Federal authorities subsequently charged Small under 18 U. S. C. §922(g)(1), which forbids "any person ... convicted in any court ... of a crime punishable by imprisonment for a term exceeding one year ... to ... possess ... any firearm." (Emphasis added.) Small pleaded guilty while reserving the right to challenge his conviction on the ground that his earlier conviction, being foreign, fell outside §922(g)(1)'s scope. The Federal District Court and the Third Circuit rejected this argument.

Held: Section 922(g)(1)'s phrase "convicted in any court" encompasses only domestic, not foreign, convictions. Pp. 2-9.

(a) In considering the scope of the phrase "convicted in any court" it is appropriate to assume that Congress had domestic concerns in mind. This assumption is similar to the legal presumption that Congress ordinarily intends its statutes to have domestic, not extraterritorial, application, see, e.g., Foley Bros., Inc. v. Filardo, 336 U. S. 281, 285. The phrase "convicted in any court" describes one necessary portion of the "gun possession" activity that is prohibited as a matter of domestic law. Moreover, because foreign convictions may include convictions for conduct that domestic laws would permit, e.g., for engaging in economic conduct that our society might encourage, convictions from a legal system that are inconsistent with American understanding of fairness, and convictions for conduct that domestic law punishes far less severely, the key statutory phrase "convicted in any court of, a crime punishable by imprisonment for a term exceeding one year" somewhat less reliably identifies dangerous individuals for the purposes of U. S. law where foreign convictions, rather than domestic convictions, are at issue. In addition, it is difficult to read the statute as asking judges or prosecutors to refine its definitional distinctions where foreign convictions are at issue. To somehow weed out inappropriate foreign convictions that meet the statutory definition is not consistent with the statute's language; it is not easy for those not versed in foreign laws to accomplish; and it would leave those previously convicted in a foreign court (say of economic crimes) uncertain about their legal obligations. These considerations provide a convincing basis for applying the ordinary assumption about the reach of domestically oriented statutes here. Thus, the Court assumes a congressional intent that the phrase "convicted in any court" applies domestically, not extraterritorially, unless the statutory language, context, history, or purpose shows the contrary. Pp. 2-5.

(b) There is no convincing indication to the contrary here. The statute's language suggests no intent to reach beyond domestic convictions. To the contrary, if read to include foreign convictions, the statute's language creates anomalies. For example, in creating an exception allowing gun possession despite a

conviction for an antitrust or business regulatory crime, §921(a)(20)(A) speaks of "Federal or State" antitrust or regulatory offenses. If the phrase "convicted in any court" generally refers only to domestic convictions, this language causes no problem. But if the phrase includes foreign convictions, the words "Federal or State" prevent the exception from applying where a foreign antitrust or regulatory conviction is at issue. Such illustrative examples suggest that Congress did not consider whether the generic phrase "convicted in any court" applies to foreign convictions. Moreover, the statute's legislative history indicates no intent to reach beyond domestic convictions. Although the statutory purpose of keeping guns from those likely to become a threat to society does offer some support for reading §922(g)(1) to include foreign convictions, the likelihood that Congress, at best, paid no attention to the matter is reinforced by the empirical fact that, according to the Government, since 1968, there have fewer than a dozen instances in which such a foreign conviction has served as a predicate for a felon-in-possession prosecution. Pp. 5–8.

333 F. 3d 425, reversed and remanded.

Breyer, J., delivered the opinion of the Court, in which Stevens, O'Connor, Souter, and Ginsburg, JJ., joined. Thomas, J., filed a dissenting opinion, in which Scalia and Kennedy, JJ., joined. Rehnquist, C. J., took no part in the decision of the case.

Justice Breyer delivered the opinion of the Court.

The question before us focuses upon the words "convicted in any court." Does this phrase apply only to convictions entered in any *domestic* court or to *foreign* convictions as well? We hold that the phrase encompasses only domestic, not foreign, convictions.

The United States Criminal Code makes it "unlawful for any person ... who has been *convicted in any court,* of a crime punishable by imprisonment for a term exceeding one year ... to ... possess ... any firearm." 18 U. S. C. §922(g)(1) (emphasis added).

The question before us focuses upon the words "convicted in any court." Does this phrase apply only to convictions entered in any *domestic* court or to *foreign* convictions as well? We hold that the phrase encompasses only domestic, not foreign, convictions.

I

In 1994 petitioner, Gary Small, was convicted in a Japanese court of having tried to smuggle several pistols, a rifle, and ammunition into Japan. Small was sentenced to five years' imprisonment.

In 1994 petitioner, Gary Small, was convicted in a Japanese court of having tried to smuggle several pistols, a rifle, and ammunition into Japan. Small was sentenced to five years' imprisonment. 183 F. Supp. 2d 755, 757, n. 3 (WD Pa. 2002). After his release, Small returned to the United States, where he bought a gun from a Pennsylvania gun dealer. Federal authorities subsequently charged Small under the "unlawful gun possession" statute here at issue. 333 F. 3d 425, 426 (CA3 2003). Small pleaded guilty while reserving the right to challenge his conviction on the ground that his earlier conviction, being a foreign conviction, fell outside the scope of the illegal gun possession statute. The Federal District Court rejected Small's argument, as did the Court of Appeals for the Third Circuit. 183 F. Supp. 2d, at 759; 333 F. 3d, at 427, n. 2. Because the Circuits disagree about the matter, we granted certiorari. Compare *United States* v. *Atkins,* 872 F. 2d 94, 96 (CA4 1989) ("convicted in any court" includes foreign convictions); *United States* v. *Winson,* 793 F. 2d 754, 757–759 (CA6 1986) (same), with *United States* v. *Gayle,* 342 F. 3d 89, 95 (CA2 2003) ("convicted in any court" does not include foreign convictions); *United States* v. *Concha,* 233 F. 3d 1249, 1256 (CA10 2000) (same).

II

A

General words, such as the word 'any,' must be limited in their application to those objects to which the legislature intended to apply them

'any' means different things depending upon the setting

The question before us is whether the statutory reference "convicted in *any* court" includes a conviction entered in a *foreign* court. The word "any" considered alone cannot answer this question. In ordinary life, a speaker who says, "I'll see any film," may or may not mean to include films shown in another city. In law, a legislature that uses the statutory phrase "'any person'" may or may not mean to include "'persons'" outside "the jurisdiction of the state." See, *e.g., United States* v. *Palmer,* 3 Wheat. 610, 631 (1818) (Marshall, C. J.) ("[G]eneral words," such as the word "'any,'" must "be limited" in their application "to those objects to which the legislature intended to apply them"); *Nixon* v. *Missouri Municipal League,* 541

U. S. 125, 132 (2004) ("'any'" means "different things depending upon the setting"); *United States* v. *Alvarez-Sanchez*, 511 U. S. 350, 357 (1994) ("[R]espondent errs in placing dispositive weight on the broad statutory reference to 'any' law enforcement officer or agency without considering the rest of the statute"); *Middlesex County Sewerage Authority* v. *National Sea Clammers Assn.*, 453 U. S. 1, 15-16 (1981) (it is doubtful that the phrase "'any statute'" includes the very statute in which the words appear); *Flora* v. *United States*, 362 U. S. 145, 149 (1960) ("[A]ny sum," while a "catchall" phase, does not "define what it catches"). Thus, even though the word "any" demands a broad interpretation, see, *e.g.*, *United States* v. *Gonzales*, 520 U. S. 1, 5 (1997), we must look beyond that word itself.

Congress ordinarily intends its statutes to have domestic, not extraterritorial, application.

That presumption would apply, for example, were we to consider whether this statute prohibits unlawful gun possession abroad as well as domestically.

In determining the scope of the statutory phrase we find help in the "commonsense notion that Congress generally legislates with domestic concerns in mind." *Smith* v. *United States*, 507 U. S. 197, 204, n. 5 (1993). This notion has led the Court to adopt the legal presumption that Congress ordinarily intends its statutes to have domestic, not extraterritorial, application. See *Foley Bros., Inc.* v. *Filardo*, 336 U. S. 281, 285 (1949); see also *Palmer, supra*, at 631 ("The words 'any person or persons,' are broad enough to comprehend every human being" but are "limited to cases within the jurisdiction of the state"); *EEOC* v. *Arabian American Oil Co.*, 499 U. S. 244, 249-251 (1991). That presumption would apply, for example, were we to consider whether this statute prohibits unlawful gun possession abroad as well as domestically. And, although the presumption against extraterritorial application does not apply directly to this case, we believe a similar assumption is appropriate when we consider the scope of the phrase "convicted in any court" here.

considered as a group, foreign convictions differ from domestic convictions in important ways... crimes punishable by more than one year's imprisonment may include a conviction for conduct that domestic laws would permit, for example, for engaging in economic conduct that our society might encourage. See, *e.g.*, Art. 153 of the Criminal Code of the Russian Soviet Federated Socialist Republic... criminalizing "Private Entrepreneurial Activity"; ...criminalizing "Speculation," which is defined as "the buying up and reselling of goods or any other articles for the purpose of making a profit"

They would include a conviction from a legal system that is inconsistent with an American understanding of fairness. See, *e.g.*, U. S. Dept. of State, Country Reports on Human Rights Practices for 2003... citing examples in which "the testimony of one man equals that of two women"

And they would include a conviction for conduct that domestic law punishes far less severely. See, *e.g.*, Singapore Vandalism Act... imprisonment for up to three years for an act of vandalism.

For one thing, the phrase describes one necessary portion of the "gun possession" activity that is prohibited as a matter of domestic law. For another, considered as a group, foreign convictions differ from domestic convictions in important ways. Past foreign convictions for crimes punishable by more than one year's imprisonment may include a conviction for conduct that domestic laws would permit, for example, for engaging in economic conduct that our society might encourage. See, *e.g.*, Art. 153 of the Criminal Code of the Russian Soviet Federated Socialist Republic, in Soviet Criminal Law and Procedure 171 (H. Berman & J. Spindler transls. 2d ed. 1972) (criminalizing "Private Entrepreneurial Activity"); Art. 153, *id.*, at 172 (criminalizing "Speculation," which is defined as "the buying up and reselling of goods or any other articles for the purpose of making a profit"); cf. *e.g.*, Gaceta Oficial de la Republica de Cuba, ch. II, Art. 103, p. 68 (Dec. 30, 1987) (forbidding propaganda that incites against the social order, international solidarity, or the Communist State). They would include a conviction from a legal system that is inconsistent with an American understanding of fairness. See, *e.g.*, U. S. Dept. of State, Country Reports on Human Rights Practices for 2003, Submitted to the House Committee on International Relations and the Senate Committee on Foreign Relations, 108th Cong., 2d Sess., 702-705, 1853, 2023 (Joint Comm. Print 2004) (describing failures of "due process" and citing examples in which "the testimony of one man equals that of two women"). And they would include a conviction for conduct that domestic law punishes far less severely. See, *e.g.*, Singapore Vandalism Act, ch. 108, §§2, 3, III Statutes of Republic of Singapore p. 258 (imprisonment for up to three years for an act of vandalism). Thus, the key statutory phrase "convicted in any court of, a crime punishable by imprisonment for a term exceeding one year" somewhat less reliably identifies dangerous individuals for the purposes of U. S. law where foreign convictions, rather than domestic convictions, are at issue.

it would leave those previously convicted in a foreign court (say of economic crimes) uncertain about their legal obligations.

In addition, it is difficult to read the statute as asking judges or prosecutors to refine its definitional distinctions where foreign convictions are at issue. To somehow weed out inappropriate foreign convictions that meet the statutory definition is not consistent with the statute's language; it is not easy for those not versed in foreign laws to accomplish; and it would leave those previously convicted in a foreign court (say of economic crimes) uncertain about their legal obligations. Cf. 1 United States Sentencing Commission, Guidelines Manual §4A1.2(h) (Nov. 2004) ("[S]entences resulting from foreign convictions are not counted" as a "prior sentence" for criminal history purposes).

We consequently assume a congressional intent that the phrase "convicted in any court" applies domestically, not extraterritorially. But, at the same time, we stand ready to revise this assumption should statutory language, context, history, or purpose show the contrary.

These considerations, suggesting significant differences between foreign and domestic convictions, do not dictate our ultimate conclusion. Nor do they create a "clear statement" rule, imposing upon Congress a special burden of specificity. See *post*, at 5 (*Thomas, J.*, dissenting). They simply convince us that we should apply an ordinary assumption about the reach of domestically oriented statutes here—an assumption that helps us determine Congress' intent where Congress likely did not consider the matter and where other indicia of intent are in approximate balance. Cf. *ibid.* We consequently assume a congressional intent that the phrase "convicted in any court" applies domestically, not extraterritorially. But, at the same time, we stand ready to revise this assumption should statutory language, context, history, or purpose show the contrary.

B

We have found no convincing indication to the contrary here. The statute's language does not suggest any intent to reach beyond domestic convictions. Neither does it mention foreign convictions nor is its subject matter special, say, immigration or terrorism, where one could argue that foreign convictions would seem especially relevant. To the contrary, if read to include foreign convictions, the statute's language creates anomalies.

An individual convicted of, say, a Canadian antitrust offense could not lawfully possess a gun... but a similar individual convicted of, say, a New York antitrust offense, could lawfully possess a gun.

For example, the statute creates an exception that allows gun possession despite a prior conviction for an antitrust or business regulatory crime. 18 U. S. C. §921(a)(20)(A). In doing so, the exception speaks of "Federal or State" antitrust or regulatory offenses. *Ibid.* If the phrase "convicted in any court" generally refers only to domestic convictions, this language causes no problem. But if "convicted in any court" includes foreign convictions, the words "Federal or State" prevent the exception from applying where a *foreign* antitrust or regulatory conviction is at issue. An individual convicted of, say, a Canadian antitrust offense could not lawfully possess a gun, Combines Investigation Act, 2 R. S. C. 1985, ch. C-34, §§61(6), (9) (1985), but a similar individual convicted of, say, a New York antitrust offense, could lawfully possess a gun.

If "convicted in any court" refers only to domestic convictions, this language creates no problem. If the phrase also refers to foreign convictions, the language creates an apparently senseless distinction between (covered) domestic relations misdemeanors committed within the United States and (uncovered) domestic relations misdemeanors committed abroad.

For example, the statute specifies that predicate crimes include "a misdemeanor crime of domestic violence." 18 U. S. C. §922(g)(9). Again, the language specifies that these predicate crimes include only crimes that are "misdemeanor[s] under Federal or State law." §921(a)(33)(A). If "convicted in any court" refers only to domestic convictions, this language creates no problem. If the phrase also refers to foreign convictions, the language creates an apparently senseless distinction between (covered) domestic relations misdemeanors committed within the United States and (uncovered) domestic relations misdemeanors committed abroad.

For example, the statute provides an enhanced penalty where unlawful gun possession rests upon three predicate convictions for a "serious drug offense." §924(e)(1) (2000 ed., Supp. II). Again the statute defines the relevant drug crimes through reference to specific federal crimes and with the words "offense under State law." §§924(e)(2)(A)(i), (ii) (2000). If "convicted in any court" refers only to domestic convictions, this language creates no problem. But if the phrase also refers to foreign convictions, the language creates an apparently senseless distinction between drug offenses committed within the United States (potentially producing enhanced punishments) and similar offenses committed abroad (not producing enhanced punishments).

This exception is presumably based on the determination that such state crimes are not sufficiently serious or dangerous so as to preclude an individual from possessing a firearm. If "convicted in any court" refers only to domestic convictions, this language creates no problem. But if the phrase also refers to foreign convictions, the language creates another apparently senseless distinction between less serious crimes (misdemeanors punishable by more than one year's imprisonment) committed within the United States (not predicate crimes) and similar offenses committed abroad (predicate crimes).

For example, the statute provides that offenses that are punishable by a term of imprisonment of up to two years, and characterized under state law as misdemeanors, are not predicate crimes. §921(20). This exception is presumably based on the determination that such state crimes are not sufficiently serious or dangerous so as to preclude an individual from possessing a firearm. If "convicted in any court" refers only to domestic convictions, this language creates no problem. But if the phrase also refers to foreign convictions, the language creates another apparently senseless distinction between less serious crimes (misdemeanors punishable by more than one year's imprisonment) committed within the United States (not predicate crimes) and similar offenses committed abroad (predicate crimes). These illustrative examples taken together suggest that Congress did not consider whether the generic phrase "convicted in any court" applies to domestic as well as foreign convictions.

The statute's lengthy legislative history confirms the fact that Congress did not consider whether foreign convictions should or should not serve as a predicate to liability under the provision here at issue. Congress did consider a Senate bill containing language that would have restricted predicate offenses to domestic offenses. See S. Rep. No. 1501, 90th Cong., 2d Sess., p. 31 (1968) (defining predicate crimes in terms of "Federal" crimes "punishable by a term of imprisonment exceeding one year" and crimes "determined by the laws of the State to be a felony"). And the Conference Committee ultimately rejected this version in favor of language that speaks of those "convicted in any court, of a crime punishable by a term of imprisonment exceeding one year." H. R. Conf. Rep. No. 1956, 90th Cong., 2d Sess., pp. 28-29 (1968). But the history does not suggest that this language change reflected a congressional view on the matter before us. Rather, the enacted version is simpler and it avoids potential difficulties arising out of the fact that States may define the term "felony" differently. And as far as the legislative history is concerned, these latter virtues of the new language fully explain the change. Thus, those who use legislative history to help discern congressional intent will see the history here as silent, hence a neutral factor, that simply confirms the obvious, namely, that Congress did not consider the issue. Others will not be tempted to use or to discuss the history at all. But cf. post, at 13 (Thomas, J., dissenting).

The statute's purpose does offer some support for a reading of the phrase that includes foreign convictions. As the Government points out, Congress sought to "'keep guns out of the hands of those who have demonstrated that they may not be trusted to possess a firearm without becoming a threat to society.'" Brief for United States 16 (quoting Dickerson v. New Banner Institute, Inc., 460 U. S. 103, 112 (1983)); see also Lewis v. United States, 445 U. S. 55, 60-62, 66 (1980); Huddleston v. United States, 415 U. S. 814, 824 (1974). And, as the dissent properly notes, post, at 12, one convicted of a serious crime abroad may well be as dangerous as one convicted of a similar crime in the United States.

As the Government points out, Congress sought to "'keep guns out of the hands of those who have demonstrated that they may not be trusted to possess a firearm without becoming a threat to society.'"

The force of this argument is weakened significantly, however, by the empirical fact that, according to the Government, since 1968, there have probably been no more than "10 to a dozen" instances in which such a foreign conviction has served as a predicate for a felon-in-possession prosecution. Tr. of Oral Arg. 32. This empirical fact reinforces the likelihood that Congress, at best, paid no attention to the matter.

C

In sum, we have no reason to believe that Congress considered the added enforcement advantages flowing from inclusion of foreign crimes, weighing them against, say, the potential unfairness of preventing those with inapt foreign convictions from possessing guns.

we conclude that the phrase "convicted in any court" refers only to domestic courts, not to foreign courts. Congress, of course, remains free to change this conclusion through statutory amendment.

In sum, we have no reason to believe that Congress considered the added enforcement advantages flowing from inclusion of foreign crimes, weighing them against, say, the potential unfairness of preventing those with inapt foreign convictions from possessing guns. See *supra,* at 4. The statute itself and its history offer only congressional silence. Given the reasons for disfavoring an inference of extraterritorial coverage from a statute's total silence and our initial assumption against such coverage, see *supra,* at 5, we conclude that the phrase "convicted in any court" refers only to domestic courts, not to foreign courts. Congress, of course, remains free to change this conclusion through statutory amendment.

For these reasons, the judgment of the Third Circuit is reversed, and the case is remanded for further proceedings consistent with this opinion.

It is so ordered.

The Chief Justice took no part in the decision of this case.

Justice Thomas, with whom Justice Scalia and Justice Kennedy join, dissenting.

In concluding that "any" means not what it says, but rather "a subset of any," the Court distorts the plain meaning of the statute and departs from established principles of statutory construction.

Gary Small, having recently emerged from three years in Japanese prison for illegally importing weapons into that country, bought a gun in the United States. This violated 18 U. S. C. §922(g)(1), which makes it unlawful for any person "who has been convicted in any court of, a crime punishable by imprisonment for a term exceeding one year" to possess a firearm in or affecting commerce. Yet the majority decides that Small's gun possession did not violate the statute, because his prior convictions occurred in a Japanese court rather than an American court. In concluding that "any" means not what it says, but rather "a subset of any," the Court distorts the plain meaning of the statute and departs from established principles of statutory construction. I respectfully dissent.

I

Thinking it unusual for a person to ship a water tank from overseas as a present... Japanese customs officials searched the heater and discovered 2 rifles, 8 semiautomatic pistols, and 410 rounds of ammunition.

In December 1992, Small shipped a 19-gallon electric water heater from the United States to Okinawa, Japan, ostensibly as a present for someone in Okinawa. App. to Brief for Appellant in No. 02-2785 (CA3), pp. 507a-510a, 530a-531a, 534a, 598a (hereinafter Appellant's App.). Small had sent two other water heaters to Japan that same year. *Id.,* at 523a-527a. Thinking it unusual for a person to ship a water tank from overseas as a present, *id.,* at 599a, Japanese customs officials searched the heater and discovered 2 rifles, 8 semiautomatic pistols, and 410 rounds of ammunition. *Id.,* at 603a-604a; *id.,* at 262a, 267a, 277a.

The Japanese Government indicted Small on multiple counts of violating Japan's weapons-control and customs laws. *Id.,* at 261a-262a. Each offense was punishable by imprisonment for a term exceeding one year. 333 F. 3d 425, 426 (CA3 2003). Small was tried before a three-judge court in Naha, Japan, Appellant's App. 554a, convicted on all counts on April 14, 1994, 333 F. 3d, at 426, and sentenced to 5 years' imprisonment with credit for 320 days served, *id.,* at 426, n. 1; Government's Brief in Support of Detention in Crim. No. 00-160 (WD Pa.), pp. 3-4. He was paroled on November 22, 1996, and his parole terminated on May 26, 1998. 333 F. 3d, at 426, n. 1.

A week after completing parole for his Japanese convictions, on June 2, 1998, Small purchased a 9-millimeter SWD Cobray pistol from a firearms dealer in Pennsylvania.

A week after completing parole for his Japanese convictions, on June 2, 1998, Small purchased a 9-millimeter SWD Cobray pistol from a firearms dealer in Pennsylvania. Appellant's App. 48a, 98a. Some time later, a search of his residence, business premises, and automobile revealed a .380 caliber Browning pistol and more than 300 rounds of ammunition. *Id.*, at 47a-51a, 98a-99a. This prosecution ensued.

II

The plain terms of §922(g)(1) prohibit Small—a person "convicted in any court of, a crime punishable by imprisonment for a term exceeding one year"—from possessing a firearm in the United States. "Read naturally, the word 'any' has an expansive meaning, that is, 'one or some indiscriminately of whatever kind.'" *United States* v. *Gonzales,* 520 U. S. 1, 5 (1997) (quoting Webster's Third New International Dictionary 97 (1976) (hereinafter Webster's 3d)); see also *Department of Housing and Urban Development* v. *Rucker,* 535 U. S. 125, 130-131 (2002) (statute making "any" drug-related criminal activity cause for termination of public housing lease precludes requirement that tenant know of the activity); *Brogan* v. *United States,* 522 U. S. 398, 400-401 (1998) (statute criminalizing "any" false statement within the jurisdiction of a federal agency allows no exception for the mere denial of wrongdoing); *United States* v. *Alvarez-Sanchez,* 511 U. S. 350, 356, 358 (1994) (statute referring to "any" law-enforcement officer includes all law enforcement officers— federal, state, or local—capable of arresting for a federal crime). No exceptions appear on the face of the statute; "[n]o modifier is present, and nothing suggests any restriction," *Lewis* v. *United States,* 445 U. S. 55, 60 (1980), on the scope of the term "court." See *Gonzales, supra,* at 5 (statute referring to "'any other term of imprisonment'" includes no "language limiting the breadth of that word, and so we must read [the statute] as referring to all 'term[s] of imprisonment'"). The broad phrase "any court" unambiguously includes all judicial bodies n1 with jurisdiction to impose the requisite conviction—a conviction for a crime punishable by imprisonment for a term of more than a year. Indisputably, Small was convicted in a Japanese court of crimes punishable by a prison term exceeding one year. The clear terms of the statute prohibit him from possessing a gun in the United States.

n1 See, *e.g.*, The Random House Dictionary of the English Language 335 (1966) (defining "court" as "a place where justice is administered," "a judicial tribunal duly constituted for the hearing and determination of cases," "a session of a judicial assembly"); The Concise Oxford Dictionary of Current English 282 (5th ed. 1964) (defining "court" as an"[a]ssembly of judges or other persons acting as tribunal"); Webster's 3d 522 (1961) (defining "court" as "the persons duly assembled under authority of law for the administration of justice," "an official assembly legally met together for the transaction of judicial business," "a judge or judges sitting for the hearing or trial of cases").

Of course, the phrase "any court," like all other statutory language, must be read in context. *E.g., Deal* v. *United States,* 508 U. S. 129, 132 (1993). The context of §922(g)(1), however, suggests that there is no geographic limit on the scope of "any court." n2 By contrast to other parts of the firearms-control law that expressly mention only state or federal law, "any court" is not qualified by jurisdiction. See 18 U. S. C. §921(a)(20) (excluding certain "Federal or State offenses" from the definition of "crime punishable by imprisonment for a term exceeding one year"); §921(a)(33)(A)(i) (defining a "misdemeanor crime of domestic violence" by reference to "Federal or State law"). n3 Congress' explicit use of "Federal" and "State" in other provisions shows that it specifies such restrictions when it wants to do so.

n2 The Court's observation that "a speaker who says, 'I'll see any film,' may or may not mean to include films shown in another city," *ante,* at 2, therefore adds nothing to the analysis. The context of that statement implies that such a speaker, despite saying "any," often means only the subset of films within an accessible distance. Unlike the context of the film remark, the context of 18 U. S. C. §922(g)(1) implies no geographic restriction.

n3 See also §921(a)(15) (defining a "fugitive from justice," who is banned from possessing firearms under §922(g)(2), as "any person who has fled from any State to avoid prosecution for a crime or to avoid giving testimony"); §924(e)(2) (defining a "serious drug offense," which can trigger an enhanced sentence, by reference to particular federal laws or "State law").

foreign convictions indicate dangerousness just as reliably as domestic convictions.

Counting foreign convictions, moreover, implicates no special federalism concerns or other clear statement rules that have justified construing "any" narrowly in the past. n4 And it is eminently practical to put foreign convictions to the same use as domestic ones; foreign convictions indicate dangerousness just as reliably as domestic convictions. See Part III-B, *infra*. The expansive phrase "convicted in any court" straightforwardly encompasses Small's Japanese convictions.

n4 *Nixon* v. *Missouri Municipal League*, 541 U. S. 125 (2004), considered a federal statute authorizing preemption of state and local laws "prohibiting the ability of any entity" to provide telecommunications services. *Id.*, at 128 (internal quotation marks omitted). The Court held that the statute did not provide the clear statement required for the Federal Government to limit the States' ability to restrict delivery of such services by their own political subdivisions. *Id.*, at 140-141; see also *id.*, at 141 (*Scalia*, J., concurring in judgment); *Raygor* v. *Regents of Univ. of Minn.*, 534 U. S. 533, 540-541 (2002) ("any" in federal statute insufficiently clear statement to abrogate state sovereign immunity); *Atascadero State Hospital* v. *Scanlon*, 473 U. S. 234, 245-246 (1985) (same). No such clear statement rule is at work here.

III

Faced with the inescapably broad text, the Court narrows the statute by assuming that the text applies only to domestic convictions, *ante*, at 5; criticizing the accuracy of foreign convictions as a proxy for dangerousness, *ante*, at 3-5; finding that the broad, natural reading of the statute "creates anomalies," *ante*, at 5; and suggesting that Congress did not consider whether foreign convictions counted, *ante*, at 7-8. None of these arguments is persuasive.

A

The Court first invents a canon of statutory interpretation—what it terms "an ordinary assumption about the reach of domestically oriented statutes," *ante*, at 5—to cabin the statute's reach. This new "assumption" imposes a clear statement rule on Congress: Absent a clear statement, a statute refers to nothing outside the United States. The Court's denial that it has created a clear statement rule is implausible. *Ibid.* After today's ruling, the only way for Congress to ensure that courts will construe a law to refer to foreign facts or entities is to describe those facts or entities specifically as foreign. If this is not a "special burden of specificity," *ibid.*, I am not sure what is.

The Court's innovation is baseless. The Court derives its assumption from the entirely different, and well-recognized, canon against extraterritorial application of federal statutes: "It is a longstanding principle of American law that legislation of Congress, unless a contrary intent appears, is meant to apply only within the territorial jurisdiction of the United States." *EEOC* v. *Arabian American Oil Co.*, 499 U. S. 244, 248 (1991) (internal quotation marks omitted). But the majority rightly concedes that the canon against extraterritoriality itself "does not apply directly to this case." *Ante*, at 3. Though foreign as well as domestic convictions trigger §922(g)(1)'s prohibition, the statute criminalizes gun possession in this country, not abroad. In prosecuting Small, the Government is enforcing a domestic criminal statute to punish domestic criminal conduct. *Pasquantino* v. *United States*, *ante*, at 20-21 (federal wire fraud statute covers a domestic scheme aimed at defrauding a foreign government of tax revenue).

The extraterritoriality cases cited by the Court, *ante*, at 3, do not support its new assumption. They restrict federal statutes from applying outside the territorial jurisdiction of the United States. See *Smith* v. *United States*, 507 U. S. 197, 203-204 (1993) (Federal Tort Claims Act does not apply to claims arising in Antarctica); *Arabian American Oil Co.*, *supra*, at 249-251 (Title VII of the Civil Rights Act of 1964 does not regulate the employment practices of American firms employing American citizens abroad); *Foley Bros., Inc.* v. *Filardo*, 336 U. S. 281, 285-286 (1949) (federal labor statute does not apply to a contract between the United States and a private contractor for construction work done in a foreign country); *United States* v. *Palmer*, 3 Wheat. 610, 630-634 (1818) (statute punishing piracy on the high seas does not apply to robbery committed on the high seas by a noncitizen on board a ship belonging exclusively to subjects of a foreign state). These straightforward applications of the extraterritoriality canon, restricting federal statutes from reaching conduct *beyond U. S. borders*, lend no support to the Court's unprecedented rule restricting a federal statute from reaching conduct *within U. S. borders*.

We have, it is true, recognized that the presumption against extraterritorial application of federal statutes is rooted in part in the "commonsense notion that Congress generally legislates with domestic concerns in mind." *Smith, supra*, at 204, n. 5. But my reading of §922(g)(1) is entirely true to that notion: Gun possession in this country is surely a "domestic concern." We have also consistently grounded the canon in the risk that extraterritorially applicable U. S. laws could conflict with foreign laws, for example, by subjecting individuals to conflicting obligations. *Arabian American Oil Co., supra*, at 248. That risk is completely absent in applying §922(g)(1) to Small's conduct. Quite the opposite, §922(g)(1) takes foreign law as it finds it. Aside from the extraterritoriality canon, which the Court properly concedes does not apply, I know of no principle of statutory construction justifying the result the Court reaches. Its concession that the canon is inapposite should therefore end this case.

Rather than stopping there, the Court introduces its new "assumption about the reach of domestically oriented statutes" *sua sponte*, without briefing or argument on the point, n5 and without providing guidance on what constitutes a "domestically oriented statut[e]." *Ante*, at 5. The majority suggests that it means all statutes except those dealing with subjects like "immigration or terrorism," *ibid.*, apparently reversing our previous rule that the extraterritoriality canon "has special force" in statutes "that may involve foreign and military affairs," *Sale* v. *Haitian Centers Council, Inc.*, 509 U. S. 155, 188 (1993) (provision of the Immigration and Nationality Act does not apply extraterritorially); cf. *Palmer, supra* (statute criminalizing piracy on the high seas does not apply to robbery by noncitizen on ship belonging to foreign subjects). The Court's creation threatens to wreak havoc with the established rules for applying the canon against extraterritoriality.

n5 Neither party mentions the quasi-extraterritoriality principle that the Court fashions. The briefs barely discuss the extraterritoriality canon itself. The only reference to that canon is a footnote in the respondent's brief pointing out that it is inapposite. Brief for United States 44, n. 31.

n6 The Court attempts to justify applying its new canon with the claim that "other indicia of intent are in approximate balance." *Ante*, at 5. This claim is false. Other indicia of intent are not in balance, so long as text counts as an indicium of intent. As I have explained, Part II, *supra*, the text of §922(g)(1) encompasses foreign convictions.

B

In support of its narrow reading of the statute, the majority opines that the natural reading has inappropriate results. It points to differences between foreign and domestic convictions, primarily attacking the reliability of foreign convictions as a proxy for identifying dangerous individuals. *Ante*, at 3-5. Citing various foreign laws, the Court observes that, if interpreted to include foreign convictions, §922(g) would include convictions for business and speech activities "that [United States] laws would permit," *ante*, at 3; convictions "from a legal system that is inconsistent with an American understanding of fairness," *ante*, at 4; and convictions "for conduct that [United States] law punishes far less severely," *ibid.* The Court therefore concludes that foreign convictions cannot trigger §922(g)(1)'s prohibition on firearm possession.

It was eminently reasonable for Congress to use convictions punishable by imprisonment for more than a year—foreign no less than domestic as a proxy for dangerousness.

The Court's claim that foreign convictions punishable by imprisonment for more than a year "somewhat less reliably identif[y] dangerous individuals" than domestic convictions, *ibid.*, is untenable. In compiling examples of foreign convictions that might trigger §922(g)(1), *ibid.*, the Court constructs a parade of horribles. Citing laws of the Russian Soviet Federated Socialist Republic, Cuba, and Singapore, it cherry-picks a few egregious examples of convictions unlikely to correlate with dangerousness, inconsistent with American intuitions of fairness, or punishable more severely than in this country. *Ibid.* This ignores countless other foreign convictions punishable by more than a year that serve as excellent proxies for dangerousness and culpability. n7 Surely a "reasonable human being" drafting this language would have considered whether foreign convictions are, on average and as a whole, accurate at gauging dangerousness and culpability, not whether the worst-of-the-worst are. Breyer, On the Uses of Legislative History in Interpreting Statutes, 65 S. Cal. L. Rev. 845, 854 (1992). The Court also ignores the facts of this very case: A week after completing his sentence for shipping two rifles, eight semiautomatic pistols, and hundreds of rounds of ammunition into Japan, Small bought a gun in this country. It was eminently reasonable for Congress to use convictions punishable by imprisonment for more than a year—foreign no less than domestic—as a proxy for dangerousness.

n7 Brottsbalk (Swedish Criminal Code), SFS 1962:700, ch. 3, §1 (murder); Criminal Code of Canada, R. S. C. ch. C-46, §244(b) (1985), as amended (discharging firearm at a person with intent to endanger life); §102(2) (making an automatic weapon); Laws of the State of Israel, Penal Law §345(b)(2) (rape by threat of firearm or cutting weapon); Penal Code of Egypt Art. 143 (giving weapons to a detained person in order to help him escape); Federal Penal Code of Mexico Art. 139 (terrorism by explosives, toxic substances, firearms, fire, flooding, or other violent means); Art. 163 (kidnaping); Firearms Offenses Act 1968 (United Kingdom), ch. 27, §18(1) (carrying firearm with intent to commit an indictable offense or to resist arrest); 7 L. Rep. of Zambia Cap. 87, ch. 19, §§200-201 (1995) (murder); ch. 24, §248 (assault occasioning actual bodily harm); ch. 25, §§251-262 (kidnaping, abduction, and buying or selling slaves).

Contrary to the majority's assertion, it makes sense to bar people convicted overseas from possessing guns in the United States.

Contrary to the majority's assertion, it makes sense to bar people convicted overseas from possessing guns in the United States. The Court casually dismisses this point with the observation that only "'10 to a dozen'" prosecutions under the statute have involved foreign convictions as predicate convictions. *Ante*, at 8 (quoting Tr. of Oral Arg. 32). The rarity of such prosecutions, however, only refutes the Court's simultaneous claim, *ante*, at 3-5, that a parade of horribles will result if foreign convictions count. Moreover, the Court does not claim that any of these few prosecutions has been based on a foreign conviction inconsistent with American law. As far as anyone is aware, the handful of prosecutions thus far rested on foreign convictions perfectly consonant with American law, like Small's conviction for international gunrunning. The Court has no answer for why including foreign convictions is unwise, let alone irrational.

C

The majority worries that reading §922(g)(1) to include foreign convictions "creates anomalies" under other firearms control provisions. *Ante*, at 5-7. It is true, as the majority notes, that the natural reading of §922(g)(1) affords domestic offenders more lenient treatment than foreign ones in some respects: A domestic antitrust or business regulatory offender could possess a gun, while a similar foreign offender could not; the perpetrator of a state misdemeanor punishable by two years or less in prison could possess a gun, while an analogous foreign offender could not. *Ibid.* In other respects, domestic offenders would receive harsher treatment than their foreign counterparts: One who committed a misdemeanor crime of domestic violence in the United States could not possess a gun, while a similar foreign offender could; and a domestic drug offender could receive a 15-year mandatory minimum sentence for unlawful gun possession, while a foreign drug offender could not. *Ante*, at 6-7.

These outcomes cause the Court undue concern. They certainly present no occasion to employ, nor does the Court invoke, the canon against absurdities. We should employ that canon only "where the result of applying the plain language would be, in a genuine sense, absurd, *i.e.*, where it is quite impossible that Congress could have intended the result . . . and where the alleged absurdity is so clear as to be obvious to most anyone." *Public Citizen* v. *Department of Justice*, 491 U. S. 440, 470-471 (1989) (*Kennedy*, J., concurring in judgment); *Nixon* v. *Missouri Municipal League*, 541 U. S. 125, 141 (2004) (*Scalia*, J., concurring in judgment) ("avoidance of unhappy consequences" is inadequate basis for interpreting a text); cf. *Sturges* v. *Crowninshield*, 4 Wheat. 122, 203 (1819) (before disregarding the plain meaning of a constitutional provision, the case "must be one in which the absurdity and injustice of applying the provision to the case, would be so monstrous, that all mankind would, without hesitation, unite in rejecting the application").

the "anomalies" to which the Court points are not absurd. They are, at most, odd; they may even be rational.

Here, the "anomalies" to which the Court points are not absurd. They are, at most, odd; they may even be rational. For example, it is not senseless to bar a Canadian antitrust offender from possessing a gun in this country, while exempting a domestic antitrust offender from the ban. Congress might have decided to proceed incrementally and exempt only antitrust offenses with which it was familiar, namely, domestic ones. In any event, the majority abandons the statute's plain meaning based on results that are at most incongruous and certainly not absurd. As with the extraterritoriality canon, the Court applies a mutant version of a recognized canon when the recognized canon is itself inapposite. Whatever the utility of canons as guides to congressional intent, they are useless when modified in ways that Congress could never have imagined in enacting §922(g)(1).

the majority's interpretation permits those convicted overseas of murder, rape, assault, kidnaping, terrorism, and other dangerous crimes to possess firearms freely in the United States.

Meanwhile, a person convicted domestically of tampering with a vehicle identification number... is barred from possessing firearms. The majority's concern with anomalies provides no principled basis for choosing its interpretation of the statute over mine.

Even assuming that my reading of the statute generates anomalies, the majority's reading creates ones even more dangerous. As explained above, the majority's interpretation permits those convicted overseas of murder, rape, assault, kidnaping, terrorism, and other dangerous crimes to possess firearms freely in the United States. *Supra*, at 9, and n. 7. Meanwhile, a person convicted domestically of tampering with a vehicle identification number, 18 U. S. C. §511(a)(1), is barred from possessing firearms. The majority's concern with anomalies provides no principled basis for choosing its interpretation of the statute over mine.

D

The Court hypothesizes "that Congress did not consider whether the generic phrase 'convicted in any court' applies to domestic as well as foreign convictions," *ante*, at 7, and takes that as license to restrict the clear breadth of the text. Whether the Court's empirical assumption is correct is anyone's guess. Regardless, we have properly rejected this method of guesswork-as-interpretation. In *Beecham* v. *United States*, 511 U.

S. 368 (1994), we interpreted other provisions of the federal firearms laws to mean that a person convicted of a federal crime is not relieved of the firearms disability unless his civil rights have been restored under federal (as opposed to state) law. We acknowledged the possibility "that the phrases on which our reading of the statute turns . . . were accidents of statutory drafting," *id.*, at 374; and we observed that some legislators might have read the phrases differently from the Court's reading, "or, more likely, . . . never considered the matter at all," *ibid.* We nonetheless adhered to the unambiguous meaning of the statute. *Ibid.;* cf. *National Organization for Women, Inc.* v. *Scheidler,* 510 U. S. 249, 262 (1994) ("The fact that [the Racketeer Influenced and Corrupt Organizations Act] has been applied in situations not expressly anticipated by Congress does not demonstrate ambiguity. It demonstrates breadth" (internal quotation marks and brackets omitted)). Here, as in *Beecham,* "our task is not the hopeless one of ascertaining what the legislators who passed the law would have decided had they reconvened to consider [this] particular cas[e]," 511 U. S., at 374, but the eminently more manageable one of following the ordinary meaning of the text they enacted. That meaning includes foreign convictions.

The Court's reliance on the absence of any discussion of foreign convictions in the legislative history is equally unconvincing.

Reliance on explicit statements in the history, if they existed, would be problematic enough. Reliance on silence in the history is a new and even more dangerous phenomenon.

The Court's reliance on the absence of any discussion of foreign convictions in the legislative history is equally unconvincing. *Ante,* at 7-8. Reliance on explicit statements in the history, if they existed, would be problematic enough. Reliance on silence in the history is a new and even more dangerous phenomenon. *Koons Buick Pontiac GMC, Inc.* v. *Nigh,* 543 U. S. 50, (2004) (*Scalia,* J., dissenting) (criticizing the Court's novel "Canon of Canine Silence").

the Senate bill that formed the basis for this legislation was amended in Conference, to change the predicate offenses from "'Federal' crimes" punishable by more than one year's imprisonment and "crimes 'determined by the laws of a State to be a felony'" to conviction "'in any court, of a crime punishable by a term of imprisonment exceeding one year.'"

I do not even agree, moreover, that the legislative history is silent. As the Court describes, the Senate bill that formed the basis for this legislation was amended in Conference, to change the predicate offenses from "'Federal' crimes" punishable by more than one year's imprisonment and "crimes 'determined by the laws of a State to be a felony'" to conviction "'in any court, of a crime punishable by a term of imprisonment exceeding one year.'" *Ante,* at 7. The Court seeks to explain this change by saying that "the enacted version is simpler and . . . avoids potential difficulties arising out of the fact that States may define the term 'felony' differently." *Ante,* at 8. But that does not explain why all limiting reference to "Federal" and "State" was eliminated. The revised provision would have been just as simple, and would just as well have avoided the potential difficulties, if it read "convicted in any Federal or State court of a crime punishable by a term of imprisonment exceeding one year." Surely that would have been the natural change if expansion beyond federal and state convictions were not intended. The elimination of the limiting references suggests that not *only* federal and state convictions were meant to be covered.

Some, of course, do not believe that any statement or text that has not been approved by both Houses of Congress and the President (if he signed the bill) is an appropriate source of statutory interpretation. But for those who do, this committee change ought to be strong confirmation of the fact that "any" means not "any Federal or State," but simply "any."

IV

The Court never convincingly explains its departure from the natural meaning of §922(g)(1). Instead, it institutes the troubling rule that "any" does not really mean "any," but may mean "some subset of 'any,'" even if nothing in the context so indicates; it distorts the established canons against extraterritoriality and absurdity; it faults without reason Congress' use of foreign convictions to gauge dangerousness and culpability; and it employs discredited methods of determining congressional intent. I respectfully dissent.

CASTLE ROCK v. GONZALES
(FULL CASE)
545 U.S. 748
March 21, 2005, Argued; June 27, 2005, Decided

GIST: Building on precedent, the Court rejects the idea that the state or its police have a mandatory duty to protect individual citizens, at least in this case of a Colorado woman with a court order of protection against her abusive and eventually homicidal husband. The restraining order did not create an enforceable property right under the 14th Amendment—which she had sued under for denial of civil rights protected there. Even though she repeatedly sought police aid and was effectively ignored, leading to the murder of her abducted three children before the abusive father was shot to death by police, she had no grounds for her complaint against the state. Nothing in federal law would prevent a state from creating such a right, but the Court argued that in creating a process available to the woman, namely to be able to call on police for enforcement under circumstances which were met in this case, it did not create a property right with ascertainable value.

The question of police discretion, especially in domestic violence cases such as this one, was a turning point, since police had traditionally "underenforced" DV calls as essentially family matters. Legislatures passed numerous mandatory enforcement laws, as did Colorado, but the Court held that police discretion still existed despite the somewhat explicit language of the statute involved. The two-Justice dissent raised a serious complaint on that point: does a law mean what is says or not? The majority countered with numerous examples of when an apparently mandatory requirement had substantial breathing room.

The case involves gunfire but has no direct nexus to the Second Amendment whatsoever, and like *DeShaney v. Winnebago* (1989), leaves a private citizen without direct legal recourse in certain violent attacks when the state does not respond. But in determining that state and federal authorities have no explicit duty to protect individual citizens, some observers question whether a responsibility or power to protect oneself exists somewhere in American law, and turn to the right to keep and bear arms as a possible affirmative answer implied to that query.

Respondent filed this suit under 42 U. S. C. §1983 alleging that petitioner violated the Fourteenth Amendment's Due Process Clause when its police officers, acting pursuant to official policy or custom, failed to respond to her repeated reports over several hours that her estranged husband had taken their three children in violation of her restraining order against him. Ultimately, the husband murdered the children. The District Court granted the town's motion to dismiss, but an en banc majority of the Tenth Circuit reversed, finding that respondent had alleged a cognizable procedural due process claim because a Colorado statute established the state legislature's clear intent to require police to enforce restraining orders, and thus its intent that the order's recipient have an entitlement to its enforcement. The court therefore ruled, among other things, that respondent had a protected property interest in the enforcement of her restraining order.

Held: Respondent did not, for Due Process Clause purposes, have a property interest in police enforcement of the restraining order against her husband. Pp. 6-19.

(a) The Due Process Clause's procedural component does not protect everything that might be described as a government "benefit": "To have a property interest in a benefit, a person ... must ... have a legitimate claim of entitlement to it." Board of Regents of State Colleges v. Roth, 408 U. S. 564, 577. Such

entitlements are created by existing rules or understandings stemming from an independent source such as state law. E.g., ibid. *Pp. 6-7.*

(b) A benefit is not a protected entitlement if officials have discretion to grant or deny it. See, e.g., Kentucky Dept. of Corrections v. Thompson, *490 U. S. 454, 462-463. It is inappropriate here to defer to the Tenth Circuit's determination that Colorado law gave respondent a right to police enforcement of the restraining order. This Court therefore proceeds to its own analysis. Pp. 7-9.*

(c) Colorado law has not created a personal entitlement to enforcement of restraining orders. It does not appear that state law truly made such enforcement mandatory. A well-established tradition of police discretion has long coexisted with apparently mandatory arrest statutes. Cf. Chicago v. Morales, *527 U. S. 41, 47, n. 2, 62, n. 32. Against that backdrop, a true mandate of police action would require some stronger indication than the Colorado statute's direction to "use every reasonable means to enforce a restraining order" or even to "arrest ... or ... seek a warrant." A Colorado officer would likely have some discretion to determine that—despite probable cause to believe a restraining order has been violated—the violation's circumstances or competing duties counsel decisively against enforcement in a particular instance. The practical necessity for discretion is particularly apparent in a case such as this, where the suspected violator is not actually present and his whereabouts are unknown. In such circumstances, the statute does not appear to require officers to arrest but only to seek a warrant. That, however, would be an entitlement to nothing but procedure, which cannot be the basis for a property interest. Pp. 9-15.*

(d) Even if the statute could be said to make enforcement "mandatory," that would not necessarily mean that respondent has an entitlement to enforcement. Her alleged interest stems not from common law or contract, but only from a State's statutory scheme. If she was given a statutory entitlement, the Court would expect to see some indication of that in the statute itself. Although the statute spoke of "protected person[s]" such as respondent, it did so in connection with matters other than a right to enforcement. Most importantly, it spoke directly to the protected person's power to "initiate" contempt proceedings if the order was issued in a civil action, which contrasts tellingly with its conferral of a power merely to "request" initiation of criminal contempt proceedings—and even more dramatically with its complete silence about any power to "request" (much less demand) that an arrest be made. Pp. 15-17.

(e) Even were the Court to think otherwise about Colorado's creation of an entitlement, it is not clear that an individual entitlement to enforcement of a restraining order could constitute a "property" interest for due process purposes. Such a right would have no ascertainable monetary value and would arise incidentally, not out of some new species of government benefit or service, but out of a function that government actors have always performed—arresting people when they have probable cause. A benefit's indirect nature was fatal to a due process claim in O'Bannon v. Town Court Nursing Center, *447 U. S. 773, 787. Here, as there, "[t]he simple distinction between government action that directly affects a citizen's legal rights ... and action that is directed against a third party and affects the citizen only ... incidentally, provides a sufficient answer to" cases finding government-provided services to be entitlements. Id., at 788. Pp. 17-19.*

366 F. 3d 1093, reversed.

Scalia, J., delivered the opinion of the Court, in which Rehnquist, C. J., and O'Connor, Kennedy, Souter, Thomas, and Breyer, JJ., joined. Souter, J., filed a concurring opinion, in which Breyer, J., joined. Stevens, J., filed a dissenting opinion, in which Ginsburg, J., joined.

Justice Scalia delivered the opinion of the Court.

We decide in this case whether an individual who has obtained a state-law restraining order has a constitutionally protected property interest in having the police enforce the restraining order when they have probable cause to believe it has been violated.

I

police officers, acting pursuant to official policy or custom, failed to respond properly to her repeated reports that her estranged husband was violating the terms of a restraining order.

The horrible facts of this case are contained in the complaint that respondent Jessica Gonzales filed in Federal District Court. (Because the case comes to us on appeal from a dismissal of the complaint, we assume its allegations are true. See *Swierkiewicz* v. *Sorema N. A.,* 534 U. S. 506, 508, n. 1 (2002).) Respondent alleges that petitioner, the town of Castle Rock, Colorado, violated the Due Process Clause of the Fourteenth Amendment to the United States Constitution when its police officers, acting pursuant to official policy or custom, failed to respond properly to her repeated reports that her estranged husband was violating the terms of a restraining order. n1

n1 Petitioner claims that respondent's complaint "did not allege ... that she ever notified the police of her contention that [her husband] was actually in violation of the restraining order." Brief for Petitioner 7, n. 2. The complaint does allege, however, that respondent "showed [the police] a copy of the [temporary restraining order (TRO)] and requested that it be enforced." App. to Pet. for Cert. 126a. At this stage in the litigation, we may assume that this reasonably implied the order was being violated. See *Steel Co.* v. *Citizens for Better Environment,* 523 U. S. 83, 104 (1998).

The restraining order had been issued by a state trial court several weeks earlier in conjunction with respondent's divorce proceedings. The original form order, issued on May 21, 1999, and served on respondent's husband on June 4, 1999, commanded him not to "molest or disturb the peace of [respondent] or of any child," and to remain at least 100 yards from the family home at all times. 366 F. 3d 1093, 1143 (CA10 2004) (en banc) (appendix to dissenting opinion of O'Brien, J.). The bottom of the pre-printed form noted that the reverse side contained "IMPORTANT NOTICES FOR RESTRAINED PARTIES AND LAW ENFORCEMENT OFFICIALS." *Ibid.* (emphasis deleted). The preprinted text on the back of the form included the following "**WARNING**":

"**A KNOWING VIOLATION OF A RESTRAINING ORDER IS A CRIME** ... . A VIOLATION WILL ALSO CONSTITUTE CONTEMPT OF COURT. **YOU MAY BE ARRESTED** WITHOUT NOTICE IF A LAW ENFORCEMENT OFFICER HAS PROBABLE CAUSE TO BELIEVE THAT YOU HAVE KNOWINGLY VIOLATED THIS ORDER." *Id.,* at 1144.

The preprinted text on the back of the form also included a "**NOTICE TO LAW ENFORCEMENT OFFICIALS**," which read in part:

"YOU SHALL USE EVERY REASONABLE MEANS TO ENFORCE THIS RESTRAINING ORDER. YOU SHALL ARREST, OR, IF AN ARREST WOULD BE IMPRACTICAL UNDER THE CIRCUMSTANCES, SEEK A WARRANT FOR THE ARREST OF THE RESTRAINED PERSON WHEN YOU HAVE INFORMATION AMOUNTING TO PROBABLE CAUSE THAT THE RESTRAINED PERSON HAS VIOLATED OR ATTEMPTED TO VIOLATE ANY PROVISION OF THIS ORDER AND THE RESTRAINED PERSON HAS BEEN PROPERLY SERVED WITH A COPY OF THIS ORDER OR HAS RECEIVED ACTUAL NOTICE OF THE EXISTENCE OF THIS ORDER." *Ibid.*

On June 4, 1999, the state trial court modified the terms of the restraining order and made it permanent. The modified order gave respondent's husband the right to spend time with his three daughters (ages 10, 9, and 7) on alternate weekends, for two weeks during the summer, and, "'upon reasonable notice,'" for a mid-week dinner visit "'arranged by the parties'"; the modified order also allowed him to visit the home to collect the children for such "parenting time." *Id.,* at 1097 (majority opinion).

When the officers arrived she showed them a copy of the TRO and requested that it be enforced and the three children be returned to her immediately. The officers stated that there was nothing they could do about the TRO and suggested that [respondent] call the Police Department again if the three children did not return home by 10:00 p.m.

According to the complaint, at about 5 or 5:30 p.m. on Tuesday, June 22, 1999, respondent's husband took the three daughters while they were playing outside the family home. No advance arrangements had been made for him to see the daughters that evening. When respondent noticed the children were missing, she suspected her husband had taken them. At about 7:30 p.m., she called the Castle Rock Police Department, which dispatched two officers. The complaint continues: "When [the officers] arrived ... , she showed them a copy of the TRO and requested that it be enforced and the three children be returned to her immediately. [The officers] stated that there was nothing they could do about the TRO and suggested that [respondent] call the Police Department again if the three children did not return home by 10:00 p.m." App. to Pet. for Cert. 126a. n2

n2 It is unclear from the complaint, but immaterial to our decision, whether respondent showed the police only the original "TRO" or also the permanent, modified restraining order that had superseded it on June 4.

At approximately 8:30 p.m., respondent talked to her husband on his cellular telephone. He told her "he had the three children [at an] amusement park in Denver." *Ibid.* She called the police again and asked them to "have someone check for" her husband or his vehicle at the amusement park and "put out an [all points bulletin]" for her husband, but the officer with whom she spoke "refused to do so," again telling her to "wait until 10:00 p.m. and see if " her husband returned the girls. *Id.,* at 126a-127a.

At approximately 10:10 p.m., respondent called the police and said her children were still missing, but she was now told to wait until midnight.

at 12:10 a.m. she was told to wait for an officer to arrive. When none came, she went to the police station at 12:50 a.m. and submitted an incident report. The officer who took the report "made no reasonable effort to enforce the TRO or locate the three children. Instead, he went to dinner."

At approximately 10:10 p.m., respondent called the police and said her children were still missing, but she was now told to wait until midnight. She called at midnight and told the dispatcher her children were still missing. She went to her husband's apartment and, finding nobody there, called the police at 12:10 a.m.; she was told to wait for an officer to arrive. When none came, she went to the police station at 12:50 a.m. and submitted an incident report. The officer who took the report "made no reasonable effort to enforce the TRO or locate the three children. Instead, he went to dinner." *Id.,* at 127a.

At approximately 3:20 a.m., respondent's husband arrived at the police station and opened fire with a semiautomatic handgun he had purchased earlier that evening. Police shot back, killing him. Inside the cab of his pickup truck, they found the bodies of all three daughters, whom he had already murdered.

At approximately 3:20 a.m., respondent's husband arrived at the police station and opened fire with a semiautomatic handgun he had purchased earlier that evening. Police shot back, killing him. Inside the cab of his pickup truck, they found the bodies of all three daughters, whom he had already murdered. *Ibid.*

On the basis of the foregoing factual allegations, respondent brought an action under Rev. Stat. §1979, 42 U. S. C. §1983, claiming that the town violated the Due Process Clause because its police department had "an official policy or custom of failing to respond properly to complaints of restraining order violations" and "tolerate[d] the non-enforcement of restraining orders by its police officers." App. to Pet. for Cert. 129a. n3 The complaint also alleged that the town's actions "were taken either willfully, recklessly or with such gross negligence as to indicate wanton disregard and deliberate indifference to" respondent's civil rights. *Ibid.*

n3 Three police officers were also named as defendants in the complaint, but the Court of Appeals concluded that they were entitled to qualified immunity, 366 F. 3d 1093, 1118 (CA10 2004) (en banc). Respondent did not file a cross-petition challenging that aspect of the judgment.

Before answering the complaint, the defendants filed a motion to dismiss under Federal Rule of Civil Procedure 12(b)(6). The District Court granted the motion, concluding that, whether construed as making a substantive due process or procedural due process claim, respondent's complaint failed to state a claim upon which relief could be granted.

A panel of the Court of Appeals affirmed the rejection of a substantive due process claim, but found that respondent had alleged a cognizable procedural due process claim. 307 F. 3d 1258 (CA10 2002). On rehearing en banc, a divided court reached the same disposition, concluding that respondent had a "protected property interest in the enforcement of the terms of her restraining order" and that the town had deprived her of due process because "the police never 'heard' nor seriously entertained her request to enforce and protect her interests in the restraining order." 366 F. 3d, at 1101, 1117. We granted certiorari. 543 U. S. 955 (2004).

The Fourteenth Amendment to the United States Constitution provides that a State shall not "deprive any person of life, liberty, or property, without due process of law."

In 42 U. S. C. §1983, Congress has created a federal cause of action for "the deprivation of any rights, privileges, or immunities secured by the Constitution and laws."

The Fourteenth Amendment to the United States Constitution provides that a State shall not "deprive any person of life, liberty, or property, without due process of law." Amdt. 14, §1. In 42 U. S. C. §1983, Congress has created a federal cause of action for "the deprivation of any rights, privileges, or immunities secured by the Constitution and laws." Respondent claims the benefit of this provision on the ground that she had a property interest in police enforcement of the restraining order against her husband; and that the town deprived her of this property without due process by having a policy that tolerated nonenforcement of restraining orders.

the so-called "substantive" component of the Due Process Clause does not "require the State to protect the life, liberty, and property of its citizens against invasion by private actors."

As the Court of Appeals recognized, we left a similar question unanswered in *DeShaney* v. *Winnebago County Dept. of Social Servs.*, 489 U. S. 189 (1989), another case with "undeniably tragic" facts: Local child-protection officials had failed to protect a young boy from beatings by his father that left him severely brain damaged. *Id.*, at 191-193. We held that the so-called "substantive" component of the Due Process Clause does not "requir[e] the State to protect the life, liberty, and property of its citizens against invasion by private actors." *Id.*, at 195. We noted, however, that the petitioner had not properly preserved the argument that—and we thus "decline[d] to consider" whether—state "child protection statutes gave [him] an 'entitlement' to receive protective services in accordance with the terms of the statute, an entitlement which would enjoy due process protection." *Id.*, at 195, n. 2.

The procedural component of the Due Process Clause does not protect everything that might be described as a "benefit"

The procedural component of the Due Process Clause does not protect everything that might be described as a "benefit": "To have a property interest in a benefit, a person clearly must have more than an abstract need or desire" and "more than a unilateral expectation of it. He must, instead, have a legitimate claim of entitlement to it." *Board of Regents of State Colleges* v. *Roth*, 408 U. S. 564, 577 (1972). Such entitlements are "'of course, ... not created by the Constitution. Rather, they are created and their dimensions are defined by existing rules or understandings that stem from an independent source such as state law.'" *Paul* v. *Davis*, 424 U. S. 693, 709 (1976) (quoting *Roth, supra*, at 577); see also *Phillips* v. *Washington Legal Foundation*, 524 U. S. 156, 164 (1998).

A

Our cases recognize that a benefit is not a protected entitlement if government officials may grant or deny it in their discretion.

Our cases recognize that a benefit is not a protected entitlement if government officials may grant or deny it in their discretion. See, *e.g.*, *Kentucky Dept. of Corrections* v. *Thompson*, 490 U. S. 454, 462-463 (1989). The Court of Appeals in this case determined that Colorado law created an entitlement to enforcement of the restraining order because the "court-issued restraining order ... specifically dictated that its terms must be enforced" and a "state statute command[ed]" enforcement of the order when certain objective conditions were met (probable cause to believe that the order had been violated and that the object of the order had received notice of its existence). 366 F. 3d, at 1101, n. 5; see also *id.*, at 1100, n. 4; *id.*, at 1104-1105, and n. 9. Respondent contends that we are obliged "to give deference to the Tenth Circuit's analysis of Colorado law on" whether she had an entitlement to enforcement of the restraining order. Tr. of Oral Arg. 52.

We will not, of course, defer to the Tenth Circuit on the ultimate issue: whether what Colorado law has given respondent constitutes a property interest for purposes of the Fourteenth Amendment. That determination, despite its state-law underpinnings, is ultimately one of federal constitutional law. "Although the underlying substantive interest is created by 'an independent source such as state law,' *federal constitutional law* determines whether that interest rises to the level of a 'legitimate claim of entitlement' protected by the Due Process Clause." *Memphis Light, Gas & Water Div.* v. *Craft*, 436 U. S. 1, 9 (1978) (emphasis added) (quoting *Roth, supra*, at 577); cf. *United States ex rel. TVA* v. *Powelson*, 319 U. S. 266, 279 (1943). Resolution of the federal issue begins, however, with a determination of what it is that state law provides. In the context of the present case, the central state-law question is whether Colorado law gave respondent a right to police enforcement of the restraining order. It is on this point that respondent's call for deference to the Tenth Circuit is relevant.

We have said that a "presumption of deference [is] given the views of a federal court as to the law of a State within its jurisdiction." *Phillips, supra*, at 167. That presumption can be overcome, however, see *Leavitt* v. *Jane L.*, 518 U. S. 137, 145 (1996) *(per curiam)*, and we think deference inappropriate here. The Tenth Circuit's opinion, which reversed the Colorado District Judge, did not draw upon a deep well of state-specific expertise, but consisted primarily of quoting language from the restraining order, the statutory text, and a state-legislative-hearing transcript. See 366 F. 3d, at 1103-1109. These texts, moreover, say nothing distinctive to Colorado, but use mandatory language that (as we shall discuss) appears in many state and federal statutes. As for case law: the only state-law cases about restraining orders that the Court of Appeals relied upon were decisions of Federal District Courts in Ohio and Pennsylvania and state courts in New Jersey, Oregon, and Tennessee. *Id.*, at 1104-1105, n. 9, 1109. n4 Moreover, if we were simply to accept the Court of Appeals' conclusion, we would necessarily have to decide conclusively a federal constitutional question (*i.e.*, whether such an entitlement constituted property under the Due Process Clause and, if so, whether petitioner's customs or policies provided too little process to protect it). We proceed, then, to our own analysis of whether Colorado law gave respondent a right to enforcement of the restraining order. n5

n4 Most of the Colorado-law cases cited by the Court of Appeals appeared in footnotes declaring them to be irrelevant because they involved only substantive due process (366 F. 3d, at 1100-1101, nn. 4-5), only statutes without restraining orders (*id.,* at 1101, n. 5), or Colorado's Government Immunity Act, which the Court of Appeals concluded applies "only to ... state tort law claims" (*id.,* at 1108-1109, n. 12). Our analysis is likewise unaffected by the Immunity Act or by the way that Colorado has dealt with substantive due process or cases that do not involve restraining orders.

n5 In something of an anyone-but-us approach, the dissent simultaneously (and thus unpersuasively) contends not only that this Court should certify a question to the Colorado Supreme Court, *post,* at 5-7 (opinion of *Stevens,* J.), but also that it should defer to the Tenth Circuit (which itself did not certify any such question), *post,* at 3-4. No party in this case has requested certification, even as an alternative disposition. See Tr. of Oral Arg. 56 (petitioner's counsel "disfavor[ing]" certification); *id.,* at 25-26 (counsel for the United States arguing against certification). At oral argument, in fact, respondent's counsel declined *Justice Stevens'* invitation to request it. *Id.,* at 53.

II
B

The critical language in the restraining order came not from any part of the order itself (which was signed by the state-court trial judge and directed to the restrained party, respondent's husband), but from the preprinted notice to law-enforcement personnel that appeared on the back of the order. See *supra,* at 2-3. That notice effectively restated the statutory provision describing "peace officers' duties" related to the crime of violation of a restraining order. At the time of the conduct at issue in this case, that provision read as follows:

"(a) Whenever a restraining order is issued, the protected person shall be provided with a copy of such order. *A peace officer shall use every reasonable means to enforce a restraining order.*

"(b) *A peace officer shall arrest, or, if an arrest would be impractical under the circumstances, seek a warrant for the arrest of a restrained person* when the peace officer has information amounting to probable cause that:

"(I) The restrained person has violated or attempted to violate any provision of a restraining order; and

"(II) The restrained person has been properly served with a copy of the restraining order or the restrained person has received actual notice of the existence and substance of such order.

"(c) In making the probable cause determination described in paragraph (b) of this subsection (3), a peace officer shall assume that the information received from the registry is accurate. *A peace officer shall enforce a valid restraining order whether or not there is a record of the restraining order in the registry.*" Colo. Rev. Stat. §18-6-803.5(3) (Lexis 1999) (emphases added).

The Court of Appeals concluded that this statutory provision—especially taken in conjunction with a statement from its legislative history, n6 and with another statute restricting criminal and civil liability for officers making arrests n7—established the Colorado Legislature's clear intent "to alter the fact that the police were not enforcing domestic abuse retraining orders," and thus its intent "that the recipient of a domestic abuse restraining order have an entitlement to its enforcement." 366 F. 3d, at 1108. Any other result, it said, "would render domestic abuse restraining orders utterly valueless." *Id.,* at 1109.

n6 The Court of Appeals quoted one lawmaker's description of how the bill "'would really attack the domestic violence problems'":

"'[T]he entire criminal justice system must act in a consistent manner, which does not now occur. The police must make probable cause arrests. The prosecutors must prosecute every case. Judges must apply appropriate sentences, and probation officers must monitor their probationers closely. And the offender needs to be sentenced to offender-specific therapy.

"'[T]he entire system must send the same message ... [that] violence is criminal. And so we hope that House Bill 1253 strats us down this road.'" 336 F. 3d, at 1107 (quoting Tr. of Colorado House Judiciary Hearings on House Bill 1253, Feb. 15, 1994) (emphases omitted).

n7 Under Colo. Rev. Stat. §18-6-803.5(5) (Lexis 1999), "[a] peace officer arresting a person for violating a restraining order or otherwise enforcing a restraining order" was not to be held civilly or criminally liable unless he acted "in bad faith and with malice" or violated "rules adopted by the Colorado supreme court."

This last statement is sheer hyperbole. Whether or not respondent had a right to enforce the restraining order, it rendered certain otherwise lawful conduct by her husband both criminal and in contempt of court. See §§18-6-803.5(2)(a), (7). The creation of grounds on which he could be arrested, criminally prosecuted, and held in contempt was hardly "valueless"—even if the prospect of those sanctions ultimately failed to prevent him from committing three murders and a suicide.

We do not believe that these provisions of Colorado law truly made enforcement of restraining orders *mandatory*. A well established tradition of police discretion has long coexisted with apparently mandatory arrest statutes.

We do not believe that these provisions of Colorado law truly made enforcement of restraining orders *mandatory*. A well established tradition of police discretion has long coexisted with apparently mandatory arrest statutes.

In each and every state there are long-standing statutes that, by their terms, seem to preclude nonenforcement by the police... However, for a number of reasons, including their legislative history, insufficient resources, and sheer physical impossibility, it has been recognized that such statutes cannot be interpreted literally.

"In each and every state there are long-standing statutes that, by their terms, seem to preclude nonenforcement by the police... . However, for a number of reasons, including their legislative history, insufficient resources, and sheer physical impossibility, it has been recognized that such statutes cannot be interpreted literally... . [T]hey clearly do not mean that a police officer may not lawfully decline to make an arrest. As to third parties in these states, the full-enforcement statutes simply have no effect, and their significance is further diminished." 1 ABA Standards for Criminal Justice 1-4.5, commentary, pp. 1-124 to 1-125 (2d ed. 1980) (footnotes omitted).

It is... simply "common sense that *all* police officers must use some discretion in deciding when and where to enforce city ordinances."

The deep-rooted nature of law-enforcement discretion, even in the presence of seemingly mandatory legislative commands, is illustrated by *Chicago* v. *Morales*, 527 U. S. 41 (1999), which involved an ordinance that said a police officer "'shall order'" persons to disperse in certain circumstances, *id.*, at 47, n. 2. This Court rejected out of hand the possibility that "the mandatory language of the ordinance ... afford[ed] the police *no* discretion." *Id.*, at 62, n. 32. It is, the Court proclaimed, simply "common sense that *all* police officers must use some discretion in deciding when and where to enforce city ordinances." *Ibid.* (emphasis added).

The practical necessity for discretion is particularly apparent in a case such as this one, where the suspected violator is not actually present and his whereabouts are unknown.

Against that backdrop, a true mandate of police action would require some stronger indication from the Colorado Legislature than "shall use every reasonable means to enforce a restraining order" (or even "shall arrest ... or ... seek a warrant"), §§18-6-803.5(3)(a), (b). That language is not perceptibly more mandatory than the Colorado statute which has long told municipal chiefs of police that they "shall pursue and arrest any person fleeing from justice in any part of the state" and that they "shall apprehend any person in the act of committing any offense ... and, forthwith and without any warrant, bring such person before a ... competent authority for examination and trial." Colo. Rev. Stat. §31-4-112 (Lexis 2004). It is hard to imagine that a Colorado peace officer would not have some discretion to determine that—despite probable cause to believe a restraining order has been violated—the circumstances of the violation or the competing duties of that officer or his agency counsel decisively against enforcement in a particular instance. n8 The practical necessity for discretion is particularly apparent in a case such as this one, where the suspected violator is not actually present and his whereabouts are unknown. Cf. *Donaldson* v. *Seattle*, 65 Wash. App. 661, 671-672, 831 P. 2d 1098, 1104 (1992) ("There is a vast difference between a mandatory duty to arrest [a violator who is on the scene] and a mandatory duty to conduct a follow up investigation [to locate an absent violator].... . A mandatory duty to investigate would be completely open-ended as to priority, duration and intensity").

n8 Respondent in fact concedes that an officer may "properly" decide not to enforce a restraining order when the officer deems "a technical violation" too "immaterial" to justify arrest. Respondent explains this as a determination that there is no probable cause. Brief for Respondent 28. We think, however, that a determination of no probable cause to believe a violation has occurred is quite different from a determination that the violation is too insignificant to pursue.

The dissent correctly points out that, in the specific context of domestic violence, mandatory-arrest statutes have been found in some States to be more mandatory than traditional mandatory-arrest statutes. *Post,* at 7-13 (opinion of *Stevens,* J.). The Colorado statute mandating arrest for a domestic-violence offense is different from but related to the one at issue here, and it includes similar though not identical phrasing. See Colo. Rev. Stat. §18-6-803.6(1) (Lexis 1999) ("When a peace officer determines that there is probable cause to believe that a crime or offense involving domestic violence ... has been committed, the officer shall, without undue delay, arrest the person suspected of its commission ..."). Even in the domestic-violence context, however, it is unclear how the mandatory-arrest paradigm applies to cases in which the offender is not present to be arrested. As the dissent explains, *post,* at 9-10, and n. 8, much of the impetus for mandatory-arrest statutes and policies derived from the idea that it is better for police officers to arrest the aggressor in a domestic-violence incident than to attempt to mediate the dispute or merely to ask the offender to leave the scene. Those other options are only available, of course, when the offender is present at the scene. See Hanna, No Right to Choose: Mandated Victim Participation in Domestic Violence Prosecutions, 109 Harv. L. Rev. 1849, 1860 (1996) ("[T]he clear trend in police practice is to arrest the batterer *at the scene* ..." (emphasis added)).

As one of the cases cited by the dissent recognized, "there will be situations when no arrest is possible, *such as when the alleged abuser is not in the home.*"

As one of the cases cited by the dissent, *post,* at 12, recognized, "there will be situations when no arrest is possible, *such as when the alleged abuser is not in the home.*" *Donaldson,* 65 Wash. App., at 674, 831 P. 2d, at 1105 (emphasis added). That case held that Washington's mandatory-arrest statute required an arrest only in "cases where the offender is on the scene," and that it "d[id] not create an on-going mandatory duty to conduct an investigation" to locate the offender. *Id.,* at 675, 831 P. 2d, at 1105. Colorado's restraining-order statute appears to contemplate a similar distinction, providing that when arrest is "impractical"—which was likely the case when the whereabouts of respondent's husband were unknown— the officers' statutory duty is to "seek a warrant" rather than "arrest." §18-6-803.5(3)(b).

Such indeterminacy is not the hallmark of a duty that is mandatory. Nor can someone be safely deemed "entitled" to something when the identity of the alleged entitlement is vague.

the seeking of an arrest warrant would be an entitlement to nothing but procedure— which we have held inadequate even to support standing

After the warrant is sought, it remains within the discretion of a judge whether to grant it, and after it is granted, it remains within the discretion of the police whether and when to execute it. Respondent would have been assured nothing but the seeking of a warrant. This is not the sort of "entitlement" out of which a property interest is created.

Respondent does not specify the precise means of enforcement that the Colorado restraining-order statute assertedly mandated—whether her interest lay in having police arrest her husband, having them seek a warrant for his arrest, or having them "use every reasonable means, up to and including arrest, to enforce the order's terms," Brief for Respondent 29-30. n9 Such indeterminacy is not the hallmark of a duty that is mandatory. Nor can someone be safely deemed "entitled" to something when the identity of the alleged entitlement is vague. See *Roth,* 408 U. S., at 577 (considering whether "certain benefits" were "secure[d]" by rule or understandings); cf. *Natale* v. *Ridgefield,* 170 F. 3d 258, 263 (CA2 1999) ("There is no reason ... to restrict the 'uncertainty' that will preclude existence of a federally protectable property interest to the uncertainty that inheres in the exercise of discretion"). The dissent, after suggesting various formulations of the entitlement in question, n10 ultimately contends that the obligations under the statute were quite precise: either make an arrest or (if that is impractical) seek an arrest warrant, *post,* at 14. The problem with this is that the seeking of an arrest warrant would be an entitlement to nothing but procedure—which we have held inadequate even to support standing, see *Lujan* v. *Defenders of Wildlife,* 504 U. S. 555 (1992); much less can it be the basis for a property interest. See *post,* at 3-4 (*Souter,* J., concurring). After the warrant is sought, it remains within the discretion of a judge whether to grant it, and after it is granted, it remains within the discretion of the police whether and when to execute it. n11

Respondent would have been assured nothing but the seeking of a warrant. This is not the sort of "entitlement" out of which a property interest is created.

n9 Respondent characterizes her entitlement in various ways. See Brief for Respondent 12 ("'entitlement' to receive protective services"); id., at 13 ("interest in police enforcement action"); id., at 14 ("specific government benefit" consisting of "the government service of enforcing the objective terms of the court order protecting her and her children against her abusive husband"); id., at 32 ("[T]he restraining order here mandated the arrest of Mr. Gonzales under specified circumstances, or at a minimum required the use of reasonable means to enforce the order").

n10 See post, at 1 ("entitlement to police protection"); post, at 2 ("entitlement to mandatory individual protection by the local police force"); ibid. ("a right to police assistance"); post, at 8 ("a citizen's interest in the government's commitment to provide police enforcement in certain defined circumstances"); post, at 18 ("respondent's property interest in the enforcement of her restraining order"); post, at 20 (the "service" of "protection from her husband"); post, at 21-22 ("interest in the enforcement of the restraining order")

n11 The dissent asserts that the police would lack discretion in the execution of this warrant, post, at 13-14, n. 12, but cites no statute mandating immediate execution. The general Colorado statute governing arrest provides that police "may arrest" when they possess a warrant "commanding" arrest. Colo. Rev. Stat. §16-3-102(1) (Lexis 1999).

Making the actions of government employees obligatory can serve various legitimate ends other than the conferral of a benefit on a specific class of people.

The serving of public rather than private ends is the normal course of the criminal law because criminal acts, "besides the injury they do to individuals, ... strike at the very being of society; which cannot possibly subsist, where actions of this sort are suffered to escape with impunity."

Even if the statute could be said to have made enforcement of restraining orders "mandatory" because of the domestic-violence context of the underlying statute, that would not necessarily mean that state law gave *respondent* an entitlement to *enforcement* of the mandate. Making the actions of government employees obligatory can serve various legitimate ends other than the conferral of a benefit on a specific class of people. See, *e.g., Sandin* v. *Conner*, 515 U. S. 472, 482 (1995) (finding no constitutionally protected liberty interest in prison regulations phrased in mandatory terms, in part because "[s]uch guidelines are not set forth solely to benefit the prisoner"). The serving of public rather than private ends is the normal course of the criminal law because criminal acts, "besides the injury [they do] to individuals, ... strike at the very being of society; which cannot possibly subsist, where actions of this sort are suffered to escape with impunity." 4 W. Blackstone, Commentaries on the Laws of England 5 (1769); see also *Huntington* v. *Attrill*, 146 U. S. 657, 668 (1892). This principle underlies, for example, a Colorado district attorney's discretion to prosecute a domestic assault, even though the victim withdraws her charge. See *People* v. *Cunefare*, 102 P. 3d 302, 311-312 (Colo. 2004) (Bender, J., concurring in part, dissenting in part, and dissenting in part to the judgment).

Respondent's alleged interest stems only from a State's *statutory* scheme.... She does not assert that she has any common-law or contractual entitlement to enforcement. If she was given a statutory entitlement, we would expect to see some indication of that in the statute itself.

The protected person's express power to "initiate" civil contempt proceedings contrasts tellingly with the mere ability to "request" initiation of criminal contempt proceedings—and even more dramatically with the complete silence about any power to "request" (much less demand) that an arrest be made.

Respondent's alleged interest stems only from a State's *statutory* scheme—from a restraining order that was authorized by and tracked precisely the statute on which the Court of Appeals relied. She does not assert that she has any common-law or contractual entitlement to enforcement. If she was given a statutory entitlement, we would expect to see some indication of that in the statute itself. Although Colorado's statute spoke of "protected person[s]" such as respondent, it did so in connection with matters other than a right to enforcement. It said that a "protected person shall be provided with a copy of [a restraining] order" when it is issued, §18-6-803.5(3)(a); that a law enforcement agency "shall make all reasonable efforts to contact the protected party upon the arrest of the restrained person," §18-6-803.5(3)(d); and that the agency "shall give [to the protected person] a copy" of the report it submits to the court that issued the order, §18-6-

803.5(3)(e). Perhaps most importantly, the statute spoke directly to the protected person's power to "initiate contempt proceedings against the restrained person if the order [was] issued in a civil action or request the prosecuting attorney to initiate contempt proceedings if the order [was] issued in a criminal action." §18-6-803.5(7). The protected person's express power to "initiate" civil contempt proceedings contrasts tellingly with the mere ability to "request" initiation of criminal contempt proceedings—and even more dramatically with the complete silence about any power to "request" (much less demand) that an arrest be made.

We conclude that Colorado has not created such an entitlement.

The creation of a personal entitlement to something as vague and novel as enforcement of restraining orders cannot "simply g[o] without saying." Post, at 17, n. 16 (Stevens, J., dissenting). We conclude that Colorado has not created such an entitlement.

C

Even if we were to think otherwise concerning the creation of an entitlement by Colorado, it is by no means clear that an individual entitlement to enforcement of a restraining order could constitute a "property" interest for purposes of the Due Process Clause.

the right to have a restraining order enforced does not "have some ascertainable monetary value"

Even if we were to think otherwise concerning the creation of an entitlement by Colorado, it is by no means clear that an individual entitlement to enforcement of a restraining order could constitute a "property" interest for purposes of the Due Process Clause. Such a right would not, of course, resemble any traditional conception of property. Although that alone does not disqualify it from due process protection, as Roth and its progeny show, the right to have a restraining order enforced does not "have some ascertainable monetary value," as even our "Roth-type property-as-entitlement" cases have implicitly required. Merrill, The Landscape of Constitutional Property, 86 Va. L. Rev. 885, 964 (2000). n12 Perhaps most radically, the alleged property interest here arises incidentally, not out of some new species of government benefit or service, but out of a function that government actors have always performed—to wit, arresting people who they have probable cause to believe have committed a criminal offense. n13

n12 The dissent suggests that the interest in having a restraining order enforced does have an ascertainable monetary value, because one may "contract with a private security firm ... to provide protection" for one's family. Post, at 2, 20, and n. 18. That is, of course, not as precise as the analogy between public and private schooling that the dissent invokes. Post, at 20, n. 18. Respondent probably could have hired a private firm to guard her house, to prevent her husband from coming onto the property, and perhaps even to search for her husband after she discovered that her children were missing. Her alleged entitlement here, however, does not consist in an abstract right to "protection," but (according to the dissent) in enforcement of her restraining order through the arrest of her husband, or the seeking of a warrant for his arrest, after she gave the police probable cause to believe the restraining order had been violated. A private person would not have the power to arrest under those circumstances because the crime would not have occurred in his presence. Colo. Rev. Stat. §16-3-201 (Lexis 1999). And, needless to say, a private person would not have the power to obtain an arrest warrant.

n13 In other contexts, we have explained that "a private citizen lacks a judicially cognizable interest in the prosecution or nonprosecution of another." Linda R. S. v. Richard D., 410 U. S. 614, 619 (1973).

The indirect nature of a benefit was fatal to the due process claim of the nursing-home residents in O'Bannon v. Town Court Nursing Center, 447 U. S. 773 (1980). We held that, while the withdrawal of "direct benefits" (financial payments under Medicaid for certain medical services) triggered due process protections, id., at 786-787, the same was not true for the "indirect benefit[s]" conferred on Medicaid patients when the Government enforced "minimum standards of care" for nursing-home facilities, id., at 787. "[A]n indirect and incidental result of the Government's enforcement action ... does not amount to a deprivation of any interest in life, liberty, or property." Ibid. In this case, as in O'Bannon, "[t]he simple distinction between government action that directly affects a citizen's legal rights ... and action that is directed against a third party and affects the citizen only indirectly or incidentally, provides a sufficient answer to" respondent's reliance on cases that found government-provided services to be entitlements. Id., at 788. The O'Bannon Court expressly noted, ibid., that the distinction between direct and indirect benefits distinguished Memphis Light, Gas &

Water Div. v. *Craft,* 436 U. S. 1 (1978), one of the government-services cases on which the dissent relies, *post,* at 19.

III

respondent did not, for purposes of the Due Process Clause, have a property interest in police enforcement of the restraining order against her husband.

We conclude, therefore, that respondent did not, for purposes of the Due Process Clause, have a property interest in police enforcement of the restraining order against her husband. It is accordingly unnecessary to address the Court of Appeals' determination (366 F. 3d, at 1110-1117) that the town's custom or policy prevented the police from giving her due process when they deprived her of that alleged interest. See *American Mfrs. Mut. Ins. Co.* v. *Sullivan,* 526 U. S. 40, 61 (1999). n14

n14 Because we simply do not address whether the process would have been adequate if respondent had had a property interest, the dissent is correct to note that we do not "contest" the point, *post,* at 2. Of course we do not *accept* it either.

the benefit that a third party may receive from having someone else arrested for a crime generally does not trigger protections under the Due Process Clause, neither in its procedural nor in its "substantive" manifestations. This result reflects our continuing reluctance to treat the Fourteenth Amendment as "a font of tort law"

Although the framers of the Fourteenth Amendment and the Civil Rights Act of 1871, 17 Stat. 13 (the original source of §1983), did not create a system by which police departments are generally held financially accountable for crimes that better policing might have prevented, the people of Colorado are free to craft such a system under state law.

In light of today's decision and that in *DeShaney,* the benefit that a third party may receive from having someone else arrested for a crime generally does not trigger protections under the Due Process Clause, neither in its procedural nor in its "substantive" manifestations. This result reflects our continuing reluctance to treat the Fourteenth Amendment as "'a font of tort law,'" *Parratt* v. *Taylor,* 451 U. S. 527, 544 (1981) (quoting *Paul* v. *Davis,* 424 U. S., at 701), but it does not mean States are powerless to provide victims with personally enforceable remedies. Although the framers of the Fourteenth Amendment and the Civil Rights Act of 1871, 17 Stat. 13 (the original source of §1983), did not create a system by which police departments are generally held financially accountable for crimes that better policing might have prevented, the people of Colorado are free to craft such a system under state law. Cf. *DeShaney,* 489 U. S., at 203. n15

n15 In Colorado, the general statutory immunity for government employees does not apply when "the act or omission causing ... injury was willful and wanton." Colo. Rev. Stat. §24-10-118(2)(a) (Lexis 1999). Respondent's complaint does allege that the police officers' actions "were taken either willfully, recklessly or with such gross negligence as to indicate wanton disregard and deliberate indifference to" her civil rights. App. to Pet. for Cert. 128a.

The judgment of the Court of Appeals is Reversed.

Justice Souter, with whom Justice Breyer joins, concurring.

I agree with the Court that Jessica Gonzales has shown no violation of an interest protected by the Fourteenth Amendment's Due Process Clause, and I join the Court's opinion. The Court emphasizes the traditional public focus of law enforcement as reason to doubt that these particular legal requirements to provide police services, however unconditional their form, presuppose enforceable individual rights to a certain level of police protection. *Ante,* at 15-16. The Court also notes that the terms of the Colorado statute involved here recognize and preserve the traditional discretion afforded law enforcement officers. *Ante,* at 11-15, and n. 8. Gonzales's claim of a property right thus runs up against police discretion in the face of an individual demand to enforce, and discretion to ignore an individual instruction not to enforce (because, say, of a domestic reconciliation); no one would argue that the beneficiary of a Colorado order like the one here would be authorized to control a court's contempt power or order the police to refrain from arresting. These considerations argue against inferring any guarantee of a level of protection or safety that could be understood as the object of a "legitimate claim of entitlement," *Board of Regents of State Colleges* v. *Roth,* 408 U. S. 564, 577 (1972), in the nature of property arising under Colorado law. n16 Consequently, the classic predicate for federal due process protection of interests under state law is missing.

n16 Gonzales does not claim to have a protected liberty interest.

Gonzales implicitly recognizes this, when she makes the following argument:

"Ms. Gonzales alleges that ... she was denied the process laid out in the statute. The police did not consider her request in a timely fashion, but instead repeatedly required her to call the station over several hours. The statute promised a process by which her restraining order would be given vitality through careful and prompt consideration of an enforcement request ... . Denial of that process drained all of the value from her property interest in the restraining order." Brief for Respondent 10.

The argument is unconventional because the state-law benefit for which it claims federal procedural protection is itself a variety of procedural regulation, a set of rules to be followed by officers exercising the State's executive power: use all reasonable means to enforce, arrest upon demonstrable probable cause, get a warrant, and so on, see *ante*, at 2-3.

When her argument is understood as unconventional in this sense, a further reason appears for rejecting its call to apply *Roth*, a reason that would apply even if the statutory mandates to the police were absolute, leaving the police with no discretion when the beneficiary of a protective order insists upon its enforcement. The Due Process Clause extends procedural protection to guard against unfair deprivation by state officials of substantive state-law property rights or entitlements; the federal process protects the property created by state law. But Gonzales claims a property interest in a state-mandated process in and of itself. This argument is at odds with the rule that "[p]rocess is not an end in itself. Its constitutional purpose is to protect a substantive interest to which the individual has a legitimate claim of entitlement." *Olim* v. *Wakinekona*, 461 U. S. 238, 250 (1983); see also *Doe by Fein* v. *District of Columbia*, 93 F. 3d 861, 868 (CADC 1996) *(per curiam); Doe by Nelson* v. *Milwaukee County*, 903 F. 2d 499, 502-503 (CA7 1990). In putting to rest the notion that the scope of an otherwise discernible property interest could be limited by related state-law procedures, this Court observed that "[t]he categories of substance and procedure are distinct... . 'Property' cannot be defined by the procedures provided for its deprivation." *Cleveland Bd. of Ed.* v. *Loudermill*, 470 U. S. 532, 541 (1985). Just as a State cannot diminish a property right, once conferred, by attaching less than generous procedure to its deprivation, *ibid.*, neither does a State create a property right merely by ordaining beneficial procedure unconnected to some articulable substantive guarantee. This is not to say that state rules of executive procedure may not provide significant reasons to infer an articulable property right meant to be protected; but it is to say that we have not identified property with procedure as such. State rules of executive procedure, however important, may be nothing more than rules of executive procedure.

in every instance of property recognized by this Court as calling for federal procedural protection, the property has been distinguishable from the procedural obligations imposed on state officials to protect it.

To accede to Gonzales's argument would therefore work a sea change in the scope of federal due process, for she seeks federal process as a substitute simply for state process.

Gonzales's claim would thus take us beyond *Roth* or any other recognized theory of Fourteenth Amendment due process, by collapsing the distinction between property protected and the process that protects it

Thus, in every instance of property recognized by this Court as calling for federal procedural protection, the property has been distinguishable from the procedural obligations imposed on state officials to protect it. Whether welfare benefits, *Goldberg* v. *Kelly,* 397 U. S. 254 (1970), attendance at public schools, *Goss* v. *Lopez,* 419 U. S. 565 (1975), utility services, *Memphis Light, Gas & Water Div.* v. *Craft,* 436 U. S. 1 (1978), public employment, *Perry* v. *Sindermann,* 408 U. S. 593 (1972), professional licenses, *Barry* v. *Barchi,* 443 U. S. 55 (1979), and so on, the property interest recognized in our cases has always existed apart from state procedural protection before the Court has recognized a constitutional claim to protection by federal process. To accede to Gonzales's argument would therefore work a sea change in the scope of federal due process, for she seeks federal process as a substitute simply for state process. (And she seeks damages under Rev. Stat. §1979, 42 U. S. C. §1983, for denial of process to which she claimed a federal right.) There is no articulable distinction between the object of Gonzales's asserted entitlement and the process she desires in order to protect her entitlement; both amount to certain steps to be taken by the police to protect her family and herself. Gonzales's claim would thus take us beyond *Roth* or any other recognized theory of Fourteenth Amendment due process, by collapsing the distinction between property protected and the process that protects it, and would federalize every mandatory state-law direction to executive officers whose performance on the job can be vitally significant to individuals affected.

The procedural directions involved here are just that. They presuppose no enforceable substantive entitlement, and *Roth* does not raise them to federally enforceable status in the name of due process.

Justice Stevens, with whom Justice Ginsburg joins, dissenting.

The issue presented to us is much narrower than is suggested by the far-ranging arguments of the parties and their *amici*. Neither the tragic facts of the case, nor the importance of according proper deference to law enforcement professionals, should divert our attention from that issue. That issue is whether the restraining order entered by the Colorado trial court on June 4, 1999, created a "property" interest that is protected from arbitrary deprivation by the Due Process Clause of the Fourteenth Amendment.

It is perfectly clear, on the one hand, that neither the Federal Constitution itself, nor any federal statute, granted respondent or her children any individual entitlement to police protection.

it is equally clear that federal law imposes no impediment to the creation of such an entitlement by Colorado law.

It is perfectly clear, on the one hand, that neither the Federal Constitution itself, nor any federal statute, granted respondent or her children any individual entitlement to police protection. See *DeShaney* v. *Winnebago County Dept. of Social Servs.*, 489 U. S. 189 (1989). Nor, I assume, does any Colorado statute create any such entitlement for the ordinary citizen. On the other hand, it is equally clear that federal law imposes no impediment to the creation of such an entitlement by Colorado law. Respondent certainly could have entered into a contract with a private security firm, obligating the firm to provide protection to respondent's family; respondent's interest in such a contract would unquestionably constitute "property" within the meaning of the Due Process Clause. If a Colorado statute enacted for her benefit, or a valid order entered by a Colorado judge, created the functional equivalent of such a private contract by granting respondent an entitlement to mandatory individual protection by the local police force, that state-created right would also qualify as "property" entitled to constitutional protection.

if respondent did have a cognizable property interest in this case, the deprivation of that interest violated due process.

she contends, the officers effectively ignored her. If these allegations are true, a federal statute, Rev. Stat. §1979, 42 U. S. C. §1983, provides her with a remedy against the petitioner, even if Colorado law does not.

I do not understand the majority to rule out the foregoing propositions, although it does express doubts. See *ante*, at 17 ("[I]t is by no means clear that an individual entitlement to enforcement of a restraining order could constitute a 'property' interest"). Moreover, the majority does not contest, see *ante*, at 18, that if respondent did have a cognizable property interest in this case, the deprivation of that interest violated due process. As the Court notes, respondent has alleged that she presented the police with a copy of the restraining order issued by the Colorado court and requested that it be enforced. *Ante*, at 2, n. 1. In response, she contends, the officers effectively ignored her. If these allegations are true, a federal statute, Rev. Stat. §1979, 42 U. S. C. §1983, provides her with a remedy against the petitioner, even if Colorado law does not. See *Cleveland Bd. of Ed.* v. *Loudermill*, 470 U. S. 532 (1985).

The central question in this case is therefore whether, as a matter of Colorado law, respondent had a right to police assistance comparable to the right she would have possessed to any other service the government or a private firm might have undertaken to provide.

The central question in this case is therefore whether, as a matter of Colorado law, respondent had a right to police assistance comparable to the right she would have possessed to any other service the government or a private firm might have undertaken to provide. See *Board of Regents of State Colleges* v. *Roth*, 408 U. S. 564, 577 (1972) ("Property interests, of course, are not created by the Constitution. Rather, they are created and their dimensions are defined by existing rules or understandings that stem from an independent source such as state law—rules or understandings that secure certain benefits and that support claims of entitlement to those benefits").

There was a time when our tradition of judicial restraint would have led this Court to defer to the judgment of more qualified tribunals in seeking the correct answer to that difficult question of Colorado law. Unfortunately, although the majority properly identifies the "central state-law question" in this case as "whether Colorado law gave respondent a right to police enforcement of the restraining order," *ante*, at 8, it has chosen to ignore our settled practice by providing its *own* answer to that question. Before identifying the flaws in the Court's ruling on the merits, I shall briefly comment on our past practice.

I

The majority's decision to plunge ahead with its own analysis of Colorado law imprudently departs from this Court's longstanding policy of paying "deference [to] the views of a federal court as to the law of a State within its jurisdiction." *Phillips* v. *Washington Legal Foundation*, 524 U. S. 156, 167 (1998); see also *Bishop* v. *Wood*, 426 U. S. 341, 346, and n. 10 (1976) (collecting cases). This policy is not only efficient, but it reflects "our belief that district courts and courts of appeal are better schooled in and more able to interpret the laws of their respective States." *Brockett* v. *Spokane Arcades, Inc.*, 472 U. S. 491, 500-501 (1985); *Hillsborough* v. *Cromwell*, 326 U. S. 620, 629-630 (1946) (endorsing "great deference to the views of the judges of those courts 'who are familiar with the intricacies and trends of local law and practice'"). Accordingly, we have declined to show deference only in rare cases in which the court of appeal's resolution of state law was "clearly wrong" or otherwise seriously deficient. See *Brockett*, 472 U. S., at 500, n. 9; accord, *Leavitt* v. *Jane L.*, 518 U. S. 137, 145 (1996) *(per curiam)*.

it is certainly *plausible* to construe "*shall* use every reasonable means to enforce a restraining order" and "*shall* arrest" ... (emphases added), as conveying mandatory directives to the police

Unfortunately, the Court does not even attempt to demonstrate that the six-judge en banc majority was "clearly wrong" in its interpretation of Colorado's domestic restraining order statute; nor could such a showing be made. For it is certainly *plausible* to construe "*shall* use every reasonable means to enforce a restraining order" and "*shall* arrest," Colo. Stat. §§18-6-803.5(3)(a)-(b) (Lexis 1999) (emphases added), as conveying mandatory directives to the police, particularly when the same statute, at other times, tellingly employs different language that suggests police discretion, see §18-6-803.5(6)(a) ("A peace officer *is authorized to* use every reasonable means to protect ..."; "Such peace officer *may* transport ..." (emphases added)). n17 Moreover, unlike today's decision, the Court of Appeals was attentive to the legislative history of the statute, focusing on a statement by the statute's sponsor in the Colorado House, *ante*, at 10, n. 6 (quoting statement), which it took to "emphasiz[e] the importance of the police's mandatory enforcement of domestic restraining orders." 366 F. 3d 1093, 1107 (CA10 2004) (en banc). Far from overlooking the traditional presumption of police discretion, then, the Court of Appeals' diligent analysis of the statute's text, purpose, and history led it to conclude that the Colorado Legislature intended precisely to abrogate that presumption in the specific context of domestic restraining orders. That conclusion is eminently reasonable and, I believe, worthy of our deference. n18

n17 The Court of Appeals also looked to other provisions of the statute to inform its analysis. In particular, it reasoned that a provision that gave police officers qualified immunity in connection with their enforcement of restraining orders, see Colo. Rev. Stat. §18-6-803.5(5) (Lexis 1999), supported the inference that the Colorado Legislature intended mandatory enforcement. See 366 F. 3d 1093, 1108 (CA10 2004) (en banc).

n18 The Court declines to show deference for the odd reason that, in its view, the Court of Appeals did not "draw upon a deep well of state-specific expertise," *ante*, at 8, but rather examined the statute's text and legislative history and distinguished arguably relevant Colorado case law. See *ante*, at 8-9, and n. 4. This rationale makes a mockery of our traditional practice, for it is precisely when there is no state law on point that the presumption that circuits have local expertise plays any useful role. When a circuit's resolution of a novel question of state law is grounded on a concededly complete review of all the pertinent state-law materials, that decision is entitled to deference. Additionally, it should be noted that this is not a case in which the Court of Appeals and the District Court disagreed on the relevant issue of state law; rather, those courts disagreed only over the extent to which a probable-cause determination requires the exercise of discretion. Compare 366 F. 3d, at 1105-1110, with App. to Pet. for Cert. 122a (District Court opinion).

II

the Colorado Supreme Court is the ultimate authority on the meaning of Colorado law, and if in later litigation it should disagree with this Court's provisional state-law holding, our efforts will have been wasted and respondent will have been deprived of the opportunity to have her claims heard under the authoritative view of Colorado law.

Even if the Court had good reason to doubt the Court of Appeals' determination of state law, it would, in my judgment, be a far wiser course to certify the question to the Colorado Supreme Court. n19 Powerful considerations support certification in this case. First, principles of federalism and comity favor giving a State's high court the opportunity to answer important questions of state law, particularly when those questions implicate uniquely local matters such as law enforcement and might well require the weighing of policy considerations for their correct resolution. n20 See *Elkins* v. *Moreno*, 435 U. S. 647, 662, n. 16 (1978) (*sua sponte* certifying a question of state law because it is "one in which state governments have the highest interest"); cf. *Arizonans for Official English* v. *Arizona*, 520 U. S. 43, 77 (1997) ("Through certification of novel or unsettled questions of state law for authoritative answers by a State's highest court, a federal court may save 'time, energy, and resources, and hel[p] build a cooperative judicial federalism'" (brackets in original)). n21 Second, by certifying a potentially dispositive state-law issue, the Court would adhere to its wise policy of avoiding the unnecessary adjudication of difficult questions of constitutional law. See *Elkins*, 435 U. S., at 661-662 (citing constitutional avoidance as a factor supporting certification). Third, certification would promote both judicial economy and fairness to the parties. After all, the Colorado Supreme Court is the ultimate authority on the meaning of Colorado law, and if in later litigation it should disagree with this Court's provisional state-law holding, our efforts will have been wasted and respondent will have been deprived of the opportunity to have her claims heard under the authoritative view of Colorado law. The unique facts of this case only serve to emphasize the importance of employing a procedure that will provide the correct answer to the central question of state law. See *Brockett*, 472 U. S., at 510 (*O'Connor, J.*, concurring) ("Speculation by a federal court about the meaning of a state statute in the absence of a prior state court adjudication is particularly gratuitous when, as is the case here, the state courts stand willing to address questions of state law on certification from a federal court"). n22

n19 See Colo. Rule App. Proc. 21.1(a) (Colorado Supreme Court may answer questions of law certified to it by the Supreme Court of the United States or another federal court if those questions "may be determinative of the cause" and "as to which it appears to the certifying court there is no controlling precedent in the decisions of the [Colorado] Supreme Court").

n20 See *City of Westminster* v. *Dogan Constr. Co.*, 930 P. 2d 585, 590 (Colo. 1997) (en banc) (in interpreting an ambiguous statute, the Colorado Supreme Court will consider legislative history and the "consequences of a particular construction"); *ibid.* ("Because we also presume that legislation is intended to have just and reasonable effects, we must construe statutes accordingly and apply them so as to ensure such results"). Additionally, it is possible that the Colorado Supreme Court would have better access to (and greater facility with) relevant pieces of legislative history beyond those that we have before us. That court may also choose to give certain evidence of legislative intent greater weight than would be customary for this Court. See, *e.g.*, Brief for Peggy Kerns et al. as *Amici Curiae* in Support of Respondent (bill sponsor explaining the Colorado General Assembly's intent in passing the domestic restraining order statute).

n21 Citing similar considerations, the Second Circuit certified questions of state law to the Connecticut Supreme Court when it was faced with a procedural due process claim involving a statute that arguably mandated the removal of children upon probable cause of child abuse. See *Sealed* v. *Sealed*, 332 F. 3d 51 (2003). The Connecticut Supreme Court accepted certification and held that the provision was discretionary, not mandatory. See *Teresa T.* v. *Ragaglia*, 272 Conn. 734, 865 A. 2d 428 (2005).

n22 The Court is correct that I would take an "anyone-but-us approach," *ante*, at 9, n. 5, to the question of *who* decides the issue of Colorado law in this case. Both options that I favor—deferring to the Circuit's interpretation or, barring that, certifying to the Colorado Supreme Court—recognize the comparative expertise of another tribunal on questions of state law. And both options offer their own efficiencies. By contrast, the Court's somewhat overconfident "only us" approach lacks any cogent justification. The fact that neither party requested certification certainly cannot be a sufficient reason for dismissing that option. As with abstention, the considerations that weigh in favor of certification—federal-state comity, constitutional avoidance, judicial efficiency, the desire to settle correctly a recurring issue of state law—transcend the interests of individual litigants, rendering it imprudent to cast them as gatekeepers to the procedure. See, *e.g.*, *Elkins* v. *Moreno*, 435 U. S. 647, 662 (1978) (certifying state-law issue absent a request from the parties); *Aldrich* v. *Aldrich*, 375 U. S. 249 (1963) *(per curiam)* (same); see also 17A C. Wright, A. Miller, & E. Cooper, Federal Practice and Procedure §4248, p. 176 (2d ed. 1988) ("Ordinarily a court will order certification on its own motion").

III

the Court gives short shrift to the unique case of "mandatory arrest" statutes in the domestic violence context; States passed a wave of these statutes in the 1980's and 1990's with the unmistakable goal of eliminating police discretion in this area.

the Court is simply wrong to assert that a citizen's interest in the government's commitment to provide police enforcement in certain defined circumstances does not resemble any "traditional conception of property"

Three flaws in the Court's rather superficial analysis of the merits highlight the unwisdom of its decision to answer the state-law question *de novo*. First, the Court places undue weight on the various statutes throughout the country that seemingly mandate police enforcement but are generally understood to preserve police discretion. As a result, the Court gives short shrift to the unique case of "mandatory arrest" statutes in the domestic violence context; States passed a wave of these statutes in the 1980's and 1990's with the unmistakable goal of eliminating police discretion in this area. Second, the Court's formalistic analysis fails to take seriously the fact that the Colorado statute at issue in this case was enacted for the benefit of the narrow class of persons who are beneficiaries of domestic restraining orders, and that the order at issue in this case was specifically intended to provide protection to respondent and her children. Finally, the Court is simply wrong to assert that a citizen's interest in the government's commitment to provide police enforcement in certain defined circumstances does not resemble any "traditional conception of property," *ante*, at 17; in fact, a citizen's property interest in such a commitment is just as concrete and worthy of protection as her interest in any other important service the government or a private firm has undertaken to provide.

the Colorado General Assembly joined a nationwide movement of States that took aim at the crisis of police underenforcement in the domestic violence sphere by implementing "mandatory arrest" statutes. The crisis of underenforcement had various causes, not least of which was the perception by police departments and police officers that domestic violence was a private, "family" matter and that arrest was to be used as a last resort.

Because these cases were considered noncriminal, police assigned domestic violence calls low priority and often did not respond to them for several hours or ignored them altogether

The purpose of these statutes was precisely to "counter police resistance to arrests in domestic violence cases by removing or restricting police officer discretion..."

In 1994, the Colorado General Assembly passed omnibus legislation targeting domestic violence. The part of the legislation at issue in this case mandates enforcement of a domestic restraining order upon probable cause of a violation, §18-6-803.5(3), while another part directs that police officers "shall, without undue delay, arrest" a suspect upon "probable cause to believe that a crime or offense of domestic violence has been committed," §18-6-803.6(1). n23 In adopting this legislation, the Colorado General Assembly joined a nationwide movement of States that took aim at the crisis of police underenforcement in the domestic violence sphere by implementing "mandatory arrest" statutes. The crisis of underenforcement had various causes, not least of which was the perception by police departments and police officers that domestic violence was a private, "family" matter and that arrest was to be used as a last resort. Sack, Battered Women and the State: The Struggle for the Future of Domestic Violence Policy, 2004 Wis. L. Rev. 1657, 1662-1663 (hereinafter Sack); *id.*, at 1663 ("Because these cases were considered noncriminal, police assigned domestic violence calls low priority and often did not respond to them for several hours or ignored them altogether"). In response to these realities, and emboldened by a well-known 1984 experiment by the Minneapolis police department, n24 "many states enacted mandatory arrest statutes under which a police officer must arrest an abuser when the officer has probable cause to believe that a domestic assault has occurred or that a protection order has been violated." Developments in the Law: Legal Responses to Domestic Violence, 106 Harv. L. Rev. 1498, 1537 (1993). The purpose of these statutes was precisely to "counter police resistance to arrests in domestic violence cases by removing or restricting police officer discretion; mandatory arrest policies would increase police response and reduce batterer recidivism." Sack 1670.

n23 See Fuller & Stansberry, 1994 Legislature Strengthens Domestic Violence Protective Orders, 23 Colo. Lawyer 2327 (1994) ("The 1994 Colorado legislative session produced several significant domestic abuse bills that strengthened both civil and criminal restraining order laws and procedures for victims of domestic violence"); *id.*, at 2329 ("Although many law enforcement jurisdictions already take a proactive approach to domestic violence, arrest and procedural policies vary greatly from one jurisdiction to another. H. B. 94-1253 mandates the arrest of domestic violence perpetrators and restraining order violaters. H. B. 94-1090 repeals the requirement that protected parties show a copy of their restraining order to enforcing officers. In the past, failure to provide a copy of the restraining order has led to hesitation from police to enforce the order for fear of an illegal arrest. The new statute also shields arresting officers from liability; this is expected to reduce concerns about enforcing the mandatory arrest requirements" (footnotes omitted)).

n24 See Sack 1669 ("The movement to strengthen arrest policies was bolstered in 1984 by the publication of the results of a study on mandatory arrest in domestic violence cases that had been conducted in Minneapolis. In this study, police handled randomly assigned domestic violence offenders by using one of three different responses: arresting the offender, mediating the dispute or requiring the offender to leave the house for eight hours. The study concluded that in comparison with the other two responses, arrest had a significantly greater impact on reducing domestic violence recidivism. The findings from the Minneapolis study were used by the U. S. Attorney General in a report issued in 1984 that recommended, among other things, arrest in domestic violence cases as the standard law enforcement response" (footnotes omitted)); see also Zorza, The Criminal Law of Misdemeanor Domestic Violence, 1970-1990, 83 J. Crim. L. & C. 46, 63-65 (1992) (tracing history of mandatory arrest laws and noting that the first such law was implemented by Oregon in 1977).

Thus, when Colorado passed its statute in 1994, it joined the ranks of 15 States that mandated arrest for domestic violence offenses and 19 States that mandated arrest for domestic restraining order violations. See Developments in the Law, 106 Harv. L. Rev., at 1537, n. 68 (noting statutes in 1993); N. Miller, Institute for Law and Justice, A Law Enforcement and Prosecution Perspective 7, and n. 74, 8, and n. 90 (2003), http://www.ilj.org/dv/dvvawa2000.htm (as visited June 24, 2005, and available in Clerk of Court's case file) (listing Colorado among the many States that currently have mandatory arrest statutes). n25

n25 See also Brief for International Municipal Lawyers Association and National League of Cities, National's Sheriff's Association, and County Sheriffs of Colorado as *Amici Curiae* in Support of Petitioner 6 ("Colorado is not alone in mandating the arrest of persons who violate protective orders. Some 19 states require an arrest when a police officer has probable cause to believe that such orders have been violated" (collecting statutes)).

Given the specific purpose of these statutes, there can be no doubt that the Colorado Legislature used the term "shall" advisedly in its domestic restraining order statute. While "shall" is probably best read to mean "may" in other Colorado statutes that seemingly mandate enforcement, cf. Colo. Rev. Stat. §31-4-112 (Lexis 2004) (police "*shall suppress* all riots, disturbances or breaches of the peace, *shall apprehend* all disorderly persons in the city ..." (emphases added)), it is clear that the elimination of police discretion was integral to Colorado and its fellow States' solution to the problem of underenforcement in domestic violence cases. n26 Since the text of Colorado's statute perfectly captures this legislative purpose, it is hard to imagine what the Court has in mind when it insists on "some stronger indication from the Colorado Legislature." *Ante*, at 12.

n26 See Note, Mandatory Arrest: A Step Toward Eradicating Domestic Violence, But is It Enough&&& 1996 U. Ill. L. Rev. 533, 542, 544-546 (describing the problems that attend a discretionary arrest regime: "Even when probable clause is present, police officers still frequently try to calm the parties and act as mediators... . Three studies found the arrest rate to range between 3% and 10% when the decision to arrest is left to police discretion. Another study found that the police made arrests in only 13% of the cases where the victim had visible injuries... . Police officers often employ irrelevant criteria such as the 'reason' for the abuse or the severity of the victim's injuries in making their decision to arrest... . Some [officers] may feel strongly that police should not interfere in family arguments or lovers' quarrels. Such attitudes make police much more likely to investigate intent and provocation, and consider them as mitigating factors, in responding to domestic violence calls than in other types of cases"); see also Walsh, The Mandatory Arrest Law: Police Reaction, 16 Pace L. Rev. 97, 98 (1995). Cf. Sack 1671-1672 ("Mandatory arrest policies have significantly increased the number of arrests of batterers for domestic violence crimes... . In New York City, from 1993, the time the mandatory arrest policy was instituted, to 1999, felony domestic violence arrests increased 33%, misdemeanor domestic violence arrests rose 114%, and arrests for violation of orders of protection were up 76%" (footnotes omitted)).

While Colorado case law does not speak to the question, it is instructive that other state courts interpreting their analogous statutes have not only held that they eliminate the police's traditional discretion to refuse enforcement, but have also recognized that they create rights enforceable against the police under state law.

While Colorado case law does not speak to the question, it is instructive that other state courts interpreting their analogous statutes have not only held that they eliminate the police's traditional discretion to refuse enforcement, but have also recognized that they create rights enforceable against the police under state law. For example, in *Nearing v. Weaver*, 295 Ore. 702, 670 P. 2d 137 (1983) (en banc), the court held that although the common law of negligence did not support a suit against the police for failing to enforce a domestic restraining order, the statute's mandatory directive formed the basis for the suit because it was "a specific duty imposed by statute for the benefit of individuals previously identified by judicial order." *Id.*, at 707, 670 P. 2d, at 140. n27 In *Matthews v. Pickett County*, 996 S. W. 2d 162 (Tenn. 1999) (on certification to the Sixth Circuit), the court confirmed that the statute mandated arrest for violations of domestic restraining orders, and it held that the "public duty" defense to a negligence action was unavailable to the defendant police officers because the restraining order had created a "special duty" to protect the plaintiff. *Id.*, at 165. See also *Campbell v. Campbell*, 294 N. J. Super. 18, 24, 682 A. 2d 272, 274 (1996) (domestic restraining order statute "allows no discretion" with regard to arrest; "[t]he duty imposed on the police officer is ministerial"); *Donaldson v. Seattle*, 65 Wash. App. 661, 670, 831 P. 2d 1098, 1103 (1992) ("Generally, where an officer has legal grounds to make an arrest he has considerable discretion to do so. In regard to domestic violence, the rule is the reverse. If the officer has the legal grounds to arrest pursuant to the statute, he has a mandatory duty to make the arrest"). To what extent the Colorado Supreme Court would agree with the views of these courts is, of course, an open question, but it does seem rather brazen for the majority to assume that the Colorado Supreme Court would repudiate this consistent line of persuasive authority from other States.

n27 The Oregon Supreme Court noted that the "widespread refusal or failure of police officers to remove persons involved in episodes of domestic violence was presented to the legislature as the main reason for tightening the law so as to require enforcement of restraining orders by mandatory arrest and custody." *Nearing*, 295 Ore., at 709, 670 P. 2d, at 142.

Indeed, the Court fails to come to terms with the wave of domestic violence statutes that provides the crucial context for understanding Colorado's law. The Court concedes that, "in the specific context of domestic violence, mandatory-arrest statutes have been found in some States to be more mandatory than traditional mandatory-arrest statutes," *ante*, at 13, but that is a serious understatement. The difference is not a matter of degree, but of kind. Before this wave of statutes, the legal rule was one of discretion; as the Court shows, the "traditional," general mandatory arrest statutes have always been understood to be "mandatory" in name only, see *ante*, at 11. The innovation of the domestic violence statutes was to make police enforcement, not "more mandatory," but simply *mandatory*. If, as the Court says, the existence of a protected "entitlement" turns on whether "government officials may grant or deny it in their discretion," *ante*, at 7, the new mandatory statutes undeniably create an entitlement to police enforcement of restraining orders.

Perhaps recognizing this point, the Court glosses over the dispositive question—whether the police enjoyed discretion to deny enforcement—and focuses on a different question—which "precise means of enforcement," *ante*, at 14, were called for in this case. But that question is a red herring. The statute directs that, upon probable cause of a violation, "a peace officer shall arrest, or, if an arrest would be impractical under the circumstances, seek a warrant for the arrest of a restrained person." Colo. Rev. Stat. §18-6-803.5(3)(b) (Lexis 1999). Regardless of whether the enforcement called for in this case was arrest or the seeking of an arrest warrant (the answer to that question probably changed over the course of the night as the respondent gave the police more information about the husband's whereabouts), the crucial point is that, under the statute, the police were *required* to provide enforcement; *they lacked the discretion to do nothing.* n28 The Court suggests that the fact that "enforcement" may encompass different acts infects any entitlement to enforcement with "indeterminacy." *Ante*, at 14. But this objection is also unfounded. Our cases have never required the object of an entitlement to be some mechanistic, unitary thing. Suppose a State entitled every citizen whose income was under a certain level to receive health care at a state clinic. The provision of health care is not a unitary thing—doctors and administrators must decide what tests are called for and what procedures are required, and these decisions often involve difficult applications of judgment. But it could not credibly be said that a citizen lacks an entitlement to health care simply because the content of that entitlement is not the same in every given situation. Similarly, the enforcement of a restraining order is not some amorphous, indeterminate thing. Under the statute, if the police have probable cause that a violation has occurred, enforcement consists of either making an immediate arrest or seeking a warrant and then executing an arrest—traditional, well-defined tasks that law enforcement officers perform every day. n29

n28 Under the Court's reading of the statute, a police officer with probable cause is mandated to seek an arrest warrant if arrest is "impractical under the circumstances," but then enjoys unfettered discretion in deciding whether to *execute* that warrant. *Ante*, at 15. This is an unlikely reading given that the statute was motivated by a profound distrust of police discretion in the domestic violence context and motivated by a desire to improve the protection given to holders of domestic restraining orders. We do not have the benefit of an authoritative construction of Colorado law, but I would think that if an estranged husband harassed his wife in violation of a restraining order, and then absconded after she called the police, the statute would not only obligate the police to seek an arrest warrant, but also obligate them to execute it by making an arrest. In any event, under respondent's allegations, by the time the police were informed of the husband's whereabouts, an arrest was practical and, under the statute's terms, mandatory.

n 29 The Court wonders "how the mandatory-arrest paradigm applies to cases in which the offender is not present to be arrested." *Ante*, at 13. Again, questions as to the *scope* of the obligation to provide enforcement are far afield from the key issue—whether there exists an entitlement to enforcement. In any event, the Court's speculations are off-base. First, this is not a case like *Donaldson* v. *Seattle*, 65 Wash. App. 661, 831 P. 2d 1098 (1992), in which the restrained person violated the order and then left the scene. Here, not only did the husband violate the restraining order by coming within 100 yards of the family home, but he continued to violate the order while his abduction of the daughters persisted. This is because the restraining order prohibited him from "molest[ing] or disturb[ing] the peace" of the daughters. See 366 F. 3d, at 1143 (appendix to dissent of O'Brien, J.). Because the "scene" of the violation was wherever the husband was currently holding the daughters, this case does not implicate the question of an officer's duties to arrest a person who has left the scene and is no longer in violation of the restraining order. Second, to the extent that arresting the husband was initially "impractical under the circumstances" because his whereabouts were unknown, the Colorado statute (unlike some other States' statutes) expressly addressed that situation—it *required* the police to seek an arrest warrant. Third, the Court is wrong to suggest that this case falls outside the core situation that these types of statutes were meant to address. One of the well-known cases that contributed to the passage of these statutes involved facts similar to this case. See *Sorichetti* v. *New York City*, 65 N. Y. 2d 461, 467, 482 N. E. 2d 70, 74 (1985) (police officers at police station essentially ignored a mother's pleas for enforcement of a restraining order against an estranged husband who made threats about their 6-year-old daughter; hours later, as the mother persisted in her pleas, the daughter was found mutilated, her father having attacked her with a fork and a knife and attempted to saw off her leg); Note, 1996 U. Ill. L. Rev., at 539 (noting *Sorichetti* in the development of mandatory arrest statutes); see also Sack 1663 (citing the police's failure to respond to domestic violence calls as an impetus behind mandatory arrest statutes). It would be singularly odd to suppose that in passing its sweeping omnibus domestic violence legislation, the Colorado Legislature did not mean to require enforcement in the case of an abduction of children in violation of a restraining order.

there is little doubt that the statute at issue in this case conferred a benefit "on a specific class of people"—namely, recipients of domestic restraining orders.

The Court similarly errs in speculating that the Colorado Legislature may have mandated police enforcement of restraining orders for "various legitimate ends other than the conferral of a benefit on a specific class of people," *ante*, at 15; see also *ibid.* (noting that the "serving of public rather than private ends is the normal course of the criminal law"). While the Court's concern would have some bite were we faced with a broadly drawn statute directing, for example, that the police "*shall suppress* all riots," there is little doubt that the statute at issue in this case conferred a benefit "on a specific class of people"—namely, recipients of domestic restraining orders. Here, respondent applied for and was granted a restraining order from a Colorado trial judge, who found a risk of "irreparable injury" and found that "physical or emotional harm" would result if the husband were not excluded from the family home. 366 F. 3d, at 1143 (appendix to dissent of O'Brien, J.). As noted earlier, the restraining order required that the husband not "molest or disturb" the peace of respondent and the daughters, and it ordered (with limited exceptions) that the husband stay at least 100 yards away from the family home. *Ibid.* n30 It also directed the police to "use every reasonable means to enforce this ... order," and to arrest or seek a warrant upon probable cause of a violation. *Id.*, at 1144. Under the terms of the statute, when the order issued, respondent and her daughters became "'protected person[s].'" §18-6-803.5(1.5)(a) ("'Protected person' means the person or persons identified in the restraining order as the person or persons for whose benefit the restraining order was issued"). n31 The statute criminalized the knowing violation of the restraining order, §18-6-803.5(1), and, as already discussed, the statute (as well as the order itself) mandated police enforcement, §§18-6-803.5(3)(a)-(b). n32

n30 The order also stated: "If you violate this order thinking that the other party or child named in this order has given you permission, you are wrong, and can be arrested and prosecuted. The terms of this order cannot be changed by agreement of the other party or the child(ren), only the court can change this order." 366 F. 3d, at 1144 (appendix to dissent of O'Brien, J.).

n31 A concern for the "'protected person'" pervades the statute. For example, the statute provides that a "peace officer may transport, or obtain transportation for, the alleged victim to shelter. Upon the request of the protected person, the peace officer may also transport the minor child of the protected person, who is not an emancipated minor, to the same shelter ... ." §18-6-803.5(6)(a).

n32 I find it neither surprising nor telling, cf. *ante*, at 15, that the statute requires the restraining order to contain, "in capital letters and bold print," a "notice" informing protected persons that they can demand or request, respectively, civil and criminal contempt proceedings. §18-6-803.5(7). While the legislature may have thought that these legal remedies were not popularly understood, a person's right to "demand" or "request" police enforcement of a restraining order simply goes without saying given the nature of the order and its language. Indeed, for a holder of a restraining order who has read the order's emphatic language, it would likely come as quite a shock to learn that she has no right to demand enforcement in the event of a violation. To suggest that a protected person has no such right would posit a lacuna between a protected person's rights and an officer's duties—a result that would be hard to reconcile with the Colorado Legislature's dual goals of putting an end to police indifference and empowering potential victims of domestic abuse.

The legislative purpose in requiring the police to enforce individual restraining orders clearly is to protect the named persons for whose protection the order is issued, not to protect the community at large by general law enforcement activity.

Because the statute's guarantee of police enforcement is triggered by, and operates only in reference to, a judge's granting of a restraining order in favor of an identified "'protected person,'" there is simply no room to suggest that such a person has received merely an "'incidental'" or "'indirect'" benefit, see *ante*, at 18. As one state court put it, domestic restraining order statutes "identify with precision when, to whom, and under what circumstances police protection must be afforded. The legislative purpose in requiring the police to enforce individual restraining orders clearly is to protect the named persons for whose protection the order is issued, not to protect the community at large by general law enforcement activity." *Nearing*, 295 Ore., at 712, 670 P. 2d, at 143. n33 Not only does the Court's doubt about whether Colorado's statute created an entitlement in a protected person fail to take seriously the purpose and nature of restraining orders, but it fails to account for the decisions by other state courts, see *supra* at 11-12, that recognize that such statutes and restraining orders create individual rights to police action.

n33 See also *Matthews* v. *Pickett County*, 996 S. W. 2d 162, 165 (Tenn. 1999) ("The order of protection in this case was not issued for the public's protection in general. The order of protection specifically identified Ms. Matthews and was issued solely for the purpose of protecting her. *Cf. Ezell* [v. *Cockrell*, 902 S. W. 2d 394, 403 (Tenn. 1995)] (statute prohibiting drunk driving does not specify an individual but undertakes to protect the public in general from intoxicated drivers)"); *Sorichetti*, 65 N. Y. 2d, at 469, 482 N. E. 2d, at 75 ("The [protective] order evinces a preincident legislative and judicial determination that its holder should be accorded a reasonable degree of protection from a particular individual").

IV

Recognizing respondent's property interest in the enforcement of her restraining order is fully consistent with our precedent. This Court has "made clear that the property interests protected by procedural due process extend well beyond actual ownership of real estate, chattels, or money."

our cases have found "property" interests in a number of state-conferred benefits and services, including welfare benefits... disability benefits... public education... utility services... government employment...

Given that Colorado law has quite clearly eliminated the police's discretion to deny enforcement, respondent is correct that she had much more than a "unilateral expectation" that the restraining order would be enforced; rather, she had a "legitimate claim of entitlement" to enforcement. *Roth*, 408 U. S., at 577. Recognizing respondent's property interest in the enforcement of her restraining order is fully consistent with our precedent. This Court has "made clear that the property interests protected by procedural due process extend well beyond actual ownership of real estate, chattels, or money." *Id.*, at 571-572. The "types of interests protected as 'property' are varied and, as often as not, intangible, 'relating to the whole domain of social and economic fact.'" *Logan* v. *Zimmerman Brush Co.*, 455 U. S. 422, 430 (1982); see also *Perry* v. *Sindermann*, 408 U. S. 593, 601 (1972) ("'[P]roperty' interests subject to procedural due process protection are not limited by a few rigid, technical forms. Rather, 'property' denotes a broad range of interests that are secured by 'existing rules or understandings'"). Thus, our cases have found "property" interests in a number of state-conferred benefits and services, including welfare benefits, *Goldberg* v. *Kelly*, 397 U. S. 254 (1970); disability benefits, *Mathews* v. *Eldridge*, 424 U. S. 319 (1976); public education, *Goss* v. *Lopez*, 419 U. S. 565 (1975); utility services, *Memphis Light, Gas & Water Div.* v. *Craft*, 436 U. S. 1 (1978); government employment, *Cleveland Bd. of Ed.* v. *Loudermill*, 470 U. S. 532 (1985); as well as in other entitlements that defy easy categorization, see, *e.g.*, *Bell* v. *Burson*, 402 U. S. 535 (1971) (due process requires fair procedures before a driver's license may be revoked pending the adjudication of an accident claim); *Logan*, 455 U. S., at 431 (due process prohibits the arbitrary denial of a person's interest in adjudicating a claim before a state commission).

Police enforcement of a restraining order is a government service that is no less concrete and no less valuable than other government services, such as education.

Colorado law *guaranteed* the provision of a certain service, in certain defined circumstances, to a certain class of beneficiaries, and respondent reasonably relied on that guarantee.

Police enforcement of a restraining order is a government service that is no less concrete and no less valuable than other government services, such as education. n34 The relative novelty of recognizing this type of property interest is explained by the relative novelty of the domestic violence statutes creating a mandatory arrest duty; before this innovation, the unfettered discretion that characterized police enforcement defeated any citizen's "legitimate claim of entitlement" to this service. Novel or not, respondent's claim finds strong support in the principles that underlie our due process jurisprudence. In this case, Colorado law *guaranteed* the provision of a certain service, in certain defined circumstances, to a certain class of beneficiaries, and respondent reasonably relied on that guarantee. As we observed in *Roth*, "[i]t is a purpose of the ancient institution of property to protect those claims upon which people rely in their daily lives, reliance that must not be arbitrarily undermined." 408 U. S., at 577. Surely, if respondent had contracted with a private security firm to provide her and her daughters with protection from her husband, it would be apparent that she possessed a property interest in such a contract. Here, Colorado undertook a comparable obligation, and respondent—with restraining order in hand—justifiably relied on that undertaking. Respondent's claim of entitlement to this promised service no less legitimate than the other claims our cases have upheld, and no less concrete than a hypothetical agreement with a private firm. n35 The fact that it is based on a statutory enactment and a judicial order entered for her special protection, rather than on a formal contract, does not provide a principled basis for refusing to consider it "property" worthy of constitutional protection. n36

n34 The Court mistakenly relies on *O'Bannon* v. *Town Court Nursing Center*, 447 U. S. 773 (1980), in explaining why it is "by no means clear that an individual entitlement to enforcement of a restraining order could constitute a 'property' interest for purposes of the Due Process Clause." *Ante*, at 17. In *O'Bannon*, the question was essentially whether certain regulations provided nursing-home residents with an entitlement to continued residence in the home of their choice. 447 U. S., at 785. The Court concluded that the regulations created no such entitlement, but there was no suggestion that Congress could not create one if it wanted to. In other words, *O'Bannon* did not address a situation in which the underlying law created an entitlement, but the Court nevertheless refused to treat that entitlement as a property interest within the meaning of the Due Process Clause.

n35 As the analogy to a private security contract demonstrates, a person's interest in police enforcement has "'some ascertainable monetary value,'" *ante*, at 17. Cf. Merrill, The Landscape of Constitutional Property, 86 Va. L. Rev. 885, 964, n. 289 (2000) (remarking, with regard to the property interest recognized in *Goss* v. *Lopez*, 419 U. S. 565 (1975), that "any parent who has contemplated sending their children to private schools knows that public schooling has a monetary value"). And while the analogy to a private security contract need not be precise to be useful, I would point out that the Court is likely incorrect in stating that private security guards could not have arrested the husband under the circumstances, see *ante*, at 17, n. 10. Because the husband's ongoing abduction of the daughters would constitute a knowing violation of the restraining order, see n. 13, *supra*, and therefore a crime under the statute, see §18-6-803.5(1), a private person who was at the scene and aware of the circumstances of the abduction would have authority to arrest. See §16-3-201 ("A person who is not a peace officer may arrest another person when any crime has been or is being committed by the arrested person in the presence of the person making the arrest"). Our cases, of course, have never recognized any requirement that a property interest possess "'some ascertainable monetary value.'" Regardless, I would assume that respondent would have paid the police to arrest her husband if that had been possible; at the very least, the entitlement has a monetary value in that sense.

n36 According to *Justice Souter,* respondent has asserted a property interest in merely a "state-mandated process," *ante,* at 3 (opinion concurring in part and concurring in judgment), rather than in a state-mandated "substantive guarantee," *ibid.* This misunderstands respondent's claim. Putting aside the inartful passage of respondent's brief that *Justice Souter* relies upon, *ante,* at 2, it is clear that respondent is in fact asserting a substantive interest in the "enforcement of the restraining order." Brief for Respondent 10. Enforcement of a restraining order is a tangible, substantive act. If an estranged husband violates a restraining order by abducting children, and the police succeed in enforcing the order, the person holding the restraining order has undeniably just received a substantive benefit. As in other procedural due process cases, respondent is arguing that the police officers failed to follow fair procedures in ascertaining whether the statutory criteria that trigger their obligation to provide enforcement—*i.e.,* an outstanding order plus probable cause that it is being violated—were satisfied in her case. Cf. *Carey* v. *Piphus,* 435 U. S. 247, 266-267 (1978) (discussing analytic difference between the denial of fair process and the denial of the substantive benefit itself). It is *Justice Souter,* not respondent, who makes the mistake of "collapsing the distinction between property protected and the process that protects it," *ante,* at 4.

Justice Souter also errs in suggesting that respondent cannot have a property interest in enforcement because she would not be authorized to instruct the police to refrain from enforcement in the event of a violation. *Ante,* at 1. The right to insist on the provision of a service is separate from the right to refuse the service. For example, compulsory attendance laws deny minors the right to refuse to attend school. Nevertheless, we have recognized that minors have a property interest in public education and that school officials must therefore follow fair procedures when they seek to deprive minors of this valuable benefit through suspension. See *Goss,* 419 U. S. 565. In the end, *Justice Souter* overlooks the core purpose of procedural due process—ensuring that a citizen's reasonable reliance is not frustrated by arbitrary government action.

V

Because respondent had a property interest in the enforcement of the restraining order, state officials could not deprive her of that interest without observing fair procedures. n37 Her description of the police behavior in this case and the department's callous policy of failing to respond properly to reports of restraining order violations clearly alleges a due process violation. At the very least, due process requires that the relevant state decisionmaker *listen* to the claimant and then *apply the relevant criteria* in reaching his decision. n38 The failure to observe these minimal procedural safeguards creates an unacceptable risk of arbitrary and "erroneous deprivation[s]," *Mathews,* 424 U. S., at 335. According to respondent's complaint—which we must construe liberally at this early stage in the litigation, see *Swierkiewicz* v. *Sorema N. A.,* 534 U. S. 506, 514 (2002)—the process she was afforded by the police constituted nothing more than a "'sham or a pretense.'" *Joint Anti-Fascist Refugee Comm.* v. *McGrath,* 341 U. S. 123, 164 (1951) (Frankfurter, J., concurring).

n37 See *Logan* v. *Zimmerman Brush Co.,* 455 U. S. 422, 432 (1982) ("'"While the legislature may elect not to confer a property interest, ... it may not constitutionally authorize the deprivation of such an interest, once conferred, without appropriate procedural safeguards"'").

n38 See *Fuentes* v. *Shevin,* 407 U. S. 67, 81 (1972) ("[W]hen a person has an opportunity to speak up in his own defense, and *when the State must listen to what he has to say,* substantively unfair and simply mistaken deprivations of property interests can be prevented" (emphasis added)); *Bell* v. *Burson,* 402 U. S. 535, 542 (1971) ("It is a proposition which hardly seems to need explication that a hearing which excludes consideration of an element essential to the decision whether licenses of the nature here involved shall be suspended does not meet [the] standard [of due process]"); *Goldberg* v. *Kelly,* 397 U. S. 254, 271 (1970) ("[T]he decisionmaker's conclusion as to a recipient's eligibility must rest solely on the legal rules and evidence adduced at the hearing"); cf. *ibid.* ("[O]f course, an impartial decision maker is essential").

Accordingly, I respectfully dissent.

District of Columbia v. Heller

(FULL CASE)
554 U. S. ____ ; 128 S. Ct. 2783; 07-290
March 18, 2008 Argued. June 26, 2008 Decided

GIST: Dick Anthony Heller was a licensed security guard working in Washington, D.C. at the Federal Judicial Center on Capitol Hill. As part of his duties in protecting federal judges, employees and property he was permitted to carry a handgun. When he applied for a permit to keep his handgun at home, he was denied under a city ordinance that only allowed the possession or carrying of registered handguns, but allowed no handgun registrations to be issued to the public after 1976 when the ordinance was enacted.

Two additional ordinances prevented even a registered gun from being useable. One allowed no loaded firearms of any type in a person's home even if needed for self defense, and the other required all firearms to be made inoperable through the use of locks or by disassembly.

Heller sued for denial of his rights under the Second Amendment, yielding the highest profile test of Second Amendment protections in the nation's history. Justice Antonin Scalia wrote the 64-page five-to-four majority opinion.

The case attracted 67 *amicus* briefs, the third highest in history (47 for Heller, and 20 for the District, including one from the Solicitor General), in the most closely followed gun-rights case on record. The D.C. Circuit Court of Appeals had found in favor of Heller, in a lengthy two-to-one decision that expressly recognized the Second Amendment as an individual right, overturning the D.C. gun-ban on constitutional grounds.

The Supreme Court affirmed the lower court's holding, adding significantly to the body of jurisprudence on the subject.

1– The Second Amendment protects an individual person's right to keep and bear arms.

2– The right to keep arms and the right to bear arms are not dependent on a person's active or potential service in a state or other organized militia.

3– Use of firearms for traditionally lawful purposes, such as self-defense within the home, is a constitutionally protected right.

4– The District's handgun ban is unconstitutional, as is the ban on functional firearms, to the extent that it prohibits defensive use of the firearm.

5– The District's total ban on handgun possession is unconstitutional because it is a prohibition on an entire class of arms that Americans overwhelmingly choose for the lawful purpose of self defense.

6–The requirement that any lawful firearm in the home be disassembled, bound by locks or unloaded, making it impossible for citizens to use the arms for the core lawful purpose of self-defense is unconstitutional.

7– The prefatory clause of the Second Amendment, which announces a militia purpose, does not expand or limit the operative clause, which expresses an individual right.

8– The District is compelled to allow Mr. Heller to register his handgun.

9– The District must issue a license for Mr. Heller to carry his handgun at home.

10– The issuance of the handgun registration and license to Mr. Heller cannot be arbitrary or capricious.

The Court's explanation of its decision included many other important points, some of which may be resolved by later decisions:

1– The Second Amendment, like almost all rights, is not a right "to keep and carry any weapon whatsoever in any manner whatsoever and for whatever purpose."

2– Some longstanding firearm restrictions are constitutionally permissible, including carry in "sensitive places" (schools and government buildings are mentioned), concealed carry, existing laws regarding felons or the mentally ill, and laws "imposing conditions and qualifications on the commercial sale of arms."

3– The Miller precedent recognized that protected arms under the Second Amendment were those "in common use at the time." The Court recognized the historical tradition of prohibiting the carrying of "dangerous and unusual" weapons, which it did not specifically define.

4– Deciding whether a particular gun-control law is an infringement on the right to keep and bear arms requires a higher standard than the suggested low "rational basis" test, or the novel "interest-balancing" test created by Justice Breyer in his dissent. Being a "specific enumerated right," the Second Amendment is in a special category with other "enumerated constitutional rights" such as freedom of speech, right to counsel and the guarantee against double jeopardy (the Court's list of examples), especially where the importance of the lawful defense of self, family, and property is most acute.

5– The handgun is the quintessential self-defense weapon.

6– None of the Court's prior decisions preclude the results reached in this case.

7– The Court's interpretation is confirmed by arms-bearing rights written into state Constitutions around the time of ratification of the Bill of Rights, and by the drafting history, as well as the Amendment's interpretation by scholars, courts and legislatures through the late 19th century.

Two dissents were filed, totalling 90 pages. Justice Stevens, joined by Justices Breyer, Ginsburg and Souter, begins by accepting the rights of the individual to arms but then argues strongly against many of the findings of the Court.

1– No common-law right to self defense is enshrined in the Constitution.

2– Neither the text of the Amendment nor the arguments advanced by its proponents evidenced the slightest interest by the Founders in limiting any legislature's authority to regulate private civilian use of arms. No new evidence since Lewis in 1980 (which mentioned the Second Amendment in a footnote) supports the view that the Amendment is intended to curtail Congress' regulation of civilian use or misuse of weapons.

3–The Amendment's preamble informs and controls the effect of the operative clause, so that the right to arms applies only to individuals in connection with militia service.

4– The "right of the people" only protects the "collective action of individuals" with a duty to serve in the militia. The Founders were essentially unconcerned with the non-military possession and use of arms.

5– In the context of the Second Amendment, the phrase "to keep and bear" is unitary and has an exclusively military meaning.

6– "The Court's announcement of a new constitutional right to own and use firearms for private purposes" is a "law-changing decision" and upsets well-established precedent.

7– "The Court would have us believe that over 200 years ago, the Framers made a choice to limit the tools available to elected officials wishing to regulate civilian uses of weapons..."

Each of Stevens' assertions are carefully addressed in the majority opinion.

Justice Breyer, joined by Justices Stevens, Ginsburg and Souter, takes a different tack in his dissent. He first agrees with Stevens that the Second Amendment protects a militia-related, not a self-defense related "interest." He then suggests that even if an individual right is found in "the right of the people to keep and bear arms," government can regulate and limit that right whenever a court finds that the government's interests outweigh its burden to protect the right, and the government has no clearly superior and less restrictive alternative.

The majority strongly disagreed with his proposed standard of review because, said the majority, the core of a constitutional right is not subject to a judicial balancing test. "A constitutional guarantee subject to future judges' assessments of its usefulness is no constitutional guarantee at all." In Breyer's minority opinion:

1– Even presuming that there is a Second Amendment right to defensive gun ownership, a ban on handguns in the home for self defense in a crime-ridden urban area does not violate the Second Amendment.

2– The District's regulation is not unreasonable, inappropriate or disproportionate to the problem it seeks to solve.

3– The D.C. law is justified since it will advance goals of great public importance, namely saving lives, preventing injury and reducing crime.

4– Revolutionary-era fire-safety laws, Boston's ban on taking a loaded gun into a building, as well as other gun laws from the early Republic, were presumably considered constitutional by the Founders, and these laws imposed at least as great a burden on self defense as did the D.C. handgun ban.

5– If there is an individual right to armed self-defense, the D.C. gun lock/disassembly/unloading laws should be judicially construed to have a self-defense exception even though they don't contain one, rather than be declared unconstitutional.

Justice Breyer devotes extensive space to grim crime statistics, deflecting challenges to the legitimacy of the stats and what conclusions to draw from them, and uses the admittedly horrifying numbers to justify rights suppression as a way of stopping murderers—against 32 years of evidence in D.C. that this approach has had the opposite effect.

As with Stevens' dissent, Breyer's arguments and concerns are carefully addressed in the majority opinion.

A good deal of acrimony is expressed by the majority at the Stevens dissent, referring to elements as "grotesque" or from a "mad hatter." That dissent repeatedly accuses the majority of hypocrisy and making "risible" or implausible arguments. The back-and-forth between Breyer and Scalia is more respectful in both directions, and in both dissents, the majority and dissenters each tell the other they cannot possibly reach the conclusions they do.

The case leaves open some questions, particularly whether the Second Amendment is "incorporated" in the Fourteenth Amendment, and thereby made enforceable against state and local governments. Almost immediately following the release of the decision, lawsuits were filed against handgun bans in Chicago and Chicago suburbs, and against the complete ban on firearms in San Francisco public housing. These cases may eventually lead to Supreme Court resolution of the incorporation issue. Both pro-rights and anti-rights proponents are forecasting reliance on *Heller* in upcoming litigation.

Syllabus
NOTE: Where it is feasible, a syllabus (headnote) will be released, as is being done in connection with this case, at the time the opinion is issued. The syllabus constitutes no part of the opinion of the Court but has been prepared by the Reporter of Decisions for the convenience of the reader. See United States v. Detroit Timber & Lumber Co., 200 U. S. 321, 337.

District of Columbia law bans handgun possession by making it a crime to carry an unregistered firearm and prohibiting the registration of handguns; provides separately that no person may carry an unlicensed handgun, but authorizes the police chief to issue 1-year licenses; and requires residents to keep lawfully owned firearms unloaded and dissembled or bound by a trigger lock or similar device.
Respondent Heller, a D. C. special policeman, applied to register a handgun he wished to keep at home, but the District refused. He filed this suit seeking, on Second Amendment grounds, to enjoin the city from enforcing the bar on handgun registration, the licensing requirement insofar as it prohibits carrying an unlicensed firearm in the home, and the trigger-lock requirement insofar as it prohibits the use of functional firearms in the home. The District Court dismissed the suit, but the D. C. Circuit reversed, holding that the Second Amendment protects an individual's right to possess firearms and that the city's total ban on handguns, as well as its requirement that firearms in the home be kept nonfunctional even when necessary for self-defense, violated that right.
Held:
1. The Second Amendment protects an individual right to possess a firearm

unconnected with service in a militia, and to use that arm for traditionally lawful purposes, such as self-defense within the home. Pp. 2–53.

(a) The Amendment's prefatory clause announces a purpose, but does not limit or expand the scope of the second part, the operative clause. The operative clause's text and history demonstrate that it connotes an individual right to keep and bear arms. Pp. 2–22.

(b) The prefatory clause comports with the Court's interpretation [554 U.S. ____ (2008) 2] of the operative clause. The "militia" comprised all males physically capable of acting in concert for the common defense. The Antifederalists feared that the Federal Government would disarm the people in order to disable this citizens' militia, enabling a politicized standing army or a select militia to rule. The response was to deny Congress power to abridge the ancient right of individuals to keep and bear arms, so that the ideal of a citizens' militia would be preserved. Pp. 22–28.

(c) The Court's interpretation is confirmed by analogous arms-bearing rights in state constitutions that preceded and immediately followed the Second Amendment. Pp. 28–30.

(d) The Second Amendment's drafting history, while of dubious interpretive worth, reveals three state Second Amendment proposals that unequivocally referred to an individual right to bear arms. Pp. 30–32.

(e) Interpretation of the Second Amendment by scholars, courts and legislators, from immediately after its ratification through the late 19th century also supports the Court's conclusion. Pp. 32–47.

(f) None of the Court's precedents forecloses the Court's interpretation. Neither United States v. Cruikshank, 92 U. S. 542, 553, nor Presser v. Illinois, 116 U. S. 252, 264–265, refutes the individual rights interpretation. United States v. Miller, 307 U. S. 174, does not limit the right to keep and bear arms to militia purposes, but rather limits the type of weapon to which the right applies to those used by the militia, i.e., those in common use for lawful purposes. Pp. 47–54.

2. Like most rights, the Second Amendment right is not unlimited. It is not a right to keep and carry any weapon whatsoever in any manner whatsoever and for whatever purpose: For example, concealed weapons prohibitions have been upheld under the Amendment or state analogues. The Court's opinion should not be taken to cast doubt on longstanding prohibitions on the possession of firearms by felons and the mentally ill, or laws forbidding the carrying of firearms in sensitive places such as schools and government buildings, or laws imposing conditions and qualifications on the commercial sale of arms. Miller's holding that the sorts of weapons protected are those "in common use at the time" finds support in the historical tradition of prohibiting the carrying of dangerous and unusual weapons. Pp. 54–56.

3. The handgun ban and the trigger-lock requirement (as applied to self-defense) violate the Second Amendment. The District's total ban on handgun possession in the home amounts to a prohibition on an entire class of "arms" that Americans overwhelmingly choose for the lawful purpose of self-defense. Under any of the standards of scrutiny the Court has applied to enumerated constitutional rights, this [554 U. S. ____ (2008) 3] prohibition—in the place where the importance of the lawful defense of self, family, and property is most acute—would fail constitutional muster. Similarly, the requirement that any lawful firearm in the home be disassembled or bound by a trigger lock makes it impossible for citizens to use arms for the core lawful purpose of self-defense and is hence unconstitutional. Because Heller conceded at oral argument that

the D. C. licensing law is permissible if it is not enforced arbitrarily and capriciously, the Court assumes that a license will satisfy his prayer for relief and does not address the licensing requirement.

Assuming he is not disqualified from exercising Second Amendment rights, the District must permit Heller to register his handgun and must issue him a license to carry it in the home. Pp. 56–64.

478 F. 3d 370, affirmed.

SCALIA, J., delivered the opinion of the Court, in which ROBERTS, C. J., and KENNEDY, THOMAS, and ALITO, JJ., joined. STEVENS, J., filed a dissenting opinion, in which SOUTER, GINSBURG, and BREYER, JJ., joined. BREYER, J., filed a dissenting opinion, in which STEVENS, SOUTER, and GINSBURG, JJ., joined. [554 U. S. ____ (2008) 1]

NOTICE: This opinion is subject to formal revision before publication in the preliminary print of the United States Reports. Readers are requested to notify the Reporter of Decisions, Supreme Court of the United States, Washington, D. C. 20543, of any typographical or other formal errors, in order that corrections may be made before the preliminary print goes to press.

DISTRICT OF COLUMBIA, ET AL., PETITIONERS *v.*
DICK ANTHONY HELLER

ON WRIT OF CERTIORARI TO THE UNITED STATES COURT OF APPEALS
FOR THE DISTRICT OF COLUMBIA CIRCUIT [June 26, 2008]

JUSTICE SCALIA delivered the opinion of the Court.

We consider whether a District of Columbia prohibition on the possession of usable handguns in the home violates the Second Amendment to the Constitution.

I

The District of Columbia generally prohibits the possession of handguns. It is a crime to carry an unregistered firearm, and the registration of handguns is prohibited.

The District of Columbia generally prohibits the possession of handguns. It is a crime to carry an unregistered firearm, and the registration of handguns is prohibited.

See D. C. Code §§7–2501.01(12), 7–2502.01(a), 7– 2502.02(a)(4) (2001). Wholly apart from that prohibition, no person may carry a handgun without a license, but the chief of police may issue licenses for 1-year periods. See §§22–4504(a), 22–4506. District of Columbia law also requires residents to keep their lawfully owned firearms, such as registered long guns, "unloaded and dissembled or bound by a trigger lock or similar device" unless they are located in a place of business or are being used for lawful recreational activities. See §7–2507.02. n1

n1 There are minor exceptions to all of these prohibitions, none of which is relevant here.

the Second Amendment protects an individual right to possess firearms and that the city's total ban on handguns, as well as its requirement that firearms in the home be kept nonfunctional even when necessary for self-defense, violated that right.

[554 U. S. ____ (2008) 2] Respondent Dick Heller is a D. C. special police officer authorized to carry a handgun while on duty at the Federal Judicial Center. He applied for a registration certificate for a handgun that he wished to keep at home, but the District refused. He thereafter filed a lawsuit in the Federal District Court for the District of Columbia seeking, on Second Amendment grounds, to enjoin the city from enforcing the bar on the registration of handguns, the licensing requirement insofar as it prohibits the carrying of a firearm in the home without a license, and the trigger-lock requirement insofar as it prohibits the use of "functional firearms within the home." App. 59a. The District Court dismissed respondent's complaint, see *Parker* v. *District of Columbia*, 311 F. Supp. 2d 103, 109 (2004). The Court of Appeals for the District of Columbia Circuit, construing his complaint as seeking the right to render a firearm operable and carry it about his home in that condition only when necessary for self-defense, n2 reversed, see *Parker* v. *District of Columbia*, 478 F. 3d 370, 401 (2007). It held that the Second Amendment protects an individual right to possess firearms and that the city's total ban on handguns, as well as its requirement that firearms in the home be kept nonfunctional even when necessary for self-defense, violated that right. See *id.*, at 395, 399–401. The Court of Appeals directed the District Court to enter summary judgment for respondent.

We granted certiorari. 552 U. S. ____ (2007).

II

We turn first to the meaning of the Second Amendment.

A The Second Amendment provides: "A well regulated Militia, being necessary to the security of a free State, the right of the people to keep and bear Arms, shall not be

n2 That construction has not been challenged here.

The Constitution was written to be understood by the voters; its words and phrases were used in their normal and ordinary as distinguished from technical meaning.

[554 U. S. ____ (2008) 3] infringed." In interpreting this text, we are guided by the principle that "[t]he Constitution was written to be understood by the voters; its words and phrases were used in their normal and ordinary as distinguished from technical meaning." *United States* v. *Sprague*, 282 U. S. 716, 731 (1931); see also *Gibbons* v. *Ogden*, 9 Wheat. 1, 188 (1824). Normal meaning may of course include an idiomatic meaning, but it excludes secret or technical meanings that would not have been known to ordinary citizens in the founding generation.

The two sides in this case have set out very different interpretations of the Amendment... it protects only the right to possess and carry a firearm in connection with militia service... it protects an individual right

The two sides in this case have set out very different interpretations of the Amendment. Petitioners and today's dissenting Justices believe that it protects only the right to possess and carry a firearm in connection with militia service. See Brief for Petitioners 11–12; post, at 1 (STEVENS, J., dissenting). Respondent argues that it protects an individual right to possess a firearm unconnected with service in a militia, and to use that arm for traditionally lawful purposes, such as self-defense within the home. See Brief for Respondent 2–4.

The Second Amendment is naturally divided into two parts: its prefatory clause and its operative clause. The former does not limit the latter grammatically, but rather announces a purpose.

The Second Amendment is naturally divided into two parts: its prefatory clause and its operative clause. The former does not limit the latter grammatically, but rather announces a purpose. The Amendment could be rephrased, "Because a well regulated Militia is necessary to the security of a free State, the right of the people to keep and bear Arms shall not be infringed." See J. Tiffany, A Treatise on Government and Constitutional Law §585, p. 394 (1867); Brief for Professors of Linguistics and English as *Amici Curiae* 3 (hereinafter Linguists' Brief). Although this structure of the Second Amendment is unique in our Constitution, other legal documents of the founding era, particularly individual-rights provisions of state constitutions, commonly included a prefatory statement of purpose. See generally Volokh, The Commonplace Second Amendment, 73 N. Y. U. L. Rev. 793, 814–821 [554 U. S. ____ (2008) 4] (1998).

apart from that clarifying function, a prefatory clause does not limit or expand the scope of the operative clause.

Logic demands that there be a link between the stated purpose and the command. The Second Amendment would be nonsensical if it read, "A well regulated Militia, being necessary to the security of a free State, the right of the people to petition for redress of grievances shall not be infringed." That requirement of logical connection may cause a prefatory clause to resolve an ambiguity in the operative clause ("The separation of church and state being an important objective, the teachings of canons shall have no place in our jurisprudence." The preface makes clear that the operative clause refers not to canons of interpretation but to clergymen.) But apart from that clarifying function, a prefatory clause does not limit or expand the scope of the operative clause. See F. Dwarris, A General Treatise on Statutes 268–269 (P. Potter ed. 1871) (hereinafter Dwarris); T. Sedgwick, The Interpretation and Construction of Statutory and Constitutional Law 42–45 (2d ed. 1874). n3 " 'It is nothing unusual in acts . . . for the enacting part to go beyond the preamble; the remedy often extends beyond the particular act or mischief which first suggested the necessity of the law.' " J. Bishop,

the settled principle of law is that the preamble cannot control the enacting part of the statute in cases where the enacting part is expressed in clear, unambiguous terms.

n3 As Sutherland explains, the key 18th-century English case on the effect of preambles, Copeman v. Gallant, 1 P. Wms. 314, 24 Eng. Rep. 404 (1716), stated that "the preamble could not be used to restrict the effect of the words of the purview." J. Sutherland, Statutes and Statutory Construction, 47.04 (N. Singer ed. 5th ed. 1992). This rule was modified in England in an 1826 case to give more importance to the preamble, but in America "the settled principle of law is that the preamble cannot control the enacting part of the statute in cases where the enacting part is expressed in clear, unambiguous terms." *Ibid.*

operative provisions should be given effect as operative provisions, and prologues as prologues.

JUSTICE STEVENS says that we violate the general rule that every clause in a statute must have effect. *Post,* at 8. But where the text of a clause itself indicates that it does not have operative effect, such as "whereas" clauses in federal legislation or the Constitution's preamble, a court has no license to make it do what it was not designed to do. Or to put the point differently, operative provisions should be given effect as operative provisions, and prologues as prologues. [554 U. S. ____ (2008) 5] Commentaries on Written Laws and Their Interpretation §51, p. 49 (1882) (quoting *Rex* v. *Marks,* 3 East, 157, 165 (K. B. 1802)). Therefore, while we will begin our textual analysis with the operative clause, we will return to the prefatory clause to ensure that our reading of the operative clause is consistent with the announced purpose. n4 n4 JUSTICE STEVENS criticizes us for discussing the prologue last. *Post*, at 8. But if a prologue can be used only to clarify an ambiguous operative provision, surely the first step must be to determine whether the operative provision is ambiguous. It might be argued, we suppose, that the prologue itself should be one of the factors that go into the determination of whether the operative provision is ambiguous—but that would cause the prologue to be used to produce ambiguity rather than just to resolve it. In any event, even if we considered the prologue *along with* the operative provision we would reach the same result we do today, since (as we explain) our interpretation of "the right of the people to keep and bear arms" furthers the purpose of an effective militia no less than (indeed, more than) the dissent's interpretation. See *infra*, at 26–27.

1. Operative Clause.

The first salient feature of the operative clause is that it codifies a "right of the people."

a. "Right of the People." The first salient feature of the operative clause is that it codifies a "right of the people."

The unamended Constitution and the Bill of Rights use the phrase "right of the people" two other times, in the First Amendment's Assembly-and-Petition Clause and in the Fourth Amendment's Search-and-Seizure Clause. The Ninth Amendment uses very similar terminology ("The enumeration in the Constitution, of certain rights, shall not be construed to deny or disparage others retained by the people"). All three of these instances unambiguously refer to individual rights, not "collective" rights, or rights that may be exercised only through participation in some corporate body. n5

JUSTICE STEVENS is dead wrong to think that the right to petition is "primarily collective in nature."

n5 JUSTICE STEVENS is of course correct, *post*, at 10, that the right to assemble cannot be exercised alone, but it is still an individual right, and not one conditioned upon membership in some defined "assembly," as he contends the right to bear arms is conditioned upon membership [554 U. S. ____ (2008) 6] in a defined militia. And JUSTICE STEVENS is dead wrong to think that the right to petition is "primarily collective in nature." *Ibid.* See *McDonald* v. *Smith*, 472 U. S. 479, 482–484 (1985) (describing historical origins of right to petition).

Nowhere else in the Constitution does a "right" attributed to "the people" refer to anything other than an individual right.

Three provisions of the Constitution refer to "the people" in a context other than "rights"—the famous preamble ("We the people"), §2 of Article I (providing that "the people" will choose members of the House), and the Tenth Amendment (providing that those powers not given the Federal Government remain with "the States" or "the people"). Those provisions arguably refer to "the people" acting collectively—but they deal with the exercise or reservation of powers, not rights. Nowhere else in the Constitution does a "right" attributed to "the people" refer to anything other than an individual right. n6

n6 If we look to other founding-era documents, we find that some state constitutions used the term "the people" to refer to the people collectively, in contrast to "citizen," which was used to invoke individual rights. See Heyman, Natural Rights and the Second Amendment, in The Second Amendment in Law and History 179, 193–195 (C. Bogus ed. 2000) (hereinafter Bogus). But that usage was not remotely uniform. See, *e.g.*, N. C. Declaration of Rights §XIV (1776), in 5 The

Federal and State Constitutions, Colonial Charters, and Other Organic Laws 2787, 2788 (F. Thorpe ed. 1909) (hereinafter Thorpe) (jury trial); Md. Declaration of Rights §XVIII (1776), in 3 *id.*, at 1686, 1688 (vicinage requirement); Vt. Declaration of Rights ch. 1, §XI (1777), in 6 *id.*, at 3737, 3741 (searches and seizures); Pa. Declaration of Rights §XII (1776), in 5 *id.*, at 3081, 3083 (free speech). And, most importantly, it was clearly not the terminology used in the Federal Constitution, given the First, Fourth, and Ninth Amendments.

What is more, in all six other provisions of the Constitution that mention "the people," the term unambiguously refers to all members of the political community, not an unspecified subset. As we said in *United States* v. *Verdugo- Urquidez*, 494 U. S. 259, 265 (1990):

"'[T]he people' seems to have been a term of art employed in select parts of the Constitution. . . . [Its uses] sugges[t] that 'the people' protected by the [554 U. S. ____ (2008) 7] Fourth Amendment, and by the First and Second Amendments, and to whom rights and powers are reserved in the Ninth and Tenth Amendments, refers to a class of persons who are part of a national community or who have otherwise developed sufficient connection with this country to be considered part of that community."

the "militia" in colonial America consisted of a subset of "the people"—those who were male, able bodied, and within a certain age range.

This contrasts markedly with the phrase "the militia" in the prefatory clause. As we will describe below, the "militia" in colonial America consisted of a subset of "the people"— those who were male, able bodied, and within a certain age range. Reading the Second Amendment as protecting only the right to "keep and bear Arms" in an organized militia therefore fits poorly with the operative clause's description of the holder of that right as "the people."

We start therefore with a strong presumption that the Second Amendment right is exercised individually and belongs to all Americans.

b. "Keep and bear Arms." We move now from the holder of the right—"the people"—to the substance of the right: "to keep and bear Arms."

Before addressing the verbs "keep" and "bear," we interpret their object: "Arms." The 18th-century meaning is no different from the meaning today. The 1773 edition of Samuel Johnson's dictionary defined "arms" as "weapons of offence, or armour of defence." 1 Dictionary of the English Language 107 (4th ed.) (hereinafter Johnson). Timothy Cunningham's important 1771 legal dictionary defined "arms" as "any thing that a man wears for his defence, or takes into his hands, or useth in wrath to cast at or strike another." 1 A New and Complete Law Dictionary (1771); see also N. Webster, American Dictionary of the English Language (1828) (reprinted 1989) (hereinafter Webster) (similar).

[554 U. S. ____ (2008) 8] The term was applied, then as now, to weapons that were not specifically designed for military use and were not employed in a military capacity. For instance, Cunningham's legal dictionary gave as an example of usage: "Servants and labourers shall use bows and arrows on *Sundays*, &c. and not bear other arms." See also, *e.g.*, An Act for the trial of Negroes, 1797 Del. Laws ch. XLIII, §6, p. 104, in 1 First Laws of the State of Delaware 102, 104 (J. Cushing ed. 1981 (pt. 1)); see generally *State* v. *Duke*, 42 Tex. 455, 458 (1874) (citing decisions of state courts construing "arms"). Although one founding-era thesaurus limited "arms" (as opposed to "weapons") to "instruments of offence *generally* made use of in war," even that source stated that all firearms constituted "arms." 1 J. Trusler, The Distinction Between Words Esteemed Synonymous in the English Language 37 (1794) (emphasis added).

Some have made the argument, bordering on the frivolous, that only those arms in existence in the 18th century are protected by the Second Amendment. We do not interpret constitutional rights that way.

the Second Amendment extends, prima facie, to all instruments that constitute bearable arms, even those that were not in existence at the time of the founding.

Some have made the argument, bordering on the frivolous, that only those arms in existence in the 18th century are protected by the Second Amendment. We do not interpret constitutional rights that way. Just as the First Amendment protects modern forms of communications, e.g., *Reno* v. *American Civil Liberties Union*, 521 U. S. 844, 849 (1997), and the Fourth Amendment applies to modern forms of search, e.g., *Kyllo* v. *United States*, 533 U. S. 27, 35–36 (2001), the Second Amendment extends, prima facie, to all instruments that constitute bearable arms, even those that were not in existence at the time of the founding.

We turn to the phrases "keep arms" and "bear arms." Johnson defined "keep" as, most relevantly, "[t]o retain; not to lose," and "[t]o have in custody." Johnson 1095. Webster defined it as "[t]o hold; to retain in one's power or possession." No party has apprised us of an idiomatic meaning of "keep Arms." Thus, the most natural reading of "keep Arms" in the Second Amendment is to "have weapons."

"Keep arms" was simply a common way of referring to possessing arms, for militiamen *and everyone else.*

[554 U. S. ____ (2008) 9] The phrase "keep arms" was not prevalent in the written documents of the founding period that we have found, but there are a few examples, all of which favor viewing the right to "keep Arms" as an individual right unconnected with militia service. William Blackstone, for example, wrote that Catholics convicted of not attending service in the Church of England suffered certain penalties, one of which was that they were not permitted to "keep arms in their houses." 4 Commentaries on the Laws of England 55 (1769) (hereinafter Blackstone); see also 1 W. & M., c. 15, §4, in 3 Eng. Stat. at Large 422 (1689) ("[N]o Papist . . . shall or may have or keep in his House . . . any Arms . . . "); 1 Hawkins, Treatise on the Pleas of the Crown 26 (1771) (similar). Petitioners point to militia laws of the founding period that required militia members to "keep" arms in connection with militia service, and they conclude from this that the phrase "keep Arms" has a militia-related connotation. See Brief for Petitioners 16– 17 (citing laws of Delaware, New Jersey, and Virginia). This is rather like saying that, since there are many statutes that authorize aggrieved employees to "file complaints" with federal agencies, the phrase "file complaints" has an employment-related connotation. "Keep arms" was simply a common way of referring to possessing arms, for militiamen *and everyone else*. n7

n7 See, *e.g.*, 3 A Compleat Collection of State-Tryals 185 (1719) ("Hath not every Subject power to keep Arms, as well as Servants in his House for defence of his Person?"); T. Wood, A New Institute of the Imperial or Civil Law 282 (1730) ("Those are guilty of *publick* Force, who keep Arms in their Houses, and make use of them otherwise than upon Journeys or Hunting, or for Sale . . ."); A Collection of All the Acts of Assembly, Now in Force, in the Colony of Virginia 596 (1733) ("Free Negros, Mulattos, or Indians, and Owners of Slaves, seated at Frontier Plantations, may obtain Licence from a Justice of Peace, for keeping Arms, &c."); J. Ayliffe, A New Pandect of *Roman* Civil Law 195 (1734) ("Yet a Person might keep Arms in his House, or on his Estate, on the Account of Hunting, Navigation, Travelling, and on the Score of Selling

At the time of the founding, as now, to "bear" meant to "carry."

When used with "arms," however, the term has a meaning that refers to carrying for a particular purpose—confrontation.

[554 U. S. ____ (2008) 10] At the time of the founding, as now, to "bear" meant to "carry." See Johnson 161; Webster; T. Sheridan, A Complete Dictionary of the English Language (1796); 2 Oxford English Dictionary 20 (2d ed. 1989) (hereinafter Oxford). When used with "arms," however, the term has a meaning that refers to carrying for a particular purpose—confrontation. In *Muscarello* v. *United States*, 524 U. S. 125 (1998), in the course of analyzing the meaning of "carries a firearm" in a federal criminal statute, JUSTICE GINSBURG wrote that "[s]urely a most familiar meaning is, as the Constitution's Second Amendment . . . indicate[s]: 'wear, bear, or carry . . . upon the person or in the clothing or in a pocket, for the purpose . . . of being armed and ready for offensive or defensive action in a case of conflict with another person.' " *Id.*, at 143 (dissenting opinion) them in the way of Trade or Commerce, or such Arms as accrued to him by way of Inheritance"); J. Trusler, A Concise View of the Common Law and Statute Law of England 270 (1781) ("if [papists] keep arms in their houses, such arms may be seized by a justice of the peace"); Some Considerations on the Game Laws 54 (1796) ("Who has been deprived by [the law] of keeping arms for his own defence? What law forbids the veriest pauper, if he can raise a sum sufficient for the purchase of it, from mounting his Gun on his Chimney Piece . . . ?"); 3 B. Wilson, The Works of the Honourable James Wilson 84 (1804) (with reference to state constitutional right: "This is one of our many renewals of the Saxon regulations. 'They were bound,' says Mr. Selden, 'to keep arms for the preservation of the kingdom, and of their own person' "); W. Duer, Outlines of the Constitutional Jurisprudence of the United States 31–32 (1833) (with reference to colonists' English rights: "The right of every individual to keep arms for his defence, suitable to his condition and degree; which was the public allowance, under due restrictions of the natural right of resistance and self-preservation"); 3 R. Burn, Justice of the Peace and the Parish Officer 88 (1815) ("It is, however, laid down by Serjeant Hawkins, . . . that if a lessee, after the end of the term, keep arms in his house to oppose the entry of the lessor, . . ."); *State* v. *Dempsey*, 31 N. C. 384, 385 (1849) (citing 1840 state law making it a misdemeanor for a member of certain racial groups "to carry about his person or keep in his house any shot gun or other arms"). [554 U. S. ____ (2008) 11] (quoting Black's Law Dictionary 214 (6th ed. 1998)). We think that JUSTICE GINSBURG accurately captured the natural meaning of "bear arms." Although the phrase implies that the carrying of the weapon is for the purpose of "offensive or defensive action," it in no way connotes participation in a structured military organization.

In numerous instances, "bear arms" was unambiguously used to refer to the carrying of weapons outside of an organized militia.

From our review of founding-era sources, we conclude that this natural meaning was also the meaning that "bear arms" had in the 18th century. In numerous instances, "bear arms" was unambiguously used to refer to the carrying of weapons outside of an organized militia. The most prominent examples are those most relevant to the Second Amendment: Nine state constitutional provisions written in the 18th century or the first two decades of the 19th, which enshrined a right of citizens to "bear arms in defense of themselves and the state" or "bear arms in defense of himself and the state." n8 It is clear from those formulations that "bear arms" did not refer only to carry-

n8 See Pa. Declaration of Rights §XIII, in 5 Thorpe 3083 ("That the people have a right to bear arms for the defence of themselves and the state. . . "); Vt.

Declaration of Rights §XV, in 6 *id.*, at 3741 ("That the people have a right to bear arms for the defence of themselves and the State. . ."); Ky. Const., Art. XII, cl. 23 (1792), in 3 *id.*, at 1264, 1275 ("That the right of the citizens to bear arms in defence of themselves and the State shall not be questioned"); Ohio Const., Art. VIII, §20 (1802), in 5 *id.*, at 2901, 2911 ("That the people have a right to bear arms for the defence of themselves and the State . . . "); Ind. Const., Art. I, §20 (1816), in 2 *id.*, at 1057, 1059 ("That the people have a right to bear arms for the defense of themselves and the State. . . "); Miss. Const., Art. I, §23 (1817), in 4 *id.*, at 2032, 2034 ("Every citizen has a right to bear arms, in defence of himself and the State"); Conn. Const., Art. I, §17 (1818), in 1 *id.*, at 536, 538 ("Every citizen has a right to bear arms in defence of himself and the state"); Ala. Const., Art. I, §23 (1819), in 1 *id.*, at 96, 98 ("Every citizen has a right to bear arms in defence of himself and the State"); Mo. Const., Art. XIII, §3 (1820), in 4 *id.*, at 2150, 2163 ("[T]hat their right to bear arms in defence of themselves and of the State cannot be questioned"). See generally Volokh, State Constitutional Rights to Keep and Bear Arms, 11 Tex. Rev. L. & Politics 191 (2006).

[554 U. S. ____ (2008) 12] ing a weapon in an organized military unit. Justice James Wilson interpreted the Pennsylvania Constitution's armsbearing right, for example, as a recognition of the natural right of defense "of one's person or house"—what he called the law of "self preservation." 2 Collected Works of James Wilson 1142, and n. x (K. Hall & M. Hall eds. 2007) (citing Pa. Const., Art. IX, §21 (1790)); see also T. Walker, Introduction to American Law 198 (1837) ("Thus the right of self-defence [is] guaranteed by the [Ohio] constitution"); see also *id.*, at 157 (equating Second Amendment with that provision of the Ohio Constitution). That was also the interpretation of those state constitutional provisions adopted by pre-Civil War state courts. n9   These provisions demonstrate—again, in the most analogous linguistic context—that "bear arms" was not limited to the carrying of arms in a militia.

n9 See *Bliss* v. *Commonwealth*, 2 Litt. 90, 91–92 (Ky. 1822); *State* v. *Reid*, 1 Ala. 612, 616–617 (1840); *State* v. *Schoultz*, 25 Mo. 128, 155 (1857); see also *Simpson* v. *State*, 5 Yer. 356, 360 (Tenn. 1833) (interpreting similar provision with "common defence" purpose); *State* v. *Huntly*, 25 N. C. 418, 422–423 (1843) (same); cf. *Nunn* v. *State*, 1 Ga. 243, 250–251 (1846) (construing Second Amendment); *State* v. *Chandler*, 5 La. Ann. 489, 489–490 (1850) (same).

The phrase "bear Arms" also had at the time of the founding an idiomatic meaning that was significantly different from its natural meaning: "to serve as a soldier, do military service, fight" or "to wage war." But it *unequivocally* bore that idiomatic meaning only when followed by the preposition "against," which was in turn followed by the target of the hostilities.

The phrase "bear Arms" also had at the time of the founding an idiomatic meaning that was significantly different from its natural meaning: "to serve as a soldier, do military service, fight" or "to wage war." See Linguists' Brief 18; *post*, at 11 (STEVENS, J., dissenting). But it *unequivocally* bore that idiomatic meaning only when followed by the preposition "against," which was in turn followed by the target of the hostilities. See 2 Oxford 21. (That is how, for example, our Declaration of Independence ¶28, used the phrase: "He has constrained our fellow Citizens taken Captive on the high Seas to bear Arms against their Country . . . .") Every example given by petitioners' *amici* for the idiomatic meaning of "bear arms" [554 U. S. ____ (2008) 13] from the founding period either includes the preposition "against" or is not clearly idiomatic. See Linguists' Brief 18–

23. Without the preposition, "bear arms" normally meant (as it continues to mean today) what JUSTICE GINSBURG's opinion in *Muscarello* said.

Giving "bear Arms" its idiomatic meaning would cause the protected right to consist of the right to be a soldier or to wage war—an absurdity that no commentator has ever endorsed... Grotesque.

In any event, the meaning of "bear arms" that petitioners and JUSTICE STEVENS propose is *not even* the (sometimes) idiomatic meaning. Rather, they manufacture a hybrid definition, whereby "bear arms" connotes the actual carrying of arms (and therefore is not really an idiom) but only in the service of an organized militia. No dictionary has ever adopted that definition, and we have been apprised of no source that indicates that it carried that meaning at the time of the founding. But it is easy to see why petitioners and the dissent are driven to the hybrid definition. Giving "bear Arms" its idiomatic meaning would cause the protected right to consist of the right to be a soldier or to wage war—an absurdity that no commentator has ever endorsed. See L. Levy, Origins of the Bill of Rights 135 (1999). Worse still, the phrase "keep and bear Arms" would be incoherent. The word "Arms" would have two different meanings at once: "weapons" (as the object of "keep") and (as the object of "bear") one-half of an idiom. It would be rather like saying "He filled and kicked the bucket" to mean "He filled the bucket and died." Grotesque.

Petitioners justify their limitation of "bear arms" to the military context by pointing out the unremarkable fact that it was often used in that context— the same mistake they made with respect to "keep arms."

those military discussions include not only "bear arms" but also "carry arms," "possess arms," and "have arms"—though no one thinks that those *other* phrases also had special military meanings.

Other legal sources frequently used "bear arms" in nonmilitary contexts.

Petitioners justify their limitation of "bear arms" to the military context by pointing out the unremarkable fact that it was often used in that context—the same mistake they made with respect to "keep arms." It is especially unremarkable that the phrase was often used in a military context in the federal legal sources (such as records of congressional debate) that have been the focus of petitioners' inquiry. Those sources would have had little occasion to use it *except* in discussions about the standing army and the militia. And the phrases used primarily in those [554 U. S. ____ (2008) 14] military discussions include not only "bear arms" but also "carry arms," "possess arms," and "have arms"—though no one thinks that those *other* phrases also had special military meanings. See Barnett, Was the Right to Keep and Bear Arms Conditioned on Service in an Organized Militia?, 83 Tex. L. Rev. 237, 261 (2004). The common references to those "fit to bear arms" in congressional discussions about the militia are matched by use of the same phrase in the few nonmilitary federal contexts where the concept would be relevant. See, *e.g.*, 30 Journals of Continental Congress 349–351 (J. Fitzpatrick ed. 1934). Other legal sources frequently used "bear arms" in nonmilitary contexts. n10 Cunningham's legal dictionary, cited above,

n10 See J. Brydall, Privilegia Magnatud apud Anglos 14 (1704) (Privilege XXXIII) ("In the 21st Year of King Edward the Third, a Proclamation Issued, that no Person should bear any Arms within London, and the Suburbs"); J. Bond, A Compleat Guide to Justices of the Peace 43 (1707) ("Sheriffs, and all other Officers in executing their Offices, and all other persons pursuing Hu[e] and Cry may lawfully bear arms"); 1 An Abridgment of the Public Statutes in Force and Use Relative to Scotland (1755) (entry for "Arms": "And if any person above described shall have in his custody, use, or bear arms, being thereof convicted before one justice of peace, or other judge competent, summarily, he shall for the first offense forfeit all such arms" (quoting 1 Geo. 1, c. 54, §1)); Statute Law of Scotland Abridged 132–133 (2d ed. 1769) ("Acts for disarming the highlands" but "exempting those who have particular licenses to bear arms"); E. de Vattel, The Law of Nations, or, Principles of the Law of Nature 144 (1792) ("Since custom has allowed persons of rank and gentlemen of the army to bear arms in time of peace, strict care should be taken that none but these should be allowed to wear swords"); E. Roche, Proceedings of a Court-Martial, Held at the Council- Chamber, in the City of Cork 3 (1798) (charge VI: "With having held traitorous conferences, and with having conspired, with the like intent, for the purpose of attacking and despoiling of the arms of several of the King's subjects, qualified by law to bear arms"); C. Humphreys, A Compendium of the Common Law in force in Kentucky 482 (1822) ("[I]n this country the constitution guaranties to all persons the right to bear arms; then it can only be a crime to exercise this right in such a manner, as to terrify people unnecessarily").

[554 U. S. ____ (2008) 15] gave as an example of its usage a sentence unrelated to military affairs ("Servants and labourers shall use bows and arrows on *Sundays*, &c. and not bear other arms"). And if one looks beyond legal sources, "bear arms" was frequently used in nonmilitary contexts. See Cramer & Olson, What Did "Bear Arms" Mean in the Second Amendment?, 6 Georgetown J. L. & Pub. Pol'y (forthcoming Sept. 2008), online at http://papers.ssrn.com/abstract=1086176 (as visited June 24, 2008, and available in Clerk of Court's case file) (identifying numerous nonmilitary uses of "bear arms" from the founding period).

JUSTICE STEVENS points to a study by *amici* supposedly showing that the phrase "bear arms" was most frequently used in the military context. Of course, as we have said, the fact that the phrase was commonly used in a particular context does not show that it is limited to that context, and, in any event, we have given many sources where the phrase was used in nonmilitary contexts.

A purposive qualifying phrase that contradicts the word or phrase it modifies is unknown this side of the looking glass

The right "to carry arms in the militia for the purpose of killing game" is worthy of the mad hatter.

JUSTICE STEVENS points to a study by *amici* supposedly showing that the phrase "bear arms" was most frequently used in the military context. See *post*, at 12–13, n. 9; Linguists' Brief 24. Of course, as we have said, the fact that the phrase was commonly used in a particular context does not show that it is limited to that context, and, in any event, we have given many sources where the phrase was used in nonmilitary contexts. Moreover, the study's collection appears to include (who knows how many times) the idiomatic phrase "bear arms against," which is irrelevant. The *amici* also dismiss examples such as " 'bear arms . . . for the purpose of killing game' " because those uses are "expressly qualified." Linguists' Brief 24. (JUSTICE STEVENS uses the same excuse for dismissing the state constitutional provisions analogous to the Second Amendment that identify private-use purposes for which the individual right can be asserted. See *post*, at 12.) That analysis is faulty. A purposive qualifying phrase that contradicts the word or phrase it modifies is unknown this side of the looking glass (except, apparently, in some courses on Linguistics). If "bear arms" means, as we think, simply the carrying of arms, a modifier can limit the purpose of the carriage ("for the purpose of self-defense" or "to make war against the King"). But if "bear arms" means, as the petitioners and the dissent think, the [554 U. S. ____ (2008) 16] carrying of arms only for military purposes, one simply cannot add "for the purpose of killing game." The right "to carry arms in the militia for the purpose of killing game" is worthy of the mad hatter. Thus, these purposive qualifying phrases positively establish that "to bear arms" is not limited to military use. n11

n11 JUSTICE STEVENS contends, *post*, at 15, that since we assert that adding "against" to "bear arms" gives it a military meaning we must concede that adding a purposive qualifying phrase to "bear arms" can alter its meaning. But the difference is that we do not maintain that "against" *alters* the meaning of "bear arms" but merely that it *clarifies* which of various meanings (one of which is military) is intended. JUSTICE STEVENS, however, argues that "[t]he term 'bear arms' is a familiar idiom; when used unadorned by any additional words, its meaning is 'to serve as a soldier, do military service, fight.' " *Post*, at 11. He therefore must establish that adding a contradictory purposive phrase can *alter* a word's meaning.

It is always perilous to derive the meaning of an adopted provision from another provision deleted in the drafting process.

JUSTICE STEVENS places great weight on James Madison's inclusion of a conscientious-objector clause in his original draft of the Second Amendment: "but no person religiously scrupulous of bearing arms, shall be compelled to render military service in person." Creating the Bill of Rights 12 (H. Veit, K. Bowling, & C. Bickford eds. 1991) (hereinafter Veit). He argues that this clause establishes that the drafters of the Second Amendment intended "bear Arms" to refer only to military service. See *post*, at 26. It is always perilous to derive the meaning of an adopted provision from another provision deleted in the drafting process. n12 In any case, what JUSTICE STEVENS would conclude from the deleted provision does not follow. It was not meant to exempt from military service those who

n12 JUSTICE STEVENS finds support for his legislative history inference from the recorded views of one Antifederalist member of the House. *Post*, at 26 n. 25. "The claim that the best or most representative reading of the [language of the] amendments would conform to the understanding and concerns of [the Antifederalists] is . . . highly problematic." Rakove, The Second Amendment: The Highest Stage of Originalism, Bogus 74, 81.

[554 U. S. ____ (2008) 17] objected to going to war but had no scruples about personal gunfights. Quakers opposed the use of arms not just for militia service, but for any violent purpose whatsoever— so much so that Quaker frontiersmen were forbidden to use arms to defend their families, even though "[i]n such circumstances the temptation to seize a hunting rifle or knife in self-defense . . . must sometimes have been almost overwhelming." P. Brock, Pacifism in the United States 359 (1968); see M. Hirst, The Quakers in Peace and War 336–339 (1923); 3 T. Clarkson, Portraiture of Quakerism 103–104 (3d ed. 1807). The Pennsylvania Militia Act of 1757 exempted from service those *"scrupling the use of arms"*—a phrase that no one contends had an idiomatic meaning. See 5 Stat. at Large of Pa. 613 (J. Mitchell & H. Flanders eds. 1898) (emphasis added). Thus, the most natural interpretation of Madison's deleted text is that those opposed to carrying weapons for potential violent confrontation would not be "compelled to render military service," in which such carrying would be required. n13

n13 The same applies to the conscientious-objector amendments proposed by Virginia and North Carolina, which said: "That any person religiously scrupulous of bearing arms ought to be exempted upon payment of an equivalent to employ another to bear arms in his stead." See Veit 19; 4 J. Eliot, The Debates in the

Several State Constitutions on the Adoption of the Federal Constitution 243, 244 (2d ed. 1836) (reprinted 1941). Certainly their second use of the phrase ("bear arms in his stead") refers, by reason of context, to compulsory bearing of arms for military duty. But their first use of the phrase ("any person religiously scrupulous of bearing arms") assuredly did not refer to people whose God allowed them to bear arms for defense of themselves but not for defense of their country.

JUSTICE STEVENS suggests that "keep and bear Arms" was some sort of term of art, presumably akin to "hue and cry" or "cease and desist." (This suggestion usefully evades the problem that there is no evidence whatsoever to support a military reading of "keep arms.")

Finally, JUSTICE STEVENS suggests that "keep and bear Arms" was some sort of term of art, presumably akin to "hue and cry" or "cease and desist." (This suggestion usefully evades the problem that there is no evidence whatsoever to support a military reading of "keep arms.") JUSTICE STEVENS believes that the unitary meaning of [554 U. S. ___ (2008) 18] "keep and bear Arms" is established by the Second Amendment's calling it a "right" (singular) rather than "rights" (plural). See *post*, at 16. There is nothing to this. State constitutions of the founding period routinely grouped multiple (related) guarantees under a singular "right," and the First Amendment protects the "right [singular] of the people peaceably to assemble, and to petition the Government for a redress of grievances." See, *e.g.*, Pa. Declaration of Rights §§IX, XII, XVI, in 5 Thorpe 3083–3084; Ohio Const., Arts. VIII, §§11, 19 (1802), in *id.*, at 2910–2911. n14 And even if "keep and bear Arms" were a unitary phrase, we find no evidence that it bore a military meaning. Although the phrase was not at all common (which would be unusual for a term of art), we have found instances of its use with a clearly nonmilitary connotation. In a 1780 debate in the House of Lords, for example, Lord Richmond described an order to disarm private citizens (not militia members) as "a violation of the constitutional right of Protestant subjects to keep and bear arms for their own defense." 49 The London Magazine or Gentleman's Monthly Intelligencer 467 (1780). In response, another member of Parliament referred to "the right of bearing arms for personal defence," making clear that no special military meaning for "keep and bear arms" was intended in the discussion. *Id.*, at 467–468. n15

n14 Faced with this clear historical usage, JUSTICE STEVENS resorts to the bizarre argument that because the word "to" is not included before "bear" (whereas it is included before "petition" in the First Amendment), the unitary meaning of "to keep and bear" is established. *Post*, at 16, n. 13. We have never heard of the proposition that omitting repetition of the "to" causes two verbs with different meanings to become one. A promise "to support and to defend the Constitution of the United States" is not a whit different from a promise "to support and defend the Constitution of the United States."

n15 Cf. 3 Geo., 34, §3, in 7 Eng. Stat. at Large 126 (1748) ("That the Prohibition contained . . . in this Act, of having, keeping, bearing, or wearing any Arms or Warlike Weapons . . . shall not extend . . . to any [554 U. S. ___ (2008) 19] Officers or their Assistants, employed in the Execution of Justice . . .").

Putting all of these textual elements together, we find that they guarantee the individual right to possess and carry weapons in case of confrontation.

it has always been widely understood that the Second Amendment, like the First and Fourth Amendments, codified a *pre-existing* right.

c. Meaning of the Operative Clause. Putting all of these textual elements together, we find that they guarantee the individual right to possess and carry weapons in case of confrontation. This meaning is strongly confirmed by the historical background of the Second Amendment. We look to this because it has always been widely understood that the Second Amendment, like the First and Fourth Amendments, codified a *pre-existing* right. The very text of the Second Amendment implicitly recognizes the pre-existence of the right and declares only that it "shall not be infringed." As we said in *United States* v. *Cruikshank*, 92 U. S. 542, 553 (1876), "[t]his is not a right granted by the Constitution. Neither is it in any manner dependent upon that instrument for its existence. The Second amendment declares that it shall not be infringed . . . ." n16

n16 Contrary to JUSTICE STEVENS' wholly unsupported assertion, *post*, at 17, there was no pre-existing right in English law "to use weapons for certain military purposes" or to use arms in an organized militia.

These experiences caused Englishmen to be extremely wary of concentrated military forces run by the state and to be jealous of their arms.

the subjects which are Protestants may have arms for their defense suitable to their conditions and as allowed by law.

It was clearly an individual right, having nothing whatever to do with service in a militia.

Between the Restoration and the Glorious Revolution, the Stuart Kings Charles II and James II succeeded in using select militias loyal to them to suppress political dissidents, in part by disarming their opponents. See J. Malcolm, To Keep and Bear Arms 31–53 (1994) (hereinafter Malcolm); L. Schwoerer, The Declaration of Rights, 1689, p. 76 (1981). Under the auspices of the 1671 Game Act, for example, the Catholic James II had ordered general disarmaments of regions home to his Protestant enemies. See Malcolm 103–106. These experiences caused Englishmen to be extremely wary of concentrated military forces run by the state and to be jealous of their arms. They accordingly obtained an assurance from William and Mary, in the Declaration of Right (which was codified as the English Bill of Rights), that Protestants [554 U. S. ____ (2008) 20] would never be disarmed: "That the subjects which are Protestants may have arms for their defense suitable to their conditions and as allowed by law." 1 W. & M., c. 2, §7, in 3 Eng. Stat. at Large 441 (1689). This right has long been understood to be the predecessor to our Second Amendment. See E. Dumbauld, The Bill of Rights and What It Means Today 51 (1957); W. Rawle, A View of the Constitution of the United States of America 122 (1825) (hereinafter Rawle). It was clearly an individual right, having nothing whatever to do with service in a militia. To be sure, it was an individual right not available to the whole population, given that it was restricted to Protestants, and like all written English rights it was held only against the Crown, not Parliament. See Schwoerer, To Hold and Bear Arms: The English Perspective, in Bogus 207, 218; but see 3 J. Story, Commentaries on the Constitution of the United States §1858 (1833) (hereinafter Story) (contending that the "right to bear arms" is a "limitatio[n] upon the power of parliament" as well). But it was secured to them as individuals, according to "libertarian political principles," not as members of a fighting force. Schwoerer, Declaration of Rights, at 283; see also *id.*, at 78; G. Jellinek, The Declaration of the Rights of Man and of Citizens 49, and n. 7 (1901) (reprinted 1979).

Blackstone... cited the arms provision of the Bill of Rights as one of the fundamental rights of Englishmen. His description of it cannot possibly be thought to tie it to militia or military service. It was, he said, "the

natural right of resistance and self-preservation," and "the right of having and using arms for self-preservation and defence"

Thus, the right secured in 1689 as a result of the Stuarts' abuses was by the time of the founding understood to be an individual right protecting against both public and private violence.

By the time of the founding, the right to have arms had become fundamental for English subjects. See Malcolm 122–134. Blackstone, whose works, we have said, "constituted the preeminent authority on English law for the founding generation," *Alden* v. *Maine*, 527 U. S. 706, 715 (1999), cited the arms provision of the Bill of Rights as one of the fundamental rights of Englishmen. See 1 Blackstone 136, 139–140 (1765). His description of it cannot possibly be thought to tie it to militia or military service. It was, he said, "the natural right of resistance and self-preservation," *id.*, at 139, and "the right of having and using arms for self-preservation and defence," *id.*, at 140; [554 U. S. ___ (2008) 21] see also 3 *id.*, at 2–4 (1768). Other contemporary authorities concurred. See G. Sharp, Tracts, Concerning the Ancient and Only True Legal Means of National Defence, by a Free Militia 17–18, 27 (3d ed. 1782); 2 J. de Lolme, The Rise and Progress of the English Constitution 886– 887 (1784) (A. Stephens ed. 1838); W. Blizard, Desultory Reflections on Police 59–60 (1785). Thus, the right secured in 1689 as a result of the Stuarts' abuses was by the time of the founding understood to be an individual right protecting against both public and private violence.

what the Stuarts had tried to do to their political enemies, George III had tried to do to the colonists.

Americans understood the "right of self-preservation" as permitting a citizen to "repe[l] force by force" when "the intervention of society in his behalf, may be too late to prevent an injury."

it is a natural right which the people have reserved to themselves, confirmed by the Bill of Rights, to keep arms for their own defence."

And, of course, what the Stuarts had tried to do to their political enemies, George III had tried to do to the colonists. In the tumultuous decades of the 1760's and 1770's, the Crown began to disarm the inhabitants of the most rebellious areas. That provoked polemical reactions by Americans invoking their rights as Englishmen to keep arms. A New York article of April 1769 said that "[i]t is a natural right which the people have reserved to themselves, confirmed by the Bill of Rights, to keep arms for their own defence." A Journal of the Times: Mar. 17, New York Journal, Supp. 1, Apr. 13, 1769, in Boston Under Military Rule 79 (O. Dickerson ed. 1936); see also, *e.g.*, Shippen, Boston Gazette, Jan. 30, 1769, in 1 The Writings of Samuel Adams 299 (H. Cushing ed. 1968). They understood the right to enable individuals to defend themselves. As the most important early American edition of Blackstone's Commentaries (by the law professor and former Antifederalist St. George Tucker) made clear in the notes to the description of the arms right, Americans understood the "right of self-preservation" as permitting a citizen to "repe[l] force by force" when "the intervention of society in his behalf, may be too late to prevent an injury." 1 Blackstone's Commentaries 145–146, n. 42 (1803) (hereinafter Tucker's Blackstone). See also W. Duer, Outlines of the Constitutional Jurisprudence of the United States 31–32 (1833).

There seems to us no doubt, on the basis of both text and history, that the Second Amendment conferred an individual right to keep and bear arms. Of course the right was not unlimited, just as the First Amendment's right of free speech was not

we do not read the Second Amendment to protect the right of citizens to carry arms for *any sort* of confrontation, just as we do not read the First Amendment to protect the right of citizens to speak for *any purpose*.

[554 U. S. ____ (2008) 22] There seems to us no doubt, on the basis of both text and history, that the Second Amendment conferred an individual right to keep and bear arms. Of course the right was not unlimited, just as the First Amendment's right of free speech was not, see, *e.g.*, *United States* v. *Williams*, 553 U. S. ___ (2008). Thus, we do not read the Second Amendment to protect the right of citizens to carry arms for *any sort* of confrontation, just as we do not read the First Amendment to protect the right of citizens to speak for *any purpose*. Before turning to limitations upon the individual right, however, we must determine whether the prefatory clause of the Second Amendment comports with our interpretation of the operative clause.

2. Prefatory Clause.

The prefatory clause reads: "A well regulated Militia, being necessary to the security of a free State . . . ."

In *United States* v. *Miller* we explained that "the Militia comprised all males physically capable of acting in concert for the common defense." That definition comports with founding-era sources.

a. "Well-Regulated Militia." In *United States* v. *Miller*, 307 U. S. 174, 179 (1939), we explained that "the Militia comprised all males physically capable of acting in concert for the common defense." That definition comports with founding-era sources. See, *e.g.*, Webster ("The militia of a country are the able bodied men organized into companies, regiments and brigades . . . and required by law to attend military exercises on certain days only, but at other times left to pursue their usual occupations"); The Federalist No. 46, pp. 329, 334 (B. Wright ed. 1961) (J. Madison) ("near half a million of citizens with arms in their hands"); Letter to Destutt de Tracy (Jan. 26, 1811), in The Portable Thomas Jefferson 520, 524 (M. Peterson ed. 1975) ("[T]he militia of the State, that is to say, of every man in it able to bear arms").

Petitioners take a seemingly narrower view of the militia, stating that "[m]ilitias are the state- and congressionally- regulated military forces described in the Militia Clauses (art. I, §8, cls. 15–16)." Brief for Petitioners 12.

the militia is assumed by Article I already to be *in existence*. Congress is given the power to "provide for calling forth the militia," and the power not to create, but to "organize" it—and not to organize "a" militia, which is what one would expect if the militia were to be a federal creation, but to organize "the" militia, connoting a body already in existence. This is fully consistent with the ordinary definition of the militia as all able-bodied men.

Although the militia consists of all able-bodied men, the federally organized militia may consist of a subset of them.

[554 U. S. ____ (2008) 23] Although we agree with petitioners' interpretive assumption that "militia" means the same thing in Article I and the Second Amendment, we believe that petitioners identify the wrong thing, namely, the organized militia. Unlike armies and navies, which Congress is given the power to create ("to raise . . . Armies"; "to provide . . . a Navy," Art. I, §8, cls. 12–13), the militia is assumed by Article I already to be *in existence*. Congress is given the power to "provide for calling forth the militia," §8, cl. 15; and the power not to create, but to "organiz[e]" it—and not to organize "a" militia, which is what one would expect if the militia were to be a federal creation, but to organize "the" militia, connoting a body already in existence, *ibid.*, cl. 16. This is fully consistent with the ordinary definition of the militia as all able-bodied men. From that pool, Congress has plenary power to organize the units that will make up an effective fighting force. That is what Congress did in the first militia Act, which specified that "each and every free able-bodied white male citizen of the respective states, resident therein, who is or shall be of the age of eighteen years, and under the age of forty-five years (except as is herein after excepted) shall severally and respectively be enrolled in the militia." Act of May 8, 1792, 1 Stat. 271. To be sure, Congress need not conscript every able-bodied man into the militia, because nothing in Article I suggests that in exercising its power to organize, discipline, and arm the militia, Congress must focus upon the entire body. Although the militia consists of all able-bodied men, the federally organized militia may consist of a subset of them.

the adjective "well-regulated" implies nothing more than the imposition of proper discipline and training

Finally, the adjective "well-regulated" implies nothing more than the imposition of proper discipline and training. See Johnson 1619 ("Regulate": "To adjust by rule or method"); Rawle 121–122; cf. Va. Declaration of Rights §13 (1776), in 7 Thorpe 3812, 3814 (referring to "a well-regulated militia, composed of the body of the people, [554 U. S. ____ (2008) 24] trained to arms").

The militia is the natural defence of a free country.

b. "Security of a Free State." The phrase "security of a free state" meant "security of a free polity," not security of each of the several States as the dissent below argued, see 478 F. 3d, at 405, and n. 10. Joseph Story wrote in his treatise on the Constitution that "the word 'state' is used in various senses [and in] its most enlarged sense, it means the people composing a particular nation or community." 1 Story §208; see also 3 *id.*, §1890 (in reference to the Second Amendment's prefatory clause: "The militia is the natural defence of a free country"). It is true that the term "State" elsewhere in the Constitution refers to individual States, but the phrase "security of a free state" and close variations seem to have been terms of art in 18th-century political discourse, meaning a " 'free country' " or free polity. See Volokh, "Necessary to the Security of a Free State," 83 Notre Dame L. Rev. 1, 5 (2007); see, *e.g.*, 4 Blackstone 151 (1769); Brutus Essay III (Nov. 15, 1787), in The Essential Antifederalist 251, 253 (W. Allen & G. Lloyd eds., 2d ed. 2002). Moreover, the other instances of "state" in the Constitution are typically accompanied by modifiers making clear that the reference is to the several States—"each state," "several states," "any state," "that state," "particular states," "one state," "no state." And the presence of the term "foreign state" in Article I and Article III shows that the word "state" did not have a single meaning in the Constitution.

There are many reasons why the militia was thought to be "necessary to the security of a free state."... First... useful in repelling invasions and suppressing insurrections. Second, it renders large standing armies unnecessary... Third, when the able-bodied men of a nation are trained in arms and organized, they are better able to resist tyranny.

There are many reasons why the militia was thought to be "necessary to the security of a free state." See 3 Story §1890. First, of course, it is useful in repelling invasions and suppressing insurrections. Second, it renders large standing armies unnecessary—an argument that Alexander Hamilton made in favor of federal control over the militia. The Federalist No. 29, pp. 226, 227 (B. Wright ed. 1961) (A. Hamilton). Third, when the able-bodied men of a nation are trained in arms and organized, they are [554 U. S. ____ (2008) 25] better able to resist tyranny.

3. Relationship between Prefatory Clause and Operative Clause

the way tyrants had eliminated a militia consisting of all the able-bodied men was not by banning the militia but simply by taking away the people's arms, enabling a select militia or standing army to suppress political opponents.

We reach the question, then: Does the preface fit with an operative clause that creates an individual right to keep and bear arms? It fits perfectly, once one knows the history that the founding generation knew and that we have described above. That history showed that the way tyrants had eliminated a militia consisting of all the able-bodied men was not by banning the militia but simply by taking away the people's arms, enabling a select militia or standing army to suppress political opponents. This is what had occurred in England that prompted codification of the right to have arms in the English Bill of Rights.

During the 1788 ratification debates, the fear that the federal government would disarm the people in order to impose rule through a standing army or select militia was pervasive in Antifederalist rhetoric.

because Congress was given no power to abridge the ancient right of individuals to keep and bear arms, such a force could never oppress the people.

It was understood across the political spectrum that the right helped to secure the ideal of a citizen militia, which might be necessary to oppose an oppressive military force if the constitutional order broke down.

The debate with respect to the right to keep and bear arms, as with other guarantees in the Bill of Rights, was not over whether it was desirable (all agreed that it was) but over whether it needed to be codified in the Constitution. During the 1788 ratification debates, the fear that the federal government would disarm the people in order to impose rule through a standing army or select militia was pervasive in Antifederalist rhetoric. See, *e.g.*, Letters from The Federal Farmer III (Oct. 10, 1787), in 2 The Complete Anti-Federalist 234, 242 (H. Storing ed. 1981). John Smilie, for example, worried not only that Congress's "command of the militia" could be used to create a "select militia," or to have "no militia at all," but also, as a separate concern, that "[w]hen a select militia is formed; the people in general may be disarmed." 2 Documentary History of the Ratification of the Constitution 508–509 (M. Jensen ed. 1976) (hereinafter Documentary Hist.). Federalists responded that because Congress was given no power to abridge the ancient right of individuals to keep and bear arms, such a force could never oppress the people. See, *e.g.*, A Pennsylvanian III (Feb. 20, 1788), in The [554 U. S. ____ (2008) 26] Origin of the Second Amendment 275, 276 (D. Young ed., 2d ed. 2001) (hereinafter Young); White, To the Citizens of Virginia, Feb. 22, 1788, in *id.*, at 280, 281; A Citizen of America, (Oct. 10, 1787) in *id.*, at 38, 40; Remarks on the Amendments to the federal Constitution, Nov. 7, 1788, in *id.*, at 556. It was understood across the political spectrum that the right helped to secure the ideal of a citizen militia, which might be necessary to oppose an oppressive military force if the constitutional order broke down.

the Second Amendment's prefatory clause announces the purpose for which the right was codified: to prevent elimination of the militia. The

prefatory clause does not suggest that preserving the militia was the only reason Americans valued the ancient right; most undoubtedly thought it even more important for self-defense and hunting.

It is therefore entirely sensible that the Second Amendment's prefatory clause announces the purpose for which the right was codified: to prevent elimination of the militia. The prefatory clause does not suggest that preserving the militia was the only reason Americans valued the ancient right; most undoubtedly thought it even more important for self-defense and hunting. But the threat that the new Federal Government would destroy the citizens' militia by taking away their arms was the reason that right—unlike some other English rights—was codified in a written Constitution. JUSTICE BREYER's assertion that individual self-defense is merely a "subsidiary interest" of the right to keep and bear arms, see *post*, at 36, is profoundly mistaken. He bases that assertion solely upon the prologue—but that can only show that self-defense had little to do with the right's *codification;* it was the *central component* of the right itself.

the historical reality that the Second Amendment was not intended to lay down a "novel principle" but rather codified a right "inherited from our English ancestors"

Besides ignoring the historical reality that the Second Amendment was not intended to lay down a "novel principl[e]" but rather codified a right "inherited from our English ancestors," *Robertson* v. *Baldwin*, 165 U. S. 275, 281 (1897), petitioners' interpretation does not even achieve the narrower purpose that prompted codification of the right. If, as they believe, the Second Amendment right is no more than the right to keep and use weapons as a member of an organized militia, see Brief for Petititioners 8—if, that is, the *organized* militia is the sole institu- [554 U. S. ___ (2008) 27] tional beneficiary of the Second Amendment's guarantee— it does not assure the existence of a "citizens' militia" as a safeguard against tyranny. For Congress retains plenary authority to organize the militia, which must include the authority to say who will belong to the organized force. n17 That is why the first Militia Act's requirement that only whites enroll caused States to amend their militia laws to exclude free blacks. See Siegel, The Federal Government's Power to Enact Color-Conscious Laws, 92 Nw. U. L. Rev. 477, 521–525 (1998). Thus, if petitioners are correct, the Second Amendment protects citizens' right to use a gun in an organization from which Congress has plenary authority to exclude them. It guarantees a select militia of the sort the Stuart kings found useful, but not the people's militia that was the concern of the founding generation.

n17 Article I, §8, cl. 16 of the Constitution gives Congress the power "[t]o provide for organizing, arming, and disciplining, the Militia, and for governing such Part of them as may be employed in the Service of the United States, reserving to the States respectively, the Appointment of the Officers, and the Authority of training the Militia according to the discipline prescribed by Congress." It could not be clearer that Congress's "organizing" power, unlike its "governing" power, can be invoked even for that part of the militia not "employed in the Service of the United States." JUSTICE STEVENS provides no support whatever for his contrary view, see *post*, at 19 n.20. Both the Federalists and Anti-Federalists read the provision as it was written, to permit the creation of a "select" militia. See The Federalist No. 29, pp. 226, 227 (B. Wright ed. 1961); Centinel, Revived, No. XXIX, Philadelphia Independent Gazetteer, Sept. 9, 1789, in Young 711, 712.

B

Pennsylvania and Vermont—clearly adopted individual rights unconnected to militia service.

Our interpretation is confirmed by analogous arms-bearing rights in state constitutions that preceded and immediately followed adoption of the Second Amendment. Four States adopted analogues to the Federal Second Amendment in the period between independence and the [554 U. S. ____ (2008) 28] ratification of the Bill of Rights. Two of them—Pennsylvania and Vermont—clearly adopted individual rights unconnected to militia service. Pennsylvania's Declaration of Rights of 1776 said: "That the people have a right to bear arms *for the defence of themselves*, and the state . . . ." §XIII, in 5 Thorpe 3082, 3083 (emphasis added). In 1777, Vermont adopted the identical provision, except for inconsequential differences in punctuation and capitalization. See Vt. Const., ch. 1, §15, in 6 *id.*, at 3741.

Many colonial statutes required individual arms-bearing for public-safety reasons

North Carolina also codified a right to bear arms in 1776: "That the people have a right to bear arms, for the defence of the State . . . ." Declaration of Rights §XVII, in *id.*, at 2787, 2788. This could plausibly be read to support only a right to bear arms in a militia—but that is a peculiar way to make the point in a constitution that elsewhere repeatedly mentions the militia explicitly. See §§14, 18, 35, in 5 *id.*, 2789, 2791, 2793. Many colonial statutes required individual arms-bearing for public-safety reasons— such as the 1770 Georgia law that "for the security and *defence of this province* from internal dangers and insurrections" required those men who qualified for militia duty individually "to carry fire arms" "to places of public worship." 19 Colonial Records of the State of Georgia 137– 139 (A. Candler ed. 1911 (pt. 2)) (emphasis added). That broad public-safety understanding was the connotation given to the North Carolina right by that State's Supreme Court in 1843. See *State* v. *Huntly*, 3 Ired. 418, 422–423.

"The liberty of the press was to be unrestrained, but he who used it was to be responsible in cases of its abuse; like the right to keep fire arms, which does not protect him who uses them for annoyance or destruction."

19th-century courts never read "common defence" to limit the use of weapons to militia service

The 1780 Massachusetts Constitution presented another variation on the theme: "The people have a right to keep and to bear arms for the common defence. . . ." Pt. First, Art. XVII, in 3 Thorpe 1888, 1892. Once again, if one gives narrow meaning to the phrase "common defence" this can be thought to limit the right to the bearing of arms in a state-organized military force. But once again the State's highest court thought otherwise. Writing for the court in an 1825 libel case, Chief Justice Parker wrote: [554 U. S. ____ (2008) 29] "The liberty of the press was to be unrestrained, but he who used it was to be responsible in cases of its abuse; like the right to keep fire arms, which does not protect him who uses them for annoyance or destruction." *Commonwealth* v. *Blanding*, 20 Mass. 304, 313–314. The analogy makes no sense if firearms could not be used for any individual purpose at all. See also Kates, Handgun Prohibition and the Original Meaning of the Second Amendment, 82 Mich. L. Rev. 204, 244 (1983) (19th-century courts never read "common defence" to limit the use of weapons to militia service).

"No freeman shall ever be debarred the use of arms [within his own lands or tenements]."

We therefore believe that the most likely reading of all four of these pre-Second Amendment state constitutional provisions is that they secured an individual right to bear arms for defensive purposes. Other States did not include rights to bear arms in their pre-

1789 constitutions— although in Virginia a Second Amendment analogue was proposed (unsuccessfully) by Thomas Jefferson. (It read: "No freeman shall ever be debarred the use of arms [within his own lands or tenements]." n18 1 The Papers of Thomas Jefferson 344 (J. Boyd ed. 1950)).

n18 JUSTICE STEVENS says that the drafters of the Virginia Declaration of Rights rejected this proposal and adopted "instead" a provision written by George Mason stressing the importance of the militia. See *post*, at 24, and n. 24. There is no evidence that the drafters regarded the Mason proposal as a substitute for the Jefferson proposal.

Between 1789 and 1820, nine States adopted Second Amendment analogues. Four of them—Kentucky, Ohio, Indiana, and Missouri— referred to the right of the people to "bear arms in defence of themselves and the State." Another three States—Mississippi, Connecticut, and Alabama—used the even more individualistic phrasing that each citizen has the "right to bear arms in defence of himself and the State." Finally, two States—Tennessee and Maine—used the "common defence" language of Massachusetts.

That of the nine state constitutional protections for the right to bear arms enacted immediately after 1789 at least seven unequivocally protected an individual citizen's right to self-defense is strong evidence that that is how the founding generation conceived of the right.

19th-century courts and commentators interpreted these state constitutional provisions to protect an individual right to use arms for self-defense.

Between 1789 and 1820, nine States adopted Second Amendment analogues. Four of them—Kentucky, Ohio, Indiana, and Missouri—referred to the right of the people to "bear arms in defence of themselves and the State." See n. 8, *supra.* Another three States— Mississippi, Connecticut, and Alabama—used the even more individualistic phrasing that each citizen has the "right to bear arms in defence of himself and the State." See *ibid.* Finally, two States—Tennessee and Maine—used the "common defence" language of Massachusetts. See Tenn. Const., Art. [554 U. S. ____ (2008) 30] XI, §26 (1796), in 6 Thorpe 3414, 3424; Me. Const., Art. I, §16 (1819), in 3 *id.*, at 1646, 1648. That of the nine state constitutional protections for the right to bear arms enacted immediately after 1789 at least seven unequivocally protected an individual citizen's right to self-defense is strong evidence that that is how the founding generation conceived of the right. And with one possible exception that we discuss in Part II–D–2, 19th-century courts and commentators interpreted these state constitutional provisions to protect an individual right to use arms for self-defense. See n. 9, *supra; Simpson* v. *State*, 5 Yer. 356, 360 (Tenn. 1833).

The historical narrative that petitioners must endorse would thus treat the Federal Second Amendment as an odd outlier, protecting a right unknown in state constitutions or at English common law, based on little more than an overreading of the prefatory clause.

The historical narrative that petitioners must endorse would thus treat the Federal Second Amendment as an odd outlier, protecting a right unknown in state constitutions or at English common law, based on little more than an overreading of the prefatory clause.

C

JUSTICE STEVENS flatly misreads the historical record

JUSTICE STEVENS relies on the drafting history of the Second Amendment—the various proposals in the state conventions and the debates in Congress. It is dubious to rely on such history to interpret a text that was widely understood to codify a pre-existing right, rather than to fashion a new one. But even assuming that this legislative history is relevant, JUSTICE STEVENS flatly misreads the historical record.

It is true, as JUSTICE STEVENS says, that there was concern that the Federal Government would abolish the institution of the state militia. See *post*, at 20. That concern found expression, however, *not* in the various Second Amendment precursors proposed in the State conventions, but in separate structural provisions that would have given the States concurrent and seemingly nonpre-emptible authority to organize, discipline, and arm the militia when the Federal Government failed to do so.[554 U. S. ____ (2008) 31] See Veit 17, 20 (Virginia proposal); 4 J. Eliot, The Debates in the Several State Conventions on the Adoption of the Federal Constitution 244, 245 (2d ed. 1836) (reprinted 1941) (North Carolina proposal); see also 2 Documentary Hist. 624 (Pennsylvania minority's proposal). The Second Amendment precursors, by contrast, referred to the individual English right already codified in two (and probably four) State constitutions. The Federalist-dominated first Congress chose to reject virtually all major structural revisions favored by the Antifederalists, including the proposed militia amendments. Rather, it adopted primarily the popular and uncontroversial (though, in the Federalists' view, unnecessary) individual-rights amendments. The Second Amendment right, protecting only individuals' liberty to keep and carry arms, did nothing to assuage Antifederalists' concerns about federal control of the militia. See, *e.g.*, Centinel, Revived, No. XXIX, Philadelphia Independent Gazetteer, Sept. 9, 1789, in Young 711, 712.

JUSTICE STEVENS has brought forward absolutely no evidence that those proposals conferred only a right to carry arms in a militia. By contrast, New Hampshire's proposal, the Pennsylvania minority's proposal, and Samuel Adams' proposal in Massachusetts unequivocally referred to individual rights, as did two state constitutional provisions at the time.

our longstanding view that the Bill of Rights codified venerable, widely understood liberties.

JUSTICE STEVENS thinks it significant that the Virginia, New York, and North Carolina Second Amendment proposals were "embedded . . . within a group of principles that are distinctly military in meaning," such as statements about the danger of standing armies. *Post*, at 22. But so was the highly influential minority proposal in Pennsylvania, yet that proposal, with its reference to hunting, plainly referred to an individual right. See 2 Documentary Hist. 624. Other than that erroneous point, JUSTICE STEVENS has brought forward absolutely no evidence that those proposals conferred only a right to carry arms in a militia. By contrast, New Hampshire's proposal, the Pennsylvania minority's proposal, and Samuel Adams' proposal in Massachusetts unequivocally referred to individual rights, as did two state constitutional provisions at the time. See Veit 16, 17 (New Hampshire proposal); 6 Documentary Hist. 1452, 1453 (J. Kaminski & G. Saladino eds. 2000) (Samuel Adams' pro- [554 U. S. ____ (2008) 32] posal). JUSTICE STEVENS' view thus relies on the proposition, unsupported by any evidence, that different people of the founding period had vastly different conceptions of the right to keep and bear arms. That simply does not comport with our longstanding view that the Bill of Rights codified venerable, widely understood liberties.

D

virtually all interpreters of the Second Amendment in the century after its enactment interpreted the amendment as we do.

We now address how the Second Amendment was interpreted from immediately after its ratification through the end of the 19th century. Before proceeding, however, we take issue with JUSTICE STEVENS' equating of these sources with postenactment legislative history, a comparison that betrays a fundamental misunderstanding of a court's interpretive task. See *post*, at 27, n. 28. "Legislative history," of course, refers to the pre-enactment statements of those who drafted or voted for a law; it is considered persuasive by some, not because they reflect the general understanding of the disputed terms, but because the legislators who heard or read those statements presumably voted with that understanding. *Ibid.* "Postenactment legislative history," *ibid.*, a deprecatory contradiction in terms, refers to statements of those who drafted or voted for the law that are made after its enactment and hence could have had no effect on the congressional vote. It most certainly does not refer to the examination of a variety of legal and other sources to determine *the public understanding* of a legal text in the period after its enactment or ratification. That sort of inquiry is a critical tool of constitutional interpretation. As we will show, virtually all interpreters of the Second Amendment in the century after its enactment interpreted the amendment as we do.

1. Post-ratification Commentary

Three important founding-era legal scholars interpreted the Second Amendment in published writings. All three understood it to protect an individual right unconnected with militia service.

Three important founding-era legal scholars interpreted [554 U. S. ____ (2008) 33] the Second Amendment in published writings. All three understood it to protect an individual right unconnected with militia service.

Tucker... "This may be considered as the true palladium of liberty . . . . The right to self-defence is the first law of nature... Wherever standing armies are kept up, and the right of the people to keep and bear arms is, under any colour or pretext whatsoever, prohibited, liberty, if not already annihilated, is on the brink of destruction."

St. George Tucker's version of Blackstone's Commentaries, as we explained above, conceived of the Blackstonian arms right as necessary for self-defense. He equated that right, absent the religious and class-based restrictions, with the Second Amendment. See 2 Tucker's Blackstone 143. In Note D, entitled, "View of the Constitution of the United States," Tucker elaborated on the Second Amendment: "This may be considered as the true palladium of liberty . . . . The right to self-defence is the first law of nature: in most governments it has been the study of rulers to confine the right within the narrowest limits possible. Wherever standing armies are kept up, and the right of the people to keep and bear arms is, under any colour or pretext whatsoever, prohibited, liberty, if not already annihilated, is on the brink of destruction." 1 *id.*, at App. 300 (ellipsis in original). He believed that the English game laws had abridged the right by prohibiting "keeping a gun or other engine for the destruction of game." *Ibid*; see also 2 *id.*, at 143, and nn. 40 and 41. He later grouped the right with some of the individual rights included in the First Amendment and said that if "a law be passed by congress, prohibiting" any of those rights, it would "be the province of the judiciary to pronounce whether any such act were constitutional, or not; and if not, to acquit the accused . . . ." 1 *id.*, at App. 357. It is unlikely that Tucker was referring to a person's being "accused" of violating a law making it a crime to bear arms in a state militia. n19

n19 JUSTICE STEVENS quotes some of Tucker's unpublished notes, which he claims show that Tucker had ambiguous views about the Second Amendment. See *post*, at 31, and n. 32. But it is clear from the notes that Tucker located the power of States to arm their militias in the *Tenth* Amendment, and that he cited the Second Amendment for the [554 U. S. ____ (2008) 34] proposition that such armament could not run afoul of any power of the federal government (since the amendment prohibits Congress from ordering disarmament). Nothing in the passage implies that the Second Amendment pertains only to the carrying of arms in the organized militia.

In 1825, William Rawle, a prominent lawyer who had been a member of the Pennsylvania Assembly that ratified the Bill of Rights, published an influential treatise, which analyzed the Second Amendment as follows:

"The first [principle] is a declaration that a well regulated militia is necessary to the security of a free state; a proposition from which few will dissent. . . .

"The corollary, from the first position is, that the right of the people to keep and bear arms shall not be infringed.

Rawle... No clause in the constitution could by any rule of construction be conceived to give to congress a power to disarm the people.

"The prohibition is general. No clause in the constitution could by any rule of construction be conceived to give to congress a power to disarm the people. Such a flagitious attempt could only be made under some general pretence by a state legislature. But if in any blind pursuit of inordinate power, either should attempt it, this amendment may be appealed to as a restraint on both." Rawle 121–122. n20

n20 Rawle, writing before our decision in *Barron ex rel. Tiernan* v. *Mayor of Baltimore*, 7 Pet. 243 (1833), believed that the Second Amendment could be applied against the States. Such a belief would of course be nonsensical on petitioners' view that it protected only a right to possess and carry arms when conscripted by the State itself into militia service.

Like Tucker, Rawle regarded the English game laws as violating the right codified in the Second Amendment.

Like Tucker, Rawle regarded the English game laws as violating the right codified in the Second Amendment. See *id.*, 122–123. Rawle clearly differentiated between the people's right to bear arms and their service in a militia:

Rawle further said that the Second Amendment right ought not "be abused to the disturbance of the public peace," such as by assembling with other armed individuals "for an unlawful purpose"—statements that make no sense if the right does not extend to *any* individual purpose.

"In a people permitted and accustomed to bear arms, we have the rudiments of a militia, which properly consists of armed citizens, divided into military bands, and instructed [554 U. S. ____ (2008) 35] at least in part, in the use of arms for the purposes of war." *Id.*, at 140. Rawle further said that the Second Amendment right ought not "be abused to the disturbance of the public peace," such as by assembling with other armed individuals "for an unlawful purpose"—statements that make no sense if the right does not extend to *any* individual purpose.

JUSTICE STEVENS suggests that "there is not so much as a whisper" in Story's explanation of the Second Amendment that favors the individual-rights view. That is wrong.

Joseph Story published his famous Commentaries on the Constitution of the United States in 1833. JUSTICE STEVENS suggests that "[t]here is not so much as a whisper" in Story's explanation of the Second Amendment that favors the individual-rights view. *Post*, at 34. That is wrong. Story explained that the English Bill of Rights had also included a "right to bear arms," a right that, as we have discussed, had nothing to do with militia service. 3 Story §1858. He then equated the English right with the Second Amendment:

"§1891. A similar provision [to the Second Amendment] in favour of protestants (for to them it is confined) is to be found in the bill of rights of 1688, it being declared, 'that the subjects, which are protestants, may have arms for their defence suitable to their condition, and as allowed by law.' But under various pretences the effect of this provision has been greatly narrowed; and it is at present in England more nominal than real, as a defensive privilege." (Footnotes omitted.)

the passage from Story, shows clearly that this right was intended... and was guaranteed to, and to be exercised and enjoyed by the citizen as such, and not by him as a soldier, or in defense solely of his political rights."

Story... "One of the ordinary modes, by which tyrants accomplish their purposes without resistance, is, by disarming the people, and making it an offence to keep arms ..."

This comparison to the Declaration of Right would not make sense if the Second Amendment right was the right to use a gun in a militia, which was plainly not what the English right protected. As the Tennessee Supreme Court recognized 38 years after Story wrote his Commentaries, "[t]he passage from Story, shows clearly that this right was intended . . . and was guaranteed to, and to be exercised and enjoyed by the citizen as such, and not by him as [554 U. S. ____ (2008) 36] a soldier, or in defense solely of his political rights." *Andrews* v. *State*, 50 Tenn. 165, 183 (1871). Story's Commentaries also cite as support Tucker and Rawle, both of whom clearly viewed the right as unconnected to militia service. See 3 Story §1890, n. 2; §1891, n. 3. In addition, in a shorter 1840 work Story wrote: "One of the ordinary modes, by which tyrants accomplish their purposes without resistance, is, by disarming the people, and making it an offence to keep arms, and by substituting a regular army in the stead of a resort to the militia." A Familiar Exposition of the Constitution of the United States §450 (reprinted in 1986).

Tiffany... "the right to keep and bear arms, also implies the right to use them if necessary in self defence; without this right to use the guaranty would have hardly been worth the paper it consumed."

Antislavery advocates routinely invoked the right to bear arms for self-defense. Joel Tiffany, for example, citing Blackstone's description of the right, wrote that "the right to keep and bear arms, also implies the right to use them if necessary in self defence; without this right to use the guaranty would have hardly been worth the paper it consumed." A Treatise on the Unconstitutionality of American Slavery 117–118 (1849); see also L. Spooner, The Unconstitutionality of Slavery 116 (1845) (right enables "personal defence"). In his famous Senate speech about the 1856 "Bleeding Kansas" conflict, Charles Sumner proclaimed:

"The rifle has ever been the companion of the pioneer and, under God, his tutelary protector against the red man and the beast of the forest. Never was this efficient weapon more needed in just self-defence, than now in Kansas, and at least one article in our National Constitution must be blotted out, before the complete right to it can in any way be impeached.

"The rifle has ever been the companion of the pioneer and, under God, his tutelary protector against the red man and the beast of the forest. Never was this efficient weapon more needed in just self-defence, than now in Kansas, and at least one article in our National Constitution must be blotted out, before the complete right to it can in any way be impeached. And yet such is the madness of the hour, that, in defiance of the solemn guarantee, embodied in the Amendments to the Constitution, that 'the right of the people to keep and bear arms shall not be infringed,'
[554 U. S. ____ (2008) 37] the people of Kansas have been arraigned for keeping and bearing them, and the Senator from South Carolina has had the face to say openly, on this floor, that they should be disarmed—of course, that the fanatics of Slavery, his allies and constituents, may meet no impediment." The Crime Against Kansas, May 19–20, 1856, in American Speeches: Political Oratory from the Revolution to the Civil War 553, 606–607 (2006).

We have found only one early 19th-century commentator who clearly conditioned the right to keep and bear arms upon service in the militia— and he recognized that the prevailing view was to the contrary.

We have found only one early 19th-century commentator who clearly conditioned the right to keep and bear arms upon service in the militia—and he recognized that the prevailing view was to the contrary. "The provision of the constitution, declaring the right of the people to keep and bear arms, &c. was probably intended to apply to the right of the people to bear arms for such [militia-related] purposes only, and not to prevent congress or the legislatures of the different states from enacting laws to prevent the citizens from always going armed. A different construction however has been given to it." B. Oliver, The Rights of an American Citizen 177 (1832).

2. Pre-Civil War Case Law

The 19th-century cases that interpreted the Second Amendment universally support an individual right unconnected to militia service. In *Houston* v. *Moore*, 5 Wheat. 1, 24 (1820), this Court held that States have concurrent power over the militia, at least where not preempted by Congress. Agreeing in dissent that States could "organize, discipline, and arm" the militia in the absence of conflicting federal regulation, Justice Story said that the Second Amendment "may not, perhaps, be thought to have any important bearing on this point. If it have, it confirms and illustrates, rather than impugns the reasoning already suggested." *Id.*, at 51–53. Of course, if the Amendment simply "protect[ed] the right of the people of each of the several States to maintain a well-regulated
[554 U. S. ____ (2008) 38] militia," *post*, at 1 (STEVENS, J., dissenting), it would have enormous and obvious bearing on the point. But the Court and Story derived the States' power over the militia from the nonexclusive nature of federal power, not from the Second Amendment, whose preamble merely "confirms and illustrates" the importance of the militia. Even clearer was Justice Baldwin. In the famous fugitive-slave case of *Johnson* v. *Tompkins*, 13 F. Cas. 840, 850, 852 (CC Pa. 1833), Baldwin, sitting as a circuit judge, cited both the Second Amendment and the Pennsylvania analogue for his conclusion that a citizen has "a right to carry arms in defence of his property or person, and to use them, if

either were assailed with such force, numbers or violence as made it necessary for the protection or safety of either."

Many early 19th-century state cases indicated that the Second Amendment right to bear arms was an individual right unconnected to militia service, though subject to certain restrictions.

Many early 19th-century state cases indicated that the Second Amendment right to bear arms was an individual right unconnected to militia service, though subject to certain restrictions. A Virginia case in 1824 holding that the Constitution did not extend to free blacks explained that "numerous restrictions imposed on [blacks] in our Statute Book, many of which are inconsistent with the letter and spirit of the Constitution, both of this State and of the United States as respects the free whites, demonstrate, that, here, those instruments have not been considered to extend equally to both classes of our population.

We will only instance the restriction upon the migration of free blacks into this State, and upon their right to bear arms." *Aldridge* v. *Commonwealth*, 2 Va. Cas. 447, 449 (Gen. Ct.). The claim was obviously not that blacks were prevented from carrying guns in the militia. n21 See also

n21 JUSTICE STEVENS suggests that this is not obvious because free blacks in Virginia had been required to muster without arms. See *post*, at 28, n. 29 (citing Siegel, The Federal Government's Power to Enact Color-Conscious Laws, 92 Nw. U. L. Rev. 477, 497 (1998)). But that could not have been the type of law referred to in *Aldridge*, because that practice had stopped 30 years earlier when blacks were excluded [554 U. S. ____ (2008) 39] entirely from the militia by the First Militia Act. See Siegel, *supra*, at 498, n. 120. JUSTICE STEVENS further suggests that laws barring blacks from militia service could have been said to violate the "right to bear arms." But under JUSTICE STEVENS' reading of the Second Amendment (we think), the protected right is the right to carry arms to the extent one is enrolled in the militia, not the right *to be in the militia*. Perhaps JUSTICE STEVENS really does adopt the full-blown idiomatic meaning of "bear arms," in which case every man and woman in this country has a right "to be a soldier" or even "to wage war." In any case, it is clear to us that *Aldridge*'s allusion to the existing Virginia "restriction" upon the right of free blacks "to bear arms" could only have referred to "laws prohibiting blacks from keeping weapons," Siegel, *supra,* at 497–498.

because free blacks were treated as a "dangerous population," "laws have been passed to prevent their migration into this State; to make it unlawful for them to bear arms; to guard even their religious assemblages with peculiar watchfulness"

"The constitution of the United States also grants to the citizen the right to keep and bear arms. But the grant of this privilege cannot be construed into the right in him who keeps a gun to destroy his neighbor. No rights are intended to be granted by the constitution for an unlawful or unjustifiable purpose."

Waters v. *State*, 1 Gill 302, 309 (Md. 1843) (because free blacks were treated as a "dangerous population," "laws have been passed to prevent their migration into this State; to make it unlawful for them to bear arms; to guard even their religious assemblages with peculiar watchfulness"). An 1829 decision by the Supreme Court of Michigan said: "The constitution of the United States also grants to the citizen the right to keep and bear arms. But the grant of this privilege cannot be construed into the right in him who keeps a gun to destroy his neighbor. No rights are intended to be granted by the constitution for an unlawful or unjustifiable purpose." *United States* v. *Sheldon*, in 5 Transactions of the Supreme Court of the Territory of Michigan 337, 346 (W. Blume ed. 1940) (hereinafter Blume). It is not possible to read this as discussing anything other than an individual right unconnected to militia service. If it did have to do with militia service, the limitation upon it would not be any "unlawful or unjustifiable purpose," but any nonmilitary purpose whatsoever.

In *Nunn* v. *State*, the Georgia Supreme Court construed the Second Amendment as protecting the "*natural* right of self-defence" and therefore struck down a ban on carrying pistols openly.

In *Nunn* v. *State*, 1 Ga. 243, 251 (1846), the Georgia Supreme Court construed the Second Amendment as protecting the "*natural* right of self-defence" and therefore struck down a ban on carrying pistols openly. Its opinion perfectly captured the way in which the operative clause of the Second Amendment furthers the purpose announced [554 U. S. ____ (2008) 40] in the prefatory clause, in continuity with the English right:

"The right of the whole people, old and young, men, women and boys, and not militia only, to keep and bear *arms* of every description, and not *such* merely as are used by the *militia,* shall not be *infringed,* curtailed, or broken in upon, in the smallest degree

"The right of the whole people, old and young, men, women and boys, and not militia only, to keep and bear *arms* of every description, and not *such* merely as are used by the *militia,* shall not be *infringed,* curtailed, or broken in upon, in the smallest degree; and all this for the important end to be attained: the rearing up and qualifying a well-regulated militia, so vitally necessary to the security of a free State. Our opinion is, that any law, State or Federal, is repugnant to the Constitution, and void, which contravenes this *right,* originally belonging to our forefathers, trampled under foot by Charles I. and his two wicked sons and successors, re-established by the revolution of 1688, conveyed to this land of liberty by the colonists, and finally incorporated conspicuously in our own Magna Charta!"

the Louisiana Supreme Court held that citizens had a right to carry arms openly: "This is the right guaranteed by the Constitution of the United States, and which is calculated to incite men to a manly and noble defence of themselves, if necessary, and of their country, without any tendency to secret advantages and unmanly assassinations."

Likewise, in *State* v. *Chandler*, 5 La. Ann. 489, 490 (1850), the Louisiana Supreme Court held that citizens had a right to carry arms openly: "This is the right guaranteed by the Constitution of the United States, and which is calculated to incite men to a manly and noble defence of themselves, if necessary, and of their country, without any tendency to secret advantages and unmanly assassinations."

"The right to keep arms involves, necessarily, the right to use such arms for all the ordinary purposes, and in all the ordinary modes usual in the country, and to which arms are adapted, limited by the duties of a good citizen in times of peace."

Those who believe that the Second Amendment preserves only a militia-centered right place great reliance on the Tennessee Supreme Court's 1840 decision in *Aymette* v. *State*, 21 Tenn. 154. The case does not stand for that broad proposition; in fact, the case does not mention the word "militia" at all, except in its quoting of the Second Amendment. *Aymette* held that the state constitutional guarantee of the right to "bear" arms did not prohibit the banning of concealed weapons. The opinion first recog- [554 U. S. ____ (2008) 41] nized that both the state right and the federal right were descendents of the 1689 English right, but (erroneously, and contrary to virtually all other authorities) read that right to refer only to "protect[ion of] the public liberty" and "keep[ing] in awe those in power," *id.*, at 158. The court then adopted a sort of middle position, whereby citizens were permitted to carry arms openly, unconnected with any service in a formal militia, but were given the right to use them only for the military purpose of banding together to oppose tyranny. This odd reading of the right is, to be sure, not the one we adopt—but it is not petitioners' reading either. More importantly, seven years earlier the Tennessee Supreme Court had treated the state constitutional provision as conferring a right "of all the free citizens of the State to keep and bear arms for their defence," *Simpson*, 5 Yer., at 360; and 21 years later the court held that the "keep" portion of the state constitutional right included the right to personal self-defense: "[T]he right to keep arms involves, necessarily, the right to use such arms for all the ordinary purposes, and in all the ordinary modes usual in the country, and to which arms are adapted, limited by the duties of a good citizen in times of peace." *Andrews*, 50 Tenn., at 178; see also *ibid.* (equating state provision with Second Amendment).

3. Post-Civil War Legislation.

In the aftermath of the Civil War, there was an outpouring of discussion of the Second Amendment in Congress and in public discourse, as people debated whether and how to secure constitutional rights for newly free slaves.

In the aftermath of the Civil War, there was an outpouring of discussion of the Second Amendment in Congress and in public discourse, as people debated whether and how to secure constitutional rights for newly free slaves. See generally S. Halbrook, Freedmen, the Fourteenth Amendment, and the Right to Bear Arms, 1866–1876 (1998) (hereinafter Halbrook); Brief for Institute for Justice as *Amicus Curiae*. Since those discussions took place 75 years after the ratification of the Second Amendment, they do not provide as much insight into its original mean- [554 U. S. ____ (2008) 42] ing as earlier sources. Yet those born and educated in the early 19th century faced a widespread effort to limit arms ownership by a large number of citizens; their understanding of the origins and continuing significance of the Amendment is instructive.

Blacks were routinely disarmed by Southern States after the Civil War. Those who opposed these injustices frequently stated that they infringed blacks' constitutional right to keep and bear arms.

"The civil law [of Kentucky] prohibits the colored man from bearing arms... Their arms are taken from them by the civil authorities... Thus, the right of the people to keep and bear arms as provided in the Constitution is *infringed*."

Blacks were routinely disarmed by Southern States after the Civil War. Those who opposed these injustices frequently stated that they infringed blacks' constitutional right to keep and bear arms. Needless to say, the claim was not that blacks were being prohibited from carrying arms in an organized state militia. A Report of the Commission of the Freedmen's Bureau in 1866 stated plainly: "[T]he civil law [of Kentucky] prohibits the colored man from bearing arms. . . . Their arms are taken from them by the civil authorities. . . . Thus, the right of the people to keep and bear arms as provided in the Constitution is *infringed*." H. R. Exec. Doc. No. 70, 39th Cong., 1st Sess., 233, 236. A joint congressional Report decried:

"in some parts of [South Carolina], armed parties are, without proper authority, engaged in seizing all firearms found in the hands of the freemen. Such conduct is in clear and direct violation of their personal rights as guaranteed by the Constitution of the United States

"in some parts of [South Carolina], armed parties are, without proper authority, engaged in seizing all firearms found in the hands of the freemen. Such conduct is in clear and direct violation of their personal rights as guaranteed by the Constitution of the United States, which declares that 'the right of the people to keep and bear arms shall not be infringed.' The freedmen of South Carolina have shown by their peaceful and orderly conduct that they can safely be trusted with fire-arms, and they need them to kill game for subsistence, and to protect their crops from destruction by birds and animals." Joint Comm. on Reconstruction, H. R. Rep. No. 30, 39th Cong., 1st Sess., pt. 2, p. 229 (1866) (Proposed Circular of Brigadier General R. Saxton).

"all men, without distinction of color, have the right to keep and bear arms to defend their homes, families or themselves."

The view expressed in these statements was widely reported and was apparently widely held. For example, 554 U. S. ____ (2008) 43] an editorial in The Loyal Georgian (Augusta) on February 3, 1866, assured blacks that "[a]ll men, without distinction of color, have the right to keep and bear arms to defend their homes, families or themselves." Halbrook 19.

Congress enacted the Freedmen's Bureau Act on July 16, 1866. Section 14 stated: "[T]he right . . . to have full and equal benefit of all laws and proceedings concerning personal liberty, personal security, and the acquisition, enjoyment, and disposition of estate, real and personal, including the constitutional right to bear arms, shall be secured to and enjoyed by all the citizens . . . without respect to race or color, or previous condition of slavery. . . . " 14 Stat. 176–177.

the founding generation "were for every man bearing his arms about him and keeping them in his house, his castle, for his own defense."

The understanding that the Second Amendment gave freed blacks the right to keep and bear arms was reflected in congressional discussion of the bill, with even an opponent of it saying that the founding generation "were for every man bearing his arms about him and keeping them in his house, his castle, for his own defense." Cong. Globe, 39th Cong., 1st Sess., 362, 371 (1866) (Sen. Davis).

"Section eight is intended to enforce the well-known constitutional provision guaranteeing the right of the citizen to 'keep and bear arms,' and provides that whoever shall take away, by force or violence, or by threats and intimidation, the arms and weapons which any person may have for his defense, shall be deemed guilty of larceny of the same."

Similar discussion attended the passage of the Civil Rights Act of 1871 and the Fourteenth Amendment. For example, Representative Butler said of the Act: "Section eight is intended to enforce the well-known constitutional provision guaranteeing the right of the citizen to 'keep and bear arms,' and provides that whoever shall take away, by force or violence, or by threats and intimidation, the arms and weapons which any person may have for his defense, shall be deemed guilty of larceny of the same." H. R. Rep. No. 37, 41st Cong., 3d Sess., pp. 7–8 (1871). With respect to the proposed Amendment, Senator Pomeroy described as one of the three "indispensable" "safeguards of liberty . . . under the Constitution" a man's "right to bear arms for the defense of himself and family and his homestead." [554 U. S. ____ (2008) 44] Cong. Globe, 39th Cong., 1st Sess., 1182 (1866).

Representative Nye thought the Fourteenth Amendment unnecessary because "[a]s citizens of the United States [blacks] have equal right to protection, and to keep and bear arms for self-defense." *Id.*, at 1073 (1866).

It was plainly the understanding in the post-Civil War Congress that the Second Amendment protected an individual right to use arms for self-defense.

It was plainly the understanding in the post-Civil War Congress that the Second Amendment protected an individual right to use arms for self-defense.

4. Post-Civil War Commentators.

Every late-19th-century legal scholar that we have read interpreted the Second Amendment to secure an individual right unconnected with militia service.

Every late-19th-century legal scholar that we have read interpreted the Second Amendment to secure an individual right unconnected with militia service. The most famous was the judge and professor Thomas Cooley, who wrote a massively popular 1868 Treatise on Constitutional Limitations. Concerning the Second Amendment it said:

"Among the other defences to personal liberty should be mentioned the right of the people to keep and bear arms. . . . The alternative to a standing army is 'a well-regulated militia,' but this cannot exist unless the people are trained to bearing arms. How far it is in the power of the legislature to regulate this right, we shall not undertake to say, as happily there has been very little occasion to discuss that subject by the courts." *Id.*, at 350.

That Cooley understood the right not as connected to militia service, but as securing the militia by ensuring a populace familiar with arms, is made even clearer in his 1880 work, General Principles of Constitutional Law. The Second Amendment, he said, "was adopted with some modification and enlargement from the English Bill of Rights of 1688, where it stood as a protest against arbitrary action of the overturned dynasty in disarming the people." *Id.*, at 270. In a section entitled "The Right in General," he continued:

"It might be supposed from the phraseology of this provision that the right to keep and bear arms was only guaranteed to the militia; but this would be an interpretation not warranted by the intent

The meaning of the provision undoubtedly is, that the people, from whom the militia must be taken, shall have the right to keep and bear arms; and they need no permission or regulation of law for the purpose.

[554 U. S. ____ (2008) 45] "It might be supposed from the phraseology of this provision that the right to keep and bear arms was only guaranteed to the militia; but this would be an interpretation not warranted by the intent. The militia, as has been elsewhere explained, consists of those persons who, under the law, are liable to the performance of military duty, and are officered and enrolled for service when called upon. But the law may make provision for the enrolment of all who are fit to perform military duty, or of a small number only, or it may wholly omit to make any provision at all; and if the right were limited to those enrolled, the purpose of this guaranty might be defeated altogether by the action or neglect to act of the government it was meant to hold in check. The meaning of the provision undoubtedly is, that the people, from whom the militia must be taken, shall have the right to keep and bear arms; and they need no permission or regulation of law for the purpose. But this enables government to have a well-regulated militia; for to bear arms implies something more than the mere keeping; it implies the learning to handle and use them in a way that makes those who keep them ready for their efficient use; in other words, it implies the right to meet for voluntary discipline in arms, observing in doing so the laws of public order." *Id.*, at 271. All other post-Civil War 19th-century sources we have found concurred with Cooley. One example from each decade will convey the general flavor:

"The purpose of the Second Amendment is to secure a well-armed militia... But a militia would be useless unless the citizens were enabled to exercise themselves in the use of warlike weapons.

"[The purpose of the Second Amendment is] to secure a well-armed militia. . . . But a militia would be useless unless the citizens were enabled to exercise themselves in the use of warlike weapons. To preserve this privilege, and to secure to the people the ability to oppose themselves in military force against the usurpa- [554 U. S. ____ (2008) 46] tions of government, as well as against enemies from without, that government is forbidden by any law or proceeding to invade or destroy the right to keep and bear arms. . . . The clause is analogous to the one securing the freedom of speech and of the press. Freedom, not license, is secured; the fair use, not the libellous abuse, is protected." J. Pomeroy, An Introduction to the Constitutional Law of the United States 152– 153 (1868) (hereinafter Pomeroy).

"As the Constitution of the United States, and the constitutions of several of the states, in terms more or less comprehensive, declare the right of the people to keep and bear arms, it has been a subject of grave discussion, in some of the state courts, whether a statute prohibiting persons, when not on a journey, or as travellers, from *wearing or carrying concealed weapons*, be constitutional. There has been a great difference of opinion on the question." 2 J. Kent, Commentaries on American Law *340, n. 2 (O. Holmes ed., 12th ed. 1873) (hereinafter Kent).

"Some general knowledge of firearms is important to the public welfare; because it would be impossible, in case of war, to organize promptly an efficient force of volunteers unless the people had some familiarity with weapons of war.

No doubt, a citizen who keeps a gun or pistol under judicious precautions, practices in safe places the use of it, and in due time teaches his sons to do the same, exercises his individual right. No doubt, a person whose residence or duties involve peculiar peril may keep a pistol for prudent self-defence."

"Some general knowledge of firearms is important to the public welfare; because it would be impossible, in case of war, to organize promptly an efficient force of volunteers unless the people had some familiarity with weapons of war. The Constitution secures the right of the people to keep and bear arms. No doubt, a citizen who keeps a gun or pistol under judicious precautions, practices in safe places the use of it, and in due time teaches his sons to do the same, exercises his individual right. No doubt, a person whose residence or duties involve peculiar peril may keep a pistol for prudent self-defence." B. Abbott, Judge and Jury: A Popular Explanation of the Leading Topics in the Law of the Land 333 (1880) (hereinafter Abbott).

"The right to bear arms has always been the distinctive privilege of freemen... It was not necessary that the right to bear arms should be granted in the Constitution, for it had always existed."

[554 U. S. ____ (2008) 47] "The right to bear arms has always been the distinctive privilege of freemen. Aside from any necessity of self-protection to the person, it represents among all nations power coupled with the exercise of a certain jurisdiction. . . . [I]t was not necessary that the right to bear arms should be granted in the Constitution, for it had always existed." J. Ordronaux, Constitutional Legislation in the United States 241–242 (1891).

E

We now ask whether any of our precedents forecloses the conclusions we have reached about the meaning of the Second Amendment.

the Second Amendment does not by its own force apply to anyone other than the Federal Government... the right "is not a right granted by the Constitution or in any manner dependent upon that instrument for its existence. The second amendment . . . means no more than that it shall not be infringed by Congress."

United States v. *Cruikshank*, 92 U. S. 542, in the course of vacating the convictions of members of a white mob for depriving blacks of their right to keep and bear arms, held that the Second Amendment does not by its own force apply to anyone other than the Federal Government. The opinion explained that the right "is not a right granted by the Constitution [or] in any manner dependent upon that instrument for its existence. The second amendment . . . means no more than that it shall not be infringed by Congress." 92 U. S., at 553. States, we said, were free to restrict or protect the right under their police powers. The limited discussion of the Second Amendment in *Cruikshank* supports, if anything, the individual-rights interpretation. There was no claim in *Cruikshank* that the victims had been deprived of their right to carry arms in a militia; indeed, the Governor had disbanded the local militia unit the year before the mob's attack, see C. Lane, The Day Freedom Died 62 (2008). We described the right protected by the Second Amendment as " 'bearing arms for a lawful purpose' " n22 and said that "the people [must] look

n22 JUSTICE STEVENS' accusation that this is "not accurate," *post*, at 39, [554 U. S. ____ (2008) 48] is wrong. It is true it was the indictment that described the right as "bearing arms for a lawful purpose." But, in explicit reference to the right described in the indictment, the Court stated that "The second amendment declares that it [*i.e.,* the right of bearing arms for a lawful purpose] shall not be infringed." 92 U. S., at 553.

for their protection against any violation by their fellow-citizens of the rights it recognizes" to the States' police power. 92 U. S., at 553. That discussion makes little sense if it is only a right to bear arms in a state militia. n23

With respect to *Cruikshank*'s continuing validity on incorporation, a question not presented by this case, we note that *Cruikshank* also said that the First Amendment did not apply against the States and did not engage in the sort of Fourteenth Amendment inquiry required by our later cases.

n23 With respect to *Cruikshank*'s continuing validity on incorporation, a question not presented by this case, we note that *Cruikshank* also said that the First Amendment did not apply against the States and did not engage in the sort of Fourteenth Amendment inquiry required by our later cases. Our later decisions in *Presser* v. *Illinois*, 116 U. S. 252, 265 (1886) and *Miller* v. *Texas*, 153 U. S. 535, 538 (1894), reaffirmed that the Second Amendment applies only to the Federal Government.

the right to keep and bear arms was not violated by a law that forbade "bodies of men to associate together as military organizations, or to drill or parade with arms in cities and towns unless authorized by law."
This does not refute the individual-rights interpretation of the Amendment; no one supporting that interpretation has contended that States may not ban such groups.

JUSTICE STEVENS' statement that *Presser* "suggested that... nothing in the Constitution protected the use of arms outside the context of a militia," is simply wrong. *Presser* said nothing about the Second Amendment's meaning or scope, beyond the fact that it does not prevent the prohibition of private paramilitary organizations.

Presser v. *Illinois*, 116 U. S. 252 (1886), held that the right to keep and bear arms was not violated by a law that forbade "bodies of men to associate together as military organizations, or to drill or parade with arms in cities and towns unless authorized by law." *Id.*, at 264–265. This does not refute the individual-rights interpretation of the Amendment; no one supporting that interpretation has contended that States may not ban such groups. JUSTICE STEVENS presses *Presser* into service to support his view that the right to bear arms is limited to service in the militia by joining *Presser*'s brief discussion of the Second Amendment with a later portion of the opinion making the seemingly relevant (to the Second Amendment) point that the plaintiff was not a member of the state militia. Unfortunately for JUSTICE STEVENS' argument, that later portion deals with the *Fourteenth Amendment*; it was the *Fourteenth Amendment* to which the plaintiff's nonmembership in the militia was relevant. Thus, JUSTICE STEVENS' statement that *Presser* "suggested that... nothing in the Constitution protected the use of arms outside the context of a militia," *post*, at 40, is simply wrong. [554 U. S. ____ (2008) 49] *Presser* said nothing about the Second Amendment's meaning or scope, beyond the fact that it does not prevent the prohibition of private paramilitary organizations.

JUSTICE STEVENS places overwhelming reliance upon this Court's decision in *United States* v. *Miller*. "Hundreds of judges," we are told, "have relied on the view of the amendment we endorsed there... respect for the well-settled views of all of our predecessors on this Court, and for the rule of law itself... would prevent most jurists from endorsing such a dramatic upheaval in the law"

JUSTICE STEVENS places overwhelming reliance upon this Court's decision in *United States* v. *Miller*, 307 U. S. 174 (1939). "[H]undreds of judges," we are told, "have relied on the view of the amendment we endorsed there," *post*, at 2, and "[e]ven if the textual and historical arguments on both side of the issue were evenly balanced, respect for the well-settled views of all of our predecessors on this Court, and for the rule of law itself . . . would prevent most jurists from endorsing such a dramatic upheaval in the law," *post*, at 4. And what is, according to JUSTICE STEVENS, the holding of *Miller* that demands such obeisance? That the Second Amendment "protects the right to keep and bear arms for certain military purposes, but that it does not curtail the legislature's power to regulate the nonmilitary use and ownership of weapons." *Post*, at 2.

Nothing so clearly demonstrates the weakness of JUSTICE STEVENS' case. *Miller* did not hold that and cannot possibly be read to have held that.

the Court's basis for saying that the Second Amendment did not apply was *not* that the defendants were "bearing arms" not "for... military purposes" but for "nonmilitary use". Rather, it was that the *type of weapon at issue* was not eligible for Second Amendment protection: "In the absence of any evidence tending to show that the possession or use of a shortbarreled shotgun at this time has some reasonable relationship to the preservation or efficiency of a well regulated militia, we cannot say that the Second Amendment guarantees the right to keep and bear *such an instrument.*"

Nothing so clearly demonstrates the weakness of JUSTICE STEVENS' case. *Miller* did not hold that and cannot possibly be read to have held that. The judgment in the case upheld against a Second Amendment challenge two men's federal convictions for transporting an unregistered short-barreled shotgun in interstate commerce, in violation of the National Firearms Act, 48 Stat. 1236. It is entirely clear that the Court's basis for saying that the Second Amendment did not apply was *not* that the defendants were "bear[ing] arms" not "for . . . military purposes" but for "nonmilitary use," *post*, at 2. Rather, it was that the *type of weapon at issue* was not eligible for Second Amendment protection: "In the absence of any evidence tending to show that the possession or use of a [shortbarreled shotgun] at this time has some reasonable relationship to the preservation or efficiency of a well regulated militia, we cannot say that the Second Amendment [554 U. S. ____ (2008) 50] guarantees the right to keep and bear *such an instrument.*" 307 U. S., at 178 (emphasis added). "Certainly," the Court continued, "it is not within judicial notice that this weapon is any part of the ordinary military equipment or that its use could contribute to the common defense." *Ibid.* Beyond that, the opinion provided no explanation of the content of the right.

This holding is not only consistent with, but positively suggests, that the Second Amendment confers an individual right to keep and bear arms (though only arms that "have some reasonable relationship to the preservation or efficiency of a well regulated militia").

Had the Court believed that the Second Amendment protects only those serving in the militia, it would have been odd to examine the character of the weapon rather than simply note that the two crooks were not militiamen.

The most JUSTICE STEVENS can plausibly claim for *Miller* is that it declined to decide the nature of the Second Amendment right

Miller stands only for the proposition that the Second Amendment right, whatever its nature, extends only to certain types of weapons.

This holding is not only consistent with, but positively suggests, that the Second Amendment confers an individual right to keep and bear arms (though only arms that "have some reasonable relationship to the preservation or efficiency of a well regulated militia"). Had the Court believed that the Second Amendment protects only those serving in the militia, it would have been odd to examine the character of the weapon rather than simply note that the two crooks were not militiamen. JUSTICE STEVENS can say again and again that *Miller* did "not turn on the difference between muskets and sawed-off shotguns, it turned, rather, on the basic difference between the military and nonmilitary use and possession of guns," *post*, at 42–43, but the words of the opinion prove otherwise. The most JUSTICE STEVENS can plausibly claim for *Miller* is that it declined to decide the nature of the Second Amendment right, despite the Solicitor General's argument (made in the alternative) that the right was collective, see Brief for United States, O. T. 1938, No. 696, Pp. 4–5. *Miller* stands only for the proposition that the Second Amendment right, whatever its nature, extends only to certain types of weapons.

It is particularly wrongheaded to read *Miller* for more than what it said

The respondent made no appearance in the case, neither filing a brief nor appearing at oral argument; the Court heard from no one but the Government (reason enough, one would think, not to make that case the beginning and the end of this Court's consideration of the Second Amendment).

The Government's *Miller* brief thus provided scant discussion of the history of the Second Amendment—and the Court was presented with no counterdiscussion... As for the text of the Court's opinion itself, that discusses *none* of the history of the Second Amendment. It assumes from the prologue that the Amendment was designed to preserve the militia, (which we do not dispute), and in particular with the nature of the arms their members were expected to possess.

Not a word *(not a word)* about the history of the Second Amendment. This is the mighty rock upon which the dissent rests its case.

It is particularly wrongheaded to read *Miller* for more than what it said, because the case did not even purport to be a thorough examination of the Second Amendment. JUSTICE STEVENS claims, *post*, at 42, that the opinion reached its conclusion "[a]fter reviewing many of the same sources that are discussed at greater length by the Court today." Not many, which was not entirely the Court's [554 U. S. ___ (2008) 51] fault. The respondent made no appearance in the case, neither filing a brief nor appearing at oral argument; the Court heard from no one but the Government (reason enough, one would think, not to make that case the beginning and the end of this Court's consideration of the Second Amendment). See Frye, The Peculiar Story of *United States* v. *Miller*, 3 N. Y. U. J. L. & Liberty 48, 65–68 (2008). The Government's brief spent two pages discussing English legal sources, concluding "that at least the carrying of weapons without lawful occasion or excuse was always a crime" and that (because of the class-based restrictions and the prohibition on terrorizing people with dangerous or unusual weapons) "the early English law did not guarantee an unrestricted right to bear arms." Brief for United States, O. T. 1938, No. 696, at 9–11. It then went on to rely primarily on the discussion of the English right to bear arms in *Aymette* v. *State*, 21 Tenn. 154, for the proposition that the only uses of arms protected by the Second Amendment are those that relate to the militia, not self-defense. See Brief for United States, O. T. 1938, No. 696, at 12–18. The final section of the brief recognized that "some courts have said that the right to bear arms includes the right of the individual to have them for the protection of his person and property," and launched an alternative argument that "weapons which are commonly used by criminals," such as sawed-off shotguns, are not protected. See *id.*, at 18–21. The Government's *Miller* brief thus provided scant discussion of the history of the Second Amendment—and the Court was presented with no counterdiscussion. As for the text of the Court's opinion itself, that discusses *none* of the history of the Second Amendment. It assumes from the prologue that the Amendment was designed to preserve the militia, 307 U. S., at 178 (which we do not dispute), and then reviews some historical materials dealing with the nature of the militia, and in particular with the nature of the arms their [554 U. S. ____ (2008) 52] members were expected to possess, *id.*, at 178–182. Not a word *(not a word)* about the history of the Second Amendment. This is the mighty rock upon which the dissent rests its case. n24

As for the "hundreds of judges"... their erroneous reliance upon an uncontested and virtually unreasoned case <*Miller*> cannot nullify the reliance of millions of Americans (as our historical analysis has shown) upon the true meaning of the right to keep and bear arms.

n24 As for the "hundreds of judges," *post*, at 2, who have relied on the view of the Second Amendment JUSTICE STEVENS claims we endorsed in *Miller*: If so, they overread *Miller*. And their erroneous reliance upon an uncontested and virtually unreasoned case cannot nullify the reliance of millions of Americans (as our historical analysis has shown) upon the true meaning of the right to keep and bear arms. In any event, it should not be thought that the cases decided by these judges would necessarily have come out differently under a proper interpretation of the right.

We may as well consider at this point (for we will have to consider eventually) *what* types of weapons *Miller* permits.

"In the colonial and revolutionary war era, [small-arms] weapons used by militiamen and weapons used in defense of person and home were one and the same."

We therefore read *Miller* to say only that the Second Amendment does not protect those weapons not typically possessed by law-abiding citizens for lawful purposes, such as short-barreled shotguns.

We may as well consider at this point (for we will have to consider eventually) *what* types of weapons *Miller* permits. Read in isolation, *Miller's* phrase "part of ordinary military equipment" could mean that only those weapons useful in warfare are protected. That would be a startling reading of the opinion, since it would mean that the National Firearms Act's restrictions on machineguns (not challenged in *Miller*) might be unconstitutional, machineguns being useful in warfare in 1939. We think that *Miller's* "ordinary military equipment" language must be read in tandem with what comes after: "[O]rdinarily when called for [militia] service [able-bodied] men were expected to appear bearing arms supplied by themselves and of the kind in common use at the time." 307 U. S., at 179. The traditional militia was formed from a pool of men bringing arms "in common use at the time" for lawful purposes like self-defense. "In the colonial and revolutionary war era, [small-arms] weapons used by militiamen and weapons used in defense of person and home were one and the same." *State* v. *Kessler*, 289 Ore. 359, 368, 614 P. 2d 94, 98 (1980) (citing G. Neumann, Swords and Blades of the American Revolution 6–15, 252–254 (1973)). Indeed, that is precisely the way in which the Second [554 U. S. ____ (2008) 53] Amendment's operative clause furthers the purpose announced in its preface. We therefore read *Miller* to say only that the Second Amendment does not protect those weapons not typically possessed by law-abiding citizens for lawful purposes, such as short-barreled shotguns. That accords with the historical understanding of the scope of the right, see Part III, *infra*. n25

Lewis v. United States... an appeal from a conviction for being a felon in possession of a firearm ... In the course of rejecting the asserted challenge, the Court commented gratuitously, in a footnote, that "[t]hese

legislative restrictions on the use of firearms are neither based upon constitutionally suspect criteria, nor do they trench upon any constitutionally protected liberties... It is inconceivable that we would rest our interpretation of the basic meaning of any guarantee of the Bill of Rights upon such a footnoted dictum in a case where the point was not at issue and was not argued.

n25 *Miller* was briefly mentioned in our decision in *Lewis* v. *United States*, 445 U. S. 55 (1980), an appeal from a conviction for being a felon in possession of a firearm. The challenge was based on the contention that the prior felony conviction had been unconstitutional. No Second Amendment claim was raised or briefed by any party. In the course of rejecting the asserted challenge, the Court commented gratuitously, in a footnote, that "[t]hese legislative restrictions on the use of firearms are neither based upon constitutionally suspect criteria, nor do they trench upon any constitutionally protected liberties. See *United States* v. *Miller* . . . (the Second Amendment guarantees no right to keep and bear a firearm that does not have 'some reasonable relationship to the preservation or efficiency of a well regulated militia')." *Id.,* at 65–66, n. 8. The footnote then cites several Court of Appeals cases to the same effect. It is inconceivable that we would rest our interpretation of the basic meaning of any guarantee of the Bill of Rights upon such a footnoted dictum in a case where the point was not at issue and was not argued.

We conclude that nothing in our precedents forecloses our adoption of the original understanding of the Second Amendment.

It should be unsurprising that such a significant matter has been for so long judicially unresolved. For most of our history, the Bill of Rights was not thought applicable to the States, and the Federal Government did not significantly regulate the possession of firearms by law-abiding citizens.

This Court first held a law to violate the First Amendment's guarantee of freedom of speech in 1931, almost 150 years after the Amendment was ratified, see *Near* v. *Minnesota* (1931), and it was not until after World War II that we held a law invalid under the Establishment Clause, see *Illinois ex rel. McCollum* v. *Board of Ed. of School Dist. No. 71, Champaign Cty.,* (1948). Even a question as basic as the scope of proscribable libel was not addressed by this Court until 1964, nearly two centuries after the founding, See *New York Times Co.* v. *Sullivan.*

It is demonstrably not true that, as JUSTICE STEVENS claims, "for most of our history, the invalidity of Second-Amendment-based objections to firearms regulations has been well settled and uncontroversial." For most of our history the question did not present itself.

We conclude that nothing in our precedents forecloses our adoption of the original understanding of the Second Amendment. It should be unsurprising that such a significant matter has been for so long judicially unresolved. For most of our history, the Bill of Rights was not thought applicable to the States, and the Federal Government did not significantly regulate the possession of firearms by law-abiding citizens. Other provisions of the Bill of Rights have similarly remained unilluminated for lengthy periods. This Court first held a law to violate the First Amendment's guarantee of freedom of speech in 1931, almost 150 years after the Amendment was ratified, see *Near* v. *Minnesota ex rel. Olson*, 283 U. S. 697 (1931), and it was not until after World War II that we held a law [554 U. S. ___ (2008) 54] invalid under the Establishment Clause, see *Illinois ex rel. McCollum* v. *Board of Ed. of School Dist. No. 71, Champaign Cty.*, 333 U. S. 203 (1948). Even a question as basic as the scope of proscribable libel was not addressed by this Court until 1964, nearly two centuries after the founding. See *New York Times Co.* v. *Sullivan*, 376 U. S. 254 (1964). It is demonstrably not true that, as JUSTICE STEVENS claims, *post*, at 41–42, "for most of our history, the invalidity of Second-Amendment-based objections to firearms regulations has been well settled and uncontroversial." For most of our history the question did not present itself.

III

Like most rights, the right secured by the Second Amendment is not unlimited. From Blackstone through the 19th-century cases, commentators and courts routinely explained that the right was not a right to keep and carry any weapon whatsoever in any manner whatsoever and for whatever purpose.

prohibitions on carrying concealed weapons were lawful under the Second Amendment or state analogues.

Although we do not undertake an exhaustive historical analysis today of the full scope of the Second Amendment, nothing in our opinion should be taken to cast doubt on longstanding prohibitions on the possession of firearms by felons and the mentally ill, or laws forbidding the carrying of firearms in sensitive places such as schools and government buildings, or laws imposing conditions and qualifications on the commercial sale of arms.

Like most rights, the right secured by the Second Amendment is not unlimited. From Blackstone through the 19th-century cases, commentators and courts routinely explained that the right was not a right to keep and carry any weapon whatsoever in any manner whatsoever and for whatever purpose. See, *e.g.*, *Sheldon*, in 5 Blume 346; Rawle 123; Pomeroy 152–153; Abbott 333. For example, the majority of the 19th-century courts to consider the question held that prohibitions on carrying concealed weapons were lawful under the Second Amendment or state analogues. See, *e.g.*, *State* v. *Chandler*, 5 La. Ann., at 489–490; *Nunn* v. *State*, 1 Ga., at 251; see generally 2 Kent *340, n. 2; The American Students' Blackstone 84, n. 11 (G. Chase ed. 1884). Although we do not undertake an exhaustive historical analysis today of the full scope of the Second Amendment, nothing in our opinion should be taken to cast doubt on longstanding prohibitions on the possession of firearms by felons and the mentally ill, or laws forbidding the carrying of firearms in sensitive places such as schools and government buildings, or laws imposing conditions and qualifications on the commercial sale of [554 U. S. ___ (2008) 55] arms. n26

n26 We identify these presumptively lawful regulatory measures only as examples; our list does not purport to be exhaustive.

We also recognize another important limitation on the right to keep and carry arms. *Miller* said, as we have explained, that the sorts of weapons protected were those "in common use at the time." We think that limitation is fairly supported by the historical tradition of prohibiting the carrying of "dangerous and unusual weapons."

We also recognize another important limitation on the right to keep and carry arms. *Miller* said, as we have explained, that the sorts of weapons protected were those "in common use at the time." 307 U. S., at 179. We think that limitation is fairly supported by the historical tradition of prohibiting the carrying of "dangerous and unusual weapons." See 4 Blackstone 148–149 (1769); 3 B. Wilson, Works of the Honourable James Wilson 79 (1804); J. Dunlap, The New-York Justice 8 (1815); C. Humphreys, A Compendium of the Common Law in Force in Kentucky 482 (1822); 1 W. Russell, A Treatise on Crimes and Indictable Misdemeanors 271–272 (1831); H. Stephen, Summary of the Criminal Law 48 (1840); E. Lewis, An Abridgment of the Criminal Law of the United States 64 (1847); F. Wharton, A Treatise on the Criminal Law of the United States 726 (1852). See also *State* v. *Langford*, 10 N. C. 381, 383–384 (1824); *O'Neill* v. *State*, 16 Ala. 65, 67 (1849); *English* v. *State*, 35 Tex. 473, 476 (1871); *State* v. *Lanier*, 71 N. C. 288, 289 (1874).

It may be objected that if weapons that are most useful in military service—M-16 rifles and the like—may be banned, then the Second Amendment right is completely detached from the prefatory clause.

It may well be true today that a militia, to be as effective as militias in the 18th century, would require sophisticated arms that are highly unusual in society at large.

it may be true that no amount of small arms could be useful against modern-day bombers and tanks. But the fact that modern developments have limited the degree of fit between the prefatory clause and the protected right cannot change our interpretation of the right.

It may be objected that if weapons that are most useful in military service—M-16 rifles and the like—may be banned, then the Second Amendment right is completely detached from the prefatory clause. But as we have said, the conception of the militia at the time of the Second Amendment's ratification was the body of all citizens capable of military service, who would bring the sorts of lawful weapons that they possessed at home to militia duty. It may well be true today that a militia, to be as effective as militias in the 18th century, would require sophisticated arms that are highly unusual in society at large. Indeed, it may be true that no amount of small arms could be useful against modern-day bombers and [554 U. S. ____ (2008) 56] tanks. But the fact that modern developments have limited the degree of fit between the prefatory clause and the protected right cannot change our interpretation of the right.

IV

We turn finally to the law at issue here. As we have said, the law totally bans handgun possession in the home. It also requires that any lawful firearm in the home be disassembled or bound by a trigger lock at all times, rendering it inoperable.

**As the quotations earlier in this opinion demonstrate, the inherent right of self-defense has been central to the Second Amendment right. The handgun ban amounts to a prohibition of an entire class of "arms" that is overwhelmingly chosen by American society for that lawful purpose.
"arms" that is overwhelmingly chosen by American society for that lawful purpose. The prohibition extends, moreover, to the home, where the need for defense of self, family, and property is most acute.**

As the quotations earlier in this opinion demonstrate, the inherent right of self-defense has been central to the Second Amendment right. The handgun ban amounts to a prohibition of an entire class of "arms" that is overwhelmingly chosen by American society for that lawful purpose. The prohibition extends, moreover, to the home, where the need for defense of self, family, and property is most acute. Under any of the standards of scrutiny that we have applied to enumerated constitutional rights, n27 banning from

JUSTICE BREYER correctly notes that this law, like almost all laws, would pass rational-basis scrutiny.

Obviously, the same test could not be used to evaluate the extent to which a legislature may regulate a specific, enumerated right, be it the freedom of speech, the guarantee against double jeopardy, the right to counsel, or the right to keep and bear arms.

If all that was required to overcome the right to keep and bear arms was a rational basis, the Second Amendment would be redundant with the separate constitutional prohibitions on irrational laws, and would have no effect.

n27 JUSTICE BREYER correctly notes that this law, like almost all laws, would pass rational-basis scrutiny. *Post*, at 8. But rational-basis scrutiny is a mode of analysis we have used when evaluating laws under constitutional commands that are themselves prohibitions on irrational laws. See, *e.g.*, *Engquist* v. *Oregon Dept. of Agriculture*, 553 U. S. ___, ___ (2008) (slip op., at 9–10). In those cases, "rational basis" is not just the standard of scrutiny, but the very substance of the constitutional guarantee. Obviously, the same test could not be used to evaluate the extent to which a legislature may regulate a specific, enumerated right, be it the freedom of speech, the guarantee against double jeopardy, the right to counsel, or the right to keep and bear arms. See *United States* v. *Carolene Products Co.*, 304 U. S. 144, 152, n. 4 (1938) ("There may be narrower scope for operation of the presumption of constitutionality [*i.e.*, narrower than that provided by rational-basis review] when legislation appears on its face to be within a specific prohibition of the Constitution, such as those of the first ten amendments. . ."). If all that was required to overcome the right to keep and bear arms was a rational basis, the Second Amendment would be redundant with the separate constitutional prohibitions on irra- [554 U. S. ____ (2008) 57] tional laws, and would have no effect.

banning from the home "the most preferred firearm in the nation to 'keep' and use for protection of one's home and family," 478 F. 3d, at 400, would fail constitutional muster.

the home "the most preferred firearm in the nation to 'keep' and use for protection of one's home and family," 478 F. 3d, at 400, would fail constitutional muster.

"A statute which, under the pretence of regulating, amounts to a destruction of the right, or which requires arms to be so borne as to render them wholly useless for the purpose of defence, would be clearly unconstitutional"

Few laws in the history of our Nation have come close to the severe restriction of the District's handgun ban. And some of those few have been struck down. In *Nunn* v. *State*, the Georgia Supreme Court struck down a prohibition on carrying pistols openly (even though it upheld a prohibition on carrying concealed weapons). See 1 Ga., at 251. In *Andrews* v. *State*, the Tennessee Supreme Court likewise held that a statute that forbade openly carrying a pistol "publicly or privately, without regard to time or place, or circumstances," 50 Tenn., at 187, violated the state constitutional provision (which the court equated with the Second Amendment). That was so even though the statute did not restrict the carrying of long guns. *Ibid.* See also *State* v. *Reid*, 1 Ala. 612, 616–617 (1840) ("A statute which, under the pretence of regulating, amounts to a destruction of the right, or which requires arms to be so borne as to render them wholly useless for the purpose of defence, would be clearly unconstitutional").

the American people have considered the handgun to be the quintessential self-defense weapon.

a handgun... can be pointed at a burglar with one hand while the other hand dials the police.

handguns are the most popular weapon chosen by Americans for self-defense in the home, and a complete prohibition of their use is invalid.

It is no answer to say, as petitioners do, that it is permissible to ban the possession of handguns so long as the possession of other firearms (*i.e.*, long guns) is allowed. It is enough to note, as we have observed, that the American people have considered the handgun to be the quintessential self-defense weapon. There are many reasons that a citizen may prefer a handgun for home defense: It is easier to store in a location that is readily accessible in an emergency; it cannot easily be redirected or wrestled away by an attacker; it is easier to use for those without the upper-body strength to lift and aim a long gun; it can be pointed at a burglar with one hand while the other hand dials the police. Whatever the reason, handguns are the most popu- [554 U. S. ____ (2008) 58] lar weapon chosen by Americans for self-defense in the home, and a complete prohibition of their use is invalid.

We must also address the District's requirement (as applied to respondent's handgun) that firearms in the home be rendered and kept inoperable at all times. This makes it impossible for citizens to use them for the core lawful purpose of self-defense and is hence unconstitutional. The District argues that we should interpret this element of the statute to contain an exception for self-defense. But we think that is precluded by the unequivocal text

We must also address the District's requirement (as applied to respondent's handgun) that firearms in the home be rendered and kept inoperable at all times. This makes it impossible for citizens to use them for the core lawful purpose of self-defense and is hence unconstitutional. The District argues that we should interpret this element of the statute to contain an exception for self-defense. See Brief for Petitioners 56–57. But we think that is precluded by the unequivocal text, and by the presence of certain other enumerated exceptions: "Except for law enforcement personnel . . . , each registrant shall keep any firearm in his possession unloaded and disassembled or bound by a trigger lock or similar device unless such firearm is kept at his place of business, or while being used for lawful recreational purposes within the District of Columbia." D. C. Code §7–2507.02. The nonexistence of a self-defense exception is also suggested by the D. C. Court of Appeals' statement that the statute forbids residents to use firearms to stop intruders, see *McIntosh* v. *Washington*, 395 A. 2d 744, 755–756 (1978). n28

n28 *McIntosh* upheld the law against a claim that it violated the Equal Protection Clause by arbitrarily distinguishing between residences and businesses. See 395 A. 2d, at 755. One of the rational bases listed for that distinction was the legislative finding "that for each intruder stopped by a firearm there are four gun-related accidents within the home." *Ibid.* That tradeoff would not bear mention if the statute did not prevent stopping intruders by firearms.

the District "may not prevent [a handgun] from being moved throughout one's house."

Respondent conceded at oral argument that he does not "have a problem with... licensing" and that the District's law is permissible so long as it is "not enforced in an arbitrary and capricious manner."

We therefore assume that petitioners' issuance of a license will satisfy respondent's prayer for relief and do not address the licensing requirement.

Apart from his challenge to the handgun ban and the trigger-lock requirement respondent asked the District Court to enjoin petitioners from enforcing the separate licensing requirement "in such a manner as to forbid the carrying of a firearm within one's home or possessed land without a license." App. 59a. The Court of Appeals did not invalidate the licensing requirement, but held only [554 U. S. ___ (2008) 59] that the District "may not prevent [a handgun] from being moved throughout one's house." 478 F. 3d, at 400. It then ordered the District Court to enter summary judgment "consistent with [respondent's] prayer for relief." *Id.*, at 401. Before this Court petitioners have stated that "if the handgun ban is struck down and respondent registers a handgun, he could obtain a license, assuming he is not otherwise disqualified," by which they apparently mean if he is not a felon and is not insane. Brief for Petitioners 58. Respondent conceded at oral argument that he does not "have a problem with . . . licensing" and that the District's law is permissible so long as it is "not enforced in an arbitrary and capricious manner." Tr. of Oral Arg. 74–75. We therefore assume that petitioners' issuance of a license will satisfy respondent's prayer for relief and do not address the licensing requirement.

JUSTICE BREYER has devoted most of his separate dissent to the handgun ban. He says that, even assuming the Second Amendment is a personal guarantee of the right to bear arms, the District's prohibition is valid.

Of the laws he cites, only one offers even marginal support for his assertion. A 1783 Massachusetts law... That statute's text and its prologue, which makes clear that the purpose of the prohibition was to eliminate the danger to firefighters posed by the "depositing of loaded Arms" in buildings, give reason to doubt that colonial Boston authorities would have enforced that general prohibition against someone who temporarily loaded a firearm to confront an intruder (despite the law's application in that case).

In any case, we would not stake our interpretation of the Second Amendment upon a single law, in effect in a single city, that contradicts the overwhelming weight of other evidence regarding the right to keep and bear arms for defense of the home.

Nothing about those fire-safety laws undermines our analysis; they do not remotely burden the right of self defense as much as an absolute ban on handguns.

Nor, correspondingly, does our analysis suggest the invalidity of laws regulating the storage of firearms to prevent accidents.

JUSTICE BREYER has devoted most of his separate dissent to the handgun ban. He says that, even assuming the Second Amendment is a personal guarantee of the right to bear arms, the District's prohibition is valid. He first tries to establish this by founding-era historical precedent, pointing to various restrictive laws in the colonial period. These demonstrate, in his view, that the District's law "imposes a burden upon gun owners that seems proportionately no greater than restrictions in existence at the time the Second Amendment was adopted." *Post*, at 2. Of the laws he cites, only one offers even marginal support for his assertion. A 1783 Massachusetts law forbade the residents of Boston to "take into" or "receive into" "any Dwelling House, Stable, Barn, Out-house, Ware-house, Store, Shop or other Building" loaded firearms, and permitted the seizure of any loaded firearms that "shall be found" there. Act of Mar. 1, 1783, ch. 13, 1783 Mass. Acts p. 218. That statute's text and its prologue, which makes clear that the purpose of the prohibition was to eliminate the danger to firefighters posed by the "depositing of [554 U. S. ___ (2008) 60] loaded Arms" in buildings, give reason to doubt that colonial Boston authorities would have enforced that general prohibition against someone who temporarily loaded a firearm to confront an intruder (despite the law's application in that case). In any case, we would not stake our interpretation of the Second Amendment upon a single law, in effect in a single city, that contradicts the overwhelming weight of other evidence regarding the right to keep and bear arms for defense of the home. The other laws JUSTICE BREYER cites are gunpowder-storage laws that he concedes did not clearly prohibit loaded weapons, but required only that excess gunpowder be kept in a special container or on the top floor of the home. *Post*, at 6–7. Nothing about those fire-safety laws undermines our analysis; they do not remotely burden the right of self defense as much as an absolute ban on handguns. Nor, correspondingly, does our analysis suggest the invalidity of laws regulating the storage of firearms to prevent accidents.

JUSTICE BREYER points to other founding-era laws that he says "restricted the firing of guns within the city limits to at least some degree"... New York law levied a fine of 20 shillings on anyone who fired a gun in certain places (including houses) on New Year's Eve and the first two days of January, and was aimed at preventing the "great Damages... frequently done on those days by persons going House to House, with Guns and other Firearms and being often intoxicated with Liquor."... JUSTICE BREYER cites a Rhode Island law that simply levied a 5- shilling fine on those who fired guns in *streets* and *taverns*, a law obviously inapplicable to this case.

JUSTICE BREYER points to other founding-era laws that he says "restricted the firing of guns within the city limits to at least some degree" in Boston, Philadelphia and New York. *Post*, at 4 (citing Churchill, Gun Regulation, the Police Power, and the Right to Keep Arms in Early America, 25 Law & Hist. Rev. 139, 162 (2007)). Those laws provide no support for the severe restriction in the present case. The New York law levied a fine of 20 shillings on anyone who fired a gun in certain places (including houses) on New Year's Eve and the first two days of January, and was aimed at preventing the "great Damages . . . frequently done on [those days] by persons going House to House, with Guns and other Firearms and being often intoxicated with Liquor." 5 Colonial Laws of New York 244–246 (1894). It is inconceivable that this law would have been enforced against a person exercising his right to self-defense on New Year's Day against such drunken [554 U. S. ___ (2008) 61] hooligans. The Pennsylvania law to which JUSTICE BREYER refers levied a fine of 5 shillings on one who fired a gun or set off fireworks in Philadelphia without first obtaining a license from the governor. See Act of Aug. 26, 1721, §4, in 3 Stat. at Large 253–254. Given Justice Wilson's explanation that the right to self-defense with arms was protected by the Pennsylvania Constitution, it is unlikely that this law (which in any event amounted to at most a licensing regime) would have been enforced against a person who used firearms for self-defense. JUSTICE BREYER cites a Rhode Island law that simply levied a 5- shilling fine on those who fired guns in *streets* and *taverns*, a law obviously inapplicable to this case. See An Act for preventing Mischief being done in the town of Newport, or in any other town in this Government, 1731, Rhode Island Session Laws. Finally, JUSTICE BREYER points to a Massachusetts law similar to the Pennsylvania law, prohibiting "discharg[ing] any Gun or Pistol charged with Shot or Ball in the Town of *Boston*." Act of May 28, 1746, ch. X, Acts and Laws of Mass. Bay 208. It is again implausible that this would have been enforced against a citizen acting in self-defense, particularly given its preambulatory reference to "the *indiscreet* firing of Guns." *Ibid.* (preamble) (emphasis added).

A broader point about the laws that JUSTICE BREYER cites: All of them punished the discharge (or loading) of guns with a small fine and forfeiture of the weapon (or in a few cases a very brief stay in the local jail), not with significant criminal penalties. n29 They are akin to modern penalties for minor public-safety infractions like speeding

n29 The Supreme Court of Pennsylvania described the amount of five shillings in a contract matter in 1792 as "nominal consideration." *Morris's Lessee* v. *Smith*, 4 Dall. 119, 120 (Pa. 1792). Many of the laws cited punished violation with fine in a similar amount; the 1783 Massachusetts gunpowder-storage law carried a somewhat larger fine of £10 (200 shillings) and forfeiture of the weapon.

[554 U. S. ____ (2008) 62] or jaywalking. And although such public-safety laws may not contain exceptions for self-defense, it is inconceivable that the threat of a jaywalking ticket would deter someone from disregarding a "Do Not Walk" sign in order to flee an attacker, or that the Government would enforce those laws under such circumstances. Likewise, we do not think that a law imposing a 5-shilling fine and forfeiture of the gun would have prevented a person in the founding era from using a gun to protect himself or his family from violence, or that if he did so the law would be enforced against him. The District law, by contrast, far from imposing a minor fine, threatens citizens with a year in prison (five years for a second violation) for even obtaining a gun in the first place. See D. C. Code §7–2507.06.

JUSTICE BREYER... criticizes us for declining to establish a level of scrutiny for evaluating Second Amendment restrictions.

He proposes, explicitly at least, none of the traditionally expressed levels (strict scrutiny, intermediate scrutiny, rational basis), but rather a judge-empowering "interest-balancing inquiry" that "asks whether the statute burdens a protected interest in a way or to an extent that is out of proportion to the statute's salutary effects upon other important governmental interests."

JUSTICE BREYER arrives at his interest-balanced answer: because handgun violence is a problem, because the law is limited to an urban area, and because there were somewhat similar restrictions in the founding period (a false proposition that we have already discussed), the interest-balancing inquiry results in the constitutionality of the handgun ban. QED.

JUSTICE BREYER moves on to make a broad jurisprudential point: He criticizes us for declining to establish a level of scrutiny for evaluating Second Amendment restrictions. He proposes, explicitly at least, none of the traditionally expressed levels (strict scrutiny, intermediate scrutiny, rational basis), but rather a judge-empowering "interest-balancing inquiry" that "asks whether the statute burdens a protected interest in a way or to an extent that is out of proportion to the statute's salutary effects upon other important governmental interests." *Post*, at 10. After an exhaustive discussion of the arguments for and against gun control, JUSTICE BREYER arrives at his interest-balanced answer: because handgun violence is a problem, because the law is limited to an urban area, and because there were somewhat similar restrictions in the founding period (a false proposition that we have already discussed), the interest-balancing inquiry results in the constitutionality of the handgun ban. QED.

We know of no other enumerated constitutional right whose core protection has been subjected to a freestanding "interest-balancing" approach. The very enumeration of the right takes out of the hands of government—even the Third Branch of Government—the power to decide on a case-by-case basis whether the right is *really worth* insisting upon.

A constitutional guarantee subject to future judges' assessments of its usefulness is no constitutional guarantee at all.

Constitutional rights are enshrined with the scope they were understood to have when the people adopted them, whether or not future legislatures or (yes) even future judges think that scope too broad.

And whatever else it leaves to future evaluation, it surely elevates above all other interests the right of law-abiding, responsible citizens to use arms in defense of hearth and home.

We know of no other enumerated constitutional right whose core protection has been subjected to a freestanding "interest-balancing" approach. The very enumeration of the right takes out of the hands of government—even the [554 U. S. ____ (2008) 63] Third Branch of Government—the power to decide on a case-by-case basis whether the right is *really worth* insisting upon. A constitutional guarantee subject to future judges' assessments of its usefulness is no constitutional guarantee at all. Constitutional rights are enshrined with the scope they were understood to have when the people adopted them, whether or not future legislatures or (yes) even future judges think that scope too broad. We would not apply an "interest-balancing" approach to the prohibition of a peaceful neo-Nazi march through Skokie. See *National Socialist Party of America* v. *Skokie*, 432 U. S. 43 (1977) *(per curiam)*. The First Amendment contains the freedom-of-speech guarantee that the people ratified, which included exceptions for obscenity, libel, and disclosure of state secrets, but not for the expression of extremely unpopular and wrong-headed views. The Second Amendment is no different. Like the First, it is the very *product* of an interest-balancing by the people—which JUSTICE BREYER would now conduct for them anew. And whatever else it leaves to future evaluation, it surely elevates above all other interests the right of law-abiding, responsible citizens to use arms in defense of hearth and home.

JUSTICE BREYER chides us for leaving so many applications of the right to keep and bear arms in doubt... But since this case represents this Court's first in-depth examination of the Second Amendment, one should not expect it to clarify the entire field

there will be time enough to expound upon the historical justifications for the exceptions we have mentioned if and when those exceptions come before us.

JUSTICE BREYER chides us for leaving so many applications of the right to keep and bear arms in doubt, and for not providing extensive historical justification for those regulations of the right that we describe as permissible. See *post*, at 42–43. But since this case represents this Court's first in-depth examination of the Second Amendment, one should not expect it to clarify the entire field, any more than *Reynolds* v. *United States*, 98 U. S. 145 (1879), our first in-depth Free Exercise Clause case, left that area in a state of utter certainty. And there will be time enough to expound upon the historical justifications for the exceptions we have mentioned if and when those exceptions come before us.

In sum, we hold that the District's ban on handgun possession in the home violates the Second Amendment, as does its prohibition against rendering any lawful firearm in the home operable for the purpose of immediate self-defense.

Assuming that Heller is not disqualified from the exercise of Second Amendment rights, the District must permit him to register his handgun and must issue him a license to carry it in the home.

[554 U. S. ____ (2008) 64] In sum, we hold that the District's ban on handgun possession in the home violates the Second Amendment, as does its prohibition against rendering any lawful firearm in the home operable for the purpose of immediate self-defense. Assuming that Heller is not disqualified from the exercise of Second Amendment rights, the District must permit him to register his handgun and must issue him a license to carry it in the home.

* * *

We are aware of the problem of handgun violence in this country, and we take seriously the concerns raised by the many *amici* who believe that prohibition of handgun ownership is a solution.

The Constitution leaves the District of Columbia a variety of tools for combating that problem, including some measures regulating handguns

But the enshrinement of constitutional rights necessarily takes certain policy choices off the table. These include the absolute prohibition of handguns held and used for self-defense in the home.

what is not debatable is that it is not the role of this Court to pronounce the Second Amendment extinct.

We are aware of the problem of handgun violence in this country, and we take seriously the concerns raised by the many *amici* who believe that prohibition of handgun ownership is a solution. The Constitution leaves the District of Columbia a variety of tools for combating that problem, including some measures regulating handguns, see *supra,* at 54–55, and n. 26. But the enshrinement of constitutional rights necessarily takes certain policy choices off the table. These include the absolute prohibition of handguns held and used for self-defense in the home. Undoubtedly some think that the Second Amendment is outmoded in a society where our standing army is the pride of our Nation, where well-trained police forces provide personal security, and where gun violence is a serious problem. That is perhaps debatable, but what is not debatable is that it is not the role of this Court to pronounce the Second Amendment extinct.

We affirm the judgment of the Court of Appeals.

It is so ordered.

STEVENS, J., dissenting

SUPREME COURT OF THE UNITED STATES

No. 07–290

DISTRICT OF COLUMBIA, ET AL., PETITIONERS *v.*
DICK ANTHONY HELLER
.ON WRIT OF CERTIORARI TO THE UNITED STATES COURT OF APPEALS
FOR THE DISTRICT OF COLUMBIA CIRCUIT
[June 26, 2008]

JUSTICE STEVENS, with whom JUSTICE SOUTER, JUSTICE GINSBURG, and JUSTICE BREYER join, dissenting.

The question presented by this case is not whether the Second Amendment protects a "collective right" or an "individual right." Surely it protects a right that can be enforced by individuals. But a conclusion that the Second Amendment protects an individual right does not tell us anything about the scope of that right.

The question presented by this case is not whether the Second Amendment protects a "collective right" or an "individual right." Surely it protects a right that can be enforced by individuals. But a conclusion that the Second Amendment protects an individual right does not tell us anything about the scope of that right.

The Second Amendment plainly does not protect the right to use a gun to rob a bank; it is equally clear that it *does* encompass the right to use weapons for certain military purposes. Whether it also protects the right to possess and use guns for nonmilitary purposes like hunting and personal self-defense is the question presented by this case.

Guns are used to hunt, for self-defense, to commit crimes, for sporting activities, and to perform military duties. The Second Amendment plainly does not protect the right to use a gun to rob a bank; it is equally clear that it *does* encompass the right to use weapons for certain military purposes. Whether it also protects the right to possess and use guns for nonmilitary purposes like hunting and personal self-defense is the question presented by this case. The text of the Amendment, its history, and our decision in *United States* v. *Miller*, 307 U. S. 174 (1939), provide a clear answer to that question.

The Second Amendment was adopted to protect the right of the people of each of the several States to maintain a well-regulated militia.

Neither the text of the Amendment nor the arguments advanced by its proponents evidenced the slightest interest in limiting any legislature's authority to regulate private civilian uses of firearms.

there is no indication that the Framers of the Amendment intended to enshrine the common-law right of self-defense in the Constitution.

The Second Amendment was adopted to protect the right of the people of each of the several States to maintain a well-regulated militia. It was a response to concerns raised during the ratification of the Constitution that the power of Congress to disarm the state militias and create a national standing army posed an intolerable [554 U. S. ____ (2008) 2] threat to the sovereignty of the several States. Neither the text of the Amendment nor the arguments advanced by its proponents evidenced the slightest interest in limiting any legislature's authority to regulate private civilian uses of firearms. Specifically, there is no indication that the Framers of the Amendment intended to enshrine the common-law right of self-defense in the Constitution.

The view of the Amendment we took in *Miller*—that it protects the right to keep and bear arms for certain military purposes, but that it does not curtail the Legislature's power to regulate the nonmilitary use and ownership of weapons—is both the most natural reading of the Amendment's text and the interpretation most faithful to the history of its adoption.

In 1934, Congress enacted the National Firearms Act, the first major federal firearms law. n1 Upholding a conviction under that Act, this Court held that, "[i]n the absence of any evidence tending to show that possession or use of a 'shotgun having a barrel of less than eighteen inches in length' at this time has some reasonable relationship to the preservation or efficiency of a well regulated militia, we cannot say that the Second Amendment guarantees the right to keep and bear such an instrument." *Miller*, 307 U. S., at 178. The view of the Amendment we took in *Miller*—that it protects the right to keep and bear arms for certain military purposes, but that it does not curtail the Legislature's power to regulate the nonmilitary use and ownership of weapons—is both the most natural reading of the Amendment's text and the interpretation most faithful to the history of its adoption.

n1 There was some limited congressional activity earlier: A 10% federal excise tax on firearms was passed as part of the Revenue Act of 1918, 40 Stat. 1057, and in 1927 a statute was enacted prohibiting the shipment of handguns, revolvers, and other concealable weapons through the United States mails. Ch. 75, 44 Stat. 1059–1060 (hereinafter 1927 Act).

Since our decision in *Miller*, hundreds of judges have relied on the view of the Amendment we endorsed there

Since our decision in *Miller*, hundreds of judges have relied on the view of the Amendment we endorsed there; n2

Until the Fifth Circuit's decision in *United States* v. *Emerson*, every Court of Appeals to consider the question had understood *Miller* to hold that the Second Amendment does not protect the right to possess and use guns for purely private, civilian purposes.

n2 Until the Fifth Circuit's decision in *United States* v. *Emerson*, 270 F. 3d 203 (2001), every Court of Appeals to consider the question had understood *Miller* to hold that the Second Amendment does not protect the right to possess and use guns for purely private, civilian purposes. See, *e.g.*, *United States* v. *Haney*, 264 F. 3d 1161, 1164–1166 (CA10 2001); *United States* v. *Napier*, 233 F. 3d 394, 402–404 (CA6 2000); [554 U. S. ____ (2008) 3] *Gillespie* v. *Indianapolis*, 185 F. 3d 693, 710–711 (CA7 1999); *United States* v. *Scanio*, No. 97–1584, 1998 WL 802060, *2 (CA2, Nov. 12, 1998) (unpublished opinion); *United States* v. *Wright*, 117 F. 3d 1265, 1271–1274 (CA11 1997); *United States* v. *Rybar*, 103 F. 3d 273, 285–286 (CA3 1996); *Hickman* v. *Block*, 81 F. 3d 98, 100–103 (CA9 1996); *United States* v. *Hale*, 978 F. 2d 1016, 1018–1020 (CA8 1992); *Thomas* v. *City Council of Portland*, 730 F. 2d 41, 42 (CA1 1984) *(per curiam); United States* v. *Johnson*, 497 F. 2d 548, 550 (CA4 1974) *(per curiam); United States* v. *Johnson*, 441 F. 2d 1134, 1136

(CA5 1971); see also *Sandidge* v. *United States,* 520 A. 2d 1057, 1058–1059 (DC App. 1987). And a number of courts have remained firm in their prior positions, even after considering *Emerson.* See, *e.g., United States* v. *Lippman,* 369 F. 3d 1039, 1043–1045 (CA8 2004); *United States* v. *Parker,* 362 F. 3d 1279, 1282–1284 (CA10 2004); *United States* v. *Jackubowski,* 63 Fed. Appx. 959, 961 (CA7 2003) (unpublished opinion); *Silveira* v. *Lockyer,* 312 F. 3d 1052, 1060–1066 (CA9 2002); *United States* v. *Milheron,* 231 F. Supp. 2d 376, 378 (Me. 2002); *Bach* v. *Pataki,* 289 F. Supp. 2d 217, 224–226 (NDNY 2003); *United States* v. *Smith,* 56 M. J. 711, 716 (C. A. Armed Forces 2001).

No new evidence has surfaced since 1980 supporting the view that the Amendment was intended to curtail the power of Congress to regulate civilian use or misuse of weapons.

we ourselves affirmed it in 1980. See *Lewis* v. *United States,* 445 U. S. 55, 65–66, n. 8 (1980). n3   No new evidence has surfaced since 1980 supporting the view that the Amendment was intended to curtail the power of Congress to regulate civilian use or misuse of weapons. Indeed, a review of the drafting history of the Amendment demonstrates that its Framers *rejected* proposals that would have broadened its coverage to include such uses.

n3 Our discussion in *Lewis* was brief but significant. Upholding a conviction for receipt of a firearm by a felon, we wrote: "These legislative restrictions on the use of firearms are neither based upon constitutionally suspect criteria, nor do they entrench upon any constitutionally protected liberties. See *United States* v. *Miller,* 307 U. S. 174, 178 (1939) (the Second Amendment guarantees no right to keep and bear a firearm that does not have 'some reasonable relationship to the preservation or efficiency of a well regulated militia')." 445 U. S., at 65, n. 8.

The opinion the Court announces today fails to identify any new evidence supporting the view that the Amendment was intended to limit the power of Congress to regulate civilian uses of weapons.

The opinion the Court announces today fails to identify any new evidence supporting the view that the Amendment was intended to limit the power of Congress to regulate civilian uses of weapons. Unable to point to any such evidence, the Court stakes its holding on a strained and [554 U. S. ____ (2008) 4] unpersuasive reading of the Amendment's text; significantly different provisions in the 1689 English Bill of Rights, and in various 19th-century State Constitutions; postenactment commentary that was available to the Court when it decided *Miller;* and, ultimately, a feeble attempt to distinguish *Miller* that places more emphasis on the Court's decisional process than on the reasoning in the opinion itself.

respect for the well-settled views of all of our predecessors on this Court, and for the rule of law itself, would prevent most jurists from endorsing such a dramatic upheaval in the law.

Even if the textual and historical arguments on both sides of the issue were evenly balanced, respect for the well-settled views of all of our predecessors on this Court, and for the rule of law itself, see *Mitchell* v. *W. T. Grant Co.,* 416 U. S. 600, 636 (1974) (Stewart, J., dissenting), would prevent most jurists from endorsing such a dramatic upheaval in the law. n4   As Justice Cardozo observed years ago, the "labor of judges would be increased almost to the breaking point if every past decision could be reopened in every case, and one could not lay one's own

Stare decisis permits society to presume that bedrock principles are founded in the law rather than in the proclivities of individuals

n4 See *Vasquez* v. *Hillery,* 474 U. S. 254, 265, 266 (1986) ("*[Stare decisis]* permits society to presume that bedrock principles are founded in the law rather than in the proclivities of individuals, and thereby contributes to the integrity of our constitutional system of government, both in appearance and in fact. While *stare decisis* is not an inexorable command, the careful observer will discern that any detours from the straight path of *stare decisis* in our past have occurred for articulable reasons, and only when the Court has felt obliged 'to bring its opinions into agreement with experience and with facts newly ascertained.' *Burnet* v. *Coronado Oil & Gas Co.,* 285 U. S. 393, 412 (1932) (Brandeis, J., dissenting)"); *Pollock* v. *Farmers' Loan & Trust Co.,* 157 U. S. 429, 652 (1895) (White, J., dissenting) ("The fundamental conception of a judicial body is that of one hedged about by precedents which are binding on the court without regard to the personality of its members. Break down this belief in judicial continuity and let it be felt that on great constitutional questions this Court is to depart from the settled conclusions of its predecessors, and to determine them all according to the mere opinion of those who temporarily fill its bench, and our Constitution will, in my judgment, be bereft of value and become a most dangerous instrument to the rights and liberties of the people").

[554 U. S. ____ (2008) 5] course of bricks on the secure foundation of the courses laid by others who had gone before him." The Nature of the Judicial Process 149 (1921).

the Amendment should not be interpreted as limiting the authority of Congress to regulate the use or possession of firearms for purely civilian purposes.

In this dissent I shall first explain why our decision in *Miller* was faithful to the text of the Second Amendment and the purposes revealed in its drafting history. I shall then comment on the postratification history of the Amendment, which makes abundantly clear that the Amendment should not be interpreted as limiting the authority of Congress to regulate the use or possession of firearms for purely civilian purposes.

I

The text of the Second Amendment is brief. It provides: "A well regulated Militia, being necessary to the security of a free State, the right of the people to keep and bear Arms, shall not be infringed."

Three portions of that text merit special focus: the introductory language defining the Amendment's purpose, the class of persons encompassed within its reach, and the unitary nature of the right that it protects.

"A well regulated Militia, being necessary to the security of a free State"

The preamble to the Second Amendment makes three important points. It identifies the preservation of the militia as the Amendment's purpose; it explains that the militia is necessary to the security of a free State; and it recognizes that the militia must be "well regulated."

The preamble to the Second Amendment makes three important points. It identifies the preservation of the militia as the Amendment's purpose; it explains that the militia is necessary to the security of a free State; and it recognizes that the militia must be "well regulated." In all three respects it is comparable to provisions in several State Declarations of Rights that were adopted roughly contemporaneously with the Declaration of Independence. n5 n5 The Virginia Declaration of Rights ¶13 (1776), provided: "That a well-regulated militia, composed of the body of the people, trained to arms, is the proper, natural, and safe defence of a free State; that Standing Armies, in time of peace, should be avoided, as dangerous to [554 U. S. ____ (2008) 6] liberty; and that, in all cases, the military should be under strict subordination to, and governed by, the civil power." 1 B. Schwartz, The Bill of Rights 235 (1971) (hereinafter Schwartz).

Maryland's Declaration of Rights, Arts. XXV–XXVII (1776), provided: "That a well-regulated militia is the proper and natural defence of a free government"; "That standing armies are dangerous to liberty, and ought not to be raised or kept up, without consent of the Legislature"; "That in all cases, and at all times, the military ought to be under strict subordination to and control of the civil power." 1 Schwartz 282.

Delaware's Declaration of Rights, §§18–20 (1776), provided: "That a well regulated militia is the proper, natural, and safe defence of a free government"; "That standing armies are dangerous to liberty, and ought not to be raised or kept up without the consent of the Legislature"; "That in all cases and at all times the military ought to be under strict subordination to and governed by the civil power." 1 Schwartz 278.

Finally, New Hampshire's Bill of Rights, Arts. XXIV–XXVI (1783), read: "A well regulated militia is the proper, natural, and sure defence of a state"; "Standing armies are dangerous to liberty, and ought not to be raised or kept up without consent of the legislature"; "In all cases, and at all times, the military ought to be under strict subordination to, and governed by the civil power." 1 Schwartz 378. It elsewhere provided: "No person who is conscientiously scrupulous about the lawfulness of bearing arms, shall be compelled thereto, provided he will pay an equivalent." *Id.,* at 377 (Art. XIII).

the need for state militias has not been a matter of significant public interest for almost two centuries

Those state provisions highlight the importance members of the founding generation attached to the maintenance of state militias; they also underscore the profound fear shared by many in that era of the dangers posed by standing armies. n6 While the need for state militias has not been

n6 The language of the Amendment's preamble also closely tracks the language of a number of contemporaneous state militia statutes, many of which began with nearly identical statements. Georgia's 1778 militia statute, for example, began, "[w]hereas a well ordered and disciplined Militia, is essentially necessary, to the Safety, peace and prosperity, of this State." Act of Nov. 15, 1778, 19 Colonial Records of the State of Georgia 103 (Candler ed. 1911 (pt. 2)). North Carolina's 1777 militia statute started with this language: "Whereas a well regulated Militia is absolutely necessary for the defending and securing the Liberties of a free State." N. C. Sess. Laws ch. 1, §I, p. 1. And Connecticut's 1782 "Acts and Laws Regulating the Militia" began, "Whereas the Defence [554 U. S. ____ (2008) 7] and Security of all free States depends (under God) upon the Exertions of a well regulated Militia, and the Laws heretofore enacted have proved inadequate to the End designed." Conn. Acts and Laws p. 585 (hereinafter 1782 Conn. Acts).

These state militia statutes give content to the notion of a "well-regulated militia." They identify those persons who compose the State's militia; they create regiments, brigades, and divisions; they set forth command structures and provide for the appointment of officers; they describe how the militia will be assembled when necessary and provide for training; and they prescribe penalties for nonappearance, delinquency, and failure to keep the required weapons, ammunition, and other necessary equipment. The obligation of militia members to "keep" certain specified arms is detailed further, n. 14, *infra*, and accompanying text.

a matter of significant public interest for almost two centuries, that fact should not obscure the contemporary concerns that animated the Framers.

the Declarations of Rights of Pennsylvania and Vermont *did* expressly protect such civilian uses at the time

The contrast between those two declarations and the Second Amendment reinforces the clear statement of purpose announced in the Amendment's preamble.

The parallels between the Second Amendment and these state declarations, and the Second Amendment's omission of any statement of purpose related to the right to use firearms for hunting or personal self-defense, is especially striking in light of the fact that the Declarations of Rights of Pennsylvania and Vermont *did* expressly protect such civilian uses at the time. Article XIII of Pennsylvania's 1776 Declaration of Rights announced that "the people have a right to bear arms for the defence *of themselves* and the state," 1 Schwartz 266 (emphasis added); §43 of the Declaration assured that "the inhabitants of this state shall have the liberty to fowl and hunt in seasonable times on the lands they hold, and on all other lands therein not inclosed," *id.*, at 274. And Article XV of the 1777 Vermont Declaration of Rights guaranteed "[t]hat the people have a right to bear arms for the defence *of themselves* and the State." *Id.*, at 324 (emphasis added). The contrast between those two declarations and the Second Amendment reinforces the clear statement of purpose announced in the Amendment's preamble. It [554 U. S. ____ (2008) 8] confirms that the Framers' single-minded focus in crafting the constitutional guarantee "to keep and bear arms" was on military uses of firearms, which they viewed in the context of service in state militias.

The preamble thus both sets forth the object of the Amendment and informs the meaning of the remainder of its text. Such text should not be treated as mere surplusage, for "it cannot be presumed that any clause in the constitution is intended to be without effect."

The preamble thus both sets forth the object of the Amendment and informs the meaning of the remainder of its text. Such text should not be treated as mere surplusage, for "[i]t cannot be presumed that any clause in the constitution is intended to be without effect." *Marbury* v. *Madison,* 1 Cranch 137, 174 (1803).

The Court today tries to denigrate the importance of this clause of the Amendment by beginning its analysis with the Amendment's operative provision and returning to the preamble merely "to ensure that our reading of the operative clause is consistent with the announced purpose."

Ante, at 5. That is not how this Court ordinarily reads such texts, and it is not how the preamble would have been viewed at the time the Amendment was adopted. While the Court makes the novel suggestion that it need only find some "logical connection" between the preamble and the operative provision, it does acknowledge that a prefatory clause may resolve an ambiguity in the text. *Ante,* at 4. n7 Without identifying any language in the

n7 The sources the Court cites simply do not support the proposition that some "logical connection" between the two clauses is all that is required. The Dwarris treatise, for example, merely explains that "[t]he general purview of a statute is not . . . *necessarily* to be restrained by any words introductory to the enacting clauses." F. Dwarris, A General Treatise on Statutes 268 (P. Potter ed. 1871) (emphasis added).

"the preamble cannot control the enacting part of a statute, which is expressed in clear and unambiguous terms, yet, if any doubt arise on the words of the enacting part, the preamble may be resorted to, to explain it."

The treatise proceeds to caution that "the preamble cannot control the enacting part of a statute, which is expressed in clear and unambiguous terms, yet, if any doubt arise on the words of the enacting part, the preamble may be resorted to, to explain it." *Id.,* at 269. Sutherland makes the same point. Explaining that "[i]n the United States preambles are not as important as they are in England," the treatise notes that in the United States "the settled principle of law is that the preamble cannot control the enacting part of the statute *in cases where the* [554 U. S. ____ (2008) 9] *enacting part is expressed in clear, unambiguous terms.*" 2A N. Singer, Sutherland on Statutory Construction §47.04, p. 146 (rev. 5th ed. 1992) (emphasis added). Surely not even the Court believes that the Amendment's operative provision, which, though only 14 words in length, takes the Court the better part of 18 pages to parse, is perfectly "clear and unambiguous."

Perhaps the Court's approach to the text is acceptable advocacy, but it is surely an unusual approach for judges to follow.

text that even mentions civilian uses of firearms, the Court proceeds to "find" its preferred reading in what is at best an ambiguous text, and then concludes that its reading is not foreclosed by the preamble. Perhaps the Court's approach to the text is acceptable advocacy, but it is surely an unusual approach for judges to follow.

"The right of the people"

The centerpiece of the Court's textual argument is its insistence that the words "the people" as used in the Second Amendment must have the same meaning, and protect the same class of individuals, as when they are used in the First and Fourth Amendments.

But the Court *itself* reads the Second Amendment to protect a "subset" significantly narrower... the Court limits the protected class to "law-abiding, responsible citizens." But the class of persons protected by the First and Fourth Amendments is *not* so limited

The Court offers no way to harmonize its conflicting pronouncements.

The centerpiece of the Court's textual argument is its insistence that the words "the people" as used in the Second Amendment must have the same meaning, and protect the same class of individuals, as when they are used in the First and Fourth Amendments. According to the Court, in all three provisions—as well as the Constitution's preamble, section 2 of Article I, and the Tenth Amendment—"the term unambiguously refers to all members of the political community, not an unspecified subset." *Ante,* at 6. But the Court *itself* reads the Second Amendment to protect a "subset" significantly narrower than the class of persons protected by the First and Fourth Amendments; when it finally drills down on the substantive meaning of the Second Amendment, the Court limits the protected class to "law-abiding, responsible citizens," *ante,* at 63. But the class of persons protected by the First and Fourth Amendments is *not* so limited; for even felons (and presumably irresponsible citizens as well) may invoke the protections of those constitutional provisions. The Court offers no way to harmonize its conflicting pronouncements.

it is only the right peaceably to assemble, and to petition the Government for a redress of grievances, that is described as a right of "the people." These rights contemplate collective action.

petitioning the Government is a right that can be exercised by individuals, it is primarily collective in nature. For if they are to be effective, petitions must involve groups of individuals acting in concert.

The Court also overlooks the significance of the way the [554 U. S. ____ (2008) 10] Framers used the phrase "the people" in these constitutional provisions. In the First Amendment, no words define the class of individuals entitled to speak, to publish, or to worship; in that Amendment it is only the right peaceably to assemble, and to petition the Government for a redress of grievances, that is described as a right of "the people." These rights contemplate collective action. While the right peaceably to assemble protects the individual rights of those persons participating in the assembly, its concern is with action engaged in by members of a group, rather than any single individual. Likewise, although the act of petitioning the Government is a right that can be exercised by individuals, it is primarily collective in nature. For if they are to be effective, petitions must involve groups of individuals acting in concert.

the words "the people" in the Second Amendment refer back to the object announced in the Amendment's preamble. They remind us that it is the collective action of individuals having a duty to serve in the militia that the text directly protects

Similarly, the words "the people" in the Second Amendment refer back to the object announced in the Amendment's preamble. They remind us that it is the collective action of individuals having a duty to serve in the militia that the text directly protects and, perhaps more importantly, that the ultimate purpose of the Amendment was to protect the States' share of the divided sovereignty created by the Constitution.

As used in the Fourth Amendment, "the people" describes the class of persons protected from unreasonable searches and seizures by Government officials. It is true that the Fourth Amendment describes a right that need not be exercised in any collective sense. But that observation does not settle the meaning of the phrase "the people" when used in the Second Amendment. For, as we have seen, the phrase means something quite different in the Petition and Assembly Clauses of the First Amendment. Although the abstract definition of the phrase "the people" could carry the same meaning in the Second Amendment as in the Fourth Amendment, the preamble of the Second Amendment suggests that the uses of the phrase in the [554 U. S. ____ (2008) 11] First and Second Amendments are the same in referring to a collective activity. By way of contrast, the Fourth Amendment describes a right *against* governmental interference rather than an affirmative right *to* engage in protected conduct, and so refers to a right to protect a purely individual interest. As used in the Second Amendment, the words "the people" do not enlarge the right to keep and bear arms to encompass use or ownership of weapons outside the context of service in a well-regulated militia.

"To keep and bear Arms"

Although the Court's discussion of these words treats them as two "phrases"—as if they read "to keep" and "to bear"—they describe a unitary right

Although the Court's discussion of these words treats them as two "phrases"—as if they read "to keep" and "to bear"—they describe a unitary right: to possess arms if needed for military purposes and to use them in conjunction with military activities.

the Court limits the Amendment's protection to the right "to possess and carry weapons in case of confrontation." No party or *amicus* urged this interpretation; the Court appears to have fashioned it out of whole cloth.

the Amendment's text *does* justify a different limitation: the "right to keep and bear arms" protects only a right to possess and use firearms in connection with service in a state-organized militia.

As a threshold matter, it is worth pausing to note an oddity in the Court's interpretation of "to keep and bear arms." Unlike the Court of Appeals, the Court does not read that phrase to create a right to possess arms for "lawful, private purposes." *Parker* v. *District of Columbia,* 478 F. 3d 370, 382 (CADC 2007). Instead, the Court limits the Amendment's protection to the right "to possess and carry weapons in case of confrontation." *Ante,* at 19. No party or *amicus* urged this interpretation; the Court appears to have fashioned it out of whole cloth. But although this novel limitation lacks support in the text of the Amendment, the Amendment's text *does* justify a different limitation: the "right to keep and bear arms" protects only a right to possess and use firearms in connection with service in a state-organized militia.

The term "bear arms" is a familiar idiom; when used unadorned by any additional words, its meaning is "to serve as a soldier, do military service, fight."

by *arms*, we understand those instruments of offence generally made use of in war; such as firearms, swords, & c. By *weapons,* we more particularly mean instruments of other kinds (exclusive of firearms), made use of as offensive, on special occasions."

The *unmodified* use of "bear arms," by contrast, refers most naturally to a military purpose, as evidenced by its use in literally dozens of contemporary texts.

The term "bear arms" is a familiar idiom; when used unadorned by any additional words, its meaning is "to serve as a soldier, do military service, fight." 1 Oxford English Dictionary 634 (2d ed. 1989). It is derived from [554 U. S. ____ (2008) 12] the Latin *arma ferre,* which, translated literally, means "to bear *[ferre]* war equipment *[arma]*." Brief for Professors of Linguistics and English as *Amici Curiae* 19. One 18thcentury dictionary defined "arms" as "weapons of offence, or armour of defence," 1 S. Johnson, A Dictionary of the English Language (1755), and another contemporaneous source explained that "[b]y *arms*, we understand those instruments of offence generally made use of in war; such as firearms, swords, & c. By *weapons,* we more particularly mean instruments of other kinds (exclusive of firearms), made use of as offensive, on special occasions." 1 J. Trusler, The Distinction Between Words Esteemed Synonymous in the English Language 37 (1794). n8 Had the Framers wished to expand the meaning of the phrase "bear arms" to encompass civilian possession and use, they could have done so by the addition of phrases such as "for the defense of themselves," as was done in the Pennsylvania and Vermont Declarations of Rights. The *unmodified* use of "bear arms," by contrast, refers most naturally to a military purpose, as evidenced by its use in literally dozens of contemporary texts. n9 The absence of any refer-

The Court's repeated citation to the dissenting opinion in *Muscarello*... borders on the risible.

n8 The Court's repeated citation to the dissenting opinion in *Muscarello* v. *United States,* 524 U. S. 125 (1998), *ante,* at 10, 13, as illuminating the meaning of "bear arms," borders on the risible. At issue in *Muscarello* was the proper construction of the word "carries" in 18 U. S. C. §924(c) (2000 ed. and Supp. V); the dissent in that case made passing reference to the Second Amendment only in the course of observing that both the Constitution and Black's Law Dictionary suggested that something more active than placement of a gun in a glove compartment might be meant by the phrase " 'carries a firearm.' " 524 U. S., at 143.

of 115 texts that employed the term, all but five usages were in a clearly military context and in four of the remaining five instances, further qualifying language conveyed a different meaning.

n9 *Amici* professors of Linguistics and English reviewed uses of the term "bear arms" in a compilation of books, pamphlets, and other sources disseminated in the period between the Declaration of Independence and the adoption of the Second Amendment. See Brief for Professors of Linguistics and English as *Amici Curiae* 23–25. *Amici* determined that of 115 texts that employed the term, all but five usages were in a clearly military context, and in four of the remaining five instances, further qualifying language conveyed a different meaning. [554 U. S. ____ (2008) 13]

The Court allows that the phrase "bear Arms" did have as an idiomatic meaning, "'to serve as a soldier, do military service, fight,'" but asserts that it "*unequivocally* bore that idiomatic meaning only when followed by the preposition 'against,' which was in turn followed by the target of the hostilities." But contemporary sources make clear that the phrase "bear arms" was often used to convey a military meaning without those additional words.

The Court allows that the phrase "bear Arms" did have as an idiomatic meaning, " 'to serve as a soldier, do military service, fight,' " *ante,* at 12, but asserts that it "*unequivocally* bore that idiomatic meaning only when followed by the preposition 'against,' which was in turn followed by the target of the hostilities," *ante,* at 12–13. But contemporary sources make clear that the phrase "bear arms" was often used to convey a military meaning without those additional words. See, *e.g.,* To The Printer, Providence Gazette, (May 27, 1775) ("By the common estimate of three millions of people in America, allowing one in five to bear arms, there will be found 600,000 fighting men"); Letter of Henry Laurens to the Mass. Council (Jan. 21, 1778), in Letters of Delegates to Congress 1774–1789, p. 622 (P. Smith ed. 1981) ("Congress were yesterday informed . . . that those Canadians who returned from Saratoga . . . had been compelled by Sir Guy Carleton to bear Arms"); Of the Manner of Making War among the Indians of North-America, Connecticut Courant (May 23, 1785) ("The Indians begin to bear arms at the age of fifteen, and lay them aside when they arrive at the age of sixty. Some nations to the southward, I have been informed, do not continue their military exercises after they are fifty"); 28 Journals of the Continental Congress 1030 (G. Hunt ed. 1910) ("That hostages be mutually given as a security that the Convention troops and those received in exchange for them do not bear arms prior to the first day of May next"); H. R. J., 9th Cong., 1st Sess., 217 (Feb. 12, 1806) ("Whereas the commanders of British armed vessels have impressed

many American seamen, and compelled them to bear arms on board said vessels, and assist in fighting their battles with nations in amity and peace with the United States"); H. R. J., 15th Cong., 2d Sess., 182–183 (Jan. 14, 1819) ("[The petitioners] state that they were residing in the British province of Canada, at the commencement of the late war, and that owing to their attachment to the United States, they refused to bear arms, when called upon by the British authorities . . .").
ence to civilian uses of weapons tailors the text of the Amendment to the purpose identified in its preamble. n10

A man in the pursuit of deer, elk, and buffaloes, might carry his rifle every day, for forty years, and, yet, it would never be said of him, that he had *borne arms,* much less could it be said, that a private citizen *bears arms,* because he has a dirk or pistol concealed under his clothes, or a spear in a cane."

n10 *Aymette* v. *State,* 21 Tenn. 154, 156 (1840), a case we cited in *Miller,* further confirms this reading of the phrase. In *Aymette,* the Tennessee Supreme Court construed the guarantee in Tennessee's 1834 Constitution that " 'the free white men of this State, have a right to keep and bear arms for their common defence.' " Explaining that the provision was adopted with the same goals as the Federal Constitution's Second Amendment, the court wrote: "The words 'bear arms' . . . have reference to their military use, and were not employed to mean wearing them about the person as part of the dress. As the object for which the right [554 U. S. ____ (2008) 14] to keep and bear arms is secured, is of general and public nature, to be exercised by the people in a body, for their *common defence,* so the *arms,* the right to keep which is secured, are such as are usually employed in civilized warfare, and that constitute the ordinary military equipment." 21 Tenn., at 158. The court elaborated: "[W]e may remark, that the phrase '*bear arms*' is used in the Kentucky Constitution as well as our own, and implies, as has already been suggested, their military use. . . . A man in the pursuit of deer, elk, and buffaloes, might carry his rifle every day, for forty years, and, yet, it would never be said of him, that he had *borne arms,* much less could it be said, that a private citizen *bears arms,* because he has a dirk or pistol concealed under his clothes, or a spear in a cane." *Id.,* at 161.
But when discussing these words, the Court simply ignores the preamble.
The Court argues that a "qualifying phrase that contradicts the word or phrase it modifies is unknown this side of the looking glass." *Ante,* at 15. But this fundamentally fails to grasp the point. The stand-alone phrase "bear arms" most naturally conveys a military meaning *unless* the addition of a qualifying phrase signals that a different meaning is intended. When, as in this case, there is no such qualifier, the most natural meaning is the military one; and, in the absence of any qualifier, it is all the more appropriate to look to the preamble to confirm the natural meaning of the text. n11 The Court's objection is particularly
n11 As lucidly explained in the context of a statute mandating a sentencing enhancement for any person who "uses" a firearm during a crime of violence or drug trafficking crime:
"To use an instrumentality ordinarily means to use it for its intended purpose. When someone asks, 'Do you use a cane?,' he is not inquiring whether you have your grandfather's silver-handled walking stick on display in the hall; he wants to know whether you *walk* with a cane. Similarly, to speak of 'using a firearm' is to speak of using it for its distinctive purpose, *i.e.,* as a weapon. To be sure, one can use a firearm in a number of ways, including as an article of exchange, just as one

can 'use' a cane as a hall decoration—but that is not the ordinary meaning of 'using' the one or the other. The Court does not appear to grasp the distinction between how a word *can be* used and how it *ordinarily* is used." *Smith* v. *United States*, 508 U. S. 223, 242 (1993) (SCALIA, J., dissenting) (some internal marks, footnotes, and citations [554 U. S. ____ (2008) 15] omitted).

puzzling in light of its own contention that the addition of the modifier "against" changes the meaning of "bear arms." Compare *ante*, at 10 (defining "bear arms" to mean "carrying [a weapon] for a particular purpose— confrontation"), with *ante*, at 12 ("The phrase 'bear Arms' also had at the time of the founding an idiomatic meaning that was significantly different from its natural meaning: to serve as a soldier, do military service, fight or to wage war. But it unequivocally bore that idiomatic meaning only when followed by the preposition 'against.' " (citations and some internal quotation marks omitted)).

The Amendment's use of the term "keep" in no way contradicts the military meaning conveyed by the phrase "bear arms" and the Amendment's preamble.

The Amendment's use of the term "keep" in no way contradicts the military meaning conveyed by the phrase "bear arms" and the Amendment's preamble. To the contrary, a number of state militia laws in effect at the time of the Second Amendment's drafting used the term "keep" to describe the requirement that militia members store their arms at their homes, ready to be used for service when necessary. The Virginia military law, for example, ordered that "every one of the said officers, noncommissioned officers, and privates, shall constantly *keep* the aforesaid arms, accoutrements, and ammunition, ready to be produced whenever called for by his commanding officer." Act for Regulating and Disciplining the Militia, 1785 Va. Acts ch. 1, §3, p. 2 (emphasis added). n12

each Person enrolled as aforesaid, shall also *keep* at his Place of Abode one Pound of good merchantable Gunpowder and three Pounds of Ball sized to his Musket or Rifle"

every person between the ages of eighteen and fifty... shall at his own expense, provide himself... with a musket or firelock, with a bayonet, a cartouch box to contain twenty three cartridges, a priming wire, a brush and six flints, all in good order

n12 See also Act for the regulating, training, and arraying of the Militia, . . . of the State, 1781 N. J. Laws, ch. XIII, §12, p. 43 ("And be it Enacted, That each Person enrolled as aforesaid, shall also *keep* at his Place of Abode one Pound of good merchantable Gunpowder and three Pounds of Ball sized to his Musket or Rifle" (emphasis added)); An Act for establishing a Militia, 1785 Del. Laws §7, p. 59 ("*And be it enacted,* That every person between the ages of eighteen and fifty . . . shall at his own expense, provide himself . . . with a musket or firelock, with a bayonet, a cartouch box to contain twenty three cartridges, a priming wire, a brush and six flints, all in good order, on or before the first day of April next, under the penalty of forty shillings, and shall *keep* the [554 U. S. ____ (2008) 16] same by him at all times, ready and fit for service, under the penalty of two shillings and six pence for each neglect or default thereof on every muster day" (second emphasis added)); 1782 Conn. Acts 590 ("And it shall be the duty of the Regional Quarter-Master to provide and *keep* a sufficient quantity of Ammunition and warlike stores for the use of their respective regiments, to be *kept* in such place or places as shall be ordered by the Field Officers" (emphasis added)).

"[K]eep and bear arms" thus perfectly describes the responsibilities of a framing-era militia member.

the clause protects only one right, rather than two. It does not describe a right "to keep arms" and a separate right "to bear arms."

Different language surely would have been used to protect nonmilitary use and possession of weapons from regulation if such an intent had played any role in the drafting of the Amendment.

This reading is confirmed by the fact that the clause protects only one right, rather than two. It does not describe a right "to keep arms" and a separate right "to bear arms." Rather, the single right that it does describe is both a duty and a right to have arms available and ready for military service, and to use them for military purposes when necessary. n13 Different language surely would have been used to protect nonmilitary use and possession of weapons from regulation if such an intent had played any role in the drafting of the Amendment.

* * *

When each word in the text is given full effect, the Amendment is most naturally read to secure to the people a right to use and possess arms in conjunction with service in a well-regulated militia.

When each word in the text is given full effect, the Amendment is most naturally read to secure to the people a right to use and possess arms in conjunction with service in a well-regulated militia. So far as appears, no more than that was contemplated by its drafters or is encompassed within its terms. Even if the meaning of the text were genuinely susceptible to more than one interpretation, the burden would remain on those advocating a departure from the purpose identified in the preamble and

n13 The Court notes that the First Amendment protects two separate rights with the phrase "the 'right [singular] of the people peaceably to assemble, and to petition the Government for a redress of grievances.' " *Ante*, at 18. But this only proves the point: In contrast to the language quoted by the Court, the Second Amendment does not protect a "right to keep *and to* bear arms," but rather a "right to keep and bear arms." The state constitutions cited by the Court are distinguishable on the same ground.

the Court's emphatic reliance on the claim "that the Second Amendment... codified a *pre-existing* right," is of course beside the point because the right to keep and bear arms for service in a state militia was also a pre-existing right.

[554 U. S. ____ (2008) 17] from settled law to come forward with persuasive new arguments or evidence. The textual analysis offered by respondent and embraced by the Court falls far short of sustaining that heavy burden. n14 And the Court's emphatic reliance on the claim "that the Second Amendment . . . codified a *pre-existing* right," *ante*, at 19, is of course beside the point because the right to keep and bear arms for service in a state militia was also a pre-existing right.

n14 The Court's atomistic, word-by-word approach to construing the Amendment calls to mind the parable of the six blind men and the elephant, famously set in verse by John Godfrey Saxe. The Poems of John Godfrey Saxe 135–136 (1873). In the parable, each blind man approaches a single elephant; touching a different part of the elephant's body in isolation, each concludes that he has learned its true nature. One touches the animal's leg, and concludes that the elephant is like a tree; another touches the trunk and decides that the elephant is like a snake; and so on. Each of them, of course, has fundamentally failed to grasp the nature of the creature.

Indeed, not a word in the constitutional text even arguably supports the Court's overwrought and novel description of the Second Amendment as "elevat[ing] above all other interests" "the right of law-abiding, responsible citizens to use arms in defense of hearth and home." *Ante,* at 63.

II

The proper allocation of military power in the new Nation was an issue of central concern for the Framers. The compromises they ultimately reached, reflected in Article I's Militia Clauses and the Second Amendment, represent quintessential examples of the Framers' "splitting the atom of sovereignty." n15

n15 By " 'split[ting] the atom of sovereignty,' " the Framers created " 'two political capacities, one state and one federal, each protected from incursion by the other. The resulting Constitution created a legal system unprecedented in form and design, establishing two orders of government, each with its own direct relationship, its own privity, its own set of mutual rights and obligations to the people who sustain it [554 U. S. ____ (2008) 18] and are governed by it.' " *Saenz* v. *Roe,* 526 U. S. 489, 504, n. 17 (1999) (quoting *U. S. Term Limits, Inc.* v. *Thornton,* 514 U. S. 779, 838 (1995) (KENNEDY, J., concurring)).

the Framers recognized the dangers inherent in relying on inadequately trained militia members... "this force, though armed, was largely untrained, and its deficiencies were the subject of bitter complaint."

Two themes relevant to our current interpretive task ran through the debates on the original Constitution. "On the one hand, there was a widespread fear that a national standing Army posed an intolerable threat to individual liberty and to the sovereignty of the separate States." *Perpich* v. *Department of Defense,* 496 U. S. 334, 340 (1990). n16 Governor Edmund Randolph, reporting on the Constitutional Convention to the Virginia Ratification Convention, explained: "With respect to a standing army, I believe there was not a member in the federal Convention, who did not feel indignation at such an institution." 3 J. Elliot, Debates in the Several State Conventions on the Adoption of the Federal Constitution 401 (2d ed. 1863) (hereinafter Elliot). On the other hand, the Framers recognized the dangers inherent in relying on inadequately trained militia members "as the primary means of providing for the common defense," *Perpich,* 496 U. S., at 340; during the Revolutionary War, "[t]his force, though armed, was largely untrained, and its deficiencies were the subject of bitter complaint." Wiener, The Militia Clause of the Constitution, 54 Harv. L. Rev. 181, 182 (1940). n17 In order to respond to those twin concerns, a

n16 Indeed, this was one of the grievances voiced by the colonists: Paragraph 13 of the Declaration of Independence charged of King George, "He has kept among us, in times of peace, Standing Armies without the Consent of our legislatures."

George Washington... warned that for Congress "to place any dependance upon Militia, is, assuredly, resting upon a broken staff." Several years later he reiterated this view in another letter to Congress: "Regular Troops alone are equal to the exigencies of modern war, as well for defence as offence . . . . *No Militia* will ever acquire the habits necessary to resist a regular force. . . . The firmness requisite for the real business of fighting is only to be attained by a constant course of discipline and service."

n17 George Washington, writing to Congress on September 24, 1776, warned that for Congress "[t]o place any dependance upon Militia, is, assuredly, resting upon a broken staff." 6 Writings of George Washington 106, 110 (J. Fitzpatrick ed. 1932). Several years later he reiterated this view in another letter to Congress: "Regular Troops alone are equal to the exigencies of modern war, as well for defence as offence . . . . *No Militia* will ever acquire the habits necessary to resist a regular force. . . . The firmness requisite for the real business of fighting is only to be attained by a constant course of discipline and service." 20 *id.,* at [554 U. S. ____ (2008) 19] 49, 49–50 (Sept. 15, 1780). And Alexander Hamilton argued this view in many debates. In 1787, he wrote:

Alexander Hamilton argued this view in many debates... "Here I expect we shall be told that the militia of the country is its natural bulwark, and would be at all times equal to the national defense. This doctrine, in substance, had like to have lost us our independence... War, like most other things, is a science to be acquired and perfected by diligence, by perseverance, by time, and by practice."

"Here I expect we shall be told that the militia of the country is its natural bulwark, and would be at all times equal to the national defense. This doctrine, in substance, had like to have lost us our independence. . . . War, like most other things, is a science to be acquired and perfected by diligence, by perseverance, by time, and by practice." The Federalist No. 25, p. 166 (C. Rossiter ed. 1961). compromise was reached: Congress would be authorized to raise and support a national Army n18 and Navy, and also to organize, arm, discipline, and provide for the calling forth of "the Militia." U. S. Const., Art. I, §8, cls. 12–16. The President, at the same time, was empowered as the "Commander in Chief of the Army and Navy of the United States, and of the Militia of the several States, when called into the actual Service of the United States." Art. II, §2. But, with respect to the militia, a significant reservation was made to the States: Although Congress would have the power to call forth, n19 organize, arm, and discipline the militia, as well as to govern "such Part of them as may be employed in the Service of the United States," the States respectively would retain the right to appoint the officers and to train the militia in accordance with the discipline prescribed by Congress. Art. I, §8, cl. 16. n20

n18 "[B]ut no Appropriation of Money to that Use [raising and supporting Armies] shall be for a longer Term than two Years." U. S. Const., Art I, §8, cl. 12

n19 This "calling forth" power was only permitted in order for the militia "to execute the Laws of the Union, suppress Insurrections and repel Invasions." *Id.,* Art. I, §8, cl. 15.

n20 The Court assumes—incorrectly, in my view—that even when a state militia was not called into service, Congress would have had the power to exclude individuals from enlistment in that state militia. See *ante,* at 27. That assumption is not supported by the text of the Militia Clauses of the original Constitution, which confer upon Congress the power to "organiz[e], ar[m], and disciplin[e], the Militia," Art. I, §8, cl. 16, but not the power to say who will be members of a state militia. It is also flatly inconsistent with the Second Amendment. The States' power to create their own militias provides an easy answer to the [554 U. S. ____ (2008) 20] Court's complaint that the right as I have described it is empty because it merely guarantees "citizens' right to use a gun in an organization from which Congress has plenary authority to exclude them." *Ante,* at 28.

But the original Constitution's retention of the militia and its creation of divided authority over that body did not prove sufficient to allay fears about the dangers posed by a standing army. For it was perceived by some that Article I contained a significant gap: While it empowered Congress to organize, arm, and discipline the militia, it did not prevent Congress from providing for the militia's *dis*armament. As George Mason argued during the debates in Virginia on the ratification of the original Constitution:

"The militia may be here destroyed by that method which has been practiced in other parts of the world before; that is, by rendering them useless—by disarming them. Under various pretences, Congress may neglect to provide for arming and disciplining the militia; and the state governments cannot do it, for Congress has the exclusive right to arm them." Elliot 379.

New Hampshire... suggested that the Constitution should more broadly protect the use and possession of weapons, without tying such a guarantee expressly to the maintenance of the militia... unsuccessful proposals in both Massachusetts and Pennsylvania would have protected a more broadly worded right... Faced with all of these options, it is telling that James Madison chose to craft the Second Amendment as he did.

This sentiment was echoed at a number of state ratification conventions; indeed, it was one of the primary objections to the original Constitution voiced by its opponents. The Anti-Federalists were ultimately unsuccessful in persuading state ratification conventions to condition their approval of the Constitution upon the eventual inclusion of any particular amendment. But a number of States did propose to the first Federal Congress amendments reflecting a desire to ensure that the institution of the militia would remain protected under the new Government. The proposed amendments sent by the States of Virginia, North Carolina, and New York focused on the importance of preserving the state militias and reiterated the dangers posed by standing armies. New Hampshire sent a proposal that differed significantly from the others; while also [554 U. S. ____ (2008) 21] invoking the dangers of a standing army, it suggested that the Constitution should more broadly protect the use and possession of weapons, without tying such a guarantee expressly to the maintenance of the militia. The States of Maryland, Pennsylvania, and Massachusetts sent no relevant proposed amendments to Congress, but in each of those States a minority of the delegates advocated related amendments. While the Maryland minority proposals were exclusively concerned with standing armies and conscientious objectors, the unsuccessful proposals in both Massachusetts and Pennsylvania would have protected a more broadly worded right, less clearly tied to service in a state militia. Faced with all of these options, it is telling that James Madison chose to craft the Second Amendment as he did.

The relevant proposals sent by the Virginia Ratifying Convention read as follows:

"17th, That the people have a right to keep and bear arms; that a well regulated Militia composed of the body of the people trained to arms is the proper, natural and safe defence of a free State. That standing armies are dangerous to liberty, and therefore ought to be avoided, as far as the circumstances and protection of the Community will admit; and that in all cases the military should be under strict subordination to and be governed by the civil power." Elliot 659.

"19th. That any person religiously scrupulous of bearing arms ought to be exempted, upon payment of an equivalent to employ another to bear arms in his stead." *Ibid*.

North Carolina adopted Virginia's proposals and sent them to Congress as its own, although it did not actually ratify the original Constitution until Congress had sent the proposed Bill of Rights to the States for ratification. 2 [554 U. S. ____ (2008) 22] Schwartz 932–933; see The Complete Bill of Rights 182– 183 (N. Cogan ed. 1997) (hereinafter Cogan).

New York produced a proposal with nearly identical language. It read:

"That the people have a right to keep and bear Arms; that a well regulated Militia, including the body of the People capable of bearing Arms, is the proper, natural, and safe defence of a free State. . . . That standing Armies, in time of Peace, are dangerous to Liberty, and ought not to be kept up, except in Cases of necessity; and that at all times, the Military should be kept under strict Subordination to the civil Power." 2 Schwartz 912.

each proposal embedded the phrase within a group of principles that are distinctly military in meaning.

Notably, each of these proposals used the phrase "keep and bear arms," which was eventually adopted by Madison. And each proposal embedded the phrase within a group of principles that are distinctly military in meaning. n21

By contrast, New Hampshire's proposal, although it followed another proposed amendment that echoed the familiar concern about standing armies, n22 described the protection involved in more clearly personal terms. Its

n21 In addition to the cautionary references to standing armies and to the importance of civil authority over the military, each of the proposals contained a guarantee that closely resembled the language of what later became the Third Amendment. The 18th proposal from Virginia and North Carolina read "That no soldier in time of peace ought to be quartered in any house without the consent of the owner, and in time of war in such manner only as the law directs." Elliott 659. And New York's language read: "That in time of Peace no Soldier ought to be quartered in any House without the consent of the Owner, and in time of War only by the Civil Magistrate in such manner as the Laws may direct." 2 Schwartz 912.

n22 "Tenth, That no standing Army shall be Kept up in time of Peace unless with the consent of three fourths of the Members of each branch of Congress, nor shall Soldiers in Time of Peace be quartered upon private Houses with out the consent of the Owners."

[554 U. S. ____ (2008) 23] proposal read:

"Twelfth, Congress shall never disarm any Citizen unless such as are or have been in Actual Rebellion." Id., at 758, 761.

The proposals considered in the other three States, although ultimately rejected by their respective ratification conventions, are also relevant to our historical inquiry. First, the Maryland proposal, endorsed by a minority of the delegates and later circulated in pamphlet form, read:

"4. That no standing army shall be kept up in time of peace, unless with the consent of two thirds of the members present of each branch of Congress.

. . . . .

"10. That no person conscientiously scrupulous of bearing arms in any case, shall be compelled personally to serve as a soldier." Id., at 729, 735.

The rejected Pennsylvania proposal, which was later incorporated into a critique of the Constitution titled "The Address and Reasons of Dissent of the Pennsylvania Minority of the Convention of the State of Pennsylvania to Their Constituents (1787)," signed by a minority of the State's delegates (those who had voted against ratification of the Constitution), id., at 628, 662, read:

7. "That the people have a right to bear arms for the defense of themselves and their own State, or the United States, or for the purpose of killing game; and no law shall be passed for disarming the people or any of them unless for crimes committed, or real danger of public injury from individuals; and as standing armies in the time of peace are dangerous to liberty, they ought not to be kept up; and that the military shall be kept under strict subordination to, and be governed by the civil powers." Id., at 665.

[554 U. S. ____ (2008) 24] Finally, after the delegates at the Massachusetts Ratification Convention had compiled a list of proposed amendments and alterations, a motion was made to add to the list the following language: "[T]hat the said Constitution never be construed to authorize Congress to . . . prevent the people of the United States, who are peaceable citizens, from keeping their own arms." Cogan 181. This motion, however, failed to achieve the necessary support, and the proposal was excluded from the list of amendments the State sent to Congress. 2 Schwartz 674–675.

Madison, charged with the task of assembling the proposals for amendments sent by the ratifying States, was the principal draftsman of the Second Amendment. He had before him, or at the very least would have been aware of, all of these proposed formulations.

Madison, charged with the task of assembling the proposals for amendments sent by the ratifying States, was the principal draftsman of the Second Amendment. n23 He had before him, or at the very least would have been aware of, all of these proposed formulations. In addition, Madison had been a member, some years earlier, of the committee tasked with drafting the Virginia Declaration of Rights. That committee considered a proposal by Thomas Jefferson that would have included within the Virginia Declaration the following language: "No freeman shall ever be debarred the use of arms [within his own lands or tenements]." 1 Papers of Thomas Jefferson 363 (J. Boyd ed. 1950). But the committee rejected that language, adopting instead the provision drafted by George Mason. n24

n23 Madison explained in a letter to Richard Peters, Aug. 19, 1789, the paramount importance of preparing a list of amendments to placate those States that had ratified the Constitution in reliance on a commitment that amendments would follow: "In many States the [Constitution] was adopted under a tacit compact in [favor] of some subsequent provisions on this head. In [Virginia]. It would have been *certainly* rejected, had no assurances been given by its advocates that such provisions would be pursued. As an honest man *I feel* my self bound by this consideration." Creating the Bill of Rights 281, 282 (H. Veit, K. Bowling, & C. Bickford eds. 1991) (hereinafter Veit).

n24 The adopted language, Virginia Declaration of Rights ¶13 (1776), read as follows: "That a well-regulated Militia, composed of the body of [554 U. S. ____ (2008) 25] the people, trained to arms, is the proper, natural, and safe defence of a free State; that Standing Armies, in time of peace, should be avoided as dangerous to liberty; and that, in all cases, the military should be under strict subordination to, and governed by, the civil power." 1 Schwartz 234.

With all of these sources upon which to draw, it is strikingly significant that Madison's first draft omitted any mention of nonmilitary use or possession of weapons.

With all of these sources upon which to draw, it is strikingly significant that Madison's first draft omitted any mention of nonmilitary use or possession of weapons. Rather, his original draft repeated the essence of the two proposed amendments sent by Virginia, combining the substance of the two provisions succinctly into one, which read: "The right of the people to keep and bear arms shall not be infringed; a well armed, and well regulated militia being the best security of a free country; but no person religiously scrupulous of bearing arms, shall be compelled to render military service in person." Cogan 169.

Madison's decision to model the Second Amendment on the distinctly military Virginia proposal is therefore revealing, since it is clear that he

considered and rejected formulations that would have unambiguously protected civilian uses of firearms.

it is reasonable to assume that all participants in the drafting process were fully aware of the other formulations that would have protected civilian use and possession of weapons and that their choice to craft the Amendment as they did represented a rejection of those alternative formulations.

Madison's decision to model the Second Amendment on the distinctly military Virginia proposal is therefore revealing, since it is clear that he considered and rejected formulations that would have unambiguously protected civilian uses of firearms. When Madison prepared his first draft, and when that draft was debated and modified, it is reasonable to assume that all participants in the drafting process were fully aware of the other formulations that would have protected civilian use and possession of weapons and that their choice to craft the Amendment as they did represented a rejection of those alternative formulations.

Madison's initial inclusion of an exemption for conscientious objectors sheds revelatory light on the purpose of the Amendment. It confirms an intent to describe a duty as well as a right, and it unequivocally identifies the military character of both. The objections voiced to the conscientious- objector clause only confirm the central meaning of the text. Although records of the debate in the Senate, which is where the conscientious-objector clause was [554 U. S. ____ (2008) 26] removed, do not survive, the arguments raised in the House illuminate the perceived problems with the clause: Specifically, there was concern that Congress "can declare who are those religiously scrupulous, and prevent them from bearing arms." n25 The ultimate removal of the clause, therefore, only serves to confirm the purpose of the Amendment—to protect against congressional disarmament, by whatever means, of the States' militias.

n25 Veit 182. This was the objection voiced by Elbridge Gerry, who went on to remark, in the next breath: "What, sir, is the use of a militia? It is to prevent the establishment of a standing army, the bane of liberty. . ... Whenever government mean to invade the rights and liberties of the people, they always attempt to destroy the militia, in order to raise an army upon their ruins." *Ibid.*

The Court also contends that because "Quakers opposed the use of arms not just for militia service, but for any violent purpose whatsoever," *ante,* at 17, the inclusion of a conscientious-objector clause in the original draft of the Amendment does not support the conclusion that the phrase "bear arms" was military in meaning. But that claim cannot be squared with the record. In the proposals cited *supra,* at 21–22, both Virginia and North Carolina included the following language: "That any person religiously scrupulous of bearing arms ought to be exempted, upon payment of an equivalent *to employ another to bear arms in his stead*" (emphasis added). n26 There is no plausible argument that the use of "bear arms" in those provisions was not unequivocally and exclusively military: The State simply does not compel its citizens to carry arms for the purpose of private "confrontation," *ante,* at 10, or for self-defense.

n26 The failed Maryland proposals contained similar language. See *supra,* at 23.

The evidence plainly refutes the claim that the Amendment was motivated by the Framers' fears that Congress might act to regulate any civilian uses of weapons.

The history of the adoption of the Amendment thus describes an overriding concern about the potential threat to state sovereignty that a federal standing army would [554 U. S. ____ (2008) 27] pose, and a desire to protect the States' militias as the means by which to guard against that danger. But state militias could not effectively check the prospect of a federal standing army so long as Congress retained the power to disarm them, and so a guarantee against such disarmament was needed. n27 As we explained in *Miller:* "With obvious purpose to assure the continuation and render possible the effectiveness of such forces the declaration and guarantee of the Second Amendment were made. It must be interpreted and applied with that end in view." 307 U. S., at 178. The evidence plainly refutes the claim that the Amendment was motivated by the Framers' fears that Congress might act to regulate any civilian uses of weapons. And even if the historical record were genuinely ambiguous, the burden would remain on the parties advocating a change in the law to introduce facts or arguments " 'newly ascertained,' " *Vasquez,* 474 U. S., at 266; the Court is unable to identify any such facts or arguments.

n27 The Court suggests that this historical analysis casts the Second Amendment as an "odd outlier," *ante,* at 30; if by "outlier," the Court means that the Second Amendment was enacted in a unique and novel context, and responded to the particular challenges presented by the Framers' federalism experiment, I have no quarrel with the Court's characterization.

III

Although it gives short shrift to the drafting history of the Second Amendment, the Court dwells at length on four other sources: the 17th-century English Bill of Rights; Blackstone's Commentaries on the Laws of England; postenactment commentary on the Second Amendment; and post-Civil War legislative history. n28 All of these

n28 The Court's fixation on the last two types of sources is particularly puzzling, since both have the same characteristics as postenactment legislative history, which is generally viewed as the least reliable source of authority for ascertaining the intent of any provision's drafters. As has been explained:

[554 U. S. ____ (2008) 28] "The legislative history of a statute is the history of its consideration and enactment. 'Subsequent legislative history'—which presumably means the *post*-enactment history of a statute's consideration and enactment—is a contradiction in terms. The phrase is used to smuggle into judicial consideration legislators' expression *not* of what a bill currently under consideration means (which, the theory goes, reflects what their colleagues understood they were voting for), but of what a law *previously enacted* means. . . . In my opinion, the views of a legislator concerning a statute already enacted are entitled to no more weight than the views of a judge concerning a statute not yet passed." *Sullivan* v. *Finkelstein,* 496 U. S. 617, 631–632 (1990) (SCALIA, J., concurring in part).

sources shed only indirect light on the question before us, and in any event offer little support for the Court's conclusion. n29

n29 The Court stretches to derive additional support from scattered state-court cases primarily concerned with state constitutional provisions. See *ante,* at 38–41. To the extent that those state courts assumed that the Second Amendment was coterminous with their differently worded state constitutional arms provisions, their discussions were of course dicta. Moreover, the cases on which the Court relies were decided between 30 and 60 years after the ratification of the Second Amendment, and there is no indication that any of them engaged in a careful textual or historical analysis of the federal constitutional provision. Finally, the interpretation of the Second Amendment advanced in those cases is not as clear as the Court apparently believes. In *Aldridge* v. *Commonwealth,* 2 Va. Cas. 447 (Gen. Ct. 1824), for example, a Virginia court pointed to the restriction on free blacks' "right to bear arms" as evidence that the protections of the State and Federal Constitutions did not extend to free blacks. The Court asserts that "[t]he claim was obviously not that blacks were prevented from carrying guns in the militia*." Ante,* at

39. But it is not obvious at all. For in many States, including Virginia, free blacks during the colonial period were prohibited from carrying guns in the militia, instead being required to "muste[r] without arms"; they were later barred from serving in the militia altogether. See Siegel, The Federal Government's Power to Enact Color-Conscious Laws: An Originalist Inquiry, 92 Nw. U. L. Rev. 477, 497–498, and n. 120 (1998). But my point is not that the *Aldridge* court endorsed my view of the Amendment—plainly it did not, as the premise of the relevant passage was that the Second Amendment applied to the States. Rather, my point is simply that the court could have understood the Second Amendment to protect a [554 U. S. ___ (2008) 29] militia-focused right, and thus that its passing mention of the right to bear arms provides scant support for the Court's position.

The English Bill of Rights

The Court's reliance on Article VII of the 1689 English Bill of Rights... is misguided

The Court's reliance on Article VII of the 1689 English Bill of Rights—which, like most of the evidence offered by the Court today, was considered in *Miller* n30 —is misguided both because Article VII was enacted in response to different concerns from those that motivated the Framers of the Second Amendment, and because the guarantees of the two provisions were by no means coextensive. Moreover, the English text contained no preamble or other provision identifying a narrow, militia-related purpose.

n30 The Government argued in its brief that:

"[I]t would seem that the early English law did not guarantee an unrestricted right to bear arms. Such recognition as existed of a right in the people to keep and bear arms appears to have resulted from oppression by rulers who disarmed their political opponents and who organized large standing armies which were obnoxious and burdensome to the people. This right, however, it is clear, gave sanction only to the arming of the people as a body to defend their rights against tyrannical and unprincipled rulers. It did not permit the keeping of arms for purposes of private defense." Brief for United States in *United States* v. *Miller,* O. T. 1938, No. 696, pp. 11–12 (citations omitted). The Government then cited at length the Tennessee Supreme Court's opinion in *Aymette,* 21 Tenn. 154, which further situated the English Bill of Rights in its historical context. See n. 10, *supra.*

the right was qualified in two distinct ways: First, it was restricted to those of adequate social and economic status ("suitable to their Condition"); second, it was only available subject to regulation by Parliament ("as allowed by Law")

The English Bill of Rights responded to abuses by the Stuart monarchs; among the grievances set forth in the Bill of Rights was that the King had violated the law "[b]y causing several good Subjects being Protestants to be disarmed at the same time when Papists were both armed and Employed contrary to Law." Article VII of the Bill of Rights was a response to that selective disarmament; it guaranteed that "the Subjects which are Protestants may have Armes for their defence, Suitable to their condition and as allowed by Law." L. Schwoerer, The Declaration of Rights, 1689 (App. 1, pp. 295, 297) (1981). This grant did [554 U. S. ___ (2008) 30] not establish a general right of all persons, or even of all Protestants, to possess weapons. Rather, the right was qualified in two distinct ways: First, it was restricted to those of adequate social and economic status ("suitable to their Condition"); second, it was only available subject to regulation by Parliament ("as allowed by Law"). n31 n31 Moreover, it was the Crown, not Parliament, that was bound by the English provision; indeed, according to some prominent historians, Article VII is best understood not as announcing any individual right to unregulated firearm ownership (after all, such a reading would fly in the face of the text), but as an assertion of the concept of parliamentary supremacy. See Brief for Jack N. Rakove et al. as *Amici Curiae* 6–9.

The Court may well be correct that the English Bill of Rights protected the right of *some* English subjects to use *some* arms for personal self-defense free from restrictions by the Crown (but not Parliament). But that right—adopted in a different historical and political context and framed in markedly different language—tells us little about the meaning of the Second Amendment.

Blackstone's Commentaries

The excerpt from Blackstone offered by the Court, therefore, is, like Article VII itself, of limited use in interpreting the very differently worded, and differently historically situated, Second Amendment.

The Court's reliance on Blackstone's Commentaries on the Laws of England is unpersuasive for the same reason as its reliance on the English Bill of Rights. Blackstone's invocation of " 'the natural right of resistance and self-preservation,' " *ante*, at 20, and " 'the right of having and using arms for self-preservation and defence' " *ibid.*, referred specifically to Article VII in the English Bill of Rights. The excerpt from Blackstone offered by the Court, therefore, is, like Article VII itself, of limited use in interpreting the very differently worded, and differently historically situated, Second Amendment.

Blackstone described an interpretive approach that gave far more weight to preambles than the Court allows.

the proeme, or preamble, is often called in to help the construction of an act of parliament."

What *is* important about Blackstone is the instruction he provided on reading the sort of text before us today. Blackstone described an interpretive approach that gave far more weight to preambles than the Court allows. [554 U. S. ____ (2008) 31] Counseling that "[t]he fairest and most rational method to interpret the will of the legislator, is by exploring his intentions at the time when the law was made, by *signs* the most natural and probable," Blackstone explained that "[i]f words happen to be still dubious, we may establish their meaning from the context; with which it may be of singular use to compare a word, or a sentence, whenever they are ambiguous, equivocal, or intricate. Thus, the proeme, or preamble, is often called in to help the construction of an act of parliament." 1 Commentaries on the Laws of England 59–60 (1765) (hereinafter Blackstone). In light of the Court's invocation of Blackstone as " 'the preeminent authority on English law for the founding generation,' " *ante*, at 20 (quoting *Alden* v. *Maine*, 527 U. S. 706, 715 (1999)), its disregard for his guidance on matters of interpretation is striking.

Postenactment Commentary

The Court also excerpts, without any real analysis, commentary by a number of additional scholars, some near in time to the framing and others post-dating it by close to a century. Those scholars are for the most part of limited relevance in construing the guarantee of the Second Amendment: Their views are not altogether clear, n32

n32 For example, St. George Tucker, on whom the Court relies heavily, did not consistently adhere to the position that the Amendment was designed to protect the

"Blackstonian" self-defense right, *ante,* at 33. In a series of unpublished lectures, Tucker suggested that the Amendment should be understood in the context of the compromise over military power represented by the original Constitution and the Second and Tenth Amendments:

"If a State chooses to incur the expense of putting arms into the Hands of its own Citizens for their defense, it would require no small ingenuity to prove that they have no right to do it, or that it could by any means contravene the Authority of the federal Govt. It may be alleged indeed that this might be done for the purpose of resisting the laws of the federal Government, or of shaking off the union: to which the plainest [554 U. S. ____ (2008) 32] answer seems to be, that whenever the States think proper to adopt either of these measures, they will not be with-held by the fear of infringing any of the powers of the federal Government. But to contend that such a power would be dangerous for the reasons above maintained would be subversive of every principle of Freedom in our Government; of which the first Congress appears to have been sensible by proposing an Amendment to the Constitution, which has since been ratified and has become part of it, viz., 'That a well regulated militia being necessary to the Security of a free State, the right of the people to keep and bear arms shall not be infringed.' To this we may add that this power of arming the militia, is not one of those prohibited to the States by the Constitution, and, consequently, is reserved to them under the twelfth Article of the ratified aments." S. Tucker, Ten Notebooks of Law Lectures, 1790's, Tucker-Coleman Papers, pp. 127– 128 (College of William and Mary).

See also Cornell, St. George Tucker and the Second Amendment: Original Understandings and Modern Misunderstandings, 47 Wm. & Mary L. Rev. 1123 (2006).

they tended to collapse the Second Amendment with Article VII of the English Bill of Rights, and they appear to have been unfamiliar with the drafting history of the Second Amendment. n33

The Court does acknowledge that at least one early commentator described the Second Amendment as creating a right conditioned upon service in a state militia... what is striking about the Court's discussion is its failure to refute Oliver's description of the meaning of the Amendment or the intent of its drafters; rather, the Court adverts to simple nose-counting to dismiss his view.

n33 The Court does acknowledge that at least one early commentator described the Second Amendment as creating a right conditioned upon service in a state militia. See *ante,* at 37–38 (citing B. Oliver, The Rights of an American Citizen (1832)). Apart from the fact that Oliver is the *only* commentator in the Court's exhaustive survey who appears to have inquired into the intent of the drafters of the Amendment, what is striking about the Court's discussion is its failure to refute Oliver's description of the meaning of the Amendment or the intent of its drafters; rather, the Court adverts to simple nose-counting to dismiss his view.

Contrary to the Court's assertions, however, Story actually supports the view that the Amendment was designed to protect the right of each of the States to maintain a well-regulated militia.

The most significant of these commentators was Joseph Story. Contrary to the Court's assertions, however, Story actually supports the view that the Amendment was designed to protect the right of each of the States to maintain a well-regulated militia. When Story used the term "palladium" in discussions of the Second Amendment, he merely echoed the concerns that animated the Framers of the Amendment and led to its adoption. An excerpt from [554 U. S. ____ (2008) 33] his 1833 Commentaries on the Constitution of the United States—the same passage cited by the Court in *Miller* n34 —merits reproducing at some length:

n34 *Miller,* 307 U. S., at 182, n. 3.

It is against sound policy for a free people to keep up large military establishments and standing armies in time of peace, both from the enormous expenses with which they are attended and the facile means which they afford to ambitious and unprincipled rulers to subvert the government, or trample upon the rights of the people.

among the American people, there is a growing indifference to any system of militia discipline, and a strong disposition, from a sense of its burdens, to be rid of all regulations.

"The importance of [the Second Amendment] will scarcely be doubted by any persons who have duly reflected upon the subject. The militia is the natural defence of a free country against sudden foreign invasions, domestic insurrections, and domestic usurpations of power by rulers. It is against sound policy for a free people to keep up large military establishments and standing armies in time of peace, both from the enormous expenses with which they are attended and the facile means which they afford to ambitious and unprincipled rulers to subvert the government, or trample upon the rights of the people. The right of the citizens to keep and bear arms has justly been considered as the palladium of the liberties of a republic, since it offers a strong moral check against the usurpation and arbitrary power of rulers, and will generally, even if these are successful in the first instance, enable the people to resist and triumph over them. And yet, though this truth would seem so clear, and the importance of a well-regulated militia would seem so undeniable, it cannot be disguised that, among the American people, there is a growing indifference to any system of militia discipline, and a strong disposition, from a sense of its burdens, to be rid of all regulations.

How it is practicable to keep the people duly armed without some organization, it is difficult to see.

How it is practicable to keep the people duly armed without some organization, it is difficult to see. There is certainly no small danger that indifference may lead to disgust, and disgust to contempt; and thus gradually undermine all the protection intended by the clause of our national bill of rights." 2 J. Story, Commentaries on the Constitution of the United [554 U. S. ____ (2008) 34] States §1897, pp. 620–621 (4th ed. 1873) (footnote omitted).

There is not so much as a whisper in the passage above that Story believed that the right secured by the Amendment bore any relation to private use or possession of weapons for activities like hunting or personal self-defense.

Story thus began by tying the significance of the Amendment directly to the paramount importance of the militia. He then invoked the fear that drove the Framers of the Second Amendment—specifically, the threat to liberty posed by a standing army. An important check on that danger, he suggested, was a "well-regulated militia," *id.,* at 621, for which he assumed that arms would have to be kept and, when necessary, borne. There is not so much as a whisper in the passage above that Story believed that the right secured by the

Amendment bore any relation to private use or possession of weapons for activities like hunting or personal self-defense.

After extolling the virtues of the militia as a bulwark against tyranny, Story went on to decry the "growing indifference to any system of militia discipline." *Ibid.* When he wrote, "[h]ow it is practicable to keep the people duly armed without some organization it is difficult to see," *ibid.*, he underscored the degree to which he viewed the arming of the people and the militia as indissolubly linked. Story warned that the "growing indifference" he perceived would "gradually undermine all the protection intended by this clause of our national bill of rights," *ibid.* In his view, the importance of the Amendment was directly related to the continuing vitality of an institution in the process of apparently becoming obsolete.

Story's exclusive focus on the militia in his discussion of the Second Amendment confirms his understanding of the right protected by the Second Amendment as limited to military uses of arms.

In an attempt to downplay the absence of any reference to nonmilitary uses of weapons in Story's commentary, the Court relies on the fact that Story characterized Article VII of the English Declaration of Rights as a " 'similar provision,' " *ante,* at 36. The two provisions were indeed similar, in that both protected some uses of firearms. But Story's characterization in no way suggests that he believed that the provisions had the same scope. To the [554 U. S. ____ (2008) 35] contrary, Story's exclusive focus on the militia in his discussion of the Second Amendment confirms his understanding of the right protected by the Second Amendment as limited to military uses of arms.

Justice Story did not view the Amendment as conferring upon individuals any "self-defense" right disconnected from service in a state militia.

Story's writings as a Justice of this Court, to the extent that they shed light on this question, only confirm that Justice Story did not view the Amendment as conferring upon individuals any "self-defense" right disconnected from service in a state militia. Justice Story dissented from the Court's decision in *Houston* v. *Moore,* 5 Wheat. 1, 24 (1820), which held that a state court "had a concurrent jurisdiction" with the federal courts "to try a militia man who had disobeyed the call of the President, and to enforce the laws of Congress against such delinquent." *Id.,* at 31– 32. Justice Story believed that Congress' power to provide for the organizing, arming, and disciplining of the militia was, when Congress acted, plenary; but he explained that in the absence of congressional action, "I am certainly not prepared to deny the legitimacy of such an exercise of [state] authority." *Id.,* at 52. As to the Second Amendment, he wrote that it "may not, perhaps, be thought to have any important bearing on this point. If it have, it confirms and illustrates, rather than impugns the reasoning already suggested." *Id.,* at 52–53. The Court contends that had Justice Story understood the Amendment to have a militia purpose, the Amendment would have had "enormous and obvious bearing on the point." *Ante,* at 38. But the Court has it quite backwards: If Story had believed that the purpose of the Amendment was to permit civilians to keep firearms for activities like personal self-defense, what "confirm[ation] and illustrat[ion]," *Houston,* 5 Wheat., at 53, could the Amendment possibly have provided for the point that States retained the power to organize, arm, and discipline their own militias? [554 U. S. ____ (2008) 36]

Post-Civil War Legislative History

The Court suggests that by the post-Civil War period, the Second Amendment was understood to secure a right to firearm use and

ownership for purely private purposes like personal self-defense... such sources are entitled to limited, if any, weight.

All of the statements the Court cites were made long after the framing of the Amendment and cannot possibly supply any insight into the intent of the Framers

The Court suggests that by the post-Civil War period, the Second Amendment was understood to secure a right to firearm use and ownership for purely private purposes like personal self-defense. While it is true that some of the legislative history on which the Court relies supports that contention, see *ante,* at 41–44, such sources are entitled to limited, if any, weight. All of the statements the Court cites were made long after the framing of the Amendment and cannot possibly supply any insight into the intent of the Framers; and all were made during pitched political debates, so that they are better characterized as advocacy than good-faith attempts at constitutional interpretation.

What is more, much of the evidence the Court offers is decidedly less clear than its discussion allows. The Court notes that "[b]lacks were routinely disarmed by Southern States after the Civil War. Those who opposed these injustices frequently stated that they infringed blacks' constitutional right to keep and bear arms." *Ante,* at 42. The Court hastily concludes that "[n]eedless to say, the claim was not that blacks were being prohibited from carrying arms in an organized state militia," *ibid.* But some of the claims of the sort the Court cites may have been just that. In some Southern States, Reconstruction-era Republican governments created state militias in which both blacks and whites were permitted to serve. Because "[t]he decision to allow blacks to serve alongside whites meant that most southerners refused to join the new militia," the bodies were dubbed "Negro militia[s]." S. Cornell, A Well-Regulated Militia 176–177 (2006). The "arming of the Negro militias met with especially fierce resistance in South Carolina. . . . The sight of organized, armed freedmen incensed opponents of Reconstruction and led to an intensified campaign of Klan terror. Leading members of the Negro militia were beaten or lynched and their weapons stolen." *Id.,* at 177.

[554 U. S. ____ (2008) 37] One particularly chilling account of Reconstruction-era Klan violence directed at a black militia member is recounted in the memoir of Louis F. Post, A "Carpetbagger" in South Carolina, 10 Journal of Negro History 10 (1925). Post describes the murder by local Klan members of Jim Williams, the captain of a "Negro militia company," *id.,* at 59, this way:

"[A] cavalcade of sixty cowardly white men, completely disguised with face masks and body gowns, rode up one night in March, 1871, to the house of Captain Williams . . . in the wood [they] hanged [and shot] him . . . [and on his body they] then pinned a slip of paper inscribed, as I remember it, with these grim words: 'Jim Williams gone to his last muster.' " *Id.,* at 61.

In light of this evidence, it is quite possible that at least some of the statements on which the Court relies actually did mean to refer to the disarmament of black militia members.

IV

The brilliance of the debates that resulted in the Second Amendment faded into oblivion during the ensuing years, for the concerns about Article I's Militia Clauses that generated such pitched debate during the ratification process and led to the adoption of the Second Amendment were short lived.

In 1792, the year after the Amendment was ratified, Congress passed a statute that purported to establish "an Uniform Militia throughout the United States." 1 Stat. 271. The statute commanded every able-bodied white male citizen between the ages of 18 and 45 to be enrolled therein and to "provide himself with a good musket or [554 U. S. ____ (2008)

38] firelock" and other specified weaponry. n35 *Ibid.* The statute is significant, for it confirmed the way those in the founding generation viewed firearm ownership: as a duty linked to military service. The statute they enacted, however, "was virtually ignored for more than a century," and was finally repealed in 1901. See *Perpich,* 496 U. S., at 341.

n35 The additional specified weaponry included: "a sufficient bayonet and belt, two spare flints, and a knapsack, a pouch with a box therein to contain not less than twenty-four cartridges, suited to the bore of his musket or firelock, each cartridge to contain a proper quantity of powder and ball: or with a good rifle, knapsack, shot-pouch and powderhorn, twenty balls suited to the bore of his rifle and a quarter of a pound of powder." 1 Stat. 271.

The Amendment played little role in any legislative debate about the civilian use of firearms for most of the 19th century

The postratification history of the Second Amendment is strikingly similar. The Amendment played little role in any legislative debate about the civilian use of firearms for most of the 19th century, and it made few appearances in the decisions of this Court. Two 19th-century cases, however, bear mentioning.

In *United States* v. *Cruikshank,* 92 U. S. 542 (1876), the Court sustained a challenge to respondents' convictions under the Enforcement Act of 1870 for conspiring to deprive any individual of " 'any right or privilege granted or secured to him by the constitution or laws of the United States.' " *Id.,* at 548. The Court wrote, as to counts 2 and 10 of respondents' indictment:

"The right there specified is that of 'bearing arms for a lawful purpose.' This is not a right granted by the Constitution. Neither is it in any manner dependent on that instrument for its existence. The second amendment declares that it shall not be infringed; but this, as has been seen, means no more than that it shall not be infringed by Congress. This is one of the amendments that has no other effect than to restrict the powers of the national government." *Id.,* at 553.

The majority's assertion that the Court in *Cruikshank* "described the right protected by the Second Amendment as '"bearing arms for a lawful purpose,"' " is not accurate. The *Cruikshank* Court explained that the defective *indictment* contained such language, but the Court did not itself describe the right, or endorse the indictment's description

[554 U. S. ____ (2008) 39] The majority's assertion that the Court in *Cruikshank* "described the right protected by the Second Amendment as ' "bearing arms for a lawful purpose," ' " *ante,* at 47 (quoting *Cruikshank,* 92 U. S., at 553), is not accurate. The *Cruikshank* Court explained that the defective *indictment* contained such language, but the Court did not itself describe the right, or endorse the indictment's description of the right.

Moreover, it is entirely possible that the basis for the indictment's counts 2 and 10, which charged respondents with depriving the victims of rights secured by the Second Amendment, was the prosecutor's belief that the victims— members of a group of citizens, mostly black but also white, who were rounded up by the Sheriff, sworn in as a posse to defend the local courthouse, and attacked by a white mob—bore sufficient resemblance to members of a state militia that they were brought within the reach of the Second Amendment. See generally C. Lane, The Day Freedom Died: The Colfax Massacre, The Supreme Court, and the Betrayal of Reconstruction (2008).

Only one other 19th-century case in this Court, *Presser* v. *Illinois,* 116 U. S. 252 (1886), engaged in any significant discussion of the Second Amendment. The petitioner in *Presser* was convicted of violating a state statute that prohibited organizations other than the Illinois National Guard from associating together as military companies or parading with arms.

Presser challenged his conviction, asserting, as relevant, that the statute violated both the Second and the Fourteenth Amendments. With respect to the Second Amendment, the Court wrote:

We think it clear that the sections under consideration... do not infringe the right of the people to keep and bear arms.

"We think it clear that the sections under consideration, which only forbid bodies of men to associate together as military organizations, or to drill or parade with arms in cities and towns unless authorized by law, do not infringe the right of the people to keep and [554 U. S. ____ (2008) 40] bear arms. But a conclusive answer to the contention that this amendment prohibits the legislation in question lies in the fact that the amendment is a limitation only upon the power of Congress and the National government, and not upon that of the States." *Id.,* at 264–265.

And in discussing the Fourteenth Amendment, the Court explained:

"The plaintiff in error was not a member of the organized volunteer militia of the State of Illinois, nor did he belong to the troops of the United States or to any organization under the militia law of the United States. On the contrary, the fact that he did not belong to the organized militia or the troops of the United States was an ingredient in the offence for which he was convicted and sentenced. The question is, therefore, had he a right as a citizen of the United States, in disobedience of the State law, to associate with others as a military company, and to drill and parade with arms in the towns and cities of the State? If the plaintiff in error has any such privilege he must be able to point to the provision of the Constitution or statutes of the United States by which it is conferred." *Id.,* at 266.

Presser, therefore, both affirmed *Cruikshank's* holding that the Second Amendment posed no obstacle to regulation by state governments, and... nothing in the Constitution protected the use of arms outside the context of a militia "authorized by law" and organized by the State or Federal Government.

Presser, therefore, both affirmed *Cruikshank's* holding that the Second Amendment posed no obstacle to regulation by state governments, and suggested that in any event nothing in the Constitution protected the use of arms outside the context of a militia "authorized by law" and organized by the State or Federal Government. n36

n36 In another case the Court endorsed, albeit indirectly, the reading of *Miller* that has been well settled until today. In *Burton* v. *Sills,* 394 U. S. 812 (1969) *(per curiam),* the Court dismissed for want of a substantial federal question an appeal from a decision of the New Jersey [554 U. S. ____ (2008) 41] Supreme Court upholding, against a Second Amendment challenge, New Jersey's gun control law. Although much of the analysis in the New Jersey court's opinion turned on the inapplicability of the Second Amendment as a constraint on the States, the court also quite correctly read *Miller* to hold that "Congress, though admittedly governed by the second amendment, may regulate interstate firearms so long as the regulation does not impair the maintenance of the active, organized militia of the states." *Burton* v. *Sills,* 53 N. J. 86, 98, 248 A. 2d 521, 527 (1968).

In 1901 the President revitalized the militia by creating the National Guard of the several States

the dominant understanding of the Second Amendment's inapplicability to private gun ownership continued well into the 20th century.

the 1934 Act prohibiting the possession of sawed-off shotguns and machine guns—were enacted over minor Second Amendment objections dismissed by the vast majority of the legislators who participated in the debates.

for most legislators they did not even raise the specter of possible conflict with the Second Amendment.

In 1901 the President revitalized the militia by creating " 'the National Guard of the several States,' " *Perpich,* 496 U. S., at 341, and nn. 9–10; meanwhile, the dominant understanding of the Second Amendment's inapplicability to private gun ownership continued well into the 20th century. The first two federal laws directly restricting civilian use and possession of firearms—the 1927 Act prohibiting mail delivery of "pistols, revolvers, and other firearms capable of being concealed on the person," Ch. 75, 44 Stat. 1059, and the 1934 Act prohibiting the possession of sawed-off shotguns and machine guns—were enacted over minor Second Amendment objections dismissed by the vast majority of the legislators who participated in the debates. n37 Members of Congress clashed over the wisdom and efficacy of such laws as crime-control measures. But since the statutes did not infringe upon the military use or possession of weapons, for most legislators they did not even raise the specter of possible conflict with the Second Amendment.

n37 The 1927 statute was enacted with no mention of the Second Amendment as a potential obstacle, although an earlier version of the bill had generated some limited objections on Second Amendment grounds; see 66 Cong. Rec. 725–735 (1924). And the 1934 Act featured just one colloquy, during the course of lengthy Committee debates, on whether the Second Amendment constrained Congress' ability to legislate in this sphere; see Hearings on House Committee on Ways and Means H. R. 9006, before the 73d Cong., 2d Sess., p. 19 (1934).

for most of our history, the invalidity of Second-Amendment-based objections to firearms regulations has been well settled and uncontroversial.

the *Miller* Court unanimously concluded that the Second Amendment did not apply to the possession of a firearm that did not have "some reasonable relationship to the preservation or efficiency of a well regulated militia."

Thus, for most of our history, the invalidity of Second-Amendment-based objections to firearms regulations has [554 U. S. ____ (2008) 42] been well settled and uncontroversial. n38 Indeed, the Second Amendment was not even mentioned in either full House of Congress during the legislative proceedings that led to the passage of the 1934 Act. Yet enforcement of that law produced the judicial decision that confirmed the status of the Amendment as limited in reach to military usage. After reviewing many of the same sources that are discussed at greater length by the Court today, the *Miller* Court unanimously concluded that the Second Amendment did not apply to the possession of a firearm that did not have "some reasonable relationship to the preservation or efficiency of a well regulated militia." 307 U. S., at 178.

The majority appears to suggest that even if the meaning of the Second Amendment has been considered settled by courts and legislatures for over two centuries, that settled meaning is overcome by

the "reliance of millions of Americans" "upon the true meaning of
the right to keep and bear arms."

Presumably... the Court means that many Americans own guns for self-
defense, recreation, and other lawful purposes, and object to government
interference with their gun ownership. I do not dispute the correctness of
this observation. But it is hard to see how Americans have "relied," in the
usual sense of the word, on the existence of a constitutional right that,
until 2001, had been rejected by every federal court
to take up the question.

n38 The majority appears to suggest that even if the meaning of the Second
Amendment has been considered settled by courts and legislatures for over two
centuries, that settled meaning is overcome by the "reliance of millions of
Americans" "upon the true meaning of the right to keep and bear arms." *Ante,* at 52,
n. 24. Presumably by this the Court means that many Americans own guns for self-
defense, recreation, and other lawful purposes, and object to government
interference with their gun ownership. I do not dispute the correctness of this
observation. But it is hard to see how Americans have "relied," in the usual sense of
the word, on the existence of a constitutional right that, until 2001, had been rejected
by every federal court to take up the question. Rather, gun owners have "relied" on
the laws passed by democratically elected legislatures, which have generally
adopted only limited gun-control measures.

Indeed, reliance interests surely cut the other way: Even apart from the
reliance of judges and legislators who properly believed, until today, that
the Second Amendment did not reach possession of firearms for purely
private activities, "millions of Americans," have relied on the power of
government to protect their safety and well-being,
and that of their families.

Indeed, reliance interests surely cut the other way: Even apart from the reliance
of judges and legislators who properly believed, until today, that the Second
Amendment did not reach possession of firearms for purely private activities,
"millions of Americans," have relied on the power of government to protect their
safety and well-being, and that of their families. With respect to the case before us,
the legislature of the District of Columbia has relied on its ability to act to "reduce
the potentiality for gun-related crimes and gun-related deaths from occurring within
the District of Columbia," H. Con. Res. 694, 94th Cong., 2d Sess., 25 (1976); see
post, at 14–17 (BREYER, J., dissenting); so, too have the residents of the District.

The key to that decision... turned, rather, on the basic difference between
the military and nonmilitary use and possession of guns.

If use for self-defense were the relevant standard, why did the Court not
inquire into the suitability of a particular weapon
for self-defense purposes?

The key to that decision did not, as the Court belatedly suggests, *ante,* at 49–51, turn
on the difference between [554 U. S. ____ (2008) 43] muskets and sawed-off shotguns; it
turned, rather, on the basic difference between the military and nonmilitary use and
possession of guns. Indeed, if the Second Amendment were not limited in its coverage to
military uses of weapons, why should the Court in *Miller* have suggested that some

weapons but not others were eligible for Second Amendment protection? If use for self-defense were the relevant standard, why did the Court not inquire into the suitability of a particular weapon for self-defense purposes?

as our decision in *Marbury* v. *Madison,* in which only one side appeared and presented arguments, demonstrates, the absence of adversarial presentation alone is not a basis for refusing to accord *stare decisis* effect to a decision of this Court.

those sources upon which the Court today relies most heavily *were* available to the *Miller* Court.

Perhaps in recognition of the weakness of its attempt to distinguish *Miller*, the Court argues in the alternative that *Miller* should be discounted because of its decisional history. It is true that the appellee in *Miller* did not file a brief or make an appearance, although the court below had held that the relevant provision of the National Firearms Act violated the Second Amendment (albeit without any reasoned opinion). But, as our decision in *Marbury* v. *Madison*, 1 Cranch 137, in which only one side appeared and presented arguments, demonstrates, the absence of adversarial presentation alone is not a basis for refusing to accord *stare decisis* effect to a decision of this Court. See Bloch, *Marbury* Redux, in Arguing *Marbury* v. *Madison* 59, 63 (M. Tushnet ed. 2005). Of course, if it can be demonstrated that new evidence or arguments were genuinely not available to an earlier Court, that fact should be given special weight as we consider whether to overrule a prior case. But the Court does not make that claim, because it cannot. Although it is true that the drafting history of the Amendment was not discussed in the Government's brief, see *ante*, at 51, it is certainly not the drafting history that the Court's decision today turns on. And those sources upon which the Court today relies most heavily *were* available to the *Miller* Court. The Government cited the English Bill of Rights and quoted a lengthy passage from *Aymette* detailing the history leading to the [554 U. S. ___ (2008) 44] English guarantee, Brief for United States in *United States* v. *Miller*, O. T. 1938, No. 696, pp 12–13; it also cited Blackstone, *id.*, at 9, n. 2, Cooley, *id.*, at 12, 15, and Story, *id.*, at 15. The Court is reduced to critiquing the number of *pages* the Government devoted to exploring the English legal sources. Only two (in a brief 21 pages in length)! Would the Court be satisfied with four? Ten?

The Court is simply wrong when it intones that *Miller* contained "*not a word*" about the Amendment's history.

The Court is simply wrong when it intones that *Miller* contained "*not a word*" about the Amendment's history. *Ante*, at 52. The Court plainly looked to history to construe the term "Militia," and, on the best reading of *Miller*, the entire guarantee of the Second Amendment. After noting the original Constitution's grant of power to Congress and to the States over the militia, the Court explained:

"With obvious purpose to assure the continuation and render possible the effectiveness of such forces the declaration and guarantee of the Second Amendment were made. It must be interpreted and applied with that end in view.

"The Militia which the States were expected to maintain and train is set in contrast with Troops which they were forbidden to keep without the consent of Congress. The sentiment of the time strongly disfavored standing armies; the common view was that adequate defense of country and laws could be secured through the Militia—civilians primarily, soldiers on occasion.

"The signification attributed to the term Militia appears from the debates in the Convention, the history and legislation of Colonies and States, and the writings of approved commentators." *Miller*, 307 U. S., at 178–179.

The majority cannot seriously believe that the *Miller* Court did not consider any relevant evidence; the majority simply does not approve of the conclusion the *Miller* Court reached on that evidence.

that is insufficient reason to disregard a unanimous opinion of this Court, upon which substantial reliance has been placed by legislators and citizens for nearly 70 years.

The majority cannot seriously believe that the *Miller* Court did not consider any relevant evidence; the majority [554 U. S. ____ (2008) 45] simply does not approve of the conclusion the *Miller* Court reached on that evidence. Standing alone, that is insufficient reason to disregard a unanimous opinion of this Court, upon which substantial reliance has been placed by legislators and citizens for nearly 70 years.

V

the right the Court announces was not "enshrined" in the Second Amendment by the Framers; it is the product of today's law-changing decision.

The Court concludes its opinion by declaring that it is not the proper role of this Court to change the meaning of rights "enshrine[d]" in the Constitution. *Ante,* at 64. But the right the Court announces was not "enshrined" in the Second Amendment by the Framers; it is the product of today's law-changing decision. The majority's exegesis has utterly failed to establish that as a matter of text or history, "the right of law-abiding, responsible citizens to use arms in defense of hearth and home" is "elevate[d] above all other interests" by the Second Amendment. *Ante,* at 64.

Until today, it has been understood that legislatures may regulate the civilian use and misuse of firearms so long as they do not interfere with the preservation of a well-regulated militia.

The Court's announcement of a new constitutional right to own and use firearms for private purposes upsets that settled understanding

the reality that the need to defend oneself may suddenly arise in a host of locations outside the home, I fear that the District's policy choice may well be just the first of an unknown number of dominoe to be knocked off the table.

Until today, it has been understood that legislatures may regulate the civilian use and misuse of firearms so long as they do not interfere with the preservation of a well-regulated militia. The Court's announcement of a new constitutional right to own and use firearms for private purposes upsets that settled understanding, but leaves for future cases the formidable task of defining the scope of permissible regulations. Today judicial craftsmen have confidently asserted that a policy choice that denies a "law-abiding, responsible citize[n]" the right to keep and use weapons in the home for self-defense is "off the table." *Ante,* at 64. Given the presumption that most citizens are law abiding, and the reality that the need to defend oneself may suddenly arise in a host of locations outside the home, I fear that the District's policy choice may well be just the first of an unknown number of dominoes to be [554 U. S. ____ (2008) 46] knocked off the table. n39

no one has suggested that the political process is not working exactly as it should in mediating the debate between the advocates and opponents of gun control.

adherence to a policy of judicial restraint would be far wiser than the bold decision announced today.

n39 It was just a few years after the decision in *Miller* that Justice Frankfurter (by any measure a true judicial conservative) warned of the perils that would attend this Court's entry into the "political thicket" of legislative districting. *Colegrove* v. *Green,* 328 U. S. 549, 556 (1946) (plurality opinion). The equally controversial political thicket that the Court has decided to enter today is qualitatively different from the one that concerned Justice Frankfurter: While our entry into that thicket was justified because the political process was manifestly unable to solve the problem of unequal districts, no one has suggested that the political process is not working exactly as it should in mediating the debate between the advocates and opponents of gun control. What impact the Court's unjustified entry into *this* thicket will have on that ongoing debate—or indeed on the Court itself—is a matter that future historians will no doubt discuss at length. It is, however, clear to me that adherence to a policy of judicial restraint would be far wiser than the bold decision announced today.

it will surely give rise to a far more active judicial role in making vitally important national policy decisions than was envisioned at any time in the 18th, 19th, or 20th centuries.

I do not know whether today's decision will increase the labor of federal judges to the "breaking point" envisioned by Justice Cardozo, but it will surely give rise to a far more active judicial role in making vitally important national policy decisions than was envisioned at any time in the 18th, 19th, or 20th centuries.

The Court would have us believe that over 200 years ago, the Framers made a choice to limit the tools available to elected officials wishing to regulate civilian uses of weapons, and to authorize this Court to use the common-law process of case-by-case judicial lawmaking to define the contours of acceptable gun control policy.

The Court properly disclaims any interest in evaluating the wisdom of the specific policy choice challenged in this case, but it fails to pay heed to a far more important policy choice—the choice made by the Framers themselves. The Court would have us believe that over 200 years ago, the Framers made a choice to limit the tools available to elected officials wishing to regulate civilian uses of weapons, and to authorize this Court to use the common-law process of case-by-case judicial lawmaking to define the contours of acceptable gun control policy. Absent compelling evidence that is nowhere to be found in the Court's opinion, I could not possibly conclude that the Framers made such a choice.

For these reasons, I respectfully dissent.

BREYER, J., dissenting

SUPREME COURT OF THE UNITED STATES

No. 07–290

DISTRICT OF COLUMBIA, ET AL., PETITIONERS *v.*
DICK ANTHONY HELLER
ON WRIT OF CERTIORARI TO THE UNITED STATES COURT OF APPEALS
FOR THE DISTRICT OF COLUMBIA CIRCUIT
[June 26, 2008]

JUSTICE BREYER, with whom JUSTICE STEVENS, JUSTICE SOUTER, and JUSTICE GINSBURG join, dissenting.

We must decide whether a District of Columbia law that prohibits the possession of handguns in the home violates the Second Amendment. The majority, relying upon its view that the Second Amendment seeks to protect a right of personal self-defense, holds that this law violates that Amendment. In my view, it does not.

I

The majority's conclusion is wrong for two independent reasons. The first reason is that set forth by JUSTICE STEVENS—namely, that the Second Amendment protects militia-related, not self-defense-related, interests.

self-defense alone, detached from any militia-related objective, is not the Amendment's concern.

The majority's conclusion is wrong for two independent reasons. The first reason is that set forth by JUSTICE STEVENS—namely, that the Second Amendment protects militia-related, not self-defense-related, interests. These two interests are sometimes intertwined. To assure 18thcentury citizens that they could keep arms for militia purposes would necessarily have allowed them to keep arms that they could have used for self-defense as well. But self-defense alone, detached from any militia-related objective, is not the Amendment's concern.

The second independent reason is that the protection the Amendment provides is not absolute. The Amendment permits government to regulate the interests that it serves... the majority's view cannot be correct unless it can show that the District's regulation is unreasonable or inappropriate in Second Amendment terms. This the majority cannot do.

The second independent reason is that the protection the Amendment provides is not absolute. The Amendment permits government to regulate the interests that it serves. Thus, irrespective of what those interests are— whether they do or do not include an independent interest [554 U. S. ____ (2008) 2] in self-defense—the majority's view cannot be correct unless it can show that the District's regulation is unreasonable or inappropriate in Second Amendment terms. This the majority cannot do.

the District's law is consistent with the Second Amendment even if that Amendment is interpreted as protecting a wholly separate interest in

individual self-defense... the presence of handguns in high-crime urban areas, represents a permissible legislative response to a serious, indeed life-threatening, problem.

In respect to the first independent reason, I agree with JUSTICE STEVENS, and I join his opinion. In this opinion I shall focus upon the second reason. I shall show that the District's law is consistent with the Second Amendment even if that Amendment is interpreted as protecting a wholly separate interest in individual self-defense. That is so because the District's regulation, which focuses upon the presence of handguns in high-crime urban areas, represents a permissible legislative response to a serious, indeed life-threatening, problem.

the law will advance goals of great public importance, namely, saving lives, preventing injury, and reducing crime

the law concerns handguns, which are specially linked to urban gun deaths and injuries, and which are the overwhelmingly favorite weapon of armed criminals

the law imposes a burden upon gun owners that seems proportionately no greater than restrictions in existence at the time the Second Amendment was adopted.

the District's law falls within the zone that the Second Amendment leaves open to regulation by legislatures.

Thus I here assume that one objective (but, as the majority concedes, *ante*, at 26, not the *primary* objective) of those who wrote the Second Amendment was to help assure citizens that they would have arms available for purposes of self-defense. Even so, a legislature could reasonably conclude that the law will advance goals of great public importance, namely, saving lives, preventing injury, and reducing crime. The law is tailored to the urban crime problem in that it is local in scope and thus affects only a geographic area both limited in size and entirely urban; the law concerns handguns, which are specially linked to urban gun deaths and injuries, and which are the overwhelmingly favorite weapon of armed criminals; and at the same time, the law imposes a burden upon gun owners that seems proportionately no greater than restrictions in existence at the time the Second Amendment was adopted. In these circumstances, the District's law falls within the zone that the Second Amendment leaves open to regulation by legislatures.

II

The Second Amendment says that: "A well regulated [554 U. S. ____ (2008) 3] Militia, being necessary to the security of a free State, the right of the people to keep and bear Arms, shall not be infringed." In interpreting and applying this Amendment, I take as a starting point the following four propositions, based on our precedent and today's opinions, to which I believe the entire Court subscribes:

(1) The Amendment protects an "individual" right—*i.e.*, one that is separately possessed, and may be separately enforced, by each person on whom it is conferred. See, *e.g.*, *ante*, at 22 (opinion of the Court); *ante*, at 1 (STEVENS, J., dissenting).

(2) As evidenced by its preamble, the Amendment was adopted "[w]ith obvious purpose to assure the continuation and render possible the effectiveness of [militia] forces." *United States* v. *Miller*, 307 U. S. 174, 178 (1939); see *ante*, at 26 (opinion of the Court); *ante*, at 1 (STEVENS, J., dissenting).

(3) The Amendment "must be interpreted and applied with that end in view." *Miller*, *supra*, at 178.

The right protected by the Second Amendment is not absolute, but instead is subject to government regulation.

(4) The right protected by the Second Amendment is not absolute, but instead is subject to government regulation. See *Robertson* v. *Baldwin*, 165 U. S. 275, 281–282 (1897); *ante*, at 22, 54 (opinion of the Court).

the Amendment, in addition to furthering a militia-related purpose, also furthers an interest in possessing guns for purposes of self-defense, at least to some degree.

My approach to this case, while involving the first three points, primarily concerns the fourth. I shall, as I said, assume with the majority that the Amendment, in addition to furthering a militia-related purpose, also furthers an interest in possessing guns for purposes of self-defense, at least to some degree. And I shall then ask whether the Amendment nevertheless permits the District handgun restriction at issue here.

I shall not assume that the Amendment contains a specific untouchable right to keep guns in the house to shoot burglars.

Although I adopt for present purposes the majority's position that the Second Amendment embodies a general concern about self-defense, I shall not assume that the Amendment contains a specific untouchable right to keep guns in the house to shoot burglars. The majority, which [554 U. S. ___ (2008) 4] presents evidence in favor of the former proposition, does not, because it cannot, convincingly show that the Second Amendment seeks to maintain the latter in pristine, unregulated form.

To the contrary, colonial history itself offers important examples of the kinds of gun regulation that citizens would then have thought compatible with the "right to keep and bear arms,"... including regulations that imposed obstacles to the use of firearms for the protection of the home.

To the contrary, colonial history itself offers important examples of the kinds of gun regulation that citizens would then have thought compatible with the "right to keep and bear arms," whether embodied in Federal or State Constitutions, or the background common law. And those examples include substantial regulation of firearms in urban areas, including regulations that imposed obstacles to the use of firearms for the protection of the home.

Boston, Philadelphia, and New York City, the three largest cities in America during that period, all restricted the firing of guns within city limits to at least some degree.

See also An Act for preventing Mischief being done in the Town of *Newport*

Boston, Philadelphia, and New York City, the three largest cities in America during that period, all restricted the firing of guns within city limits to at least some degree. See Churchill, Gun Regulation, the Police Power, and the Right to Keep Arms in Early America, 25 Law & Hist. Rev. 139, 162 (2007); Dept. of Commerce, Bureau of Census, C. Gibson, Population of the 100 Largest Cities and Other Urban Places in the United States: 1790 to 1990 (1998) (Table 2), online at http://www.census.gov/population/documentation/twps0027/tab02.txt (all Internet materials as visited June 19, 2008, and available in Clerk of Court's case file). Boston in 1746 had a law prohibiting the "discharge" of "any Gun or Pistol charged with Shot or Ball in the Town" on penalty of 40 shillings, a law that was later revived in 1778. See Act of May 28, 1746, ch. 10; An Act for Reviving and Continuing

Sundry Laws that are Expired, and Near Expiring, 1778 Massachusetts Session Laws, ch. 5, pp. 193, 194. Philadelphia prohibited, on penalty of 5 shillings (or two days in jail if the fine were not paid), firing a gun or setting off fireworks in Philadelphia without a "governor's special license." See Act of Aug. 26, 1721, §4, in 3 Mitchell, Statutes at Large of Pennsylvania 253–254. And New York City banned, on penalty of a 20-shilling fine, the firing of guns (even in [554 U. S. ____ (2008) 5] houses) for the three days surrounding New Year's Day. 5 Colonial Laws of New York, ch. 1501, pp. 244–246 (1894); see also An Act to Suppress the Disorderly Practice of Firing Guns, & c., on the Times Therein Mentioned, 8 Statutes at Large of Pennsylvania 1770–1776, pp. 410– 412 (1902) (similar law for all "inhabited parts" of Pennsylvania). See also An Act for preventing Mischief being done in the Town of *Newport*, or in any other Town in this Government, 1731, Rhode Island Session Laws (prohibiting, on penalty of 5 shillings for a first offense and more for subsequent offenses, the firing of "any Gun or Pistol . . . in the Streets of any of the Towns of this Government, or in any Tavern of the same, after dark, on any Night whatsoever").

several towns and cities (including Philadelphia, New York, and Boston) regulated, for fire-safety reasons, the storage of gunpowder, a necessary component of an operational firearm.

Boston's gunpowder law imposed a £10 fine upon "any Person" who "shall take into any Dwelling-House, Stable, Barn, Out-house, Ware-house, Store, Shop, or other Building, within the Town of Boston, any . . . Fire-Arm, loaded with, or having Gun-Powder."

Furthermore, several towns and cities (including Philadelphia, New York, and Boston) regulated, for fire-safety reasons, the storage of gunpowder, a necessary component of an operational firearm. See Cornell & DeDino, A Well Regulated Right, 73 Fordham L. Rev. 487, 510–512 (2004). Boston's law in particular impacted the use of firearms in the home very much as the District's law does today. Boston's gunpowder law imposed a £10 fine upon "any Person" who "shall take into any Dwelling-House, Stable, Barn, Out-house, Ware-house, Store, Shop, or other Building, within the Town of Boston, any . . . Fire-Arm, loaded with, or having Gun-Powder." An Act in Addition to the several Acts already made for the prudent Storage of Gun- Powder within the Town of Boston, ch. XIII, 1783 Mass. Acts 218–219; see also 1 S. Johnson, A Dictionary of the English Language 751 (4th ed. 1773) (defining "firearms" as "[a]rms which owe their efficacy to fire; guns"). Even assuming, as the majority does, see *ante*, at 59–60, that this law included an implicit self-defense exception, it would nevertheless have prevented a homeowner from keeping in his home a gun that he could immediately pick up and use against an intruder. Rather, the homeowner [554 U. S. ____ (2008) 6] would have had to get the gunpowder and load it into the gun, an operation that would have taken a fair amount of time to perform. See Hicks, United States Military Shoulder Arms, 1795–1935, 1 Am. Military Hist. Foundation 23, 30 (1937) (experienced soldier could, with specially prepared cartridges as opposed to plain gunpowder and ball, load and fire musket 3-to-4 times per minute); *id.*, at 26– 30 (describing the loading process); see also Grancsay, The Craft of the Early American Gunsmith, 6 Metropolitan Museum of Art Bulletin 54, 60 (1947) (noting that rifles were slower to load and fire than muskets).

the law would, as a practical matter, have prohibited the carrying of loaded firearms anywhere in the city, unless the carrier had no plans to enter any building or was willing to unload or discard his weapons before going inside.

Moreover, the law would, as a practical matter, have prohibited the carrying of loaded firearms anywhere in the city, unless the carrier had no plans to enter any building or was willing to unload or discard his weapons before going inside. And Massachusetts residents must have believed this kind of law compatible with the provision in the Massachusetts Constitution that granted "the people . . . a right to keep and to bear arms for the common defence"— a provision that the majority says was interpreted as "secur[ing] an individual right to bear arms for defensive purposes." Art. XVII (1780), in 3 The Federal and State Constitutions, Colonial Charters, and Other Organic Laws 1888, 1892 (F. Thorpe ed. 1909) (hereinafter Thorpe); *ante*, at 28–29 (opinion of the Court).

Although it is unclear whether these laws, like the Boston law, would have prohibited the storage of gunpowder inside a firearm, they would at the very least have made it difficult to reload the gun to fire a second shot unless the homeowner happened to be in the portion of the house where the extra gunpowder was required to be kept.

"Until 1835 all small arms were single-shot weapons, requiring reloading by hand after every shot"

The New York City law, which required that gunpowder in the home be stored in certain sorts of containers, and laws in certain Pennsylvania towns, which required that gunpowder be stored on the highest story of the home, could well have presented similar obstacles to in-home use of firearms. See Act of April 13, 1784, ch. 28, 1784 N. Y. Laws p. 627; An Act for Erecting the Town of Carlisle, in the County of Cumberland, into a Borough, ch. XIV, §XLII, 1782 Pa. Laws p. 49; An Act for Erecting the Town of Reading, in the County of Berks, into a Borough, ch. LXXVI, §XLII, 1783 Pa. Laws p. 211. Although it is un- [554 U. S. ____ (2008) 7] clear whether these laws, like the Boston law, would have prohibited the storage of gunpowder inside a firearm, they would at the very least have made it difficult to reload the gun to fire a second shot unless the homeowner happened to be in the portion of the house where the extra gunpowder was required to be kept. See 7 United States Encyclopedia of History 1297 (P. Oehser ed. 1967) ("Until 1835 all small arms [were] single-shot weapons, requiring reloading by hand after every shot"). And Pennsylvania, like Massachusetts, had at the time one of the self-defense-guaranteeing state constitutional provisions on which the majority relies. See *ante*, at 28 (citing Pa. Declaration of Rights, Art. XIII (1776), in 5 Thorpe 3083).

the majority's assumption that such exceptions existed relies largely on the preambles to these acts—an interpretive methodology that it elsewhere roundly derides.

the gunpowder-storage laws would have *burdened* armed self-defense, even if they did not completely *prohibit* it.

The majority criticizes my citation of these colonial laws. See *ante*, at 59–62. But, as much as it tries, it cannot ignore their existence. I suppose it is possible that, as the majority suggests, see *ante*, at 59–61, they all in practice contained self-defense exceptions. But none of them expressly provided one, and the majority's assumption that such exceptions existed relies largely on the preambles to these acts—an interpretive methodology that it elsewhere roundly derides. Compare *ibid.* (interpreting 18th-century statutes in light of their preambles), with *ante*, at 4–5, and n. 3 (contending that the operative language of an 18thcentury enactment may extend beyond its preamble). And in any event, as I have shown, the gunpowder-storage laws would have *burdened* armed self-defense, even if they did not completely *prohibit* it.

This historical evidence demonstrates that a self-defense assumption is the *beginning*, rather than the *end*, of any constitutional inquiry. That the District law impacts self-defense merely raises *questions* about the law's constitutionality. But to answer the questions that are raised (that is, to see whether the statute is unconstitutional) requires us to focus on practicalities, the statute's rationale, the problems that called it into being, its rela- [554 U. S. ___ (2008) 7] tion to those objectives—in a word, the details. There are no purely logical or conceptual answers to such questions. All of which to say that to raise a self-defense question is not to answer it.

III

How is a court to determine whether a particular firearm regulation (here, the District's restriction on handguns) is consistent with the Second Amendment? What kind of constitutional standard should the court use? How high a protective hurdle does the Amendment erect?

I therefore begin by asking a process-based question: How is a court to determine whether a particular firearm regulation (here, the District's restriction on handguns) is consistent with the Second Amendment? What kind of constitutional standard should the court use? How high a protective hurdle does the Amendment erect?

It certainly would not be unconstitutional under, for example, a "rational basis" standard, which requires a court to uphold regulation so long as it bears a "rational relationship" to a "legitimate governmental purpose."

The law at issue here, which in part seeks to prevent gun-related accidents, at least bears a "rational relationship" to that "legitimate" life-saving objective.

The question matters. The majority is wrong when it says that the District's law is unconstitutional "[u]nder any of the standards of scrutiny that we have applied to enumerated constitutional rights." *Ante*, at 56. How could that be? It certainly would not be unconstitutional under, for example, a "rational basis" standard, which requires a court to uphold regulation so long as it bears a "rational relationship" to a "legitimate governmental purpose." *Heller* v. *Doe*, 509 U. S. 312, 320 (1993). The law at issue here, which in part seeks to prevent gun-related accidents, at least bears a "rational relationship" to that "legitimate" life-saving objective. And nothing in the three 19thcentury state cases to which the majority turns for support mandates the conclusion that the present District law must fall. See *Andrews* v. *State*, 50 Tenn. 165, 177, 186– 187, 192 (1871) (striking down, as violating a *state* constitutional provision adopted in 1870, a *statewide* ban on a carrying a broad class of weapons, insofar as it applied to revolvers); *Nunn* v. *State*, 1 Ga. 243, 246, 250–251 (1846) (striking down similarly broad ban on openly carrying weapons, based on erroneous view that the Federal Second Amendment applied to the States); *State* v. *Reid*, 1 Ala. 612, 614–615, 622 (1840) (*upholding* a concealed-weapon ban against a *state* constitutional challenge). These cases [554 U. S. ___ (2008) 9] were decided well (80, 55, and 49 years, respectively) after the framing; they neither claim nor provide any special insight into the intent of the Framers; they involve laws much less narrowly tailored that the one before us; and state cases in any event are not determinative of federal constitutional questions, see, *e.g.*, *Garcia* v. *San Antonio Metropolitan Transit Authority*, 469 U. S. 528, 549 (1985) (citing *Martin* v. *Hunter's Lessee*, 1 Wheat. 304 (1816)).

Respondent proposes that the Court adopt a "strict scrutiny" test, which would require reviewing with care each gun law to determine whether it is "narrowly tailored to achieve a compelling governmental interest."

the majority implicitly, and appropriately, rejects that suggestion by broadly approving a set of laws... whose constitutionality under a strict scrutiny standard would be far from clear.

Respondent proposes that the Court adopt a "strict scrutiny" test, which would require reviewing with care each gun law to determine whether it is "narrowly tailored to achieve a compelling governmental interest." *Abrams* v. *Johnson*, 521 U. S. 74, 82 (1997); see Brief for Respondent 54–62. But the majority implicitly, and appropriately, rejects that suggestion by broadly approving a set of laws—prohibitions on concealed weapons, forfeiture by criminals of the Second Amendment right, prohibitions on firearms in certain locales, and governmental regulation of commercial firearm sales—whose constitutionality under a strict scrutiny standard would be far from clear. See *ante*, at 54.

adoption of a true strict-scrutiny standard for evaluating gun regulations would be impossible... because almost every gun-control regulation will seek to advance (as the one here does) a "primary concern of every government—a concern for the safety and indeed the lives of its citizens."

the Court has in a wide variety of constitutional contexts found such public-safety concerns sufficiently forceful to justify restrictions on individual liberties

any attempt *in theory* to apply strict scrutiny to gun regulations will *in practice* turn into an interest-balancing inquiry

Indeed, adoption of a true strict-scrutiny standard for evaluating gun regulations would be impossible. That is because almost every gun-control regulation will seek to advance (as the one here does) a "primary concern of every government—a concern for the safety and indeed the lives of its citizens." *United States* v. *Salerno*, 481 U. S. 739, 755 (1987). The Court has deemed that interest, as well as "the Government's general interest in preventing crime," to be "compelling," see *id.,* at 750, 754, and the Court has in a wide variety of constitutional contexts found such public-safety concerns sufficiently forceful to justify restrictions on individual liberties, see *e.g.*, *Brandenburg* v. *Ohio*, 395 U. S. 444, 447 (1969) *(per curiam)* (First Amendment free speech rights); *Sherbert* v. *Verner*, 374 U. S. 398, 403 (1963) (First Amendment religious [554 U. S. ____ (2008) 10] rights); *Brigham City* v. *Stuart*, 547 U. S. 398, 403–404 (2006) (Fourth Amendment protection of the home); *New York* v. *Quarles*, 467 U. S. 649, 655 (1984) (Fifth Amendment rights under *Miranda* v. *Arizona*, 384 U. S. 436 (1966)); *Salerno*, *supra*, at 755 (Eighth Amendment bail rights). Thus, any attempt *in theory* to apply strict scrutiny to gun regulations will *in practice* turn into an interest-balancing inquiry, with the interests protected by the Second Amendment on one side and the governmental public-safety concerns on the other, the only question being whether the regulation at issue impermissibly burdens the former in the course of advancing the latter.

I would simply adopt such an interest-balancing inquiry explicitly.

"where a law significantly implicates competing constitutionally protected interests in complex ways," the Court generally asks whether the statute burdens a protected interest in a way or to an extent that is out of proportion to the statute's salutary effects upon other important governmental interests.

Contrary to the majority's unsupported suggestion that this sort of "proportionality" approach is unprecedented, the Court has applied it in various constitutional contexts, including election-law cases, speech cases, and due process cases.

I would simply adopt such an interest-balancing inquiry explicitly. The fact that important interests lie on both sides of the constitutional equation suggests that review of gun-control regulation is not a context in which a court should effectively presume either constitutionality (as in rational-basis review) or unconstitutionality (as in strict scrutiny). Rather, "where a law significantly implicates competing constitutionally protected interests in complex ways," the Court generally asks whether the statute burdens a protected interest in a way or to an extent that is out of proportion to the statute's salutary effects upon other important governmental interests. See *Nixon* v. *Shrink Missouri Government PAC*, 528 U. S. 377, 402 (2000) (BREYER, J., concurring). Any answer would take account both of the statute's effects upon the competing interests and the existence of any clearly superior less restrictive alternative. See *ibid.* Contrary to the majority's unsupported suggestion that this sort of "proportionality" approach is unprecedented, see *ante*, at 62, the Court has applied it in various constitutional contexts, including election-law cases, speech cases, and due process cases. See 528 U. S., at 403 (citing examples where the Court has taken such an approach); see also, *e.g., Thompson* v. *Western States Medical Center*, 535 U. S. 357, 388 [554 U. S. ____ (2008) 11] (2002) (BREYER, J., dissenting) (commercial speech); *Burdick* v. *Takushi*, 504 U. S. 428, 433 (1992) (election regulation); *Mathews* v. *Eldridge*, 424 U. S. 319, 339–349 (1976) (procedural due process); *Pickering* v. *Board of Ed. of Township High School Dist. 205, Will Cty.*, 391 U. S. 563, 568 (1968) (government employee speech).

In applying this kind of standard the Court normally defers to a legislature's empirical judgment in matters where a legislature is likely to have greater expertise and greater institutional factfinding capacity. See *Turner Broadcasting System, Inc.* v. *FCC*, 520 U. S. 180, 195–196 (1997); see also *Nixon, supra*, at 403 (BREYER, J., concurring). Nonetheless, a court, not a legislature, must make the ultimate constitutional conclusion, exercising its "independent judicial judgment" in light of the whole record to determine whether a law exceeds constitutional boundaries. *Randall* v. *Sorrell*, 548 U. S. 230, 249 (2006) (opinion of BREYER, J.) (citing *Bose Corp.* v. *Consumers Union of United States, Inc.*, 466 U. S. 485, 499 (1984)).

hundreds of gun-law decisions issued in the last half-century by Supreme Courts in 42 States, which courts with "surprisingly little variation," have adopted a standard more deferential than strict scrutiny. While these state cases obviously are not controlling, they are instructive.

The above-described approach seems preferable to a more rigid approach here for a further reason. Experience as much as logic has led the Court to decide that in one area of constitutional law or another the interests are likely to prove stronger on one side of a typical constitutional case than on the other. See, *e.g., United States* v. *Virginia*, 518 U. S. 515, 531–534 (1996) (applying heightened scrutiny to gender-based classifications, based upon experience with prior cases); *Williamson* v. *Lee Optical of Okla., Inc.*, 348 U. S. 483, 488 (1955) (applying rational-basis scrutiny to economic legislation, based upon experience with prior cases). Here, we have little prior experience. Courts that *do* have experience in these matters have uniformly taken an approach that treats empirically-based legislative judgment with a degree of deference. See Winkler, Scrutinizing the Second Amendment, 105 Mich. L. Rev. 683, 687, 716–718 (2007) (describing hundreds of [554 U. S. ____ (2008) 12] gun-law decisions issued in the last half-century by Supreme Courts in 42 States, which courts with "surprisingly little variation," have adopted a standard more deferential than strict scrutiny). While these state cases obviously are not controlling, they are instructive. Cf., *e.g.*, *Bartkus* v. *Illinois*, 359 U. S. 121, 134 (1959) (looking to the "experience of state courts" as informative of a constitutional question). And they thus provide some comfort regarding the practical wisdom of following the approach that I believe our constitutional precedent would in any event suggest.

IV

I, like the majority, see no need to address the constitutionality of the licensing requirement.

The present suit involves challenges to three separate District firearm restrictions. The first requires a license from the District's Chief of Police in order to carry a "pistol," *i.e.*, a handgun, anywhere in the District. See D. C. Code §22–4504(a) (2001); see also §§22–4501(a), 22–4506. Because the District assures us that respondent could obtain such a license so long as he meets the statutory eligibility criteria, and because respondent concedes that those criteria are facially constitutional, I, like the majority, see no need to address the constitutionality of the licensing requirement. See *ante*, at 58–59.

because I see nothing in the District law that would *preclude* the existence of a background common-law self-defense exception, I would avoid the constitutional question by interpreting the statute to include it.

The second District restriction requires that the lawful owner of a firearm keep his weapon "unloaded and disassembled or bound by a trigger lock or similar device" unless it is kept at his place of business or being used for lawful recreational purposes. See §7–2507.02. The only dispute regarding this provision appears to be whether the Constitution requires an exception that would allow someone to render a firearm operational when necessary for self-defense (*i.e.*, that the firearm may be operated under circumstances where the common law would normally permit a self-defense justification in defense against a criminal charge). See *Parker* v. *District of Columbia*, 478 [554 U. S. ____ (2008) 13] F. 3d 370, 401 (2007) (case below); *ante*, at 57–58 (opinion of the Court); Brief for Respondent 52–54. The District concedes that such an exception exists. See Brief for Petitioners 56–57. This Court has final authority (albeit not often used) to definitively interpret District law, which is, after all, simply a species of federal law. See, *e.g.*, *Whalen* v. *United States*, 445 U. S. 684, 687–688 (1980); see also *Griffin* v. *United States*, 336 U. S. 704, 716–718 (1949). And because I see nothing in the District law that would *preclude* the existence of a background common-law self-defense exception, I would avoid the constitutional question by interpreting the statute to include it. See *Ashwander* v. *TVA*, 297 U. S. 288, 348 (1936) (Brandeis, J., concurring).

I am puzzled by the majority's unwillingness to adopt a similar approach. It readily reads unspoken self-defense exceptions into every colonial law, but it refuses to accept the District's concession that this law has one.

I am puzzled by the majority's unwillingness to adopt a similar approach. It readily reads unspoken self-defense exceptions into every colonial law, but it refuses to accept the District's concession that this law has one. Compare *ante*, at 59–61, with *ante*, at 57–58. The one District case it cites to support that refusal, *McIntosh* v. *Washington*, 395 A. 2d 744, 755–756 (1978), merely concludes that the District Legislature had a rational basis for applying the trigger-lock law in homes but not in places of business. Nowhere does that case say that the statute precludes a self-defense exception of the sort that I have just described. And even if it did, we are not bound by a lower court's interpretation of federal law.

Because registration is a prerequisite to firearm possession, the effect of this provision is generally to prevent people in the District from possessing handguns... I shall ask how the statute seeks to further the governmental interests that it serves... The ultimate question is whether the statute imposes burdens that, when viewed in light of the statute's legitimate objectives, are disproportionate.

The third District restriction prohibits (in most cases) the registration of a handgun within the District. See §7– 2502.02(a)(4). Because registration is a prerequisite to firearm possession, see §7–2502.01(a), the effect of this provision is generally to prevent people in the District from possessing handguns. In determining whether this regulation violates the Second Amendment, I shall ask how the statute seeks to further the governmental interests that it serves, how the statute burdens the interests [554 U. S. ____ (2008) 14] that the Second Amendment seeks to protect, and whether there are practical less burdensome ways of furthering those interests. The ultimate question is whether the statute imposes burdens that, when viewed in light of the statute's legitimate objectives, are disproportionate. See *Nixon*, 528 U. S., at 402 (BREYER, J., concurring).

A

No one doubts the constitutional importance of the statute's basic objective, saving lives. But there is considerable debate about whether the District's statute helps to achieve that objective.

No one doubts the constitutional importance of the statute's basic objective, saving lives. See, *e.g.*, *Salerno*, 481 U. S., at 755. But there is considerable debate about whether the District's statute helps to achieve that objective. I begin by reviewing the statute's tendency to secure that objective from the perspective of (1) the legislature (namely, the Council of the District of Columbia) that enacted the statute in 1976, and (2) a court that seeks to evaluate the Council's decision today.

1

the major substantive goal of the District's handgun restriction is "to reduce the potentiality for gun-related crimes and gun-related deaths from occurring within the District of Columbia."

The committee concluded, on the basis of "extensive public hearings" and "lengthy research," that "the easy availability of firearms in the United States has been a major factor contributing to the drastic increase in gun-related violence and crime over the past 40 years."

First, consider the facts as the legislature saw them when it adopted the District statute. As stated by the local council committee that recommended its adoption, the major substantive goal of the District's handgun restriction is "to reduce the potentiality for gun-related crimes and gun-related deaths from occurring within the District of Columbia." Hearing and Disposition before the House Committee on the District of Columbia, 94th Cong., 2d Sess., on H. Con. Res. 694, Ser. No. 94–24, p. 25 (1976) (herinafter DC Rep.) (reproducing, *inter alia,* the Council committee report). The committee concluded, on the basis of "extensive public hearings" and "lengthy research," that "[t]he easy availability of firearms in the United States has been a major factor contributing to the drastic increase in gun-related violence and crime over the past 40 years." *Id.,* at 24, 25. It reported to the Council "startling statistics," *id.,* at 26, regarding gun-related crime, acci- [554 U. S. ____ (2008) 15] dents, and deaths, focusing particularly on the relation between handguns and crime and the proliferation of handguns within the District. See *id.,* at 25–26.

according to the committee, "for every intruder stopped by a homeowner with a firearm, there are 4 gun-related accidents within the home."

The committee informed the Council that guns were "responsible for 69 deaths in this country each day," for a total of "[a]pproximately 25,000 gun-deaths . . . each year," along with an additional 200,000 gun-related injuries. *Id.*, at 25. Three thousand of these deaths, the report stated, were accidental. *Ibid.* A quarter of the victims in those accidental deaths were children under the age of 14. *Ibid.* And according to the committee, "[f]or every intruder stopped by a homeowner with a firearm, there are 4 gun-related accidents within the home." *Ibid.*

The committee also stated that, "contrary to popular opinion on the subject, firearms are more frequently involved in deaths and violence among relatives and friends than in premeditated criminal activities."... the committee reported that "most murders are committed by previously law-abiding citizens, in situations where spontaneous violence is generated by anger, passion or intoxication, and where the killer and victim are acquainted."

In respect to local crime, the committee observed that there were 285 murders in the District during 1974—a record number. *Id.*, at 26. The committee also stated that, "[c]ontrary to popular opinion on the subject, firearms are more frequently involved in deaths and violence among relatives and friends than in premeditated criminal activities." *Ibid.* Citing an article from the American Journal of Psychiatry, the committee reported that "[m]ost murders are committed by previously law-abiding citizens, in situations where spontaneous violence is generated by anger, passion or intoxication, and where the killer and victim are acquainted." *Ibid.* "Twenty-five percent of these murders," the committee informed the Council, "occur within families." *Ibid.*

handguns... had "become easy for juveniles to obtain," even despite then-current District laws prohibiting juveniles from possessing them

The committee report furthermore presented statistics strongly correlating handguns with crime. Of the 285 murders in the District in 1974, 155 were committed with handguns. *Ibid.* This did not appear to be an aberration, as the report revealed that "handguns [had been] used in roughly 54% of all murders" (and 87% of murders of law enforcement officers) nationwide over the preceding several years. *Ibid.* Nor were handguns only linked to murders, as statistics showed that they were used in roughly [554 U. S. ____ (2008) 16] 60% of robberies and 26% of assaults. *Ibid.* "A crime committed with a pistol," the committee reported, "is 7 times more likely to be lethal than a crime committed with any other weapon." *Id.*, at 25. The committee furthermore presented statistics regarding the availability of handguns in the United States, *ibid.*, and noted that they had "become easy for juveniles to obtain," even despite then-current District laws prohibiting juveniles from possessing them, *id.*, at 26.

It recommended that the Council adopt a restriction on handgun registration to reflect "a legislative decision that, at this point in time and due to the gun-control tragedies and horrors enumerated previously" in the committee report, "pistols... are no longer justified in this jurisdiction."

a policy decision that handguns... have no legitimate use in the purely urban environment of the District"

In the committee's view, the current District firearms laws were unable "to reduce the potentiality for gun-related violence," or to "cope with the problems of gun control in the District" more generally. *Ibid.* In the absence of adequate federal gun legislation, the committee concluded, it "becomes necessary for local governments to act to protect their citizens, and certainly the District of Columbia as the only totally urban statelike jurisdiction should be strong in its approach." *Id.,* at 27. It recommended that the Council adopt a restriction on handgun registration to reflect "a legislative decision that, at this point in time and due to the gun-control tragedies and horrors enumerated previously" in the committee report, "pistols . . . are no longer justified in this jurisdiction." *Id.,* at 31; see also *ibid.* (handgun restriction "denotes a policy decision that handguns . . . have no legitimate use in the purely urban environment of the District").

The District's special focus on handguns thus reflects the fact that the committee report found them to have a particularly strong link to undesirable activities in the District's exclusively urban environment. See *id.,* at 25– 26. The District did not seek to prohibit possession of other sorts of weapons deemed more suitable for an "urban area." See *id.,* at 25. Indeed, an original draft of the bill, and the original committee recommendations, had sought to prohibit registration of shotguns as well as handguns, but the Council as a whole decided to narrow the prohibi- [554 U. S. ____ (2008) 17] tion. Compare *id.,* at 30 (describing early version of the bill), with D. C. Code §7–2502.02).

2

Petitioners, and their *amici,* have presented us with more recent statistics that tell much the same story that the committee report told 30 years ago.

Next, consider the facts as a court must consider them looking at the matter as of today. See, *e.g., Turner,* 520 U. S., at 195 (discussing role of court as factfinder in a constitutional case). Petitioners, and their *amici,* have presented us with more recent statistics that tell much the same story that the committee report told 30 years ago. At the least, they present nothing that would permit us to second-guess the Council in respect to the numbers of gun crimes, injuries, and deaths, or the role of handguns.

From 1993 to 1997, there were 180,533 firearm-related deaths in the United States, an average of over 36,000 per year. Fifty-one percent were suicides, 44% were homicides, 1% were legal interventions, 3% were unintentional accidents, and 1% were of undetermined causes.

From 1993 to 1997, there were 180,533 firearm-related deaths in the United States, an average of over 36,000 per year. Dept. of Justice, Bureau of Justice Statistics, M. Zawitz & K. Strom, Firearm Injury and Death from Crime, 1993–97, p. 2 (Oct. 2000), online at http://www.ojp.usdoj.gov/bjs/pub/pdf/fidc9397.pdf (hereinafter Firearm Injury and Death from Crime). Fifty-one percent were suicides, 44% were homicides, 1% were legal interventions, 3% were unintentional accidents, and 1% were of undetermined causes. See *ibid.* Over that same period there were an additional 411,800 nonfatal firearm-related injuries treated in U. S. hospitals, an average of over 82,000 per year. *Ibid.* Of these, 62% resulted from assaults, 17% were unintentional, 6% were suicide attempts, 1% were legal interventions, and 13% were of unknown causes. *Ibid.*

More male teenagers die from firearms than from all natural causes combined.

The statistics are particularly striking in respect to children and adolescents. In over one in every eight firearm-related deaths in 1997, the victim was someone under the age of 20. American Academy of Pediatrics, Firearm-Related Injuries Affecting the Pediatric Population, 105 Pediatrics 888 (2000) (hereinafter Firearm-Related Injuries). Firearm-related deaths account for 22.5% of all [554 U. S. ____ (2008) 18] injury deaths between the ages of 1 and 19. *Ibid.* More male teenagers die from firearms than from all natural causes combined. Dresang, Gun Deaths in Rural and Urban Settings, 14 J. Am. Bd. Family Practice 107 (2001). Persons under 25 accounted for 47% of hospital-treated firearm injuries between June 1, 1992 and May 31, 1993. Firearm-Related Injuries 891.

Handguns are involved in a majority of firearm deaths and injuries in the United States. *Id.,* at 888. From 1993 to 1997, 81% of firearm-homicide victims were killed by handgun. Firearm Injury and Death from Crime 4; see also Dept. of Justice, Bureau of Justice Statistics, C. Perkins, Weapon Use and Violent Crime, p. 8 (Sept. 2003), (Table 10), http://www.ojp.usdoj.gov/bjs/pub/pdf/wuvc01. pdf (hereinafter Weapon Use and Violent Crime) (statistics indicating roughly the same rate for 1993–2001). In the same period, for the 41% of firearm injuries for which the weapon type is known, 82% of them were from handguns. Firearm Injury and Death From Crime 4. And among children under the age of 20, handguns account for approximately 70% of all unintentional firearm-related injuries and deaths. Firearm-Related Injuries 890. In particular, 70% of all firearm-related teenage suicides in 1996 involved a handgun. *Id.,* at 889; see also Zwerling, Lynch, Burmeister, & Goertz, The Choice of Weapons in Firearm Suicides in Iowa, 83 Am. J. Public Health 1630, 1631 (1993) (Table 1) (handguns used in 36.6% of all firearm suicides in Iowa from 1980–1984 and 43.8% from 1990–1991).

Handguns also appear to be a very popular weapon among criminals.

Handguns also appear to be a very popular weapon among criminals. In a 1997 survey of inmates who were armed during the crime for which they were incarcerated, 83.2% of state inmates and 86.7% of federal inmates said that they were armed with a handgun. See Dept. of Justice, Bureau of Justice Statistics, C. Harlow, Firearm Use by Offenders, p. 3 (Nov. 2001), online at http:// [554 U. S. ____ (2008) 19] www.ojp.usdoj.gov/bjs/pub/pdf/fuo.pdf; see also Weapon Use and Violent Crime 2 (Table 2) (statistics indicating that handguns were used in over 84% of nonlethal violent crimes involving firearms from 1993 to 2001). And handguns are not only popular tools for crime, but popular objects of it as well: the FBI received on average over 274,000 reports of stolen guns for each year between 1985 and 1994, and almost 60% of stolen guns are handguns. Dept. of Justice, Bureau of Justice Statistics, M. Zawitz, Guns Used in Crime, p. 3 (July 1995), online at http://www.ojp.usdoj.gov/bjs/pub/pdf/guic.pdf. Department of Justice studies have concluded that stolen handguns in particular are an important source of weapons for both adult and juvenile offenders. *Ibid.*

Statistics further suggest that urban areas, such as the District, have different experiences with gun-related death, injury, and crime, than do less densely populated rural areas.

Homicide appears to be a much greater issue in urban areas; from 1985 to 1993, for example, "half of all homicides occurred in 63 cities with 16% of the nation's population."

rural areas appear to have a higher rate of firearm suicide

Statistics further suggest that urban areas, such as the District, have different experiences with gun-related death, injury, and crime, than do less densely populated rural areas. A disproportionate amount of violent and property crimes occur in urban areas, and urban criminals are more likely than other offenders to use a firearm during the commission of a violent crime. See Dept. of Justice, Bureau of Justice Statistics, D. Duhart, Urban, Suburban, and Rural Victimization, 1993–98, pp. 1, 9 (Oct. 2000), online at http://www.ojp.usdoj.gov/bjs/pub/pdf/ usrv98.pdf. Homicide appears to be a much greater issue in urban areas; from 1985 to 1993, for example, "half of all homicides occurred in 63 cities with 16% of the nation's population." Wintemute, The Future of Firearm Violence Prevention, 282 JAMA 475 (1999). One study concluded that although the overall rate of gun death between 1989 and 1999 was roughly the same in urban than rural areas, the urban homicide rate was three times as high; even after adjusting for other variables, it was still twice as high. Branas, Nance, Elliott, Richmond, & Schwab, Urban-Rural Shifts in Intentional Firearm Death, 94 Am. J. Public Health 1750, 1752 (2004); see also ibid. (noting that [554 U. S. ____ (2008) 20] rural areas appear to have a higher rate of firearm suicide). And a study of firearm injuries to children and adolescents in Pennsylvania between 1987 and 2000 showed an injury rate in urban counties 10 times higher than in nonurban counties. Nance & Branas, The Rural-Urban Continuum, 156 Archives of Pediatrics & Adolescent Medicine 781, 782 (2002).

Studies to date generally support the hypothesis that the greater number of rural gun deaths are from rifles or shotguns, whereas the greater number of urban gun deaths are from handguns."

Finally, the linkage of handguns to firearms deaths and injuries appears to be much stronger in urban than in rural areas. "[S]tudies to date generally support the hypothesis that the greater number of rural gun deaths are from rifles or shotguns, whereas the greater number of urban gun deaths are from handguns." Dresang, supra, at 108. And the Pennsylvania study reached a similar conclusion with respect to firearm injuries—they are much more likely to be caused by handguns in urban areas than in rural areas. See Nance & Branas, supra, at 784.

3

Respondent and his many amici for the most part do not disagree about the figures set forth in the preceding subsection, but they do disagree strongly with the District's predictive judgment that a ban on handguns will help solve the crime and accident problems that those figures disclose... they provide facts and figures designed to show that it has not done so in the past, and hence will not do so in the future.

Respondent and his many amici for the most part do not disagree about the figures set forth in the preceding subsection, but they do disagree strongly with the District's predictive judgment that a ban on handguns will help solve the crime and accident problems that those figures disclose. In particular, they disagree with the District Council's assessment that "freezing the pistol . . . population within the District," DC Rep., at 26, will reduce crime, accidents, and deaths related to guns. And they provide facts and figures designed to show that it has not done so in the past, and hence will not do so in the future.

First, they point out that, since the ban took effect, violent crime in the District has increased, not decreased.

First, they point out that, since the ban took effect, violent crime in the District has increased, not decreased. See Brief for Criminologists et al. as Amici Curiae 4–8, 3a (hereinafter Criminologists' Brief); Brief for Congress of Racial Equality as Amicus Curiae 35–36; Brief for National Rifle Assn. et al. as Amici Curiae 28–30 (hereinafter [554 U. S. ____ (2008) 21] NRA Brief). Indeed, a comparison with 49 other major cities reveals that the District's homicide rate is actually substantially higher relative to these other cities than it was before the handgun restriction went into effect. See Brief for Academics as Amici Curiae 7–10 (hereinafter Academics' Brief); see also Criminologists' Brief 6–9, 3a– 4a, 7a. Respondent's amici report similar results in comparing the District's homicide rates during that period to that of the neighboring States of Maryland and Virginia (neither of which restricts handguns to the same degree), and to the homicide rate of the Nation as a whole. See Academics' Brief 11–17; Criminologists' Brief 6a, 8a.

Second, respondent's *amici* point to a statistical analysis that... strict gun laws are correlated with *more* murders, not fewer... a reduction in the number of guns does not lead to a reduction in the amount of violent crime.

Second, respondent's *amici* point to a statistical analysis that regresses murder rates against the presence or absence of strict gun laws in 20 European nations. See Criminologists' Brief 23 (citing Kates & Mauser, Would Banning Firearms Reduce Murder and Suicide? 30 Harv. J. L. & Pub. Pol'y 649, 651–694 (2007)). That analysis concludes that strict gun laws are correlated with *more* murders, not fewer. See Criminologists' Brief 23; see also *id.,* at 25–28. They also cite domestic studies, based on data from various cities, States, and the Nation as a whole, suggesting that a reduction in the number of guns does not lead to a reduction in the amount of violent crime. See *id.,* at 17–20. They further argue that handgun bans do not reduce suicide rates, see *id.,* at 28–31, 9a, or rates of accidents, even those involving children, see Brief for International Law Enforcement Educators and Trainers Assn. et al. as *Amici Curiae* App. 7–15 (hereinafter ILEETA Brief).

Third, they point to evidence indicating that firearm ownership does have a beneficial self-defense effect... there were 2.2-to-2.5 million defensive uses of guns (mostly brandishing, about a quarter involving the actual firing of a gun) annually

Another study estimated that for a period of 12 months ending in 1994, there were 503,481 incidents in which a burglar found himself confronted by an armed homeowner, and that in 497,646 (98.8%) of them, the intruder was successfully scared away.

A third study suggests that gun-armed victims are substantially less likely than non-gun-armed victims to be injured in resisting robbery or assault.

Third, they point to evidence indicating that firearm ownership does have a beneficial self-defense effect. Based on a 1993 survey, the authors of one study estimated that there were 2.2-to-2.5 million defensive uses of guns (mostly brandishing, about a quarter involving the actual firing of a gun) annually. See Kleck & Gertz, [554 U. S. ____ (2008) 22] Armed Resistance to Crime, 86 J. Crim. L. & C. 150, 164 (1995); see also ILEETA Brief App. 1–6 (summarizing studies regarding defensive uses of guns). Another study estimated that for a period of 12 months ending in 1994, there were 503,481 incidents in which a burglar found himself confronted by an armed homeowner, and that in 497,646 (98.8%) of them, the intruder was successfully scared away. See Ikida, Dahlberg, Sacks, Mercy, & Powell, Estimating Intruder-Related Firearms Retrievals in U. S. Households, 12 Violence & Victims 363 (1997). A third study suggests that gun-armed victims are substantially less likely than non-gun-armed victims to be injured in resisting robbery or assault. Barnett & Kates, Under Fire, 45 Emory L. J. 1139, 1243–1244, n. 478 (1996). And additional evidence suggests that criminals are likely to be deterred from burglary and other crimes if they know the victim is likely to have a gun. See Kleck, Crime Control Through the Private Use of Armed Force, 35 Social Problems 1, 15 (1988) (reporting a substantial drop in the burglary rate in an Atlanta suburb that required heads of households to own guns); see also ILEETA Brief 17–18 (describing decrease in sexual assaults in Orlando when women were trained in the use of guns).

Fourth, respondent's *amici* argue that laws criminalizing gun possession are self-defeating, as evidence suggests that they will have the effect only of restricting law-abiding citizens, but not criminals, from acquiring guns.

Fourth, respondent's *amici* argue that laws criminalizing gun possession are self-defeating, as evidence suggests that they will have the effect only of restricting law-abiding citizens, but not criminals, from acquiring guns. See, *e.g.*, Brief for President *Pro Tempore* of Senate of Pennsylvania as *Amicus Curiae* 35, 36, and n. 15. That effect, they argue, will be especially pronounced in the District, whose proximity to Virginia and Maryland will provide criminals with a steady supply of guns. See Brief for Heartland Institute as *Amicus Curiae* 20.

In the view of respondent's *amici*, this evidence shows that other remedies—such as *less* restriction on gun ownership, or liberal authorization of law-abiding citizens to carry concealed weapons— better fit the problem.

at a minimum the District fails to show that its *remedy,* the gun ban, bears a reasonable relation to the crime and accident *problems* that the District seeks to solve.

In the view of respondent's *amici*, this evidence shows that other remedies—such as *less* restriction on gun ownership, or liberal authorization of law-abiding citizens to [554 U. S. ____ (2008) 23] carry concealed weapons—better fit the problem. See, *e.g.*, Criminologists' Brief 35–37 (advocating easily obtainable gun licenses); Brief for Southeastern Legal Foundation, Inc. et al. as *Amici Curiae* 15 (hereinafter SLF Brief) (advocating "widespread gun ownership" as a deterrent to crime); see also J. Lott, More Guns, Less Crime (2d ed. 2000). They further suggest that at a minimum the District fails to show that its *remedy,* the gun ban, bears a reasonable relation to the crime and accident *problems* that the District seeks to solve. See, *e.g.*, Brief for Respondent 59–61.

These empirically based arguments may have proved strong enough to convince many legislatures, as a matter of legislative policy, not to adopt total handgun bans. But the question here is whether they are strong enough to destroy judicial confidence in the reasonableness of a legislature that rejects them. And that they are not.

For one thing, they can lead us more deeply into the uncertainties that surround any effort to reduce crime, but they cannot prove either that handgun possession diminishes crime or that handgun bans are ineffective.

The statistics do show a soaring District crime rate. And the District's crime rate went up after the District adopted its handgun ban. But, as students of elementary logic know, *after it* does not mean *because of it.* What would the District's crime rate have looked like without the ban? Higher? Lower? The same? Experts differ; and we, as judges, cannot say.

These empirically based arguments may have proved strong enough to convince many legislatures, as a matter of legislative policy, not to adopt total handgun bans. But the question here is whether they are strong enough to destroy judicial confidence in the reasonableness of a legislature that rejects them. And that they are not. For one thing, they can lead us more deeply into the uncertainties that surround any effort to reduce crime, but they cannot prove either that handgun possession diminishes crime or that handgun bans are ineffective. The statistics do show a soaring District crime rate. And the District's crime rate went up after the District adopted its handgun ban. But, as students of elementary logic know, *after it* does not mean *because of it.* What would the District's crime rate have looked like without the ban? Higher? Lower? The same? Experts differ; and we, as judges, cannot say.

What about the fact that foreign nations with strict gun laws have higher crime rates? Which is the cause and which the effect? The proposition that strict gun laws *cause* crime is harder to accept than the proposition that strict gun laws in part grow out of the fact that a nation already has a higher crime rate.

What about the fact that foreign nations with strict gun laws have higher crime rates? Which is the cause and which the effect? The proposition that strict gun laws *cause* crime is harder to accept than the proposition that strict gun laws in part grow out of the fact that a nation already has a higher crime rate. And we are then left with the same question as before: What would have happened to crime without the gun laws—a question that respon- [554 U. S. ____ (2008) 23] dent and his *amici* do not convincingly answer.

suppose that respondent's *amici* are right when they say that householders' possession of loaded handguns help to frighten away intruders. On that assumption, one must still ask whether that benefit is worth the potential death-related cost.

Further, suppose that respondent's *amici* are right when they say that householders' possession of loaded handguns help to frighten away intruders. On that assumption, one must still ask whether that benefit is worth the potential death-related cost. And that is a question without a directly provable answer.

Finally, consider the claim of respondent's *amici* that handgun bans *cannot* work; there are simply too many illegal guns already in existence for a ban on legal guns to make a difference. In a word, they claim that, given the urban sea of pre-existing legal guns, criminals can readily find arms regardless. Nonetheless, a legislature might respond, we want to make an effort to try to dry up that urban sea, drop by drop. And none of the studies can show that effort is not worthwhile.

They succeed in proving that the District's predictive judgments are controversial. But they do not by themselves show that those judgments are incorrect

In a word, the studies to which respondent's *amici* point raise policy-related questions. They succeed in proving that the District's predictive judgments are controversial. But they do not by themselves show that those judgments are incorrect; nor do they demonstrate a consensus, academic or otherwise, supporting that conclusion.

the District and its *amici* support the District's handgun restriction with studies of their own. One in particular suggests that, statistically speaking, the District's law has indeed had positive lifesaving effects.

Others suggest that firearm restrictions as a general matter reduce homicides, suicides, and accidents in the home.

Still others suggest that the defensive uses of handguns are not as great in number as respondent's *amici* claim.

Thus, it is not surprising that the District and its *amici* support the District's handgun restriction with studies of their own. One in particular suggests that, statistically speaking, the District's law has indeed had positive lifesaving effects. See Loftin, McDowall, Weirsema, & Cottey, Effects of Restrictive Licensing of Handguns on Homicide and Suicide in the District of Columbia, 325 New England J. Med. 1615 (1991) (hereinafter Loftin study). Others suggest that firearm restrictions as a general matter reduce homicides, suicides, and accidents in the home. See, *e.g.,* Duggan, More Guns, More Crime, 109 J. Pol. Econ. 1086 (2001); Kellerman, Somes, Rivara, Lee, & Banton, Injuries and Deaths Due to Firearms in the Home, 45 J. Trauma, Infection & Critical Care 263 (1998); [554 U. S. ____ (2008) 25] Miller, Azrael, & Hemenway, Household Firearm Ownership and Suicide Rates in the United States, 13 Epidemiology 517 (2002). Still others suggest that the defensive uses of handguns are not as great in number as respondent's *amici* claim. See, *e.g.,* Brief for American Public Health Assn. et al. as *Amici Curiae* 17–19 (hereinafter APHA Brief) (citing studies).

Respondent and his *amici* reply to these responses; and in doing so, they seek to discredit as methodologically flawed the studies and evidence relied upon by the District... And, of course, the District's *amici* produce counter-rejoinders, referring to articles that defend their studies.

Respondent and his *amici* reply to these responses; and in doing so, they seek to discredit as methodologically flawed the studies and evidence relied upon by the District. See, *e.g.,* Criminologists' Brief 9–17, 20–24; Brief for Assn. Am. Physicians and Surgeons, Inc. as *Amicus Curiae* 12–18; SLF Brief 17–22; Britt, Kleck, & Bordua, A Reassessment of the D.C. Gun Law, 30 Law & Soc. Rev. 361 (1996) (criticizing the Loftin study). And, of course, the District's *amici* produce counter-rejoinders, referring to articles that defend their studies. See, *e.g.,* APHA Brief 23, n. 5 (citing McDowall, Loftin, & Wiersema et al., Using Quasi-Experiments to Evaluate Firearm Laws, 30 Law & Soc. Rev. 381 (1996)).

The upshot is a set of studies and counterstudies that, at most, could leave a judge uncertain about the proper policy conclusion.

legislators, not judges, have primary responsibility for drawing policy conclusions from empirical fact.

The upshot is a set of studies and counterstudies that, at most, could leave a judge uncertain about the proper policy conclusion. But from respondent's perspective any such uncertainty is not good enough. That is because legislators, not judges, have primary responsibility for drawing policy conclusions from empirical fact. And, given that constitutional allocation of decision-making responsibility, the empirical evidence presented here is sufficient to allow a judge to reach a firm *legal* conclusion.

this Court, in First Amendment cases applying intermediate scrutiny, has said that our "sole obligation" in reviewing a legislature's "predictive judgments" is "to assure that, in formulating its judgments," the legislature "has drawn reasonable inferences based on substantial evidence."

the District legislature's predictive judgments satisfy that legal standard. That is to say, the District's judgment, while open to question, is nevertheless supported by "substantial evidence."

In particular this Court, in First Amendment cases applying intermediate scrutiny, has said that our "sole obligation" in reviewing a legislature's "predictive judgments" is "to assure that, in formulating its judgments," the legislature "has drawn reasonable inferences based on substantial evidence." *Turner,* 520 U. S., at 195 (internal quotation marks omitted). And judges, looking at the [554 U. S. ___ (2008) 26] evidence before us, should agree that the District legislature's predictive judgments satisfy that legal standard. That is to say, the District's judgment, while open to question, is nevertheless supported by "substantial evidence."

the District's decision represents the kind of empirically based judgment that legislatures, not courts, are best suited to make.

deference to legislative judgment seems particularly appropriate here, where the judgment has been made by a local legislature, with particular knowledge of local problems and insight into appropriate local solutions.

Different localities may seek to solve similar problems in different ways, and a "city must be allowed a reasonable opportunity to experiment with solutions to admittedly serious problems."

There is no cause here to depart from the standard set forth in *Turner,* for the District's decision represents the kind of empirically based judgment that legislatures, not courts, are best suited to make. See *Nixon,* 528 U. S., at 402 (BREYER, J., concurring). In fact, deference to legislative judgment seems particularly appropriate here, where the judgment has been made by a local legislature, with particular knowledge of local problems and insight into appropriate local solutions. See *Los Angeles* v. *Alameda Books, Inc.,* 535 U. S. 425, 440 (2002) (plurality opinion) ("[W]e must acknowledge that the Los Angeles City Council is in a better position than the Judiciary to gather an evaluate data on local problems"); cf. DC Rep., at 67 (statement of Rep. Gude) (describing District's law as "a decision made on the local level after extensive debate and deliberations"). Different localities may seek to solve similar problems in different ways, and a "city must be allowed a reasonable opportunity to experiment with solutions to admittedly serious problems." *Renton* v. *Playtime Theatres, Inc.,* 475 U. S. 41, 52 (1986) (internal quotation marks omitted). "The Framers recognized that the most effective democracy occurs at local levels of government, where people with firsthand knowledge of local problems have more ready access to public officials responsible for dealing with them." *Garcia* v. *San Antonio Metropolitan Transit Authority,* 469 U. S. 528, 575, n. 18 (1985) (Powell, J., dissenting) (citing The Federalist No. 17, p. 107 (J. Cooke ed. 1961) (A. Hamilton)). We owe that democratic process some substantial weight in the constitutional calculus.

I conclude that the District's statute properly seeks to further the sort of life-preserving and public-safety interests that the Court has called "compelling."

For these reasons, I conclude that the District's statute properly seeks to further the sort of life-preserving and [554 U. S. ___ (2008) 27] public-safety interests that the Court has called "compelling." *Salerno,* 481 U. S., at 750, 754.

B

I next assess the extent to which the District's law burdens the interests that the Second Amendment seeks to protect.

I next assess the extent to which the District's law burdens the interests that the Second Amendment seeks to protect. Respondent and his *amici,* as well as the majority, suggest that those interests include: (1) the preservation of a "well regulated Militia"; (2) safeguarding the use of firearms for sporting purposes, *e.g.*, hunting and marksmanship; and (3) assuring the use of firearms for self-defense. For argument's sake, I shall consider all three of those interests here.

1

The District's statute burdens the Amendment's first and primary objective hardly at all.

The District's statute burdens the Amendment's first and primary objective hardly at all. As previously noted, there is general agreement among the Members of the Court that the principal (if not the only) purpose of the Second Amendment is found in the Amendment's text: the preservation of a "well regulated Militia." See *supra*, at 3. What scant Court precedent there is on the Second Amendment teaches that the Amendment was adopted "[w]ith obvious purpose to assure the continuation and render possible the effectiveness of [militia] forces" and "must be interpreted and applied with that end in view." *Miller*, 307 U. S., at 178. Where that end is implicated only minimally (or not at all), there is substantially less reason for constitutional concern. Compare *ibid.* ("In the absence of any evidence tending to show that possession or use of a 'shotgun having a barrel of less than eighteen inches in length' at this time has some reasonable relationship to the preservation or efficiency of a well regulated militia, we cannot say that the Second Amendment guarantees the right to keep and bear such an instrument").

the present case has nothing to do with *actual* military service... The District does not consider him <Heller>, at 66 years of age, to be a member of its militia.

[554 U. S. ____ (2008) 28] To begin with, the present case has nothing to do with *actual* military service. The question presented presumes that respondent is "*not* affiliated with any state-regulated militia." 552 U. S. __ (2007) (emphasis added). I am aware of no indication that the District either now or in the recent past has called up its citizenry to serve in a militia, that it has any inkling of doing so anytime in the foreseeable future, or that this law must be construed to prevent the use of handguns during legitimate militia activities. Moreover, even if the District were to call up its militia, respondent would not be among the citizens whose service would be requested. The District does not consider him, at 66 years of age, to be a member of its militia. See D. C. Code §49–401 (2001) (militia includes only male residents ages 18 to 45); App. to Pet. for Cert. 120a (indicating respondent's date of birth).

as some *amici* claim, the statute might interfere with training in the use of weapons, training useful for military purposes... the Second Amendment protects "learning to handle and use arms in a way that makes those who keep them ready for their efficient use" during militia service.

"private ownership of firearms makes for a more effective fighting force" because "military recruits with previous firearms experience and training are generally better marksmen, and accordingly, better soldiers."

"well-regulated militia—whether *ad hoc* or as part of our organized military—depends on recruits who have familiarity and training with firearms—rifles, pistols, and shotguns."

"civilians who are familiar with handgun marksmanship and safety are much more likely to be able to safely and accurately fire a rifle or other firearm with minimal training upon entering military service"

Nonetheless, as some *amici* claim, the statute might interfere with training in the use of weapons, training useful for military purposes. The 19th-century constitutional scholar, Thomas Cooley, wrote that the Second Amendment protects "learning to handle and use [arms] in a way that makes those who keep them ready for their efficient use" during militia service. General Principles of Constitutional Law 271 (1880); *ante*, at 45 (opinion of the Court); see also *ante*, at 45–46 (citing other scholars agreeing with Cooley on that point). And former military officers tell us that "private ownership of firearms makes for a more effective fighting force" because "[m]ilitary recruits with previous firearms experience and training are generally better marksmen, and accordingly, better soldiers." Brief for Retired Military Officers as *Amici Curiae* 1–2 (hereinafter Military Officers' Brief). An *amicus* brief filed by retired Army generals adds that a "well-regulated militia—whether *ad hoc* or as part of our organized military—depends on recruits who have familiarity and training with firearms—rifles, pistols, and shotguns." Brief for [554 U. S. ____ (2008) 29] Major General John D. Altenburg, Jr., et al. as *Amici Curiae* 4 (hereinafter Generals' Brief). Both briefs point out the importance of handgun training. Military Officers' Brief 26–28; Generals' Brief 4. Handguns are used in military service, see *id.,* at 26, and "civilians who are familiar with handgun marksmanship and safety are much more likely to be able to safely and accurately fire a rifle or other firearm with minimal training upon entering military service," *id.,* at 28.

the District's law does not seriously affect military training interests. The law permits residents to engage in activities that will increase their familiarity with firearms. They may register (and thus possess in their homes) weapons other than handguns, such as rifles and shotguns (only weapons that cannot be registered are sawed-off shotguns, machine guns, short-barreled rifles, and pistols not registered before 1976)

Regardless, to consider the military-training objective a modern counterpart to a similar militia-related colonial objective and to treat that objective as falling within the Amendment's primary purposes makes no difference here. That is because the District's law does not seriously affect military training interests. The law permits residents to engage in activities that will increase their familiarity with firearms. They may register (and thus possess in their homes) weapons other than handguns, such as rifles and shotguns. See D. C. Code §§7–2502.01, 7–2502.02(a) (only weapons that cannot be registered are sawed-off shotguns, machine guns, short-barreled rifles, and pistols not registered before 1976); compare Generals' Brief 4 (listing "*rifles,* pistols, and *shotguns*" as useful military weapons; emphasis added). And they may operate those weapons within the District "for lawful recreational purposes." §7–2507.02; see also §7–2502.01(b)(3) (nonresidents "participating in any lawful recreational firearm-related activity in the District, or on his way to or from such activity in another jurisdiction" may carry even weapons not registered in the District). These permissible recreations plainly include actually using and firing the weapons, as evidenced by a specific D. C. Code provision contemplating the existence of local firing ranges. See §7–2507.03.

while the District law prevents citizens from training with handguns *within the District*, the District consists of only 61.4 square miles of urban area. The adjacent States do permit the use of handguns for target practice, and those States are only a brief subway ride away.

And while the District law prevents citizens from training with handguns *within the District*, the District consists [554 U. S. ____ (2008) 30] of only 61.4 square miles of urban area. See Dept. of Commerce, Bureau of Census, United States: 2000 (pt. 1), p. 11 (2002) (Table 8). The adjacent States do permit the use of handguns for target practice, and those States are only a brief subway ride away. See Md. Crim. Law Code Ann. §4–203(b)(4) (Lexis Supp. 2007) (general handgun restriction does not apply to "the wearing, carrying, or transporting by a person of a handgun used in connection with," *inter alia*, "a target shoot, formal or informal target practice, sport shooting event, hunting, [or] a Department of Natural Resources-sponsored firearms and hunter safety class"); Va. Code Ann. §18.2–287.4 (Lexis Supp. 2007) (general restriction on carrying certain loaded pistols in certain public areas does not apply "to any person actually engaged in lawful hunting or lawful recreational shooting activities at an established shooting range or shooting contest"); Washington Metropolitan Area Transit Authority, Metrorail System Map, http://www.wmata.com/ metrorail/systemmmap.cfm.

Of course, a subway rider must buy a ticket, and the ride takes time. It also costs money to store a pistol, say, at a target range, outside the District. But given the costs already associated with gun ownership and firearms training, I cannot say that a subway ticket and a short subway ride (and storage costs) create more than a minimal burden.

I conclude that the District's law burdens the Second Amendment's primary objective little, or not at all.

Of course, a subway rider must buy a ticket, and the ride takes time. It also costs money to store a pistol, say, at a target range, outside the District. But given the costs already associated with gun ownership and firearms training, I cannot say that a subway ticket and a short subway ride (and storage costs) create more than a minimal burden. Compare *Crawford* v. *Marion County Election Bd.*, 553 U. S. ___, ___ (2008) (slip op., at 3) (BREYER, J., dissenting) (acknowledging travel burdens on indigent persons in the context of voting where public transportation options were limited). Indeed, respondent and two of his coplaintiffs below may well use handguns outside the District on a regular basis, as their declarations indicate that they keep such weapons stored there. See App. to Pet. for Cert. 77a (respondent); see also *id.*, at 78a, 84a (coplaintiffs). I conclude that the District's law burdens the Second Amendment's primary objective little, or not at [554 U. S. ____ (2008) 31] all.

2

any inability of District residents to hunt near where they live has much to do with the jurisdiction's exclusively urban character and little to do with the District's firearm laws... I reach a similar conclusion, namely, that the District's law burdens any sports-related or hunting-related objectives that the Amendment may protect little, or not at all.

The majority briefly suggests that the "right to keep and bear Arms" might encompass an interest in hunting. See, *e.g.*, *ante*, at 26. But in enacting the present provisions, the District sought "to take nothing away from sportsmen." DC Rep., at 33. And any inability of District residents to hunt near where they live has much to do with the jurisdiction's exclusively urban character and little to do with the District's firearm laws. For reasons similar to those I discussed in the preceding subsection—that the District's law does not prohibit possession of rifles or shotguns, and the presence of opportunities for sporting activities in nearby States—I reach a similar conclusion, namely, that the District's law burdens any sports-related or hunting-related objectives that the Amendment may protect little, or not at all.

3

As the Court of Appeals noted, statistics suggest that handguns are the most popular weapon for self defense... To that extent the law burdens to some degree an interest in self-defense that for present purposes I have assumed the Amendment seeks to further.

The District's law does prevent a resident from keeping a loaded handgun in his home. And it consequently makes it more difficult for the householder to use the handgun for self-defense in the home against intruders, such as burglars. As the Court of Appeals noted, statistics suggest that handguns are the most popular weapon for self defense. See 478 F. 3d, at 400 (citing Kleck & Gertz, 86 J. Crim. L. & C., at 182–183). And there are some legitimate reasons why that would be the case: *Amici* suggest (with some empirical support) that handguns are easier to hold and control (particularly for persons with physical infirmities), easier to carry, easier to maneuver in enclosed spaces, and that a person using one will still have a hand free to dial 911. See ILEETA Brief 37–39; NRA Brief 32– 33; see also *ante*, at 57. But see Brief for Petitioners 54– 55 (citing sources preferring shotguns and rifles to hand- [554 U. S. ____ (2008) 32] guns for purposes of self-defense). To that extent the law burdens to some degree an interest in self-defense that for present purposes I have assumed the Amendment seeks to further.

C

"existence of a clearly superior, less restrictive alternative" can be a factor in determining whether a law is constitutionally proportionate. Here I see none.

In weighing needs and burdens, we must take account of the possibility that there are reasonable, but less restrictive alternatives. Are there *other* potential measures that might similarly promote the same goals while imposing lesser restrictions? See *Nixon*, 528 U. S., at 402 (BREYER, J., concurring) ("existence of a clearly superior, less restrictive alternative" can be a factor in determining whether a law is constitutionally proportionate). Here I see none.

allowing a law enforcement officer immediately to assume that *any* handgun he sees is an *illegal* handgun. And there is no plausible way to achieve that objective other than to ban the guns.

The reason there is no clearly superior, less restrictive alternative to the District's handgun ban is that the ban's very objective is to reduce significantly the number of handguns in the District, say, for example, by allowing a law enforcement officer immediately to assume that *any* handgun he sees is an *illegal* handgun. And there is no plausible way to achieve that objective other than to ban the guns.

the very attributes that make handguns particularly useful for self-defense are also what make them particularly dangerous.

That they are small and light makes them easy to steal, and concealable, suggesting that concealed-weapon bans are constitutional.

It does not help respondent's case to describe the District's objective more generally as an "effort to diminish the dangers associated with guns." That is because the very attributes that make handguns particularly useful for self-defense are also what make them particularly dangerous. That they are easy to hold and control means that they are easier for children to use. See Brief for American Academy of Pediatrics et al. as *Amici Curiae* 19 ("[C]hildren as young as three are able to pull the trigger of most handguns"). That they are maneuverable and permit a free hand likely contributes to the fact that they are by far the firearm of choice for crimes such as rape and robbery. See Weapon Use and Violent Crime 2 (Table 2). [554 U. S. ____ (2008) 33] That they are small and light makes them easy to steal, see *supra*, at 19, and concealable, cf. *ante*, at 54 (opinion of the Court) (suggesting that concealed-weapon bans are constitutional).

any measure less restrictive in respect to the use of handguns for self-defense will, to that same extent, prove less effective in preventing the use of handguns for illicit purposes.

If a resident has a handgun in the home that he can use for self-defense, then he has a handgun in the home that he can use to commit suicide or engage in acts of domestic violence.

If it is indeed the case, as the District believes, that the number of guns contributes to the number of gun-related crimes, accidents, and deaths, then, although there may be less restrictive, *less effective* substitutes for an outright ban, there is no less restrictive *equivalent* of an outright ban.

This symmetry suggests that any measure less restrictive in respect to the use of handguns for self-defense will, to that same extent, prove less effective in preventing the use of handguns for illicit purposes. If a resident has a handgun in the home that he can use for self-defense, then he has a handgun in the home that he can use to commit suicide or engage in acts of domestic violence. See *supra*, at 18 (handguns prevalent in suicides); Brief for National Network to End Domestic Violence et al. as *Amici Curiae* 27 (handguns prevalent in domestic violence). If it is indeed the case, as the District believes, that the number of guns contributes to the number of gun-related crimes, accidents, and deaths, then, although there may be less restrictive, *less effective* substitutes for an outright ban, there is no less restrictive *equivalent* of an outright ban.

Licensing restrictions would not similarly reduce the handgun population, and the District may reasonably fear that even if guns are initially restricted to law-abiding citizens, they might be stolen and thereby placed in the hands of criminals.

Licensing restrictions would not similarly reduce the handgun population, and the District may reasonably fear that even if guns are initially restricted to law-abiding citizens, they might be stolen and thereby placed in the hands of criminals. See *supra*, at 19. Permitting certain types of handguns, but not others, would affect the commercial market for handguns, but not their availability. And requiring safety devices such as trigger locks, or imposing safe-storage requirements would interfere with any self-defense interest while simultaneously leaving operable weapons in the hands of owners (or others capable of acquiring the weapon and disabling the safety device) who might use them for domestic violence or other crimes.

the fact that as many as 41 States may pre-empt local gun regulation suggests that the absence of more regulation like the District's may perhaps have more to do with state law than with a lack of locally perceived need for them.

The absence of equally effective alternatives to a complete prohibition finds support in the empirical fact that other States and urban centers prohibit particular types of [554 U. S.

_____ (2008) 34] weapons. Chicago has a law very similar to the District's, and many of its suburbs also ban handgun possession under most circumstances. See Chicago, Ill., Municipal Code §§8–20–030(k), 8–20–40, 8–20–50(c) (2008); Evanston, Ill., City Code §9–8–2 (2007); Morton Grove, Ill., Village Code §6–2–3(C) (2008); Oak Park, Ill., Village Code §27–2–1 (2007); Winnetka, Ill., Village Ordinance §9.12.020(B) (2008); Wilmette, Ill., Ordinance §12–24(b) (2008). Toledo bans certain types of handguns. Toledo, Ohio, Municipal Code, ch. 549.25 (2007). And San Francisco in 2005 enacted by popular referendum a ban on most handgun possession by city residents; it has been precluded from enforcing that prohibition, however, by state-court decisions deeming it pre-empted by state law. See *Fiscal* v. *City and County of San Francisco*, 158 Cal. App. 4th 895, 900–901, 70 Cal. Rptr. 3d 324, 326–328 (2008). (Indeed, the fact that as many as 41 States may pre-empt local gun regulation suggests that the absence of more regulation like the District's may perhaps have more to do with state law than with a lack of locally perceived need for them. See Legal Community Against Violence, Regulating Guns in America 14 (2006), http://www. lcav.org/Library/reports_analyses/National_Audit_Total_ 8.16.06.pdf.

there may be no substitute to an outright prohibition in cases where a governmental body has deemed a particular type of weapon especially dangerous.

In addition, at least six States and Puerto Rico impose general bans on certain types of weapons, in particular assault weapons or semiautomatic weapons. See Cal. Penal Code §12280(b) (West Supp. 2008); Conn. Gen. Stat. §§53–202c (2007); Haw. Rev. Stat. §134–8 (1993); Md. Crim. Law Code Ann. §4–303(a) (Lexis 2002); Mass. Gen. Laws, ch. 140, §131M (West 2006); N. Y. Penal Law Ann. §265.02(7) (West Supp. 2008); 25 Laws P. R. Ann. §456m (Supp. 2006); see also 18 U. S. C. §922(o) (federal machinegun ban). And at least 14 municipalities do the same. See Albany, N. Y., Municipal Code §193–16(A) (2005); Aurora, Ill., Ordinance §29–49(a) (2007); Buffalo, [554 U. S. _____ (2008) 35] N. Y., City Code §180–1(F) (2000); Chicago, Ill., Municipal Code §8–24–025(a), 8–20–030(h); Cincinnati, Ohio, Admin. Code §708–37(a) (Supp. 2008); Cleveland, Ohio, Ordinance §628.03(a) (2008); Columbus, Ohio, City Code §2323.31 (2007); Denver, Colo., Municipal Code §38–130(e) (2008); Morton Grove, Ill., Village Code §6–2–3(B); N. Y. C. Admin. Code §10–303.1 (2007); Oak Park, Ill., Village Code §27–2-1; Rochester, N. Y., Code §47–5(f) (2008); South Bend, Ind., Ordinance §§13–97(b), 13–98 (2008); Toledo, Ohio, Municipal Code §549.23(a). These bans, too, suggest that there may be no substitute to an outright prohibition in cases where a governmental body has deemed a particular type of weapon especially dangerous.

D

the District's objectives are compelling; its predictive judgments as to its law's tendency to achieve those objectives are adequately supported; the law does impose a burden upon any self-defense interest that the Amendment seeks to secure; and there is no clear less restrictive alternative.

I turn now to the final portion of the "permissible regulation" question: Does the District's law *disproportionately* burden Amendment-protected interests? Several considerations, taken together, convince me that it does not.

The upshot is that the District's objectives are compelling; its predictive judgments as to its law's tendency to achieve those objectives are adequately supported; the law does impose a burden upon any self-defense interest that the Amendment seeks to secure; and there is no clear less restrictive alternative. I turn now to the final portion of the "permissible regulation" question: Does the District's law *disproportionately* burden Amendment-protected interests? Several considerations, taken together, convince me that it does not.

First, the District law is tailored to the life-threatening problems it attempts to address. The law concerns one class of weapons, handguns, leaving residents free to possess shotguns and rifles, along with ammunition.

there is no less restrictive way to achieve the problem-related benefits that it seeks.

First, the District law is tailored to the life-threatening problems it attempts to address. The law concerns one class of weapons, handguns, leaving residents free to possess shotguns and rifles, along with ammunition. The area that falls within its scope is totally urban. Cf. *Lorillard Tobacco Co.* v. *Reilly*, 533 U. S. 525, 563 (2001) (varied effect of statewide speech restriction in "rural, urban, or suburban" locales "demonstrates a lack of narrow tailoring"). That urban area suffers from a serious handgun-fatality problem. The District's law directly aims at that compelling problem. And there is no less restrictive way [554 U. S. ____ (2008) 36] to achieve the problem-related benefits that it seeks.

Second, the self-defense interest in maintaining loaded handguns in the home to shoot intruders is not the *primary* interest, but at most a subsidiary interest, that the Second Amendment seeks to serve.

Second, the self-defense interest in maintaining loaded handguns in the home to shoot intruders is not the *primary* interest, but at most a subsidiary interest, that the Second Amendment seeks to serve. The Second Amendment's language, while speaking of a "Militia," says nothing of "self-defense." As JUSTICE STEVENS points out, the Second Amendment's drafting history shows that the language reflects the Framers' primary, if not exclusive, objective. See *ante*, at 17–28 (dissenting opinion). And the majority itself says that "the threat that the new Federal Government would destroy the citizens' militia by taking away their arms was *the* reason that right . . . was codified in a written Constitution." *Ante*, at 26 (emphasis added). The *way* in which the Amendment's operative clause seeks to promote that interest—by protecting a right "to keep and bear Arms"— may *in fact* help further an interest in self-defense. But a factual connection falls far short of a primary objective. The Amendment itself tells us that militia preservation was first and foremost in the Framers' minds. See *Miller*, 307 U. S., at 178 ("With obvious purpose to assure the continuation and render possible the effectiveness of [militia] forces the declaration and guarantee of the Second Amendment were made," and the amendment "must be interpreted and applied with that end in view").

Further, any self-defense interest at the time of the Framing could not have focused exclusively upon urban-crime related dangers.

Americans, many living on the frontier, would likely have thought of self-defense primarily in terms of outbreaks of fighting with Indian tribes, rebellions such as Shays' Rebellion, marauders, and crime-related dangers to travelers on the roads, on footpaths, or along waterways.

They are unlikely then to have thought of a right to keep loaded handguns in homes to confront intruders in urban settings as *central*.

Further, any self-defense interest at the time of the Framing could not have focused exclusively upon urban-crime related dangers. Two hundred years ago, most Americans, many living on the frontier, would likely have thought of self-defense primarily in terms of outbreaks of fighting with Indian tribes, rebellions such as Shays' Rebellion, marauders, and crime-related dangers to travelers on the roads, on footpaths, or along waterways. See Dept. of Commerce, Bureau of Census, Population: 1790 to 1990 (1998) (Table 4), online at http://www.census.gov/ [554 U. S. ____ (2008) 37] population/censusdata/table-4.pdf (of the 3,929,214 Americans in 1790, only 201,655—about 5%—lived in urban areas). Insofar as the Framers focused at all on the tiny fraction of the population living in large cities, they would have been aware that these city dwellers were subject to firearm restrictions that their rural counterparts were not. See *supra*, at 4–7. They are unlikely then to have thought of a right to keep loaded handguns in homes to confront intruders in urban settings as *central*. And the subsequent development of modern urban police departments, by diminishing the need to keep loaded guns nearby in case of intruders, would have moved any such right even further away from the heart of the amendment's more basic protective ends. See, *e.g.*, Sklansky, The Private Police, 46 UCLA L. Rev. 1165, 1206–1207 (1999) (professional urban police departments did not develop until roughly the mid-19th century).

Nor, for that matter, am I aware of any evidence that *handguns* in particular were central to the Framers' conception of the Second Amendment.

Nor, for that matter, am I aware of any evidence that *handguns* in particular were central to the Framers' conception of the Second Amendment. The lists of militia-related weapons in the late 18th-century state statutes appear primarily to refer to other sorts of weapons, muskets in particular. See *Miller*, 307 U. S., at 180–182 (reproducing colonial militia laws). Respondent points out in his brief that the Federal Government and two States at the time of the founding had enacted statutes that listed handguns as "acceptable" militia weapons. Brief for Respondent 47. But these statutes apparently found them "acceptable" only for certain special militiamen (generally, certain soldiers on horseback), while requiring muskets or rifles for the general infantry. See Act of May 8, 1792, ch. XXXIII, 1 Stat. 271; Laws of the State of North Carolina 592 (1791); First Laws of the State of Connecticut 150 (1784); see also 25 Journals of the Continental Congress, Pp. 1774–1789 741–742 (1922).

Samuel Adams, who lived in Boston, advocated a constitutional amendment that would have precluded the Constitution from ever being "construed" to "prevent the people of the United States, who are peaceable citizens, from keeping their own arms."

he doubtless knew that Massachusetts law prohibited Bostonians from keeping loaded guns in the house. So how could Samuel Adams have advocated such protection *unless* he thought that the protection was *consistent* with local regulation that seriously impeded urban residents from using their arms against intruders?

it seems unlikely that the Framers thought about *urban* gun control at all.

Third, irrespective of what the Framers *could have* [554 U. S. ____ (2008) 38] *thought,* we know what they *did think.* Samuel Adams, who lived in Boston, advocated a constitutional amendment that would have precluded the Constitution from ever being "construed" to "prevent the people of the United States, who are peaceable citizens, from keeping their own arms." 6 Documentary History of the Ratification of the Constitution 1453

(J. Kaminski & G. Saladino eds. 2000). Samuel Adams doubtless knew that the Massachusetts Constitution contained somewhat similar protection. And he doubtless knew that Massachusetts law prohibited Bostonians from keeping loaded guns in the house. So how could Samuel Adams have advocated such protection *unless* he thought that the protection was *consistent* with local regulation that seriously impeded urban residents from using their arms against intruders? It seems unlikely that he meant to deprive the Federal Government of power (to enact Boston-type weapons regulation) that he know Boston had and (as far as we know) he would have thought constitutional under the Massachusetts Constitution. Indeed, since the District of Columbia (the subject of the Seat of Government Clause, U. S. Const., Art. I, §8, cl. 17) was the only *urban* area under direct federal control, it seems unlikely that the Framers thought about *urban* gun control at all. Cf. *Palmore* v. *United States*, 411 U. S. 389, 397–398 (1973) (Congress can "legislate for the District in a manner with respect to subjects that would exceed its powers, or at least would be very unusual, in the context of national legislation enacted under other powers delegated to it").

I cannot agree with the majority that these laws are largely uninformative because the penalty for violating them was civil, rather than criminal... a constitutional right can be burdened by penalties far short of jail time.

Of course the District's law and the colonial Boston law are not identical. But the Boston law disabled an even wider class of weapons (indeed, all firearms). And its existence shows at the least that local legislatures could impose (as here) serious restrictions on the right to use firearms. Moreover, as I have said, Boston's law, though highly analogous to the District's, was not the *only* colo- [554 U. S. ___ (2008) 39] nial law that could have impeded a homeowner's ability to shoot a burglar. Pennsylvania's and New York's laws could well have had a similar effect. See *supra*, at 6–7. And the Massachusetts and Pennsylvania laws were not only thought consistent with an *unwritten* common-law gun-possession right, but also consistent with *written* state constitutional provisions providing protections similar to those provided by the Federal Second Amendment. See *supra*, at 6–7. I cannot agree with the majority that these laws are largely uninformative because the penalty for violating them was civil, rather than criminal. *Ante*, at 61–62. The Court has long recognized that the exercise of a constitutional right can be burdened by penalties far short of jail time. See, *e.g.*, *Murdock* v. *Pennsylvania*, 319 U. S. 105 (1943) (invalidating $7 per week solicitation fee as applied to religious group); see also *Forsyth County* v. *Nationalist Movement*, 505 U. S. 123, 136 (1992) ("A tax based on the content of speech does not become more constitutional because it is a small tax").

we must look, not to what 18th-century legislatures actually *did* enact, but to what they would have thought they *could* enact.

It is similarly "treacherous" to reason from the fact that colonial legislatures *did not* enact certain kinds of legislation an unalterable constitutional limitation on the power of a modern legislature *cannot* do so.

Regardless, why would the majority require a precise colonial regulatory analogue in order to save a modern gun regulation from constitutional challenge? After all, insofar as we look to history to discover how we can constitutionally regulate a right to self-defense, we must look, not to what 18th-century legislatures actually *did* enact, but to what they would have thought they *could* enact. There are innumerable policy-related reasons why a legislature might not act on a particular matter, despite having the power to do so. This Court has "frequently cautioned that it is at best treacherous to find in congressional silence alone the adoption of a controlling rule of law." *United States* v. *Wells*, 519 U. S.

482, 496 (1997). It is similarly "treacherous" to reason from the fact that colonial legislatures *did not* enact certain kinds of legislation an unalterable constitutional limitation on the power of a modern legislature *cannot* do so. The question should not [554 U. S. ____ (2008) 40] be whether a modern restriction on a right to self-defense *duplicates* a past one, but whether that restriction, when compared with restrictions originally thought possible, enjoys a similarly strong justification. At a minimum that similarly strong justification is what the District's modern law, compared with Boston's colonial law, reveals.

The decision will encourage legal challenges to gun regulation throughout the Nation. Because it says little about the standards used to evaluate regulatory decisions, it will leave the Nation without clear standards for resolving those challenges

litigation over the course of many years, or the mere specter of such litigation, threatens to leave cities without effective protection against gun violence and accidents during that time.

Fourth, a contrary view, as embodied in today's decision, will have unfortunate consequences. The decision will encourage legal challenges to gun regulation throughout the Nation. Because it says little about the standards used to evaluate regulatory decisions, it will leave the Nation without clear standards for resolving those challenges. See *ante*, at 54, and n. 26. And litigation over the course of many years, or the mere specter of such litigation, threatens to leave cities without effective protection against gun violence and accidents during that time.

the majority's decision threatens severely to limit the ability of more knowledgeable, democratically elected officials to deal with gun-related problems.

I can understand how reasonable individuals can disagree about the merits of strict gun control as a crime-control measure

I cannot understand how one can take from the elected branches of government the right to decide whether to insist upon a handgun-free urban populace in a city now facing a serious crime problem and which, in the future, could well face environmental or other emergencies that threaten the breakdown of law and order.

As important, the majority's decision threatens severely to limit the ability of more knowledgeable, democratically elected officials to deal with gun-related problems. The majority says that it leaves the District "a variety of tools for combating" such problems. *Ante*, at 64. It fails to list even one seemingly adequate replacement for the law it strikes down. I can understand how reasonable individuals can disagree about the merits of strict gun control as a crime-control measure, even in a totally urbanized area. But I cannot understand how one can take from the elected branches of government the right to decide whether to insist upon a handgun-free urban populace in a city now facing a serious crime problem and which, in the future, could well face environmental or other emergencies that threaten the breakdown of law and order.

V

The majority derides my approach as "judge-empowering." *Ante*, at 62. I take this criticism seriously, but I do not think it accurate. As I have previously ex- [554 U. S. ____ (2008) 41] plained, this is an approach that the Court has taken in other areas of constitutional law. See *supra*, at 10–11. Application of such an approach, of course, requires judgment, but the very nature of the approach—requiring careful identification of the relevant interests and evaluating the law's effect upon them—limits the judge's choices; and the method's necessary transparency lays bare the judge's reasoning for all to see and to criticize.

The majority's methodology is, in my view, substantially less transparent than mine. At a minimum, I find it difficult to understand the reasoning that seems to underlie certain conclusions that it reaches.

In the majority's view, the Amendment also protects an interest in armed personal self-defense, at least to some degree. But the majority does not tell us precisely what that interest is.

The majority spends the first 54 pages of its opinion attempting to rebut JUSTICE STEVENS' evidence that the Amendment was enacted with a purely militia-related purpose. In the majority's view, the Amendment also protects an interest in armed personal self-defense, at least to some degree. But the majority does not tell us precisely what that interest is. "Putting all of [the Second Amendment's] textual elements together," the majority says, "we find that they guarantee the individual right to possess and carry weapons in case of confrontation." *Ante*, at 19. Then, three pages later, it says that "we do not read the Second Amendment to permit citizens to carry arms for *any sort* of confrontation." *Ante*, at 22. Yet, with one critical exception, it does not explain which confrontations count. It simply leaves that question unanswered.

How can citations such as these support the far-reaching proposition that the Second Amendment's primary concern is not its stated concern about the militia, but rather a right to keep loaded weapons at one's bedside to shoot intruders?

The majority does, however, point to one type of confrontation that counts, for it describes the Amendment as "elevat[ing] above all other interests the right of law-abiding, responsible citizens to use arms in defense of hearth and home." *Ante*, at 63. What is its basis for finding that to be the core of the Second Amendment right? The only historical sources identified by the majority that even appear to touch upon that specific matter consist of an 1866 newspaper editorial discussing the [554 U. S. ____ (2008) 42] Freedmen's Bureau Act, see *ante*, at 43, two quotations from that 1866 Act's legislative history, see *ante*, at 43–44, and a 1980 state court opinion saying that in colonial times the same were used to defend the home as to maintain the militia, see *ante*, at 52. How can citations such as these support the far-reaching proposition that the Second Amendment's primary concern is not its stated concern about the militia, but rather a right to keep loaded weapons at one's bedside to shoot intruders?

Nor is it at all clear to me how the majority decides *which* loaded "arms" a homeowner may keep.

This definition conveniently excludes machineguns, but permits handguns, which the majority describes as "the most popular weapon chosen by Americans for self-defense in the home."

According to the majority's reasoning, if Congress and the States lift restrictions on the possession and use of machineguns, and people buy machineguns to protect their homes, the Court will have to reverse

course and find that the Second Amendment *does*, in fact, protect the individual self-defense-related right to possess a machinegun.

if tomorrow someone invents a particularly useful, highly dangerous self-defense weapon, Congress and the States had better ban it immediately, for once it becomes popular Congress will no longer possess the constitutional authority to do so.

the majority determines what regulations are permissible by looking to see what existing regulations permit. There is no basis for believing that the Framers intended such circular reasoning.

Nor is it at all clear to me how the majority decides *which* loaded "arms" a homeowner may keep. The majority says that that Amendment protects those weapons "typically possessed by law-abiding citizens for lawful purposes." *Ante*, at 53. This definition conveniently excludes machineguns, but permits handguns, which the majority describes as "the most popular weapon chosen by Americans for self-defense in the home." *Ante*, at 57; see also *ante*, at 54–55. But what sense does this approach make? According to the majority's reasoning, if Congress and the States lift restrictions on the possession and use of machineguns, and people buy machineguns to protect their homes, the Court will have to reverse course and find that the Second Amendment *does*, in fact, protect the individual self-defense-related right to possess a machinegun. On the majority's reasoning, if tomorrow someone invents a particularly useful, highly dangerous self-defense weapon, Congress and the States had better ban it immediately, for once it becomes popular Congress will no longer possess the constitutional authority to do so. In essence, the majority determines what regulations are permissible by looking to see what existing regulations permit. There is no basis for believing that the Framers intended such circular reasoning.

I am similarly puzzled by the majority's list... Why these?
The majority fails to cite any colonial analogues.

I am similarly puzzled by the majority's list, in Part III of its opinion, of provisions that in its view would survive Second Amendment scrutiny. These consist of (1) "prohi- [554 U. S. ____ (2008) 43] bitions on carrying concealed weapons"; (2) "prohibitions on the possession of firearms by felons"; (3) "prohibitions on the possession of firearms by . . . the mentally ill"; (4) "laws forbidding the carrying of firearms in sensitive places such as schools and government buildings"; and (5) government "conditions and qualifications" attached "to the commercial sale of arms." *Ante*, at 54. Why these? Is it that similar restrictions existed in the late 18th century? The majority fails to cite any colonial analogues. And even were it possible to find analogous colonial laws in respect to all these restrictions, why should these colonial laws count, while the Boston loaded-gun restriction (along with the other laws I have identified) apparently does not count? See *supra*, at 5–6, 38–39.

Assume, for argument's sake, that the Framers did intend the Amendment to offer a degree of self-defense protection. Does that mean that the Framers also intended to guarantee a right to possess a loaded gun near swimming pools, parks, and playgrounds? That they would not have cared about the children who might pick up a loaded gun on their parents' bedside table?

At the same time the majority ignores a more important question: Given the purposes for which the Framers enacted the Second Amendment, how should it be applied to modern-day circumstances that they could not have anticipated? Assume, for argument's sake, that the Framers did intend the Amendment to offer a degree of self-defense protection. Does that mean that the Framers also intended to guarantee a right to possess a loaded gun near swimming pools, parks, and playgrounds? That they would not have cared about the children who might pick up a loaded gun on their parents' bedside table? That they (who certainly showed concern for the risk of fire, see *supra*, at 5–7) would have lacked concern for the risk of accidental deaths or suicides that readily accessible loaded handguns in urban areas might bring? Unless we believe that they intended future generations to ignore such matters, answering questions such as the questions in this case requires judgment—judicial judgment exercised within a framework for constitutional analysis that guides that judgment and which makes its exercise transparent. One cannot answer those questions by combining inconclusive historical research with judicial *ipse dixit*. [554 U. S. ____ (2008) 44]

Far more important are the unfortunate consequences that today's decision is likely to spawn.

the decision threatens to throw into doubt the constitutionality of gun laws throughout the United States. I can find no sound legal basis for launching the courts on so formidable and potentially dangerous a mission... there simply is no untouchable constitutional right guaranteed by the Second Amendment to keep loaded handguns in the house in crime-ridden urban areas.

The argument about method, however, is by far the less important argument surrounding today's decision. Far more important are the unfortunate consequences that today's decision is likely to spawn. Not least of these, as I have said, is the fact that the decision threatens to throw into doubt the constitutionality of gun laws throughout the United States. I can find no sound legal basis for launching the courts on so formidable and potentially dangerous a mission. In my view, there simply is no untouchable constitutional right guaranteed by the Second Amendment to keep loaded handguns in the house in crime-ridden urban areas.

VI

I conclude that the District's measure is a proportionate, not a disproportionate, response to the compelling concerns that led the District to adopt it.

I would find the District's measure consistent with the Second Amendment's demands.

For these reasons, I conclude that the District's measure is a proportionate, not a disproportionate, response to the compelling concerns that led the District to adopt it. And, for these reasons as well as the independently sufficient reasons set forth by JUSTICE STEVENS, I would find the District's measure consistent with the Second Amendment's demands.

With respect, I dissent.

Kopel on Heller

In 1974, after President Gerald Ford took the Oath of Office, he spoke to the American people: "My fellow Americans, our long national nightmare is over. Our Constitution works; our great Republic is a government of laws and not of men. Here the people rule."

His words are apt today. The 32-year nightmare of the law-abiding citizens of Washington, D.C., is over. They can legally use firearms in defense of their homes against violent predators. Soon, the good citizens of Washington will be able to purchase handguns for lawful defense.

For nearly seven decades the U.S. Supreme Court stood idle while lower federal courts nullified the Second Amendment. This year, our Independence Day celebrations were especially joyful, as the Supreme Court finally vindicated America's first freedom.

It was wonderful to have the opportunity to play a part in one of the most important Supreme Court cases in American history. On the morning of Thursday, June 26, I felt like Sam Gamgee, in *The Lord of the Rings*, when he finally saw the evil ring falling to its destruction in the volcano at Mount Doom. And now, the foundations of Barad Dûr are beginning to crack, with the end of the handgun bans in Morton Grove and Wilmette.

Everyone who played a role in Second Amendment activism over the last 35 years can feel proud of what we have accomplished together.

There is still much to be done to restore Second Amendment rights in the United States. And those rights will never be secure as long as the United Nations continues its relentless attacks. Those attacks will stop when enough governments in other nations change their policies, and demand that they stop. So over the long term, American human rights advocates need to help their friends in other nations begin to change the political culture in those nations, as we have changed the political culture in the United States in the last decade-and-a-half. Justice Scalia's opinion reminds us that the right to arms and the right of self-defense are not granted to Americans by the Second Amendment. Rather, they are inherent natural rights which belong to everyone.

A new chapter has opened in the story of mankind's struggle for freedom. Working with groups like the Second Amendment Foundation, the Independence Institute, and the National Rifle Association, together we can seize the historic opportunity in the early 21st century to protect and to advance in our nation and in our world the eternal truths of the Declaration of Independence.

The View from the Counsel Table
DATELINE: Colorado, Mar. 31, 2008, Oral Argument in *D.C. v. Heller*

On March 18, I joined the lawyers for Dick Heller at the counsel table for oral argument in *District of Columbia v. Heller*. The counsel table has four seats, and there were three lawyers representing Mr. Heller, so Alan Gura, the lead lawyer in the case, invited me to sit with them at the counsel table.

The practical function of the lawyers who are not presenting the oral argument is to write notes for the arguing lawyer, in case a tangential issue comes up. During the presentations by Walter Dellinger (for D.C.) and Paul Clement (for the Solicitor General), Justice Stevens asked questions which pointed out that of the Founding Era state constitutions, only two (Pennsylvania and Vermont) specifically mentioned self-defense as one of the purposes for the right to arms. So I gave Gura a note pointing out that courts in Massachusetts and North Carolina had interpreted their state constitution "for the common defence" language as an encompassing a right to arms for legitimate purposes, including defense against criminals. During Gura's presentation, Justice Stevens raised the point again, and Gura began to detail the case law, but Justice Stevens waved him off, stating that he was interested only in the constitutional texts.

After oral argument in any case, it's always possible to think about how a particular answer could have been given better; but I think that Alan Gura did an excellent job. He was solid, well-informed, and persuasive.

Some observations from a first-timer in the Supreme Court:

The counsel table is quite near the Bench. It's an interesting experience to see the Justices up close and personal, after having spent so many months trying to discern their modes of thought.

It is indeed awe-inspiring to hear the Marshal of the Court announce: "Oyez! Oyez! Oyez! All persons having business before the Honorable, the Supreme Court of the United States, are admonished to draw near and give their attention, for the Court is now sitting. God save the United States and this Honorable Court!"

Before the argument, Walter Dellinger, a true Southern gentleman, came over to shake our hands. He graciously told Gura that Gura would do "great," and said that his own very first oral argument had been his best.

Also awe-inspiring are the Court's chambers, with a beautiful high ceiling, and friezes on all four walls depicting great law-givers, as well as mythical characters personifying law-related virtues such as wisdom.

Based on the oral argument, it is possible to identify a few of the *amicus* briefs that were particularly influential. As Respondent, Gura would have been foolhardy to argue that the Court's leading precedent, *United States v. Miller* needed to be altered in any respect. That argument was instead in Nelson Lund's excellent brief for the Second Amendment Foundation, and was apparently adopted by Justice Kennedy.

Justice Kennedy's view that the militia clause of the Second Amendment emphasizes the importance of the militia, but does not limit the rights clause was supported not only by Gura's brief, but also by a careful textual analysis in the Lund brief, and by a strong historical presentation in the Academics for the Second Amendment brief, written by David Hardy and Joseph Olson.

Gura was asked at one point if there was any contemporaneous evidence indicating that self-defense was a purpose of the Second Amendment. He began by pointing to the 1787 Dissent from the Pennsylvania ratifying convention, which had urged that the proposed U.S. Constitution be amended to state: "That the people have a right to bear arms for the defence of themselves and their own state, or the United States, or for the purpose of killing game; and no law shall be passed for disarming the people or any of them, unless for crimes committed, or real danger of public injury from individuals; and as standing armies in the time of peace are dangerous to liberty, they ought not to be kept up: and that the military shall be kept under strict subordination to and be governed by the civil powers."

Justice Souter retorted that the Pennsylvania Dissent was only concerned about the militia. Given the text of what the Pennsylvanians said, I find this view implausible; the better argument on D.C.'s side (made by, among others, Dennis Henigan of the Brady Center) seemed to be that if James Madison wanted to protect more than militia-only uses of firearms, he could have copied Pennsylvania's language, but he chose not to.

Nevertheless, Justice Souter seemed to have been persuaded by arguments in a historians' brief by Carl Bogus, which cited the law review scholarship about Pennsylvania by Nathan Kozuskanich. Kozuskanich was also cited in D.C.'s briefs, and in several of D.C.'s *amicus* briefs.

Michael Bane's Down Range TV has a collection of various lawyers, academics, and other Second Amendment advocates, discussing the oral argument. He also has a link to the oral argument audio. C-Span's Real Video coverage of the press conference after the brief (about 21 minutes, equally divided between the two sides) is on the Internet. A 15 minute iVoices.org podcast in which I'm interviewed about the oral argument is also posted online.

For over a quarter-century, pro-Second Amendment lawyers such as Stephen Halbrook, Bob Dowlut, Don Kates, and David Hardy had dedicated their careers to making March 18, 2008, possible. Moreover, without the work of millions of pro-Second Amendment activists over the years, there would have been no chance of victory, however persuasive the evidence of original meaning might be. If the gun-prohibition lobby had succeeded in its plans to use the 1976 D.C. ban to pass handgun bans in many cities and several states, it is doubtful that the Supreme Court would have had the institutional will to strike down so many laws. And it also seems unlikely that most of the Justices who might have been appointed by a President Kerry, Dukakis, Mondale, or Carter would have been willing to declare even the D.C. ban unconstitutional.

Yet while the work of millions of citizens made March 18 possible, it was Alan Gura who had to finish the job alone. Our young Skywalker performed magnificently, and I hope that by the Fourth of July, the law-abiding citizens of our nation's capital will once again enjoy their rights to own handguns, and to use firearms in defense of their homes and families.

A Tremendous Victory

From reasononline (Reason Magazine), Thu., June 26, 2008 (reprinted with permission)

Heller is a tremendous victory for human rights and for libertarian ideals. Today's majority opinion provides everything which the lawyers closely involved in the case, myself included, had hoped for. Of course I would have preferred a decision which went much further in declaring various types of gun control to be unconstitutional. But Rome was not built in a day, and neither is constitutional doctrine.

For most of our nation's history, the U.S. Supreme Court did nothing to protect the First Amendment; it was not until the 1930s when a majority of the Court took the first steps towards protecting freedom of the press. It would have been preposterous to be disappointed that a Court in, say, 1936, would not declare a ban on flag-burning to be unconstitutional. It took decades for the Supreme Court to build a robust First Amendment doctrine strong enough to protect even the free speech rights of people as loathsome as flag-burners or American Nazis.

Likewise, the Equal Protection clause of the Fourteenth Amendment was, for all practical purposes, judicially nullified from its enactment until the 1930s. When the Court in that decade started taking Equal Protection seriously, the Court began with the easiest cases—such as Missouri's banning blacks from attending the University of Missouri

Law School, while not even having a "separate but equal" law school for them. It was three decades later when, having constructed a solid foundation of Equal Protection cases, the Court took on the most incendiary racial issue of all, and struck down the many state laws which banned inter-racial marriage.

So too with the Second Amendment. From the Early Republic until the present, the Court has issued many opinions which recognize the Second Amendment as an individual right. Yet most of these opinions were in *dicta*. After the 1939 case of *United States v. Miller*, the Court stood idle while lower federal courts did the dirty work of nullifying the Second Amendment, by over-reading *Miller* to claim that only National Guardsmen are protected by the Amendment.

Today, that ugly chapter in the Court's history is finished. *Heller* is the first step on what will be a long journey. Today, the Court struck down the most freakish and extreme gun-control law in the nation; only in D.C. was home self-defense with rifles and shotguns outlawed. *Heller* can be the beginning of a virtuous circle in which the political branches will strengthen Second Amendment rights (as in the 40 states which now allow all law-abiding, competent adults to obtain concealed-handgun carry permits), and the courts will be increasingly willing to declare unconstitutional the ever-rarer laws which seriously infringe the right to keep and bear arms.

As the political center of gravity moves step by step in a pro-rights direction, gun-control laws which today might seem (to most judges) to be constitutional will be viewed with increasing skepticism. The progress that the pro-Second Amendment movement has made in the last 15 years has been outstanding. As long as gun owners and other pro-Second Amendment citizens stay politically active, the next 15, 30, and 45 years can produce much more progress, and the role of the judiciary in protecting Second Amendment rights will continue to grow.

Dave Kopel is Research Director at the Independence Institute, in Golden, Colorado. He was one of three lawyers at the counsel table who assisted Alan Gura at the oral argument on March 18. His brief for the International Law Enforcement Educators and Trainers Association was cited four times in the Court's opinions.

Conservative Activists Key to DC Handgun Decision
From *Human Events*, Fri., June 27, 2008 (reprinted with permission)

The human rights victory in today's Supreme Court decision in *District of Columbia v. Heller* could never happened without *Human Events* and the other pillars of the conservative and libertarian movements.

The 5-4 margin shows that Supreme Court appointments and Senate confirmations really do matter. Had a President Mondale, Dukakis,

Gore, or Kerry been appointing Justices, the result today would have been different, and the Second Amendment would have been nullified. Had just a few 2002 and 2004 U.S. Senate races turned out differently—had Second Amendment citizen activists worked just a little less hard—the nomination of Samuel Alito would have been filibustered to death.

Citizen activism is no less important this year. A President Obama would appoint Justices who would ensure that *Heller* was the last case in which the Second Amendment was enforced. Whether the Second Amendment even applies to state and local governments, through "incorporation" in the Fourteenth Amendment, is unresolved.

Soon there will be challenges to the handgun bans in Chicago and its suburbs, which will present the incorporation issue squarely. Obama Justices and the Obama U.S. Department of Justice would fight energetically against recognizing the Second Amendment as a limit on state or local gun bans.

A second influence of the conservative and libertarian movements could be seen in the dissent authored by Justice Stevens. The Scalia majority and the Stevens dissent are both argued mostly in terms of original meaning and textualism. Both Scalia and Stevens delve very deeply into 18th and 19th century sources on the meaning of words, and the original public understanding of the Second Amendment. At least in terms of the Second Amendment, we are all originalists now.

It was not too distant past, constitutional originalism was beyond the pale in polite circles of the left-leaning legal elite. No longer.

There was much conflict in the early stages of the D.C. gun-law case between Alan Gura (the lead lawyer for Heller) and the National Rifle Association. The NRA was worried about bringing a case to a Supreme Court on which Justice O'Connor would have had the decisive vote. Especially in light of the Ginsburg-O'Connor 1994 concurring opinion in *Staples v. United States* noting "the 'widespread lawful gun ownership' Congress and the States have allowed to persist in this country." (emphasis added).

But by the time the *Heller* case reached the Supreme Court, the NRA engaged everything it had to help the case. Among the fruits of the massive NRA effort was an *amicus* brief written by the country's most experienced Second Amendment litigator, Stephen Halbrook, which was joined by 55 Senators, 250 U.S. Representatives, and by Richard Cheney in his role as President of the Senate.

More broadly, *Heller* could not have been won today if handgun prohibition were not abnormal in the United States. When the 1976 D.C. handgun ban was being enacted, some city council members openly acknowledged that the ban would accomplish little, but they hoped that it would be the start of a trend toward a national handgun ban.

But the handgun-ban virus spread only to Chicago (1982) and five Chicago suburbs. The NRA and other pro-rights activists crushed statewide handgun-ban initiatives in both Massachusetts (1976) and California (1982). The NRA successfully pushed for pre-emption laws in almost every state in the country, to prevent local governments from banning handguns.

No matter how powerful the arguments of Gura and other pro-rights lawyers about the original meaning of the Second Amendment, it is very doubtful that the Supreme Court would have had the nerve to declare handgun prohibition unconstitutional if handgun bans were on the books in a dozen states and in scores of cities.

Alan Gura's great legal skills—and the skills of *amici* lawyers such as Stephen Halbrook—were of course essential to the victory in *Heller*. But the best pro-Second Amendment lawyers in America had the chance to win because the conservative and libertarian movements—including publications like *Human Events* and groups like the NRA—worked for decades to make sure that handgun prohibition was freakishly rare in American life, that originalism was a respectable mode of constitutional interpretation, and that the Supreme Court included five Justices who considered the right to own a handgun in one's home for family defense to be a legitimate part of American freedom.

Dave Kopel is Research Director at the Independence Institute, in Golden, Colorado. He was one of three lawyers at the counsel table who assisted Alan Gura at the oral argument on March 18. His brief for the International Law Enforcement Educators and Trainers Association was cited four times in today's opinions. www.davekopel.org

Miller, Colt .45s and Natural Law
From *SCOTUSblog.com*, Fri., June 27, 2008 (used with permission)

The first thing that should be said about *Heller* is that it was a well-lawyered case on both sides. What a contrast to *United States v. Miller*—which, as detailed in a law review article cited by the Scalia majority, was apparently a collusive test case, in which the passive defense attorney and a compliant federal district judge did the bidding of the U.S. Attorney to bring the weakest possible Second Amendment case before the Court, and then to ensure that only the U.S. Attorney's side even presented a brief. (Frye, The Peculiar Story of United States v. Miller, 3 N. Y. U. J. L. & Liberty 48 (2008).)

Alan Morrison's opening brief for D.C. did about the best job possible with the available materials in arguing against the Standard Model of the Second Amendment. His supplemental argument that the Second Amendment, even under the Standard Model, does not apply to the

District of Columbia was a long shot that, ultimately, did not work; but it was worth trying, given the uphill fight that D.C. faced in defeating the Standard Model or in getting a Court majority to declare a handgun ban valid.

Carl Bogus's historical brief also did a fine job of assembling historical materials, and arguing against the Standard Model. The brief was obviously an important resource for Justice Stevens' dissent.

Although I don't agree with some of the claims in Alan's and Carl's commentaries here on Scotusblog, today isn't the day to continue those arguments; the various briefs filed on both sides provide plenty of material thereon.

The speculation about the post-*Heller* scope of permissible gun controls is interesting, and both sides of the debate will use the same words of the majority's language to argue for or against bans on various classes of guns, such as small handguns, big .50 caliber rifles, and so on. Whatever the results of those arguments, it does seem clear at least one type of gun ban is going to have a very tough time passing judicial review.

D.C. outlaws any self-loading rifle or handgun for which there exists a magazine holding more than 12 rounds. For example, the Colt .45 handgun has been, since its invention in 1911, one of the most common American handguns. The Colt .45 comes with a standard 7-round ammunition magazine. It's possible, if you search long enough, to buy a 15- or 20-round magazine for the Colt. Except as a novelty, these magazines have no use on a Colt .45. They make the handgun much too large to carry, and they extend so far below the grip that they make the gun awkward to handle.

In the District of Columbia (but nowhere else in the United States), the Colt .45 is banned. Not just banned if you have a 20-round magazine for the gun, but banned even if you only have the standard 7-round magazine. Preposterously, the D.C. ordinance classifies the 7-round Colt as a "machine gun," and outlaws civilian possession of these so-called "machine guns."

Heller says that there may not be bans on guns "typically possessed by law-abiding citizens for lawful purposes." This surely encompasses the Colt .45, and the thousands of other models banned by D.C.'s overbroad "machine gun" law. The D.C. ordinance prohibits about three-quarters of the handguns made in the U.S. in a typical year, and a very large fraction of rifles, including low-powered .22 caliber rifles from venerable companies like Winchester.

The D.C. City Council would do well to re-write its machine-gun ban so that it applies only to real machine guns. If not, it will be a close contest to see whether the ordinance is removed first by Congress or by the courts.

One aspect of the *Heller* majority opinion that has not yet attracted the attention of commentariat, but may be greatly important of the long run, is the presence of natural law.

Heller reaffirms a point made in the 1876 *Cruikshank* case. The right to arms (unlike, say, the right to grand jury indictment) is not a right which is granted by the Constitution. It is a pre-existing natural right which is recognized and protected by the Constitution:

"it has always been widely understood that the Second Amendment, like the First and Fourth Amendments, codified a pre-existing right. The very text of the Second Amendment implicitly recognizes the pre-existence of the right and declares only that it 'shall not be infringed.' As we said in *United States v. Cruikshank*, 92 U. S. 542, 553 (1876), "[t]his is not a right granted by the Constitution. Neither is it in any manner dependent upon that instrument for its existence. The Second amendment declares that it shall not be infringed..."

This is consistent with Blackstone's language, quoted by the majority, that the right to arms protects the "natural right of resistance and self-preservation." The majority writes that "Justice James Wilson interpreted the Pennsylvania Constitution's arms bearing right, for example, as a recognition of the natural right of defense 'of one's person or house' — what he called the law of 'self preservation.'"

Likewise quoted with approval is the 1846 Georgia Supreme Court decision *Nunn v. State*, which "construed the Second Amendment as protecting the 'natural right of self-defence'." Similarly, "A New York article of April 1769 said that '[i]t is a natural right which the people have reserved to themselves, confirmed by the Bill of Rights, to keep arms for their own defence." *A Journal of the Times*: Mar. 17, *New York Journal*, Supp. 1, Apr. 13, 1769...

Self-defense has generally been highly regarded by the American public, and it can be argued that self-defense is the epitome of an unenumerated Ninth Amendment right. See Nicholas J. Johnson, "Self-Defense?" *12 Journal of Law, Economics & Policy* 187 (2006). But some federal and state courts have been hostile to self-defense as a right (rather than as a mere privilege which can be withdrawn by government, or even forbidden).

Heller moves self-defense from the shadowy limbo of the Ninth Amendment into the bright uplands of the Second Amendment. It is now beyond dispute, in an American court, that self-defense is an inherent right, and that it is protected by the United States Constitution.

American constitutional law has a long record of infiltrating into other civilized nations. American protection for freedom of speech and freedom of the press, as well as American anti-discrimination laws, have had significant influence in our fellow democracies. Sometimes that influence is direct, with foreign courts citing American precedents. But more influential, in the long run, is the effect that the American example has on the rights-consciousness of the public in those nations.

The right to arms has already shown that it travels. In 2006, the people of Brazil overwhelmingly rejected a referendum to ban gun ownership, and proponents of the referendum noted with dismay the success of anti-referendum advertising which urged Brazilians not to surrender their rights.

The idea that self-defense is a natural right long predates the European discovery of the New World. Yet in some nations today, such at the United Kingdom and the Netherlands, the principle that there is a right even of unarmed self-defense is in grave danger—at least among the judiciary and the rest of the governing elites.

So while we wonder whether *Heller* will affect the often-capricious enforcement of New York City's pistol-licensing laws, perhaps one of the greatest influences of *Heller* (and, I hope, its progeny) will be in other nations, where the explicit affirmation of the natural right of self-defense by the most influential court in the world will bolster our democratic brothers and sisters in their efforts to preserve and strengthen their own natural right of resistance and self-preservation.

If you are interested in the topic of a natural-law right of self-defense (and the derivative right of defensive arms), you might be interested in: Kopel, Gallant, & Eisen, "The Human Right of Self-Defense," 22 BYU Journal of Public Law 43 (2008).

This post was authored by David Kopel, Research Director of the Independence Institute, who filed an amicus *brief in* Heller *in support of the respondents on behalf of the International Law Enforcement Educators and Trainers Association and others.*

The First Dominos Fall: Morton Grove and Wilmette Handgun Bans

From *The Volokh Conspiracy*, June 29, 2008 (used with permission)

After the D.C. city council banned handguns in 1976, and the voters of Massachusetts overwhelmingly rejected a handgun-ban initiative that same year, the next U.S. jurisdiction to enact a handgun ban was the Chicago suburb of Morton Grove, in 1981. Chicago did the same in 1982, and then four other Chicago suburbs, including Wilmette, later followed suit.

The Mayor of Morton Grove has announced that he will propose repeal of the handgun ban. Wilmette, meanwhile, has suspended enforcement of its handgun ban.

Both Morton Grove and Wilmette were among the cities sued on Friday (6/27/08) by the NRA. Their decisions are sensible. While the issue of Second Amendment incorporation is still unresolved, Richard Daley's government in Chicago can spend its own funds to fight the issue all the way to the Supreme Court. If Daley wins, the suburbs can re-institute their bans. If Daley loses (an outcome that seems more likely than not if the Supreme Court takes the case), then Wilmette and Morton Grove have saved themselves hundreds of thousands of dollars of attorney's fees, since they would have to pay their own lawyers, and have to pay the plaintiffs' lawyers for bringing a successful civil rights claim.

Morton Grove was the site of perhaps the worst legal defeat for the Second Amendment in American history. The lawsuit against the ban lost 2-1 in the Seventh Circuit, and then 4-3 in the Illinois Supreme Court (notwithstanding specific legislative history from the 1966 Illinois constitutional convention that the right to arms provision would prevent handgun bans). The U.S. Supreme Court denied *certiorari* in the federal case. Attorneys Stephen Halbrook and Don Kates were closely involved in the Morton Grove litigation.

In *Heller*, the Morton Grove cases were the strongest precedents which plainly supported the constitutionality of a complete handgun ban, even under an individual right to arms.

Ironically, Morton Grove proved very helpful to pro-Second Amendment forces in other states. The case received much national attention, and Morton Grove's ban was the key example used by NRA lobbyists to promote state preemption laws all over the country in the 1980s. These state laws eliminated or restricted many local gun controls, and always outlawed local handgun bans. The preemption laws were important in stopping the spread of local handgun prohibition. As a result, when the time came for the U.S. Supreme Court to hear *Heller*, handgun bans remained freakish exceptions to the national norm.

It is very pleasing to see constitutional rights being re-established in the site of one of their most notorious defeats.

Heller's Kitchen
From *The New York Sun*, Mon., June 30, 2008 (used with permission)

When the case of *District of Columbia v. Heller* was before the Supreme Court, Mayor Bloomberg filed a brief in support of the District's handgun ban, arguing that a militia-only interpretation of the Second Amendment was necessary to keep New York City's gun laws intact. On Thursday, when the Supreme Court ruled against Mr. Bloomberg's position, the mayor claimed that the ruling was a "benefit" and would not affect any New York City laws. His claim was half-right.

It is a benefit, but it's unlikely that it will not affect any New York City laws. In most of America, *Heller* will have little effect on state and local laws, because the vast majority of states already have an individual right to arms in their state Constitutions. Illinois and California are two of the states that don't have a right to handguns; suits have already been filed challenging the handgun ban in Chicago and the S.F. ban on firearms possession by public-housing residents. Those cases will help decide whether the Second Amendment is enforceable against state and local governments or only against the federal government.

New York's state Constitution has no right to arms, but the Civil Rights Law does. The Civil Rights Law begins with a Bill of Rights. Article 4 declares: "A well regulated militia being necessary to the security of a free state, the right of the people to keep and bear arms cannot be infringed." It is identical to the Second Amendment of the United States Constitution, except that New York follows modern standards for capitalization and punctuation, and says "cannot" instead of "shall not."

As a Monroe County court accurately observed in the 1994 case *Citizens for a Safer Community v. City of Rochester*, "The Courts of this State have concluded that the language of federal law interpreting the Second Amendment (which is identical in its language to Article 2, section 4 of the Civil Rights Law) should be used in interpreting the provisions of this state law."

Some New York courts have interpreted the New York right to arms restrictively, but these decisions were explicitly based on misunderstanding of the same language in the Second Amendment. The cases treating the Civil Rights Law as almost meaningless are of dubious validity now that *Heller* has made is clear that "the right of the people to keep and bear arms" is a broad and important individual right.

The New York City law which most obviously violates the right to arms is the complete ban on air guns. The venerable Daisy Red Ryder BB gun is contraband. *Heller* and the Supreme Court's previous major Second Amendment precedent, *United States v. Miller* (1939) forbid the prohibition of arms "typically possessed by law-abiding citizens for lawful purposes."

Air guns are ubiquitous almost everywhere except New York City, and are used almost exclusively for law-abiding purposes. Pursuant to *Heller*, regulation of air guns might be fine, but prohibition of all air guns is not.

Unlike firearms, air guns (which shoot small BBs or pellets) can be safely used inside an apartment or house. An old sofa cushion is a safe backstop. In a city where target ranges are few and expensive, air guns offer a practical way for people to practice safely with a gun. The right to arms necessarily includes the right to practice arms safety.

New York City bans magazines ("detachable rectangular boxes which hold a gun's ammunition") which hold more than 17 rounds. Whether the ban is consistent with *Heller* is debatable. Clearly inconsistent is the ban on any magazine which protrudes below the grip of the gun. The most common handgun in the United States is the Colt 1911 pistol, and the variants made by many other companies. The pistol's magazine holds seven rounds. Some after-market magazine companies make slightly larger ones, which hold eight or nine rounds. These magazines extend a half-inch or less below the grip.

There's no public-safety benefit to allowing guns with 17 rounds stored within the grip, but banning guns with 8 rounds because of a quarter-inch protrusion below the grip.

Regarding gun carrying, *Heller* might, arguably, mean that New York City would have to follow a similar policy to Connecticut (and 39 other states): issue permits to carry a concealed handgun for lawful defense if the applicant is over 21, and passes a fingerprint-based background check and a safety class.

At the least, *Heller* indicates that gun-carry licensing may not be "enforced in an arbitrary and capricious manner." This is a problem for New York State's carry-licensing law, as Suzanne Novak detailed in a 1998 article in the Fordham Urban Law Journal. New York state law sets essentially no standards to guide local officials in deciding whether to issue carry permits.

The problem is acute in New York City. Celebrities, the ultra-wealthy, and the politically influential get carry permits. But many of the people who need them the most — such as stalking victims, or crime witnesses who have been threatened by the criminal's friends — often do not. Even if New York City is not required to go as far as Connecticut, the City does need much less favoritism and much more objectivity in its administration of carry permits.

Mr. Kopel is an associate policy analyst with the Cato Institute, in Washington, D.C., and has taught the "Gun Control and Gun Rights" course at New York University Law School. He was part of the team of four lawyers presenting the oral argument to the Supreme Court in District of Columbia v. Heller.

The Natural Right of Self-Defense: *Heller's* Lesson for the World

By David B. Kopel[1]

The following is an article by Dave Kopel in the Syracuse Law Review, Volume 59, No. 2. That issue is a special Symposium on the Heller decision, and will also include the following articles: Linda Greenhouse on Justice Breyer's dissent, reflecting on what his opinion says about his jurisprudence; Michael Dorf on incorporation; Richard Epstein on the application of Epstein's individual-rights scholarship to the Court's evolving jurisprudence; Carl Bogus and Paul Finkelman on Heller's place within the historical context of gun litigation; Richard Schragger on the case's implications for our Living Constitution; Nelson Lund on the difference between the Supreme Court's approach to incorporation and the approach taken by the lower courts; and Michael O'Shea on the standard of review to be applied in future litigation. The symposium issue is expected to be published by early 2009. Copies of the symposium issue are available from the Syracuse Law Review, Syracuse University College of Law, Syracuse, New York 13244-1030, 315-443-3680.

One of the most important elements of the *District of Columbia v. Heller* decision is the natural law. Analysis of natural law in *Heller* shows why Justice Stevens' dissent is clearly incorrect, and illuminates a crucial weakness in Justice Breyer's dissent. The constitutional recognition of the natural law right of self-defense has important implications for American law, and for foreign and international law.

I. The Natural Law in Right of Armed Defense

A. In the *Heller* Case

Heller reaffirms a point made in the 1876 *Cruikshank* case. The right to arms (unlike, say, the right to grand jury indictment) is *not* a right which is granted by the Constitution. It is a pre-existing natural right which is recognized and protected by the Constitution:

> it has always been widely understood that the Second Amendment, like the First and Fourth Amendments, codified a pre-existing right. The very text of the Second Amendment

implicitly recognizes the pre-existence of the right and declares only that it "shall not be infringed." As we said in United States v. Cruikshank, 92 U. S. 542, 553 (1876), "[t]his is not a right granted by the Constitution. Neither is it in any manner dependent upon that instrument for its existence. The Second amendment declares that it shall not be infringed..."[2]

As *Heller* pointed out, the 1689 English Declaration of Right (informally known as the English Bill of Rights) was a "predecessor of our Second Amendment."[3] According to the Declaration: "[T]he subjects which are Protestants may have arms for their defense suitable to their conditions and as allowed by law."[4] The Convention Parliament which wrote the Declaration of Right stated that the right to arms for defense was a "true, ancient, and indubitable right." Yet as Joyce Malcolm has detailed, 1689 was the first time that the right to arms had been formally protected by a positive enactment of English law.[5]

The explanation is simple. The Convention Parliament did not believe that it was creating new rights, but simply recognizing established ones. Although previous Parliaments had not enacted a statute specifically to protect the right of armed self-defense, British case law since 1330 had long recognized an absolute right to use deadly force against home invaders.[6] The right to self-defense itself, along with its necessary implication of the right to use appropriate arms for self-defense, was considered to be firmly established by natural law.

Thus, *Heller* quoted Blackstone's treatise (which was by far the most influential legal treatise in the Early American Republic[7]) explaining that the Declaration of Right protected "the natural right of resistance and self-preservation," which was effectuated by "the right of having and using arms for self-preservation and defence."[8]

Some other parts of the *Heller* opinion include citations to sources describing the right of armed self-defense as a "natural" or "inherent" right. The majority writes that "Justice James Wilson interpreted the Pennsylvania Constitution's arms bearing right, for example, as a recognition of the natural right of defense 'of one's person or house' — what he called the law of 'self preservation.'"[9]

Likewise quoted with approval is the 1846 Georgia Supreme Court decision *Nunn v. State*, which "construed the Second Amendment as protecting the '*natural* right of self-defence'."[10] Similarly, "A New York article of April 1769 said that '[i]t is a natural right which the people have reserved to themselves, confirmed by the Bill of Rights, to keep arms for their own defence."[11]

Thus, the *Heller* opinion concludes: "As the quotations earlier in this opinion demonstrate, the inherent right of self-defense has been central to the Second Amendment right."[12] *Heller's* recognition self-defense as a natural right was consistent with the same view in *The Federalist*,[13] in most state constitutions,[14] and in case law from before the Civil War to modern times.[15]

B. Roots of the Right

Although some modern scholars deny that natural law exists, there is no dispute that the Founders strongly believed in it.[16] In a constitutional sense, the natural law basis of the right to armed self-defense is part of the original public meaning of the Second Amendment. That human rights were inherent, and not granted by government, was, after all, the basis on which the nation was created: "We hold these truths to be self-evident: that all men are endowed by their Creator with certain unalienable rights."[17]

"Natural law" as a term of legal art was originally based on Catholic legal thought. In the twelfth century, Gratian's "Treatise of the Discordant Canons" consolidated and synthesized disparate sources in various canon laws (church laws). He began with an explanation of natural law:

> Natural law is common to all nations because it exists everywhere through natural instinct, not because of any enactment. It includes the union of men and women, the succession and rearing of children, the identical liberty of all in the acquisition of those things, which I omit, which are taken from the earth or at sea, the return of a thing deposited or of money entrusted, and the repelling of violence by force. This, and anything similar, is never regarded as unjust but is held to be natural and equitable.[18]

Gratian's formulation of the natural right of "repelling violence by force" was similar to an expression of the same principle in Roman Law.[19]

In the five centuries from Gratian to the American Constitution, the concept of natural law, including natural rights, was developed by Catholic Scholars such as Thomas Aquinas, Francisco de Vitoria, Juan de Mariana, and Francisco Suárez (who called self-defense "the greatest of all rights"). From the personal right of self-defense against lone criminals, they derived the people's right of self-defense against criminal, tyrannical governments.[20]

Few Americans were familiar with these Catholic scholars, except for Aquinas. The Anglo-Americans learned the language of natural rights, including the natural right of self-defense, from Protestant thinkers who had adopted the Catholic self-defense theories. The first of these writers were the persecuted Protestants of sixteenth-century

France and England, including Theodore Beza, Peter Martyr Vermigli, and Christopher Goodman. For the Americans, the most influential were John Poynet, author of *A Shorte Treatise of Politike Power* (1556), and the pseudonymous Marcus Junius Brutus, who wrote *Vindiciae Contra Tyrannos* (Vindication Against Tyrants) in 1579.[21] According to John Adams, *Vindiciae* was one of the leading books by which England's and America's "present liberties have been established."[22] Adams wrote that there were three key periods in English history where scholars addressed the problems of tyranny and the proper structure of governments. The first of these, according to Adams, was the English reformation; next, when John Poynet put forth "all the essential principles of liberty, which were afterward dilated on by Sidney and Locke."[23]

The Founders were also familiar with the great writers of international law, who based their entire system on the foundation of the natural right of self-defense. Hugo Grotius, the most important writer of all time in international law, built the laws of international warfare by extrapolation from the natural right of personal defense.[24] Samuel von Puffendorf, who extended and elaborated Grotius's work on international law and political philosophy, called self-defense the foundation of civilized society.[25]

The Declaration of Independence affirms that governments are created for the purpose of protecting natural rights.[26] Accordingly, a necessary feature of a legitimate government will be the protection of natural rights. As the Supreme Court explained in *Cruikshank*, the right to assemble and the right to keep and bear arms were, each, "found wherever civilization exists."[27] Although personal self-defense is not specifically mentioned in the Declaration of Independence, that natural right is the intellectual foundation, in Western philosophy, of the right of the people to defend all their natural rights by using force to overthrow a tyrant.[28]

II. The Natural Right's Implications for the *Heller* Dissents

A. Natural Right and the Stevens Dissent

Justice Stevens' dissent does about as well as possible, given the facts available, on issues such as how much weight to give to the Second Amendment's preamble, and whether "bear arms" must necessarily mean the carrying of guns *only* while in military service. Throughout the opinion, he argues passionately for his interpretation, although that interpretation requires the reader to view the evidence from very selectively; the dissent is like the argument that a sheet of paper has only one dimension, because if you look at it from just the right angle, it appears to be a straight line. Vast amounts of evidence have to be willfully ignored. For example, one treatise by Justice Story describes the Second Amendment in terms which are, at least arguably, not necessarily incompatible with Stevens' militia-only view.[29] But another treatise by Story, which quoted by the majority, describes the Second Amendment in terms which fit the *Heller* majority's view, and which are plainly contrary to the Stevens militia-only theory.[30] The majority opinion discusses both treatises,[31] but Stevens writes at length about the first treatise, ignores the existence of the second treatise, and provides no explanation for having done so.[32]

Justice Stevens dismisses the English Declaration of Right, and Blackstone's description thereof, by contending that they addressed issues which were not of concern to the Founders, who according to Stevens were only thinking about the state ratification debates involving state vs. federal powers over the militia.[33] Stevens' view is contrary to that of James Madison, the author of the Second Amendment. In Madison's notes for his speech introducing the Bill of Rights into the House of Representatives, he described arms rights amendment a remedying two crucial defects in the English Declaration of Right: that the right included only the Protestant population, and that the right was, as a statutory enactment, efficacious against the king, but not against the actions of later Parliaments.[34]

But even without reference to Madison's notes, the Stevens theory that the Second Amendment does not include the right of self-defense simply collapses when one gets to the word "the".

The Second Amendment does not purport to grant a right, but instead declares that "the right...shall not be infringed." Thus, the Second Amendment guarantees a pre-existing right. The *Heller* majority says so,[35] and Stevens concedes the point.[36] What was that pre-existing right? There are only two possibilities. One, as explicated by Scalia (consistent with Madison), is that the right is the English/Blackstone/natural right of arms for self-defense. Stevens, however, contends that "the" right is the right to serve in an armed militia. Only if he is correct about this point can his dissent as a whole be correct that the Second Amendment is purely about a right to have arms while in militia service.

There is not a shred of evidence from 1789, or from anytime before 1789, that militia service was a "right." As Justice Scalia pointed out, the Stevens claim that "the" pre-existing right in the Second Amendment was a pre-existing right to service in the militia is unsupported by any evidence. There is simply no document or other source, from the 18th, 17th, or 16th centuries (or indeed from any century until the 21st, when the claim was invented as part of the *Heller* litigation) that the Second Amendment was preceded somewhere in Anglo-American law by a right to serve in the militia, or to have arms solely while in the militia. Rather, this novel theory appears in the *Heller* amicus brief filed by the Brady Center.[37] The brief too is unadorned by any citation for its claim.

Natural Right and the Breyer Dissent

Most of the Breyer dissent lays out an interest-balancing test, in which Justice Breyer argues that there is *some* social science evidence in favor of the D.C. handgun ban, and therefore a judge cannot say as a matter of law that the ban is unconstitutional.[38] A crucial step in that interest-balancing test is the weight of the interest on each side. Justice Breyer points out that preservation of arms ownership for use in a citizen militia was a major concern of the Second Amendment.[39] Accordingly, he disputes the majority's statement that the right of self-defense is "central" to the Second Amendment, and that the "core" of the Second Amendment is armed self-defense of the home.[40]

Justice Scalia responded by explaining why interest-balancing was inappropriate for a core constitutional right, but he did not directly address Breyer's question about why self-defense should be considered part of the core in the first place. However, the answer is fairly clear from the natural law perspective which is incorporated in the majority opinion. Blackstone describes the right to personal defensive arms (protected but not created by the 1689 English Declaration of Right) as a "natural" right. Other sources in the majority opinion make the same point that the Second Amendment protects a "natural" right.

Even if balancing were appropriate, Justice Breyer's scales are inaccurate, because they underweight the importance of self-defense. Surely nothing could be more fundamental than a natural right. The Declaration of Independence, after all, did not begin with a statement of the importance of rights which were created by government (e.g., the right of a citizen to be assisted by his nation's consular offices when he is traveling in a foreign country). Rather, the Declaration starts with natural, inherent rights, and states that the very purpose of government is to protect these rights. By the Declaration's principles, the time that is most appropriate for rigorous judicial review is when a government infringes on one of the natural rights which the very government was established to protect.

From Grotius, Pufendorf, and many other sources, the Founders could see that self-defense had been protected under the laws of Ancient Rome and Ancient Greece, and from the very inception of the Hebrew nation.[41] The historical episodes when the right of armed self-defense was endangered—the persecution of the disarmed Huguenots in France, the gun bans of the power-mad Stuarts monarchs in England, the 1775 confiscation of privately-owned from the people of

Boston by General Gage's army—were precisely the episodes of tyranny which the Founders aimed to ensure would never again take place in the United States of America. From the Founders' perspective, the right to arms truly was found "wherever civilization exists."

III. The Natural Right's Implication for Future Legal Developments

A. Implications for American Law

Self-defense has generally been highly regarded by the American public, and Nicholas Johnson has persuasively argued that self-defense is the epitome of an unenumerated Ninth Amendment right.[42] In contrast, some commentary has denigrated self-defense as a privilege, not a right.[43]

Heller moves self-defense from the shadowy limbo of the Ninth Amendment into the bright uplands of the Second Amendment. It is now beyond dispute, in an American court, that self-defense is an inherent right, and that it is protected by the United States Constitution.

The constitutional history of the right of self-defense is similar to that of the right of association. The right of association is not formally stated in the Constitution. But it is easy to see how if the right did not exist, many of the core purposes of the First Amendment might be defeated. For example, if people could not voluntarily associate in groups such as the NAACP, then their practical ability to petition the government for redress of grievances, to assemble, and to speak out effectively on issues of public importance would be greatly diminished. Thus, starting in 1958, the Supreme Court recognized a constitutional right of association, finding it rooted in the First and Fourteenth Amendments.[44] Over the subsequent half-century, the Court has fleshed out that right, and applied it in many contexts far distant from the original cases involving Jim Crow state governments attempting to suppress the NAACP.

In a series of cases in the late nineteenth and early twentieth centuries, the Supreme Court strongly defended the right of self-defense—holding, for example, that carrying a gun for lawful protection was not evidence of murderous intent, and that a crime victim was not required to retreat or to avoid any place where he had a right to be before he could exercise his right to use deadly force in self-defense.[45] Likewise, the defensive actions of crime-victims should not be subjected to judicial second-guessing; as Justice Holmes memorably put it: "Detached reflection cannot be demanded in the presence of an uplifted knife."[46]

These cases were decided as matters of federal common law, most of them arising out of death sentences improperly imposed on people in the Indian Territory of Oklahoma for use of a gun in self-defense.[47] Now that *Heller* has made it clear that self-defense is part of the Constitution, and not just part of federal common law, there may be plausible arguments that the rules of the Self-Defense Cases are likewise required as a matter of constitutional law.

Should the Second Amendment be incorporated against the states, a few jurisdictions might have to change hostile procedural rules against self-defense. For example, until recently, Arizona required that a defendant asserting self-defense must carry the burden of proof.[48] The few states which require retreat by a crime victim in her own home might lose constitutional challenges to those laws. If a judge prohibited a criminal defense lawyer during voir dire from asking potential jurors about whether they had moral objections to self-defense, a criminal conviction from such a jury might be invalid.[49]

B. Implications for Foreign Law

Heller of course only applies as binding law within the jurisdiction of the United States. However, American constitutional law has a long record of infiltrating into other civilized nations. American protection for freedom of speech and freedom of the press, as well as American anti-discrimination laws, have had significant influence in our fellow democracies. Sometimes that influence is direct, with foreign courts citing American precedents. But more important, in the long run, is the effect that the American example has on the rights-consciousness of the public in those nations.

The right to arms has already shown that it travels. In 2006, the people of Brazil overwhelmingly rejected a referendum to ban gun ownership, and proponents of the referendum noted with dismay the success of anti-referendum advertising which urged Brazilians not to surrender their rights.[50]

For the last decade, the United Nations has led a concerted global campaign against citizen gun ownership. The global prohibitionists have, to the extent they have acknowledged any American interest in protecting American laws, claimed that the Second Amendment protects no individual right of gun ownership, but is only a "collective" right which no individual has a right to exercise. All nine Justices in *Heller* rejected that claim, and affirmed that the Second Amendment guarantees an individual right. As a fallback position, some advocates have stated that the American Second Amendment is unique, and that its very absence shows the permissibility of gun prohibition in other nations.[51]

The latter argument was never really correct as a matter of constitutional law. Three nations besides the United States have a constitutional right to arms, and twenty nations have a formal constitutional recognition of self-defense.[52]

Heller's natural law explication of the inherent right of armed self-defense teaches another very relevant lesson. The right of self-defense is *not* culturally contingent, and it does not depend on national law. The right of self-defense is a universal, fundamental, natural and inherent human right.

Of course there will be many governments which have ignored that right, and will continue to do so. For example, in the United Kingdom and the Netherlands, the principle that there is a right even of *unarmed* self-defense has been in grave danger—at least among the judiciary and the rest of the governing elites.[53]

Yet because *Heller* was not written solely in terms of positive American law, but rather which explicit recognition of pre-existing natural rights, the case may play a role in reminding the people of the world that they too have "the natural right of resistance and self-preservation," a right which is necessarily effectuated by "the right of having and using arms for self-preservation and defence."[54]

On the one side of the debate are the Kenyans who say that the central government, which is manifestly unable and unwilling to protect the tribespeople, should rescind its prohibition on their possession of arms.[55] On the other side is the United Nations, which claims that self-defense is not a right, but is a violation of the right of the criminal attacker, which seeks to outlaw all defensive ownership of firearms, and which has declared that laws in the United States and other nations which allow use of deadly force against rapists and other violent predators are a human rights violation.[56]

Heller points to a resolution of the conflict. Long before there was a United Nations, or a United States of America, there were inherent natural rights. The recognition of those rights is as old as civilization itself. Perhaps one of the greatest influences of *Heller* (and, I hope, its progeny) will be in other nations, where the explicit affirmation of the natural right of self-defense by the most influential court in the world will bolster our global brothers and sisters in their efforts to preserve and strengthen their own natural right of resistance and self-preservation.

FOOTNOTES

[1] Research Director, Independence Institute, Golden, Colorado. Associate Policy Analyst, Cato Institute, Washington, D.C. J.D., University of Michigan, 1985. In Heller, Kopel wrote the amicus brief for the International Law Enforcement

Educators & Trainers Association, and other law enforcement organizations and leaders; the brief was cited four times in Justice Breyer's opinion. Kopel was one of three lawyers who joined Alan Gura at the Supreme Court counsel table on March 18, 2008, to assist Gura in his presentation of the oral argument.

[2] District of Columbia v. Heller, 554 U.S.---, 128 S.Ct. 2783, 2797-98 (2008).

[3] *Id.* at 2798.

[4] 1 W. & M., c. 2, §7 (1689).

[5] JOYCE MALCOLM, TO KEEP AND BEAR ARMS: THE ORIGINS OF AN ANGLO-AMERICAN RIGHT 117-18 (1994).

[6] David Caplan & Susan Wimmershoff-Caplan, *Postmodernism and the Model Penal Code*, 73 UMKC L. REV. 1080 (2005).

[7] "Blackstone, whose works, we have said, 'constituted the preeminent authority on English law for the founding generation,' *Alden* v. *Maine*, 527 U. S. 706, 715 (1999), cited the arms provision of the Bill of Rights as one of the fundamental rights of Englishmen." Heller at 2798.

[8] Slip op. at 20, quoting 1 WILLIAM BLACKSTONE, COMMENTARIES ON THE LAWS OF ENGLAND *139–40 (1765); *see also* Heller at 2792, n. 7: "W. Duer, Outlines of the Constitutional Jurisprudence of the United States 31–32 (1833) (with reference to colonists' English rights: 'The right of every individual to keep arms for his defence, suitable to his condition and degree; which was the public allowance, under due restrictions of the natural right of resistance and self-preservation')."

[9] Heller at 2793.

[10] *Id.* at 2809.

[11] *Id.* at 2799, *quoting* A Journal of the Times: Mar. 17, New York Journal, Supp. 1, Apr. 13, 1769.

[12] *Id.* at 2817. The opinion includes other statements that self-defense is a right. *Id.* at 2820 ("It is inconceivable that this law would have been enforced against a person exercising his right to self-defense on New Year's Day against such drunken hooligans."), at 2801 ("JUSTICE BREYER's assertion that individual self-defense is merely a 'subsidiary interest' of the right to keep and bear arms, see post, at 36, is profoundly mistaken. He bases that assertion solely upon the prologue—but that can only show that self defense had little to do with the right's codification; it was the central component of the right itself.").

[13] THE FEDERALIST, no. 28 (Alexander Hamilton) ("that original right of self-defense which is paramount to all positive forms of government");

[14] David B. Kopel, Paul Gallant, & Joanne D. Eisen, *The Human Right of Self-Defense*, 22 BYU J. PUB. L. 43, 101-02, 128 (2008) (35 U.S. state constitutions affirm that human rights are inherent, natural, or created by God; 37 state constitutions affirm a right of self-defense, sometimes, but not always, articulated in the same clause as right to arms).

[15] *See, e.g.*, People v. Young, 825 P.2d 1004, 1007 (Colo. App., 1991) (citing the 1960 Colorado Supreme Court decision *Vigil v. People* that "self-defense is a

natural right which is based on the law of self-preservation"); Finch v. State, 445 So. 2d 964, 966 (Ala. Crim. App., 1983) ("We agree with proposition expounded in Blankenship, supra, that: 'Self-defense is a common instinct and a natural right, and, as we understand it, means standing one's ground and repelling, as a means of self-protection, unprovoked force with force.'"); Miller v. State, 119 N.W. 850, 857 (Wis. 1909) ("the divine right of self-defense"). Hummel v. State, 69 Okla. Crim. 38, 99 P.2d 91 (Okla. Crim. App., 1940) ("the law adopts the natural right of self-defense, because it considers the future process of law an inadequate remedy for present injuries accompanied with force."); National Life & Acc. Ins. Co. v. Turner, 174 So. 646, (La. App., 1937) ("The right of self-defense is a natural right."); Allen v. Currie, 8 La. App. 30 (La. App., 1928) ("even men of mature years will, in the exercise of their natural right of self-defense, meet or repulse any aggressor who may attempt to encroach on their rights. This is unquestionably true."); People v. Burns, 300 Ill. 361, 366, 133 N.E. 263 (Ill. 1921) ("When a citizen exercises the right of self-defense, he is not taking the law into his own hands. He is simply exercising a natural right which the law recognizes and protects."); State v. Arnett, 258 Mo. 253, 167 S.W. 526 (Mo., 1914) (If statute against exhibiting a weapon in an angry manner "was designed to abrogate the right of self-defense, and if its effect be to do so, it is then more than possible that its constitutional validity might well be questioned, for that it whittles away a part of that 'natural right to life, liberty and the enjoyment of the gains of their own industry,' which is vouchsafed to the citizen by the organic law. Section 4, art. 2, Const. Mo."); People v. Watson, 165 Cal. 645, 133 P. 298 (1913) ("While defendant's conduct with the woman was immoral, it did not take away from him the natural right of self-defense…"); Railroad Commission of Ohio v. Hocking Valley R. Co. 82 Ohio St. 25, 91 N.E. 865 (1910) ("By universal consent self-defense is recognized as a natural right of every individual and of every collection of individuals."); Robinson v. Territory, 16 Okla. 241, 85 P. 451 (Indian Terr., 1905) ("The right of self-defense is founded upon the natural right of a man to protect himself against the unlawful assault upon him by another."); St. Louis Southwestern Ry. Co. v. Berger, 64 Ark. 613, 44 S.W. 809 (1898) (Railroad cannot be sued because of an employee's act of lawful self-defense. The employee's self-defense is "not within any employment he may make, being a natural right which he can neither surrender, nor gratify by any contractual act…"); Thornton v. Taylor, 19 Ky. L. Rptr. 320, 39 S.W. 830 (Ky., 1897) ("The right of self-defense is a natural right…); State v. McGonigle, 14 Wash. 594, 45 P. 20 (1896) ("The plea of self-defense rests on the natural right."); Konigsberger v. Harvey, 12 Or. 286, 7 P. 114 (1885) ("The law upon that subject is the same as it was 500 years ago. The right of self-defense is a natural right, inherent in mankind…"); Isaacs v. State, 25 Tex. 174, 177 (1860) (" It is the necessity of the case, and that only which justifies a killing--on that necessity the right to kill rests, and when the necessity ceases, the right no longer exists. This limitation, which the law puts on the right of self-defense, is founded on the same law of nature and reason which gives the right of defense; and it does not restrain it, but protects it and prevents its abuse by those who would, under its color and the pretense of defense, seek to gratify revenge or an occasion to kill.").

Even in the South on the eve of the Civil War, the natural right of self-defense guaranteed the right to a free black to use violence against a white law enforcement officer:

The conviction of the defendant may involve the proposition that a free negro is not justified, under any circumstances, in striking a white man. To this, we cannot yield our assent...

...

An officer of the town having a notice to serve on the defendant, without any authority whatever, arrests him and attempts to tie him!! Is not this gross oppression? For what purpose was he to be tied? What degree of cruelty might not the defendant reasonably apprehend after he should be entirely in the power of one who had set upon him in so highhanded and lawless a manner? Was he to submit tamely?--Or, was he not excusable for resorting to the natural right of self-defense?

Upon the facts stated, we think his Honor ought to have instructed the jury to find the defendant not guilty. There is error. Venire de novo.

State v. Davis, 52 N.C. 52 (7 Jones) (1859).

A decision from a few decades earlier shows the connections with the English and American common law natural right:

the right of necessary defence, in the protection of a man's person or property, is derived to him from the law of nature, and should never be unnecessarily restrained by municipal regulation. However proper it may be for every well ordered community to be tender of the public peace, and careful of the lives of its citizens, there can be neither policy or propriety in extending this tenderness and care so far as to protect the robber, the burglar and the nocturnal thief, by an unnecessary restraint of the honest citizen's natural right of self-defence. Sir Matthew Hale, in speaking on this subject, says, "the right of self-defence in these cases is founded in the law of nature, and is not, nor can be superceded by the law of society. Before societies were formed, the right of self defence resided in individuals, and since, in cases of necessity, individuals incorporated into society, can not resort for protection to the law of society, that law with great propriety and strict justice considereth them as still, in that instance, under the protection of the law of nature."

Gray vs. Combs, 30 Ky. 478 (1832). Hale was Lord Chief Justice of England from 1671-76, and one of the most influential of all common law judges and treatise authors. The quote actually appears to be from MICHAEL FOSTER, CROWN CASES AND CROWN LAW 273-74 (1762). Foster was a judge of the Court of King's Bench from 1745 to 1763, and was much respected by Blackstone. The quote, with attribution to Foster, appears in the 1847 American annotated edition of MATTHEW HALE, 1 HISTORY OF THE PLEAS OF THE CROWN 478 n.1 (W.A. Stokes & A. Ingersoll eds., Phil., 1847) (1732) (note added by editor). Because the 1847 "first American edition" of Hale post-dates the 1832 Kentucky court decision, it seems probable that the Kentucky court was using an English edition of Hale which also included an editor's annotation with the Foster language.

To muddy the trail a little further, part of the quote appears in Parrish v. Commonwealth, 81 Va. 1 (1884), citing to Hale as quoted in "Rutherforth Institutes"—which means THOMAS RUTHERFORTH, INSTITUTES OF NATURAL LAW: BEING THE SUBSTANCE OF A COURSE OF LECTURES ON GROTIUS DE JURE BELLI ET PACIS READ IN ST. JOHN'S COLLEGE, CAMBRIDGE ch. 16 (1st pub. 1754-56) (a series of English-language lectures on Grotius [*infra*] and natural law; Rutherforth's treatise was very popular in the United States in the 18th and 19th centuries). *Cf.* Commonwealth v. Riley, Thacher's Crim. Cas. 471, 474-75 (Boston Mun.Ct., Mass., 1837) (citing Foster: "In the case of justifiable self-defence, the injured party may repel force by force in defence of his person, habitation, or property, against one who manifestly intendeth and endeavors by violence or surprise, to commit a known felony upon either. It is justly considered that the right in such case, is founded in the law of nature, and is not, nor can be superseded by any law of society. There being at the time no protection from society, the individual is remitted for protection to the law of nature.").

[16] *See, e.g.,* JOHN HART ELY, DEMOCRACY AND DISTRUST: A THEORY OF JUDICIAL REVIEW (1980). Ely, who denies natural law, argues that judicial review should be limited to situations where the ordinary democratic process has failed to protect the rights of minorities. His theory would lead to same result in *Heller*. Every state legislature in the United States includes representatives from urban, suburban, and rural districts. The diversity of constituencies helps ensure that legislators have a diversity of life experiences, and makes it possible to legislators to explain to their colleagues aspects of daily life which may be unfamiliar. For example, a rural legislator may not understand from personal experience how big-city traffic jams waste so much time for suburban parents who are picking up children school or daycare, and shuttling them to sports or music lessons; but the rural legislator can learn about the problem by talking to her suburban colleagues. Similarly, an urban legislator may have no personal understanding of the traditional role of the shooting sports in American life, but a rural legislator can explain it to her. The District of Columbia, however, is a compact and densely-populated city. Its members represent only urban areas, so the Council necessarily suffers from a unique lack of intellectual and life-experience diversity, compared to state legislators. Moreover, the current Council's predecessors worked to eradicate the culture of legitimate firearms usage within the District; zoning rules outlaw indoor shooting ranges throughout the District. Because of the urban-only structure of the District's government, it is uniquely susceptible to bigotry and irrational prejudice against law-abiding gun owners. To cite but one example, the District was the only government in the United States which forbade legal firearms owners from using their guns for self-defense in the home.

[17] United States, Declaration of Independence, para. 2 (1776).

[18] GRATIAN, THE TREATISE ON LAWS (DECRETUM DD. 1-20) WITH THE ORDINARY GLOSS 6 (Augustine Thompson & James Gordley trans., Catholic U. Pr. of America, 1993) (approx. 1150) (Distinction One, case 7, § 2). In the original:

Ius naturale est commune omnium nationum, eo quod ubique instinctu naturae, non constitutione aliqua habetur, ut uiri et feminae coniunctio, liberorum successio et educatio, communis omnium possessio et omnium una libertas, acquisitio eorum, quae celo, terra marique capiuntur; item depositae rei uel commendatae pecuniae restitutio, uiolentiae per uim repulsio. Nam hoc, aut si quid huic simile est, numquam iniustum, sed naturale equumque habetur.

Like self-defense, the natural law right of marriage and child-raising is not enumerated in the United States Constitution, but is a constitutionally-protected fundamental right. *See, e.g.*, Zablocki v. Redhail 434 U.S 374 (1978) (marriage as fundamental right); Meyer v. Nebraska, 262 U.S. 390 (1923) (raising children).

[19] The key Roman law rules for self-defense rule were "arms may be repelled by arms" and "it is permissible to repel force by force." DIG. 43.16.1.27 (Ulpian, Edict 69) ("Cassius writes that it is permissible to repel force by force, and this right is conferred by nature. From this it appears, he says, that arms may be repelled by arms.").

[20] *See* David B. Kopel, *The Catholic Second Amendment*, 29 HAMLINE L. REV. 519 (2006) (Aquinas and Mariana); David B. Kopel, Paul Gallant, & Joanne D. Eisen, *The Human Right of Self-Defense*, 22 BYU J. PUB. L. 43 (2008) (Vitoria and Suárez); *see also* David B. Kopel, *Self-defense in Asian Religions*, 2 LIBERTY L. REV. 79 (2007) (Hinduism, Sikhism, Confucianism, Taoism, and [in practice] Buddhism all respect self-defense as an inherent right; that the Asian religions have, in this regard, quite similar attitudes to Western religions provides an important data point in support of the theory that natural law is a real phenomenon).

[21] *See* MARCUS JUNIUS BRUTUS, VINDICIAE, CONTRA TYRANNOS: OR, CONCERNING THE LEGITIMATE POWER OF A PRINCE OVER THE PEOPLE, AND OF THE PEOPLE OVER A PRINCE (George Garnett ed., 1994) (1st Pub. 1579); DOUGLAS F. KELLY, THE EMERGENCE OF LIBERTY IN THE MODERN WORLD: THE INFLUENCE OF CALVIN ON FIVE GOVERNMENTS FROM THE 16TH THROUGH 18TH CENTURIES 44 (1992) (explaining *Vindiciae*'s debt to Catholic thought); JOHN DALBERG ACTON, THE HISTORY OF FREEDOM AND OTHER ESSAYS 82 (1993) ("the greater part of the political ideas" of John Milton and John Locke "may be found in the ponderous Latin of Jesuits who were subjects of the Spanish Crown," such as Mariana and Suárez).

[22] JOHN ADAMS, 3 A DEFENCE OF THE CONSTITUTIONS OF THE UNITED STATES OF AMERICA 210-11 (Union, N.J.: The Lawbook Exchange, 2001) (1st pub. Philadelphia, 1797).

[23] *Id.*, at 210. Jefferson described John Locke, Algernon Sidney, Aristotle, and Cicero as the four major sources of the American consensus on rights and liberty, which Jefferson distilled into the Declaration of Independence. Thomas Jefferson, letter to Henry Lee, May 8, 1825.

[24] HUGO GROTIUS, THE RIGHTS OF WAR AND PEACE (Liberty Fund 2005) (reprint of 1737 English translation by John Morrice of the 1724 annotated French translation by Jean Barbeyrac) (1625).

[25] SAMUEL PUFENDORF, OF THE LAW OF NATURE AND NATIONS (The Lawbook Exchange 2005) (reprint of 1726 London edition of the 1706–07 Barbeyrac French translation and annotation, with English translation by Mr. Carew) (1672).

[26] "That to secure these rights, Governments are instituted among Men, deriving their just powers from the consent of the governed, --That whenever any Form of Government becomes destructive of these ends, it is the Right of the People to alter or to abolish it, and to institute new Government, laying its foundation on such principles and organizing its powers in such form, as to them shall seem most likely to effect their Safety and Happiness." United States, Declaration of Independence, para. 2 (1776).

[27] The right to assemble, with which the right to arms was construed *in pari materia*:

> existed long before the adoption of the Constitution of the United States. In fact, it is, and always has been, one of the attributes of citizenship under a free government. It "derives its source," to use the language of Chief Justice Marshall, in Gibbons v. Ogden, 9 Wheat. 211, "from those laws whose authority is acknowledged by civilized man throughout the world." It is found wherever civilization exists. It was not, therefore, a right granted to the people by the Constitution. The government of the United States when established found it in existence, with the obligation on the part of the States to afford it protection.

United States v. Cruikshank, 92 U.S. 542, 551-53 (1876) (including similar analysis regarding the "The right... of 'bearing arms for a lawful purpose.' This is not a right granted by the Constitution. Neither is it in any manner dependent upon that instrument for its existence.")

[28] Even if one claims that there is no such thing as natural law, the right of self-defense is so well-established in the common law and in long-standing American tradition that it is precisely the type of unemunerated right which requires constitutional recognition. *See, e.g.*, Lawrence v. Texas, 539 U.S. 558, 588 (2003) (Scalia, J., dissenting), *citing* Washington v. Glucksberg, 521 U.S. 702 (1997) (unenumerated rights should be constitutionally recognized if they are "deeply rooted in this Nation's history and tradition"); Montana v. Egelhoff, 518 U.S. 37, 56 (1996) (Scalia, J., plurality op.) ("the right to have a jury consider self-defense evidence" has strong support in the "historical record" and may be "fundamental"); Eugene Volokh, *State Constitutional Rights to Keep and Bear Arms*, 11 Tex. Rev. L. & Pol. 191 (2006) (many state right to arms provisions explicitly mention self-defense).

[29] 3 Joseph Story, Commentaries on the Constitution of the United States § 1858 (1833)

[30] Joseph Story, A Familiar Exposition of the Constitution of the United States § 450 (1840) ("One of the ordinary modes, by which tyrants accomplish their purposes without resistance, is, by disarming the people, and making it an offence to keep arms, and by substituting a regular army in the stead of a resort to the militia.").

[31] Heller, at 2798, 2800, 2806-07

[32] *Id.* at 2839-40 (Stevens, J., dissenting).

[33] *Id.* at 2837-38 (Stevens, J., dissenting).

[34] "They [the proposed Bill of Rights] relate 1st. to private rights-- . . . fallacy on both sides--espec[iall]y as to English Decln. of Rts--1. mere act of parl[iamen]t. 2. no freedom of press--Conscience . . . attainders--arms to Protest[an]ts." James Madison, *Notes for Speech in Congress Supporting Amendments* (June 8, 1789), *in* 12 The Papers of James Madison 193-94 (Charles F. Hobson et. al. eds., 1979). One can only speculate about the *Heller* majority did not mention Madison's notes. The notes were certainly discussed in one of the most important amicus briefs. Brief of Academics for the Second Amendment, at 34-35, District of Columbia v. Heller, http://www.gurapossessky.com/news/parker/documents/07-290bsacAcademicsforSecondAmendment.pdf. Oral argument made it clear that,

at least, Justice Kennedy had read that brief. Perhaps Justice Scalia was being absolutely faithful to the "original public meaning" theory of interpretation. That is, consider what the public thought the constitutional language meant; do not try to divine "original intent" two centuries later by looking at diaries of the Founders.

[35] Heller, at 2797-98.

[36] *Id.* at 2831 (Stevens, J., dissenting).

[37] Amicus brief for the Brady Center to Prevent Gun Violence et al., 18 n. 6, District of Columbia v. Heller, http://www.gurapossessky.com/news/parker/documents/07-290tsacBradyCenter.pdf (pointing out that the state militia systems pre-dated the Constitution, but providing no evidence that militia service was a right). For history of militia litigation in the United States, and the near-total absence of the Second Amendment therefrom, *see* J. Norman Heath, *Exposing the Second Amendment: Federal Preemption of State Militia Legislation*, 79 U. DET. MERCY L. REV. 39 (2001).

[38] Justice Breyer supported the argument by pointing to gun restrictions in a few cities in early America. The centerpiece of the argument was a Massachusetts law which prevented taking loaded guns into buildings in Boston. Heller, at 2849 (Breyer, J., dissenting) (Providing a fine for any person who "shall take into any Dwelling-House, Stable, Barn, Out-house, Ware-house, Store, Shop, or other Building, within the Town of Boston, any . . . Fire-Arm, loaded with, or having Gun-Powder."). Justice Breyer took the case as standing for the possibility constitutionality of bans on self-defense guns in the home: "Even assuming, as the majority does, *see ante*, at 59–60, that this law included an implicit self-defense exception, it would nevertheless have prevented a homeowner from keeping in his home a gun that he could immediately pick up and use against an intruder. Rather, the homeowner would have had to get the gunpowder and load it into the gun, an operation that would have taken a fair amount of time to perform." Justice Breyer appears to have misread the statute, which only outlawed the *taking* of guns into buildings. The statute did *not* prohibit loading a gun within one's own home or business, and keeping it loaded therein.

[39] The balancing test is offered *arguendo*, since Justice Breyer explains that he is also joining the Stevens dissent, which argues that there is an individual Second Amendment right, but that right has no application outside of militia service. Heller, at 2847-48 (Breyer, J., dissenting).

[40] Heller, at 2866 (Breyer, J., dissenting) ("at most a subsidiary interest").

[41] *See* Kopel, *The Human Right of Self-Defense*; *see also* David B. Kopel, *The Torah and Self-Defense*, 109 PENN STATE L. REV. 17 (2004); David B. Kopel, *The Religious Roots of the American Revolution and the Right to Keep and Bear Arms*, 17 J. FIREARMS & PUB. POL'Y 167 (2005) (early Americans' views of ancient Israel as their role model).

[42] *See* Nicholas J. Johnson, *Self-Defense?* 12 J. LAW, ECON. & POL'Y 187 (2006).

[43] *E.g.*, Vera Bergelson, *Rights, Wrongs, and Comparative Justifications.* 28 CARDOZO L. REV. 2481, 2488 (2007) ("All public officials--a policeman performing a valid arrest, a sheriff taking possession of the debtor's property

pursuant to a court judgment, or an executioner giving the prisoner a lethal injection in accordance with the execution order--act under the right to act that way. In contrast, people acting in self-defense, or pursuant to necessity or parental authority act merely under a privilege.")

[44] NAACP v. Alabama ex rel. Patterson, 357 U.S. 449 (1958).

[45] *See* David B. Kopel, *The Self-Defense Cases: How the United States Supreme Court Confronted a Hanging Judge in the Nineteenth Century and Taught Some Lessons for Jurisprudence in the Twenty-first*, 27 AM. J. CRIM. L. 293 (2000).

[46] Brown v. United States, 256 U.S. 335, 343 (1921) (also declaring there is no duty to retreat).

[47] Kopel, *The Self-Defense Cases*, *supra*.

[48] *E.g.*, State v. Farley, 199 Ariz. 542, 544-545, 19 P.3d 1258, 1260-1261 (Ariz. App. 2001) (upholding statutory requirement that criminal defendant prove self-defense by preponderance of evidence).

[49] Black v. State, 829 N.E.2d 607 (Ind. App., 2005) (based on self-defense right in Indiana Constitution).

[50] *See* David Morton, *Gunning For the World: The National Rifle Association has found that its message—loving freedom means loving guns—translates into almost every language*, FOR. POL., July 5, 2006:

> If you asked people in Bosnia, Botswana, or, for that matter, Brazil, what the Second Amendment of the U.S. Constitution stands for, most of them would probably have no idea. But the unexpected defeat of Brazil's proposed gun prohibition suggests that, when properly packaged, the "right to keep and bear arms" message strikes a chord with people of very different backgrounds, experiences, and cultures, even when that culture has historically been anti-gun. In fact, the Second Amendment may be a more readily exportable commodity than gun control advocates are willing to accept, especially in countries with fresh memories of dictatorship. When it is coupled with a public's fear of crime—a pressing concern in most of the developing world—the message is tailored for mass consumption.

[51] *Accord* Thomas Gabor, *Firearms and Self-Defence: A Comparison of Canada and the United States*, Working Document, Dept. of Just., Canada, July 1997, at 20, http://www.cfc-cafc.gc.ca/pol-leg/res-eval/publications/reports/1997/pdfs/selfdef_en.pdf.

[52] Kopel, *The Human Right of Self-defense*, at 138-41. Self-defense is in the constitutions of Antigua & Barbuda, the Bahamas, Barbados, Belize, Cyprus, Grenada, Guyana, Haiti, Honduras, Jamaica, Malta, Mexico, Nigeria, Peru, Samoa, St. Kitts & Nevis, Saint Lucia, Saint Vincent and the Grenadines, Slovakia, and Zimbabwe. The right to arms is explicit in the Constitutions of Guatemala, Haiti, Mexico, and the United States. *Id.*

[53] Following years of public pressure, the government of the U.K. in July 2008 amended the self-defense law to clarify and protect some self-defense rights for the victims of home invasions. *See* Criminal Justice and Immigration Act 2008, 2008 ch. 4, § 76: reasonableness use of the force is to be judged according to the circumstances as the defender perceived them; and must consider "(a) that a

person acting for a legitimate purpose may not be able to weigh to a nicety the exact measure of any necessary action; and (b) that evidence of a person's having only done what the person honestly and instinctively thought was necessary for a legitimate purpose constitutes strong evidence that only reasonable action was taken by that person for that purpose."; *see also* Richard Edwards, Crime Correspondent and Chris Hope, *"Have-a-go heroes" get legal right to defend themselves*, THE TELEGRAPH (London), July 16, 2008.

[54] A right of self-defense without a right to at least some defensive arms would be a right of little practical utility. It is arms—especially, firearms—which allow a weaker person to defend herself against a stronger attacker or group of attacker. It is the firearm which best makes a deterrent threat of self-defense, while allowing the victim to remain beyond the grasping distance of the stronger assailant(s).

[55] Paul Letiwa, *Why Herders Won't Surrender Their Firearms Just Yet*, THE NATION (Kenya), April 30, 2008

http://allafrica.com/stories/200804300138.html ("'How can the Government ask us to surrender our guns when we know very well that there is no security for us? If we give out our firearms, say today, who will protect us when the neighbouring tribes strike? How about our stolen livestock? Who is going to return them to us?' Mr Lengilikwai talks with bitterness."); Ng'ang'a Mbugua, *Law Should Be Changed to Free Guns*, THE NATION (Nairobi), Apr. 25, 2008, http://allafrica.com/stories/printable/200804251276.html (Noting success of armed defense program of the people of the Keiro Valley, "In the past, critics of liberalising access to firearms have argued that they would put ordinary people's lives in peril because even squabbles in the streets or the bedroom would be resolved by bullets. Incidentally, such incidents are few and far between in the Kerio Valley despite the easy accessibility of AK- 47s as well as the relatively low levels or education and social sophistication....If Kenya is to achieve long-lasting stability, it ought to borrow a leaf from the US, whose constitution gives the people the right to bear arms and form militias for their own defence should the armed forces fail them, as happened in Kenya after the December elections."). *See generally* David B. Kopel, Paul Gallant & Joanne D. Eisen, *Human Rights and Gun Confiscation*, 26 QUINNIPIAC L. REV. 383 (2008) (describing gun policies in Kenya, Uganda, and South Africa).

[56] 6. *See* U.N. Human Rights Council, Sub-Comm'n on the Promotion and Prot. of Human Rights, 58th Sess., *Adoption of the Report on the Fifty-eighth Session to the Human Rights Council*, U.N. Doc. A/HRC/Sub.1/58/L.11/Add.1 (Aug. 24, 2006), *available at* http://hrp.cla.umn.edu/documents/ A.HRC.Sub.1.58.L.11. Add.1.pdf. The United Nations report on self-defense in analyzed in detail in Kopel, *The Human Right of Self-Defense*, *supra*.

The Experts Speak

Bob Levy

In *District of Columbia v. Heller*, the Court was faced with four key questions: (1) Does the Second Amendment secure an individual or collective right? (2) Is the D.C. gun ban unconstitutional? (3) What is the scope of the right? And (4) what standard of review will the Court apply in examining other gun control regulations?

On the first question, the Court decided 5-4 that the Second Amendment secures an individual right, not necessarily tied to militia service—a right that extends at least as far as private possession of ordinary firearms in the home for self defense. If the Court had ruled otherwise, the Second Amendment would be a dead letter. On the second question, the Court held that D.C.'s ban on all functional firearms in the home is unconstitutional—"under any of the standards of scrutiny the Court has applied to enumerated constitutional rights."

Both holdings were clear victories for Mr. Heller, who had asked the Court to reach those conclusions even if it did not choose to resolve the third and fourth questions concerning the scope of the right and the standard of review in future cases.

On the scope question, the Court was more circumspect. Because Heller had not challenged D.C.'s licensing requirements, the Court did not resolve whether those requirements are constitutional. But the Court did volunteer that some regulations would likely be sustained— including "longstanding prohibitions on the possession of firearms by felons and the mentally ill, or laws forbidding the carrying of firearms in ... schools and government buildings, or laws imposing conditions and qualifications on the commercial sale of arms."

Moreover, stated Justice Antonin Scalia, under *United States v. Miller*— which the Court correctly interpreted to address the type of weapons that the Second Amendment protects, not whether an individual is part of a militia—"the carrying of dangerous and unusual weapons" can probably be barred.

Finally, the Court was reluctant to provide precise guidelines regarding the standard of review that it would apply in dealing with the deluge of Second Amendment challenges that have already begun winding their way through the judicial system. The Court may ultimately give *Heller* less than the "strict scrutiny" standard he had suggested.

On the other hand, the Court categorically rejected "rational basis" scrutiny, which has been a rubber-stamp for virtually all legislative enactments. And the Court also rejected Justice Stephen Breyer's "interest-balancing" test, which is no more than a repeat of the process that legislatures undertake in crafting regulations. Something higher is demanded, said Scalia, when an express constitutional right is at issue. That means, at a minimum, the Court will adopt the "intermediate" level of scrutiny urged by Solicitor General Paul Clement in his brief for the Justice Department.

All in all, the *Heller* opinion was a major victory for the Constitution. It's not everything we could have hoped for, but it lays a solid foundation for step-by-step dismantlement of unconstitutional gun-control regimes in a handful of U.S. jurisdictions.

Robert A. Levy is senior fellow in constitutional studies at the Cato Institute, co-counsel to Mr. Heller, and co-author of The Dirty Dozen: How Twelve Supreme Court Cases Radically Expanded Government and Eroded Freedom *(Penguin/Sentinel, May 2008).*

Alan Gura

Yesterday's decision is a huge victory for liberty. First, we saved the Second Amendment. That much should be obvious from the opinion. Yesterday, federal courts in 47 states were telling Americans they had no Second Amendment rights. The score is now 50–0, plus the capital, in the other direction.

For budding lawyers, "individual right" is now the correct answer on the Multi-State Bar Exam. The movement to end private firearm owner-ship in America is dead and buried. Yes, we've got some work to do to make sure it stays that way. It will.

The case is "narrow but broad." Narrow, in the sense that our objective was merely to secure the individual nature of Second Amendment rights, and demonstrate—with a judgment—that the right has substance. Broad, in the sense that this simple principle can now be applied in other contexts.

This is not just about flat-out gun bans in Washington, D.C. homes. All regulations that touch upon Second Amendment rights will get a well-deserved constitutional look.

Instant background checks and felon-in-possession laws will survive. Laws meant to harass gun possession, while at best advancing only a hypothetical public benefit, will not. The Second Amendment is now a normal part of the Bill of Rights.

It's not realistic to expect one Second Amendment case to answer all right-to-arms questions for all time, just as we have no one decision telling us what a Fourth Amendment "reasonable search" is in all circumstances. We may not win every case. We'll win a good number of them. The next step is obviously 14th Amendment incorporation. I'm looking forward to leading that fight. Learn more: chicagoguncase.com.

Libertarians can be impatient. Would anyone prefer the quick certainty of *Kelo*? Or *McConnell v. FEC*? It may be a tough slog to restore the Takings Clause and to free political speech. Restoring the Second Amendment will take time, too. Today, with the right to keep and bear arms, we start from a position of strength.

Alan Gura argued District of Columbia v. Heller *before the Supreme Court. He is a partner at Gura & Possessky. This article originally appeared in reasononline (Reason Magazine) and is reproduced with permission.*

The following is edited from a presentation by Mr. Gura to The Virginia Citizens Defense League on July 17, 2008. It may be viewed here: http://www.vcdl.org/Heller/VCDL_Gura.mov

We are changing the way law students and lawyers and judges and most importantly legislators are thinking about the Second Amendment.

The landscape has changed dramatically. Every city council or state legislature or even Congress, whenever they think of or propose a gun law, they need to start thinking—are we going to get sued over this, what's it going to cost, is this law that we're proposing really going to have a public safety purpose, does it make sense, is it respectful of the individual right to bear arms, or is this just a gimmick that's designed to harass people and make gun ownership expensive or impossible or difficult. If it's in the first category it's going to survive. If it's in the second category it's just going to make me and my friends a little wealthier (laughter).

The Supreme Court did its job. The Supreme Court and the courts in general are the place we go as individuals when the political process fails us. The Court is there not to worship and give deference to the political branches, the Court is there to enforce the constitutional rights when the political branches fail us. Some people call that activism, I prefer to call that engagement. If activism means we're going to actively enforce the Bill of Rights against the government when it oversteps its bounds, that's a great thing, and we need more of it.

In this case we had a law that was really quite drastic. When I would tell people what this law actually did, a lot of folks would say, "Really? Was the law really that crazy?"

This was a law that banned all handguns—you couldn't have a handgun in your house. If you had a rifle or shotgun, it had to be at all times unloaded and either disassembled or bound by a trigger lock, with no exception for home self defense. If the bad guys busted in, and you happened to have one of these registered shotguns, the only thing you could do with it would be whack the intruder over the head or throw it at the intruder. You couldn't actually ever render that shotgun operable for self defense.

We argued to the courts, and the courts agreed with us, that if you have the right to arms, you have the right to arms that actually work.

The case was designed to take the craziest, most extreme gun laws in America, and hold them out as an example of why the individual right should survive. If you have any sort of individual right under the Second Amendment, at the very absolute minimum, it means you have the right to have a working handgun inside your house, for self defense, if you're a law-abiding, normal, non-psychopathic person. And the Court agreed with us. The case was not designed to solve every single question that might come out under the Second Amendment.

Remember, the Second Amendment is a normal part of the Bill of Rights. Just like other parts of the Bill of Rights, we don't have one case that tells us for all time what a reasonable search is under the Fourth Amendment, or one case that for all circumstances tells us what free speech is and when you can or can't exercise it. Same with the right to keep and bear arms. We found out at least in the home you can have a gun. I suspect other permutations of this right are applicable as well.

There are going to be all kinds of laws that will no longer survive and there will be all kinds of laws that will survive.

Even back in the days of the Revolution, the right to arms was denied certain people—primarily Tory loyalists. If you were going to be supportive of King George they were going to take away your guns, although interestingly, oftentimes they let people keep their pistols, they would take away their muskets and their rifles. Those were the assault weapons of the day (laughter).

Had I gotten in front of the Supreme Court and said, "No law means no law," and "Shall not be infringed.." well, that's a good way to lose.

We did win a very broad and very powerful Second Amendment from the Supreme Court. The Supreme Court made it very clear that the Second Amendment will have the same standard of review protection, the same level of constitutional protection, that traditionally has been afforded other enumerated constitutional rights, such as the First Amendment.

We just wanted to show that the right had substance and meaning, that at least *something* is unconstitutional under the Second Amendment, and give us a clue that yes, it is a meaningful amendment, and that's what the Court did.

Don B. Kates

The gun bans *Heller* overturned reflected falsehoods like, "most homicides are not committed by the 'hardened' criminal who would seek out a gun or other lethal weapon whether or not it was legal, but rather by ordinary, 'law abiding' citizens who kill on impulse rather than by intent [because a firearm was available in a moment of ungovernable anger]."

Though such falsehoods routinely appear in purportedly scholarly articles, these *never* supply supporting references—for there are none! Perpetrator data dating back to the 19th century invariably show that "most murderers differ little from other major *criminals.*" Far from being law abiding responsible adults:

- "The vast majority of persons involved in life-threatening violence have a long criminal record with many prior contacts with the justice system"

- "Homicide is usually part of a pattern of violence, engaged in by people who are known... as violence prone.'"

- Psychological studies find 80-100% of juvenile murderers are psychotic or have psychotic symptoms.

- Though only 15% of Americans have criminal records, roughly 90 percent of adult murderers have adult records (exclusive or their often extensive juvenile records), with an average adult crime career of six or more years, including four major felonies.

- *The New York Times* study of the 1,662 NYC murders in 2003-2005 found, "More than 90 percent of the killers had criminal records ..."

- "Some 95% of homicide offenders... [in a Kennedy School study had been] arraigned at least once in Massachusetts courts before they [murdered],... On average... homicide offenders had been arraigned for 9 prior offenses..."

- "A history of domestic violence was present in 95.8%" of the intra-family homicides studied.

- Of Illinois murderers in 1991-2000, the great majority had prior felony records.

- Eighty percent of 1997 Atlanta murder arrestees had previously been arrested at least once for a drug offense; and 70% had three or more prior drug arrests—in addition to all their arrests for other crimes.

- Baltimore police records show that 92% of 2006 murder suspects had criminal records.

In sum, guns or no guns, the vast majority of murderers are simply not law abiding responsible adults—despite vociferous inaccurate assertions of the anti-gun-rights coalition. So firmly is this established by perpetrator studies that it is a "criminological axiom."

The policy implications are obvious: Since ordinary people do not commit gun crimes there is no point to disarming them. Rather, doing so is counter-productive since it leaves innocent victims defenseless against violent predators.

This material is drawn from an article by Don B. Kates & Gary Mauser, "Would Banning Firearms Reduce Murder and Suicide: A Review of International Evidence," 30 Harvard Journal of Law & Public Policy 651-694 (2007) (footnotes omitted), reprinted by permission of Mr. Kates.

Don B. Kates is a retired professor of criminal and constitutional law and a criminologist. He was deeply involved in the Heller *case in filing* amicus *briefs and in focusing the* amicus *effort for the NRA.*

Gary Mauser is professor emeritus in the Institute for Canadian Urban Research Studies, and the Faculty of Business Administration at Simon Fraser University in Canada. His academic research for over 20 years has involved studying firearms and crime.

Clayton Cramer

A Crucial Reminder That Politics Matter

Those of us who contributed to the scholarly research for *Heller* can congratulate ourselves about how important it was to helping the Court make the right decision—and it is very satisfying to see your name in a Supreme Court decision. (Page 15 of Scalia's opinion, in my case.) We can also take some comfort in seeing how the dissenting opinions declined to fully embrace the collective rights view of the Second Amendment—which for most of the latter half of the twentieth century was the dominant view in law schools, the federal bench, and generally, elite opinion. That's progress!

But before we get too proud of how our historical and legal scholarship defeated the forces of gun control and elitism, I think it is worthwhile to remember what *really* happened here. Most of the five Justices that voted with us seem to believe in originalism—that they recognize an obligation to put the original meaning of the Constitution above their personal preferences about what the law should be. Justice Thomas' opinions—and more often his dissents—show that he understands that originalism matters, and he does his best to follow it.

This is true even for laws that Thomas agreed were "uncommonly silly," such as the sodomy law struck down in *Lawrence v. Texas* (2003). Chief Justice Roberts' remarks during oral arguments about the modernity and non-constitutional nature of standards of review give me some confidence that he understands the ahistorical nature of much of what passes for judicial reasoning these last few decades. (Justice Scalia, as much as I admire his intellect, does not seem to be *quite* as consistent an originalist as Thomas, apparent in the *Raich* case.)

But Justice Kennedy? He voted with us, and made clear during oral arguments that he was on our side—but the same week as *Heller*, he wrote the opinion in *Kennedy v. Louisiana* (2008), ruling that capital punishment for child rape was "cruel and unusual punishment" using an "evolving standards" approach—a profoundly anti-originalist approach. I'm glad that Kennedy was on our side in *Heller*, but it is pretty clear that he was on our side because he opposes absurdly restrictive gun control—not because he feels any obligation to follow the Constitution's original meaning.

How will Justice Kennedy vote if California's assault-weapon ban comes before the Court? I have considerable confidence that Justices Thomas, Scalia, Roberts, and Alito will look at original meaning, and vote to strike it down. But Justice Kennedy? Who knows? Do you want to flip a coin?

And this is why politics *still* matters. Imagine if John Kerry had been elected President in 2004. Does anyone seriously think that originalists like Roberts or Alito would have ended up on the Supreme Court? Does anyone seriously think that *Heller* would have been decided 5-4 in our favor? Reading the confused and sometimes factually erroneous dissents in *Heller* tells me that President Kerry's appointments would have helped write a 6-3 decision that found that the Second Amendment was essentially meaningless.

Heller isn't the last word on the meaning of the Second Amendment. It is really the *first* word. Chief Justice Roberts sets great value on what he calls "judicial modesty"—judges not getting too arrogant in their authority to second-guess legislative bodies. When in doubt as to the constitutionality of a law, judges should defer to the people and their elected representatives. I suspect that for this reason, Chief Justice Roberts may have also been part of why the majority in *Heller* did not go beyond the question that they were supposed to be deciding here: was D.C.'s handgun ban contrary to the Second Amendment?

Consequently, Justice Scalia's opinion was careful not to lay down what standard of review should be used—pointing out that D.C.'s law would fail the test under *any* standard of review. But that also means that there is still considerable uncertainty as to how the Second Amendment should be applied to a variety of different questions.

Will the Court find that the Fourteenth Amendment incorporates the Second Amendment against the states, requiring California, Chicago, Massachusetts, New Jersey, and a few other benighted places to strike down most of their gun-control laws? Some of us are working on that case now, and the historical evidence is even stronger for this than it was for the Second Amendment—but that case won't reach the Supreme Court for several years.

What about location? Can Congress ban guns in National Parks? What about federal buildings? Will local licensing in Puerto Rico, the U.S. Virgin Islands and other federal territories survive?

What types of arms are protected? Handguns, clearly, are protected. What about semiautomatic "assault weapons"? Are machine guns protected arms, perhaps under a more stringent regulatory scheme than ordinary small arms? What distinguishes a category of protected arms which might be subject to additional regulation (such as machine guns) from a category that may be banned completely (such as chemical weapons or artillery)?

What classes of persons may be prohibited from possessing arms? Felons don't seem to be in dispute. Could Chicago solve their "problem" with *Heller* by making it unlawful for anyone convicted of a parking violation to possess handguns? Probably not, but somewhere between parking tickets and murder, the Court is going to have to draw a line and say, "Yes, the federal and state governments can prohibit arms possession by this class of criminals—but not this class."

All these questions are going to be resolved through a series of lawsuits in the next few years—and the types of justices that sit on the Supreme Court are going to make a world of difference. That's why as much as I don't particularly like John McCain, I don't see that I have much choice as to who to vote for in November. I know what sort of justices Barack Obama is likely to appoint—and they are likely to be *less* sympathetic to the individual rights' version of the Second Amendment than Justices Stevens, Souter, Ginsburg, and Breyer.

Clayton E. Cramer is a software engineer and historian. His most recent book was Armed America: The Remarkable Story of How and Why Guns Became as American as Apple Pie *(Nelson Current, 2006).*

Eugene Volokh

1. There's no substitute for winning elections. The 5-4 conservative-liberal lineup (admittedly, with one of the four being a Bush, Sr. appointee) shows this. These issues aren't just about winning elections, as I'll note below. But winning is part of it. My guess is that, if the McCain campaign is smart about this, it can make this an important linchpin of its fundraising ("imagine what would happen to your rights if Justices Scalia and Kennedy retire soon and are replaced by Barack

Obama"), of its attempts to energize the base, and of its attempts to bring over swing voters in swing states where the middle of the electorate tends to be pro-gun.

Naturally, the Obama campaign can try the same, as I'm sure it will be doing as to abortion rights. My guess is that such Obama strategies will be less effective than a McCain strategy of hitting the gun-rights point (of course, in ads targeted to particular subsets of the voters): My sense is that pro-gun-ban voters are less dedicated to this view than are pro-gun-rights voters, and that the pro-abortion-rights voters are less likely to be swing voters in swing states. But in any case, both approaches might make sense—McCain may hit the gun-rights issue hard in some places, and Obama the abortion-rights issue hard mostly in other places (and especially to energize his base, including Hillary Clinton partisans who might otherwise have been lukewarm towards Obama).

2. In some situations, academic writings make a big difference. My sense is that thirty or even twenty years ago, even most conservative Justices wouldn't have accepted the individual-rights view. After all, support for anti-crime laws has long been a traditional conservative principle. Chief Justice Burger was famously a supporter of the states' rights view of the Second Amendment. And judges, including conservative judges, tend to be influenced by solid bodies of law created by other judges (even lower-court judges), and back then the unanimous view of federal circuit courts was to dismiss the individual rights view as something of a crank perspective.

I think that the scholarly work on the Second Amendment, starting with Don Kates' seminal *Handgun Prohibition and the Original Meaning of the Second Amendment* (Michigan Law Review, 1983) and continuing with the work of Nelson Lund, Sandy Levinson, Joyce Malcolm, Stephen Halbrook, Glenn Harlan Reynolds, Akhil Reed Amar (though his position was a bit more ambiguous), and others, dramatically changed the landscape.

At least, the scholarship led conservative judges—starting with prominent circuit judges and moving on to Supreme Court Justices—to look seriously at the issue, and pointed them to historical evidence that they might have otherwise missed. (Note, by the way, that Kates, Halbrook, and Clayton Cramer, another important historical writer in this field, a co-written article of whose was cited in the opinion, are not professors, though their articles are academic works. Note also that not all these authors were cited by the Court, but they were certainly cited in the briefs, and their work was relied on by later writers.)

Naturally, the scholarship wouldn't have succeeded without the underlying evidence, and the 5-4 division on the Court shows that it wouldn't have succeeded without Justices who were sympathetic to the argument. But I doubt that the Justices would have been as sympathetic, or would have looked closely at all the right evidence, without the work of scholars.

Eugene Volokh teaches free-speech law, criminal law, religious-freedom law, and church-state-relations law at UCLA Law School. He clerked for Justice Sandra Day O'Connor on the U.S. Supreme Court, has written three textbooks and more than 50 law-review articles, and his work is cited in the majority opinion in Heller.

Daniel Schmutter

Substantial Victory for American Gun Owners?

Having submitted an *amicus curiae* brief on the side of Respondent Heller, I cannot help but conclude that today's decision represents a substantial victory for American gun owners. Yet, to read the press releases of various anti-gun interest groups and government officials, you would think that the other side won today.

This is because the majority opinion clearly provides room for the survival of gun laws that do not offend the fundamental self-defense purpose of the Second Amendment. Thus, as with other rules of law, the real meat and potatoes, so to speak, will be found in the lawsuits to come. Accordingly, anti-gun groups have already taken up the gauntlet and broadly asserted that today's decision affirms the validity of "reasonable" efforts by government to control crime. Well, not so fast.

What the decision does recognize is that the right to keep and bear arms is not absolute. So far that's nothing controversial. Notwithstanding the fact that some folks would have liked a decision that swept away gun laws *en masse*, I doubt that anyone seriously expected there was any real likelihood of that. Instead, those watching this issue were keenly interested in the scope of the right and the standard of review to be applied. Well, we got some information on both of those.

For instance, we know that outright handgun bans are now off the table (federally, at least—for now). We also know that self defense is a key linchpin of the right to keep and bear arms. We also know that, at some level, the types of weapons protected by the Second Amendment bear some relationship to the extent to which they are in common use.

Similarly, we know that the Court views certain types of laws as likely valid, such as laws prohibiting possession of firearms by felons or the mentally ill, or in school and government buildings. Yet these are hardly the laws that proponents of gun control are usually talking about when they refer to "reasonable" laws.

Typically, proponents of "reasonable" gun laws mean something far more aggressive. Thus, when anti-gun groups hail today's decision as affirming the right to enact "reasonable" gun measures, they take a giant leap into what is truly a massive area of uncertainty. The vast chasm between "ban on handguns" and "ban on felons with handguns" is fertile ground for decades of litigation.

To be sure, *Heller* represents a very good decision establishing a strong right to keep and bear arms. Yet it will require years of litigation to define that right before it is of any firm degree of utility to either side. What is clearly true from the majority opinion, however, is that no matter what happens, there will be a substantial realm that will always remain solidly in the political arena. Considerable room has been left for presumptively valid gun laws, and both sides will have plenty to keep them busy going forward.

Mr. Schmutter is a litigation attorney based in New Jersey, practicing before federal and state trial and appellate courts, administrative tribunals and arbitration panels in New Jersey and New York. He represented Jews for the Preservation of Firearms Ownership as amicus curiae *before the Supreme Court in* Heller.

David T. Hardy

Justice Stevens in Dissent: The Fine Art of Misreading Cases

When discussing *Heller*, we must pay some attention to the dissenters' theories. After all, they did come within one vote of winning!

That they came so close is shocking—and Justice Stevens' dissent is nothing that deserved to come that close. It begins with an embarrassing error. Stevens' major argument is that a) the 1939 decision in *United States v. Miller* is the key precedent, b) he applies it correctly, and c) the majority does not.

In researching a prior court ruling, the *very first thing* an attorney or judge looks at is the procedural question: what happened in that case? Did the lower court dismiss a case at its outset, or did it end in a verdict, or maybe the jury entered a verdict and then the judge set it aside? Did the higher court uphold the lower court, or reverse it? With that in mind, you can make sense of the case.

Justice Stevens describes the National Firearms Act of 1934 and then turns to *Miller* saying, "Upholding a conviction under that Act, this Court held..."

There are only two problems: Jack Miller was never convicted, and the Supreme Court did not uphold anything! The lower court *dismissed the indictment* against Miller before trial, and the Supreme Court *reversed* that dismissal.

It's the type of error that leaves you wondering whether Justice Stevens actually understood the *Miller* decision. All he had to do was look at the title. "*United States v. Miller*" tells you that the first party, the United States, was *appealing*—it had lost in the lower court.

The first paragraph in *Miller* says: "The District Court held that section 11 of the Act violates the Second Amendment. It accordingly sustained the demurrer and quashed the indictment." *Miller* ends with "the challenged judgment must be reversed."

To be fair, the majority voices the same error—perhaps one responded in haste to the other's argument without doing the legwork.

Regardless, it's not the only glaring error in the dissent. In discussing the militia, Stevens refers to a 1990 Supreme Court decision, *Perpich v. Dodd*. Citing to it, Stevens says "In 1901 the President revitalized the militia by creating the 'National Guard of the several States...'"

But if you read *Perpich*, it doesn't say that. Instead, it says that President Teddy Roosevelt in 1901 called for revitalizing the militia, but it was Congress, not the President, that created the federal Guard... in 1903.

Such errors suggest Justice Stevens perhaps just skimmed cases before expounding upon them. All you have to do is read *Perpich* to understand who did what and when. Obvious questions—how would a President find the legal power to create a new military organization?— never popped into his mind.

Justice Stevens then turns to his central theme: "The Second Amendment was adopted to protect the right of the people of each of the several States to maintain a well-regulated militia."

But every provision of the Bill of Rights must be given meaning. The Framers didn't list among our most vital rights things that were meaningless or trivial.

Stevens adopts D.C.'s line. He argues that certain Americans were concerned that Congress would not enact a militia law requiring militiamen to be armed, and this would "disarm" the militia system unless the States had the power to do so. Thus, he argues, the Second Amendment was only meant to protect a "right" to have arms if your State ordered you to have them after Congress neglected to do so.

Stevens writes: "It [the Second Amendment] was a response to concerns raised during the ratification of the Constitution that the power of Congress to disarm the state militias and create a national standing army posed an intolerable threat to the sovereignty of the several States."

Justice Stevens' theory is here utterly untenable. Worse, he completely omits the fact that a brief submitted to the Court showed that this theory was absolutely worthless.

In the brief for Academics for the Second Amendment, Joe Olson and I demonstrated:

1. Yes, there were Framers concerned about the militia being left unarmed, but they weren't pushing for the future Second Amendment. They wanted a different and additional guarantee that "each state respectively shall have the power to provide for organizing, arming, and disciplining its own militia, whensoever Congress shall omit or neglect to provide for the same." The Framers used clear English to say what they wanted.

2. That additional guarantee (in the above words) was put into the Virginia ratifying convention's demands for a bill of rights, together with the ancestor of the Second Amendment. They were *two separate ideas*.

3. When James Madison drafted the Bill of Rights, he worked from the Virginia ratifying convention's proposals. He put the Second Amendment in. *He omitted the separate clause* on States arming the militia.

4. When the first Senate debated the Bill of Rights, Virginia senators moved to put the militia-arming clause back in. The first Senate *voted the idea down*. We found this in the Journal of the First Senate:

> On motion, To add the following clause to the Articles of Amendment to the Constitution ... to wit: 'That each State respectively shall have the power to provide for organizing, arming, and disciplining its own militia, whensoever Congress shall omit or neglect to provide for the same...'

It passed in the negative, i.e., it was voted down.

In short, there were Framers concerned about having States able to arm their militias. But they weren't calling for the Second Amendment, but for a different provision entirely. And they lost. James Madison scrapped their idea, and Congress rejected their second try.

Just to cap it off, when the First Congress later debated a militia act, an amendment was proposed that could have been read as allowing States to provide for militia armament. James Madison himself led the opposition: "It was said it would be destructive of the bill, as it would leave it optional with the States, or individuals, whether the militia should be armed or not. This motion was lost by a great majority."

We may never know how four Justices were willing to sign on to such flawed work—ideology? sloth? inattention?—but their signatures do nothing to make it more credible.

Stevens' conclusion has a logical problem as well. As the majority noted, the Bill of Rights was intended to be a check on Congress and the new national government. But the Constitution had given Congress the power to organize the militia. If the right to arms only covers the militia, and Congress can define who is in the militia, then the right is no check on Congress at all. It would be as if freedom of the press were limited to the Government Printing Office. Stevens replies thusly:

The Court assumes—incorrectly, in my view—that even when a state militia was not called into service, Congress would have had the power to exclude individuals from enlistment in that state militia. That assumption is not supported by the text of the Militia Clauses of the original Constitution, which confer upon Congress the power to "organiz[e], ar[m], and disciplin[e], the Militia," Art. I, §8, cl. 16, but not the power to say who will be members of a state militia.

Stevens again must ignore the *amicus* briefs and authorities they cite. Our Academics brief had cited to legal studies by J. Norman Heath. Heath tracked early Supreme Court decisions and found they ruled that, once Congress legislated (no matter how inadequately, the Court added) regarding the militia, the States lost all power to regulate it. Moreover, Heath found a State decision holding specifically that a State could not include within its definition of militia any person who was outside the Federal definition. Stevens' claim was settled by the Court two hundred years ago, in cases he apparently doesn't know existed!

So if the right to arms is limited to militiamen, the Second Amendment is indeed no check on the national government. The right to arms belongs to you only if Congress lets you have it!

The Stevens dissent, in sum, mis-cites major cases so grossly as to suggest its author never really read them. Its historical theory of intent was demolished by the briefs filed—indeed, so thoroughly that D.C. abandoned the point in its last brief. Its argument for purpose was rejected by the Court two centuries ago, in opinions Stevens never found. And four Justices signed on to it nonetheless!

Attorney David T. Hardy graduated from the University of Arizona College of Law in 1975, and practices law in Tucson. He is the author of fourteen law review articles, ten on the right to arms or firearms laws, which have been cited as authority by the U.S. Supreme Court and eleven of the U.S. Circuit Courts of Appeals. In D.C. v. Heller, he co-authored the amicus *brief for Academics for the Second Amendment.*

Glenn Reynolds

• From *reasononline (Reason Magazine),* used with permission: My first thought on *Heller* is that many gun-rights supporters never thought they'd live to see a Supreme Court opinion to the effect that "The Second Amendment protects an individual right to possess a firearm unconnected with service in a militia, and to use that arm for tradition-ally lawful purposes, such as self-defense within the home." Bob Levy, who brought the case against the advice of many gun-rights supporters, should feel very good about that.

My second thought is that this is a gift to the Obama campaign. While this won't take the gun issue off the table, it also won't energize the gun-rights crowd (which cost Al Gore the election in 2000 when he failed to carry Tennessee, largely because of his support for gun control) the way a contrary opinion would have. Obama's record of strong support for sweeping gun control would hurt him much more if gun owners felt more vulnerable.

My third thought is that whether this has much impact on the real world depends on how the next several cases proceed. In the 1990s the Supreme Court announced a major shift in Commerce Clause doctrine that offered the hope of paring back federal power considerably. But right-leaning public interest law groups didn't take up the challenge and bring carefully selected cases to advance the principle, leading it to be characterized by some (including me) as a constitutional revolution where nobody showed up. Gun-rights advocates are already talking about follow-on challenges in places like Chicago or Morton Grove. How well those are brought will have a lot to do with whether the *Heller* opinion is a milestone, or just a speed bump.

• *From Instapundit* (Reynolds' blog): I'm writing a short piece on *Heller* for Northwestern, and something became clear to me as soon as I started writing: What's most striking about *Heller* is that absolutely everybody—majority and dissents—says the Second Amendment protects an individual right.

It's true that the dissenters' view of that right is somewhere between "minimalist" (to be charitable) and "incoherent" (to be accurate). But nonetheless, all nine Justices specifically said the right is individual, and thus rejected the "collective right" position on the Second Amendment, a position that's been the mainstay of gun-control groups, newspaper editorialists, and lower federal courts for decades, and one that was presented by those adherents as so obviously correct that those arguing for an individual right were called "frauds" and shills for the NRA.

Yet the collective right theory could not command a single vote on the Court when actually tested. It was, it seems, a paper tiger all along.

• *Excerpted from* Northwestern University Law Review Colloquy, *Vol. 102, No. 406 (2008) used with permission (footnotes omitted): (online at law.northwestern.edu/lawreview/colloquy/2008/23)*

Heller's Future in the Lower Courts
by Glenn H. Reynolds and Brannon P. Denning

Abstract: The Supreme Court's recent decision in *District of Columbia v. Heller* not only established an individual right to gun ownership, but also overturned—by a 9-0 margin—lower-court caselaw based on a "collective right" interpretation of the Second Amendment. This article looks at how *Heller* is likely to fare in the lower courts, based on experience with other recent Supreme Court decisions, and incorporates new scholarship on decision rules and the so-called "new doctrinalism."

The Supreme Court has released its long-awaited opinion in *District of Columbia v. Heller*, and the buzz has been considerable. Though much has been made of the majority's historic ruling and of the narrowness of that majority, many commentators have missed an important point. What *Heller* is most notable for is its complete and unanimous rejection of the "collective rights" interpretation that for nearly seventy years held sway with pundits, academics, and—most significantly—lower courts.

The repudiation of this extensive body of case law suggests that the real test of *Heller* will occur once the lower courts, traditionally hostile to an individual rights interpretation of the Second Amendment, face the inevitable follow-up cases challenging other restrictive gun laws. Experience with other seemingly groundbreaking Supreme Court decisions in recent years, such as *United States v. Lopez*, suggests that lower-court foot-dragging may limit *Heller*'s reach, though this time around there will likely be considerably more scrutiny and more vigorous litigation efforts.

If the lower courts present a challenge to the implementation of *Heller*, they also provide litigants with an opportunity. Given the fact that the *Heller* majority declined to give a detailed accounting of the proper standard of review to be used in subsequent Second Amendment cases, litigants have a rare opportunity to write on a *tabula* much more *rasa* than is ordinarily the case in constitutional litigation, making use of recent scholarship on the crafting of constitutional decision rules that implement constitutional provisions.

In the pages that follow, we take a look at these aspects of *Heller*. The triumph of the Standard Model of the Second Amendment is examined in Part I. Part II asks whether *Heller* is merely the opening volley in the coming judicialization of the gun control debate, or whether like the Court's attempt to rein in congressional power under the Commerce Clause, *Heller* will ultimately be seen as largely symbolic. Finally, in Part III, we discuss the possibility that recent scholarship on constitutional doctrine might play a role in separating permissible from impermissible gun controls post-*Heller*.

I. Individual and Collective Rights

Pre-*Heller* discussions of the Second Amendment noted the conflict between an individual rights model in which the Amendment confers a right to arms on individual citizens, who are entitled to use the courts to resist infringements in the same fashion as other constitutional rights such as free speech or privacy, and a collective rights model in which they are not...

II. The Lower Courts and the *Heller* Decision

It is impossible to review the Second Amendment jurisprudence from the federal courts of appeals (excepting only *Parker v. District of*

Columbia, the lower-court version of *Heller*, and *United States v. Emerson*) without noting two things: a significant hostility toward individual-rights arguments, and a surprisingly deep investment in their own case law, despite its rather tenuous anchor in the Supreme Court's decisions. This raises the question: what will they do when presented with gun-rights cases post-*Heller*?...

Will *Heller* suffer *Lopez's* fate, serving more as casebook fodder than as actual authority? On the surface, there are some analogies between the Commerce Clause and the Second Amendment that suggest that, like *Lopez*, *Heller* itself may end up as so much sound and fury, signifying nothing—or at least nothing much.

First, there are the institutional prejudices of the courts of appeals, favoring the status quo and possessing a desk-clearing mentality. Like the bureaucrats they increasingly resemble, the members of the appellate judiciary don't like to rock the boat. In addition, the Courts of Appeal have a history of more-or-less open hostility to claims of a private right to arms. The vast majority of cases to date suggest that, to the extent they can, they will try to rule against such a right.

Second, as was true following *Lopez*, there are few federal firearms laws that are vulnerable under *Heller*. Indeed, Justice Scalia's opinion took some pains to make clear what the Court was not calling into question:

> [N]othing in our opinion should be taken to cast doubt on longstanding prohibitions on the possession of firearms by felons and the mentally ill, or laws forbidding the carrying of firearms in sensitive places such as schools and government buildings, or laws imposing conditions and qualifications on the commercial sale of arms.

Indeed the very enumeration of "presumptively lawful regulatory measures" seemed calculated to reduce expectations among, for example, felons convicted of possessing firearms in violation of federal law, that *Heller* represented a "Get Out of Jail Free" card.

Third, the *Heller* majority's refusal to be pinned down on a specific standard of review might also leave an opening for lower courts to confine *Heller* to its facts. For example, a court might read *Heller* as standing for the proposition that anything less than an absolute ban could pass muster. Even if a reviewing court adopts the kind of intermediate standard of review urged by the Solicitor General, it might simply apply the standard in a way that defers to governmental judgments about the necessity of regulation. A more explicit articulation of the standard to be employed could have discouraged lower court evasion of *Heller*, or at least made such evasion somewhat easier to detect, if the Court was inclined to monitor lower courts for compliance, something that it did not do following *Lopez*.

Fourth, because the majority preemptively (perhaps "peremptorily" is a better word) signaled its view that a number of federal gun control laws would *not* be called into question by *Heller*, the most promising targets—local gun bans similar to the District's and restrictive state gun laws—lie beyond the immediate scope of *Heller*, since the Second Amendment remains outside those provisions of the Bill of Rights that have been incorporated through the Fourteenth Amendment and applied to states. Thus, the true test of *Heller's* reach will turn on whether the Court will be willing to entertain one of the proliferating number of cases challenging these laws. If the Court does not, then, like *Lopez, Heller* may end up having all the robustness of a "but see" cite...

Finally, despite the unanimity of the Court in its conclusion that the Second Amendment protected *some* individual right, the alternative limiting implementations of that right were expressed as dissents, as opposed to partial concurrences. Thus, there aren't any narrow concurring opinions whose authors essentially control the outcome of future cases; the alternative approaches of the dissenters are, well, *dissents*. Imagine a situation, though, in which Justice Breyer's "interest-balancing" approach was a concurring opinion; lower courts seeking to limit *Heller* might choose Justice Breyer's standard of review in the absence of anything definite in the majority opinion...

Though the civics-book formulation provides that the Supreme Court establishes clear principles which lower courts should conscientiously apply, reality is considerably more complex and frequently less satisfying. Unfortunately, as many lawyers can attest, the Supreme Court often formulates principles which are not clear, and sometimes it fails to establish principles at all. Lower courts, meanwhile, are not always conscientious in following the Supreme Court's lead, whether for reasons of bureaucratic rigidity or because they have their own agendas. Given the Supreme Court's light caseload, and the enormous number of cases in the lower courts, the path taken by the federal judiciary can diverge considerably from that established by the Supreme Court.

Will *Heller* be such a case? As we've noted before, this depends—upon the behavior of litigants, upon the predilections of lower court judges, and upon the degree and nature of scrutiny that the process receives. For us, at least, it offers an opportunity to continue our study of how Supreme Court precedent influences lower courts in an entirely new context, for which we are properly grateful.

Glenn H. Reynolds is the Beauchamp Brogan Distinguished Professor of Law, University of Tennessee. Brannon P. Denning is a Professor of Law and Director of Faculty Development, Cumberland School of Law, Samford University.

Robert J. Cottrol

Some Immediate Post-Heller Thoughts

When Alan Korwin asked me if I would write something to be included in this book, I naturally leapt at the chance. *Heller* is the Supreme Court's most important examination of the Second Amendment, the first time the nation's highest tribunal has heard a fully litigated case on the central question of the meaning of the constitutional provision. Alan Korwin is a well-respected publisher in the area of firearms law. As a legal historian and as one who has devoted a considerable amount of time and energy to writing on the Second Amendment I was eager to be included in this "first draft of history," this early round of commentary on such an important case.

After the decision came out I must confess to a case of cold feet with respect to my participation. *Heller's* historic importance cannot be overstated and Alan remains an important commentator on firearms law, but I was beginning to wonder if my background was adequate to the task. I saw the decision as stating a very modest protection for Second Amendment rights, namely the right to have a firearm in the home for home defense. This was at most an affirmation of the bare minimum that the Second Amendment might be read as protecting. I don't criticize the majority for that decision. Courts decide the cases in front of them and that is all Dick Heller was asking for. Mr. Heller got the relief he was seeking and the Court affirmed that the Second Amendment protected the rights of individuals. That was sufficient, indeed quite good.

What gave me pause was the reaction of long time firearms-prohibition advocates. To say that the reaction was hysterical would be to exhaust my powers of understatement. The modest, careful opinion authored by Justice Scalia engendered apocalyptic screeds by editorial writers of some of the nation's leading newspapers including *The Washington Post, Chicago Tribune* and reliably enough *The New York Times*, which the next day ran an editorial entitled "Lock and Load." Its horrible predictions of the consequences of *Heller* made Chicken Little seem like an optimist.

Not to be outdone by the nation's editorial writers, Chicago Mayor Richard Daley opined, "Then why don't we do away with the court system and go back to the Old West, you have a gun and I have a gun and we'll settle it in the streets." After that I wasn't sure about gun-control legislation but I was certainly open to the idea of self-control legislation.

My perusal of reactions by gun-prohibition advocates also led me to a letter to the editor in *The Washington Post*. The letter writer was denouncing the gun lobby for bringing the case (the gun lobby or NRA was actually somewhat wary of the case at first, but that's another story). The writer went on to indicate that the decision spoiled Washington, a lovely city with tree-lined streets. I have listened to and participated in many a debate on the gun issue, but until that point I was never aware that the state of gun legislation had any appreciable impact on whether or not a city had tree-lined streets. You do learn something new every day.

In any event these reactions made me think. Perhaps as a legal historian I am somewhat out of my depth as a commentator on *Heller*. The hysteria, the vehemence of the reaction, led me to think that perhaps this is an area better left to those with training in psychiatry or at the very least some work in abnormal psychology. A person trained to study issues like the Framers' intentions, or the importance of legal precedent seemed somewhat besides the point in the face of these initial commentaries.

So I was prepared to withdraw from the project, leaving the field to those trained in the therapeutic disciplines who seemed more suited to explaining the mass hysteria that swept some quarters in the wake of *Heller*. Still I did promise Alan and I wanted to be included in the book so I thought perhaps some brief comments on the decision, or at least one aspect of it would be appropriate.

One of the aspects of the case that I find curious is Justice Stevens' dissent and particularly his use of the three cases, *United States v. Miller* (1939), *Presser v. Illinois* (1886) and *United States v. Cruikshank* (1876), in which the Supreme Court had previously considered Second Amendment claims. Justice Stevens has written a long dissent in which he presents an historical narrative considerably at odds with the one presented by Justice Scalia. It is instructive to look at how Justice Stevens handled those precedents.

Supreme Court Justices are not historians, at least not professional historians, and although they are often called upon to use or interpret history, we do not expect them to necessarily have historical expertise. But we should expect that they are expert at reading and understanding the Court's prior decisions before applying them to new cases. And yet Stevens' opinion is especially problematic on this score. Justice Stevens makes quite a lot of *Miller,* the Court's most important pronouncement on the Second Amendment before *Heller*, and the Court's only consideration of the issue in the twentieth century. He argues that the decision restricts the Second Amendment's protections to the possession and bearing of arms for militia purposes only. This is simply incorrect.

The treatment of the Court's decision in *Cruikshank* is little better. *Cruikshank* involved federal prosecution of members of a white mob who attacked a group of black men who were attempting to vote in

Reconstruction-era Louisiana. Members of the mob were prosecuted for violating the civil rights of the black men including their First Amendment right to peaceable assembly and their Second Amendment right to keep and bear arms. Justice Stevens wants to enlist *Cruikshank* as authority for the proposition that the Second Amendment does not protect the right to arms for any lawful purpose. And yet the actual opinion in *Cruikshank* does not support this proposition. Instead, as it was applied to the protections of the First and Second Amendments, it placed a limit on Congress' ability to protect individuals against private deprivations of civil rights.

Equally unsatisfactory was Justice Stevens' handling of the 1886 decision in *Presser*. That decision involved an appeal from a conviction under an Illinois statute for parading with arms while not being a member of the organized state militia. The Court in *Presser* upheld the conviction and dismissed the Second Amendment claim, not on the grounds that the Second Amendment did not protect the right of individuals, or that the right could only be exercised within the context of an organized militia. It did so on the grounds that the Second Amendment limited only the federal and not the state governments. This was standard constitutional doctrine in the late nineteenth century. The Court would only begin the business of *incorporation,* or applying the Bill of Rights to the states, in the twentieth century. Justice Stevens' efforts to enlist the case in a militia-only reading of the Second Amendment represents a severe misreading.

I bring up Justice Stevens' misreadings in these three cases not to nit pick (although that is a major occupation of lawyers and particularly law professors) but to indicate that his whole dissent rests on a very selective reading both of the history generally and most especially of Supreme Court precedent, an area where we might expect the Justice to have considerable expertise. Let me suggest it is an area worthy of meticulous examination and critique by students of the Court and students of the Second Amendment.

In any event I am glad that Alan invited me to participate in this project. Let me return for just a second to my earlier concerns. With the ferocity of the reaction to this decision in anti-gun (and anti-gun-owner) circles, I do hope that one of the participants in this project is going to give us a brief or perhaps extensive discussion of the psychological dimension of the reaction.

Robert J. Cottrol is the Harold Paul Green Research Professor of Law, and Professor of History and Sociology at George Washington University. He has written extensively on the Second Amendment and was co-counsel on a brief filed by the Congress of Racial Equality supporting the individual rights view of the Second Amendment.

Bruce N. Eimer, Ph.D., A.B.P.P.

The Psychology of the Left Wing's Reaction to Heller

Gun-control advocates responded with great disappointment to the *Heller* decision, with reactions ranging from outrage to denial of the decision's importance. Some leftist commentators said *Heller* was no surprise—and that it would have little effect on future efforts to restrict the "unhealthy" spread of guns throughout society.

People who wish to believe that the Second Amendment guarantees no individual's right to keep and bear arms hold a whole set of consistent underlying core beliefs. They tend to hold to a statist view that only the police and the military are capable or should be allowed to keep and bear arms. They fear that civilians cannot be trusted to responsibly handle firearms. Perhaps most tellingly, they do not trust themselves to bear arms and they project this distrust onto everyone else everywhere.

By extension, they hold extreme anti-self-defense beliefs. They do not believe people should be allowed to defend themselves against deadly force, because they are in psychological denial. That is, their highly polarized belief system does not allow them to perceive any justifiable need for individual personal defense.

People with such highly polarized views tend to see things in black or white—very good or very bad. Therefore, anything in *Heller* that conflicts with their deep-seated feelings seems very bad, and must be discounted or railed against.

The core beliefs about gun rights on both sides of the debate are held with a lot of emotion. These beliefs are also tied to lifestyle. A person's lifestyle is a filter for both receptive and expressive data. We all tend to see the world in terms of our core beliefs and our lifestyle.

What happens when one's lifestyle is threatened? The answer is that people react extremely—as if their very life is being threatened. That is what we have been observing in many of the extreme left's reactions to *Heller*. But there is more to it.

Anti-gun-rights people (so-called "gun-control" advocates) tend to be hoplophobic. That is, they tend to be irrationally afraid of firearms and hence, they see physical threats everywhere there are firearms. *Heller* exacerbates this fear for them, and they act out that fear.

One compensation for this mortal fear some people feel is to externalize the responsibility for their own safety (which they do not perceive as their own in the first place). They project this onto government. They do not see it as possible for them to be responsible for their own self defense. They cannot discriminate between people who are sufficiently responsible to own and maintain firearms and those who are not. By definition, for them, nobody (except a parental-substitute in the police or military) is capable of such a life-sustaining task. All firearm owners are lumped into the one simplistic derogatory category, "gun nuts," with the potential—a projection of their own fears and feelings of inadequacy—to explode, wreak havoc and commit atrocities.

The feeling was expressed to me recently by a doctor and a lawyer, who both stated (in different contexts) that they could not own a gun because if they did, they would eventually get angry and use it! They then classically projected this fear, and concluded that no one should have the right to keep and bear arms for the same compelling reasons. Yet with an adult-child paradigm, they managed to rationalize arms in the hands of violence-trained warrior "guardians" (soldiers and police).

The very strong emotional reactions from a hoplophobic, anti-gun-rights, nanny-state control contingent to the *Heller* ruling is related to the violation of their core beliefs and schemas. Their conscious and subconscious fears of firearms have now been activated and in some cases have gone wild. Never mind that *Heller* was highly qualified, narrowly crafted, of limited scope and tempered to allow local jurisdictions to retain power to levy "reasonable" restrictions on firearm ownership and use.

Gun-control advocates tend to be quite left-of-center in their political beliefs in general. Their firearm fears typically coalesce with a host of other leftist-socialist, liberal beliefs about people and government, particularly that government can and should solve most if not all of society's problems. This stands in stark contrast to the more mature individual-responsibility model of a typical gun owner, which helped mold the American character.

Because the gun-reluctant segment of society generally believes that all "non-official" gun ownership is dangerous and hence a threat, any decision such as *Heller*, favoring individual gun ownership and human rights, is viewed as a grave threat to their life and lifestyle. On this, they act out accordingly, as we have seen.

Deadly force is only legally justified under the narrowest of circumstances, basically, in the face of an immediate, unprovoked, illegal and genuine threat to life or limb. The gun-control left, enveloped in irrational morbid fears, view the *Heller* decision as if it were an immediate and unavoidable threat to their life and limb, an artifact of their own hoplophobia. This helps explain some of the irrational "Wild West" and blood-in-the-streets fears we've seen expressed in the news.

Bruce N. Eimer, Ph.D., A.B.P.P. is a board certified, licensed clinical psychologist, a certified school psychologist, and an NRA Certified Firearms Instructor (Pistol, Shotgun, Personal Defense). He is the co-

author of the Essential Guide to Handguns: Firearm Instruction for Personal Defense and Protection *(Looseleaf Law Publications, 2006) and numerous books in the field of clinical psychology.*

Joyce Lee Malcolm

What a great day for individual rights. The majority of the Supreme Court retrieved the original intent of the Second Amendment to permit individuals the right and ability to defend themselves. For thirty years those convinced that ordinary people can't be trusted with guns have dominated the discussion. In order to ban civilian ownership of weapons, the original meaning of the Second Amendment had to be reinterpreted, and unfortunately with its awkward language—which was well-understood at the time—that wasn't too difficult.

Generations of law students have been taught that the Second Amendment merely protected the right of states to have a militia, a right already incorporated into the body of the Constitution. The nearly complete control over the militia by the federal government was not altered in any way by the amendment, but no mind.

The linguistic efforts to deny an individual right were quite inventive— "the people" only in this amendment meant a group, not an individual, "bear arms" implied an exclusively military context, that awkward word "keep" was to be erased by linking it with "bear" in order to make it exclusively military, and so on. And it all nearly worked. But not quite.

Thanks to the scholarly efforts of many people, the overwhelming evidence for an individual right to keep and have weapons for self-defense was uncovered and published. It was that evidence that the justices relied upon.

My only disappointment with an otherwise great decision was how narrow it was. Four justices ignored the evidence in order to preserve the gun-control measures meant to deny individuals the right to be armed. In the process, they were prepared to erase a basic right and uphold the stringent and ineffective D.C. gun ban, a law that went so far as to forbid reassembling a gun at home in the case of a break-in.

Still, it was a great day for every American, one that will ensure a safer America than any number of gun bans ever could.

Joyce Lee Malcolm is professor of legal history at George Mason University School of law. She is the author of To Keep and Bear Arms: The Origins of an Anglo-American Right. *This article originally appeared in reasononline (Reason Magazine), used with permission.*

Michael P. Anthony, Esq.

A New Standard for Constitutional Gun-Control Laws

In the landmark *Heller* decision, the Supreme Court directly addressed the meaning of the Second Amendment to the U.S. Constitution.

Heller decided conclusively that the District of Columbia may not ban the possession of an operable handgun in the home for self defense, by a person who is not a prohibited possessor. The decision hints strongly that its reasoning applies to the States and creates constitutional limitations on legislation beyond the D.C. gun ban. However, the application of *Heller* to the States and to other gun-control laws remains for future resolution, and is not examined here.

The unresolved issue addressed here is defining which of the common constitutional "standards of review" or "tests" should be applied to Second Amendment cases. *Heller* arguably creates a new, separate standard of review for Second Amendment cases. This article is meant to introduce that standard as a test to be applied to future Second Amendment challenges to gun-control laws.

Heller does not adopt any of the common standards of review for constitutional cases. At footnote 27, *Heller* rejects the "rational-basis scrutiny" test for its review of the long-standing D.C. gun ban. Footnote 27 expresses the majority's view that no "rational basis" or "interest-balancing" test applies to Second Amendment cases (noting that such tests do not apply to the other protections of the Bill of Rights). However, the *Heller* majority does not expressly state what "standard of review" applies to Second Amendment cases. Many argue over the meaning and impact of footnote 27, and many more argue over what common standard of review should apply. This argument is unnecessary—because *Heller* in effect creates a new, practical Second Amendment standard of review.

A principle larger than "standard of review" lies at the foundation of *Heller*—the inherent or God-given right of self-defense or self-protection. *Heller* expressly recognizes this right of self-defense as a "core" purpose of the Second Amendment. In so doing, *Heller* goes a long way toward setting a new test for determining whether a gun-control law is constitutional.

Heller contains an exhaustive discussion of the meaning of the words in the Second Amendment. But, *Heller* looked to *the purpose* of the Second Amendment to determine whether the District of Columbia's gun-control laws are constitutional. *Heller* expressly acknowledged a larger, "core" purpose for the Second Amendment that goes beyond a right to possess a firearm. *Heller* recognizes a fundamental, inherent right of self defense:

"[T]he inherent right of self-defense has been central to the Second Amendment right. The [D.C.] handgun ban amounts to a prohibition of an entire class of 'arms' that is overwhelmingly chosen by American society for that lawful purpose. The prohibition extends, moreover, to the home, where the need for defense of self, family, and property is most acute. Under any of the standards of scrutiny that we have applied to enumerated constitutional rights, [see note 27] banning from the home 'the most preferred firearm in the nation to 'keep' and use for protection of one's home and family,' *Parker v. District of Columbia*, 478 F.3d 370, 400 (2007), would fail constitutional muster." *Heller* majority at pg. 56, citing D.C. Court of Appeals decision in *Heller* (emphasis added).

In its discussion, the Supreme Court elevates this central Second Amendment purpose for keeping guns (i.e., for self-defense) into a test for determining whether a gun-control law is permissible. The Court applied this test in a practical manner that should become a standard in future cases. Indeed, applying such a practical test would circumvent one of the sticky issues otherwise left unresolved—under what standard are such laws to be reviewed?

Heller declared unconstitutional the District of Columbia's ban on operable handguns in the home because such a ban "makes it impossible for citizens to use them [handguns] for the core lawful purpose of self-defense..." *Heller*, pg. 58. (*Heller* is not the first case in which the U.S. Supreme Court has spoken of this "right" of self-defense. For other cases where this right is mentioned, see Kopel, Halbrook and Korwin, *Supreme Court Gun Cases* (Bloomfield Press 2003).

The Court's pronouncement that D.C. cannot constitutionally ban this "core lawful purpose of self-defense" is clear and penetrating. Under this standard, there is no need to search for a rational basis for the D.C. gun ban. Nor is there a need to search for a compelling governmental interest to support a strict-scrutiny test. *Heller's* reasoning, combined with its rejection of the "rational basis" test at footnote 27, sets the stage for application of the *Heller* "inherent right of self defense" test to all gun-control statutes.

By creating a standard of review that is specifically tailored to the Second Amendment, *Heller* renders standards such as strict scrutiny and rational basis unnecessary and superfluous in such cases. Indeed, if the underlying purpose of the Second Amendment is to be achieved, application of a standard that recognizes that purpose is vitally important. In fact, courts have for centuries strived to interpret laws to satisfy their intent. No less noble objective should be applied to interpreting the right of the people to keep and bear arms.

In it simplest terms, the *Heller* standard of review will require a court in any Second Amendment case to ask the question: *Does this gun-control law deny people their core, inherent, lawful right of self-defense?* A law that denies that right should be unconstitutional under *Heller*.

Going forward, the question should be: How much can the government regulate this core, inherent, lawful right of self-defense? This will require legislators, judges and a future Supreme Court to determine the meaning of *infringe*. If that word is given its plain meaning (an approach *Heller* supports), the government's ability to regulate firearms as related to self-defense should be limited to regulations that do not infringe that right. The discussion in *Heller* includes *dicta* that allows existing gun-purchasing, concealed-carry and other gun laws that are in place across the U.S. But, *Heller* does not attempt to list permissible and impermissible gun laws.

The task ahead for judges is to follow the *Heller* test to limit government from infringing upon the fundamental right of self-defense. In view of the hostility that some judges and legislators have expressed toward this right, *Heller* will challenge them to abandon their personal prejudices and follow the significant precedent that *Heller* represents.

Under *Heller*, our government has a constitutional duty to recognize and protect our inherent, core rights of self-defense by limiting gun regulations to measures that do not infringe upon that right. In view of the vast array of gun-control laws that have been adopted over decades without constitutional restraint (See, e.g., Korwin and Anthony, *Gun Laws of America*, Bloomfield Press 2007), *Heller* will be the parent of many offspring. Hopefully, those offspring will consistently apply the test laid down in *Heller* to protect the human and civil right of self-defense underlying the Second Amendment from unconstitutional infringement.

Michael Anthony is a trial lawyer with the Phoenix firm of Carson Messinger Elliott Laughlin & Ragan, P.L.L.C., where he concentrates on complex civil litigation and appellate cases. He is licensed to practice before the United States Supreme Court, the Ninth Circuit Court of Appeals, the U.S. Court of Military Appeals and the Supreme Courts of Texas and Arizona.

Sandy Froman

The Supreme Court's decision in *D.C. vs. Heller* is a landmark. It will shape gun rights for decades to come, and could determine the outcome of the presidential election...

In one sense this is a tremendous victory for gun owners. For a long time there was a consensus among liberal professors that the Second Amendment was not a private right. Historical research, legal precedent and analysis of the amendment's language proved otherwise, and this week the Court decided that it was always intended to secure individual rights.

In another sense this was less about victory and more about avoiding defeat. Had Justice Kennedy voted the other way, it would have been catastrophic for gun owners. Such a ruling could mean critical loss of support for the individual-rights view in just one generation.

Many questions are left open by this decision. The first is whether it is incorporated—meaning that it applies against state and local laws—by the Fourteenth Amendment. The Bill if Rights only limits the federal government, and it applies directly to Washington, D.C. But whether it controls the states and anti-gun cities like Chicago and New York remains to be litigated...

This is like the NCAA basketball tournament. This wasn't the championship game. We haven't even reached the Sweet Sixteen. All we did was win the first tournament round. *Heller* is the first case in what could be 30 years of litigation over the nature and scope of this right.

That means the future of gun rights will turn on who wins the White House. John McCain promises to appoint Supreme Court justices like John Roberts and Sam Alito, who today voted in favor of an individual right. Barack Obama promises to appoint justices like Ruth Bader Ginsburg, who today voted to uphold D.C.'s handgun ban, saying that the Second Amendment protects no individual rights whatsoever.

Heller is now the *Roe vs. Wade* of gun rights. All gun legislation will now be tested in court, and the biggest battles over firearms will hereafter be won or lost in the Supreme Court. Gun owners need to ask candidates one question: What kind of justices will you appoint?

Sandy Froman is a Tucson-based attorney and past president of the National Rifle Association. This article originally appeared in The Arizona Republic, *June 28, 2008, used with permission.*

Nick Dranias

1. The Goldwater Institute *amicus* brief in *Heller* was necessitated by the Justice Department's unexpected request for the Supreme Court to adopt a middling level of judicial scrutiny and kick-the-can avoidance of the issue. This was a stunningly adverse position from a supposedly pro-gun-rights administration. More than anything else, the Justice Department's position threatened to take away one of the five votes that would otherwise likely support the right result. I don't have direct or indirect proof, but I suspect the Goldwater Institute crucially helped Justice Scalia hold the line on reaching a 5-4 decision affirming the Second Amendment.

2. I was satisfied with the result in *Heller*. I think the result reached was all that could reasonably be expected at this stage. More was established about the nature of the Second Amendment's protections in this case than was established in a half-century of cases following the

case that first enforced the First Amendment. Most importantly, Justice Scalia locked-in the core protections of the Second Amendment (self-defense in the home and defense against tyranny) and pointed the way to the originalist method of interpreting and enforcing rights.

In this method, you toss aside the scrutiny tests, and the subjective balancing of interests they entail, and instead examine what was meant by the right in question when it was framed and ratified, what that meaning implies for the fact pattern in question, and once this is established, either enforce the right or hold that the right does not exist in this specific factual context. My hope is that the scrutiny tests, if they remain in use, will ultimately be reserved solely for those occasions where the meaning and/or application of a particular constitutional right is genuinely indeterminate when considered within a given fact pattern.

3. I thought the public reaction was terrific. The media coverage was plentiful, which was good. I don't know of any media reporting that was more biased than usual—I just didn't watch enough of it to form an opinion.

4. Incorporation of the Second Amendment to the States is the next step. Justice Scalia's ironic reference to *United States v. Cruikshank*, which refused incorporation, is the key. Justice Scalia takes the time to discuss first how extending the right to keep and bear arms to blacks was a central focus of Congressional action leading up to the Fourteenth Amendment. He then discusses how *Cruikshank* overturned the convictions of a white mob for depriving an African-American of his Second Amendment rights.

The purpose of the discussion is obviously not to embrace the anti-incorporation aspect of the decision. It was meant to highlight the unchallenged premise that the Second Amendment was understood as an individual right, to distinguish its holding (which was merely that the U.S. Constitution does not restrict private action), and to throw the outrageous facts of the case in the face of the dissenters—reminding so-called liberal Justices that their opinion would deprive a minority group of a constitutional right they were plainly meant to enjoy.

Although incorporation was not reached, I think Justice Scalia's decision to focus on this case and the facts leading up to it is a strong hint that he believes the Fourteenth Amendment was meant to enforce the Second Amendment against the States. Hopefully, the majority that produced *Heller* will take the recently-filed Chicago or San Francisco cases and rule that the Second Amendment is incorporated to the states through the privileges or immunities clause of the Fourteenth Amendment. This would also restore the privileges or immunities clause to its rightful place in the Constitution as the legal authority for enforcing the Bill of Rights against the States, and return the due process clause to its

primary function of ensuring procedures are in accord with fundamental fairness.

*Nick Dranias is the Director of the Center for Constitutional
Government at the Goldwater Institute in Phoenix, Ariz. Prior to joining
Goldwater, he was an attorney with the Institute for Justice.*

Frederick R. Bieber, Ph.D.

The Supreme Court's majority opinion in *Heller* is scholarly and well
reasoned. It reflects a deep respect for individual rights. While pleased
with the outcome I am somewhat surprised by the narrow majority.

It is particularly gratifying that the majority makes settled law that
individual rights of gun ownership are guaranteed under the 2nd
Amendment as preexisting rights. That is, our Constitution does not
give, but rather guarantees that, the preexisting natural right to keep and
bear arms "shall not be infringed."

It is both sad and disappointing to read the slanted media coverage of
the *Heller* decision, especially the editorials in *The New York Times*,
Washington Post, and the Chicago newspapers. I wonder if the reporters
and editors have even read the *Heller* decision. It is particularly disturbing that the mainstream media has not produced a critical analysis of
either the deeply thoughtful majority opinion or the dissenting ones.

The level of gun-related crime is a serious matter that must be
addressed by all who share a natural concern about suicides and homicides committed with firearms. Indeed, Washington, D.C., Chicago,
and New York are among the most dangerous cities in the world,
outside of Kabul and Baghdad. What many fail to recognize or admit is
that the great majority of gun-related crime is committed by those
already in unlawful possession of firearms or who would have no
chance of lawful possession under existing federal or state statutes or
under *Heller*.

Our *amicus* brief, and others, in support of respondent Heller, provided
data summaries showing there is no clear relationship between the level
of lawful gun ownership and documented crime rates, in America or
elsewhere. It seems clear that the Justices did read and benefit from all
the *amicus* briefs submitted.

Going forward, the *Heller* majority decision now inspires a careful
study of all state, municipal, and city firearms laws and regulations, as it
appears that many would not withstand scrutiny under *Heller*. For
example, here where I work in the Commonwealth of Massachusetts,
under M.G.L. Chapter 140, lawful possession of all types of firearms is
complicated, expensive and unduly burdensome.

The Massachusetts laws relating to firearms storage, while perhaps well-
intentioned, essentially prevent homeowners from rapid access in times

of need for self defense. In Massachusetts and in most other states we must meet with legislators, mayors and attorneys general to draft amended legislation that is respectful of individual rights and that conforms to *Heller*. Failing in such efforts, formal court challenges to consolidate *Heller* at the state and local levels will most certainly follow.

Among the questions not addressed or settled under *Heller* are those relating to regulation of ownership and possession of specific types of firearms not directly mentioned. Such issues will be clarified in the coming wave of amendments and challenges to existing statutes.

It is noteworthy that in *Heller* the Court refers to their prior ruling in the *Miller* decision, in which the Court explained that the sorts of weapons protected by the 2nd Amendment were those "in common use at the time." Police agencies, including their SWAT teams, are in fact comprised of civilians who commonly use semi-automatic pistols and rifles in their work, including high-power rifles chambered in rounds such as .308, .50 BMG and .338 Lapua. Such firearms are also used by non-sworn civilians for private use in sport and hunting and would be useful in activities of formal or impromptu militias for the common defense.

Therefore it will be important to protect and defend, through formal court action if necessary, individual rights of the people to ownership and possession of all manner of such firearms in common use.

Frederick R. Bieber, Ph.D., is an Associate Professor of Pathology at Harvard Medical School, and contributed to the amicus *brief for Criminologists, Social Scientists, Other Distinguished Scholars and the Claremont Institute.*

Richard Stevens

Supporters of self-defense rights can see the *Heller* decision in two key ways. First: the highest court in the land declared as true what we have said for decades. In other words, we were right about: the individual right to arms preexisting government, the meaning of "militia," the nature of the militia clause in the Second Amendment, and that laws requiring defense-blocking trigger locks or banning home-defense weapons are unconstitutional.

We should use the *Heller* decision constantly in writings and media as strongly supporting our position. Our position on the Second Amendment was logical, factual and correct—we were right, case closed. A whole generation of Americans should grow up understanding the historical and philosophical truth we have been proclaiming.

Second: the *Heller* decision may lull Americans into a false confidence that self-defense rights are now eternally protected. The opposite is true because: (1) it is not certain the courts will hold *Heller* applies to state and local laws; and (2) the Second Amendment's phrase "shall not be infringed" was scarcely analyzed in *Heller*. If resolved against the individual right to arms, these uncertainties may render *Heller* a constitutional truism with no real teeth.

I have long counseled RKBA people against putting too much stock in litigation to protect the 2A. I have been pretty much alone in that position, although Aaron Zelman fully concurred. My argument is this:

1. Litigation that runs against the popular/establishment legal grain is a thankless and worthless waste of money in most cases.

2. Even if you "win," the win has to set a precedent, and the precedent has to be on a point broad enough to affect other cases, else it can be legally distinguished and not applied by lower courts. Otherwise, the win is symbolic and pyrrhic, not practical.

3. The only way RKBA survives in this country is for hearts and minds of Americans to be moved to understand RKBA as an obvious mandatory result of the right to self-defense against aggression.

So, with *Heller*, we risk getting all worked up about the courtroom battles, and thereby miss the opportunity to move American hearts and minds toward our camp. I counsel people to use *Heller* as a teaching tool. Proclaim we are right—the Supreme Court said so—and keep proclaiming it and teaching it and trumpeting the moral high ground. We need a shift in the culture.

The defense of human freedom never ends. *Heller* helps by strongly supporting defense rights, but the job will not be finished until the very idea of victim-disarmament laws elicits the same hissing derision as chattel slavery and human sacrifice.

Attorney Richard Stevens is the author of Dial 911 and Die *and former editor of* The Bill of Rights Sentinel, *published by JPFO.*

Chuck Michel

From the Second Amendment Foundation news release, on the lawsuit against San Francisco's gun ban in public housing: "As with the advancement of any civil right throughout history, subsequent litigation is essential in order to establish both the parameters of the Second Amendment's protections, and initially to establish that the Second Amendment restricts state and local governments from infringing on your right to self defense." He adds:

To do that, the NRA is leading a coalition of like minded self-defense civil-rights groups into strategic litigation. San Francisco's ban on firearm possession in public housing is one of several local ordinances in the country that presents an opportunity to establish that initial "incorporation" principle to stop Second Amendment infringement by state and local governments. In the process, we hope to restore the right of public housing residents to chose to own a gun to defend themselves and their families.

Publicly, the gun control lobby's leaders are putting on a brave face and putting a new spin on their post-*Heller* arguments. But many gun banners know at heart that the incremental approach they have advocated doesn't work. It was a means to advance their covert, if not really secret, desire: complete civilian disarmament. So one consequence of the Supreme Court's decision should be that those who publicly advocated an incremental gun control approach—while actually harboring an extreme prohibition agenda—realize they can never achieve their true goal. They can never win gun prohibition while *Heller* stands. Hopefully, many lose heart and give up the fight.

One more nice little thing about *Heller*. Now no one questions me when I tell them I'm a civil-rights lawyer. Now we are all unquestionably self-defense civil-rights activists.

C.D. "Chuck" Michel is Managing Partner of Trutanich-Michel, LLP, a boutique Los Angeles law firm specializing in land use and firearms law. His clients include corporations, the NRA, the firearms industry, gun ranges and individuals. He was formerly a criminal prosecutor and Staff Counsel to the "Christopher Commission" investigating the LAPD in the wake of the Rodney King incident. He was co-counsel with Dave Kopel on the Heller amicus brief filed on behalf of ILEETA and other law enforcement leaders.

Craig Cantoni

So if my reading is correct, the narrow *Heller* decision was that the Second Amendment is an individual right, not a collective one, so a citizen can keep an operable gun at home for self-defense, period. (Had I lived in DC, I would have done so anyway.) I find it fascinating then that in *Helvering v. Davis* (1937), the Court ruled that citizens don't have an individual right to their money—that their money belongs to the collective, to be taken from them and doled out to others as the legislature so deems.*

Of course they prettied up the decision with fancy language, but that was the essence. As a result, I find myself in the bizarre situation in which I have a narrow individual right of self defense, but no individual right whatsoever to my money. Worse, unlike a gun, I can't hide my money from the government. In fact, if I try to hide my money from the tax man, the government can send armed agents to my house to take it, and I have no right to use a gun to stop them.

My chances of being robbed by the government are far, far greater than being robbed by a burglar, but the Court has ruled that I can't do anything about the former and can do something about the latter. Boy, I feel a lot better now.

Thomas Carlyle said, "In the long run every government is the exact symbol of its people, with their wisdom and unwisdom." Translation: You're screwed.

*The Institute for Justice recently summarized this case saying it, "allowed the federal government to tax and spend for the 'general welfare,' thereby opening the floodgates of the redistributive state— taking money from some and giving it to others, without any meaningful constitutional constraints."

Craig J. Cantoni is a thinker, writer and activist. His many credits include two books, a long-running newspaper column, seven op-eds in the Wall Street Journal, *guest editorials and scholarly works in national publications, and the former presidency of a 5,000-member grassroots group that fought and won against government overreach.*

The Pro-Rights Groups

National Rifle Association

U. S. Supreme Court Strikes Down D.C. Gun Ban! Declares That the Second Amendment Guarantees an Individual Right to Keep and Bear Arms. June 26, 2008

FAIRFAX, Va.—Leaders of the National Rifle Association (NRA) praised the Supreme Court's historic ruling overturning Washington, D.C.'s ban on handguns and on self-defense in the home, in the case of *District of Columbia v. Heller.*

"This is a great moment in American history. It vindicates individual Americans all over this country who have always known that this is their freedom worth protecting," declared NRA Executive Vice President Wayne LaPierre. "Our founding fathers wrote and intended the Second Amendment to be an individual right. The Supreme Court has now acknowledged it. The Second Amendment as an individual right now becomes a real permanent part of American constitutional law."

Last year, the District of Columbia appealed a Court of Appeals ruling affirming that the Second Amendment to the Constitution guarantees an individual right to keep and bear arms, and that the District's bans on handguns, carrying firearms within the home and possession of functional firearms for self-defense violate that fundamental right.

"Anti-gun politicians can no longer deny that the Second Amendment guarantees a fundamental right," said NRA chief lobbyist Chris W. Cox. "All law-abiding Americans have a fundamental, God-given right to defend themselves in their homes. Washington, D.C. must now respect that right."

Second Amendment Foundation

Second Amendment Triumph: Justices Uphold Individual Right!

BELLEVUE, Wash.—With this morning's ruling on the case of *District of Columbia v. Heller*, America has begun "its long march back toward liberty under a Second Amendment that means what it says," the Second Amendment Foundation said.

"Today's ruling by the Supreme Court should forever put to rest any contention that the right to keep and bear arms is not a fundamental, individual civil right," said SAF founder Alan M. Gottlieb. "For six decades, anti-gun-rights extremists have engaged in a monumental fraud that has been unfortunately perpetuated by activist judges who erroneously insisted that the right to keep and bear arms applies only to service in a militia.

"Wisdom and truth have triumphed over hysteria and falsehood," he continued. "This decision makes it clear that a right 'of the people' is a right enjoyed by, and affirmed for, all citizens. It destroys a cornerstone of anti-gun rights elitism, which has fostered—through years of deceit and political demagoguery—the erosion of this important civil right.

"This ruling also makes it abundantly clear that laws which ban the possession of firearms, or make it simply impossible through regulation for citizens to exercise their right to keep and bear arms, are unconstitutional and cannot stand," Gottlieb stated. "Today, America has taken a small but significant step toward restoring the Second Amendment to its proper place in our Bill of Rights.

"For too many years," he observed, "Americans have seen this fundamental civil right under constant and unrelenting attack. We are hopeful that today's decision will halt an insidious campaign for citizen disarmament through legislation and regulations that have made our neighborhoods less safe, our cities less secure and our people less self-reliant, which is the trait that has made America unique among nations.

"But this fight is hardly over," Gottlieb concluded. "Today's ruling is a stepping stone, the foundation upon which we can rebuild this important individual right. Our work has only just begun."

National Shooting Sports Foundation

Firearms Industry Hails Victory in Supreme Court 2nd Amendment Case

NEWTOWN, Conn.—The National Shooting Sports Foundation (NSSF)—the trade association for the firearms industry—hailed today's United States Supreme Court 5-4 decision written by Justice Scalia that determined authoritatively that the Second Amendment of the U.S. Constitution guarantees an individual right to keep and bear arms.

"Today's decision by the U.S. Supreme Court is a major victory for all Americans," said NSSF President Steve Sanetti. "The *Heller* decision reaffirms the wisdom of our founding fathers in creating the Bill of Rights to protect and preserve individual rights, the cornerstone of our democracy. Furthermore, this decision solidifies an historical fact, the commonsense understanding that governments have powers, not rights—rights are reserved exclusively for individuals."

Demonstrating the strong grassroots support for the individual rights thesis, the nation's leading gun-control group, the Brady Campaign to Prevent Gun Violence, conceded victory prior to the High Court's ruling. In an interview with ABC News last week, Brady Campaign President Paul Helmke noted, "We've lost the battle on what the Second Amendment means. Seventy-five percent of the public thinks it's an individual right." The U.S. Supreme Court agrees that the public is correct.

The importance of having a uniform and legally accepted definition of the Second Amendment is particularly important to the firearms industry, as noted by Sanetti. "The products that our industry manufactures are the means through which our Second Amendment rights are realized. Clearly sportsmen, hunters, responsible firearms owners and the industry are all heavily vested in this groundbreaking ruling."

Though the *Heller* decision is the first time that the High Court has declared in absolute terms that the Second Amendment is an individual right, the nation's leading historians, legal scholars and constitutional experts have long been on record supporting such a conclusion. Renowned scholars, including Lawrence Tribe of Harvard, Akhil Reed Amar of Yale, William Van Alstyne of Duke and Sanford Levinson of the University of Texas, have been vocal in their assertion that the Second Amendment, like all the other rights of the people recognized in the Bill of Rights, secures an individual's right to keep and bear arms.

"Today's decision lays to rest the specious argument that the Second Amendment is not an individual right and marks the beginning of the end of repressive gun laws that have infringed upon individual liberty and done nothing to make America safer," said Lawrence G. Keane, NSSF senior vice president and general counsel.

Gun Owners of America

The Heller Earthquake Resonates in Bradyville, by Erich Pratt

With one stroke of the pen, the Supreme Court not only vetoed the most draconian ban on guns in the country, it refuted a myriad of myths that have been peddled in the gun-control utopia of "Bradyville" for so many years, sending shockwaves through the gun-hating legal community. Now, groups like the Brady Campaign are scrambling for new talking points, since the Justices effectively dismantled their mythical assertions in the 64-page majority opinion.

Gun Owners of America submitted an *amicus* brief in the *Heller* case and, among other things, urged the Court *not* to use it as a springboard to resolve the constitutionality of all of the nation's firearms laws.

If the Court had done that, it could have been a disaster. After all, the majority stated its opinion should "not be taken to cast doubt" on at least some prohibited persons' restrictions, gun-free-school-zones bans and dealer-licensing requirements. This *dicta* implies that courts might go further than the Constitution allows in upholding some gun restrictions in the future. Thankfully, this *dicta* is just that—it's editorializing by the Justices, which is non-binding on future courts. We're lucky it's not more expansive than it is.

Still, though people talk about the Supreme Court being the final word, we must exercise great caution, since activists don't mind overturning the Court when it suits their whims and they are able. Consider what Frank Lautenberg did after the Supreme Court struck down the gun-free-school-zones ban in 1995. Remember that? Lautenberg came right back with language that changed only a few words and got it passed again, thus nullifying (in effect) the Supreme Court's *Lopez* decision. The High Court's pronouncements are neither immutable nor indelible.

The GOA brief was the only one making the request not to rule on these other gun issues, thus upholding judicial restraint. We were most pleased to see that the Justices heeded our admonition to limit the Court's holding to the case before it.

In so doing, the Court followed GOA's request to shoot down both the D.C. government and the Bush Administration on one important point—the mistaken idea that the Court should set a "standard" to "balance" our liberties against the government's interest in enforcing restrictions.

To be sure, the Court's ruling opens the door to future lawsuits that take direct aim at many kinds of gun-control laws around the country:

(1) Gun bans. By stating that handgun bans are unconstitutional at the federal level, the Court has given pro-gun activists the green light to challenge the types of bans—or de facto bans—that exist in cities like San Francisco, Chicago and New York City.

(2) Lock up your safety laws. Trigger locks, and other similar laws, are another type of restriction that could fall like dominos. The Court struck down DC's requirement that honest citizens lock up their guns, because it prevents or delays the ability of gun owners to defend themselves.

(3) Licensure laws. The Court's opinion effectively "punted" on this issue, simply stating that Heller's attorney had conceded this point during oral arguments. The Court clearly said it would "not address the licensing requirement."

The GOA *amicus* brief was the only one that heavily emphasized the last four words of the Second Amendment—emphasizing that the right to keep and bear arms "shall not be infringed." Now that the Court has ruled the amendment protects an individual right, gun-rights supporters can take the argument to the next step, stressing that this "enumerated constitutional right" (in the words of the Court) cannot be infringed without violating the constitutional text.

Truly, it is a sad day for the residents of Bradyville, because they have continuously put all their hopes and dreams in the opinions of the courts. And for now, the Supreme Court has turned its back on them.

Erich Pratt, Director of Communications for the 300,000-member Gun Owners of America, appears regularly on national radio and TV programs such as NBC's Today Show, MSNBC, CNN and Fox Cable News. He is the author of a civil government textbook, The Constitutional Recipe for Freedom: Twelve Principles of Liberty Today's Politicians Don't Want You to Know.

Jews for the Preservation of Firearms Ownership

Will Heller *be Heaven or Hell for Gun Owners?* by Aaron Zelman

The *Heller* Supreme Court majority opinion means we *won a rhetorical battle* for Second Amendment Freedoms—but are *still losing the greater gun-control war.* The harsh reality is *sinister ambiguities* in the ruling will create more "gun control" schemes than ever before in America.

The gun prohibitionists are fully energized and gearing up for a D-Day assault on the Second Amendment. The FBI is opposed to the ruling, making malicious and stupid claims it will interfere with fighting crime and terrorism. Further, FBI director Robert Mueller fears his grandkids will not be able to attend a gun-free college campus. In short, *the FBI along with dozens of other federal, state, local agencies and politicians wants you defenseless.* The mass media, as always, is ready and willing to distort the truth. As always, Hollywood is boosting all these anti-freedom attacks.

Heller does not stop BATFE thuggery nor the *confiscation of firearms during a national disaster* by your local law-enforcement agency.

Prepare yourself for massive efforts to overthrow *Heller.* Get ready for the new Supreme Court to swing a leftist majority followed by a set-up case to overthrow *Heller.* It could easily be *just months away*—no matter who wins the presidential and congressional elections.

Heller is a perfect example of how *dangerously hopeless* it can be when looking solely to the courts for justice. If legions of gun owners fail to see how *Heller* will be used to promote harsher "gun control" schemes—and don't aggressively fight those schemes—you and your loved ones could be victimized by the most sweeping power grab in American history.

We must win in the court of public opinion if we are going to win at all.

JPFO has the solution to that vital goal... Watch for *our free, high-impact film* on the Internet educating mainstream America about the six things Americans should know about the Second Amendment. We live in a technological age. If we do not use the same weapons our enemies use—then we lose.

Aaron Zelman founded JPFO in 1989 and molded it into an aggressive civil-rights organization. He has co-authored books on life insurance, the growing police state, gun control, genocide, the Gran'pa Jack *illustrated booklets, a documentary film* (Innocents Betrayed) *proving the gun-control-genocide connection, and* The Gang, *exposing criminal behavior of the BATFE.*

The Firearms Coalition

The length to which the dissenting Justices are willing to twist history and contort language in attempts to justify their outrageous positions is nothing less than staggering. The intellectual gymnastics engaged in by the Justices in their efforts to support their idiotic, fore drawn conclusions should seriously shake the faith of the most trusting citizen. It is simply outrageous that men and women of intellect and learning would take up a position and then selectively sort through history for tiny threads of support for that position while completely ignoring the full, rich tapestry which displays a clear picture of an absolutely opposite position.

The intellectual dishonesty displayed by the dissenting Justices—and to a much lesser degree by the majority—should be deeply disturbing to every thinking American. These are not trivial matters that are being dealt with by the Court. These are issues that reach down to the basic founding principles of our Republic. How can we entrust matters of such great import to people who demonstrate a willingness to contort history to their own personal beliefs and philosophies rather than examining evidence and drawing rational conclusions based on that evidence.

The fact is, many judges, Justices included, know little to nothing about guns. To them guns are scary and dangerous things and they are uncomfortable with the idea of, "just anyone" having them. It's clear that those who were fearful of sending *any* Second Amendment case up to the Supreme Court had plenty to be concerned about.

This is not the time for complacency. It's by no means the end of the war. Many more court battles will be fought in the coming years, and those cases will be decided by federal judges—judges who are appointed for life by the President and confirmed by the Senate. *Voting matters!*

Founded on July 4th, 1984 by the legendary hero of the gun-rights movement, Neal Knox, The Firearms Coalition is, as the name implies, a coalition of organizations and individuals committed to the restoration and defense of firearms civil rights.

The Anti-Rights Camp

Brady Center to Prevent Gun Violence

Statement Of Brady President Paul Helmke

Our fight to enact sensible gun laws will be undiminished by the Supreme Court's decision in the *Heller* case. While we disagree with the Supreme Court's ruling, which strips the citizens of the District of Columbia of a law they strongly support, the decision clearly suggests that other gun laws are entirely consistent with the Constitution.

For years, the gun lobby has used fear of government gun confiscation to thwart efforts to pass sensible gun laws, arguing that even modest gun laws will lead down the path to a complete ban on gun ownership. Now that the Court has struck down the District's ban on handguns, while making it clear that the Constitution allows for reasonable restrictions on access to dangerous weapons, this "slippery slope" argument is gone.

The Court also rejected the absolutist misreading of the Second Amendment that some use to argue "any gun, any time for anyone," which many politicians have used as an excuse to do nothing about the scourge of gun violence in our country and to block passage of common sense gun laws. Lifesaving proposals such as requiring Brady background checks on all gun sales, limiting bulk sales of handguns, and strengthening the power of federal authorities to shut down corrupt gun dealers can now be debated on their merits without distractions of fear or ideology.

The *Heller* decision, however, will most likely embolden criminal defendants, and ideological extremists, to file new legal attacks on existing gun laws. With the help of the Brady Center's legal team, those attacks can, and must, be successfully resisted in the interest of public safety.

After the *Heller* ruling, as before, approximately 80 Americans will continue to die from guns every day. Our weak or non-existent gun laws contribute to the thousands of senseless gun deaths and injuries in this country that occur each year. We must continue to fight for sensible gun laws to help protect our families and our communities.

The Brady Center to Prevent Gun Violence is a national non-profit organization working to reduce the tragic toll of gun violence in America, through education, research, and legal advocacy. The programs of the Brady Center complement the legislative and grassroots mobilization of its sister organization, the Brady Campaign to Prevent Gun Violence with its dedicated network of Million Mom March Chapters.

Sarah Brady

With Your Help, Brady Center Will Defend America's Gun Laws

Just hours ago, the U.S. Supreme Court handed down its ruling on the most significant Second Amendment case in our country's history, *District of Columbia v. Heller.* I want you to know that we have hit the ground running. Our fight to enact and defend strong gun laws to save lives will be undiminished.

The *Heller* decision will no doubt embolden ideological extremists to file new legal attacks on existing gun laws. But with the help of the Brady Center's legal team, those attacks can, and must, be successfully resisted in the interest of public safety.

That is why we need your help now. This fight is so critical that we need to raise $50,000 by June 30. Your gift to our Brady Gun Law Defense Fund will be fully tax-deductible! We also have an opportunity and we plan to seize it.

We disagree with the Court's decision giving individuals a right to possess guns for private purpose. However, what is critically important is that all nine Justices agreed that a wide variety of gun laws are constitutional, including restrictions on carrying concealed weapons, guns in schools and other sensitive places, and bans on "dangerous and unusual" weapons.

For years, the gun lobby has used fear of confiscation by the government to block efforts to pass sensible gun laws, arguing that even modest gun laws would lead down the path to a complete ban on gun ownership. Since the Court has overturned the District's ban on handguns, this "slippery slope" argument is gone.

The Court also rejected the "absolutist" view of the Second Amendment that some use to argue "any gun, any time for any one." Now, politicians will no longer have these arguments to justify opposition to universal background checks and other common sense measures to prevent dangerous people from getting dangerous weapons.

As a result, gun control should no longer be a "wedge" issue in politics. We can move forward with finding sensible solutions to gun violence. So with your help we will be ready to defend current gun laws that protect you, your family and community—from the long-standing machine-gun ban, to the 1968 Gun Control Act, to the Brady background check law, to your local and state laws—like the ones in Chicago and New York—as well as the laws in California and New Jersey banning military-style assault weapons, and many more.

Your Brady Center will defend these laws in the courts as we have done so many times in the past against the attacks of the gun lobby. Please give generously today. Sincerely, Sarah Brady, Chair

Sarah Brady became the nation's most outspoken anti-gun advocate after her husband Jim, who was press secretary for Ronald Reagan at the time, was shot and disabled in 1981 during an assassination attempt on the President. She heads the organization that bears her name.

Violence Policy Center

On Supreme Court Ruling in District of Columbia v. Heller Overturning DC Handgun Ban; Supreme Court Ruling Overturning DC Handgun Ban Should Allow Ban on Semiautomatic Handguns to Stand

WASHINGTON, D.C.—Following today's 5-4 Supreme Court opinion authored by 2007 Sport Shooting Ambassador Award winner Antonin Scalia overturning Washington, DC's handgun ban, but apparently allowing for the retention of the law's ban on most semiautomatic weapons, including semiautomatic handguns, VPC Legislative Director Kristen Rand states:

"Today's opinion turns legal logic and common sense on its head. As measured in gun death and injury, handguns are our nation's most lethal category of firearm: accounting for the vast majority of the 30,000 Americans who die from guns each year. Handguns are our nation's leading murder and suicide tool. Yet the majority opinion offers the greatest offender the strongest legal protection. It's analogous to the Court carving out special constitutional protection for child pornography in a First Amendment case.

"In its ruling, the Court has ignored our nation's history of mass shootings, assassinations, and unparalleled gun violence. It has instead accepted an abstract academic argument with dangerous real-world results for residents of the District of Columbia. Thankfully, because the plaintiff in *Heller* did not challenge the District's ban on "machine guns," Washington, DC's ban on most semiautomatic weapons, including semiauto handguns, should be unaffected."

The Court's ruling today does not appear to affect the District's ban on "machine guns," which under DC law includes any gun "which shoots, is designed to shoot, or can be readily converted or restored to shoot semiautomatically, more than 12 shots without manual reloading." This definition would include virtually all semiautomatic handguns. As a result, the District's ban can remain in force for those types of handguns, commonly known as pistols. In essence, the Court's ruling for the most part will only affect revolvers and derringers.

Semiautomatic guns fire one shot per trigger pull, have greater ammunition capacity, and can be quickly and easily reloaded. They are the weapon of choice in mass shootings and police killings, and are the most common type of handgun manufactured in America, representing 73 percent of the 1,403,329 handguns manufactured in the United States in 2006 (the last year for which figures are available). In contrast, revolvers hold only five to six ammunition rounds, fire more slowly, take time to reload, and represent only 27 percent of the handguns manufactured in 2006.

The Violence Policy Center is a national non-profit educational foundation that conducts research on violence in America and works to develop violence-reduction policies and proposals. The Center examines the role of firearms in America, conducts research on firearms violence, and explores new ways to decrease firearm-related death and injury.

American Bar Association President William H. Neukom

[Note: The American Bar Association refused to grant permission to reproduce the public statement of its president, William H. Neukom (which you can read on their website), because *The Heller Case: Gun Rights Affirmed* is a "commercial venture." The ABA filed *amicus* in support of the District's gun ban that the High Court overturned.]

The association's public statement suggests that the ruling will allow a "vast body of regulation" to exist and grow, notes limitations and restrictions the decision "appears to support," and makes little mention of the rights protections that appear to be the main holdings of the Court. Among the limits the ABA is "gratified" to see and focuses upon are allowable firearm types, unusual and dangerous weapons, licensing schemes, carry restrictions, and general limits for public safety, the needs of law enforcement, government powers for legitimate public interests, restrictions already enacted, and whatever might be based upon "reason and practicality."

American Civil Liberties Union

[Note: The ACLU did not file *amicus* for either side in the *Heller* case, and posted no comment when the landmark constitutional case was decided. The group's position, used in its advertising, is, "We're the ACLU. We stand up for the Constitution. And we will not yield."]

In personal correspondence to its national and local leadership (Anthony D. Romero, Exec. Dir.; Nadine Strossen, Pres.; Robert O. Meitz, PhD., Ariz. Chap. Pres.) after *Heller* was granted *cert*, Kitt Barrett, the Member Services Coordinator, responded for the organization thus:

"Thank you for your email of December 28, 2007 to the American Civil Liberties Union. As I'm sure you are aware, the National ACLU is neutral on the issue of gun control. We believe the Second Amendment does not confer an unlimited right upon individuals to own guns or other weapons, nor does it prohibit reasonable regulation of gun ownership, such as licensing and registration... Today, we defend the rights guaranteed by the Constitution and the Bill of Rights, and we reject the Bush administration's claim that we must give up our fundamental American liberties if we want to keep our country safe."

Their position is clarified on their website, quoted here in part, as fair use for educational purposes:

"The ACLU has often been criticized for "ignoring the Second Amendment" and refusing to fight for the individual's right to own a gun or other weapons. This issue, however, has not been ignored by the ACLU. The national board has in fact debated and discussed the civil liberties aspects of the Second Amendment many times.

"We believe that the constitutional right to bear arms is primarily a collective one... In today's world, that idea is somewhat anachronistic... The ACLU therefore believes that the Second Amendment does not confer an unlimited right upon individuals to own guns or other weapons nor does it prohibit reasonable regulation of gun ownership, such as licensing and registration...

"The national ACLU is neutral on the issue of gun control. We believe that the Constitution contains no barriers to reasonable regulations of gun ownership. If we can license and register cars, we can license and register guns...

"Most opponents of gun control concede that the Second Amendment certainly does not guarantee an individual's right to own bazookas, missiles or nuclear warheads. Yet these, like rifles, pistols and even submachine guns, are arms... The question therefore is not whether to restrict arms ownership, but how much to restrict it... there is no constitutional impediment to the regulation of firearms... Unless the Constitution protects the individual's right to own all kinds of arms, there is no principled way to oppose reasonable restrictions on handguns, Uzis or semi-automatic rifles...

"If indeed the Second Amendment provides an absolute, constitutional protection for the right to bear arms in order to preserve the power of the people to resist government tyranny, then it must allow individuals to possess bazookas, torpedoes, SCUD missiles and even nuclear warheads, for they, like handguns, rifles and M-16s, are arms... as soon as we allow governmental regulation of any weapons, we have broken the dam of Constitutional protection. Once that dam is broken, we are not talking about whether the government can constitutionally restrict arms, but rather what constitutes a reasonable restriction..."

Late breaking news: ACLU has posted a blog comment: "The ACLU interprets the Second Amendment as a collective right. Therefore, we disagree with the Supreme Court's decision in *D.C. v. Heller*. While the decision is a significant and historic reinterpretation of the right to keep and bear arms, the decision leaves many important questions unanswered that will have to be resolved in future litigation, including what regulations are permissible, and which weapons are embraced by the Second Amendment right that the Court has now recognized."

Within a week it had attracted more than 750 scathing comments and articulate repudiations, including a flood of member resignations.

The Rev. Jesse Jackson

"More people will die from gunshots due to the decision of five right-wing Supreme Court justices... To reach their ruling, the gang of five had to distort the clear meaning of the words of the Second Amendment and reinvent the intent of the Founders. They had to trample the wishes of a popularly elected local government and throw out a 32-year-old law. They had to ignore 69 years of Supreme Court precedents holding that the Second Amendment applied, as its words say, to the rights of states to sustain a militia... they demonstrated the extent to which they are activist, conservative ideologues, quite willing to legislate from the bench... This has already begun to generate a flood of new cases, as the gun nut lobby tries to overturn gun-control laws across the country.

"Here's the reality that the gang of five simply ignored. Cities such as Chicago desperately need strong gun control laws... Chicago needs laws that require extensive background checks of potential buyers, and that limit the number of guns someone can buy. Straw buyers purchase guns by the dozens and then resell them to street gangs. There is no possible reason a gun owner needs to buy more than one gun a month.

"Similarly, Chicago and other cities need limits on the kind of weapons sold... assault weapons aren't necessary to defend your home. They aren't useful in hunting deer or shooting doves. They are killer guns, putting police at risk. And worse, in an age of terror, they provide the capacity to shoot down airplanes, or shoot up shopping centers... The decision of the gang of five is a boon to the gun industry and a nightmare to neighborhoods across America..."

Adrian Fenty, Mayor, District of Columbia
"I am disappointed in the court's ruling and believe that more handguns in the District of Columbia will only lead to more handgun violence."

Marion Barry, Former Mayor, District of Columbia
"This sends the wrong message and will create more opportunity for thefts of legal handguns that can ultimately be used in the commission of crimes."

Richard M. Daley, Mayor, Chicago

"a very frightening decision... Does this lead to everyone having a gun in our society?... The old West—you have a gun and I have a gun and we'll settle on the street."

Michael Bloomberg, Mayor, New York City

"Eighty people a day die at the hands of guns. We have got to stop that. The court clearly ruled that reasonable regulations are permitted under that decision."

Gavin Newsom, Mayor, San Francisco

The ruling, "just flies in the face of reality. You just wish the Supreme Court could spend a week in public housing and then come out with this decision. It's very easy and comfortable to stand there with security guards and metal detectors and make these decisions."

Vince Gray, Chairman of the D.C. City Council

Regarding opening a gun store in D.C., which has none currently, so residents can buy a firearm or have one shipped in from an out-of-state dealer: "First of all, I don't want them anywhere. But if we're going to have them, we'll look at things, like keeping them away from schools and churches."

Nancy Pelosi, Speaker of the U.S. House of Representative

"I think it still allows the District of Columbia to come forward with a law that's less pervasive. I think the court left a lot of room to run in terms of concealed weapons and guns near schools."

Dianne Feinstein, Senator (D, CA)

"open(s) the doors to litigation against every gun-safety law that states have passed—assault weapons bans, trigger locks and all the rest of it."

Frank Lautenberg, Senator (D-NJ)

"Today, President Bush's radical Supreme Court justices put rigid ideology ahead of the safety of communities in New Jersey and across the country. This decision illustrates why I have strongly opposed extremist judicial nominees and will continue to do so in the future."

Robert Mueller, Director, FBI

The ruling, "does throw a lot of things up in the air." Referring to his grandchildren bound for college, he hopes, "those campuses will be weapons free." "I tend to believe weapons harm people and more often than not they harm the people carrying them."

Tom Barwin, Village Manager, Oak Park, Ill.

"It's just completely befuddling that our Supreme Court would be in alliance with the gangbangers." (as quoted on National Public Radio)

Selected Media Coverage

The New York Times

Justices Rule for Individual Gun Rights
By Linda Greenhouse, June 27, 2008
(Brief excerpt reprinted as fair use for review and commentary)

"WASHINGTON—The Supreme Court on Thursday embraced the long-disputed view that the Second Amendment protects an individual right to own a gun for personal use, ruling 5 to 4 that there is a constitutional right to keep a loaded handgun at home for self-defense.

"The landmark ruling overturned the District of Columbia's ban on handguns, the strictest gun-control law in the country, and appeared certain to usher in a fresh round of litigation over gun rights throughout the country. The court rejected the view that the Second Amendment's "right of the people to keep and bear arms" applied to gun ownership only in connection with service in the "well regulated militia" to which the amendment refers.

"Justice Antonin Scalia's majority opinion, his most important in his 22 years on the court, said the justices were 'aware of the problem of handgun violence in this country' and 'take seriously' the arguments in favor of prohibiting handgun ownership. 'But the enshrinement of constitutional rights necessarily takes certain policy choices off the table,' he said, adding: 'It is not the role of this court to pronounce the Second Amendment extinct.'"...

The New York Times (Editorial)

Lock and Load, June 27, 2008
(Brief excerpt reprinted as fair use for review and commentary)

Thirty-thousand Americans are killed by guns every year — on the job, walking to school, at the shopping mall. The Supreme Court on Thursday all but ensured that even more Americans will die senselessly with its wrongheaded and dangerous ruling striking down key parts of the District of Columbia's gun-control law...

This is a decision that will cost innocent lives, cause immeasurable pain and suffering and turn America into a more dangerous country. It will also diminish our standing in the world, sending yet another message that the United States values gun rights over human life... [A]s early as 1939, it [the Court] made clear that the Second Amendment only protects the right of people to carry guns for military use in a militia...

The gun lobby will now trumpet this ruling as an end to virtually all gun restrictions, anywhere, at all times. That must not happen. And today's decision still provides strong basis for saying it should not...

That last part is the final indignity of the decision: when the justices go to work at the Supreme Court, guns will still be banned. When most Americans show up at their own jobs, they will not have that protection...

This audaciously harmful decision, which hands the far right a victory it has sought for decades, is a powerful reminder of why voters need to have the Supreme Court firmly in mind when they vote for the president this fall...

The Chicago Tribune (Editorial)
(Brief excerpt reprinted as fair use for review and commentary)

Repeal the 2nd Amendment.

No, we don't suppose that's going to happen any time soon. But it should. The 2nd Amendment to the U.S. Constitution is evidence that, while the founding fathers were brilliant men, they could have used an editor.

A well regulated Militia, being necessary to the security of a free State, the right of the people to keep and bear Arms, shall not be infringed.

If the founders had limited themselves to the final 14 words, the amendment would have been an unambiguous declaration of the right to possess firearms. But they didn't and it isn't. The amendment was intended to protect the authority of the states to organize militias. The inartful wording has left the amendment open to public debate for more than 200 years. But in its last major decision on gun rights, in 1939, the U.S. Supreme Court unanimously found that that was the correct interpretation.

On Tuesday, five members of the court edited the 2nd Amendment. In essence, they said: Scratch the preamble, only 14 words count. In doing so, they have curtailed the power of the legislatures and the city councils to protect their citizens...

Repeal the 2nd Amendment? Yes, it's an anachronism. We won't repeal the amendment, but at least we can have that debate. Want to debate whether crime-staggered cities should prohibit the possession of handguns? The Supreme Court has just said, forget about it.

The Wall Street Journal

Silver Bullet, June 27, 2008
(Brief excerpt reprinted as fair use for review and commentary)

The 2008 Supreme Court term ended with a bang yesterday as the Justices issued their most important ruling ever in upholding an individual right to bear arms. The dismaying surprise is that the Second Amendment came within a single vote of becoming a dead constitutional letter...

Justice Scalia shreds the collective interpretation as a matter of both common law and Constitutional history. He writes that the Founders, as well as nearly all Constitutional scholars over the decades, believed in the individual right. Many Supreme Court opinions invoke the Founders, but this one is refreshing in its resort to first American principles and its affirmation of a basic liberty...

Justice Scalia illuminates a main fault line on this current Supreme Court. The four liberals are far more willing to empower the government and judges to restrict individual liberty, save on matter of personal life style (abortion, gay rights) or perhaps crime. The four conservatives are far more willing to defend individuals against government power—for example, in owning firearms, or private property (the 2005 *Kelo* case on eminent domain). Justice Anthony Kennedy swings both ways, and in *Heller* he sided with the people.

Heller leaves many questions unanswered. Contrary to the worries expressed by the Bush administration in its embarrassing *amicus* brief, the ruling does not bar the government from regulating machine guns or other heavy weapons; or from limiting gun ownership by felons or the mentally ill...

Heller reveals the High Court at its best, upholding individual liberty as the Founders intended. Yet it is also precarious because the switch of a single Justice would have rendered the Second Amendment a nullity. With the next President likely to appoint as many as three Justices, the right to bear arms has been affirmed but still isn't safe.

Daily News (New York)

"Now Americans have a brand-new right they did not explicitly have before. We think it's a dubious new right. We think the five justices are off the wall."

The Salt Lake Tribune

"No fair reading of the plain language of the amendment or its history could have reached the conclusion the court announced."

Contrarian Views

The Heller Misdirection, by William Norman Grigg

"A nation of slaves is always prepared to applaud the clemency of their master, who, in the abuse of absolute power, does not proceed to the last extremes of injustice and oppression.
–Edward Gibbon, *Decline and Fall of the Roman Empire*

Like the inhabitants of other formerly free societies, Americans are content to define "freedom" in terms of those liberties we are permitted to exercise. The Supreme Court ruling in *District of Columbia v. Heller* is perfectly in harmony with this self-defeating concept of "freedom."

It is entirely appropriate that the decision was written by Antonin Scalia, the most reliably authoritarian and consistently liberty-aversive member of the Court. With an air of regal condescension, Scalia allows that the Second Amendment acknowledges and protects an individual right to armed self-defense. He then explicitly limits the extent to which that "right" can be exercised, redefining it as a State-conferred privilege.

We can't really expect a statist creature like Antonin Scalia to embrace the view that the right to keep and bear arms includes the right of citizens, acting either individually or collectively, to kill agents of the state when such action is necessary and morally justified. Any other view of the Second Amendment is worse than useless; this is certainly true of the view that emerges in Scalia's *Heller* opinion.

"The Second Amendment protects an individual right to possess a firearm unconnected with service in a militia, and to use that arm for traditionally lawful purposes, such as self-defense *within the home*," summarizes Scalia at the beginning of his opinion. [emphasis added]

A few paragraphs later Scalia elaborates a bit on the implied limitations of the "right" he describes. Insisting that previous Court rulings effectively limit "the type of weapon to which the right applies to those used by the militia, i.e., those in common use for lawful purposes," he asserts: "Like most rights, the Second Amendment right is not unlimited. It is *not a right to keep and carry any weapon whatsoever in any manner whatsoever and for whatever purpose.... Miller's* holding that the sorts of weapons protected are those 'in common use at the time' finds support in the historical tradition of prohibiting the carrying of dangerous and unusual weapons." [emphasis added]

Nothing "dangerous and unusual" here: Combat-armed occupation troops patrol Katrina-ravaged New Orleans as part of an operation that included disarmament of law-abiding citizens.

When government grants a liberty and then restricts the manner in which it can be used, the result is not a right, but a limited, conditional license. Scalia's passage cited above will inevitably be seen as a license from the Court for legislative bodies to enact, or fortify, laws against "dangerous and unusual" weapons—such as the scary-looking guns ritually denounced as "assault weapons," for example. And other even more troubling portions of his opinion will abet further restrictions on the purposes for which firearms can be used.

At various points in his opinion, Scalia brushes up against the radical origins of the Second Amendment. For example: "The Antifederalists feared that the Federal Government would disarm the people in order to disable [the] citizens' militia, enabling a politicized standing army or a select militia to rule. The response was to deny Congress power to abridge the ancient right of individuals to keep and bear arms, so that the ideal of a citizens' militia would be preserved." (Pg. 2; also 22–28)

The clear implication here is that the "ancient right of individuals" to armed self-defense includes the right to organize for the purpose of insurrection against a tyrannical government. Scalia revisits that theme in reviewing efforts by George III's government to disarm American colonists (pg. 21). Discussing the ancient origins of the right, Scalia notes that "the Stuart Kings Charles II and James II succeeded in using select militias loyal to them to suppress political dissidents, in part by disarming their opponents" (pg. 19). He quite usefully admits that "when able-bodied men of a nation are trained in arms and organized, they are better able to resist tyranny" (pp. 24–25), without teasing any specific application from that provocative observation.

Although he draws only scantily from the vast corpus of insurrectionary writings by the Founders that deal with the right to armed self-defense (the most notable being Madison's endorsement, in Federalist essay 46, of direct military action against a tyrannical central government), Scalia does cite some interesting literature of that sort from mid-19th century.

For instance, he quotes John Norton Pomeroy's 1868 book *An Introduction to the Constitutional Law of the United States*, which stated that the Second Amendment would make no sense unless it enables citizens "to exercise themselves in the use of warlike weapons. To preserve this privilege, and *to secure to the people the ability to oppose themselves in military force against the usurpations of government*, as well as against enemies from without, that government is forbidden by any law or proceeding to invade or destroy the right to keep and bear arms..." [emphasis added]

[Photo caption: Given the chance, they'll grab your guns: A house-to-house gun grab in New Orleans; *photo on website*]

From the foregoing it's clear that Scalia is aware of the insurrectionary origins and purpose of the Second Amendment. Passages of that sort are scattered through the 67-page opinion and left without significant elaboration.

What's even odder is the fact that Scalia, drawing on Joseph Story's immensely influential Commentaries, asserts that the "free state" to be defended by the people under arms is not the individual state they inhabit—as the Founders would have understood—but rather the unitary nation created as a result of the Union victory in the War Between the States (pg. 24).

Scalia appears to be saying that while the right to bear arms was associated with the colonial and state militias, that right does not exist exclusively to carry out that function. But he also seems to assert that since the modern "militia" is an institution controlled by the central government and devoted to its protection, *there's no longer a legitimate right to armed self-defense against the government.*

On this point, Scalia's analysis is difficult to distinguish from that offered by the dissenting judges, who would simply dispense with the right to bear arms entirely, rather than paying lip-service to it while denying its chief purpose and encouraging various encumbrances on it, as Scalia does.

[Photo caption: Your friendly neighborhood stormtrooper on patrol in New Orleans: If they were really the Good Guys, would they dress like this? *Shows hooded, riot-geared agents in camo; photo on website*]

"Undoubtedly some think that the Second Amendment is outmoded in a society where our standing army is the pride of our Nation, where well-trained police forces provide personal security, and where gun violence is a serious problem," Scalia concludes. "That is perhaps debatable, but what is not debatable is that it is not the role of this Court to pronounce the Second Amendment extinct."

Indeed not: Scalia's opinion suggests the role of the Court is to placate key elements of the Republican coalition while suggesting alternative routes to those who seek the eventual abolition of the right that was once protected by the Second Amendment. While Scalia's ruling reinforces one of the few effective rallying points for the demoralized Republican Party ("This year's election is all about the judges!"), it does nothing of substance to defer the day when some judge or president will be able to pronounce the Second Amendment extinct.

This point simply can't be emphasized too often: *The innate right of armed self-defense exists whether any government chooses to recognize it.* What made the Second Amendment unique was its recognition of the fact that in the constitutional scheme, the government does not have a monopoly on the legitimate use of force. Scalia, like many statist jurists before him, insists that the permissible civilian uses of firearms are all defined within that government-exercised monopoly on force;

they are temporary concessions that can be redefined by our rulers at whim.

In a genuinely free society, citizens would enjoy the unqualified liberty to acquire weapons of any sort, in any quantity they pleased, for the specific purpose of being able to out-gun the government and its agents when such action would be justified.

Most Americans, as ignorant of our heritage of principled insurrection as they are well-versed in the ephemera of degenerate pop culture, would find such sentiments abhorrent. In that fact we see that—whatever may be the status of our current "right" to keep and bear arms—the intellectual and psychological disarmament of our population is nearly complete.

William Norman Grigg writes the Pro Libertate blog. His photos are posted at http://www.lewrockwell.com/grigg/grigg-w32.html

Anonymous

We could hardly have hoped for a better conclusion to the *Heller* debacle. We give up nothing in the Supreme Court's ritualized formalization of an "individual right" under the Second Amendment, for we always knew that was the truth of the matter. Abandoning our old, worn-out, unconvincing and unsupportable arguments in fact frees us to pursue more opportunistic goals in the march toward finally disarming the entire American public.

The need to recant those old positions doesn't even arise, we simply stand behind the new model and proceed as if nothing happened. Waste no energy apologizing or humbly confessing to error. The true advance of collectivism doesn't need some sacred collectivist doctrine enshrined in centuries old parchment to prevail.

The greatest achievement here, already embraced and vigorously promoted with the success of the concealed-carry-permit program, is that the public is increasingly receptive, willing, even eager to adopt gun registration as a norm. This is the great irony. We predicted this as early as the 1960s (to great skepticism as you'll recall). While the "freedom" crowd is ignorantly celebrating a "win" we advance our agenda flawlessly. A mere four decades ago such a possibility was nonexistent and unthinkable.

Immediately upon release of the decision, that portion of the public *most* attached to its guns and so-called gun rights, began aching to be registered. It took little prodding to convince Mayor Fenty, Police Chief Lanier and their minions to waste no time in establishing a registration system. The foot-dragging years-to-implementation approach fell quickly when the higher goals were recognized.

Even the exorbitant fees sought by some of the money-hungry bureaucrats were easily defeated in favor of low-barrier-to-entry small annual fees. There will be time aplenty in the future to ratchet those tax levels up to where they need to be, to advance the voluntary component of disarmament similar to the FFL shakeout. The sooner the gun toters are registered and licensed, the sooner the taxes can begin to flow, the lists can grow, and the acceptance of gun lists can become standardized in the American psyche.

Swift implementation has the side benefit of making the authorities appear cooperative, which will have public relations value as the net grows larger and tighter around the gun owners we seek to subjugate.

Inclusion of vague language about banning weapons that are "unusual and dangerous" could not have been better had we written it ourselves. I dare say none of us would have dared attempt that had we the power to do so, it would have seemed impossible to slip in such fungible terms—and then it is dropped in our laps. The fates indeed smile upon us. "Unusual" can be drawn upon to eliminate any weapons of any sort developed in the future which are, by definition and lack of prior existence, unusual. Nothing need make them morph into usual weapons for the public.

"Dangerous" on the other hand is a true thing of beauty. What is a gun, blade or any weapon but dangerous by its very definition. In this we have a seed planted that can, with time and effort, and cooperation from our friends in media and high places, grow into a tree of imaginary peace, whose leaves offer no shade to anything more dangerous than a pea shooter. Already, D.C. is talking about derringers as suitable for registration. Derringers! This is playing out better than any of us thought it could even ten years ago.

Our best estimates suggest the major players in the gun lobby will continue to support registration schemes, as long as a carrot of gun possession is attached. It has even been boldly suggested that the gun lobby could become the biggest promoter of such plans, playing into our efforts seamlessly. Those useful idiots are actually battling now for state-to-state registration compliance (they call it reciprocity, a term we should adopt as well in appearing to resist it), in which any gun owner moving between state lines must be identified in national databases instantly accessible to any law-enforcement personnel.

A framework for firearm possession without the lock-grip registrations isn't even on the drawing board. Thanks to our effort to manipulate the playing field, such an approach is widely seen as unobtainable and not worth the political capital. And why bother, when you can get all you think you want at the mere acceptance of a little paperwork.

Even the preemption laws, which we carefully gave the appearance of resisting until they had been enacted in 41 states, work in our favor.

While on the surface, these assumptions of gun protection power at the state legislative level prevent us from attacking gun possession piecemeal and locally, when control of state bodies is completed in the estimated 5 to 7 years (as projected under 2006-B1), we can trample private gun possession like Sherman marching to the sea. Sheriffs, the only other significant obstacle before us, will be powerless to resist short of insurrection.

Right now, three teams are busy at work milking *Heller* for additional levers that can be applied to achieve the ultimate solution. Principles expressed in the dissents, especially Justice Breyer's circuitous logic are yielding fruit we will harvest shortly. Allies nationally are aligning to advance the most promising aspects of those studies, and there are several. One of our projections foresees the Mullenix case against ATF crashing to defeat with *Heller* as a citation. Several high-confidence gun-lobby lawsuits appear poised to backfire in our favor.

The greatest surprise of the whole affair remains that no voices have been seriously raised objecting to the global gun-registration potentials. The best and brightest just fall in line. Our enemies may be less bright than we give them credit for, or perhaps we've just been lucky.

Only minor and fringe elements have even considered pressing for permitless carry, or destruction of extant databases and other efforts to derail national registration. Proposals for national carry all include, nay rely upon, permit-registration elements, and even these calls died away after we got that in place for off-duty and retired police.

The loudest voice for dismantling registration and permits, now that GOA has subdued its rhetoric, is perhaps Jews for the Preservation of Firearms Ownership, but they are so far out of the mainstream they are taken seriously by none of the major players with whom we must contend. From their perspective, "the NRA is the leading gun-control group in the world," a perspective we can privately agree with. Would they be willing to issue the permits themselves, as JPFO sardonically intones? We know that opportunity will reside elsewhere.

One other fringe element bears watching. Two wildcat activists, Russ Howard and Brian Pucket, q.v., are proposing an alternative to the NICS background check. NICS as you know is central to our national database of gun owners and other miscreants. The BIDS system would decentralize background checks while effectively screening out criminals from retail gun sales, and because it is hundreds of millions of dollars less expensive, this makes it dangerous to us. In that are the seeds of a problem. Though the effort is limited at present to a few obscure web postings (and some rather flaky implementation ideas), it bears watching.

This anonymous essay imagines a strategic analysis of Heller *from the anti-gun viewpoint.*

Summary of All *Amicus* Briefs

Heller has the third highest number of friend-of-the-court briefs ever filed, at 67 (47 for Heller and 20 for D.C., including the Solicitor General's). The top was 107 in the affirmative action case *Grutter* (539 U.S. 306 in 2003), and then 78 for the abortion case *Webster* (492 U.S. 490 in 1989).

Never in the Court's long history has any brief been filed with a majority of both Houses of Congress as signatories. That occurred for the pro-rights position in Vice President Cheney's brief, written by Stephen P. Halbrook (250 Representatives and 55 Senators). In contrast, 18 Representatives and no Senators signed onto one of the anti-rights briefs.

As a matter of standard form, an *amicus* brief must include at its beginning a summary of the arguments it will make. While these short remarks do little to express the full content and reasoning of the brief, they do make clear the position of the parties, and provided a convenient way for us to summarize the mountain of data presented to the Court before oral arguments were made. To read the briefs themselves, use the Supreme Court link on the home page at gunlaws.com.

Briefs for the Respondent, Mr. Heller: The Pro-Rights Positions

Academics
I. Comparing the District's murder rate to murder rates of other jurisdictions
A. The Fifty Largest Cities
B. Comparison to Maryland and Virginia
C. Comparison to the United State's murder rates
D. The District's Homicide Rate
II. Notes on Other Claims
Conclusion: This Court should affirm the judgment of the Court of Appeals.

Academics for the Second Amendment
I. Petitioners' attempt to explain the purpose of the Second Amendment misreads the historical record, mistakes the relationship between arms and militia duty, and improperly applies the very interpretative principle it invokes
A. The one certainty in the historical record is that Madison and the First Congress did not intend to protect the power of states to arm the militia if Congress failed to do so
1. In drafting the Bill of Rights, Madison discarded proposals to provide for state arming of the militia
2. The First Congress considered, and voted down, a motion to add Virginia's militia-arming proposal to the Bill of Rights

3. The First Congress considered militia armament a key federal power, and rejected attempts to allow states to provide or to require it

B. Petitioners' position mistakes the relationship between militia organization and arms: the framing generation had unorganized militiamen, and required them to keep arms

C. Petitioners' position misapplies the principles of construction it espouses

II. Citizen arms, citizen armies: the intellectual foundations of the Second Amendment

III. The right to arms in early American statecraft

IV. The ratification process and proposals for a Bill of Rights

A. The conflict over ratification; of armies and citizens' arms

B. Proposals for a Bill of Rights

V. The drafting of the American Bill of Rights

A. Background to the drafting process

B. Madison's crafting of the right to arms

C. The First Congress and the Second Amendment

VI. The original public meaning of the Second Amendment incorporated the arms amendments Proposed in the various state ratifying conventions

Conclusion: The operative clause of the Second Amendment is as unambiguous as any command of the First Amendment. Read in light of its preamble, it is meant to guarantee the existence of an armed citizenry, the militia infrastructure from which the Republic could obtain (and would be more likely to create) a well regulated militia. Rather than giving effect to both the Amendment's clauses, Petitioners propose that this Court give effect to neither. Under its reading, there is no duty to create a well-regulated militia, and absent that, the people have no right to arms, either.

Petitioners' interpretation of the Second Amendment moreover disregards its history: Madison and Congress rejected language creating a power of the States to arm the militia, just as they rejected language limiting it to a right "for the common defense." The decision of the Court of Appeals should be affirmed.

The Alaska Outdoor Council, Alaska Fish And Wildlife Conservation Fund, Sitka Sportsman's Assoc., Juneau Rifle And Pistol Club, Juneau Gun Club, And Alaska Territorial Sportsmen, Inc.

I. The District's claim that the Second Amendment does not protect an individual right "to keep and bear arms" is not supported by a logical analysis of the text of the Amendment

A. The District's argument overlooks the fact that the word "Militia" has an entirely different meaning from the phrase "a well regulated militia"

B. The District's Assertion that the words "keep and bear" in the Second Amendment simply mean "keeping" arms for the purpose of "bearing" them in a context is without foundation

C. The District's notion that the nature of a right specifically guaranteed by the Constitution should be understood by an intended purpose of the guarantee is mistaken

II. The District's claim that the Second Amendment does not protect an individual right "to keep and bear arms" is not supported by the principal purpose of the Amendment

III. The "collective right" interpretation of the Second Amendment rests on an imported ideology taken from German social and political thought and stands wholly outside American political thought and traditions

IV. If the Second Amendment protects the right of individuals who are not affiliated with any state-regulated militia "to keep and bear" firearms, then each of the District's laws under review violate Mr. Heller's Second Amendment rights

A. The Second Amendment recognizes a pre-existing "right of the people to keep and bear arms"

B. The "right of the people to keep and bear arms" encompasses the common law right of self-defense and its corollary, the "right to keep and bear arms" for self-defense

C. The right to keep and bear arms for self-defense is a fundamental right

D. The District's three laws under review are per se violations of Mr. Heller's Second Amendment rights

E. Alternatively, if there is no per se Second Amendment violation here, then the correct standard of review of the District's laws is strict scrutiny

F. The District has failed to carry its burden of proof as required by the standard of strict scrutiny

Conclusion: For the foregoing reasons, the judgment of the United States Court of Appeals for the District of Columbia should be affirmed.

The American Center for Law and Justice

I. The Bill of Rights, including the Second Amendment right of the people to keep and bear arms, binds both Congress and the District council

A. Whether legislating nationally or merely locally for the District of Columbia, Congress is at all times subject to the constitutional restraints imposed upon it by the Bill of Rights

B. The District of Columbia Council, exercising legislative authority pursuant to a delegation of power by Congress, is likewise bound by the guarantees of the Bill of Rights

II. The Second Amendment secures the inherent, individual and private right of the people to keep and bear arms

A. The Bill of Rights secures pre-existing individual rights of the American people

B. The text of the Second Amendment protects and secures the individual right to keep and bear arms for private uses

Conclusion: This Court should affirm the decision below that the D.C. Code provisions at issue infringe the Second Amendment right of individual citizens to keep and bear arms.

American Civil Rights Union

I. This case easily satisfies all of the classic criteria for granting a writ of certiorari

II. Petitioner does not correctly state the question presented by this case

III. The text of the Second Amendment plainly protects a right of each individual citizen to keep and bear arms

IV. The District of Columbia's gun control laws have not been effective in reducing crime, and may have been counterproductive

Conclusion: For all of the foregoing reasons, *Amicus Curiae* American Civil Rights Union respectfully submits that this Court should grant the requested Writ of Certiorari, and affirm the decision of the District of Columbia Circuit below.

American Legislative Exchange Council

I. The text of the Second Amendment supports the right to keep arms in the home

II. The history of the adoption of the Second Amendment supports the right to keep arms in the home

III. Past and current state guarantees support the right to keep arms in the home

Conclusion: The laws under review sweep too broadly. A complete handgun ban is an unconstitutional infringement regardless of the standard of review. The Parker decision should be affirmed because it is supported by the do not infringe command of the Second Amendment. It is also supported by the national consensus that the Constitution guarantees an individual right to keep arms, and by the national consensus that handguns should not be banned.

Association of American Physicians and Surgeons, Inc.

I. The interpretation of the Constitution cannot depend on politicized views of medicine

II. The Petitioner's medical amici briefs are fatally flawed in ignoring undeniable benefits of firearms

A. The primary use of guns is defensive, having a beneficial effect

B. The AAP amici brief relies on flawed studies and unjustified conclusions

C. The APHA Amici Brief Ignores the Greater Benefits of Gun Ownership

III. The Right to Bear Arms has an essential role in deterring tyranny, terrorism and genocide

Conclusion: The decision below should be affirmed.

Buckeye Firearms Foundation LLC, National Council For Investigation And Security Services, Ohio Association Of Private Detective Agencies, Inc., DBA Ohio Association Of Security And Investigation Services (Oasis), Michigan Council Of Private Investigators, Indiana Association Of Professional Investigators, And Kentucky Professional Investigators Association

I. The District of Columbia Metropolitan Police Department has failed to adequately protect the citizens of Washington, D.C.

A. Washington, D.C. has a significant crime problem

B. The MPD has a significant problem hiring and retaining qualified police officers

C. The MPD has a significant history of mismanagement

D. The District's "911 system is a joke"

E. The MPD has a significant history of corruption

F. The MPD has stifled private security and mismanaged the industry's regulation

II. The citizens of Washington, D.C. have no legal recourse against the Metropolitan Police Department for these failures

III. When the police fail to protect the citizens and the courts immunize the police for these same failures, the Second Amendment must be interpreted as a private right to keep and bear firearms for the defense of self and others

Conclusion: The United States Court of Appeals for the District of Columbia Circuit should be affirmed.

The Cato Institute and History Professor Joyce Lee Malcolm

I. The English right to have and use arms belonged to individuals broadly, regardless of militia service, and particularly protected their "keeping" of guns for self-defense.

A. The English right was, by well before the founding, a broadly applicable right of individuals, not depending on militia service.

B. The core of the English right, settled by at least the 1730s, was the right of ordinary subjects to "keep" firearms for defense of their homes and families.

C. Rather than interfering with the freedom of individuals to keep firearms for self-defense, English law in the 1700s protected the peace by directly punishing belligerent uses of those arms.
II. The Second Amendment secures at least the individual right inherited from England, as early American authorities demonstrate.
A. Authorities before the Second Amendment's adoption recognized the right inherited from England and, due to the revolution, that it facilitated not only self-defense but also a militia of the people.
B. Authorities soon after the Second Amendment's adoption recognized it as securing—and expanding—the right inherited from England, with the additional purpose of facilitating a militia of the people.
C. Early American authorities likewise adopted the English focus on directly punishing belligerent uses of arms, rather than interfering with the freedom of individuals to keep them for defense of home and family.

Conclusion: The District of Columbia laws violate the core of the right to arms inherited from England and secured by the Second Amendment. The Court should affirm.

Center for Individual Freedom

I. Supreme Court precedent does not establish a collective right of states to keep and bear arms, nor does it reject an individual right to keep and bear arms
A. The Supreme Court in *United States v. Miller* was unable to determine whether the defendants' Second Amendment rights had been violated
B. Subsequent lower courts have misconstrued the holding in *United States v. Miller*
II. Adopting Petitioners' collective right view would trigger radical, unexpected, and disruptive consequences
A. A collective right ruling would create a cause of action for states to litigate that right in federal court
B. A collective right to keep and bear arms would contradict other constitutional provisions, call the National Guard into question, and collide with existing federal firearms laws
1. A collective right decision would contradict other provisions of the Constitution
2. A collective right holding could immediately call federal firearms laws into question
3. A decision establishing a collective right would immediately open the National Guard as presently constituted to legal challenge

Conclusion: For each of the foregoing reasons, *Amicus* respectfully submits that the decision below should be affirmed, and that the Second Amendment to the United States Constitution confers an individual right of the people to keep and bear arms.

Organizations and Scholars Correcting Myths and Misrepresentations Commonly Deployed by Opponents of an Individual-Rights-Based Interpretation of the Second Amendment (Citizens Committee for the Right to Keep and Bear Arms)

I. The District falsely claims that the right to keep and bear arms is only for militia
A. The District takes United States v. Cruikshank out of context to argue that the right to keep and bear arms is not constitutionally protected
B. The Brady brief turns the 1181 Assize of Arms and the English Bill of Rights on their heads
C. The District falsely claims that the right to keep and bear arms is exclusively for the common defense

D. The District falsely claims that the right to keep and bear arms is only for the military, ignoring the original definition of the "militia" as the body of the people

E. The District falsely claims that Congress can change the Constitution by adopting a limited definition of the term "militia" and that Congress did so

F. The District falsely claims that the Pennsylvania Declaration of Rights does not include keeping arms for self-defense

G. The District misuses the Oxford English Dictionary to support an artificially narrow definition of "arms"

H. The Linguist's *amicus* brief misuses Webster's 1828 Dictionary to project a military meaning on the Second Amendment

I. The District denies the sovereignty of the people by falsely claiming that the Second Amendment permits them to be disarmed in favor of an exclusive military class

II. The District makes numerous historical, legal, and statistical misrepresentations in attempting to justify disarming its people

A. The District falsely claims that its law permits people to assemble and load long guns for self-defense

B. The District falsely asserts that other jurisdictions' laws are comparable to the District's law

C. The District relies on deeply flawed research and evidence taken out of context to claim that its handgun ban has reduced homicide rates

D. The District falsely asserts that handguns are deadlier than long guns

E. The District incorrectly asserts that handguns are dangerous in the hands of ordinary citizens

F. The District falsely asserts that accidental handgun deaths of children are frequent

G. The District overstates the impact of handguns in the schools

H. The District falsely claims that state law permitted significant gun control in an early period

1. Massachusetts
2. Alabama
3. Indiana
4. Tennessee
5. Georgia

I. The Appleseed brief mis-cites state cases to argue that it is constitutional to ban an entire class of weapons

Conclusion: The decision of the court below should be affirmed.

Congress of Racial Equality

I. Gun control measures have been and are used to disarm and oppress blacks and other minorities

A. Gun control in slave codes

B. Black codes, Reconstruction and the Fourteenth Amendment: a fundamental individual right to keep and bear arms

C. Post-Reconstruction

D. United States v. Cruikshank

E. Gun control in the Twentieth Century

II. Current gun control efforts: a legacy of racism

A. By prohibiting the possession of firearms, the State discriminates against minority and poor citizens

B. The enforcement of gun prohibitions spur increased civil liberties violations, especially in regard to minorities and the poor

III. The District's gun control laws have been a disaster

Conclusion: Gun control laws like the ones at issue in this case bear especially hard on the poor and minorities. Enforcement of gun control laws, like the ones at issue, will have a disparate impact on minorities and the poor.

Judgment below should be upheld.

Criminologists, Social Scientists, Other Distinguished Scholars and The Claremont Institute

I. There is no evidence that the District's gun prohibitions have produced good results

A. Following the enactment of the District's handgun ban, the District has not been made safer—indeed, the District has only become an even more dangerous place to live

b. Studies relied upon by the District and amici to try to explain away the District's substantial increase in murder during the handgun ban period are unreliable

1. The Loftin study

2. The Kellermann study

II. Criminological evidence from the United States and from foreign jurisdictions discredits the notion that "more guns equals more murder."

A. United States statistics show that increased gun availability does not increase the number of murders

B. The Duggan study relied on by the District and amici is fundamentally flawed

C. Foreign criminological evidence discredits the notion that more guns equals more murder

III. Even national gun bans fail to reduce violence

IV. Handgun bans do not reduce suicide rates

V. The District's ban of armed home defense admits of no implied exception

vi. Whatever benefits gun control offers can be accomplished by a permit or background check system

Conclusion: In this case, the facts simply do not fit the rhetoric behind the District's gun ban. Such bans do not produce good results. Rather, such bans irrationally strip law-abiding citizens of the most effective means of defending themselves and their loved ones—and, if the evidence indicates anything, it is that criminals take full advantage. *Amici* respectfully submit that the judgment of the Court of Appeals was correct and should be affirmed.

Disabled Veterans for Self-Defense and Kestra Childers

I. Moral authority

II. Legal authority – common law

III. Independence

IV. The right of self-defense

V. D.C. Code §§7-2502.02(A)(4); 22-4504(A), and 7-2507.02 violate the Second Amendment rights of individuals who are not affiliated with any state-regulated militia, but who wish to keep handguns and other firearms for private use in their homes

A. The collective right interpretation is wrong

B. The Second Amendment protects an individual right

1. Contemporaries thought that the Second Amendment protected an individual right
2. The colonial experience gave the framers cause to protect an individual right

Conclusion: The Court should affirm the judgment of the Court of Appeals for the D.C. Circuit. Amici realize that the language of the Second Amendment can be construed in two ways. However, Amici believe that this Court should affirm the judgment of the Circuit Court for several reasons.

Affirming the judgment would construe the Second Amendment to protect an individual right. If there was any authority, contemporaneous with the ratification of the Bill of Rights which did not believe that this was the intent of James Madison when he wrote it, of the Congress when they offer it for ratification, or the states when they ratified it, we have not found it.

The rights of Englishman under the common law are protected in the Constitution and the Bill of Rights. The three absolute rights protected in the due process clauses of the Fifth and Fourteenth Amendments. The first auxiliary right is protected in Article I of the Constitution. The second auxiliary right is protected by the Tenth Amendment. The third auxiliary right is protected by Article III of the Constitution and by the First, Fourth, Fifth, Sixth, Seventh and Eighth Amendments. The fourth auxiliary right is protected by the First Amendment. Where is the fifth auxiliary right? This Court has observed that "... the rights of life and personal liberty are natural rights of man." United States v. Cruikshank, 92 U.S. 542, 543 (1875). Not one of the rights which were so carefully protected in the Bill of Rights could be enjoyed unless one's life were first preserved. The confiscation of privately owned firearms in Boston was listed, in the Declaration of July 6, 1775, as one of the causes impelling us to take up arms. Would such men, under such circumstances, have left the fifth auxiliary right unprotected? All contemporary authorities appear to have thought not. They thought that it was protected in the Second Amendment.

Affirming the judgment would change very little in America. Most Americans who are not part of the organized militia already have the right to keep and bear functional firearms, including handguns, in their homes. The decision we seek from this Court would merely strengthen the protection of this right.

However, for residents of the District of Columbia, and any other jurisdiction which prohibits private ownership of handguns, it will make a large difference in a number of ways. First, the current situation creates a safety hazard which the District Government appears not to have considered.

As noted above, in every federal Circuit in which a convicted felon sought to offer a defense of justification for possession of a firearm in violation of 18 U.S.C. §922(g), it has been recognized. In the Fourth Circuit, for example, in United States v. Crittenden, 883 F.2d 326, 330 (4th Cir. 1989), the court established a four prong test for justification in the face of such charges. The defendant must produce evidence which would allow the factfinder to conclude he (1) was under unlawful and present threat of death or serious bodily injury; (2) did not recklessly place himself in a situation where he would be forced to engage in criminal conduct; (3) had no reasonable legal alternative (to both the criminal act and the avoidance of the threatened harm); and (4) there is a direct causal relationship between the criminal action and the avoidance of the threatened harm. These are, essentially, the same criteria which one who is not a prohibited person would have to show to justify shooting a dangerous attacker.

As things stand now, a District resident may keep a rifle or shotgun in his home. It would be unlawful to keep one's firearm fully assembled and loaded, but the government may not check to see if one is complying with the requirements of D.C. Code §7-2507.02 without probable cause. The District authorities will never know that one is in violation unless one actually shoots an intruder in self-defense. In that case, if the shooting is justified, one must assume that the violation of the D.C. Code will also meet the criteria for justification.

While this means that a D.C. resident would run very little risk of prosecution for keeping a loaded rifle in his home, society would be much better off if he could keep a loaded handgun instead:

Consider penetration: even the .44 magnum, the most powerful of all handguns, penetrates no more than thirteen inches in wood, while revolvers in the far more commonly owned .32 to .38 calibers range from two to seven inches of penetration.

The reason for the difference in penetration is relative velocity. A 158 grain bullet from a .38 special revolver will leave the muzzle at 755 feet per second. A 150 grain bullet from a .30-06 hunting rifle, will leave the muzzle at 2920 feet per second. The relative dangers are obvious, a handgun would be much better suited for home defense.

The District of Columbia is a densely populated urban environment. A rifle or shotgun is much more likely to have an accidental discharge as a handgun for a number of reasons. But assume that there is a justified shooting. The problem over penetration still endangers innocents with a rifle far more than with a handgun. Further, a rifle or a shotgun would be awkward to use for home defense because of the size. If awkward for a healthy person, it may approach impossible in a confined space for a person who is bound to a wheel chair.

If District residents were permitted to have functional handguns in their homes, it is unlikely that this would lead to an increase in violent crime. The people who are inclined to commit violent crimes already have handguns. To see how honest people in the District will respond to having the right to keep and bear a functional handgun in their homes, we can look at jurisdictions in which there is a state constitutional right to arms for self-defense.

The constitutions of New Hampshire, South Dakota and Vermont each protects a right to have arms for self-defense. During the five years 2002-2006, according to the F.B.I. Uniform Crime Reports there were 208 homicides in these states. Their combined population, as of July 1, 2007, was 2,733,296. During that same period the District of Columbia, population 588,292, had 1,099 homicides. The rate per 100,000 population during this five year period, for the three states was 1.54. For the District of Columbia, it was 38. One might safely conclude that if honest people living in the District were allowed to have functional firearms, including handguns, in their homes, this would be unlikely to increase the rate of violent crime. One speculates that the prediction of Cesare Beccaria, cited above, that disarming the honest emboldens the dishonest, might be proven to be correct.

There are, in the District of Columbia, people who are elderly or disabled, as are many members of the Amici, Disabled Vets, as well as Amici Kestra Childers. An affirmation of the judgment would be great help to give security to those of diminished physical capacity. On their behalf, Amici ask:

Suppose a strong and vigorous man strikes me with his fist, and I am a poor fellow who cannot stand up to him with a fist. May I defend myself with a sword?

For the reasons presented, Amici pray that this Court will affirm the judgment of the Circuit Court.

Eagle Forum Education & Legal Defense Fund

I. The Second Amendment guarantees an individual right to keep and bear arms
A. The Second Amendment's operative clause guarantees "the people" the "right" to keep and bear arms
B. The right "to keep and bear arms" protects private conduct
C. The historical record demonstrates that the Second Amendment guaranteed an individual right to bear arms
II. The prefatory clause of the Second Amendment does not limit the rights of individuals who are not affiliated with a state-regulated militia
A. The Second Amendment's operative language protecting the right of "the people" is not controlled or limited by the Amendment's prefatory clause
B. The Second Amendment's prefatory clause refutes petitioners' "collective rights" view
III. While the appropriate standard of review is not before the court, the Second Amendment guarantees a fundamental right and alleged violations of the Amendment are therefore subject to strict scrutiny

Conclusion: For the foregoing reasons, the Court of Appeals' decision should be affirmed.

Former Senior Officials of the Department of Justice

I. The current Administration properly recognized that the Second Amendment secures an individual right
A. Prior to *United States v. Miller*, the executive branch repeatedly recognized that the Second Amendment secures an individual right
B. The position of the United States in *Miller* did not signal an abandonment of the individual rights view of the Second Amendment
C. The collective rights analysis offered by the Johnson Administration in support of its gun control initiatives was flawed and incomplete
D. Subsequent Twentieth Century executive interpretations were cursory and often equivocal
E. In definitively affirming that the Second Amendment secures an individual right, the current Administration fulfilled its obligation to uphold the Constitution
II. Interpreting the Second Amendment to secure an individual right does not call into question the Constitutionality of existing federal firearms laws
III. The court need not address the Solicitor General's proposal for a multi-tiered standard of Second Amendment review to affirm the decision below, nor is this case a suitable vehicle for doing so

Conclusion: For the foregoing reasons, the decision of the Court of Appeals should be affirmed.

The Foundation for Free Expression

I. The text of the Second Amendment supports an individual right to bear arms
A. The Second Amendment protects both the right of the people to participate in government and their right to be free from improper government interference
B. A well-regulated militia is composed of the entire people, prepared to defend themselves and others using their individually owned arms
1. The militia has always been broadly defined as an amorphous body of the people
2. A militia is "well-regulated" when citizens are prepared to act defensively in emergencies, using their lawfully possessed weapons; formal organization is not required

C. "A free state" is a political entity in which citizens are secure in their homes and travel freely because they have the means to defend themselves against criminal attacks or oppressive government

1. "A free state" is a general reference to a political unit; it is not a synonym for one of the states of the United States

2. The right to bear arms is broader in scope than the need to maintain a well-regulated militia

3. People are not free when they are not at liberty to move about the community without fear of criminal attacks

D. To "bear" arms is to carry or wear them on the person for the purpose of defensive action in appropriate circumstances

E. To "keep" arms is to retain possession of them

F. Arms is a broad, indefinite term that must be understood in the context of the Second Amendment's purposes

G. "The people" is a term of art used in the Constitution to describe the individual citizens of the United States

1. "The people" has a collective aspect but that aspect is not exclusive

2. "The people" have "rights" and "powers" under the Constitution; governments have "powers" but never "rights"

3. Ordinary citizens have the right to participate in the defense of their communities and country

II. The Second Amendment protects an individual right consistent with America's founding documents and other basic legal principles

A. The Declaration of Independence acknowledges inalienable rights to life and liberty; the Second Amendment guarantees an auxiliary right to protect these primary rights

B. The Bill of Rights consistently guarantees individual rights of "the people"

1. The organizational structure of the Bill of Rights and placement of the Second Amendment are contrary to the "states rights" position

2. Individual rights are sometimes exercised by a group of individuals

C. Courts should be consistent when interpreting the Constitution and guarding the Constitutional rights of American

D. Defense of self or others has long been recognized as a natural right and a complete defense to criminal or civil charges

1. Law-abiding citizens frequently use guns to save lives and halt the escalation of violent crime

2. Gun control laws do not contribute to the government's interest in preserving human life

III. The individual right to bear arms is confirmed by history, commentators, early state constitutions, and early case law

A. England's Bill of Rights guaranteed the individual right to bear arms for self-defense

B. American government departed from the traditions of other countries, where governments did not trust the people to bear arms

C. The legislative history of the Second Amendment supports the understanding that an individual right was guaranteed

D. The Constitutional ratification process confirms the understanding of early Americans that individuals had the right to be armed

E. State constitutions, state laws, and early American legal commentators all agreed that the American people retained the right to bear arms

1. State laws and constitutions guarded the individual right to bear arms

2. Early American commentators unanimously agreed that the Second Amendment guaranteed an individual right
F. Nineteenth Century case law and other judicial sources affirm an individual rights interpretation of the Second Amendment
G. The U.S. Senate Judiciary Committee and U.S. Justice Department have adopted the individual rights position

Conclusion: This Court should uphold the individual right to keep and bear arms guaranteed to Americans, so they might lawfully defend themselves and their communities.

Foundation for Moral Law

I. The Constitutionality of the D.C. handgun provisions should be decided according to the unaltered text of the Second Amendment
II. The history behind the Second Amendment reveals a healthy American fear of government tyranny and the need for self-defense through the bearing of arms
A. The right to keep and bear arms in English history
B. The right to keep and bear arms in early American history
C. The right to keep and bear arms in the debate on the Constitution
D. James Madison and the right to keep and bear arms
III. The text of the Second Amendment recognizes an individual right to keep and bear arms
A. The "militia" clause
B. "[T]he people" to whom the right belongs
C. "[T]o keep and bear arms"
D. The text and reasonable restrictions

Conclusion: For the reasons stated, this Honorable Court should affirm the decision of the District of Columbia Court of Appeals and invalidate the D.C. code provisions at issue as blatant violations of the Second Amendment.

Georgiacarry.org, inc.

I. Gun control in the District of Columbia
II. Gun control in the United States
A. Pre-Civil War gun control
B. Reconstruction Era gun control
C. Late Reconstruction/Industrial Age gun control
D. Atlanta Race Riots resulted in black disarmament
III. Modern application of gun control

Conclusion: American history, from colonial times to the immediate past, is replete with evidence that gun control has frequently been implemented with a nefarious purpose of subjugating blacks and other minorities. Even today's gun control laws are often vestiges of, or the continuation of, the nation's Jim Crow past. At best, many such laws have greater effects on minorities and the economically disadvantaged. As the parties and other *amici* no doubt will argue, the Framers put into place a constitutional guarantee that the right of the people to keep and bear arms shall not be infringed. It clearly was the intent of the drafters of the Fourteenth Amendment to ensure that this guarantee applied to all people and against the states as well as the federal government.

This Court should apply the Second Amendment as it was intended, and eradicate any vestiges of Jim Crow in the District of Columbia's firearms laws.

The Goldwater Institute

I. The Second Amendment right deserves protection equivalent to other fundamental individual rights enumerated in the Bill of Rights, not the "intermediate" scrutiny proposed by the government

A. The D.C. Circuit applied the proper standard of scrutiny for fundamental individual rights, and did not apply a "per se" or "categorical" rule

B. Core Second Amendment rights should be accorded the full protection due other individual rights enumerated in the Constitution

C. Strict scrutiny will not automatically invalidate federal firearms regulation

D. No basis exists for adopting an "intermediate" level of scrutiny for Second Amendment rights

II. This case should not be remanded to the Court of Appeals

A. No remand is necessary if the Court applies strict scrutiny

B. No remand would be necessary even if the Court applied the Government's proposed standard of review

1. A remand would be inconsistent with this Court's customary practice

2. A remand would undermine this Court's role in giving guidance to the federal judiciary

Conclusion: For the foregoing reasons, the judgment below should be affirmed.

Grass Roots of South Carolina, Inc.

I. The right to keep and bear arms in the privacy of the home is a natural right unabridged by the Constitution

II. The preexisting right to keep and bear arms is protected by the right to privacy emanating from the Second Amendment

III. The right to keep and bear arms in the privacy of the home extends to the District of Columbia

Conclusion: For the foregoing reasons, Grass Roots of South Carolina, Inc. respectfully requests that this Court affirm the judgment of the Court of Appeals.

Gun Owners of America, Inc., Gun Owners Foundation, Maryland Shall Issue, Inc., Virginia Citizens Defense League, Gun Owners Of California, Inc., Lincoln Institute For Research And Education, and Conservative Legal Defense And Education Fund

I. The Court should address only the precise firearms issues before it, not firearms laws generally as the Solicitor General has urged

II. The Second Amendment secures the individual and unalienable right of the American people to keep and bear arms

A. The Bill of Rights, as a whole, rests upon the governing principle that the people embody the nation's sovereignty

B. The individual right of the people to keep and bear arms is ultimately necessary to secure the uniquely American right of the sovereign people to reconstitute their government

C. The right of the people to keep and bear arms is an individual right, not a state's right to arm its militia

D. The American Revolution was precipitated by threats to the colonists' right to keep and bear arms

III. The challenged D.C. code provisions impermissibly infringe on Respondent's protected Second Amendment right to the private ownership and use of a handgun in his home

A. The Amendment's preamble establishes the standard of review

B. D.C. code provisions impermissibly classify persons eligible to possess a firearm

C. D.C. code provisions impermissibly classify weaponry

Conclusion: For the foregoing reasons, the decision of the United States Court of Appeals for the District of Columbia Circuit should be affirmed.

The Heartland Institute

I. The Second Amendment manifests the right of self-defense that American law has always embraced

A. English antecedents

B. Philosophical underpinnings

C. The Federalist debates

D. Early interpretations of the Second Amendment

E. Early state constitutional provisions

F. Early state case law

II. The Second Amendment prohibits unreasonable interference with the right of individuals to possess, in their homes, arms commonly used for self defense

A. The *Miller* framework provides the starting point for modern Second Amendment jurisprudence

B. The Self-Defense Test

C. The Self-Defense Test permits reasonable regulation

III. The challenged laws violate the Second Amendment as unreasonable interferences with the individual right to possess arms commonly used for self-defense

A. The District's gun control laws effectively outlaw private handgun ownership

B. Handguns are the epitome of arms commonly used for self-defense

C. The District's limited allowance for shotguns and rifles cannot shield its handgun ban from constitutional challenge

D. The link between handguns and crime is a constitutional red herring

E. The District's handgun ban should be struck down in this proceeding; remand is not necessary here

Conclusion: The court should affirm the judgment below.

The Institute for Justice

I. The history and adoption of the Fourteenth Amendment is a valuable and proper source for construing the right to keep and bear arms protected by the Second Amendment

II. The history and adoption of the Fourteenth Amendment confirms and establishes that the right to keep and bear arms is an individual right

A. State violation of freedmen's right to keep and bear arms was a central evil to be remedied by the Fourteenth Amendment

B. Legislative responses to Southern recalcitrance and violations of the right to keep and bear arms

C. The Fourteenth Amendment and enforcement of the Second Amendment against the states

D. Lessons from the background, history, and adoption of the Fourteenth Amendment

III. Incorporation and the Second Amendment in the Supreme Court

Conclusion: For the reasons above, this Court should affirm the judgment of the Court of Appeals for the District of Columbia Circuit.

The International Law Enforcement Educators And Trainers Association (ILEETA), The International Association Of Law Enforcement Firearms Instructors (IALEFI), Maryland State Lodge, Fraternal Order Of Police, Southern States Police Benevolent Association, 29 Elected California District Attorneys, San Francisco Veteran Police Officers Association, Long Beach Police Officers Association, Texas Police Chiefs Association, Texas Municipal Police Association, New York State Association Of Auxiliary Police, Mendocino County, Calif., Sheriff Thomas D. Allman, Oregon State Rep. Andy Olson, National Police Defense Foundation, Law Enforcement Alliance of America, and the Independence Institute

I. The efficacy and social benefits of armed self-defense
A. Burglary
B. Deterrence
C. The frequency of defensive gun use
D. Natural experiments
E. 911 is insufficient
F. Self-defense does not make victims worse off
G. Law enforcement benefits of citizen self-defense
II. The invidious conflation of law-abiding gun owners with incipient murderers
A. Domestic violence
B. Juveniles
C. Body count statistics
D. Accidents
III. Long guns are inadequate substitutes
IV. The handgun and self-defense bans violate precedent and original intent

Conclusion: "I don't intend to run this government around the moment of survival," declared D.C. Councilman David A. Clarke, chairman of the committee that created the handgun and self-defense ban. The Second Amendment forbids banning the tools of survival. Petitioners' dangerous laws deprive the public and law enforcement of the life-saving, crime reducing effects of gun ownership which are apparent in the 50 states.

International Scholars
I. A Fundamental Right to Self-Defense
A. The Common Law Tradition
B. International Law
II. International Comparisons
III. Foreign Gun Laws
A. Austrian Laws
1. Possession
2. Storage
3. Self-Defense
B. Canadian Laws
1. Possession
2. Storage
3. Self-Defense
C. French Laws
1. Possession
2. Storage
3. Self-Defense
D. German Laws
1. Possession

2. Storage
3. Self-Defense
E. Italian Laws
1. Possession
2. Storage
3. Self-Defense

Conclusion: Petitioners' firearm laws are an extreme departure from international norms, are not justified by any legitimate interest of Petitioners and infringe upon the fundamental right of self-defense. For the foregoing reasons, the decision below should be affirmed.

Jeanette M. Moll

I. Second Amendment as an individual right
A. Only "people" have rights, government has authority
B. The Second Amendment as a collective right results in the loss of an amendment in the Bill of Rights
II. A man's home is his castle
A. Governmental presence, whether tangible or intangible, has no place in our homes
B. English origins of the Fourth Amendment and the sanctity of one's home

Conclusion: For the reasons set forth above, the Court should affirm the judgment of the Court of Appeals.

Jews for the Preservation of Firearms Ownership

The Court should affirm the judgment of the Court of Appeals because an individual right to keep and bear arms, separate from state regulated militia service, is fundamental to prevent the risk of tyranny and genocide

Conclusion: For the foregoing reasons, the judgment of the Court of Appeals should be affirmed.

The President *Pro Tempore* of the Senate of Pennsylvania, Joseph B. Scarnati, III

I. Pennsylvania's constitutional history supports the existence of an individual right to bear arms in self-defense
A. The Pennsylvania Constitution
B. Pennsylvania Colonial History
1. Early Proprietorship
2. Quaker Aversion to a militia and Original Associator Movement
3. Early Stages of French & Indian War
4. 1755 Militia Act
5. End of French & Indian War, 1757 Militia Act, and role of Pennsylvania's earliest official fighting forces
6. Strife during interwar years
C. Revolutionary War onset
D. Development of 1776 Constitution
E. Actions of constitutional government and remainder of the Revolutionary War
F. Pennsylvania's ratification of the U.S. Constitution and the dissent of the minority
II. Second Amendment adoption
III. The individual right to keep firearms for self-defense is as important today as ever

IV. The Second Amendment provides an individual, and fundamental, right to keep handguns and other firearms for self-defense

Conclusion: *Amicus curiae* requests that this Court affirm the decision of the U.S. Court of Appeals for the District of Columbia Circuit.

The Libertarian National Committee, Inc.

I. The Solicitor General misinterprets the standard it proposes

II. The standard proposed is and should be restricted to the unique area of regulation of certain electoral activities

III. Even if the proposed standard were adopted, the appropriate result would be affirmance, not remand

Conclusion: The Solicitor General cites certain precedent of this court without noting that they are applicable only to a narrow subset of first amendment situations – those involving access to the ballot. This, in turn, involves the unique situation in which a first amendment right can only be exercised, in a practical manner, with extensive government regulation. Even if those standards were applied here, strict scrutiny would be required, and the ruling below therefore affirmed. To Americans of the framing period, the Second Amendment was no "second class right." On the contrary, St. George tucker described it as "the true palladium of liberty." *Blackstone's Commentaries, With Notes Of Reference To The Constitution And Laws* 300 (1803). Its infringement here, by an ordinance outlawing possession of a large class of arms by citizens, no matter how law-abiding, clearly requires strict scrutiny.

The ruling of the District of Columbia circuit should be affirmed.

Liberty Legal Institute

I. Introduction

II. An outright ban on traditional firearms is the equivalent of an unconstitutional ban on all First Amendment activity

III. The regulation of core Second Amendment rights demands the same exacting scrutiny, strict scrutiny, as the regulation of core political or religious speech

IV. Weapons beyond the scope of this case should not serve as a basis for lowering the standard of scrutiny for all bans on firearms

Conclusion: The D.C. Circuit, in keeping with the limited issues presented in *Parker*, provided a precedent-rich analysis helpful for determining both the nature of the "arms" covered by the Second Amendment and the proper response to an outright ban on any of these arms. Amici encourage the Court to draw upon its vast experience in First Amendment jurisprudence to inform its analysis and formulation of the legal framework for resolving this case. The Court should affirm that the Second Amendment secures the individual right to own and use firearms and affirm the court below.

Major General John D. Altenburg, Jr., Lieutenant General Charles E. Dominy, Lieutenant General Tom Fields, Lieutenant General Jay M. Garner, General Ronald H. Griffith, General William H. Hartzog, Lieutenant General Ronald V. Hite, Major General John. G. Meyer, Jr., Honorable Joe R. Reeder, Lieutenant General Dutch Shoffner, General John Tilelli, And The American Hunters And Shooters Association

I. Military pre-training is critical to the national defense

A. Marksmanship facilitates military training

1. The framers of the Second Amendment inherited a tradition of legally mandated pre-induction weapons training
2. Colonial America emulated the English experience and promoted small arms proficiency among its citizens
B. Congress promotes small-arms marksmanship among the civilian population
1. Congress creates the civilian small-arms marksmanship training programs
2. Training and marksmanship programs prove highly successful
II. The District of Columbia gun law impedes small-arms training and undermines military preparedness
III. The District of Columbia gun law impedes the federal government's function of training citizens for national defense and therefore, is barred by the D.C. home rule act

Conclusion: For the foregoing reasons, the judgment below should be affirmed.

Maricopa County Attorney's Office and Other Prosecutor Agencies

I. Speculation on how this Court's decision may impact existing regulations on firearms is irrelevant
II. The Second Amendment protects an individual right to keep and bear arms
A. Textual analysis of the operative and prefatory clauses, in tandem, supports the adoption of the individual rights model
1. The operative clause
2. The prefatory clause
B. Historically, and as construed by this court in *Miller*, the term "militia" as used in the Second Amendment presupposed that militia-members would arm themselves
III. Not only is the right individual, it is fundamental; laws infringing the right should therefore be subject to strict scrutiny
A. The right to bear arms is "deeply rooted in the nation's history"
B. Its inclusion within the Bill of Rights is also significant
IV. Recognition of the right as individual, fundamental and subject to heightened scrutiny does not threaten the validity of all gun control regulations
V. D.C. code §§ 7-2502.02(a)(4), 22-4504(a), and 7-2507.02 do not pass constitutional muster
A. D.C. Code § 7-2507.02
B. D.C. Code § 22-4504
C. D.C. Code § 7-2507.02

Conclusion: For these reasons, the Maricopa County Attorney's Office and the other amici prosecutor agencies request that this Court affirm the decision of the D.C. Circuit below.

55 Members of United States Senate, the President of the United States Senate, and 250 Members of United States House Of Representatives

I. Original intent and early interpretation
A. The Text: Rights of the People vs. State Powers
B. Drafting the Amendment in 1789
C. The Freedmen's Bureau Act of 1866
II. Continuation of a consistent reading
A. Regulation in the District of Columbia
B. The Property Requisition Act of 1941
C. The Firearms Owners' Protection Act of 1986
III. Legislation in the 21st century

A. Protection of Lawful Commerce in Arms Act
B. Disaster Relief & Emergency Assistance Act Amendment
C. The D.C. Personal Protection Act Bill
IV. A handgun ban is unreasonable on its face, rendering a remand for further proceedings unnecessary

Conclusion: This Court should affirm the judgment of the Court of Appeals.

[Editors Note: The members of Congress joining this brief included <u>Senators</u> A. Wayne Allard (CO, R), John A. Barrasso (WY, R), Max S. Baucus (MT, D), Robert F. Bennett (UT, R), Christopher S. Bond (MO, R), Samuel D. Brownback (KS, R), James P. D. Bunning (KY, R), Richard M. Burr (NC, R), Robert P. Casey, Jr. (PA, D), C. Saxby Chambliss (GA, R), Thomas A. Coburn (OK, R), W. Thad Cochran (MS, R), Norman Coleman, Jr. (MN, R), Susan M. Collins (ME, R), Robert P. Corker, Jr. (TN, R), John Cornyn, III (TX, R), Larry E. Craig (ID, R), Michael D. Crapo (ID, R), James W. DeMint (SC, R), Elizabeth H. Dole (NC, R), Pete V. Domenici (NM, R), Michael B. Enzi (WY, R), Russell D. Feingold (WI, D), Lindsey O. Graham (SC, R), Charles E. Grassley (IA, R), Judd A. Gregg (NH, R), Charles T. Hagel (NE, R), Orrin G. Hatch (UT, R), Kay Bailey Hutchison (TX, R), James M. Inhofe (OK, R), John H. Isakson (GA, R), Timothy P. Johnson (SD, D), Jon L. Kyl (AZ, R), Blanche L. Lincoln (AR, D), Melquiades R. Martinez (FL, R), John S. McCain, III (AZ, R), A. Mitchell McConnell (KY, R), Lisa A. Murkowski (AK, R), E. Benjamin Nelson (NE, D), C. Patrick Roberts (KS, R), Kenneth L. Salazar (CO, D), Jefferson B. Sessions, III (AL, R), Richard C. Shelby (AL, R), Gordon H. Smith (OR, R), Olympia J. Snowe (ME, R), Arlen Specter (PA, R), Theodore F. Stevens (AK, R), John E. Sununu (NH, R), Jon Tester (MT, D), John R. Thune (SD, R), David B. Vitter (LA, R), George V. Voinovich (OH, R), James H. Webb, Jr. (VA, D) and Roger F. Wicker (MS, R); and <u>Representatives</u> Robert B. Aderholt (AL-04, R), W. Todd Akin (MO-2, R), Rodney M. Alexander (LA-5, R), Jason Altmire (PA-4, D), Michael A. Arcuri (NY-24, D), Joe Baca (CA-43, D), Michele M. Bachmann (MN-6, R), Spencer T. Bachus, III (AL-6, R), Brian Baird (WA-3, D), Richard H. Baker (LA-6, R), J. Gresham Barrett (SC-3, R), John J. Barrow (GA-12, D), Roscoe G. Bartlett (MD-6, R), Joe L. Barton (TX-6, R), Marion Berry (AR-1, D), Judith B. Biggert (IL-13, R), Brian P. Bilbray (CA-50, R), Gus M. Bilirakis (FL-9, R), Robert W. Bishop (UT-1, R), Sanford D. Bishop (GA-2, D), Marsha W. Blackburn (TN-7, R), Roy D. Blunt (MO-7, R), John A. Boehner (OH-8, R), Josiah R. Bonner, Jr. (AL-1, R), Mary Bono Mack (CA-45, R), John N. Boozman (AR-3, R), D. Daniel Boren (OK-2, D), Leonard L. Boswell (IA-3, D), Frederick C. Boucher (VA-9, D), Charles W. Boustany, Jr. (LA-7, R), F. Allen Boyd, Jr. (FL-2, D), Nancy Boyda (KS-2, D), Kevin P. Brady (TX-8, R), Paul C. Broun (GA-10, R), Henry E. Brown, Jr. (SC-1, R), Virginia Brown-Waite (FL-5, R), Vernon G. Buchanan (FL-13, R), Michael C. Burgess (TX-26, R), Danny L. Burton (IN-5, R), Stephen E. Buyer (IN-4, R), Kenneth S. Calvert (CA-44, R), David L. Camp (MI-4, R), John B. T. Campbell, III (CA-48, R), Christopher B. Cannon (UT-3, R), Eric I. Cantor (VA-7, R), Shelley M. Capito (WV-2, R), Dennis A. Cardoza (CA-18, D), Christopher P. Carney (PA-10, D), John R. Carter (TX-31, R), Steven J. Chabot (OH-1, R), A. Benjamin Chandler, III (KY-6, D), J. Howard Coble (NC-6, R), Stephen I. Cohen (TN-9, D), Thomas J. Cole (OK-4, R), K. Michael Conaway (TX-11, R), James H. S. Cooper (TN-5, D), Joseph D. Courtney (CT-2, D), Jerry F. Costello (IL-12, D), Robert E. Cramer, Jr. (AL-5, D), Ander Crenshaw (FL-4, R), Barbara L. Cubin (WY-AL, R), R. Enrique Cuellar (TX-28, D), John A. Culberson (TX-7, R), Artur G. Davis (AL-7, D), David Davis (TN-1, R), Geoffrey C. Davis (KY-4, R), Lincoln E. Davis (TN-4, D), Thomas M. Davis, III (VA-11, R), J. Nathan Deal (GA-9, R), Peter A. DeFazio (OR-4, D), Charles W. Dent (PA-15, R), Lincoln Diaz-Balart (FL-21, R), Mario Diaz-Balart (FL-25, R), John D. Dingell

(MI-15, D), Joseph S. Donnelly (IN-2, D), John T. Doolittle (CA-4, R), David T. Dreier (CA-26, R), Thelma D. Drake (VA-2, R), John J. Duncan, Jr. (TN-2, R), T. Chester Edwards (TX-17, D), Brad Ellsworth (IN-8, D), Jo Ann H. Emerson (MO-8, R), Philip S. English (PA-3, R), R. Terry Everett (AL-2, R), Mary C. Fallin (OK-5, R), Thomas C. Feeney, III (FL-24, R), Jeff Flake (AZ-6, R), J. Randy Forbes (VA-4, R), Jeffrey L. Fortenberry (NE-1, R), Virginia A. Foxx (NC-5, R), Trent Franks (AZ-2, R), Elton W. Gallegly (CA-24, R), E. Scott Garrett (NJ-5, R), James W. Gerlach (PA-6, R), Gabrielle Giffords (AZ-8, D), Kirsten R. Gillibrand (NY-20, D), J. Phillip Gingrey (GA-11, R), Louis B. Gohmert, Jr. (TX-1, R), Virgil H. Goode, Jr. (VA-5, R), Robert W. Goodlatte (VA-6, R), Barton J. Gordon (TN-6, D), Kay M. Granger (TX-12, R), Samuel B. Graves, Jr. (MO-6, R), R. Eugene Green (TX-29, D), Ralph M. Hall (TX-4, R), Richard N. Hastings (WA-4, R), Robin C. Hayes (NC-8, R), Dean Heller (NV-2, R), T. Jeb Hensarling (TX-5, R), Walter W. Herger (CA-2, R), Stephanie M. Herseth Sandlin (SD-AL, D), Brian M. Higgins (NY-27, D), Baron P. Hill (IN-9, D), David L. Hobson (OH-7, R), Paul W. Hodes (NH-2, D), Peter Hoekstra (MI-2, R), T. Timothy Holden (PA-17, D), Kenny C. Hulshof (MO-9, R), Duncan L. Hunter (CA-52, R), Robert D. Inglis (SC-4, R), Darrell E. Issa (CA-49, R), R. Samuel Johnson (TX-3, R), Timothy V. Johnson (IL-15, R), Walter B. Jones, Jr. (NC-3, R), James D. Jordan (OH-4, R), Steven L. Kagen (WI-8, D), Paul E. Kanjorski (PA-11, D), Richard A. Keller (FL-8, R), Ronald J. Kind (WI-3, D), Steven A. King (IA-5, R), John H. Kingston (GA-1, R), John P. Kline, Jr. (MN-2, R), Joseph C. Knollenberg (MI-9, R), J. Randy Kuhl, Jr. (NY-29, R), Douglas L. Lamborn (CO-5, R), Nicholas V. Lampson (TX-22, D), Thomas P. Latham (IA-4, R), Steven C. LaTourette (OH-14, R), Robert E. Latta (OH-5, R), C. Jeremy Lewis (CA-41, R), Ron E. Lewis (KY-2, R), John E. Linder (GA-7, R), Frank D. Lucas (OK-3, R), Daniel E. Lungren (CA-3, R), Cornelius H. McGillicuddy, IV (FL-14, R), Timothy E. Mahoney (FL-16, D), Donald A. Manzullo (IL-16, R), Kenny E. Marchant (TX-24, R), James C. Marshall (GA-8, D), James D. Matheson (UT-2, D), Kevin O. McCarthy (CA-22, R), Michael T. McCaul (TX-10, R), Thaddeus G. McCotter (MI-11, R), James O. McCrery, III (LA-4, R), Patrick T. McHenry (NC-10, R), John M. McHugh (NY-23, R), D. Carmichael McIntyre, II (NC-7, D), Howard P. McKeon (CA-25, R), Cathy McMorris Rodgers (WA-5, R), Malcolm R. Melancon (LA-3, D), John L. Mica (FL-7, R), Michael H. Michaud (ME-2, D), Candice S. Miller (MI-10, R), Gary G. Miller (CA-42, R), Jefferson B. Miller (FL-1, R), Harry E. Mitchell (AZ-5, D), Alan B. Mollohan (WV-1, D), Jerry Moran (KS-1, R), Timothy F. Murphy (PA-18, R), John P. Murtha, Jr. (PA-12, D), Marilyn N. Musgrave (CO-4, R), Sue W. Myrick (NC-9, R), Robert R. Neugebauer (TX-19, R), Devin G. Nunes (CA-21, R), James L. Oberstar (MN-8, D), Solomon P. Ortiz (TX-27, D), Ronald E. Paul (TX-14, R), Stevan E. Pearce (NM-2, R), Michael R. Pence (IN-6, R), Collin C. Peterson (MN-7, D), John E. Peterson (PA-5, R), Thomas E. Petri (WI-6, R), Charles W. Pickering, Jr. (MS-3, R), Joseph R. Pitts (PA-16, R), Todd R. Platts (PA-19, R), L. Ted Poe (TX-2, R), Earl R. Pomeroy (ND-AL, D), Jon C. Porter, Sr. (NV-3, R), Thomas E. Price (GA-6, R), Deborah D. Pryce (OH-15, R), Adam H. Putnam (FL-12, R), George P. Radanovich (CA-19, R), Nick J. Rahall, II (WV-3, D), Dennis R. Rehberg (MT-AL, R), David G. Reichert (WA-8, R), Richard G. Renzi (AZ-1, R), Silvestre Reyes (TX-16, D), Thomas M. Reynolds (NY-26, R), Ciro D. Rodriguez (TX-23, D), Harold D. Rogers (KY-5, R), Michael D. Rogers (AL-3, R), Michael J. Rogers (MI-8, R), Dana T. Rohrabacher (CA-46, R), Peter J. Roskam (IL-6, R), Ileana C. Ros-Lehtinen (FL-18, R), Michael A. Ross (AR-4, D), Edward R. Royce (CA-40, R), Paul D. Ryan (WI-1, R), Timothy J. Ryan (OH-17, D), John T. Salazar (CO-3, D), William T. Sali (ID-1, R), Jean Schmidt (OH-2, R), F. James Sensenbrenner, Jr. (WI-5, R), Peter A. Sessions (TX-32, R), John B. Shadegg (AZ-3, R), John M. Shimkus (IL-

19, R), J. Heath Shuler (NC-11, D), William F. Shuster (PA-9, R), Michael K. Simpson (ID-2, R), Adrian M. Smith (NE-3, R), Lamar S. Smith (TX-21, R), Mark E. Souder (IN-3, R), Zachary T. Space (OH-18, D), Clifford B. Stearns (FL-6, R), Bart T. Stupak (MI-1, D), John M. Sullivan (OK-1, R), Thomas G. Tancredo (CO-6, R), John S. Tanner (TN-8, D), G. Eugene Taylor (MS-4, D), Lee R. Terry (NE-2, R), W. McClellan Thornberry (TX-13, R), W. Todd Tiahrt (KS-4, R), Patrick J. Tiberi (OH-12, R), Michael R. Turner (OH-3, R), Frederick S. Upton (MI-6, R), Timothy Walberg (MI-7, R), Gregory P. Walden (OR-2, R), James T. Walsh (NY-25, R), Timothy J. Walz (MN-1, D), Zachary P. Wamp (TN-3, R), David J. Weldon, Jr. (FL-15, R), Gerald C. Weller (IL-11, R), Lynn A. Westmoreland (GA-3, R), W. Edward Whitfield (KY-1, R), Charles A. Wilson (OH-6, D), Heather A. Wilson (NM-1, R), Addison G. Wilson (SC-2, R), Robert J. Wittman (VA-1, R), Frank R. Wolf (VA-10, R), Donald E. Young (AK-A).]

Mountain States Legal Foundation

I. The philosophical underpinnings of the Second Amendment include the right to self-defense and the ability to guard against government tyranny

II. These philosophical underpinnings of the Second Amendment are satisfied only if the right to keep and bear arms is an individual right

III. The values underlying the Second Amendment are present in the history, culture, and jurisprudence of the American West

A. The possession and use of arms for self-defense is of fundamental importance in the history and culture of the West

B. The possession and use of arms as a defense against tyranny to preserve individual liberty is a fundamental value in Western history and culture

C. The possession and use of arms for self-defense and defense against tyranny to preserve individual liberty is viewed as a fundamental right in Western culture, as evidenced by arms jurisprudence

Conclusion: The judgment of the Court of Appeals should be affirmed.

The National Rifle Association and the NRA Civil Rights Defense Fund

I. The Second Amendment guarantees an individual right to keep and bear arms

II. Laws infringing Second Amendment rights should be subject to strict scrutiny and facial invalidation where overly broad

III. The District's handgun ban and licensing and trigger-lock provisions are unconstitutional infringements of Second Amendment rights

Conclusion: For the foregoing reasons, the holding of the D.C. Circuit should be affirmed.

The National Shooting Sports Foundation, Inc.

I. Firearms were a principal and ubiquitous tool of survival in colonial America

II. The British tried and failed to disarm the colonists during the American Revolution

A. At the earliest hostilities, colonists asserted their pre-existing individual right to keep and bear arms

B. Britain tried to subdue Boston by disarming its residents

C. Colonists outside Massachusetts successfully resisted disarmament

III. Because the Second Amendment derives from the Americans' refusal to be disarmed, it must be read to protect an individual's right to keep and bear arms

A. The Constitution's "militia clause" renewed fears of disarmament

B. Seeking to allay fears of disarmament, Federalists argued that the Constitution
   would not permit disarmament of "the people"
C. The Second Amendment was proposed and designed to guarantee individuals
   their right to keep and bear arms

Conclusion: In accordance with the intent of the framers that the Second
Amendment protect an individual right to "keep and bear arms," this Court should
affirm the decision below of the United States Court of Appeals for the District of
Columbia Circuit.

The Paragon Foundation, Inc.

I. "The right of the people" to keep and bear arms existed before the formation of
   any government and exists not because of government but is preserved by it
II. The Second Amendment must be interpreted in conjunction with the historical
    use of arms by individuals for self-defense, hunting, and other practical purposes
III. An individual right to keep and bear arms is good public policy

Conclusion: The Court should affirm the judgment of the Court of Appeals.

Pink Pistols and Gays and Lesbians for Individual Liberty

I. The Second Amendment guarantees LGBT individuals the right to keep and bear
   arms to protect themselves in their homes
A. Recognition of an individual right to keep and bear arms is literally a matter of
   life or death for members of the LGBT community
B. The police have no duty to protect and do not adequately protect LGBT
   individuals from hate violence that occurs in their homes
II. LGBT individuals have a Second Amendment right to possess firearms to protect
    themselves from hate violence in their homes
A. The Bill of Rights protects the rights of individuals from governmental
   encroachment
B. The Second Amendment guarantees the right to possess firearms for self-defense
C. The Second Amendment guarantees the right to possess firearms in one's home
III. The Second Amendment must recognize an individual right of "the people" to
     avoid disqualifying LGBT individuals from any enjoyment of that right
A. If the right recognized in the Second Amendment is conditioned upon
   membership in state and Congressionally regulated military forces, LGBT
   individuals, and others, are excluded from the right to bear arms
B. Because the government defines eligibility for service in regulated military
   forces, interpreting the Second Amendment as a right conditioned upon
   membership in a regulated military force, prevents the Amendment from
   constraining government action
C. Conditioning Second Amendment rights upon membership in a regulated
   military force, which excludes LGBT and other individuals from enjoying the
   right to self-defense, is contrary to the intentions of the framers

Conclusion: For the foregoing reasons, *amicus* respectfully request that this Court
affirm the decision of the Court of Appeals and confirm that LGBT individuals have
a Second Amendment right to keep firearms in their homes for their own self-
protection.

Retired Military Officers

I. The District's "states' rights" view of the Second Amendment is inconsistent with
   its place in the Constitutional plan

II. The right to individual ownership of firearms protected by the Second Amendment is essential to national defense
A. The United States military benefits from the ability to recruit from a pool of civilians experienced in the use of firearms
1. Military recruits with firearms training and experience make better soldiers
2. The United States government has a long history of promoting civilian firearms ownership and training
3. Handgun training is beneficial to military effectiveness and national defense
B. Armed civilians are an effective deterrent to and defense against foreign invasion
1. The American experience
2. The Swiss example

Conclusion: For all of these reasons, the judgment of the Court of Appeals should be affirmed.

The Rutherford Institute

I. The framers of the Constitution intended the Second Amendment to apply to individuals to serve as a guarantor against tyrannical government
II. The militarization of police forces represents a modern-day standing army
III. African-American experiences show the necessity of the individual right to bear arms
A. Historical abuses
B. Modern-day abuses

Conclusion: The District of Columbia's ban on handguns strikes at the very heart of the fundamental right of the individual—enshrined in the Second Amendment—to keep and bear arms. To argue or insinuate that the Second Amendment is only a collective right is a grave misreading of the Framers' intentions, while subverting the very basis upon which our rights as a free people depends.

For the aforementioned reasons, therefore, the Court should affirm Respondent's claim and uphold the Court of Appeals for the District of Columbia's ruling.

Second Amendment Foundation

I. Petitioners' interpretation of the Second Amendment is untenable, and the legal test suggested in *United States v. Miller* is unworkable
II. The text of the Second Amendment establishes that the Constitutional right extends beyond militia-related weapons and activities
A. The grammatical structure of the Second Amendment does not imply that the purpose of the Constitutional right is limited to fostering a well regulated militia
B. The term "bear Arms" in the Second Amendment's operative clause does not imply that the Amendment has an exclusively military purpose
C. "The people" referred to in the Second Amendment has always been a much larger body of individuals than the militia
III. The nature and history of the Second Amendment confirm that its purpose cannot be confined to fostering a well regulated militia
A. The Second Amendment contributes to a well regulated militia by preventing a specific misuse of Congress' Article I authorities, including its authority to regulate the militia
B. The Second Amendment's background and drafting history confirm that the Constitutional right is not limited to militia-related purposes
C. This Court has recognized that the Constitution contains declaratory language that does not change the legal effects that the Constitution would have had without that language

IV. The purpose of the Second Amendment includes protection of the fundamental natural right of self defense against criminal violence

Conclusion: The judgment of the Court of Appeals should be affirmed.

Southeastern Legal Foundation, Inc., Second Amendment Sisters, Inc., Women Against Gun Control, 60 Plus Association, Inc., Robert B. Smith, J.D., Christie Davies, M.A., Ph.D., Joe Michael Cobb, and Mrs. Minnie Lee Faulkner

I. The brief 's structure

II. Empirical research illustrates the use of the individual right of armed self-defense embodied in the Second Amendment for the benefit of women, the elderly and the physically disabled

A. Empirical research supports the common sense argument that the use of handguns protects women, the elderly and the physically disabled from greater physical threat

B. The amici curiae brief filed by violence policy center in support of appellants incorrectly characterizes the value of the handgun as an effective means of self-defense

III. The historical context of the Second Amendment conclusively demonstrates the preexisting right of personal armed self-defense

Iv. Anecdotal evidence and declarations illustrate the critical importance of the individual right of armed self-defense embodied in the Second Amendment for women, the elderly and the physically disabled

A. Recent anecdotes effectively illustrate the importance of the personal right of armed self-defense for women, the elderly and the physically disabled

1. Home invasions

2. Parking lot incidents

B. Nancy Hart and Minnie Lee Faulkner: historical and present day illustrations of how firearms deter assailants

1. Nancy Hart: revolutionary war notable used firearms for personal and family security

2. Minnie Lee Faulkner: a modern illustration that the use of a firearm deters an attacker

Conclusion: For the foregoing reasons, Southeastern Legal Foundation, Inc., Second Amendment Sisters, Inc., Women Against Gun Control, 60 Plus Association, Inc., Professor Robert B. Smith, Dr. Christie Davies, Professor Joe Michael Cobb and Minnie Lee Faulkner respectfully submit that the judgment of the Court of Appeals should be affirmed.

State Firearm Associations

I. The private possession of firearms was functionally significant to the founding of the United States

II. The Constitution, together with the Bill of Rights, represents a profound national commitment to both individual liberty and state sovereignty

A. The federal government is a government of limited powers that do not include the power to directly regulate firearm ownership or possession

B. The Bill of Rights, as a whole, further reaffirmed Congress' confinement to the areas of specific authority enumerated in Article I, Section 8

C. The Second Amendment simply confirmed a right that already existed

III. This Court and Congress have both recognized the limits to federal power

A. This court's precedent forecloses a wandering application of the commerce power in this arena

B. Congress' limited role in regulating the private ownership of firearms is an historic fact

IV. Congress has acknowledged its role of supporting private ownership of firearms among the citizenry

V. The federal government's power over the District of Columbia is subject to specific constitutional limitations

Conclusion: For the foregoing reasons, the decision of the court below should be affirmed.

The states of Texas, Alabama, Alaska, Arkansas , Colorado , Florida, Georgia, Idaho, Indiana, Kansas, Kentucky, Louisiana, Michigan, Minnesota, Mississippi, Missouri, Montana, Nebraska, New Hampshire, New Mexico, North Dakota, Ohio, Oklahoma, Pennsylvania, South Carolina, South Dakota, Utah, Virginia, Washington, West Virginia, and Wyoming

I. The Court of Appeals correctly held that the Second Amendment guarantees an individual right to keep and bear arms

A. The Second Amendment's text guarantees an individual right to keep and bear arms

1. The "right of the people" is an individual right

2. The District misinterprets the meaning of "keep" and "bear arms"

3. The Second Amendment's introductory clause does not convert an individual right into a "collective" or "quasi-collective" right

B. The Court's precedent supports the principle that the Second Amendment guarantees an individual right

C. The weight of scholarly commentary also supports the conclusion that the Second Amendment guarantees an individual right to keep and bear arms

D. The Second Amendment's history demonstrates that it guarantees an individual right to arms

II. The Court of Appeals correctly held that the District of Columbia's firearms regulations are unconstitutional

A. The Court of Appeals's decision should be affirmed because statutes effectively prohibiting any citizen from keeping and bearing "arms" are unconstitutional

1. The D.C. code provisions concern "arms" protected under the Second Amendment

2. The Court of Appeals correctly concluded that the District's statutes are unconstitutional

B. The Court of Appeals's decision should be affirmed because the District's firearms prohibitions also cannot withstand scrutiny under the standard of review recommended by the United States

C. The unreasonableness of the District's statutory scheme is further evidenced by the fact that it runs counter to the regulatory approach of all fifty states

III. None of the federal firearms regulations discussed in the United States's brief is jeopardized by the Court of Appeals's decision

Conclusion: The Court should affirm the judgment of the Court of Appeals.

Virginia1774.org

The Second Amendment to the United States Constitution is a self-executing provision that preserves both a well regulated militia and the right of the people or individuals to keep and bear arms for their own self-defense, self-preservation, or any other lawful purpose

A. The People are the militia

B. The individual right to keep and bear arms

Conclusion: For all the foregoing reasons, *Amicus Curiae*, Virginia1774.org respectfully submits that this Court should affirm the judgment of United States Court of Appeals District of Columbia Circuit below.

126 Women State Legislators And Academics

I. The time has long passed when social conditions mandated that all women equally depend upon the protection of men for their physical security

A. The defense of women as men's sole prerogative and responsibility

B. Changing demographics heighten the need for many women to provide their own physical security

II. Equal protection in Washington, D.C. now means that women are equally free to defend themselves from physical assault without the most effective means to truly equalize gender-based physical differences

A. Violence against women in the District of Columbia and the District's response

B. The benefits of handguns for women facing grave threat

C. Women may not depend upon the District's law enforcement services

D. Congress speaks: the Violence Against Women Act of 1994

III. Gender characteristics should at least be considered before barring law-abiding women handguns, the most suitable means for their self-protection

Conclusion: Upholding the lower court's decision will not eliminate sexual discrimination as it manifests itself most forcefully in violence against women. No ruling from this Court or any legislation should be expected to accomplish that. Moreover, many women will choose not to exercise the right to own a firearm. Even fewer will be presented the agonizing decision to actually use a handgun in the defense of themselves or their children. A large segment of women were likewise averse, moderately supportive or even downright indifferent to female suffrage and women's reproductive choice. However, the fact that only some will choose to exercise their right to self-defense should in no way prove a legal impediment to those women for whom owning a firearm is necessary to their ability to determine the course of their lives and consequently their place in society. The Court should therefore consider the effect the District's handgun ban has on women who have no other significant options when facing a life and death situation. While the basis of the Court's decision should of course revolve around its determination that the Second Amendment guarantees for all D.C. residents the ability to own a handgun in their own homes, this case presents a special opportunity for the Court to advance its gender-related jurisprudence. *Amicae* therefore pray that the Court upholds the decision of the Court of Appeals for the District of Columbia.

Briefs for the Petitioner, District of Columbia and Mayor Adrian M. Fenty: The Anti-Rights Positions

The American Academy of Pediatrics, the Society for Adolescent Medicine, the Children's Defense Fund, Women Against Gun Violence and Youth Alive!

I. Handguns are more lethal than other types of firearms and are particularly dangerous to children and youth

A. Handguns in the home are deadly to children

B. The District of Columbia handgun law is a reasonable restriction because children cannot be taught gun safety

C. The District of Columbia handgun law is a reasonable restriction because handguns make suicide more likely and suicide-attempts more injurious to children and adolescents

D. The District of Columbia's handgun law is a reasonable restriction because handguns increase the likelihood and deadliness of accidents involving children

E. The District of Columbia handgun law is a reasonable restriction because firearms and especially handguns increase homicide and nonfatal assault rates among America's youth

II. Comparing the experience of children and youth in foreign countries

III. The District's handgun law is a reasonable restriction because of the economic, societal and psychological costs of handgun violence upon children

Conclusion: Because of the proven harm attributable to handguns and especially because of the unique risk handguns create for children and adolescents, the District of Columbia reasonably enacted legislation to mitigate a pervasive public health crisis. The reasonableness of the District of Columbia's attempt to preserve the public's health is confirmed by both domestic and foreign data. Neither the precedents of this Court, nor the intention of the framers of the Constitution support striking down the District of Columbia's ordinance. These *amici* respectfully request that the judgment of the Court of Appeals be reversed and judgment be entered for petitioners.

The American Bar Association

I. The decision below undermines the rule of law by failing to provide special justifications for abandoning consistent and longstanding precedent upon which legislators, regulators, and the public have relied

A. The decision below conflicts with a vast body of precedent

B. The decision below jeopardizes an extensive regulatory framework that was predicated on longstanding judicial precedent

1. Federal legislation on firearms

2. State and local firearm regulations

II. The determinations required by the decision below would compound the disruption of the regulatory system developed in reliance on judicial precedent

A. The decision below does not create an objective, reliable, and intelligible definition of "arms"

B. The decision below will entangle courts in factual and policy determinations more appropriately left to state and local legislatures

Conclusion: The American Bar Association respectfully requests that the Court reverse the decision below.

American Public Health Association, American College of Preventive Medicine, American Trauma Society, and American Association of Suicidology

I. Public health research may be relevant to assessing the Constitutionality of the statutes at issue

II. Guns in the home increase the risk of suicide, homicide, and death from accidental shooting

A. Suicide risk is greater in homes with guns, and in communities with a higher prevalence of guns

B. Homicide risk is greater in homes with guns, and in communities with a higher prevalence of guns

C. The risk of death from accidental shooting is greater in homes with guns, and in communities with a higher prevalence of guns

III. The District of Columbia's laws banning most handguns and requiring safe storage of all firearms are consistent with public health research and data demonstrating the risks associated with handguns and the benefits of the laws themselves

A. Banning handguns in Washington D.C. appears to have reduced suicide and homicide rates, as handguns pose a particular public health risk

B. Safe storage practices appear to reduce gun deaths

Conclusion: As illustrated above, firearm-related homicide, suicide, and fatal accidental shootings are a major public health problem in the United States today. The public health approach seeks to illuminate policy options by examining the environmental, not just individual, causes of violence and injuries. State and local legislators must be able to respond to the science as it develops. We thus urge the Court to take the evidence presented in this brief into consideration as it analyzes these important legal issues.

Brady Center to Prevent Gun Violence, International Association of Chiefs of Police, Major Cities Chiefs, International Brotherhood of Police Officers, National Organization of Black Law Enforcement Executives, Hispanic American Police Command Officers Association, National Black Police Association, National Latino Peace Officers Association, School Safety Advocacy Council, and Police Executive Research Forum

I. The Second Amendment guarantees no right to possess firearms unless in connection with service in a state-regulated militia

A. Read to give meaning to all its words, the Amendment connects the right guaranteed to the well regulated militia

B. *United States v. Miller* establishes that the Amendment's expressed militia purpose limits the scope of the right guaranteed

C. The "well regulated militia" is an organized military force, not an unorganized collection of individuals

D. The phrase "keep and bear arms" has an exclusively military meaning

1. The Second Amendment was drafted to respond to anti-federalist fears that Congress would fail to arm the militia

2. Madison's initial proposal treated "bearing arms" as synonymous with "rendering military service"

3. The debates in the first Congress reflect the framers' view that the Second Amendment related only to militia use

4. The phrase "keep and bear arms" refers to possession and use of weapons for military purposes

E. The guarantee of the right to "the people" is entirely consistent with the "militia purpose" interpretation

II. The court should continue to entrust gun regulation to elected legislative bodies as it has for more than two hundred years

A. Federal, state, and local legislatures have regulated gun ownership in the interest of public safety since the founding

B. This court should exercise caution before giving the judiciary unprecedented authority over issues like gun control historically addressed by legislatures

Conclusion: For the foregoing reasons, the decision of the court below should be reversed.

The City Of Chicago and the Board Of Education of the City of Chicago

I. The Second Amendment should not be incorporated against the states

A. Because the Second Amendment is a federalism provision, it should not be incorporated against the states

1. The Second Amendment's text identifies it as a federalism provision

2. The Second Amendment's historical context confirms that it is a federalism provision

3. The practice of state and local governments for two centuries confirms the Second Amendment as a federalism provision

B. This court's selective-incorporation doctrine confirms that the Second Amendment should not apply to the states

1. The history of the Second Amendment demonstrates that any private right to own guns outside of a militia context is not fundamental

2. A private right for persons not associated with any state militia even arguably exists in the Constitution of at most one of the original states

3. Many later state constitutions do not preclude gun regulation, and state and local governments have implemented myriad gun control regulations with strong popular support

4. The federalist purpose of the Second Amendment further confirms that even if incorporation were a theoretical possibility, the court should nonetheless affirm Presser.

II. In any event, state or local handgun bans—and the District's handgun ban—are constitutional.

Conclusion: The judgment of the Court of Appeals should be reversed.

American Jewish Committee, Anti-Defamation League, Baptist Peace Fellowship of North America, Ceasefire NJ, Central Conference of American Rabbis, Citizens for a Safer Minnesota, Methodist Federation for Social Action, Clifton Kirkpatrick in his capacity as the stated Clerk of the Presbyterian Church (U.S.A.), Educational Fund to Stop Gun Violence, Freedom States Alliance, American Jewish Congress, Friends Committee on National Legislation, Gray Panthers, Gunfreekids.Org, Illinois Council Against Handgun Violence, Illinoisvictims.Org, Iowans for the Prevention of Gun Violence, Jenna Foundation for Nonviolence, Inc., Karla Zimmerman Memorial Foundation, National Association for the Advancement Of Colored People, National Council of Jewish Women, New England Coalition to Prevent Gun Violence, New Yorkers Against Gun Violence, DC Statehood Green Party, North Carolinians Against Gun Violence Education Fund, Ohio Coalition Against Gun Violence, Renée Olumbuni Rondeau Peace Foundation, Root (Reaching Out to Others Together) Inc., Union for Reform Judaism, Virginia Center for Public Safety, Wisconsin Anti-Violence Effort, and certain individual victims and families of victims of gun violence

I. The Second Amendment is rooted in the protection of individual liberty provided by federalism
A. Text and history confirm that the Second Amendment protects state autonomy by creating militia-related rights
1. Text and structure make clear that the Second Amendment is a militia-and federalism-based protection
2. The contemporaneous debates confirm the Second Amendment's purpose
II. Pre- and post-ratification events confirm that the Second Amendment embodies federalism principles
A. State laws enacted before and after the Second Amendment's adoption confirm that it reinforces federalism
B. The role of state militias in modern times cannot alter the Constitution's meaning
III. The practices of nations sharing our common-law heritage confirm the Second Amendment's unique roots in American federalism
A. England and Canada have handgun bans that closely parallel D.C.'s
B. Australia, New Zealand, and South Africa all strictly regulate firearms
Conclusion: The judgment of the Court of Appeals should be reversed.

DC Appleseed Center for Law and Justice, D.C. Chamber of Commerce, D.C. for Democracy, D.C. League of Women Voters, Federal City Council, and Washington Council of Lawyers

I. Any private right to keep and bear arms must be subject to reasonable regulation in furtherance of public safety
A. In reviewing regulations under the Second Amendment, the court should accord substantial deference to local officials' exercise of their police powers
B. The right to keep and bear arms has always been subject to reasonable regulation
C. Deference is warranted in light of the myriad different ways in which the possession, use, and safe handling of weapons may be regulated in the interests of public safety
II. The statutes at issue strike a reasonable balance between the exercise of the police power and any legitimate private right to self-defense in the home
A. There is no unlimited right to keep and bear any arms for any purpose
B. The District's regulation is reasonable because it restricts access to only one category of weapons while still permitting use of other firearms in self-defense if safely stored
Conclusion: For the foregoing reasons, and those set forth in the briefs of petitioners, the judgment of the Court of Appeals should be reversed.

District Attorneys

I. The Court should reverse the decision below
II. The Court should limit its opinion to the narrow question presented by the three D.C. statutes at issue
A. The Court should not unintentionally provoke constitutional challenges of criminal gun laws nationwide by introducing uncertainty into a well settled area of the law
1. Gun laws have been in effect for centuries
2. Criminal firearms laws have withstood repeated Second Amendment challenges in state and federal courts
3. An affirmance of the lower court's decision could generate substantial uncertainty and spur a wave of Second Amendment litigation nationwide

4. Constitutional challenges have already begun, and more are being planned
B. The Court should not needlessly hinder prosecutors' ability to enforce criminal firearms laws by injecting uncertainty about their constitutionality
C. The Court should tailor its opinion to the three D.C. code provisions at issue

Conclusion: For all the foregoing reasons, *Amici* respectfully submit that the decision below should be reversed and that the Court's opinion be strictly limited to the narrow question presented.

Former Department of Justice Officials

The Second Amendment does not protect firearms possession or use that is unrelated to participation in a well-regulated militia
A. Congress has enacted a series of statutes regulating firearms possession and use
B. For decades the Department of Justice maintained the position that the Second Amendment only prohibits those laws that interfere with the operation of a well-regulated militia
1. The government's brief in *United States v. Miller*
2. This Court's *Miller* decision
3. Post-*Miller* developments
C. The Office of Legal Counsel repeatedly took the position that the Second Amendment does not protect a right to keep and bear arms for private purposes
D. The Department of Justice changes its position
E. The Department's change in position was unjustified and unwise

Conclusion: The judgment of the Court of Appeals should be reversed.

Jack N. Rakove, Saul Cornell, David T. Konig, William J. Novak, Lois G. Schwoerer et al. (Historians)

Even after the parliamentary Bill of Rights of 1689 allowed certain classes of Protestant subjects to keep arms, British constitutional doctrine and practice subjected the limited right therein recognized to extensive legal regulation and limitation.
The first American Bills of Rights made no mention of a private right to keep arms
By proposing to transfer authority over the militia from the states to Congress, the Constitution radically challenged conventional republican thinking about the nature of the militia
Anti-Federalist objections to the Militia Clause preponderantly evoked the traditional fear of standing armies and its corollary endorsement of the value of the militia
Explicit Anti-Federalist references to a private right to arms were conspicuously few in number and failed to generate political support
James Madison's original draft of the Second Amendment does not support an individual rights interpretation
The final revisions of the Second Amendment reflected the Federalists' determination to preserve Congressional authority over the organization of the militia
The Second Amendment is best understood as an affirmation of federalism values, which helps to explain why the "insurrectionist" theory of its origins is fallacious
A historically-grounded analysis of what was actually debated in 1787-1789 can only conclude that the status of the militia was always what was in dispute, and not the private rights of individuals

Conclusion: For all the foregoing reasons, the judgment of the United States Court of Appeals for the District of Columbia should be reversed.

Major American Cities, The United States Conference of Mayors, and Legal Community Against Violence

I. America's cities face substantial costs from gun violence and must have the flexibility to regulate guns to protect against loss of life, threats to public safety, killing of police officers, and crippling health care and economic costs posed by certain types of guns and gun access

II. The Second Amendment does not limit the options available to cities to address the problem of gun violence

Conclusion: American cities need flexibility to respond to the serious threat of gun violence facing their communities. Although the Court need not address this issue in this case, nothing in the Second Amendment restrains the authority of States or their political subdivisions to meet this threat through the regulation of firearms within their borders. The Second Amendment applies to the federal government alone. It does not constrain firearms regulations in the District of Columbia or in the States or their political subdivisions. The Court of Appeals decision was in error and should be reversed.

Members of Congress

I. Interpretation of the Second Amendment to resolve this case should be informed by Congress's legislative activities and role as a constitutional interpreter

Ii. The decision below breaks with this Court's precedent and fails to accord appropriate deference to legislative judgments about the nature and boundaries of any rights conferred by the Second Amendment

A. The decision below is an unwarranted departure from this Court's precedent

B. Even if Second Amendment rights were implicated, the Court of Appeals failed to apply an appropriate level of scrutiny

C. Disputes regarding Second Amendment constraints on federal laws relating to the use or possession of "arms" generally should be deemed nonjusticiable

Conclusion: For the foregoing reasons, the decision of the Court of Appeals should be reversed.

[Editor's Note: The members of Congress joining this brief included Representatives Robert A. Brady (PA-01), John Conyers, Jr. (MI-14), Danny K. Davis (IL-07), Keith Ellison (MN-05), Sam Farr (CA-17), Chaka Fattah (PA-02, served as lead member), Al Green (TX-09), Raúl M. Grijalva (AZ-07), Michael Honda (CA-15), Zoe Lofgren (CA-16), Carolyn McCarthy (NY-04) , Gwen Moore (WI-04), James P. Moran (VA-08), Eleanor Holmes Norton (DC), Bobby L. Rush (IL-01), Maxine Waters (CA-35), Lynn C. Woolsey (CA-06) and Albert R. Wynn (MD-04). No Senators joined.]

The NAACP Legal Defense & Educational Fund, Inc.

I. A radical departure from the court's Second Amendment jurisprudence is not warranted

A. The Second Amendment does not protect an individual right to "keep and bear arms" for purely private purposes

B. The clear and established understanding of the Second Amendment should not be disturbed

1. Abandoning the clear and established understanding of the Second Amendment would produce substantial upheaval in the manner in which firearms are regulated nationwide

2. Abandoning the clear and established understanding of the Second Amendment unduly limits the ability of States and municipalities struggling to address the

problem of gun violence, a problem of particular interest to this nation's African-
American community
3. Abandoning the clear and established understanding of the Second Amendment
   would not address racial discrimination in the administration of criminal justice
   in general or the administration of firearm restrictions in particular

Conclusion: This Court, all but two of the federal Courts of Appeals, and the
various State appellate courts have consistently held that the Second Amendment
does not protect an individual right to "keep and bear Arms" for purely private
purposes. Prior to the decision below, no federal court had ever found a statute
facially invalid under the Second Amendment without subsequently being
reversed. While evolution in the understanding of a Constitutional provision is
sometimes warranted, nothing has changed in regard to the Second Amendment
that would justify this Court in radically departing from its jurisprudence here; if
anything, the lethal nature of the modern handgun and the epidemic of handgun
violence and its attendant effects on the African-American community in this
country should cast doubt on the radical reinterpretation of the Second
Amendment proffered by the D.C. Circuit.

**National Network to End Domestic Violence, National Network to End Domestic Violence
Fund, District Of Columbia Coalition Against Domestic Violence, Alabama Coalition Against
Domestic Violence, Arizona Coalition Against Domestic Violence, Arkansas Coalition
Against Domestic Violence, California Partnership To End Domestic Violence, Connecticut
Coalition Against Domestic Violence, Delaware Coalition Against Domestic Violence,
Family Violence Prevention Fund, Florida Coalition Against Domestic Violence, Georgia
Coalition Against Domestic Violence, Hawaii State Coalition Against Domestic Violence,
Idaho Coalition Against Sexual & Domestic Violence, Indiana Coalition Against Domestic
Violence, Inc., Iowa Coalition Against Domestic Violence, Kansas Coalition Against Sexual
and Domestic Violence, Kentucky Domestic Violence Association, Legal Momentum,
Louisiana Coalition Against Domestic Violence, Inc., Jane Doe Inc. (The Massachusetts
Coalition Against Sexual Assault and Domestic Violence), Michigan Coalition Against
Domestic and Sexual Violence, Mississippi Coalition Against Domestic Violence, Montana
Coalition Against Domestic and Sexual Violence, National Alliance to End Sexual Violence,
National Center on Domestic and Sexual Violence, Nevada Network Against Domestic
Violence, New Hampshire Coalition Against Domestic and Sexual Violence, New Jersey
Coalition for Battered Women, North Carolina Coalition Against Domestic Violence, North
Dakota Council on Abused Women's Services/Coalition Against Sexual Assault in North
Dakota, Action Ohio, Ohio Domestic Violence Network, Oregon Coalition Against Domestic
and Sexual Violence, Pennsylvania Coalition Against Domestic Violence, Puerto Rico
Coalition Against Domestic Violence and Sexual Assault (Coordinadora Paz Para La Mujer,
Inc.), Rhode Island Coalition Against Domestic Violence, South Carolina Coalition Against
Domestic Violence And Sexual Assault, South Dakota Coalition Against Domestic Violence
and Sexual Assault, Tennessee Coalition Against Domestic and Sexual Violence, Vermont
Network Against Domestic and Sexual Violence, Washington State Coalition Against
Domestic Violence, West Virginia Coalition Against Domestic Violence, Wisconsin Coalition
Against Domestic Violence, Wyoming Coalition Against Domestic Violence and Sexual
Assault**

I. Domestic violence is a serious crime that leaves millions of women and children
   nationwide scarred both physically and emotionally
II. Firearms exacerbate an already deadly crisis

III. The statute plainly survives constitutional scrutiny

Conclusion: For the foregoing reasons, the Court of Appeals erred in finding that D.C. Code §§ 7-2502.02(a)(4), 22-4504(a), and 7-2507.02 violate the Second Amendment, and the opinion of the Court of Appeals for the District of Columbia Circuit should be REVERSED.

New York, Hawaii, Maryland, Massachusetts, New Jersey, and Puerto Rico

I. The Second Amendment does not apply to state laws

II. The states have established workable rules to protect an individual right to bear arms

Conclusion: This Court should reaffirm the principle that the laws of the several States are outside the domain of the Second Amendment.

Law Professors Erwin Chemerinsky and Adam Winkler

I. Reasonable restrictions on the right to keep and bear arms are constitutionally permissible

A. The vast majority of weapons safety regulations are unquestionably legitimate, and thus the predicate for heightened scrutiny is absent

1. The vast majority of weapons regulations are clearly legitimate

2. Weapons safety laws are a difficult and technical matter for which legislatures, not courts are best equipped to make the necessary tradeoffs

B. Assuming an individual right unrelated to militia service, the text of the Second Amendment and the history of the right to bear arms support the application of reasonableness review

1. A reasonableness test is consistent with the text of the Second Amendment, which explicitly acknowledges the necessity of government regulation for public safety and security

2. There is a long, established history and tradition of legislative authority to reasonably regulate the right to keep and bear arms

A. Gun control in the founding era

B. The tradition of legislative authority to regulate dangerous weapons

C. Federalism values support the adoption of a reasonable regulation standard consistent with current state constitutional law

II. Even if the right to private ownership of weapons is a fundamental right, reasonable regulations of the right remain constitutionally permissible

A. Fundamental rights do not universally trigger heightened review

B. Guns are a form of property subject to deferential scrutiny

Conclusion: The Founders' original understanding that the right to keep and bear arms did not prohibit even onerous weapons safety laws, the long history of firearms regulation in America, and the consistent federal and state constitutional law principle of reasonableness review all recommend against this Court adopting a heightened form of scrutiny for the Second Amendment. For the foregoing reasons, amici respectfully request that, if this Court reads the Second Amendment to protect a right to possess guns for private purposes, the standard of review applicable to weapons regulation should be the reasonable regulation test used uniformly by the states.

Professors of Criminal Justice

1. The D.C. gun law is an effective mechanism for reducing handgun violence

A. There is a proven correlation between the availability of handguns and incident s of violence

B. The effectiveness of the D.C. gun control law demonstrates its reasonableness

C. The D.C. gun control law effectively reduces the supply of handguns in the District

2. Stricter gun control laws in adjacent jurisdictions would make individual gun control laws more effective

Conclusion: The judgment of the Court of Appeals should be reversed.

Professors of Linguistics and English Dennis E. Baron, Ph.D., Richard W. Bailey, Ph.D. and Jeffrey P. Kaplan, Ph.D.

I. The Second Amendment's absolute construction functions as a sentence modifier

II. The Amendment's unmistakably military language protects the right of the people to serve in a well regulated militia and keep arms for such service

A. Because a well regulated militia is necessary

B. The right of the people to keep and bear arms shall not be infringed

C. Perpetuation of a "well regulated" militia is the purpose of the Amendment

Conclusion: For all of the foregoing reasons, judgment of the Court of Appeals should be reversed.

Violence Policy Center and the Police Chiefs for the Cities of Los Angeles, Minneapolis, and Seattle

I. The Second Amendment permits reasonable restrictions on the right to bear arms

II. The District of Columbia's handgun ban is a reasonable restriction on any private right to bear arms

A. The District's handgun ban was a manifestly reasonable restriction at the time it was enacted

B. The reasonableness of the District's handgun ban is increasingly evident in today's handgun environment

1. The handgun industry has shifted production from revolvers to high-capacity semiautomatic pistols

2. The modern handgun is designed for superior lethality

a. The ammunition capacity of handguns has increased dramatically

b. Handguns have higher caliber ammunition designed for increased lethality

c. Handguns used today are more concealable

C. The handgun ban is reasonable because handguns are much more commonly used in acts of violence than other firearms

1. Handguns continue to be responsible for a disproportionately high number of homicides, including mass shootings

2. Handguns are used in firearm suicides at a disproportionately high rate

3. Handguns are used in non-lethal crimes at a disproportionately high rate

4. Handguns kill far more police officers than any other firearm

D. The handgun ban is reasonable because handguns are less effective for self-defense than other firearms

Conclusion: The District of Columbia's handgun ban is an eminently reasonable restriction on any private right to bear arms for persons unaffiliated with a militia, given the manifest dangers to the public safety that handguns present. The Court should reverse the judgment of the Court of Appeals.

Brief for the United States:
The Federal Government's Position

A. The Second Amendment protects an individual right to possess firearms, including for purposes unrelated to militia operations

1. The text of the Second Amendment, and its placement within the Bill of Rights, strongly indicate that the amendment protects an individual right

2. The Second Amendment's reference to the necessity of a "well regulated militia" does not limit the substantive right that the amendment secures

B. Like rights conferred by surrounding provisions of the Bill of Rights, the individual right guaranteed by the Second Amendment is subject to reasonable restrictions and important exceptions

1. Congress has authority to prohibit particular types of firearms, such as machineguns

2. Congress has substantial authority to ban the private possession of firearms by persons whom Congress deems unfit to keep such weapons

3. Congress has authority to regulate the manufacture, sale, and flow of firearms in commerce

C. The Court should remand this case to the lower courts to permit them to analyze the constitutionality of the D.C. laws at issue under the proper constitutional inquiry

Conclusion: The Court should affirm that the Second Amendment, no less than other provisions of the Bill of Rights, secures an individual right, and should clarify that the right is subject to the more flexible standard of review described above. If the Court takes those foundational steps, the better course would be to remand.

Summaries of the First 92 Gun-Related Cases to Reach the U.S. Supreme Court

When *Supreme Court Gun Cases* first came out in 2003, it contained text from all 92 firearm-related cases the Court had heard up to that time. The 44 most important cases were included in their entirety, and 48 others were excerpted for the gun-related portions. More than 1,000 key quotations were highlighted, and each case entry began with a plain-English gist to get to the heart of the matter. Those gists are collected here, so this volume continues to represent the entire body of work from the Supreme Court on the subject.

The original book, with the cases reproduced, will continue to remain available while supplies last, after which it will be offered as a downloadable and searchable pdf file. The official versions of the cases of course can be easily obtained on the Internet and are all linked from gunlaws.com, but the highlighted quotes and extensive support material in the original book provide significant additional value and enjoyment.

HOUSTON v. MOORE
18 U.S. 1; 5 L. Ed. 19; 5 Wheat. 1
FEBRUARY, 1820 Term

The High Court's first known mention of the 2nd Amendment occurs in a very lengthy decision, as a brief remark in a dissent.

After a man named Houston failed to appear when summoned for militia duty during the War of 1812, he was tried and convicted by the State of Pennsylvania for violating a Pennsylvania statute against failing to perform federal militia service. Houston argued that the Pennsylvania legislature could not enact such a statute, because the statute was inconsistent with federal powers over the militia, since Congress had passed a law providing punishment for people who failed to perform federal militia service. The majority of the Supreme Court disagreed, and ruled that the state and federal statutes could co-exist.

In dissent, Justice Joseph Story (a great advocate of federal power) argued that the federal statute left no room for a state statute on the same subject. In a hypothetical discussion over whether a state statute might be constitutional if there were no federal statute, Justice Story commented that the 2nd Amendment (he says Fifth but quotes the Second, in perhaps the most notable typographical error in all these cases) would probably have no important bearing on the point. The 2nd Amendment played no role in the majority opinions, and was only mentioned in a cursory way in a dissent. The Court's treatment of the 2nd Amendment in this case—it is not present in the lengthy discussion—suggests that the Amendment was not primarily viewed as a guarantee of state government powers to control state militias.

DRED SCOTT v. SANDFORD
60 U.S. 393; 15 L. Ed. 691; 19 HOW 393
DECEMBER, 1856, Term

The second gun case in the High Court's history is widely known and extensively studied for its social impact, and as a sobering reflection on our nation's past. It has not, until this time, been thought of by many as a gun case, *per se*. But a mere few paragraphs within its copious length show a sense of gun rights that is simultaneously abhorrent to modern thought, and is as illustrative of the understanding of gun rights at this early point in our history, as any other entry in *Supreme Court Gun Cases*.

This is the infamous case from the pre-Civil War era involving a slave's suit for his freedom. In it, the Court states that if a slave were entitled to the rights and privileges secured by the Constitution, he would have the right to keep and carry arms wherever he went, the same as other citizens, and it certainly "cannot be supposed" that the states "intended to secure to them" such rights.

Later, discussing congressional power over Territories that had not yet become States, the Court said Congress could not deprive Territorial citizens of the protections of the Bill of Rights, including the right to keep and bear arms, or other important rights, such as the right to a jury trial.

It came as quite a surprise to find that *Dred Scott* would turn out to provide a key element in understanding what the 2nd Amendment intended to say, and that blacks, in being denied their rights, helped define what those rights are. After the War Between the States, there were efforts to both secure and to deny the right to keep arms and the right to bear arms for newly freed slaves. This became the focus of local and state activity nationally, and the innards of the 14th Amendment to the U.S. Constitution.

EX PARTE MILLIGAN
71 U.S. 2; 18 L. Ed. 281; 4 Wall. 2
DECEMBER, 1866, Term

Milligan, a citizen of Indiana, was sentenced to death by a military court martial during the Civil War because of his sympathies for the Confederate cause. He brought a petition for a writ of habeas corpus, arguing that military tribunals could not displace civil courts in states that were not in rebellion. The Supreme Court unanimously agreed. While the Court's opinion did not discuss the 2nd Amendment, lawyers on both sides of the case used the 2nd Amendment to argue by analogy, with arguments recognizing the 2nd Amendment as a right belonging to free citizens. As was the norm for 19th century cases, the official report of the case included the attorneys' arguments, preserving their thinking for posterity (and this book). Note how they consistently refer to the various "articles," reminding us that the Bill of Rights was a single amendment with twelve articles, ten of which were ratified.

Milligan also claimed he could not be guilty of violating the laws of war since he was not in the military, or "in the militia in actual service," and the Court again agreed. The distinction between citizens, and citizens called into active militia service, is pronounced in this case. The idea expressed repeatedly is that the militia, when not called into federal service, are just people and hence subject to civil courts, not military tribunals. Milligan's involvement with arms without being an activated militia member is never called into question.

CUMMINGS v. MISSOURI
71 U.S. 277; 18 L. Ed. 356; 4 Wall. 277
DECEMBER, 1866, Term

This case involved the conviction of a Catholic priest for teaching and preaching without having taken an oath required by the Missouri Constitution. In formulating its opinion, the Court identifies bearing arms as an example of a civil right, and says suspension or deprivation of such rights is punishment.

UNITED STATES v. CRUIKSHANK
92 U.S. 542; 23 L. Ed. 588; 2 Otto 542
OCTOBER, 1875 Term

Often thought of as the first real Supreme Court gun case, we now see that *Cruikshank* is only fifth in line.

William Cruikshank was a Ku Klux Klan leader in the South following the Civil War. He led a band of rioters in Louisiana who burned down a courthouse in which a group of armed blacks had taken refuge, all part of a disputed election. Cruikshank and his white followers were brought to trial—efforts such as theirs to disarm Freedmen were a hot national issue.

The federal Enforcement Act of May, 1870 made it illegal to band together or conspire to deprive people of their rights under the Constitution. It was an expression in statute of principles found in the new 14th Amendment, and created misdemeanor and felony offenses. In order to determine if the defendants were guilty, the Court had to decide if the rights allegedly deprived were actually rights granted by the Constitution.

The Court found that certain basic human rights in that document existed prior to when the Constitution was written, that the rights are fundamental to civilization, and were recognized but not created by the Constitution. All the Constitution did was guarantee against any federal government interference in those extant rights. These rights included free speech, the right to assemble for redress of grievances, and the right to bear arms, among others.

The federal prosecution was for conspiracy to prevent black people from the free exercise and enjoyment of rights and privileges granted and secured to them by the Constitution and laws of the United States. The Court famously stated here that the 2nd Amendment did not create a right to bear arms, but instead recognized and guaranteed a preexisting fundamental human right. Construing the 1st Amendment the same way, the Court held that the indictment against Cruikshank was defective, because the rights of assembly and of bearing arms were not granted or secured by the Constitution; rather, the 1st and 2nd Amendments merely limited the power of Congress to restrict those preexisting rights.

The defendants, charged with 32 counts of oppressing blacks in Louisiana, had been acquitted of murder at the lower court level, and were now exonerated of the remaining charges and released.

PRESSER v. ILLINOIS

116 U.S. 252; 6 S. Ct. 580; 29 L. Ed. 615
Argued November 23, 24, 1885. January 4, 1886, Decided

Herman Presser was indicted and pled guilty to a charge of drilling and parading an armed company of men without permission from the Governor, as required by Illinois law. He marched his company of about 400 men, part of a society called the Lehr und Wehr Verein, through the streets of Chicago, they carrying rifles, and he on horseback with a cavalry sword. In this appeal, Presser argued that the Illinois Military Code, under which he was charged, was in conflict with the United States Constitution.

Presser made constitutional claims against numerous parts of the Code, and the Court sidestepped most, saying it needn't review the entire code to cleanly and legally separate the parts he was charged under. A summary of that code is provided. The contentions made on behalf of Presser by Lyman Trumbull make compelling reading but are not part of the Court's opinion, and in fact the Court found against the plaintiff and his pleadings.

The 2nd Amendment was one basis of Presser's claim. The Court held that the 2nd Amendment is not violated by a ban on armed parades, and that the organizing and drilling of armed units is the prerogative of governments and not of individual citizens. After quoting the Amendment completely for reference, the Court singled out the right of the people to keep and bear arms in its discussions of state vs. federal powers. The Court also said that the 2nd Amendment (like the rest of the Bill of Rights, under the Court's thinking at the time) limited only the federal government, not state governments.

LOGAN v. UNITED STATES

144 U.S. 263; 12 S. Ct. 617; 36 L. Ed. 429
Argued January 26, 27, 1892. April 4, 1892, Decided

Logan marks the beginning of a series of cases in which the Supreme Court sets out the principles of self defense. As was the style at the time, the decisions include graphic depictions of the facts of each case. When it comes to the twelve self-defense cases of the 1890s, these read like good cowboy Westerns. One additional case occurred in 1921, and in 1995, a police use-of-force case (*Tennessee v. Garner*) addressed the tangential self-defense issue of *chase* or stopping a fleeing felon. All 16 self-defense cases are indicated by a "△" marker in the Chronological List of Cases and the Descriptive Index. In addition, the introductory essay by Korwin includes a chart assigning the basic principles of self defense to the cases that address them.

The five Marlow brothers were indicted in Texas for larceny in Indian Country. They were out on bail and living at a farm 12 miles from the courthouse. One of the brothers, Boone, was also wanted for murder.

The county sheriff, with a deputy named Collier, rode out one day to serve the murder warrant. As soon as Boone stepped outside, without warning, Collier fired at him. Boone returned fire but missed and ended up killing the sheriff. Boone took off, never to be seen again.

The angry townsfolk, motivated by the killing of their beloved sheriff, went out to the farm and hauled the remaining four brothers off to the local jail. After an angry assault in the jail, repulsed by the Marlows, Collier (who was now the sheriff), arranged with the County Attorney to take the prisoners to an adjacent county jail for safekeeping. Deep in the dark of night, they assembled a three-vehicle convoy, bristling with armed guards, with the prisoners in the lead wagon.

Instead of heading to another jail, the Marlows were driven by their captors into an ambush by a mob a few miles out of town. Though shackled in pairs, they managed to jump out of the hack they were in when the shooting began, grabbed guns from their "guards" and attackers, and drove off the perpetrators in what must have been a scene to rival anything Hollywood has ever produced. The facts of the incident are included in the case below. Two of the Marlows and two of the conspirators were shot dead in the ambush, and people on both sides were wounded.

The two surviving Marlow brothers, wounded and bleeding, managed to unshackle themselves from their dead kin in order to get away, and were eventually taken to federal court in Dallas, by a deputy U.S. Marshal, and tried and acquitted. The Logan case wrestled with their rights while in custody.

A federal statute of the time prohibited conspiracies to injure or threaten a citizen in the exercise of a right secured by the United States Constitution. Similar language can be found in current federal law under 18 USC §§241 and 242. In a rambling decision, the Court states that some rights, such as the right to assemble peacefully, and the right of the people to keep and bear arms, are not guaranteed by the Constitution, they are simply recognized by it as pre-existing rights and in that sense are more fundamentally inherent than those rights granted by the Constitution. These rights are outside of Congress' authority to act, or of any congressional ability to require the states to act. Such rights are part of the "natural and inalienable rights of man," and "the fundamental rights which belong to every citizen as a member of society."

The Court had to decide if the prisoners, even though betrayed by their legal guards, were entitled constitutionally to protection while they were kept defenseless in custody. The Court acknowledged several times that, as prisoners, they were denied the exercise of self defense.

The Justices found that because the United States had the power to punish crimes against the laws of the United States, it necessarily had the power to arrest and safely detain people accused of such crimes while they, as prisoners, are denied the usual means of self defense. This power to detain, they argued, implies a right of the person detained to be protected from unlawful violence.

Where, as here, the right is created by the Constitution, the United States may legislate to protect the right from infringement by individuals and states. Where the right is preexisting and the Constitution merely recognizes it (as with the 1st and 2nd Amendments), the United States is itself barred from infringing the right and is not empowered by the 14th Amendment to legislate to protect it from infringement by states or individuals.

Logan was named as one of the shooters by a wounded Marlow and by others, in testimony that was not without conflicts. It seems that Logan was supposed to be a guard that night, got himself excused by the leaders of the convoy (who were in on the ambush plan), and then tipped off the mob, all of whom were conspirators to deny the prisoners their rights. Along with two other perpetrators, Logan was convicted of the conspiracy charge. No one was found guilty of the murders, and the remaining defendants were acquitted.

GOURKO v. UNITED STATES
153 U.S. 183; 14 S. Ct. 806; 38 L. Ed. 680
Submitted November 17, 1893. April 16, 1894, Decided

Gourko marks the beginning of a string of self-defense cases arising from a single district courthouse. The dreaded "Hanging Judge" Isaac Parker can rightly be seen today as the unintended champion of armed self defense, a right he fought against at that time. Responsible for 88 death sentences and hangings, his hostility toward the idea of self defense afforded the Supreme Court the perfect opportunity to examine and clarify the common law surrounding self defense, in the years from 1893 to 1896. Based in Ft. Smith, Arkansas, where his court is now a National Historic Site, the lawless reaches of Parker's jurisdiction included neighboring Oklahoma, which was then Indian Territory, largely under federal law, and a hotbed of Wild West violence.

As the cases show, Parker consistently misled juries and obtained guilty verdicts. On appeal, the High Court reversed so often that Parker and the Justices were in an open feud. The full story is told in an article by David Kopel in the Summer 2000 edition of the *American Journal of Criminal Law* (posted at davekopel.org). The Supreme Court's cases publicly chastised the court from the Western District of Arkansas and Judge Parker personally, a rare occurrence in Supreme Court decisions.

Civil libertarians of today may find new cause to admire the Court of Chief Justice Fuller, known primarily for its unfortunate racism in *Plessy v. Fergusson*. It was this same Court however, standing against the abuses of Judge Parker, that defended the often poor, uneducated ethnic minorities— American Indians, blacks, immigrants, even people of mixed blood whose jurisdiction itself was in doubt—who carried guns for self defense and had even killed white men in saving their own lives.

John Gourko was a peaceable, frail young Polish immigrant miner who had been repeatedly threatened by Peter Carbo, a physically strong 200-pound "dangerous character." Carbo had loudly and publicly accused Gourko and his brother of stealing some mined coal from him.

After an altercation in which Carbo threatened to "shoot John like a dog," Gourko armed himself with a pistol. Later, Gourko killed Carbo and was convicted of murder. The High Court overturned his conviction and ruled unanimously that if Gourko believed Carbo intended to kill or seriously harm him, he was justified in arming himself. If Gourko later killed Carbo in circumstances where Gourko was not justified on self-defense grounds, the mere fact that Gourko had armed himself defensively did not turn the killing into premeditated murder. The Court takes for granted that personally arming yourself in the face of a serious threat is a normal, understandable, reasonable response to a known danger.

MILLER v. STATE OF TEXAS
153 U.S. 535; 14 S. Ct. 874; 38 L. Ed. 812
Submitted April 23, 1894. May 14, 1894, Decided

Frank Miller, a convicted murderer from Dallas, appealed his death sentence, arguing in part that the Texas law prohibiting carrying weapons on yourself was in violation of his 2nd Amendment rights, and that this was made enforceable against the states by the 14th Amendment. (Unbeknownst to most people who absorb cultural information from TV, Texas has basically not allowed the carrying of handguns in the state from just after the Civil War until 1995, when a right-to-carry permit-and-fee system was implemented in place of the near-absolute ban.)

Miller also argued that search and seizure of his firearm without a warrant under Texas law was likewise unconstitutional. It's almost a crime that these fundamental constitutional issues—and this one could have been a blockbuster—are so often framed in the context of the worst elements of society, but such is the nature of this business.

The Court closed the door on Miller and rejected his appeal because he had not raised this argument prior to his Supreme Court appeal. Perhaps the Justices recognized it as a desperate last gasp of a doomed man but their hands were tied. The Court delicately sidestepped a landmine of an issue, fell back comfortably on a non-committal procedural way out, and without reading between the lines, simply said he got his paperwork out of order and sent him to his death. The Court appeared to consider the 14th Amendment issue of applying the Bill of Rights to the States to be an unresolved matter of law.

For a discussion of this case in great detail, see the *Journal of Law and Policy* article (Vol. 9, 2001) by Leonardatos, Kopel and Halbrook, on the Internet at davekopel.org.

STARR v. UNITED STATES
153 U.S. 614; 14 S. Ct. 919; 38 L. Ed. 841
Submitted March 5, 1894. May 14, 1894, Decided

Henry Starr, a teenaged Cherokee Indian, was wanted for stealing horses, and was laying low in the high country, aware the authorities were looking for him. Deputy U.S. Marshall Henry Dickey had summoned Floyd Wilson as his posse to help him serve a warrant on the young man. After a chase on horseback, when they got within talking range of Starr, Wilson whipped out his rifle and started firing. Starr shot back, downing Wilson, who then went for his revolver and fired four shots wildly. Starr rushed forward and fired again at point-blank range, killing Wilson and ending the assault. Witnesses confirmed that Wilson fired first, but Starr was sentenced to hang, in part because it was an officer of the law he had killed. The facts preserved in this case read like a good Western thriller.

Starr appealed his murder conviction on the grounds that, although the deputy and posse were legally serving a warrant, they failed to identify themselves properly and simply opened fire, so Starr had a right of self defense intact. The 2nd Amendment is not directly implicated unless you take into account the Court's complete ease with the fact that people carry guns and use them in natural and lawful personal protection, and there is an extended discussion on the law of self defense.

The Court unanimously reversed the conviction and remanded for a new trial because district Judge Parker's jury instructions too narrowly characterized the defendant's right of self defense against an attack by a person he did not know was an officer lawfully trying to arrest him. Although Starr was a wanted man, his right to defend against an attack did not evaporate. The Supreme Court also scolded the lower court for its handling of the case, and for launching into a tirade in the jury instruction.

THOMPSON v. UNITED STATES
155 U.S. 271; 15 S. Ct. 73; 39 L. Ed. 146
Submitted October 18, 1894. December 3, 1894, Decided

The defendant, an Indian boy about 17 years old, was charged with and convicted of murder after killing a man, Charles Hermes, who had previously threatened to "chop his head open." The Arkansas trial court of Judge Parker instructed the jury that, since the boy had deliberately armed himself after an earlier confrontation, a charge of murder would apply.

Thompson had delivered a package for the woman with whom he was boarding, using the only road leading to his destination. On the way, he passed a field where Hermes was working, and was threatened by Hermes directly. Fearing for his safety, Thompson thought it best to arm himself, so he borrowed a Winchester rifle before returning by that same road. Sure enough, a gun fight ensued and Hermes was killed, with the details described in the decision.

The Supreme Court unanimously disagreed with the lower court, holding that deliberately arming yourself after a dispute is not by itself sufficient to make a subsequent homicide into a premeditated murder. They cite related self-defense principles already established under *Gourko*. The Court accepted as routine the concept that firearms are owned by the general public and are used in lawful self defense—lawful firearm possession by individuals is as unremarkable as possession of pens. In understated and ironic judicial style the Court criticized Judge Parker's worst conclusions by repeatedly referring to him as "learned."

BEARD v. UNITED STATES
158 U.S. 550; 15 S. Ct. 962; 39 L. Ed. 1086
Submitted March 13, 1895. May 27, 1895, Decided

This case examines the underpinnings of personal self defense. Presented in colorful detail are the facts of a confrontation between neighbors and relatives over a cow.

Beard used the shotgun he normally carried with him when he was traveling, to defend himself against the three men he encountered on his return, who were trying to take the cow off his property. The men, brothers, had a long-term angry dispute with Beard, and were carrying concealed handguns in their pockets. When the first one made a move as if to draw, Beard hit him over the head with the shotgun, so he wouldn't have to shoot him, according to the testimony. But the blow crushed the skull and proved lethal. Using the shotgun, Beard managed to disarm the other two brothers, without firing a shot.

While it's easy to visualize the sequence of events described in many of the Court's self-defense cases, the descriptions in *Beard* resist visualization— how three armed men, positioned as they were, could be defeated without a hostile shot fired. Taunted by the Jones brothers that his shotgun wasn't loaded, Beard fired a blast into the air. He claimed he had "ten cartridges in the magazine," probably as a boast, since a shotgun with a ten-round magazine didn't exist at the time.

The case touched on numerous aspects of self defense: public threats of harm, reasonable belief of an imminent mortal threat, provocation and mutual combat, equal force, necessity, your rights at home, standing your ground, bad jury instructions, and the differences between murder and manslaughter. Included is some of the longest-winded bombast in this book—extended tracts from Judge Parker's charge to the jury, quoted in the decision. Look for the opening and closing quote marks to avoid the sleep-inducing effect of these lengthy portions.

A strong position is carved out here by the Court, concerning "the ancient doctrine" of a duty to retreat when attacked, saying the "American mind" is very strongly against enforcement of any such rule. The Court found the idea of "retreat to the wall" had medieval English roots, which may have made sense in days of hand-to-hand villainy with clubs and edged weapons, but made no sense in a world of long-distance repeating rifles. The Court determined, with 18 supporting citations, that under the circumstances in this case—a man threatened and attacked on his own property near his home— there was no duty to retreat in acting to save his own life.

ALLISON v. UNITED STATES
160 U.S. 203; 16 S. Ct. 252; 40 L. Ed. 395
Submitted November 20, 1895. December 16, 1895, Decided

In this self-defense case, 20-year-old defendant John Allison shot and killed his abusive father William, with a hunting rifle, when it appeared that his father was reaching for the concealed pistol he was known to carry. In the week before the killing, the father had threatened to blow the family's brains out, and he had recently been released from prison for firing a shot at them during an argument.

Trial Judge Isaac Parker, of the Western District of Arkansas, injected all sorts of bias and erroneous interpretation of the law in order to force a conviction. The High Court's decision includes lengthy quotes of the judge's statements and charge to the jury (including Parker's subtle swipe at the High Court for being "technical and hair splitting"). Parker seemed to feel that if a man is threatened, the man then automatically harbors a grudge, and the grudge is a motivation in the homicide. Parker downplayed the character witnesses and prior threats. He said you can't trust the testimony of a person on trial for his life, because anyone in that position will lie. It was a perfect stage for the Supreme Court to set the record straight on armed self defense in America.

The Supreme Court unanimously reversed the murder conviction and called for a new trial. The Justices found that Judge Parker had inappropriately denigrated the right of self defense in his jury instructions, and in other ways misled the jury. The Justices' frustration with Parker was increasing, and they lambasted his actions in their published conclusion. The case hinged on reasonable belief and grounds for that belief, as well as the nature of threats and the character of the adversary, which are jury decisions, not matters of law. As it turned out, the father was not armed as he usually was, when he reached as if to draw and was fatally shot by his son. The son's testimony was the only evidence for key parts of what actually occurred.

BROWN v. WALKER
161 U.S. 591; 16 S. Ct. 644; 40 L. Ed. 819
Argued January 23, 1896. March 23, 1896, Decided

This case involves the 5th Amendment privilege against self incrimination as it applies to a grand jury witness. Brown declined to answer grand jury questions on self incrimination grounds, was held in contempt, and appealed. The Court rejected Brown's claim that he could not be compelled to testify. The majority opinion of Justice Brown referred to the first eight amendments of the Bill of Rights as incorporating "certain principles of natural justice." Justice Field's dissenting opinion refers to the right to bear arms as one of the essential and inseparable features of English liberty.

WALLACE v. UNITED STATES
162 U.S. 466; 16 S. Ct. 859; 40 L. Ed. 1039
Submitted March 2, 1896. April 20, 1896, Decided

Jerry Wallace lived with his wife Jane on a piece of land she owned in Kansas. Her father Alexander Zane disputed the boundary of her land with his own, and he eventually picked a lethal fight over it. Wallace, described as a quiet, peaceful man with poor eyesight, managed to take down Zane, a known troublemaker, with a single blast. He was charged with and subsequently convicted of murder.

This is a self-defense case—the only one in this time period that is not from Judge Parker in Arkansas. The Court unanimously held that if the defendant started the dispute with the intent of killing the victim, then the killing was murder. If the defendant had no such intent, and the killing was necessary to avoid serious and imminent danger to himself, the fact that the defendant started the dispute did not preclude him from employing deadly force—a double-barreled shotgun in this case—in self defense. The facts involved are a drama of family land ownership, boundary disputes, death threats, getting drunk to build a fence with your buddies on disputed land, a mild mannered defendant, a butcher-knife wielding bully, and a confrontation that soured quickly.

ALBERTY v. UNITED STATES
162 U.S. 499; 16 S. Ct. 864; 40 L. Ed. 1051
Submitted March 4, 1896. April 20, 1896, Decided

Here you have two young men interested in the same woman. The defendant, Alberty, is her husband. Duncan, the deceased, paid enough attention to her to get her to move to a room of her own at Lipe's, where she worked. One night, from the yard where Alberty worked (also at Lipe's), he saw a man trying to climb into his wife's bedroom window. He approached in the pitch dark, apparently unaware of who the person was, and in an ensuing confrontation, shot Duncan to death while trying to avoid Duncan's apparently drawn knife. Mind reeling, Alberty left the body and ran away.

The case opens with a remarkable discussion of race, in a lengthy effort to determine proper jurisdiction over the parties. If they were both Indians in Indian country, the federal court would have no jurisdiction. The Court concluded that Alberty, a black man born in slavery, was a "member of the Cherokee Nation, but not an Indian," and Duncan, the illegitimate child of a male Choctaw and a black slave, was a "colored citizen of the United States." In the midst of this racially charged decade, the Supreme Court was hearing and defending the rights of the most repressed classes.

Alberty appealed his murder conviction and death sentence, claiming errors were made in the charge to the jury, and in the inference to be drawn from his flight after shooting Duncan to death. The Court discussed in some detail the right of self defense and the duty to retreat. The Court held that, contrary to District Judge Parker's detailed description to the jury, there was no duty to retreat in a case such as this, and that you may stand your ground against such an assault. The Court touched indirectly on the point of matching force with force.

Disagreeing with Judge Parker's jury instruction that Alberty provoked the fight by going over to investigate, the High Court held that it was "perfectly natural" to investigate in such a circumstance, and that responding to any aggression offered was permissible.

Years had passed before Alberty was caught, in St. Louis, turned in by a former prisoner who recognized him. While the lower court insisted that running away after the fact was a pretty sure sign of guilt, the High Court rejected that idea rather eloquently by listing all sorts of reasons why an innocent person might flee after an incident, including among others, the humiliation, annoyance and expense of defense. Granted a new trial, Alberty was acquitted and moved back to St. Louis.

ACERS v. UNITED STATES
164 U.S. 388; 17 S. Ct. 91; 41 L. Ed. 481
Submitted October 22, 1896. November 30, 1896, Decided

It's hard to miss the biblical overtones of this self-defense case, in which Acers smashed Owens on the head with a big rock and fractured his skull. The two men had been at odds over their business affairs. Unlike Abel, Owens survived. Acers tried to slide out of the charge of assault-with-intent-to-kill by claiming self defense. Acers said he thought Owens was about to draw a pistol, but there was no corroborating evidence, and no pistol ever turned up. That may be the most tenuous link to guns for a case that has made it into *Supreme Court Gun Cases*, though it is right on target for related self-defense information.

"Hanging Judge" Isaac Parker in Arkansas convicted Acers of murder. The Supreme Court agreed completely, saying you need the elements of self defense present before you can avail yourself of its protections. In doing so the Court described conditions of justifiable self defense, by agreeing with the statements made by Judge Parker. Self defense requires a reasonable perception and belief that there is a present danger of deadly violence. Simple fear is not enough justification.

The Court also said that anything (the rock in this case) can be a deadly weapon depending upon how it is used. Based on the size of this rock (9 by 3 by 2 inches), the force used (enough to crack a skull), and the area attacked (the head), this stone was a deadly weapon. Statutes today often distinguish between a deadly weapon—something designed for lethal use—and a dangerous object, something that could be used lethally but is not so designed. Finally, the Court took yet another slap at the District Court for the Western District of Arkansas, for carelessness in its work.

ALLEN v. UNITED STATES
164 U.S. 492; 17 S. Ct. 154; 41 L. Ed. 528
Submitted October 23, 1896. December 7, 1896, Decided

The Court expressed some displeasure with this appeal—the third time it had considered the case—of a murder conviction from Arkansas Judge Parker. Yet while the High Court had easily overturned Parker in the past, here they were confronted not with a justifiable homicide, but with a true murder. They upheld the conviction, and the murderer was sent to prison for life. Alexander Allen, the 14-year-old defendant (they call him the prisoner) had gone through a fence, called out to his adversary, 18-year-old Phillip Henson, punched him in the face, and then shot him twice, once in the back.

The Court described conditions necessary to show premeditation and intent to kill, they defined manslaughter and self defense, and they pointed out that words alone are insufficient to justify an assault. They also indicated that while flight after the fact might suggest guilt it does not prove it. Allen had fled after the incident.

Judge Parker gained a legacy in this case. The High Court approved his instruction to a deadlocked jury, that jurors should each listen to the other side's arguments with a disposition to be convinced. Parker got the language from state courts in Massachusetts and Connecticut. Known as the "Allen charge," *Black's Law Dictionary* notes that it is illegal in some states. It is also known as a dynamite charge, a shotgun instruction, and a third degree instruction.

ROWE v. UNITED STATES
164 U.S. 546; 17 S. Ct. 172; 41 L. Ed. 547
Submitted October 22, 1896. November 30, 1896, Decided

Here is one of the best Wild West dramas contained in Supreme Court gun-related self-defense cases, and the last one from Judge Isaac Parker, who retired soon after. Rowe traveled 20 horse-drawn miles to town with his wife to go shopping. Later, he met another man, Bozeman, at the dinner table of a hotel and they exchanged some hostile words. Rowe bragged he was armed.

After dinner they met again in the hotel lobby. Bozeman grossly insulted Rowe, who kicked at him lightly and then stepped back and leaned on a counter. Bozeman then lurched at Rowe and began slicing his face with a knife, so Rowe pulled his pistol and killed his assailant with a single shot. Naturally, the prosecution and defense disagreed on who said what or when. Rowe was convicted of manslaughter, got five years and a $500 fine.

The Justices declared that you can be involved in starting a difficulty, which would normally deny you any claim of self defense, and regain your right to self defense by honestly withdrawing from the conflict you may have begun. They placed great emphasis on determining the sincerity of your withdrawal. The Court also flatly rejected the notion that you should or must shoot to only wound during a deadly struggle, if you are able.

It's interesting to see how the defendant, a Cherokee Indian, kept his gun with him for the long ride to town, but then felt secure enough once in town to leave the gun at the livery stable until before he prepared to journey home again. Also of note, the decision described how the fired shot hit Bozeman near the right elbow and then traveled through his body from right to left. In the conclusion, in addition to having dismissed Parker's shoot-to-wound conjecture, the Court spoke of the folly of trying to wing an assailant's arm to paralyze it and thus hope to stop him, while fighting for your life during mortal combat.

ROBERTSON v. BALDWIN
165 U.S. 275; 17 S. Ct. 326; 41 L. Ed. 715
Argued December 15, 1896. January 25, 1897, Decided

This is an appeal from dismissal of a petition for writ of habeas corpus. The petitioners were seamen who claimed that their detention, to enforce their service contract, was in violation of the 13th Amendment, which forbids involuntary servitude. The Court affirmed the dismissal of the petition, and explained that all the rights in the Constitution were subject to preexisting common-sense exceptions. In abstractly discussing limits on rights, they said the right of the people to keep and bear arms was not infringed by laws prohibiting concealed carry. In the same sentence they said freedom of speech and of the press did not permit publication of blasphemous or indecent articles, or other publications injurious to public morals. They pointed out that the Bill of Rights didn't invent new rights, it protected existing ones.

ANDERSEN v. UNITED STATES
170 U.S. 481; 18 S. Ct. 689; 42 L. Ed. 1116
Argued April 11, 1898. May 9, 1898, Decided

Andersen, a ship's cook, appealed his conviction for murdering the ship's mate on the high seas. This case reads like a good novel—a small ship in 1879, a cruel captain, a murderous cook running around with three pistols, two bodies dumped overboard, and the ship set ablaze—quite a remarkable tale, and true.

The opening indictment is possibly the worst English in *Supreme Court Gun Cases*. A single 624-word sentence, it is all but indecipherable to a modern reader and was perhaps even worse when written. It uses mind-numbing redundancy and pompous grandiosity of the like, "then and there had and held, then and there piratically, feloniously, wilfully and of his malice aforethought did discharge and shoot off to, against and upon the said William Wallace Saunders, sometimes called William Saunders, with intent him, the said William Wallace Saunders, sometimes called William Saunders, then and there to kill and murder..."

The case itself goes on at length, however, in very readable style, describing the lurid details of the crime and aftermath, with testimony from the shipmates and the defendant. The crew are remarkably uniform in their tale condemning Andersen's actions, who cries out against them for abandoning him, yet on the ship they agreed it was self defense, or so he says.

The fascinating story, taken as a whole, seems to describe Andersen's sure guilt. The Court agreed, rejecting his claims of provocation and self defense. In rejecting Andersen's claims, the Court lays out the precise conditions required for a self-defense claim to win the day, none of which Andersen had. In a bizarre defense tactic, Andersen suggested that since the Mate had been shot and then quickly thrown overboard, the exact cause of death could not be determined. It fell on predictably deaf ears.

Although Anderson apparently committed two murders (the captain and the first mate), he was only tried for the mate's murder. This is because a) there were eye witnesses, b) his self-defense claim in the Captain's quarters, where the first homicide took place, could be an obstacle to the government's case against him, and c) the time between the Captain's murder and the mate's allowed sufficient time to show premeditation at least in the second killing.

MAXWELL v. DOW

176 U.S. 581; 20 S. Ct. 448; 44 L. Ed. 597
Argued December 4, 1899. February 26, 1900, Decided

In a state court, Maxwell was charged by information rather than by grand jury indictment, and was later convicted by an eight-person jury on a charge of robbery. The Court rejected Maxwell's contention that he had a right to indictment by a grand jury and trial by a twelve-person jury under the 14th Amendment. Decided in 1900, this case occurred long before the Court, in piecemeal fashion, made most of the Bill of Rights enforceable against the states via the Due Process clause of the 14th Amendment.

Justice Peckham cited several prior cases holding various portions of the Bill of Rights inapplicable to the states. Among the cases was *Presser v. Illinois*, which held that the 2nd Amendment restrained only Congress. Justice Harlan, dissenting, argued that the framers of the 14th Amendment did indeed intend to make the personal rights contained in the Bill of Rights effective against the states. His charming description of the adoption of the Bill of Rights, and his careful reasoning for incorporating the Bill of Rights against the states foreshadowed the Court's later decisions, when concern for state sovereignty would dissolve and federal guarantees for citizens would be mandated more broadly.

While this case, as recently as 1900, flatly says the separate states are unencumbered by the Bill of Rights, today we take it for granted that the protections of the Bill of Rights cannot be abrogated by the states. One of the glaring exceptions of course is in the 2nd Amendment, where incorporation against the states has not been formally addressed under the due-process doctrine.

KEPNER v. UNITED STATES

195 U.S. 100; 24 S. Ct. 797; 49 L. Ed. 114
Argued April 22, 1904. May 31, 1904

This case is an appeal from a criminal conviction in the Philippines, at that time a territory of the United States. Kepner was tried without a jury and acquitted in November 1901. The judgment of acquittal was reversed on appeal, and Kepner was retried and convicted. Kepner appealed on the ground that his second trial was in violation of both the territorial law and the U.S. Constitutional provision against twice putting a person in jeopardy for the same offense. At issue was whether the laws of the territory put in place by Congress were intended to adopt the Spanish civil law interpretation of double jeopardy that existed prior to U.S. rule in the Philippines, or the U.S. interpretation of double jeopardy. In making this determination, Justice Day refers to the near-total adoption of the Bill of Rights into the governing law of the Philippines. He notes that the "right of the people to bear arms" is one of two rights omitted (the other was the right to a jury trial).

TRONO v. UNITED STATES

199 U.S. 521; 26 S. Ct. 121; 50 L. Ed. 292
Argued October 31, 1905. December 4, 1905 Decided

This is another double jeopardy case on appeal from the territorial courts of the Philippines. The Court held that there was no constitutional violation when the defendant was acquitted at trial of the highest charge but convicted of a lesser included offense, appealed the conviction, and was subsequently convicted of the highest charge. Discussing the incorporation of most of the Bill of Rights into the law of the Philippines, the Court noted that the right of the people to bear arms was omitted.

TWINING v. NEW JERSEY

211 U.S. 78; 29 S. Ct. 14; 53 L. Ed. 97
Argued March 19, 20, 1908. November 9, 1908, Decided

This appeal asked the Court to require the states to recognize, through the 14th Amendment, the 5th Amendment right against self-incrimination. The Court held the right was neither one of the privileges and immunities of national citizenship, nor was it implicit in the Privileges and Immunities clause of the 14th Amendment. Indicative of the times, the Court draws distinctions between "National citizenship" and associated federal rights, and "citizens of the United States" and rights under the aegis of the individual states. The Court included in its discussion a statement that the right to bear arms guaranteed by the 2nd Amendment, one of the safeguards of personal rights in the first eight Articles of Amendment to the Federal Constitution, is not one of the privileges and immunities secured against state action.

PATSONE v. PENNSYLVANIA

232 U.S. 138; 34 S. Ct. 281; 58 L. Ed. 539
Argued November 4, 1913. January 19, 1914

This case is a 14th Amendment challenge to a Pennsylvania law prohibiting nonresident aliens from hunting. State law made possession of shotguns and rifles by an alien for hunting unlawful, and subject to a fine and confiscation of the firearms. An Italian was convicted of such an offense, and brought an action on denial of due process since he was singled out as a class. The Court held the law was not in conflict with the United States Constitution because states could classify crimes and were free to properly do so. The Court also noted that wild game in a state belongs to the state, and the state may do with it as they wish.

On the challenge of violating an 1871 treaty with the Kingdom of Italy, the Court noted that weapons such as pistols that may be needed occasionally for self defense were not banned by the state. On the point about affecting trade and commerce under the treaty, the Justices wryly replied that when a case comes up about an Italian possessing a stock of guns for purposes of trade they will deal with that then.

The case begins below (after the syllabus in italics) with the published claims of the plaintiff's attorney, worded to seem quite reasonable, but these were rejected as invalid in the Court's decision.

STEARNS v. WOOD

236 U.S. 75; 35 S. Ct. 229; 59 L. Ed. 475
Argued December 18, 1914. January 18, 1915

Major Stearns, in the Inspector General Dept. of the Ohio National Guard, was facing a ceiling on his career, because the Secretary of War had required all state Adjutants General to limit the attainable rank in such departments to Lieutenant Colonel. Stearns sued his AG, Wood, and in the appeal asked the Supreme Court to assess all sorts of subjects he (and we) would like to see interpreted.

This opinion dismissed Stearns' challenge of the Secretary of War's general order affecting the organization of the Ohio National Guard. Stearns was unable to satisfy the requirement that anyone bringing a case needs constitutional "standing," a sufficiently concrete personal stake in a case or controversy. Accordingly, the Court never addressed Stearns' petition that they interpret the 2nd Amendment, or anything else in the long list he sought opinions on, tersely remarking that they had better things to do with their time.

BROWN v. UNITED STATES

256 U.S. 335; 41 S. Ct. 501; 65 L. Ed. 961
Argued November 19, 1920. May 16, 1921

Twenty-five years after "Hanging Judge" Parker's self-defense cases occupied the Court's attention, one more self-defense issue arrived, concerning defense at a place of work.

Evidence showed there had been trouble between defendant Brown and Hermes for a long time, and that Hermes had already assaulted Brown twice with a knife. On the day of the incident Brown had brought a handgun to work in his coat pocket—he was doing excavation for a Post Office—fearing recent threats Hermes had made. Sure enough, Hermes showed up with a bad attitude and a blade. Brown ran over to get his coat, retrieved the gun and shot four times as Hermes struck with the knife. He fired his final shot after Hermes was down.

The Court overturned Brown's murder conviction from the lower court, saying, first, if you have a right to be where you are, you have a right to stand your ground against an assailant; there was no automatic duty to retreat. Secondly, the Court remarked that in the heat of mortal combat a late shot does not in and of itself prevent a self-defense claim, and the issue is a point the jury must decide. Finally, the Court indicated that the right to stand your ground was roughly equivalent in your home, on your land or at work discharging your duties. It was in this case Justice Oliver Wendell Holmes made his famous remark:

> "Detached reflection cannot be demanded
> in the presence of an uplifted knife."

UNITED STATES v. SCHWIMMER

279 U.S. 644; 49 S. Ct. 448; 73 L. Ed. 889
April 12, 1929, Argued. May 27, 1929, Decided

Schwimmer was a Hungarian-born pacifist who sought to become a naturalized citizen of the United States. Her reservations about taking up arms in defense of the United States were held to be sufficient grounds for rejection of her petition, even though, as a 49-year-old female, she would probably never be asked to bear arms for national defense. Among other things, the Court reasoned that, as a pacifist, she might attempt to dissuade other people from performing their duties to bear arms and so she would detract from the country's strength and safety. The Justices state unequivocally that taking up arms when necessary in the nation's defense is a citizen's duty. The Court's quotation of the 2nd Amendment has seven typographical differences from the handwritten parchment version in the rotunda of the National Archives.

HAMILTON v. REGENTS OF THE UNIVERSITY OF CALIFORNIA

293 U.S. 245; 55 S. Ct. 197; 79 L. Ed. 343
October 17, 18, 1934, Argued. December 3, 1934, Decided

This case arises out of a challenge brought by a student who wanted to attend a state university but did not want to attend the required military instruction. Hamilton's argument that the state law was in violation of the 14th Amendment was rejected. The Court cited the 2nd Amendment to support the proposition that states could impose military training on their citizens, so long as the training did not violate federal law or rights.

SONZINSKY v. UNITED STATES

300 U.S. 506; 57 S. Ct. 554; 81 L. Ed. 772
March 12, 1937, Argued. March 29, 1937, Decided

Congressional debate surrounding the passage of the National Firearms Act of 1934 showed a marked concern against legislating in the domain of the 2nd Amendment, which was practically nonexistent up until that time (see the "Growth In Federal Gun Law" chart in *Gun Laws of America*, listed at gunlaws.com). Congress had passed a few restrictions on hunting in National Parks in the late 1890s and early 1900s, a ban on mailing concealable guns through the Post Office, and the original militia act in 1792, which required able-bodied citizens to keep arms, but that was pretty much all they had ever done. The NFA was an unprecedented giant leap into the nascent field of federal gun law.

It was only highly publicized gangland rub-outs during the Prohibition Era that prompted Congress to find some way to control the firearms that bootleggers were partial to, like the submachine gun. Fearful that any direct legislation would be unconstitutional, Congress decided to use its taxing authority. The requirements of the NFA, when placed in the statutes, went not into the criminal code, but into the tax code.

Sonzinsky challenged the constitutional authority of the United States government to enforce the National Firearms Act. The Court held that Congress could use its taxing power to impose heavy taxes on certain types of firearms and on firearms dealers, a significant increase in power. The Court explained that it would pay no attention to whether the tax was really designed to raise revenue, or was a subterfuge to impose laws which would otherwise be beyond congressional power.

UNITED STATES v. MILLER
307 U.S. 174; 59 S. Ct. 816; 83 L. Ed. 1206
March 30, 1939, Argued. May 15, 1939, Decided

The most commonly cited gun case in all of the Supreme Court's decisions, the *Miller* case frequently carries a characterization that can now be seen as less than accurate, such as "one of the Court's few pronouncements on the subject." It has been discussed in scores of law review articles without arriving at any consensus. *Miller* is unusual in several ways.

First, the two defendants who were charged with illegal possession of an unregistered short-barreled shotgun ran off before the High Court case and were not heard from in court again (except for a plea agreement described below). Second, no one represented their side before the Supreme Court that day, what the Court refers to as "no appearance for appellees," so only the government's arguments were heard. Third, since the lower court took no evidence concerning the nature or usability of a short shotgun, and the Supreme Court does not take evidence, the case has no record on a central point—the usefulness of this type of firearm. Finally, the short decision can be termed a "wobbler," easily interpreted to support disparate points of view. Anyone who follows these matters knows that the main factions in the gun debate all point to *Miller* as supporting their position.

It seems that the Court managed to tiptoe around some crucial elements, upholding the tax law in question. The Justices provided some interesting dicta, historical research about the militia and the 2nd Amendment from the time of the country's founding, and concluded that without better evidence, it could not make a better determination.

The National Firearms Act of 1934 had restricted, among other things, possession of short shotguns unless the guns were federally registered and a hefty tax was paid. The district court easily held the NFA unconstitutional on its face, on 2nd Amendment grounds, and released Miller and his co-defendant Layton. Interestingly, the federal government missed its deadline for filing an appeal, so the district court's decision had effectively invalidated the NFA. Recognizing their oversight later, the government actually re-indicted Miller and Layton, and when the case was dismissed a second time, filed a timely appeal to bring it to the Supreme Court.

After the Supreme Court took the case and the government filed its brief, Miller's lawyer telegraphed the Court that he had no money to file a brief or to come to Washington, D.C., to argue the case, and suggested that the Court rely on the brief of the United States. This would be considered legal malpractice today, in that the defendant's attorney invited the Court to adopt the prosecution's arguments.

The Supreme Court found that it was premature for any court to conclude whether or not the NFA violated the 2nd Amendment, so they remanded the case back to the district court for further proceedings. The Court reasoned that because the case had not presented any evidence of the military usefulness of the weapon, there was no way to say that there was a reasonable relationship between possession of a short-barreled shotgun and "the preservation or efficiency of a well regulated militia."

Meanwhile, Miller (a former bank robber) had been murdered before the decision. After the case was remanded, Layton pled guilty in a plea-bargain agreement with the government. Thus, no evidentiary hearing was ever held on whether a short-barreled shotgun was a militia-type weapon and protected from registration and taxation by the 2nd Amendment.

TOT v. UNITED STATES
319 U.S. 463; 63 S. Ct. 1241; 87 L. Ed. 1519
April 5, 6, 1943, Argued. June 7, 1943, Decided

The Federal Firearms Act included a clause that said if a person with a prior conviction for a crime of violence, or a fugitive, was found in possession of a firearm, that person was presumed to have obtained the gun in interstate commerce (which would give Congress jurisdiction). The Court decided this was not a rational conclusion, and that this did not provide sufficient facts to establish guilt. In other words, the law cannot presume a gun had just been in interstate commerce just because it was possessed by a felon. The law at the time was seen to affect only receipt of firearms or ammunition as a part of interstate transportation. It did not reach receipt of a gun or ammo in an intrastate transaction, which at some prior time had been transported interstate. That distinction was later addressed in *Bass*, *Barrett*, and *Scarborough*.

The lower court case (131 F.2d 261) that began the road to this appeal was found by Attorney Stephen Halbrook to be the original source of the "collective rights" conjecture used by anti-rights advocates in modern times. That case purports to be based on the intent of the Framers, but none of the references cited deny that the 2nd Amendment protects an individual right. Subsequent cases that make use of the collectivist argument merely string cite to cases ultimately traceable to *Tot*.

ADAMSON v. CALIFORNIA
332 U.S. 46; 67 S. Ct. 1672; 91 L. Ed. 1903; 171 A.L.R. 1223
January 15-16, 1947, Argued. June 23, 1947, Decided

This decision reaffirmed earlier cases holding that various provisions of the Bill of Rights, including the 5th Amendment privilege against self incrimination, were not binding on the states through the 14th Amendment. Justice Black, in a dissenting opinion joined by Douglas, quoted the legislative history of the 14th Amendment at length. He argued that it was intended to incorporate the Bill of Rights, including the 2nd Amendment, against the states. Justices Murphy and Rutledge agreed with this view, but would not have limited the content of the 14th Amendment Due Process Clause only to the provisions in the Bill of Rights.

JOHNSON v. EISENTRAGER
339 U.S. 763; 70 S. Ct. 936; 94 L. Ed. 1255
April 17, 1950, Argued. June 5, 1950, Decided

German nationals were arrested in China for violations of the laws of war. After Germany's unconditional surrender, these men continued to gather intelligence on U.S. forces and their movements for the Japanese. They were given a military trial in China and then transferred to Germany to serve out their sentences. While confined in Germany, 21 of them petitioned a U.S. district court for a writ of habeas corpus ordering their release.

They argued that their trial and imprisonment was contrary to provisions of the United States Constitution. It's a novel approach—Nazis captured in China and convicted of spying on the U.S. claim their imprisonment violates their constitutional rights. The Supreme Court held that these nonresident enemy aliens were not entitled to access U.S. Courts during wartime, so their petitions for habeas corpus were dismissed. Supporting the argument, Justice Jackson, writing for six Justices, reasoned if constitutional rights extended to nonresident enemy aliens, the absurd result would be that the aliens could require U.S. courts to assure them freedoms of speech, press, and assembly as in the 1st Amendment, and the right to bear arms as in the 2nd Amendment

KNAPP v. SCHWEITZER
357 U.S. 371; 78 S. Ct. 1302; 2 L. Ed. 2d 1393
March 6, 10, 1958, Argued. June 30, 1958, Decided

The issue in this New York union racketeering case was the scope of the privilege against self-incrimination. A witness had been granted immunity against state prosecution in exchange for his testimony, but, believing he might still be subject to federal prosecution for his testimony, he refused to testify. He was held in contempt of the NY court. Justice Frankfurter, for six members of the Court, held that the 5th Amendment limits only the federal government and not the states. Once the witness has been granted immunity from state prosecution, the state could compel him to testify (which could expose him to separate federal action). In rejecting Knapp's case, the Court pointed to the great historic divide between federal and state law enforcement powers. The Court cited the right to keep and bear arms as one of the rights previously held inapplicable to the states.

KONIGSBERG v. STATE BAR OF CALIFORNIA
366 U.S. 36; 81 S. Ct. 997; 6 L. Ed. 2d 105
December 14, 1960, Argued. April 24, 1961, Decided

Konigsberg applied for admission to the California Bar. He declined to answer any questions relating to his membership in the Communist Party on the grounds that the questions infringed his right of free association and expression under the 1st Amendment. His application was rejected and this challenge followed. The Court held that his 1st Amendment rights, as incorporated against the states through the 14th Amendment, were not violated. In the course of its discussion, the Court rejected the contention that the seemingly absolute language of the 1st Amendment ("Congress shall make no law...") required an absolute interpretation, and listed many examples of well-established exceptions, such as libel, slander, perjury, false advertising, solicitation of crime and more. The Court then draws a comparison to the "equally unqualified command" of the 2nd Amendment. The dissent argues there can be no such minor tinkering.

POE v. ULLMAN
367 U.S. 497; 81 S. Ct. 1752; 6 L. Ed. 2d 989
March 1-2, 1961, Argued. June 19, 1961, Decided

This was a challenge under the 14th Amendment to a Connecticut law banning the use of and the giving of advice for the use of contraceptive devices. Only once since it was enacted in 1879 was anyone charged under the law, but in that case the Connecticut Supreme Court upheld the law. Because there was no apparent risk of prosecution, the Court dismissed the case because there was not a sufficient controversy to merit adjudication. Dissenting, Justice Harlan mentioned the right to keep and bear arms along with other constitutional liberties, in a quote that would be repeatedly used by later Courts, on the breadth of liberty guaranteed by the 14th Amendment.

MALLOY v. HOGAN
378 U.S. 1; 84 S. Ct. 1489; 12 L. Ed. 2d 653
March 5, 1964, Argued. June 15, 1964, Decided

This case touches upon how much of the Bill of Rights applies against the states through the 14th Amendment, which in some measure forbids depriving people of their rights as national citizens. A constant fire has burned on this point since enactment of that Amendment in 1868. Early Courts flatly refused to impose the Bill of Rights on the states, as encroachments on state autonomy and sovereignty, and then experienced wholesale turnabouts in more recent years. The Court held, in the context of a gambling prosecution, that the 5th Amendment privilege against self incrimination applies against the states through the 14th Amendment, in the same way the 5th Amendment applies to the federal government.

Recounting the history of "incorporation" of the rights secured by the first eight amendments, the Court cited numerous prior decisions that called for full inclusion, no inclusion, and unpersuasive results. The list of cases holding that the Bill of Rights did not apply to the states includes *Presser,* which found the 2nd Amendment was a federal restriction and did not restrict the states. Today *Presser* stands out as one of the rare cases in which a portion of the Bill of Rights is still not explicitly incorporated under the 14th Amendment, for lack of a case addressing the point since that one in 1886. In this particular regard, the High Court could fairly be characterized as having said little on the subject.

MARYLAND v. UNITED STATES
381 U.S. 41; 85 S. Ct. 1293; 14 L. Ed. 2d 205
March 15, 1965, Argued. May 3, 1965, Decided

Several people died when a Maryland Air National Guard pilot in a jet trainer collided with an airliner. At issue was whether the pilot was in his military or civilian capacity at the time of the accident. The Court held that regardless of whether the pilot was in his civilian or military capacity, he was a state employee, so the federal government was not liable for the accident. Citing the militia clauses of Article I, section 8 of the Constitution, but not citing the 2nd Amendment, the Court wrote "The National Guard is the modern Militia reserved to the States."

GRISWOLD v. CONNECTICUT
381 U.S. 479; 85 S. Ct. 1678; 14 L. Ed. 2d 510
March 29-30, 1965, Argued. June 7, 1965, Decided

The Court ruled that a Connecticut statute forbidding the use of contraceptives violates a constitutional right to marital privacy. Although such a right is not specifically mentioned anywhere in the Constitution, the Justices perceived the right in the outer shadows (the "penumbra") of the Bill of Rights, as well as in the 9th Amendment's protection of rights not specifically listed in the document. Though the 2nd Amendment is not specifically named in the case, Justice Goldberg's concurring opinion, in which the Chief Justice and Justice Brennan joined, contains repeated reference to fundamental rights guaranteed to the people in the first eight amendments of the Bill of Rights, which is where the right to keep and bear arms resides.

MIRANDA v. ARIZONA
384 U.S. 436; 86 S. Ct. 1602; 16 L. Ed. 2d 694
February 28-March 1, 1966, Argued. June 13, 1966, Decided

This well-known case led to the now familiar verbal warning for criminal suspects, "You have the right to remain silent…". Without that warning, most custodial interrogations would be deemed coercive and thus inadmissible as a violation of the 5th Amendment privilege against self incrimination.

Miranda's basic principles are only tangential to the infringement issues continually arising over the right to keep arms and the right to bear arms, and *Miranda* is by no stretch a gun case itself *per se*. But it is in a special category of cases that is cited frequently in terms of the general rights involved in firearms rights.

A reader who feels that the inclusion of this case goes too far afield of the *Supreme Court Gun Cases* theme (and case count) will be pleased to note that the following seven cases have not been included for that very reason:

Marbury v. Madison, 5 U.S. 137 1803
"an act of the legislature repugnant to the constitution is void."

Boyd v. United States, 116 U.S. 616 1886
"It is the duty of courts to be watchful for the constitutional rights of the citizen, and against any stealthy encroachments thereon."

Norton v. Shelby County, 118 U.S. 425 1886
"An unconstitutional act is not law; it confers no rights; it imposes no duties; affords no protection; it creates no office; it is in legal contemplation as though it had never been passed."

Olmstead v. United States, 277 U.S. 438 1928
"Experience should teach us to be most on our guard to protect liberty when the government's purposes are beneficent. Men born to freedom are naturally alert to repel invasion of their liberty by evil-minded rulers. The greatest dangers to liberty lurk in insidious encroachment by men of zeal, well meaning but without understanding." (Note: quoted from dissent.)

Murdock v. Pennsylvania, 319 U.S. 105 1943
"A state may not impose a charge for the enjoyment of a right granted by the Federal Constitution."

"a person cannot be compelled 'to purchase, through a license fee or a license tax, the privilege freely granted by the Constitution.'"

Staub v. Baxley, 355 U.S. 313 1958
"It is settled by a long line of recent decisions of this Court that an ordinance which, like this one, makes the peaceful enjoyment of freedoms which the Constitution guarantees contingent upon the uncontrolled will of an official— as by requiring a permit or license which may be granted or withheld in the

discretion of such official—is an unconstitutional censorship or prior restraint upon the enjoyment of those freedoms."

Shuttlesworth v. City of Birmingham Alabama, 394 U.S. 147 1969
"And our decisions have made clear that a person faced with such an unconstitutional licensing law may ignore it and engage with impunity in the exercise of the right of free expression for which the law purports to require a license."

It's probably a good idea to keep in mind that the axiom described in these cases—an unconstitutional law is void—has an important corollary. Even an unconstitutional law is the law, and stays in place with full force and effect, until it is declared unconstitutional by a court of competent jurisdiction, or until removed by the legislature. People are arrested, prosecuted and imprisoned under unconstitutional laws all the time. Some get off later. That can be summed up with a piece of street wisdom: The law means what the officer with the gun in your ear says it means.

HAYNES v. UNITED STATES
390 U.S. 85; 88 S. Ct. 722; 19 L. Ed. 2d 923
October 11, 1967, Argued. January 29, 1968, Decided

This case applied the 5th Amendment privilege against self incrimination to the National Firearms Act registration requirements. The Court held the privilege to be a complete defense to a charge of failing to register possession of an NFA firearm or possession of an unregistered NFA firearm. The law in question was written in such a way that you were guilty if you failed to fill out the form, and guilty if you filled it out accurately, a forced self incrimination which the Court could not let stand. The Court stated that Congress' authority to regulate in this area was not at issue, only the 5th Amendment implications of registration of certain NFA weapons. Federal statutes were subsequently amended to address the problem identified in *Haynes*, allowing ongoing registration of NFA weapons. The statutory changes Congress hoped would correct the situation came before the High Court in 1971 in *U.S. v. Freed*, and were upheld.

DUNCAN v. LOUISIANA
391 U.S. 145; 88 S. Ct. 1444; 20 L. Ed. 2d 491
January 17, 1968, Argued. May 20, 1968, Decided

The Court ruled that the 6th Amendment right to a jury trial applied against the states through the 14th Amendment. Justice Black, concurring with Justice Douglas, quoted from the 14th Amendment ratification debates, including a reference to the right to keep and bear arms as one of the "personal rights guarantied and secured by the first eight amendments of the Constitution."

TERRY v. OHIO
392 U.S. 1; 88 S. Ct. 1868; 20 L. Ed. 2d 889
December 12, 1967, Argued. June 10, 1968, Decided

This famous case authorized what has become known as a "Terry frisk," a limited protective non-invasive search for weapons, made by a peace officer under specially defined circumstances.

Terry and his two accomplices were observed apparently casing a jewelry store, by plainclothes Cleveland police detective Martin McFadden, a 39-year police veteran. The suspects walked past the shop and peered in the window a dozen times, after which McFadden approached them, sensing they were up to no good. When they mumbled instead of identifying themselves, after McFadden had identified himself as a policeman, he grabbed Terry, spun him around and patted down the outside of his clothes. He felt a pistol under Terry's overcoat, then found a pistol in the outer pocket of Chilton, one of the accomplices, and nothing on the third man they were with. The officer had a police wagon called to the scene and Terry and Chilton, who hadn't visibly committed any crime in front of him, were subsequently charged with concealed weapons violations based on McFadden's search.

The defendants moved to have the charges against them dropped, claiming the evidence against them had been seized illegally. Officer McFadden, they argued, had no "probable cause" to suspect a crime had been committed when he made the search that found the guns. Without probable cause, they claimed the pat-down violated their protection from unreasonable search and seizure.

In this critically important 4th Amendment case the High Court held that such a "stop and frisk" is a seizure of the person, and a search, conducted without a warrant, but that it could be allowed under the 4th Amendment if it was reasonable. There is an immediate interest of the police officer in taking steps to neutralize a threat of physical harm. Discretion of the officer at the scene, and an evaluation of the facts afterwards by a court determine reasonableness. An arrest would require the higher standard of probable cause, and would justify a full search of the suspect. The more limited Terry frisk, in order to avoid violating the right to be free from unreasonable search and seizure, does not allow a full search, but only a superficial pat down for the safety of the officer and others nearby. The Court recognizes a potential for abuse, especially in populations that complain of police harassment, and that even a frisk of outer clothing for weapons is a severe intrusion upon cherished personal security.

In a lone dissent, Justice Douglas is dismayed at the elimination of the long-held probable-cause requirement that an officer would have to be able to express later, or that a judge would need to issue a warrant. He says such a change, if needed to combat modern forms of lawlessness, is a "long step down the totalitarian path" and should require a choice of the people through an amendment to the Constitution.

In subsequent years, the *Terry* decision has been used to justify a wide variety of frisks, pat-downs and other intermediate searches, often under conditions that have little to do with the officer-safety rationale used here.

BURTON v. SILLS
394 U.S. 812; 89 S. Ct. 1486; 22 L. Ed. 2d 748
April 28, 1969, Decided

The Supreme Court of New Jersey upheld the constitutionality of a state gun licensing law. This law required a firearm purchaser to have an identification card issued by the local chief of police. Issuance of the identification cards left some discretion in the hands of the police chief. The New Jersey Supreme Court relied on cases holding the 2nd Amendment inapplicable to the states and on selected secondary sources interpreting the 2nd Amendment as not guaranteeing an individual right. The Court dismissed the appeal for want of a substantial federal question.

UNITED STATES v. FREED
401 U.S. 601; 91 S. Ct. 1112; 28 L. Ed. 2d 356
January 11, 1971, Argued. April 5, 1971, Decided

Although the general public could be compelled to register certain firearms under the National Firearms Act, a felon could not be compelled to do so because it would violate the 5th Amendment guarantee against self incrimination. The Court reached this unexpected result in *Haynes v. U.S.*, and Congress promptly rewrote the law to cure the problem. In *Freed*, under the newly amended statute, the Court rejects a 5th Amendment challenge, establishing the legitimacy of the ingenious new licensing scheme, summarized succinctly in Justice Douglas' third paragraph.

NFA "firearms" aren't guns as most people think of the term, they include a special class of weapons better known as "destructive devices"—bombs, missiles, incendiaries, machine guns, sawed-off rifles and shotguns, and in Freed's case, hand grenades—which the Act refers to collectively (and somewhat confusingly) as "firearms" and regulates under tax law.

UNITED STATES v. BASS
404 U.S. 336; 92 S. Ct. 515; 30 L. Ed. 2d 488
October 18, 1971, Argued. December 20, 1971, Decided

Bass was convicted of violating the federal ban on possession of a firearm by a convicted felon. The felon-in-possession ban, like the rest of the Gun Control Act of 1968, was enacted on the basis of Congress' power to regulate interstate commerce. On appeal, Bass argued that the government failed to show that his firearms possession had a nexus with interstate commerce. Interpreting the language Congress used, the Court held that an interstate commerce nexus must be shown for all three offenses: receiving, possessing, and transporting firearms by a felon. The Court went on to say that proof that the firearm in question had previously traveled in interstate commerce, which would be true of most firearms, would be sufficient to satisfy the nexus for possession.

Government prosecutors had not attempted to show this connection at trial, thinking it unnecessary, based on the omission of a single comma in the law (they made other arguments too, but the comma became key, see the discussion at Roman numeral "I"). That cost them the case, freed the defendant, and put the onus on the government to prove this in all future cases (it's not a tremendously difficult proof to make).

The government's arguments here seek easier convictions. On one hand that would be desirable to help take criminals out of circulation, but on the other hand, it is undesirable to the extent it could more easily lead to convictions of the innocent, or be abused by the authorities. The Court actually rebukes Congress mildly for not making the statute more clear.

UNITED STATES v. BISWELL
406 U.S. 311; 92 S. Ct. 1593; 32 L. Ed. 2d 87
March 28, 1972, Argued. May 15, 1972, Decided

Biswell was a pawn shop owner and federally licensed firearms dealer. He got a visit one day from a local police officer and a federal agent from the Treasury Dept. After identifying themselves, they asked to look in his locked gun storeroom. He asked if they had a warrant. They said no, but showed him instead the statute authorizing unannounced searches for licensed dealers. Biswell replied, "Well, that's what it says so I guess it's okay." Inside, they found two sawed-off rifles, and he was arrested and convicted for dealing in National Firearms Act firearms without paying the required special occupational tax.

This is a 4th Amendment case in which the Court held that no warrant is required for the government to conduct an unannounced search of a federal firearms licensee's business, under 18 U.S.C. §923 (g), and to confiscate illegally possessed weapons. A dealer who "chooses to engage in this pervasively regulated business" knows the requirement, and effective inspection is a necessary deterrent to criminal activity. This is also the first case in which the word "sporting" appears in connection with firearms, in an inaccurate reference to the defendant being "federally licensed to deal in sporting weapons," since a dealer license makes no such distinction.

ADAMS v. WILLIAMS
407 U.S. 143; 92 S. Ct. 1921; 32 L. Ed. 2d 612
April 10, 1972, Argued. June 12, 1972, Decided

This is a 4th Amendment case with a discussion of carrying guns and the justification needed for a police officer to frisk someone for weapons. At 2:15 a.m. in a high-crime area, a police officer received a tip from an informant he knew that a man was sitting in a nearby car with drugs and a gun at his waist. The officer tapped on the car window, asking Williams to open the door. When Williams rolled down the window, the officer reached in and pulled a revolver from Williams' waistband. After Williams was arrested for unlawful possession of the gun, drugs were found on Williams and in the car. Williams challenged the sufficiency of the justification for the stop and frisk.

The Court held that Williams' 4th Amendment rights were not violated. Compare this case with *J.L. v. Florida*, where a similar tip made anonymously was found insufficient to support a stop and frisk. In dissent, Justice Douglas, joined by Justice Marshall, called for sweeping gun control, psychological tests for gun owners, and a ban on pistols for everyone but the police. He would prefer, he says, to "water down" the 2nd Amendment.

LAIRD v. TATUM
408 U.S. 1; 92 S. Ct. 2318; 33 L. Ed. 2d 154
March 27, 1972, Argued. June 26, 1972, Decided

This case arose out of a challenge to domestic surveillance conducted by Army Intelligence, in assisting local authorities in Detroit, immediately following riots in 1967. Five members of the Court held that the 1st Amendment claims did not present a sufficient controversy for adjudication, as there was no showing of present or future harm. Dissenting, Justices Douglas and Marshall emphasized the importance of civilian control over the military. In support of this argument, they pointed to the role of the 2nd Amendment "specifically authorizing a decentralized militia, guaranteeing the right of the people to keep and bear arms."

ROE v. WADE

410 U.S. 113; 93 S. Ct. 705; 35 L. Ed. 2d 147
December 13, 1971, Argued. January 22, 1973, Decided

This is the well-known abortion case striking down a Texas abortion law, because it infringed rights protected by the 9th and 14th Amendments. Concurring, Justice Stewart quoted Justice Harlan's list of liberties protected by the Bill of Rights, including the right to keep and bear arms, from *Poe v. Ullman*.

HUDDLESTON v. UNITED STATES

415 U.S. 814; 94 S. Ct. 1262; 39 L. Ed. 2d 782
November 7, 1973, Argued. March 26, 1974, Decided

William Huddleston pawned his wife's Winchester 30-30 for $25 at a pawnshop in Oxnard, California. He later hocked her Russian 7.62 and a Remington .22, and then redeemed them a few months later. He filled out and signed the 4473 federal firearms transfer form inaccurately. His story is told in this case rather well, and you get a glimpse of how a defendant moves through the system.

This is a case interpreting the Gun Control Act of 1968 as it applies to redemption of guns from a pawn shop by a felon who had pawned them. Huddleston argued that the GCA wasn't intended to apply to pawn transactions, that he retained title in the pawn and didn't "acquire" the guns when they were redeemed. The Court disagreed, holding that the Act applied to pawn the same as sales from dealers, to fulfill Congress' intent to keep guns out of the hands of felons, fugitives, juveniles and the mentally defective. The Court recognized a congressional intent to prohibit firearms to individuals whose possession would be contrary to the public interest.

UNITED STATES v. POWELL

423 U.S. 87; 96 S. Ct. 316; 46 L. Ed. 2d 228
Argued October 6, 1975. December 2, 1975 Decided

This is an appeal from a conviction for mailing a firearm capable of being concealed on the person. Based on one of the oldest federal gun laws, enacted in 1927, the statute outlawed such mail in order to remove the U.S. Post Office as a vehicle for criminals to arm themselves. Powell advanced both a statutory construction argument and an argument that the statute was unconstitutionally vague. In particular, she claimed the law did not ban mailing a 10-inch barrel, 22-inch overall sawed off shotgun. The Court rejected her arguments, holding that the statute did not apply only to handguns, and that the statute gave adequate notice of the prohibited conduct.

BARRETT v. UNITED STATES

423 U.S. 212; 96 S. Ct. 498; 46 L. Ed. 2d 450
Argued November 4, 1975. January 13, 1976 Decided

Pearl Barrett was caught and convicted of housebreaking, a felony in Kentucky, and received a two-year sentence. Five years later, he walked into an auto parts store, owned by the local dentist in Booneville, Ky., his home town, and bought a .32 caliber Smith and Wesson revolver. The dentist knew him, and skipped filling out the required 4473 form. Within an hour, Barrett had gotten himself liquored up and arrested for driving while intoxicated; the county sheriff who made the arrest found Barrett's fully loaded gun lying on the floorboard on the driver's side.

This time, Barrett was convicted of receiving a firearm that had been shipped in interstate commerce. Barrett tried to wiggle out of his conviction by claiming he was outside the scope of the law because he bought the gun at a local dealer in his state of residence. He suggested that Congress had only meant to reach felons who were acting in some interstate way, not merely intrastate transactions with a gun that might have, at some time in the past, traveled across state lines. The gun had been made in Massachusetts, shipped to a distributor in North Carolina, and then to the Kentucky dentist.

The Court had little difficulty rejecting it. The Court held that the government need not prove the defendant had participated in the interstate shipment of the firearm. Rather, the government need only prove that at some point the firearm had crossed state lines. Because Barrett had not filled out a 4473 form, he faced no issues related to making false statements.

MOORE v. CITY OF EAST CLEVELAND

431 U.S. 494; 97 S. Ct. 1932; 52 L. Ed. 2d 531
Argued November 2, 1976. May 31, 1977 Decided

This case is a substantive due process case challenging a zoning regulation that prohibited certain family members from living together. In discussing the scope of the 14th Amendment Due Process Clause, both the majority and the dissent quote Justice Harlan's dissent in *Poe v. Ullman* listing the right to keep and bear arms among other constitutional liberties.

SCARBOROUGH v. UNITED STATES

431 U.S. 563; 97 S. Ct. 1963; 52 L. Ed. 2d 582
Argued March 2, 1977. June 6, 1977 Decided; as amended

This case involves the interpretation of the Gun Control Act's prohibition of firearms possession "in commerce or affecting commerce" by a convicted felon. The Court held that if the firearm had once traveled in interstate commerce, no matter how long ago, that was sufficient to make a case against a violator. The defendant, a convicted drug dealer, also argued that the gun moved in commerce before he was convicted. The Court rejected this argument as any sort of defense, taking a very broad view of the needed nexus between commerce and any gun in question. As with previous Gun Control Act cases, the case was about statutory construction, not whether the Gun Control Act was a constitutionally proper exercise of the interstate commerce power.

In dissent by himself, Justice Stewart wrestles with a problem the Court's decision creates. A person who legally possesses firearms becomes guilty automatically of a serious crime if ever convicted of any felony, as a felon in possession of firearms. The government argues it would be reasonable about this, and that "prosecutorial discretion" would take care of the problem. Proper construction of a criminal statute though, Stewart says, cannot depend upon the good will of those who must enforce it.

SIMPSON v. UNITED STATES
435 U.S. 6; 98 S. Ct. 909; 55 L. Ed. 2d 70
November 1, 1977, Argued. February 28, 1978, Decided

Armed bank robbers got away with $40,000 from a bank in Kentucky, and then two months later hit a branch of the same bank on the other side of town for about the same amount. They were caught, tried and convicted of both crimes, and received lengthy sentences. Their sentences were increased for using guns in the commission of the crimes, under both the federal bank robbery statute (18 USC §2113) and the federal felony-with-a-firearm statute (18 USC §924). Wrestling with the question of double jeopardy, the Court applied the "Blockburger test," which they describe below, and other reasoning, to decide that the sentences cannot be enhanced under both statutes for the same crime.

LEWIS v. UNITED STATES
445 U.S. 55; 100 S. Ct. 915; 63 L. Ed. 2d 198
January 7, 1980, Argued. February 27, 1980, Decided

George Lewis appealed his conviction for "possession of a firearm by a convicted felon" on the grounds that his prior conviction was unconstitutional under the 6th Amendment. He had been found guilty of a Florida breaking-and-entering felony 16 years earlier without being represented by a lawyer, before this arrest for gun possession in 1977. The Court held that a defendant may not contest the validity of a prior felony conviction at his trial for unlawful possession of a firearm. A felony conviction, even one apparently unconstitutional, was found to be a sufficient basis for a conviction of possession of a firearm by a convicted felon.

The Court repeatedly notes Congress' intent to ban gun possession by people deemed specifically dangerous, and Congress' expressed intent to leave the rights of the innocent untouched. The Court says the "fact of conviction must deprive the person of a right to a firearm," implying the right must exist in the first place, since it can be removed. In a footnote, Justice Blackmun's majority opinion comes close to endorsing the anti-individual interpretation of the 2nd Amendment.

BUSIC v. UNITED STATES
446 U.S. 398; 100 S. Ct. 1747; 64 L. Ed. 2d 381
February 27, 1980, Argued. May 19, 1980, Decided

Michael Busic and Anthony LaRocca, Jr., arranged to sell $30,000 of narcotics to a man they didn't realize was a DEA undercover agent. When the agent showed up with the money, they tried to rob him instead. The agent called in his backup, LaRocca fired a few shots but hit no one, and the pair were taken into custody and disarmed (Busic had a gun tucked under his belt). The pair were convicted and received stiff prison terms, part of which came from a sentence enhancement under 18 USC §111 for armed assault of a federal officer, and also from 18 USC §924, for committing a federal felony with a firearm. For reasons similar to the *Simpson* decision, the Court held that the sentences could be increased only under the provision of the armed assault law.

DICKERSON v. NEW BANNER INSTITUTE
460 U.S. 103; 103 S. Ct. 986; 74 L. Ed. 2d 845
November 29, 1982, Argued. February 23, 1983, Decided

This case involves the interpretation of the federal prohibition on possession of firearms by anyone who has been convicted of a crime punishable by more than a year in prison. The Court held that a person who pled guilty to such a crime, was given probation and a deferred judgment, and later had the record of the deferred judgment expunged was still "convicted" for the purpose of applying the federal statute and keeping the prohibition in place.

UNITED STATES v. ONE ASSORTMENT OF 89 FIREARMS
465 U.S. 354; 104 S. Ct. 1099; 79 L. Ed. 2d 361
November 30, 1983, Argued. February 22, 1984, Decided

Patrick Mulcahey was charged with dealing in firearms without a federal license, a serious crime. When brought to trial, he claimed he had been entrapped into making the illegal transactions, and the jury acquitted him. Despite being found not guilty, the government moved to confiscate his firearms, suing the guns, not Mulcahey, in an *in rem* civil procedure.

Mulcahey argued the matter was settled with his acquittal, and that the 5th Amendment protection against being charged twice for the same crime prevented the government from taking his property. The issues decided by the Court do not involve the right to bear arms, as Mulcahey did not raise the 2nd Amendment in his defense.

The Court upheld the forfeiture, deciding that acquittal of criminal charges does not automatically bar a subsequent civil proceeding. The forfeiture was remedial in nature, not criminal, and thus not a violation of double jeopardy. The lower threshold of evidence needed to win in a civil proceeding allowed the government to make its case and confiscate the firearms. Although the defendant was not found guilty of dealing without a license, the guns were destined to be sold in violation of law and therefore could be seized. In making their decision, they overturned *Coffey v. U.S.* which, since 1886, had suggested a civil forfeiture could not constitutionally proceed after acquittal on related criminal charges. This weakening of the protections against double jeopardy contributes to the risk citizens now face of federal, state, criminal and civil trials for the same offense.

This turned out to be a major case setting the stage for massive use of civil forfeiture of people's property in subsequent decades. Congress limited the government's firearms forfeitures abuses somewhat by enacting the Firearms Owners' Protection Act soon afterwards in 1986. However, *One Assortment* remains a major pro-forfeiture precedent in many other judicial contexts.

TENNESSEE v. GARNER

471 U.S. 1; 105 S. Ct. 1694; 85 L. Ed. 2d 1
October 30, 1984, Argued. March 27, 1985, Decided

Common law in existence from before the Bill of Rights, explicit statutes of nearly half the states, and the law in Tennessee at the time of this case allowed police officers to shoot a fleeing felony suspect if it was the only way to prevent the person from escaping. Many arguments exist for and against such a long-standing and widely held policy, and they are examined in this case. The Court decided that such open-ended authorization of the use of deadly force is an unreasonable form of seizure under the 4th Amendment.

This is the only High Court case touching upon the fringe self-defense issue of pursuit. While deadly force is recognized as legitimate in responding to a potentially deadly attack, its use to stop a suspect from getting away is much less reliable justification.

Typically viewed in legal circles as a deadly force case, or a 4th Amendment case, to many police officers *Garner* is the quintessential gun case because it illuminates the question of when you can draw and use your sidearm. Additional conditions must be present now before deadly force is permissible for officers dealing with a fleeing suspect. Conditions include whether the suspect poses a threat to the community, or threatens the officer with a weapon, or if there is probable cause to believe the suspect has committed a crime involving the infliction or threatened infliction of serious physical harm. An officer must also give some warning if feasible.

Memphis police officer Elton Hymon, responding to a residential burglary call, found a jimmied window and then heard the back door slam. In the junk-strewn backyard he saw a figure crouching near a fence. He shouted a police warning and ordered the individual to freeze. The shadowy figure jumped up on the fence and was one leap from escape when the officer took him into custody and prevented his escape, with a revolver shot to the back of the head. The officer acted under authority of Tennessee law written to prevent such escapes, and fifteen-year-old Edward Garner, unarmed, died on the way to the hospital.

The High Court decided that Tennessee's law was unconstitutional and rewrote the requirements for use of deadly force by the police. It is important to keep in mind that the conditions discussed in here apply to the authorities, or a person called to assist the authorities, but not to the general public, who are not addressed in this regard at the Supreme Court level. Common wisdom holds that its better for a criminal to get away than to have a lien on your home from legal bills after shooting someone running away with your TV or the family jewels. State laws vary widely about citizen use of deadly force against fleeing felons, and of course, a person is only determined to be a felon after a conviction.

Justice Sandra Day O'Conner, writing in dissent for a minority of three, agrees that shooting a fleeing suspect is a "seizure" for constitutional purposes, but the dissenters characterize the majority's decision as a new right for burglary suspects to blithely leave the scene of a crime, and argue that the 4th Amendment contains no such right. The dissent takes the position that using deadly force to apprehend a fleeing burglar under the circumstances of this case is not unreasonable.

UNITED STATES v. GALIOTO
477 U.S. 556; 106 S. Ct. 2683; 91 L. Ed. 2d 459
March 26, 1986, Argued. June 27, 1986, Decided

Galioto brought an equal protection challenge to the federal prohibition on selling a firearm to a person who had been adjudicated mentally defective or involuntarily committed. He argued there was no rational basis for distinguishing felons, who could have their civil rights restored and regain the legal ability to buy firearms, from former mental patients, who had no provision for restoring their legal ability to buy firearms. Between the time the district court of New Jersey ruled in Galioto's favor, finding the arrangement in violation of the Constitution, and when the Supreme Court heard the case, Congress amended the law to create a remedy for former mental patients. Thus, the Court dismissed the equal protection challenge as moot.

DeSHANEY v. WINNEBAGO COUNTY DEPT. OF SOCIAL SERVICES
489 U.S. 189; 109 S. Ct. 998; 103 L. Ed. 2d 249
November 2, 1988, Argued. February 22, 1989, Decided

At the center of the gun issue is the question of whether the state is ultimately responsible for providing you personally with security and safety, especially when those in government know you are under a specific threat. In *DeShaney* the Court affirms the state is not responsible for your safety, concluding, among other things, that the 14th Amendment was intended "to protect the people from the State, not to ensure that the State protected them from each other."

The case hinges on a claim that Winnebago County violated a young boy's civil rights by failing to protect him from a father the Department of Social Services knew was abusive. Young Joshua was beaten nearly to death and will have to be institutionalized for life. The Court rejected his claim that his constitutional rights were violated, holding that the substantive component of the 14th Amendment Due Process Clause is a limitation on undue government action against life, liberty or property, not a guarantee that the state will protect its citizens from private violations of life, liberty or property. In a dissent, three Justices chastise the government for providing protective services and displacing private sources of protection, and then, at the critical moment, abandoning the victims and shrugging their shoulders.

UNITED STATES v. VERDUGO-URQUIDEZ
494 U.S. 259; 110 S. Ct. 1056; 108 L. Ed. 2d 222
November 7, 1989, Argued. February 28, 1990, Decided

Rene Martin Verdugo-Urquidez was the kind of drug lord who makes the newspapers. A resident and citizen of Mexico, the suspect had been captured in Mexico and brought to the United States. Some evidence against him was obtained by searching his Mexican residence after arrest, all with the cooperation of the two nations' authorities. He tried to get off by claiming the evidence was the result of an illegal search and seizure, and hence inadmissible. Upon this ignoble specimen rests an important 4th Amendment decision in which the Court held that a suspected drug lord of Mexican citizenship did not have 4th Amendment rights against unreasonable search and seizure with respect to his property in a foreign country. (This man was subsequently convicted, in a separate prosecution, of the highly publicized torture-murder of DEA Special Agent Enrique Camarena Salazar.)

In reaching its decision, the Court wrestled with the meaning of the phrase, "the people," and decided it is a term of art in the Constitution, referring to a class of persons who are part of the national community. In this light Verdugo-Urquidez had insufficient ties to the United States to be one of "the people." The Court compared the words and phrases chosen by the Framers for various clauses in the Constitution, noting that "the people" which the 2nd Amendment "protects" are the same class of persons mentioned in the Constitution's Preamble, and protected by the 1st, 4th, 9th and 10th Amendments, as well as Article 1, §2, cl.1, which specifies that Representatives are to be chosen by "the people."

PERPICH v. DEPARTMENT OF DEFENSE
496 U.S. 334; 110 S. Ct. 2418; 110 L. Ed. 2d 312
March 27, 1990, Argued. June 11, 1990, Decided

This was a challenge brought by the Governor of Minnesota to a change in federal law that allowed the federal government to call up members of the National Guard for duty or training overseas without the Governor's consent.

The Court unanimously ruled that the militia clauses in Article I did not require consent of the state governor, as the federal power is supreme over military affairs. Despite intense deliberation on the nature of and the state's power over its own militia, the arguments center entirely on Article 1 clauses of the Constitution and related statutes, and fail to include any reference to the 2nd Amendment. It is difficult to reconcile the absence of the 2nd Amendment in this case if, as proposed by recent commentators, that amendment conveys power to the states to organize their militias. In that regard, it seems impossible to reconcile this new "collectivist" view of the right to keep and bear arms with the Court's entire history.

The case provides a detailed historical view of the development of the militia, from its humble beginnings with quotations from Alexander Hamilton and from the first militia law, through the various separate and distinct elements it contains today. President Teddy Roosevelt is credited with declaring in 1901 that the 1792 militia law was worthless, and thus began the process of distinguishing between an unorganized militia composed of the citizenry at large, and a highly organized militia known today as the National Guard. It was the Dick Act of 1903 that created this separation and distinction, and of course a statute is incapable of rewriting the Constitution.

The Court also expresses comfort with the dual enlistment system, which since 1933 has required state National Guard members to simultaneously enroll in the National Guard of the United States, which is the national armed forces reserves. State members of the Guard lose their status as members of the State militia during any period of active federal duty and regain it when they muster out of federal duty. The relationship of the various parts of our armed strength is the heart of the discussion in this case.

UNITED STATES v. THOMPSON/CENTER ARMS COMPANY
504 U.S. 505; 112 S. Ct. 2102; 119 L. Ed. 2d 308
January 13, 1992, Argued. June 8, 1992, Decided

Thompson/Center challenged the government's assessment that its Contender pistol fell under the scope of the National Firearms Act of 1934 if it was possessed along with a kit that could be used to convert the Contender into a rifle. With the kit, a person could turn the Contender pistol into an ordinary rifle (entirely legal) or could put a rifle stock on the gun, while leaving the pistol barrel in place. Under federal law, this would create a short-barreled rifle, which would be illegal unless the gun were registered and the special National Firearms Act tax were paid.

The question in the case is whether a regulated firearm (the short rifle) has been "made" merely by possessing a Contender pistol and the conversion kit which could be used for legal or illegal conversions. The Court held that the statutory language was ambiguous, and because the NFA is a tax statute carrying criminal sanctions with no additional requirement of willfulness, the disputed term should be resolved in favor of the respondent, Thompson/Center, under the well-established principle of lenity.

The Court discussed that in many instances, having a collection of parts that assembles into an NFA "firearm" constitutes having one (silencers, machine guns, a gun and a machine-gun-conversion kit for it, etc.). In an interesting use of language, part of this decision relies upon the word "gun" to mean a regular firearm, such as any store might carry, and "firearm," to refer to an NFA weapon, which includes short-barreled long guns, disguised firearms like pen guns, cane guns and wallet guns, and heavier armament like explosives, bombs, rockets, mortars, incendiaries and more.

Attorney Stephen Halbrook was the lead attorney on this case and made the winning oral arguments before the Justices.

PLANNED PARENTHOOD v. CASEY
505 U.S. 833; 112 S. Ct. 2791; 120 L. Ed. 2d 674
April 22, 1992, Argued. June 29, 1992, Decided

This important case upholds certain abortion restrictions, while affirming abortion as a constitutional right. The Court's opinion—jointly written by O'Connor, Kennedy, and Souter—quotes a Supreme Court precedent from *Poe v. Ullman*, on the full scope of liberties guaranteed by the 14th Amendment, including language about the right to keep and bear arms along with other constitutional rights and liberties.

DEAL v. UNITED STATES
508 U.S. 129; 113 S. Ct. 1993; 124 L. Ed. 2d 44
March 1, 1993, Argued. May 17, 1993, Decided

This case involves interpretation of a federal statute prescribing a 5-year prison sentence for using a gun in a crime during a crime of violence and a 20-year sentence for a second or subsequent offense. The Court held that the second conviction may occur at the same trial as the first conviction. Deal, convicted at trial of six separate armed bank robberies, was sentenced to five years for the first and 20 years for robberies two through five.

SMITH v. UNITED STATES

508 U.S. 223; 113 S. Ct. 2050; 124 L. Ed. 2d 138
March 23, 1993, Argued. June 1, 1993, Decided

The Court was called upon to interpret a federal statute prescribing a mandatory sentence for "using" a firearm during and in relation to a drug-trafficking crime. Smith offered to trade his MAC-10, converted to full auto, to an undercover agent for drugs. The Court held that using a weapon, within the meaning of the drug statute, did not require using the firearm as a weapon. Any manner of facilitating the crime, including barter, was sufficient to trigger the mandatory sentence—30 years in Smith's case. The Court made an exception for a firearm that in no way furthered the crime, such as one used to scratch your head. Many colorful and unusual hypotheticals such as that are strewn throughout this case and in the dissent by three of the Justices.

STINSON v. UNITED STATES

508 U.S. 36; 113 S. Ct. 1913; 123 L. Ed. 2d 598
March 24, 1993, Argued. May 3, 1993, Decided

At trial, three-time loser Terry Stinson was convicted as a career offender on the basis of a court decision that possession of a firearm by a convicted felon was a crime of violence. The issue in the case was whether the commentary to the U.S. Sentencing Guidelines is binding on the federal courts. The Court held that the commentary is indeed binding on federal courts, and thus an amendment to the Guidelines that specifically excluded firearms possession by a felon from the definition of "crime of violence" should have been applied.

ALBRIGHT v. OLIVER

510 U.S. 266; 114 S. Ct. 807; 127 L. Ed. 2d 114
October 12, 1993, Argued. January 24, 1994, Decided

This case rejected Albright's argument that the 14th Amendment Due Process Clause protects a right to be free of malicious prosecution. In dissent, Justices Stevens and Blackmun argued for a more expansive reading of the Due Process Clause, listing the right to keep and bear arms as a liberty guaranteed by the Constitution, by quoting the decision in *Poe v. Ullman*.

BEECHAM v. UNITED STATES

511 U.S. 368; 114 S. Ct. 1669; 128 L. Ed. 2d 383
March 23, 1993, Argued. May 16, 1994, Decided

Federal law makes it illegal for a convicted felon to possess a firearm, but a felon who has had civil rights restored is no longer under that disability. The Court held that a state restoration of civil rights does not eliminate the federal disability; the jurisdiction that convicted the person must be the one that restores the civil rights. The Court notes that a person cannot restore those rights currently at the federal level, but that this leaves the person no worse off than in states (it names eleven) that also have no current provision for restoring these lost rights.

CUSTIS v. UNITED STATES

511 U.S. 485; 114 S. Ct. 1732; 128 L. Ed. 2d 517
February 28, 1994, Argued. May 23, 1994, Decided

Custis was convicted at trial of possession of a firearm by a felon. The government used two state convictions to enhance his sentence under the Armed Career Criminal Act of 1984. Custis challenged the use of the state convictions on the grounds that his constitutional rights were violated during those trials. The Court held that a defendant may not challenge the validity of a prior conviction in a federal sentencing hearing.

STAPLES v. UNITED STATES

511 U.S. 600; 114 S. Ct. 1793; 128 L. Ed. 2d 608
November 30, 1993, Argued. May 23, 1994, Decided

Possession of an unregistered machine gun is illegal under the National Firearms Act of 1934. Staples was charged under this law when officers discovered his semiautomatic AR-15 rifle, that had been modified to enable automatic fire. The Court held that a conviction under this law requires proof that the defendant knew that the rifle was capable of automatic fire. The Court expresses discomfort several times with the government's zeal in prosecuting gun owners who have no guilty state of mind, or *mens rea,* just possession of a weapon they either do not know the characteristics of, or do not recognize as a specially regulated type of device. The Court takes the stance that, because guns are so commonly owned in this country, and so widely held historically to be legal at state and federal levels, that people would not automatically equate a gun with wrongdoing, as the government suggests. They reject the argument that dangerousness automatically implies regulatory control.

In concurrence, Justice Ginsburg, joined by O'Connor, implies that widespread legal gun ownership exists because Congress and the states have allowed it to persist. In dissent, Justices Stevens and Blackmun take some of the most anti-rights positions in all these cases, and condone the possibility of some injustice in protecting the public safety.

The case has particular significance in the number of times and certainty with which the Court states that gun ownership is and has always been widespread and lawful in the United States.

UNITED STATES v. LOPEZ

514 U.S. 549; 115 S. Ct. 1624; 131 L. Ed. 2d 626
November 8, 1994, Argued. April 26, 1995, Decided

To exert control over increasingly broad swaths of activity, Congress has used its constitutional power to regulate commerce between the states. The Congressional commerce power has been the primary tool used for implementing federal gun law in recent history. In the early Republic, Congress did comparatively little with this power, and was challenged infrequently. In more recent times, the interstate Commerce Clause has been held to control everything from growing and eating your own wheat, to possession of a firearm on or near any local school—which is the kernel of this case of a Texas 12th grader who brought a .38 caliber revolver and ammo to school.

The Supreme Court used this challenge of a gun-ban law—The Gun-Free School Zones Act of 1990—to draw in the reins of an increasingly powerful Congress, and to partially reestablish boundaries for Congress' enumerated power over interstate commerce. It was the first significant attenuation of congressional commerce power in decades.

The Court chides the federal government for proposing standards so broad that they could basically use the Commerce Clause to remove any limitation on federal power over the states and the public, right down to a direct national police force, and even in areas where states historically have enjoyed sovereignty. When asked at oral argument what limits the government's interpretation of the Commerce Clause would provide, the government's attorneys were speechless. The dissenting opinion also could not find a single example of where federal power would end if the notion was allowed to stand that everything, basically, has some connection to interstate commerce, as the four Justices in the minority argued to establish.

In this five-to-four decision the Court found the Gun-Free School Zone law to be a criminal statute that had nothing to do with "commerce" or any sort of economic enterprise, however broadly one might define those terms. The majority put the brakes on a potentially huge increase in federal power. The dissent makes a good case though that schools are indeed an economic enterprise and are directly connected in myriad ways to interstate commerce, and that violence in general and guns in particular interfere with the educational process. They posit that guns have no place in a school environment (without limiting that sentiment to illegally possessed guns), and that Congress should have the power to ban guns outright, at least in this setting.

There is a good examination in this case of what Congress can and cannot do, as a function of federalism and the Commerce Clause, and the history leading us to present conditions.

Although the commerce power is where the federal government hangs its hat in these arguments, it is police power at the local level that it would have obtained if it had been successful. The net effect, if the Court would have decided the other way, would be to empower federal authorities to make and enforce law at every level, in the name of influencing commerce. Justice Thomas suggests that a review of the Court's recent doctrine behind commerce-clause power is in need of review due to the unintended consequences of changes made in the last 60 years.

As soon as the law was invalidated as an unconstitutional exercise of authority, Congress waltzed around the decision by reenacting the law, adding brief verbiage about interstate commerce in an effort to surmount the Supreme Court's objections, and placed it back on the books where the old law had just been removed (18 USC §922(q)). The Gun-Free School Zone law thus stands unless challenged again at some future time.

Questions came up about including this lengthy case unedited, since large sections of it are not directly related to guns per se. Seeing, however, that Congress has relied almost exclusively on this broad grant of power to implement its firearm (and other) controls across the country in recent decades, the enormous significance of *Lopez* argued for its full inclusion. The case is discussed in detail in an article in the *Connecticut Law Review* (Volume

30, 1997), available on davekopel.org, and in the book *Gun Laws of America*, available at gunlaws.com.

BAILEY v. UNITED STATES
516 U.S. 137; 116 S. Ct. 501; 133 L. Ed. 2d 472
October 30, 1995, Argued. December 6, 1995, Decided

The Court interprets a federal statute that imposes an additional five-year prison term on anyone who uses or carries a firearm during and in relation to a drug-trafficking crime. Cases of this sort have long been thought of as really a statutory interpretation case, or a drug case, or a sentencing case, or an instruction on police procedure case. The Court's deep examination of what precisely constitutes use of a firearm makes it relevant to the theme of *Supreme Court Gun Cases.*

Two drug dealers' cases are consolidated in this decision. Bailey and Robinson were caught red-handed with cocaine and arrested, and in the subsequent searches, each was found to have a gun. The government argued that the presence of the gun constituted "use" for the purpose of enhancing the sentence. The only problem with the government's argument was that Bailey's loaded pistol was in a bag locked in his trunk, and Robinson's unloaded .22 caliber Derringer was holstered in a locked trunk in her bedroom closet. The defendants argued that this did not amount to "use" under the law.

The Court agreed with them, and held that to be convicted for using a gun in a drug-trafficking crime, you must in some way actively employ the gun, not merely possess it somewhere. Congress later amended the law to reach anyone who, "in furtherance of any such crime, possesses a firearm," described as a higher standard than possession "during and in relation to" the crime.

The concept "use a firearm" is described here only in relation to a specific penalty enhancement for a type of drug offense. If ever a question comes up concerning "use" of a firearm in another context, this case will become an obvious reference point.

UNITED STATES v. URSERY
518 U.S. 267; 116 S. Ct. 2135; 135 L. Ed. 2d 549
April 17, 1996, Argued. June 24, 1996, Decided

Guy Ursery was caught growing marijuana for personal use in and around his house in a heavily wooded area in Michigan. In addition to convicting him on drug charges, the government moved to confiscate his home, alleging it had been used to facilitate illegal drug transactions. The lengthy case addresses complex issues concerning the Constitution's double jeopardy clause, and civil asset forfeiture law. The Court holds that the taking of this man's house by the government is a civil forfeiture, not an additional penalty for committing a crime, and is remedial in nature. If the forfeiture had been found instead to be punitive, double jeopardy would prohibit it after a criminal conviction on the same set of facts. They describe a history of treating *in rem* cases (which are taken against a thing instead of a person), as being remedial.

In rem cases have a certain awkwardness to them, first evident by their very names, because they resort to a legal fiction invented to find property guilty "as though it were conscious instead of inanimate and insentient."

Some key precedents relied upon in *Ursery* were set by the *in rem* case of *U.S. v. One Assortment of 89 Firearms,* which established a two-stage test for allowable forfeitures. There's nothing uniquely important about guns per se in *Ursery,* and indeed, the other two precedent-setting cases concerned smuggled emeralds in 1972, and a liquor still in 1931 during Prohibition. So while this is "only" a drug case, and a double jeopardy case, and an asset forfeiture case, and a congressional intent case, it mentions firearms 54 times and could hardly be excluded. In delivering its opinion, the Court discusses what it did in *89 Firearms* in concise terms, a case that took away a man's inventory of firearms, after he was acquitted on the same set of facts, for the alleged commission of a separate crime.

The Court came to the conclusion that civil actions against property are not punishment in a criminal sense, and so they do not violate the double jeopardy clause of the 5th Amendment, and a person can effectively be tried twice for the same event. In a lone dissent, Justice Stevens says what he finds obvious—that of course confiscating Ursery's house was punishment, that the historical record speaks frequently of forfeiture as punishment, and that the logic the Court uses here implies that the federal government could have, during Prohibition, confiscated the homes of everyone who drank alcohol during those interesting times, called it remedial, and cut deeply into guarantees our Founders found fundamental.

UNITED STATES v. GONZALES
520 U.S. 1; 117 S. Ct. 1032; 137 L. Ed. 2d 132
December 11, 1996, Argued. March 3, 1997, Decided

The drug bust started to sour when two of the perps pulled guns on undercover police during a sting operation. The suspects wound up convicted in New Mexico courts and were serving their sentences when the federal government tried and convicted them of similar charges based on the same set of facts from the same sting. This case involves interpretation of a federal statute that requires a mandatory five-year sentence for using or carrying a gun during and in relation to a drug-trafficking offense. The statute says the prison sentence must run consecutively with any other sentence, so that it adds to the total time served. The Court ruled that the law means what it says, and that a federal judge may not order that this sentence run concurrently with a state-imposed sentence. Being tried twice for the same criminal act, by both state and federal authorities, and the seemingly apparent 5th Amendment violation this implies against double jeopardy, was not at issue.

PRINTZ v. UNITED STATES
521 U.S. 898; 117 S. Ct. 2365; 138 L. Ed. 2d 914
December 3, 1996, Argued. June 27, 1997, Decided

The Sheriffs of two counties, first Mack in Arizona, and then Printz in Montana, challenged the portion of the Brady law that commanded the chief law enforcement officer of the region to conduct a background check before approving the sale of a handgun. The Court held on 10th Amendment grounds that the federal government may not command state officers to implement a federal regulatory scheme. A concurring opinion by Justice Thomas suggested that the Brady law might violate the 2nd Amendment.

Sometimes called the Brady-law case, and therefore a gun case, this is actually a detailed study of the balance of power between the states and the central government. The Court used its review of this federal law to protect state authorities from federal incursions on a state's sovereignty. The sweeping limitations the Court describes for federal mandates were in response to a temporary provision in the Brady law, a provision that expired in 1998, five years after enactment.

The federal government, seeking a "highly attractive power," claims that the nation's earliest cases support direct federal use of state resources. The Court, acknowledging this as critically important in the operation of the country, concludes that, although impositions have been made on state courts in the past and are in limited ways permissible, the same is not generally true for the executive power in a state, which is responsible for enforcing the laws. Thus, the Brady requirement that local officials conduct background checks for the federal government's gun control plan was unconstitutional. The majority opinion says nothing about whether subjecting gun buyers themselves to the Brady scheme is constitutional.

The Court comes close to rebuking the federal government for pushing the envelope so far, referring to nearly two centuries of Congressional avoidance of compelling states to act. Justice Thomas' concurrence makes bold statements about the 2nd Amendment's relevance as an individual right, and cites an impressive list of scholarly publications that provide historical evidence.

The dissent in this case is among the most strident of all the gun cases. A single vote separates the Court in this 5 to 4 decision, between diametrically opposed positions, and an ideological schism of epic proportion. If the Court's four dissenting liberal Justices had the extra vote, the federal government would be empowered to use local officials for implementing federal regulatory programs, without federal cost, and with a significant shift in the historic character of federalism—the balance between state and central authority. The dissenters vigorously support their position, deriding the majority repeatedly.

Both sides accuse the other of inventing new law, ignoring or misreading precedent, taking quotes deceptively out of context and more. The dissent hinges much of its position on Congress' presumed power to act for the benefit of the public, especially during emergencies, or at other times if the action is temporary, and when the impact on traditional separations of powers are only, as the dissenters characterize this case: a modest obligation, minimal requirement, minimal request, trivial burden, modest burden, minor burden, and a minimal temporary imposition. They give examples of prior federal mandates they see as roughly equivalent, such as: enlisting air-raid wardens during WWII, inoculations to prevent epidemics, a military draft, and international terrorist threats. The two sides hurl Madison and Hamilton quotes at each other, and come to opposite conclusions drawn from the same historical record.

The problem, sometimes referred to as *unfunded mandates*, was resolved (sort of) according to the Court, with the passage of a law that allowed the feds to simply use state resources as long as the cost of each program was under a $50 million threshold.

The dissent accuses the majority of activism, though the majority points to more than two centuries of precedent. Justice Souter argues separately that if Congress cannot force local sheriffs to implement federal programs because it is just too great an affront to state sovereignty, the federal government will instead have to grow to implement its program, and the net affront to state sovereignty is worse.

Attorney Stephen Halbrook represented Sheriff Printz, and successfully argued the case before the Supreme Court. Attorney David Kopel assisted in the amicus brief filed by Colorado Attorney General Gale Norton on behalf of states seeking to uphold their 10th Amendment powers. For further details on this case, see the *George Mason University Civil Rights Law Journal* (Volume 7, 1999), posted at davekopel.org.

ROGERS v. UNITED STATES
522 U.S. 252; 118 S. Ct. 673; 139 L. Ed. 2d 686
November 5, 1997, Argued. January 14, 1998, Decided

When is a firearm not a firearm? When it is a National Firearms Act firearm, a special category of weapons such as silencers, hand grenades and machine guns, which have been strictly controlled by federal tax law since the 1930s. When this case says "firearm" it is generally referring to the nine-inch silencer the defendant was accused of possessing illegally. At issue was the application of *Staples v. United States*. In *Staples*, "knowing possession" of an NFA "firearm" was interpreted to require that the defendant not only knew he possessed the object but that he knew it had all the characteristics that made it a specially-regulated "firearm." The Court sidestepped the issue by dismissing this appeal, because the record in the case did not clearly present a constitutional issue to be decided. In effect, the Justices said they never should have taken the case in the first place (their consent was "improvidently granted.")

SPENCER v. KEMNA
523 U.S. 1; 118 S. Ct. 978; 140 L. Ed. 2d 43
November 12, 1997, Argued. March 3, 1998, Decided

The Court dismissed as moot Spencer's challenge to two felony convictions because his sentence had already expired and he failed to demonstrate any continuing injury. Justice Stevens, dissenting, would have found continuing injury for Spencer because the felony record results in the loss of the right to vote and to bear arms, as well as the possibility of an enhanced sentence for any future crime.

BOUSLEY v. UNITED STATES
523 U.S. 614; 118 S. Ct. 1604; 140 L. Ed. 2d 828
March 3, 1998, Argued. May 18, 1998, Decided

Bousley pled guilty to using a firearm during and in relation to a drug-trafficking crime. This case challenges the constitutionality of the guilty plea, arguing that under *Bailey v. United States*, there was no factual basis for Bousley's guilty plea, because he did not "use" the firearm as defined by law. The Court held that if Bousley were able to demonstrate that he did not "use" a firearm in relation to the drug offense, he would be entitled to challenge the guilty plea.

MUSCARELLO v. UNITED STATES
524 U.S. 125; 118 S. Ct. 1911; 141 L. Ed. 2d 111
Argued March 23, 1998. June 8, 1998, Decided

The Court was again called upon to interpret the federal gun law imposing a
mandatory 5-year sentence for using or carrying a firearm in relation to a drug-
trafficking crime. Three drug dealers had brought guns along to their deals, but
weren't "packing" (the Court's word), they kept the guns in their cars. As a
defense, they claimed they weren't actually "carrying," and the Court
examined the language of the statute. The Court held that the phrase "carries a
firearm" is not limited to carrying a gun on yourself, and includes guns carried
in a trunk or locked compartment of your car. They found no difference in the
dangerousness of a drug dealer with a gun tucked in a pocket, and a drug
dealer with a gun in the trunk.

The clearest legal error detected in any of the Court's decisions compiled in
Supreme Court Gun Cases appears in this case. Five paragraphs from the end,
the majority, relying upon a citation that is off by a single character (the (4) in
18 U.S.C. 921(a)(4)(A) should be a (3)), incorrectly define firearms as
destructive devices (grenades, bombs, missiles, rockets and similar), and draw
a wholly erroneous conclusion on that basis. The error though, falls in a minor
additional argument for their case, and had no discernable effect on the
outcome.

In one of the juiciest dissents in all the cases in this book, two quite liberal
Justices (Ginsburg and Souter) join two quite conservative Justices (Rehnquist
and Scalia) to mock the majority's use of the Bible, great authors and
newspaper clippings to make its argument. While the majority holds that the
use of the word "carry" in this case is clearly defined, the dissenters carry on
until they pretty clearly prove it's not that clear. The citation from the TV show
"M*A*S*H" is a contender for one of the most striking phrases in any decision
in *Supreme Court Gun Cases* (and perhaps in much of TV too).

Finally, the case includes what may be the most remarkable remark by a
politician whose comments enjoyed the unusual honor of inclusion in a
published majority decision. Rep. Poff, the chief legislative sponsor of the
section about carrying guns while drug trafficking, said in 1968 that the
provision seeks "to persuade the man who is tempted to commit a Federal
felony to leave his gun at home." The Court was sufficiently enamored of this
line to say it six times (three by Poff, and three by other Congressmen). In
reply, the dissenters point out that Poff's very next sentence, omitted by the
majority, erases the conclusion the Court drew. You just gotta love it.

BRYAN v. UNITED STATES
524 U.S. 184; 118 S. Ct. 1939; 141 L. Ed. 2d 197
March 31, 1998, Argued. June 15, 1998, Decided

The term *willfully* has many meanings in law. In this case, the Court interprets
in great detail what willfully means in the context of a federal gun law that
prohibits willfully dealing in firearms without a federal license. The Court held
that a person willfully violates this law by knowing the conduct is unlawful.
No specific knowledge of the federal license requirement is needed. A
legislative history of the 1968 Gun Control Act is included, which mentions
the need to subsequently enact the 1986 Firearm Owners' Protection Act
(amending the Gun Control Act), to protect law-abiding citizens from flagrant

federal abuse with respect to getting, having and using guns for lawful purposes.

CARON v. UNITED STATES
524 U.S. 308; 118 S. Ct. 2007; 141 L. Ed. 2d 303
April 21, 1998, Argued. June 22, 1998, Decided

Under federal law, a person previously convicted of an offense punishable by a penalty of at least one year in jail may not possess any firearm, and a person previously convicted of three or more such serious offenses is subject to a mandatory five-year enhanced penalty. A prior conviction no longer counts however, if the state has restored the defendant's civil rights, unless the restoration of rights expressly provides that the person may not possess firearms.

Caron had a long rap sheet, including four felony priors. Three of these were in Massachusetts, which had automatically restored most of his civil rights after five years and issued him a firearms permit for rifles, shotguns and handguns, but subject to a restriction that he may only possess the handguns in his home or business. This criminal tried to skate by claiming the limited state restoration was a complete remedy, but the Court wasn't buying. The Court held that if the defendant remains subject to any restriction on firearms ownership—that the state considers him too dangerous to have handguns while out and about—the federal government can count the offenses toward application of the enhanced sentence.

The decision comes close to a precarious position that federal controls are fine, tied to a novel though undefined concept of excessive degree of dangerousness. Contrast this concept of dangerousness with one typical of firearms experts who assert that guns are supposed to be dangerous, and wouldn't be much good if they weren't dangerous (Massad Ayoob), and that a gun that's safe isn't worth anything (Col. Jeff Cooper).

In a well-reasoned dissent, three justices argue that it is "bizarre" for the Court to subject a person to an enhanced penalty for behavior their state law allows.

PENNSYLVANIA BOARD OF PROBATION AND PAROLE v. SCOTT
524 U.S. 357; 118 S. Ct. 2014; 141 L. Ed. 2d 344
March 30, 1998, Argued. June 22, 1998, Decided

The exclusionary rule of the 4th Amendment prohibits the use of illegally obtained evidence at a trial. It serves, in part, as a deterrent to official misconduct. This is a 4th Amendment case in which the Court held that the exclusionary rule does not require exclusion of illegally seized evidence at a parole revocation hearing.

Firearms seized from Keith Scott's home in violation of his 4th Amendment rights were therefore properly admitted into evidence at his parole revocation hearing, and his goose was cooked. Scott, a felon on parole (he had just served ten years in prison for third degree murder), had been caught at his mother's home, where he lived, with five firearms, a compound bow and some arrows. He got three more years.

FLORIDA v. J. L.
529 U.S. 266; 120 S. Ct. 1375; 146 L. Ed. 2d 254
February 29, 2000, Argued. March 28, 2000, Decided

This case relates to the 4th Amendment protection against an arbitrary search. Acting on an anonymous tip, police searched a man and found an unlawfully possessed gun. Because anonymous tips are known to be less reliable information, and because such tips, if allowable as grounds for a frisk could be severely abused by anyone with a grudge, the Court decided such a search was not permissible under the 4th Amendment.

Florida, and the federal government in an amicus brief, also argued that guns are so dangerous a special exemption should be made for allegations of an illegal gun from an anonymous tipster. The Court specifically rejected this request to carve out a firearm exception to the established general rule, that a tip must be reliable in its assertions of illegality, and in its assertions of identity.

Dave Kopel was one of the attorneys who filed an amicus brief in this case. That brief is posted at davekopel.org.

CASTILLO v. UNITED STATES
530 U.S. 120; 120 S. Ct. 2090; 147 L. Ed. 2d 94
April 24, Argued. June 5, 2000, Decided

The infamous assault by the Bureau of Alcohol, Tobacco and Firearms, that resulted in the deaths of several federal agents and more than 80 members of the Branch Davidian religious group based near Waco, Texas, lead to this very narrowly focused case on a question of statutory interpretation, and a factor to be used in sentencing based on the type of firearm used. The Court concluded that the type of firearm used in a Gun Control Act violation is an element of the offense and not a mere sentencing factor, which means it must be alleged in the indictment and decided by the jury, not by a judge.

Attorney Stephen Halbrook, representing the surviving Branch Davidians charged in this case, made the winning oral arguments before the Justices.

HARRIS v. UNITED STATES
No.536 U.S. 545; 122 S. Ct. 2406; 153 L. Ed. 2d 524
March 25, 2002, Argued. June 24, 2002, Decided

This is a statutory construction case, an appeal from a conviction for brandishing a firearm during a drug-trafficking offense. The operator of a pawn shop, who routinely wore a gun at his place of business, was dealing small amounts of pot to his friends on the side. In the dissenting opinion, we learn that Harris did not actually wave his gun around, but was nonetheless charged with brandishing, which forces a higher sentence than merely possessing under the same circumstance. Progressively long sentences attach to possession, brandishing and shooting, respectively.

If a condition in a statute is an "element" of a crime, a jury must decide if it has been proven beyond a reasonable doubt, but if the condition is a sentencing "factor" a judge may decide. Harris argued that, because of the extra penalty, it was a separate offense, should have been charged in the indictment (it had not been), and a jury would have had to decide. He faced a mandatory additional seven-year minimum sentence. The Court disagreed and let the additional sentence stand. In a dissent, three of the Court's liberal justices join with a conservative to point out several interesting holes in the Court's reasoning.

UNITED STATES et al. v. BEAN
537 U.S. 71, 123 S.Ct. 584; 154 L. Ed. 2d 483
October 16, 2002, Argued. December 10, 2002, Decided

U.S. law allows a person to regain the right to arms, if the right has been lost due to a legal disability, such as a prior felony conviction (see 18 USC §925). The Secretary of the Treasury (acting through the Bureau of Alcohol, Tobacco and Firearms), is to decide if the person is fit to have those rights restored. Since 1992 however, Congress has refused to give BATF any funding with which to investigate requests for restoration of rights (every congressional funding denial is cited in this case) and the process has ground to a halt.

Thomas Bean, a gun dealer attending a gun show in Laredo, Texas, went to dinner with some of his associates after the show, across the border in Nuevo Laredo, Mexico. At the border, a single box of ammunition was found in his car, and a Mexican court convicted him of importing ammunition, a felony with a five-year sentence. He served six months in Mexican detention, and was then transferred to a U.S. facility and immediately paroled.

Devoid of any reflection about his character or intentions, the Mexican felony nonetheless effectively stripped Bean of his American gun rights. He applied for relief to BATF, who returned his application unprocessed, citing Congress' prohibition on spending any money to provide relief. Relying on a judicial-review provision of the rights-restoration law, Bean sued for relief in federal court, and won at the District and Appeals Courts. Some observers believed this heralded a long overdue correction to the rights-restoration problem.

The High Court unanimously overturned the lower courts, observing that the determination of fitness to have gun rights restored was: 1) best handled by BATF, 2) by law had to be handled by BATF, 3) that courts lacked competence to perform the determination, and 4) that without a dispositive denial, the issues the courts were empowered to address were necessarily missing. A failure to process Bean's request did not constitute a denial, so there were no grounds for judicial review, and Bean, along with many other citizens, was plain out of luck. And that was the Supreme Court's last word about your gun rights, as we went to press with this book, six years after we began the project.

THE NEXT CASE
(From Sep., 2003) As sure as the sun rises, you know there will be more cases on guns, the militia, the right to keep arms, the right to bear arms, self defense, gun crimes and more. To keep this book current, Bloomfield Press plans to post new cases on our website, gunlaws.com.

While we were finishing this book, the 5th Circuit's *Emerson* case, and the *Silveira* case from the 9th Circuit both seemed poised for possible review, and both involved the 2nd Amendment head on (Emerson is now off the burner but Silveira is poised to possibly move up). Adding to the tension, the 5th and 9th Circuits take opposite positions on the gun rights protected in the 2nd Amendment (the 5th Circuit says you have rights, the 9th Circuit says you do not; lower courts have been in disarray on this for a long while).

The *Silveira* case is of particular concern because it takes the no-rights position, and in the words of the dissent in that case, "...the panel misses the mark by interpreting the Second Amendment right to keep and bear arms as a collective right, rather than as an individual right. Because the panel's decision abrogates a constitutional right, this case should have been reheard *en banc*." In addition, "About twenty percent of the American population, those who live in the Ninth Circuit, have lost one of the ten amendments in the Bill of Rights. And, the methodology used to take away the right threatens the rest of the Constitution. The most extraordinary step taken by the panel opinion is to read the frequently used constitutional phrase, "the people," as conferring rights only upon collectives, not individuals."

This is not unexpected from the San Francisco-based 9th Circuit, the nation's most liberal and least frequently upheld federal appeals court. The High Court can let a split in the Circuits fester for decades, or take it up before the ink in this book dries, and other cases are in the judiciary pipeline that keeps on flowing and flowing. We'll just have to wait and see.

(Aug., 2008) It's five years later and we've had four more cases: *Brosseau, Small, Castle Rock* and of course *Heller*, all of which are covered in this book the same as the first 92 were originally covered in *Supreme Court Gun Cases*. The likelihood there will be additional cases is one of the safest bets on the planet. *U.S. v. Hayes*, concerning gun-rights denial in domestic violence cases was granted *cert* on Mar. 24, 2008, so it's not even a bet, it's a sure thing, as long as the sun doesn't cool. *Arizona v. Johnson* is currently going through the motions, concerning a pat-down search for weapons during a traffic stop. Dick Heller himself is back in court, seeking reasonable treatment from the government that denied his (and everyone's) rights for 32 years. Judging by D.C.'s initial unreasonable responses (and well-documented animus towards the civil right to arms), that case could find its way appealed to the top for resolution. Evan Nappen has a case brewing in New Jersey, and suits were filed immediately after *Heller* in Chicago and San Francisco. Reports of *Heller* citings are pouring in like water into the Titanic. We live in interesting times.

Sandy Froman was the first to say to me, while I was still buzzed from the success of *Heller*, that we were in for decades of litigation. In retrospect, it's an unfortunately obvious conclusion I had missed in the early heady delirium of "*Affirmed!*" My guts had leaped when I saw that word come through on SCOTUSblog.

I'm brought back to an opening line from this book. "One of the biggest problems with law today is that there is so much of it." With new law and precedent flowing forth at unprecedented speed and volume, how long will it be before we drown under the waves? Why can't our rights be simply sacrosanct, follow the contours of the freedom-loving side of America, and be done with it? It might mean no more of these books for us to write and publish. I would gladly seek other work.

Descriptive Index of Cases
by Alan Korwin

All 96 Supreme Court gun cases are posed here as answered questions to help you locate specific proceedings. [Dissents and dismissals appear in brackets.] Only questions related to firearms or self defense are listed even if, as is often the case, they are not the core issues. Many other questions are often addressed in the cases and, because of the terseness of the posed questions, you should rely on the full actual cases for an understanding of the significance of each one. Think of this index as a navigation tool, a memory jogger, and a good read. Page numbers are for SCGC; numbers for this book are marked "HC".

• Indicates the 44 cases included in their entirety in *Supreme Court Gun Cases;* all cases in this book (HC) are unedited. △ Indicates the 16 self-defense cases.

Name	Date	Citation	Page
Acers v. United States • △	1896	164 U.S. 388	238

Is fear of a deadly attack, without reasonable demonstrated grounds for the fear, sufficient to support a claim of self defense [NO]; Must the danger be immediate [YES]; Can any object be considered as a deadly weapon depending on how it was used [YES].

Adams v. Williams	1972	407 U.S. 143	363

Can a peace officer conduct a limited protective search for concealed weapons, if there is reason to believe a suspect is armed and dangerous [YES]; Are 4th Amendment guarantees violated by such a stop and frisk [NO].

Adamson v. California	1947	332 U.S. 46	310

[The dissenting opinion in a 5th Amendment case argues that the 14th Amendment was intended to incorporate the Bill of Rights, including the 2nd Amendment, against the states].

Alberty v. United States • △	1896	162 U.S. 499	231

If a husband sees another man trying to get into his wife's room window at night is it natural for him to investigate further [YES]; Is the husband under a duty to retreat when attacked with a knife under such circumstances [NO]; May the husband use only as much force as is necessary to repel the assault [YES]; If in an ensuing confrontation the husband shoots and kills the other man, then flees, must his flight in and of itself be seen as evidence of his guilt [NO].

Albright v. Oliver	1994	510 U.S. 266	481

[The dissenting opinion in a case involving freedom from malicious prosecution cites the right to keep and bear arms as among freedoms guaranteed by the Constitution].

Allen v. United States • △	1896	164 U.S. 492	241

Are words alone sufficient provocation to justify an assault [NO]; Are words alone sufficient to reduce murder to manslaughter [NO]; Can premeditation and intent to kill be determined from your actions [YES]; Although flight after a possibly criminal event may suggest guilt, does it prove it conclusively [NO].

Allison v. United States • △ .... 1895 .... 160 U.S. 203 216
Is it reasonable to believe that you're in immediate deadly danger if a person, known to be abusive, known to carry a pistol, and who has made public threats against your life, makes a motion as if to draw down on you, even if it turns out he wasn't armed at the time [YES]; If there is no corroborating evidence besides your testimony, may the jury decide to take your word for it and acquit based on your credibility [YES]; If you have your deer rifle with you while visiting a friend's house and your adversary shows up, and in an ensuing confrontation you shoot him, can the judge instruct the jury that you're guilty of murder if you armed yourself to go hunt down your adversary, when there is no evidence to support this claim [NO].

Andersen v. United States △ .... 1898 .... 170 U.S. 481 255
If an indictment is brought charging that a defendant shot and then threw a victim's body into the sea, so the exact cause of death cannot be known, is the indictment flawed and invalid [NO]; Do the elements of self defense have to be present for an accused person to successfully claim self defense [YES].

Bailey v. United States • .... 1995 .... 516 U.S. 137 542
Can the sentence for a drug offense be increased for using a gun, if the defendant possessed a gun at the time of the offense but did not actively employ it [NO]; Is the "inert presence of a firearm" sufficient to indicate "use" for the purpose of enhancing certain drug offenses [NO]; Does storing a gun with drugs or drug money constitute "use" for this purpose [NO]; Does hiding a gun where it can be grabbed and used if necessary constitute use [NO]; If the gun is not disclosed or mentioned is it used [NO].

Barrett v. United States • .... 1976 .... 423 U.S. 212 382
Is the Gun Control Act violated by a convicted felon acquiring a gun that has at some point moved in interstate commerce, even if the felon's acquisition and possession occurred entirely within one state [YES].

Bass, United States v., • .... 1971 .... 404 U.S. 336 351
To convict a felon of illegal firearm possession under federal law, does the prosecution need to show, in addition to possession, that the firearm had a connection to interstate commerce [YES]; Does the same apply to receiving, and transporting, a firearm [YES]; Would showing that the firearm had at some time previously traveled in interstate commerce be a sufficient nexus [YES].

Bean, United States v., • .... 2002 .... 01-704 643
If BATF fails to act on a request for restoration of the right to bear arms, but does not actually deny the request, are there actionable grounds for judicial review to get those rights restored [NO].

Beard v. United States • △ .... 1895 .... 158 U.S. 550 208
Can you stand your ground with a shotgun against an unprovoked armed attack on your property near your home [YES]; Is there a greater duty to retreat on your own property than in your house [NO].

Beecham v. United States • .... 1994 .... 511 U.S. 368 482
Does reinstatement of a federal felon's civil right to keep and bear arms by a state court remove the federal disability against felons bearing arms [NO]; Does the fact that Congress currently provides no way for a felon to restore the right to keep and bear arms matter in this regard [NO].

Biswell, United States v., ... 1972 .... 406 U.S. 311 361
Is the 4th Amendment violated when a federally licensed firearms dealer's business is searched under 18 USC §923(g) without a warrant, and illegally possessed guns are seized [NO]; When a dealer "chooses to engage in this pervasively regulated business" and to accept a federal license, does he do so with the knowledge that his business will be subject to effective inspection [YES].

Bousley v. United States .... 1998 .... 523 U.S. 614 599
Does a defendant need to understand what constitutes "use" of a firearm in relation to a drug-trafficking crime, in order to enter a constitutionally valid guilty plea [YES].

Brosseau v. Haugen • .... 2004 .... 543 U.S. 194..... HC101
If a police officer shoots a known criminal in the back through a vehicle window, while the person is trying to escape, is the officer protected from a lawsuit by the person under the doctrine of qualified immunity? [YES].

Brown v. United States • △ .... 1921 .... 256 U.S. 335 285
Is there a duty to retreat when attacked by a man with a knife [NO]; Believing you're in a mortal conflict, if you fire a shot in the heat of combat, which in cool reflection later may be seen as unnecessary, may you still be acquitted on grounds of self defense [YES]; Is your right of self defense roughly similar in your home, on your land, and at your work [YES]; Can detached reflection be demanded in the presence of an uplifted knife [NO].

Brown v. Walker .... 1896 .... 161 U.S. 591 223
Is the object of the first eight amendments to the Constitution to incorporate into the fundamental law of the land certain principles of natural justice [YES]; Are the first eight amendments limitations only upon the powers of Congress and the Federal courts, and not applicable to the several States, except so far as the 14th Amendment may have made them applicable [YES].

Bryan v. United States • .... 1998 .... 524 U.S. 184 613
Are you committing the crime of "willfully" dealing in firearms without a license, if you know your actions are illegal but do not know the licensing law you are violating [YES]; Was the Firearms Owners' Protection Act enacted to protect law-abiding citizens who might inadvertently violate the law [YES].

Burton v. Sills • .... 1969 .... 394 U.S. 812 344
[The New Jersey Supreme Court rejected a 2nd Amendment suit against a discretionary firearm licensing law, citing cases that held the 2nd Amendment inapplicable to the states; the U.S. Supreme Court dismissed the appeal for want of a substantial federal question.]

Busic v. United States .... 1980 .... 446 U.S. 398 410
Can an assault sentence, increased under the armed-assault-of-a-federal-officer law, also be increased under the separate federal armed-felony law [NO].

Caron v. United States .... 1998 .... 524 U.S. 308 623
Can a three-time violent-felony loser avoid a five-year mandatory penalty enhancement for carrying a gun in a subsequent crime he commits, if a state court had partially restored his right to keep and bear arms [NO]; If a state

restores a convicted felon's right to keep and bear long guns but not handguns, is the federal ban for felons on possession on all guns removed [NO].

Castillo v. United States • .... 2000 .... 530 U.S. 120 629
Is the type of firearm used in a Gun Control Act violation an element of the offense that must be determined by a jury [YES]; Is the type of firearm used in a GCA violation a sentencing factor that may be determined by a judge [NO].

Castle Rock v. Gonzalez • .... 2005 .... 545 U.S. 748 .... HC118
Do police have a mandatory duty to protect a woman with a court order of protection, against the abusive spouse named in the court order, if the spouse abducts the woman's three children and the women repeatedly requests aid and shows probable cause that a crime has been committed? [NO]. Does the woman have a cause of action after the spouse shoots the children to death, for denial of civil rights under the 14th amendment? [NO].

Cruikshank, United States v., • .... 1875 .... 92 U.S. 542 159
Does the right to bear arms for a lawful purpose depend on the Constitution for its existence [NO]; Does the 2nd Amendment have no other effect than to restrict the powers of the national government, and prevent Congress from infringing on the right to bear arms [YES].

Cummings v. Missouri .... 1866 .... 71 U.S. 277 158
Is deprivation or suspension of a person's civil rights, including the right to bear arms, a form of punishment [YES].

Custis v. United States .... 1994 .... 511 U.S. 485 485
Can a defendant at a federal sentencing hearing (in this case under the Armed Career Criminal Act of 1984) attack the validity of prior state convictions that are used to enhance his sentence [NO].

Deal v. United States .... 1993 .... 505 U.S. 129 469
When a statute calls for quadrupling the prison sentence for subsequent crimes of violence involving use of a gun, can a defendant suffer the enhanced penalty if the subsequent and original charges are all proven during a single trial [YES].

DeShaney v. Winnebago County Dept. of Social Services . 1989 .... 489 U.S. 189 441
Does the 14th Amendment guarantee that a state must protect its citizens from private violations of life, liberty or property [NO].

Dickerson v. New Banner Institute • .... 1983 .... 460 U.S. 103 411
If a state criminal conviction, which removes your ability to bear arms under federal law, is expunged at the state level, is your federal disability from bearing arms automatically removed [NO]; Is it constitutional to deny your right to arms after your conviction has been expunged [YES].

District of Columbia v. Heller • △ .... 2008 .... 07-290 .... HC141
Does the Second Amendment to the U.S. Constitution guarantee a pre-existing right to keep and bear arms to individual citizens? [YES]. Do the citizens have to be part of a state or any other organized militia to exercise this right? [NO]. Is a requirement to unload, lock up, disassemble or otherwise make a firearm inoperable at home to prevent its use for self defense unconstitutional? [YES]. Is the District of Columbia's gun ban discussed in this case overturned? [YES]. Is the use of legal firearms for lawful purposes such as self defense at home a

constitutionally protected right? [YES]. Does the Second Amendment protect a right to own weapons that are "in common use for lawful purposes"? [YES]. Is a handgun the quintessential self-defense weapon? [YES]. Is an absolute handgun ban impermissible because it is unconstitutional? [YES]. Is the right to keep and bear arms a "specific enumerated right" similar to freedom of speech, right to counsel and the guarantee against double jeopardy? [YES]. Does the Amendment's prefatory clause, which announces a purpose, limit or expand the scope of the second part, the operative clause? [NO].

Must the District of Columbia issue a license and registration to Dick Heller and other D.C. residents for them to keep operable firearms at home? [YES]. Does this create a license and registration requirement elsewhere? [NO]. Can laws limiting the carriage of weapons that are "dangerous and unusual" be permissible? [YES]. Are acceptable weapons delineated? [NO]. Can some "longstanding restrictions" on what you can carry, where you can carry (e.g., schools and government buildings), concealed carry, existing laws regarding felons or the mentally ill, and laws "imposing conditions and qualifications on the commercial sale of arms" be permissible? [YES].

Does the individual right recognized in the Second Amendment allow a person to own an atom bomb, cruise missle, F-16 or similar? [NO]. Are "collective rights" arguments concerning the meaning of the phrase "the people" mentioned in the Second Amendment correct? [NO]. Do the history, precedents, scholarship and wording of the Second Amendment support the Court's decision? [YES]. Do analogous arms-bearing rights in state Constitutions that preceded and immediately followed the Second Amendment's adoption confirm the Court's findings? [YES]. Do any of the Court's precedents foreclose the Court's interpretation? [NO]. Does this case answer all significant questions about the Second Amendment? [NO].

Dred Scott v. Sandford.. 1856 .... 60 U.S. 393 149
Do blacks have the rights of other American citizens, including the right to keep and bear arms [NO]; Can Congress deny to the people in federal Territories the right to keep and bear arms [NO].

Duncan v. Louisiana .... 1968 .... 391 U.S. 145 333
Is the right to keep and bear arms one of the personal rights guaranteed and secured by the first eight amendments of the Constitution [YES].

Ex Parte Milligan .... 1866 .... 71 U.S. 2 150
[The published legal arguments on both sides of this case, involving trial of a civilian by court martial, both make reference to the 2nd Amendment as an individual right belonging to the people, but a right not belonging to slaves or rebels; a man cannot violate the laws of war if he is not in the military or in the militia in actual service.]

Florida v. J. L. .... 2000 .... 529 U.S. 266 627
Is a vague and anonymous tip sufficient grounds to conduct a search of a person on the street alleged to be illegally carrying a gun [NO].

Freed, United States v., • .... 1971 .... 401 U.S. 601 345
Does the regulatory scheme of the amended National Firearms Act violate the 5th Amendment protection against self incrimination, or violate a person's right to due process of law [NO].

Galioto, United States v., • .... 1986 .... 477 U.S. 556 439
[Court dismisses as moot the constitutionality of allowing felons a means to
restore their right to obtain firearms but not allowing the same for former mental
patients, because Congress, while this case was in process, changed the law to
allow any person with firearms disabilities to apply for relief.]

Gonzales, United States v., ... 1997 .... 520 U.S. 1 552
May the federal five-year-sentence enhancement for using or carrying a gun
during a drug trafficking crime run concurrently with a state sentence [NO].

Gourko v. United States • △ .... 1894 .... 153 U.S. 183 189
If you shoot someone who has repeatedly threatened you, and the
circumstances of the shooting are not found to be justifiable as self defense,
does the fact that you armed yourself in response to the threat automatically
make the shooting murder (as opposed to manslaughter) [NO].

Griswold v. Connecticut .... 1965 .... 381 U.S. 479 322
Do the first eight amendments to the Constitution protect fundamental rights of
the people [YES].

Hamilton v. Regents of the University of California ...... 1934 .... 293 U.S. 245 294
Do the states have the authority to train their able-bodied male citizens of
suitable age, to develop fitness to serve in the state militia [YES]; Is the state the
sole judge of the means and amount of training as long as it doesn't conflict
with federal law [YES].

Harris v. United States .... 2002 .... 00-10666 634
Is brandishing a gun during a specified drug-trafficking crime a sentencing
factor to be determined by a judge, and not an element of the crime to be
determined by a jury [YES].

Haynes v. United States • .... 1968 .... 390 U.S. 85 326
Does Congress have the authority to regulate the manufacture, transfer, and
possession of firearms, subject to constitutional limitations, and to tax unlawful
activities [YES]; Did the registration requirements of the National Firearms Act
violate the defendant's 5th Amendment privilege against self incrimination
[YES]; Was a proper claim of 5th Amendment protection a complete defense
against failure to register or possession of an unregistered NFA weapon [YES].
(Note that Congress redrafted the relevant statute to overcome these findings
and continue to require NFA registration.)

Houston v. Moore .... 1820 .... 18 U.S. 1 147
[The first mention of the 2nd Amendment in a High Court decision occurs as a
brief remark in a dissent in this case, postulating that the amendment would
have little effect on the legitimacy of a state running and arming its militia in the
absence of, or subordinate to Congressional regulation. It implies that the
amendment was not primarily viewed as a guarantee of state government
powers to control state militias.]

Huddleston v. United States • .... 1974 .... 415 U.S. 814 369
Is the return of a gun from a pawnbroker subject to the same requirements as
the sale of a gun from a dealer under the Gun Control Act of 1968 [YES]; Is the
intention of the GCA to deprive guns to unauthorized juveniles, fugitives,
criminals and the mentally incompetent [YES]; Are hunting, target practice, gun

collecting, and the legitimate use of guns for individual protection allowed under the GCA [YES]; Did Congress require commerce in firearms to be channeled through a federalized network of dealers in an effort to halt illegal mail-order and interstate consumer traffic in firearms [YES].

Johnson v. Eisentrager .... 1950 .... 339 U.S. 763 313
Does the Constitution confer to Nazi spies captured in China during WWII, subsequently convicted of spying on the U.S. and serving their sentences in post-war Germany, the rights it confers to U.S. citizens [NO]; Do the rights of U.S. citizens include among others the right to bear arms as in the 2nd Amendment [YES].

Kepner v. United States .... 1904 .... 195 U.S. 100 274
Did the adoption in the Philippines of most of the U.S. Bill of Rights omit the right to a trial by jury and the right of the people to bear arms [YES].

Knapp v. Schweitzer .... 1958 .... 357 U.S. 371 314
Do all the first eight amendments of the Bill of Rights apply to the states [NO].

Konigsberg v. State Bar of California .... 1961 .... 366 U.S. 36 315
Does absolute verbiage ("shall make no law," "shall not be infringed") in the 1st and 2nd Amendments allow for some level of regulation, some of which is well established and widely recognized [YES].

Laird v. Tatum .... 1972 .... 408 U.S. 1 368
Was the 2nd Amendment added to the Constitution to authorize a decentralized militia, guaranteeing the right of the people to keep and bear arms [YES].

Lewis v. United States • .... 1980 .... 445 U.S. 55 401
If a person is prohibited from possessing firearms due to a prior felony conviction, does it matter if the prior conviction was unconstitutional [NO].

Logan v. United States △ .... 1892 .... 144 U.S. 263 180
Does the 2nd Amendment guarantee a preexisting right recognized by the Constitution, and not a right created by the Constitution [YES]; Is a prisoner in legal custody entitled to protection "while he is deprived of the ordinary means of defending and protecting himself" [YES].

Lopez, United States v., • .... 1995 .... 514 U.S. 549 506
Does the Interstate Commerce Clause give Congress the power to regulate personal possession of firearms near local schools [NO]; Is possession of a gun in a school zone an economic activity [NO].

Malloy v. Hogan .... 1964 .... 378 U.S. 1 319
Is it unsettled as to whether the 14th Amendment applies the first eight amendments to the Bill of Rights against the states [YES]; Did *Presser v. Illinois* find that the particular guarantees of the 2nd Amendment were not safeguarded from state action [YES].

Maryland v. United States .... 1965 .... 381 U.S. 41 320
For the purpose of determining liability in an air crash involving a National Guard and commercial aircraft, are National Guard members state employees, and not federal employees, if not specifically called into federal service [YES]; Does it matter if the members were military or civilian members [NO].

Maxwell v. Dow .... 1900 .... 176 U.S. 581 269
Did the court decide in *Presser v. Illinois* that the 2nd Amendment is only a
limitation on federal power [YES]. Would incorporation of the privileges and
immunities of U.S. citizens against the states entirely destroy the sovereignty of
the states [YES]. (Dissent suggests the Bill of Rights should apply to the states.)

Miller v. State of Texas • .... 1894 .... 153 U.S. 535 194
Will the Court accept a 2nd Amendment issue on appeal if it wasn't raised in
court prior to the appeal [NO].

Miller, United States v., • .... 1939 .... 307 U.S. 174 300
Without the presentation of evidence or testimony, can the Court determine
whether a short-barreled shotgun, as defined in the 1934 NFA law, is a militia
weapon and therefore an arm protected by the 2nd Amendment [NO]; Is
possession of arms by the people related to the preservation and efficiency of a
well regulated militia [YES].

Miranda v. Arizona .... 1966 .... 384 U.S. 436 325
Where rights secured by the Constitution are involved, can there be any rule
making or legislation that would abrogate them [NO].

Moore v. E. Cleveland .... 1976 .... 431 U.S. 494 390
Is the right to keep and bear arms among the type of individual rights
enumerated in the Bill of Rights [YES].

Muscarello v. United States • .... 1998 .... 524 U.S. 125 600
With regard to a mandatory penalty increase for carrying a firearm in relation to
a drug trafficking crime, does "carry" include in the trunk of a car [YES]; Is a
drug dealer with a gun in her pocket more dangerous than a drug dealer with a
gun in her car trunk [NO].

One Assortment of 89 Firearms, United States v., • ..... 1984 .... 465 U.S. 354 422
Does acquittal from criminal charges for dealing in firearms without a license
prevent the government from conducting a separate civil forfeiture action and
confiscating the firearms involved [NO]; Is such confiscation a violation of the
protection against double jeopardy [NO]; Can the lower threshold of guilt
(preponderance of the evidence) allow the government to prevail in the
forfeiture, where it could not against the higher threshold (beyond a reasonable
doubt) in criminal proceedings [YES]; Is the gun confiscation scheme in the law
primarily a civil, non-criminal, remedial action [YES].

Patsone v. Pennsylvania • .... 1914 .... 232 U.S. 138 279
Can a state prohibit possession of rifles or shotguns for hunting by nonresident
aliens without violating due process guarantees [YES]; Does such a prohibition
violate specified treaty conditions with Italy [NO].

Pennsylvania Bd. of Probation and Parole v. Scott .... 1998 .... 524 U.S. 357 626
Are firearms seized in a warrantless search of a paroled felon's residence
admissible as evidence at a parole revocation hearing, even if the seizure
violated the 4th Amendment [YES].

Perpich v. Department of Defense • .... 1990 .... 496 U.S. 334 446
Can members of a state's organized militia be called into federal service, for
training outside the United States, without an imminent emergency and without

the state Governor's permission [YES]; When members of the state National Guard are federalized, are they still members of their state militia [NO]; When they muster out of federal service do they regain their state status [YES].

Planned Parenthood v. Casey .... 1992 .... 505 U.S. 833 468
Do the protections of the 14th Amendment extend beyond the specifics in the Bill of Rights—such as free speech, press, religion, the right to keep and bear arms and more—and to a freedom from all arbitrary impositions [YES]; Is the right to keep and bear arms among the type of individual rights enumerated in the Bill of Rights [YES].

Poe v. Ullman .... 1961 .... 367 U.S. 497 317
(Justices Douglas and Harlan filed dissenting opinions, asserting that the 14th Amendment applies the Bill of Rights to the states, a position that was later adopted into law.)

Powell, United States v., • .... 1975 .... 423 U.S. 87 378
Is a 22-inch-long sawed-off shotgun capable of being concealed on the person and hence illegal to ship through the U.S. Post Office [YES].

Presser v. Illinois • .... 1886 .... 116 U.S. 252 172
Are all citizens capable of bearing arms the reserve military force in the country [YES]; Can the states deny citizens the right to keep and bear arms, thus depriving the United States of calling forth the militia [NO]; Can states regulate firearms as required for public order [YES].

Printz/Mack v. United States • .... 1997 .... 521 U.S. 898 556
Does the 10th Amendment prohibit the federal government from commanding local police authorities to implement federal police mandates, and conduct background checks on prospective handgun purchasers (the Brady case) [YES].

Robertson v. Baldwin .... 1897 .... 165 U.S. 275 254
Does the Bill of Rights protect "guarantees and immunities" which existed long before the Constitution was adopted [YES]; Are there well-recognized limits on these rights [YES]; Can a state prohibit concealed carry without violating the 2nd Amendment [YES].

Roe v. Wade .... 1973 .... 410 U.S. 113 369
Is the full scope of liberty protected by the 14th Amendment more than a series of isolated points that includes the right to keep and bear arms [YES].

Rogers v. United States • .... 1998 .... 522 U.S. 252 594
[A writ to consider "knowing possession" of an NFA "firearm" (a silencer in this case) is dismissed because the case fails to present the issue sufficiently clearly to merit review.]

Rowe v. United States • △ .... 1896 .... 164 U.S. 546 247
If a man is provoked into making a minor assault on someone, and then backs off in good faith, is his right to self defense restored if the person he assaulted attacks him with a deadly weapon? [YES]; Is he required to retreat under such circumstances [NO]; Is he under an obligation to try to only wound an attacker when fighting for his life [NO]; Can either party in a mutual combat claim self defense [NO].

Tennessee v. Garner △ .... 1985 .... 471 U.S. 1 428
Is the use of deadly force by police to prevent the escape of all felony suspects
constitutionally unreasonable [YES]; Is the use of deadly force by a police
officer permissible under the 4th Amendment, if necessary to prevent the
escape of a felony suspect who threatens the officer with a weapon, or if there
is probable cause to believe that the suspect has committed a crime involving
the infliction or threatened infliction of serious physical harm, if, where feasible,
some warning has been given [YES].

Terry v. Ohio .... 1968 .... 392 U.S. 1 334
Is a limited, protective, non-invasive "pat-down" search for weapons, known as
a "stop and frisk," a reasonable search and seizure under the 4th Amendment if
an officer observes suspicious behavior and believes it's necessary for the safety
of the officer or others nearby [YES]; Is the higher standard of probable cause
needed to conduct such a search for weapons [NO]; Is a more complete search
reasonable under these conditions [NO]; Is such a stop and frisk a severe but
allowable intrusion upon cherished personal security [YES].

Thompson v. United States △ .... 1894 .... 155 U.S. 271 203
Does arming yourself after being threatened, and then traveling the only road in
the area, where you know your adversary may be, turn a subsequent shooting
of the adversary during a confrontation into murder? [NO]; Is arming yourself
for legitimate self defense premeditation [NO].

Thompson/Center Arms Co., U.S. v., • .... 1992 .... 504 U.S. 505 458
Is the definition of "making" an NFA firearm sufficiently clear to require
registration and payment of the $200 NFA tax on a parts kit that can be
assembled into a legal carbine or into a must-be-registered-to-be-legal short-
barreled rifle [NO]; Is a carbine together with all the parts needed to convert it
to a machinegun a machinegun [YES]; Is an unassembled silencer a silencer
[YES]; Is an unassembled machinegun a machinegun [YES]; Is a pistol and
attachable shoulder stock found in different drawers of the same dresser a short-
barreled rifle [YES].

Tot v. United States • .... 1943 .... 319 U.S. 463 306
Does possession of a pistol by a person who has a prior felony conviction
constitute proof that the person acquired the gun in interstate commerce, or
acquired it after the date of the act that would outlaw such possession [NO].

Trono v. United States .... 1905 .... 199 U.S. 521 276
Is the right of the people to bear arms omitted in the Act of Congress of July 1,
1902, concerning people in the Philippines [YES].

Twining v. New Jersey • .... 1908 .... 211 U.S. 78 277
Are the right of trial by jury, guaranteed by the 7th Amendment, and the right to
bear arms, guaranteed by the 2nd Amendment, among the privileges and
immunities of citizens of the United States guaranteed by the 14th Amendment
against abridgment by the States [NO].

United States v. (various names)
Cases beginning with "United States" are listed alphabetically by the named
party, q.v., Bass, Bean, Biswell, Cruikshank, Freed, Galioto, Gonzales, Lopez,
Miller, One Assortment of 89 Firearms, Powell, Schwimmer, Thompson/Center
Firearms Co., Ursery, Verdugo-Urquidez.

Ursery, United States v., ... 1996 .... **518 U.S. 267** 549
Was the confiscation of guns in the U.S. v. One Assortment of 89 Firearms case
remedial, and not criminal in nature, and thus not prohibited under double
jeopardy protections [YES].

Verdugo-Urquidez, United States v., ... 1990 .... **494 U.S. 259** 444
Does the phrase "the people" used in the 2nd Amendment refer to individual
members of the American society, the same as it does in the Constitution's
preamble, and its 1st, 4th, 9th and 10th Amendments [YES]; Does the 2nd
Amendment protect "the right of the people to keep and bear arms." [YES].

Wallace v. United States • △ .... 1896 .... **162 U.S. 466** 224
Is it up to the jury to decide whether a homicide is murder, manslaughter or
justifiable [YES]; Does a perfect right of self defense require blamelessness in
the confrontation and an act of necessity only [YES]; Can you claim self defense
if you had intentionally brought about a lethal conflict [NO]; Is it up to the jury
to decide whether you armed yourself defensively or otherwise [YES]; Is it
murder if you enter a quarrel without felonious or malicious intent, and then,
under reasonable belief of imminent mortal danger, you kill the assailant [NO];
Does the fact that you deliberately go and arm yourself, for self defense or other
innocent purpose, turn a subsequent shooting necessarily from manslaughter to
murder [NO].

Chronological List of the 96 Gun Cases

Houston v. Moore, 1820
Dred Scott v. Sandford, 1856
Ex Parte Milligan, 1866
Cummings v. Missouri, 1866
United States v. Cruikshank, 1875 •
Presser v. Illinois, 1886 •
Logan v. United States, 1892 △
Gourko v. United States, 1894 △ •
Miller v. State of Texas, 1894 •
Starr v. United States, 1894 △
Thompson v. United States, 1894 △
Beard v. United States, 1895 △ •
Allison v. United States, 1895 △ •
Brown v. Walker, 1896 △ •
Wallace v. United States, 1896 △ •
Alberty v. United States, 1896 △ •
Acers v. United States, 1896 △ •
Allen v. United States, 1896 △ •
Rowe v. United States, 1896 △ •
Robertson v. Baldwin, 1897
Andersen v. United States, 1898 △
Maxwell v. Dow, 1900
Kepner v. United States, 1904
Trono v. United States, 1905
Twining v. New Jersey, 1908 •
Patsone v. Pennsylvania, 1914 •
Stearns v. Wood, 1915 •
Brown v. United States, 1921 △ •
United States v. Schwimmer, 1929 •
Hamilton v. Regents of U. of Cal., 1934
Sonzinsky v. United States, 1937 •
United States v. Miller, 1939 •
Tot v. United States, 1943 •
Adamson v. California, 1947
Johnson v. Eisentrager, 1950
Knapp v. Schweitzer, 1958
Konigsberg v. State Bar of Calif., 1961
Poe v. Ullman, 1961
Malloy v. Hogan, 1964
Maryland v. United States, 1965
Griswold v. Connecticut, 1965
Miranda v. Arizona, 1966
Haynes v. United States, 1968 •
Duncan v. Louisiana, 1968
Terry v. Ohio, 1968
Burton v. Sills, 1969 •
United States v. Freed, 1971 •
United States v. Bass, 1971 •
United States v. Biswell, 1972

Adams v. Williams, 1972
Laird v. Tatum, 1972
Roe v. Wade, 1973
Huddleston v. United States, 1974 •
United States v. Powell, 1975 •
Barrett v. United States, 1976 •
Moore v. City of E. Cleveland, 1977
Scarborough v. United States, 1977 •
Simpson v. United States, 1978
Lewis v. United States, 1980 •
Busic v. United States, 1980
Dickerson v. New Banner Inst., 1983 •
United States v. One Assortment of 89
  Firearms, 1984 •
Tennessee v. Garner, 1985 △ •
United States v. Galioto, 1986 •
DeShaney v. Winnebago County Dept.
of Social Services, 1989
U.S. v. Verdugo-Urquidez, 1990
Perpich v. Dept. of Defense, 1990 •
United States v. Thompson/Center Arms
  Company, 1992 •
Planned Parenthood v. Casey, 1992
Deal v. United States, 1993
Smith v. United States, 1993 •
Stinson v. United States, 1993
Albright v. Oliver, 1994
Beecham v. United States, 1994 •
Custis v. United States, 1994
Staples v. United States, 1994 •
United States v. Lopez, 1995 •
Bailey v. United States, 1995 •
United States v. Ursery, 1996
United States v. Gonzales, 1997
Printz v. United States, 1997 •
Rogers v. United States, 1998 •
Spencer v. Kemna, 1998
Bousley v. United States, 1998
Muscarello v. United States, 1998 •
Bryan v. United States, 1998 •
Caron v. United States, 1998
Pennsylvania Board of Probation and
  Parole v. Scott, 1998
Florida v. J. L., 2000
Castillo v. United States, 2000 •
Harris v. United States, 2002
United States et al. v. Bean, 2002 •
Brosseau v. Haugen, 2004 •
Small v. United States, 2005 •
Castle Rock v. Gonzales, 2005 •
District of Columbia v. Heller, 2008 △ •

Alan Korwin, author of three books and co-author of eight others, is a full-time freelance writer, consultant and businessman with a twenty-five-year track record. He is a founder and two-term past president of the Arizona Book Publishing Association, which has presented him with its Visionary Leadership award, named in his honor, the Korwin Award. He has received national awards for his publicity work as a member of the Society for Technical Communication, and is a past board member of the Arizona chapter of the Society of Professional Journalists.

Mr. Korwin wrote the business plan that raised $5 million in venture capital and launched the in-flight catalog *SkyMall;* he did the publicity for Pulitzer Prize cartoonist Steve Benson's fourth book; working with American Express, he wrote the strategic plan that defined their worldwide telecommunications strategy for the 1990s; and he had a hand in developing ASPED, Arizona's economic strategic plan. Korwin's writing appears nationally regularly.

Korwin turned his first book, *The Arizona Gun Owner's Guide,* into a self-published best-seller, now in its 23rd edition. With his wife Cheryl he operates Bloomfield Press, which has grown into the largest publisher and distributor of gun-law books in the country. It is built around eight books he has completed on the subject, including the unabridged federal guide, *Gun Laws of America,* an expanding line of related items, and countless radio and TV appearances. His 12th book, on the rapidly growing limits to free speech, is underway.

Alan Korwin is originally from New York City, where his clients included IBM, AT&T, NYNEX and others, many with real names. He is a pretty good guitarist and singer, with a penchant for parody (his current band is The Cartridge Family). In 1986, finally married, he moved to the Valley of the Sun. It was a joyful and successful move.

David B. Kopel is Research Director of the Independence Institute, a public policy research organization in Golden, Colorado. He is also an Associate Policy Analyst with the Cato Institute, in Washington, D.C. Kopel is the author of over five dozen articles in law reviews and other scholarly journals, and of 10 books. He is co-author of the only university textbook on firearms policy, *Gun Control and Gun* Rights (NYU Press, 2002). In the *Heller* case, Kopel authored an *amicus* brief for the International Law Enforcement Educators & Trainers Association (ILEETA) and a large coalition of law enforcement organizations and district attorneys. The brief was cited four times in the Court's opinions. At the Supreme Court, Kopel was one of three lawyers who joined Alan Gura at the counsel table on March 18, 2008, to assist him in the presentation of the oral argument in the *Heller* case.

Among Kopel's many books on firearms law and policy: *No More Wacos: What's Wrong with Federal Law Enforcement, and How to Fix It* (with Paul Blackman), which won the Thomas S. Szasz Award for Outstanding Contributions to the Cause of Civil Liberties; *Guns: Who Should Have Them?;* and *The Samurai, the Mountie, and the Cowboy: Should America Adopt the Gun Controls of Other Democracies?* which was named Book of the Year by the American Society of Criminology, Division of International Criminology.

NATIONAL GUN LAWS

It doesn't make sense to own a gun and not know the rules.

GUN LAWS OF AMERICA
Every federal gun law on the books, with plain-English summaries
by Alan Korwin with Michael P. Anthony, 352 pgs., #GLOA
$19.95. Like a complete gun-law library in your hand! The first
and only unabridged compilation of federal gun law—everything Congress has done on guns and the right to arms, and
every law is clearly described in plain English! Covers citizens, dealers, collectors, Militia, National Guard, manufactur-
ers, global disarmament, "proper" authorities, types of guns,
the lost national right to carry, the National Transportation
Guarantee, much more. Good laws, bad laws, 70 pages of
juicy intro, and the plain-English summaries make it so easy.
You'll pick it up again and again. Settles arguments big time.
Widely endorsed. *"Outstanding"* –former Arizona Attorney General Bob Corbin.

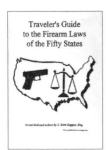

TRAVELER'S GUIDE TO THE FIREARM LAWS OF THE 50 STATES
by Attorney J. Scott Kappas, 68 pgs., #TG $12.95. Because you are sub-
ject to arrest for simply traveling from state to state with a personal
firearm, some sort of guide has been badly needed for years. This excellent book covers all the basics for armed travel: vehicles, glove box,
open carry, permits, loaded or not, weapon types, even Canada and
Mexico and more. An indispensable tool if you want to travel armed and
know the basic rules at the next state line. Ranks each state on its relative freedom too. Before you pack your bags and go, get and read this
book. **Includes the Nationwide Concealed Carry Reciprocity List!**

LICENSED TO CARRY
Guide to 30 "Shall Issue" States' Concealed-Carry Laws
by Greg Jeffrey, 74 pgs., #LTC $19.95.
Shows 30 states' requirements for eligibility, background checks, training, permitted weapons, permit forms, waiting periods, reciprocity,
penalties for unlicensed carry, who issues the license, cost, renewal
fees, prohibited places and more. Packed with charts and graphs comparing how your rights are managed and restricted from state to state,
then ranked for strictness in seven categories. Includes the number of
licenses issued and revoked.

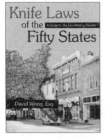

KNIFE LAWS OF THE 50 STATES
David Wong. 200 pgs. #KL $24.95. Knife-collector attorney has done a
tremendous job finding and explaining knife laws for all 50 states. Text
and charts show each state's rules for Folders, Fixed blades, Dirks,
Daggers, Stilettos, Automatics (switchblades), Balisongs (butterfly
knives), and more! Each state's primary statutes included word-for-
word, plus federal knife laws and selected court cases too! Well organized, extensive resources listed. Large format 8.5 x 11 inches. Most
gun-savvy people carry a knife—some prefer it since it's often easier
to carry legally. This book takes away the guesswork.

BLOOMFIELD PRESS • GUNLAWS.COM • 1-800-707-4020

NATIONAL GUN LAWS

It doesn't make sense to own a gun and not know the rules.

SUPREME COURT GUN CASES

Two Centuries of Gun Rights Revealed by David Kopel, Stephen P. Halbrook, Ph.D., Alan Korwin, 672 pgs. #SCGC $24.95. Nearly 100 Supreme Court gun cases demolish the myths that they've said little and you have no rights. The key 44 cases are unedited, the rest carefully excerpted. Every case has a plain-English gist, and fascinating passages are highlighted. In a landmark essay, Kopel finds that, "Supreme Court opinions dealing with the 2nd Amendment come from almost every period in the Court's history, and almost all of them assume or are consistent with the proposition that the 2nd Amendment is an individual right." Groundbreaking, superb reference. **Ask about the special supplement on the *D.C. v. Heller* gun-ban case.**

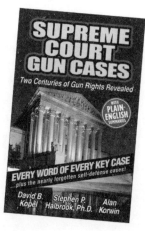

YOU & THE POLICE

What should you do if you're stopped by the police?

Do you have to tell if you have a gun with you?

Should you consent to a search if they ask? Is it required?

What's the best way to carry a gun, at the ready, in a car?

Can you talk your way out of a traffic ticket?

What are the rules at home, on foot or in your vehicle?

Boston T. Party, 168 pgs. #YATP $16.00. This book was written to answer these questions. It has frank discussion and practical ideas for how to handle a traffic stop with dignity, deny a request to search you, and deal with officers so you come out on top. Very well researched, quotes actual cases that control what police can and cannot do. Call, write or go to our secure website for your copy today.

THE CONCEALED HANDGUN MANUAL

Chris Bird, 524 pgs. #CHM $22.95.
A standard for people who keep or carry guns for self defense. Bird has 40 years experience as handgunner on 3 continents, and is a former crime reporter. Detailed accounts of self-defense incidents, latest info on laws and licenses, with the nitty gritty on picking and packing a gun, advanced shooting technique, street-wise tactics, how to see trouble coming and avoid it. What to expect after you have shot someone. Updated edition covers Virginia Tech and Katrina—"authorities" cannot protect you. This is a national best seller that answers the questions concealed-carry licensees need to know. **Includes a 50-state CCW-law guide & reciprocity lists.**

BLOOMFIELD PRESS • GUNLAWS.COM • 1-800-707-4020